America's top ski gui

"For anyone wanting to find out about an⟨...⟩ American skiing, ... Ski America & Canada ⟨...⟩ I can use while traveling, for booking a room or dinner. Is this too much to ask? Charles Leocha puts his readers first. Other guides would be better if they followed his example."
—*The Sunday Telegraph*

"...a no-holds-barred look at ski resorts. Unlike snazzy brochures that claim their respective resorts are perfect for everyone, this guide offers the lowdown on which places are better for families, singles, honeymooners, beginners and experts."
—The Gannett Newspapers

"Ski vacationers will want to look at Skiing America and Ski Europe."
—*Consumer Reports Travel Letter*

"...a personal-experience feel, with insider tips."
—*USA Today*

"...convenient, indepth and portable...provides the down and dirty basics on major resorts." —*Skiing Magazine*

"It provides independent evaluation of the ski terrain and offers more extensive information than found in other guides."
—*Skier News*

"If you're planning a ski vacation . . . this guide should serve you well."
—*Ski Magazine*

"Up-to-the-minute info, so accurate that even ski resort personnel peruse these pages . . . The only guidebook you'll ever need. The latest edition is packed chockablock with detailed information about the ski experience at every major resort in the United States and Canada."
—*Robb Report*

"Charlie Leocha is first a skier, then a writer. He shuns the party line of the big ski corporations, preferring instead to talk to locals. *Ski America's* perspective is direct, credible, and no-holds-barred."
—*Daily Record*, NJ

"The flavor, feel and personality of each resort."
—*The Boston Globe*

Thanks

No project as complex as this can be completed by
a single person or team without help from others.

•

Thank you to the public relations personnel at each of the ski resorts
reviewed in these pages: they carefully check facts,
phone numbers, prices and programs
even though they don't always agree with our reviews.

•

Thank you to Southwest Airlines for their help in getting our staffers
to ski resorts across the U.S.A. Southwest Vacations offers packages
to many of the resorts listed in this book.

•

Thank you to Auto Europe for arranging automobile rentals
for the Ski America & Canada and Ski Europe staff
whenever they travel to Canada or Europe.
If you are planning to rent a car abroad,
this company is a secret all travelers
should know about—(800) 223-5555.

•

And thank you to the Greater Québec Area Tourism and Convention Bureau,
the Charlevoix Region Tourist Association,
Monte-Saint-Anne, Stoneham, and Le Massif
for hosting our editorial conferences.

SKI AND SNOWBOARD AMERICA AND CANADA

by Charles A. Leocha

Susan Graham Staples, Editor

Hilary Nangle, Eastern Editor

with

Steve Giordano, Lynn Rosen

Peggy McKay Shinn, Karen Cummings

Jeannie Patton, Claudia Carbone,

James Kitfield, Andrew Bill,

Chris Elliott, Kari Haugeto

Bob Aubrey, Karuna Eberl

Erica Williams, Ammon Smith

Diane Slezak Scholfield, Vanessa Reese

WORLD LEISURE CORPORATION

Hampstead, NH

Help us do a better job

Research for this book is an ongoing process. We have been at it for more than a decade. Each year we revisit many of these resorts, and every winter we speak with locals from every resort.

If you find a new restaurant, hotel, bar or dance club that you feel we should include, please let us know. If you find anything in these pages that is misleading or has changed, please let us know. If we use your suggestion, we will send you a copy of next year's edition.

Send your suggestions and comments to:

Charlie Leocha, *Ski America & Canada*
World Leisure, Corporation
Box 160, Hampstead NH 03841, USA
or send e-mail to editor@worldleisure.com

Distributed to the trade in the U.S.A. by
Midpoint Trade Books, Inc., 27 W. 20th Street, Suite 1102,
New York, NY 10011, Tel. (212) 727-0190, fax (212) 727-0195.
Internet: www.midpt.com; E-mail sales: midpointny@aol.com

Distributed to the trade in U.K. by
Portfolio, Unit 5, Perivale Industrial Park, Perivale, Middlesex UB6 7RL
Tel. (020) 8997-9000, fax (020) 8997-9097.
Internet: www.portfoliobooks.com

Distributed to the trade in Canada by
Hushion House, 36 Northline Road, Toronto, Ontario, M4B 3E2, Canada
Tel. (416) 287-3146 fax (416) 287-0081 Internet: www.hushion.com.

Mail Order, Catalog, other International sales and rights, and Special Sales by
World Leisure Corporation, PO Box 160, Hampstead, NH 03841.
Tel. (877) 863-1966, fax (603) 947-0838.
E-mail: admin@worldleisure.com; Internet: www.worldleisure.com.

ISBN: 0-915009-78-1   ISSN: 1072-8988   LCCN: 93-643936

Contents by geographical regions

We have organized this table of contents by geography—the way a skier might see geography. We start with the Rocky Mountains, stretching from Canada to New Mexico. We then cover California and several resorts in Nevada. Descriptions then follow about the Pacific Northwest resorts that include Alaska, British Columbia, Washington and Oregon. Finally, we shift to the East covering resorts from Quebec, Canada, in the north to Snowshoe, West Virginia, in the south.

Within these four main sections, where resorts seem more logically organized according to geography rather than the alphabet, we have done so. For instance: Summit County with Breckenridge, Keystone and Copper Mountain, or Mt. Washington Valley that includes five or six resorts, depending on how one counts them.

Eastern Resorts

Contributors to *Ski America and Canada*

Charlie Leocha has skied virtually every major international resort. He writes about travel and skiing for magazines, newspapers and the Web. Charlie is a black-diamond skier, but a double-diamond après-skier. The rest of us bow to his energy and dancing ability. He's also the only *Ski America & Canada* staffer who knows which resorts have the best wine lists *and* the best bacon-and-eggs breakfasts. He is a member of the North American Snowsports Journalists Association (NASJA).

Susan Graham Staples lives in northern Vermont, where a day at the office often means sampling on-mountain conditions. She skis in the woods and launches off ledges with gusto. She first met Charlie when she was forced to zip down the trail edge to get a taste of the powder line that he was stealing. Susan, a former editor for *Snow Country* and *Snow Country Business*, is a member of NASJA. She also is Senior Web Editor for our Web site, www.resortspace.com, recently named a *Forbes* "Best of the Web" skiing site.

Hilary Nangle dropped out of grad school to work at a ski area. She is a member of NASJA and the Society of American Travel Writers (SATW) and writes regularly for ski and travel magazines. She has contributed to more than a dozen Fodor's Travel Guides. She has visited just about every B&B and country inn in Maine. A Mainer through and through, she believes the ideal skier's lunch is a bowl of lobster stew.

Steve Giordano is a veteran ski and travel journalist whose work has appeared in newspapers, magazines, books, radio and television. He used to be a ski patroller, but switched to ski journalism after pulling one too many drunks out of snowy creeks. A skier for more than 20 years, he switched to snow-boarding a few years ago. He is a member of NASJA and SATW. He's also married to Lynn Rosen, and they make sure our Northwest entries are up-to-date.

Lynn Rosen is an Emmy award-winning broadcaster, producer and writer at "border station" KVOS-TV in Bellingham. That's just her day job. She's also a theater critic and travel/ski writer. Mountain scenery is quite dramatic, so it's fitting that Lynn belongs to the American Theater Critics Association as well as NASJA. She also is one of the staff champion shoppers, a pushover for unique jewelry and clothing.

Peggy McKay Shinn, a Westerner at heart, is now a resident Vermonter. She has skied at most major U.S. resorts, where she seeks out terrain that makes the rest of us grow weak in the knees. A NASJA member, she cast aside a graduate degree in environmental engineering to write full-time. She gives us the real scoop on child care and nursery facilities. Much to her mother's dismay, Peggy has vowed not to let motherhood slow her down.

Diane Slezak Scholfield, a near-native Southern Californian, remembers when getting off the chair lift without falling was her biggest challenge. She now skis black diamonds, but only on sunny spring days. She's our best scout for beginner and intermediate trails, mellow après-ski, microbrews on tap, and bagel-and-coffee breakfasts. She edits SnowLink.com and has won NASJA's Excellence in Snowsports Journalism–Writing award three times.

Karen Cummings has been writing about skiing for more than a decade. She lives life, balanced between Boston and Maine, with a smile. Karen began skiing at the tender age of 25 and immediately discovered après-ski—her specialty. These days her nightlife forays are "research." Karen is an expert shopper and has bought something at every resort she visits. She is also our cross-country aficionado who loves a workout with skating skis.

Claudia Carbone lives in the woods, minutes from Breckenridge in her native state of Colorado. For her, a great day is dancing through knee-deep Rocky Mountain powder. Claudia writes for many publications. Her groundbreaking book, *WomenSki*, established her as a national authority on women's skiing. Claudia is a founder of Snow Sports Association for Women and is the recipient of the Lowell Thomas Award from Colorado Ski Country and NASJA's Excellence in Snowsports Journalism–Writing award. She also is the president of NASJA.

Andrew Bill has worked as a travel journalist for nearly 20 years, contributing to leading consumer magazines and newspapers on both sides of the Atlantic. Andy writes about adventure travel and alcoholic potables—such as, "The Best Bars Of The World" supplement for *Newsweek International* and so, ski writing was a natural progression. Our staff's witty Brit describes himself as "an avid if erratic skier."

Jeannie Patton was first published in 8th grade and she still sees life as a kid. She lived in Steamboat Springs as a ski bum, then worked for the ski area as Director of Public Relations. Author of hundreds of articles and a former editor at *Ski Magazine*, she knows that all good things come to those who hang out in high places.

James Kitfield is an expert après-skier who first met Charlie dancing in a conga line through a bar in Verbier, Switzerland. Life has been downhill since, at least as often as he can manage trips to the mountains. On the slopes he points his skis down double diamonds. Amazingly, he has a serious side. He has been awarded the Gerald R. Ford prize twice for distinguished defense reporting, and the Jesse H. Neal award for excellence in reporting.

Kari Haugeto, Aren Elliott and **Christopher Elliott** live in Key Largo, Florida, but spend all winter dreaming about powder days in the mountains. Kari writes about après-ski and nightlife activities as the editor of Cocktail.com. Aren, age 1, specializes in researching day-care facilities at ski resorts. And Christopher, who writes about consumer travel issues for publications such as *National Geographic Traveler* and *USA Today*, covers mountain activities.

Mitch Kaplan took up the pen to support his inexhaustible ski habit and has been covering skiing, adventure and family travel ever since. He currently holds the unofficial New Jersey state record for the most consecutive days spent dreaming about playing in the snow. The author of several books and a member of NASJA, SATW and ASJA, he lives with his non-skiing wife, Penny, two college-age children who won't empty the nest and a gorgeous mutt named Callie.

Bob Aubrey is a snowboarder pure and simple. If there's snow piling up in the Rockies, you'll be sure to find him out riding. He's been just about everywhere you'd want to go on a board, and prides himself on the knowledge he's picked up over his 15+ years of riding.

Karuna Eberl started snowboarding in the Colorado high country in 1988, before the hoards, and later took a sabbatical from college to be a snowboard bum in Utah. She now works from her home in Rollinsville, Colorado, as a full-time freelance writer, photographer and editor—that is, when she's not out showing up the guys on the hill. She's also a member of NASJA.

Erica Williams hung up her skis and turned to the dark side in 1995. An AASI-certified instructor, she's taught at Sunday River and Jackson Hole, where she learned the rules of the steep, deep and cliff drops. After a solo cross-country journey to spend a week flailing off Windell's Kickers on Mt. Hood Meadows, she returned to Maine. In the off-season, she works days as a landscaper, evenings at a gym where she enjoys heckling the guys, and finds time to wakeboard, rider her motorcycle and toss back a few on the beach.

Ammon Smith lives in Maine and loves to ride, catch air and play in terrain parks. He's worked on parks and pipe crews at Sunday River and Jackson Hole, which makes him an ideal rider to evaluate eastern parks. When he's not riding, he's carving gravestones (honest!).

Vanessa Reese considers herself to be the world's first "black-diamond virtual skier." She has worked on *Ski America & Canada* and *Ski Europe* and helped develop our Web site. Until two years ago, the closest this Harvard graduate had ever come to a ski slope was Boston's blizzard of '78. Now she's visited Vail and Beaver Creek and taken her first halting glides on cross-country skis and discovered snow tubing.

Katy Keck, our gourmet consultant, is recognized as one of the Top 30 Women Chefs in The World. **Scott Staples,** a ski patroller, happily accompanies his wife Susan on her trips to assess resorts; this season he contributed to the new chapter on Fernie Alpine Resort, BC. Avid snowboarders **Gavin Forbes Ehringer, Wade Nelson** and **Marie Daigle Thompson** also wrote some of our snowboarding coverage.

Plan your winter vacation with Ski America and Canada

Here's a book to help you branch out and to find the perfect ski resort (plus accommodations, restaurants and nightlife) to match your ability, your pocketbook and your interests. For overseas skiers, *Ski America and Canada* offers insights to help you locate the region and then the resort that matches your dream of an American ski vacation.

Not surprisingly, people take ski vacations for different reasons—for a romantic getaway, to have quality time with the family, to ski all-out with buddies, to ski a little and maybe shop a lot. And what happens when a hotshot skier travels with a never-ever or beginner? The average ski resort's brochure indicates that their resort is all things to all skiers—this is definitely not the case.

Ski America and Canada is as straightforward and honest a guide to North America's top resorts as you can buy. Our goal is to match you with the right vacation spot. Our staff includes experts and intermediates (including some who learned as adults), Generation Xers and Baby Boomers, skiers and snowboarders, eggs-and-bacon breakfast eaters and gourmet-coffee-and-bagel fans. Each skier and snowboarder has various likes and dislikes, and resorts have different personalities. We recognize this—that's why we include our opinions and personal observations. We detail the personality of each resort: where we found the best skiing and snowboarding, where we liked to eat and where we enjoyed the liveliest off-slope fun. And we give you the facts and current prices, plus hotel and restaurant descriptions, lift ticket and lesson prices, child care programs, nightlife hot spots, and where to call, fax, e-mail or write for more information.

A note about prices and older editions of this book

We make every attempt to include prices for the current ski season. Unfortunately, as of mid-August many resorts had not announced their new prices. Current prices have the 2002/03 notation. Where there is no notation, assume prices are from last season (2001/02). In recent years, ski resorts have created lift ticket prices for every occasion—prices for various age groups, various days, various times of the season, supermarket discounts, ad infinitum. It's getting to be just as complicated to purchase lift tickets as it is to buy your airline tickets.

Prices provided in this guidebook are in no way official and are subject to change at any time. In fact, prices do change with high and low seasons; and resorts sometimes announce one price in July, change it by November, and change prices again during the season.

Ski America and Canada is published every fall, but sometimes bookstores have older copies in their inventory. If you are reading this book in the fall of 2003 or after, get the latest edition. It can be found in most major bookstores or order it through www.worldleisure.com, www.amazon.com, or www.barnesandnoble.com. Or, send a check for $24.95 plus $3.00 for shipping and handling to World Leisure, PO Box 160, Hampstead, NH 03841.

What's new in this edition

Of course, prices, programs, lessons and facilities have been updated to provide the most accurate information available at press time about each resort. Some of these resorts have been completely transformed through new developments and new hotels.

We have added new chapters on Fernie Alpine Resort and Kicking Horse Mountain Resort, both in the Canadian Rockies of British Columbia. The chapter covering Québec City Region and its resorts—Mont-Sainte-Anne, Stoneham, and Le Massif—has been completely rewritten and expanded after our staff held its annual editorial meeting there this past winter. We continue to expand our snowboarding coverage for the major resorts, telling you where to ride, where the flats are and whether the terrain parks and features are any fun.

Keeping up with area code, resort, hotel, restaurant and price changes always keeps us busy. There are literally thousands of changes to the book each year. We continue to add Web site addresses that will help you in your planning.

Using the Internet—www.resortspace.com

The development of the Internet has significantly changed the way people research and make reservations at ski resorts. Virtually every world-class resort now has a Web site with basic information including statistics, lift tickets, ski school prices, and how to contact them; you can even book online on some of the more savvy sites.

We have gathered more information than we can possibly stuff into this guidebook, so if you want to know more about any of the resorts we review here, visit our Web site, www.resortspace.com. There you'll find additional facts, advice and words of wisdom; often you'll find out more about a resort than at the resort's own site. Indeed, few resorts work to promote the surrounding areas, but www.resortspace.com offers details about the surrounding areas as well as much more economical lodging and dining options. As prices change at each resort, we'll post that information.

During the coming months, many of the more popular resort writeups *Skiing America & Canada* as well as *Ski Europe* will be made available for purchase by the chapter through our Web site. Check online for details.

We have included the Web addresses for every resort listed in this book. Use them as well as www.resortspace.com to get the information you need.

Chapter organization

Each resort chapter has several sections. We begin by sketching the personality of the place—is it old and quaint, or modern and high-rise? Clustered at the base of the slopes, or a few miles down the road? Remote and isolated, or freeway-close? Family-oriented or catering to singles? Filled with friendly faces or an aloof herd of "beautiful" skiers?

The basic statistics of each resort include **addresses and phone numbers:** postal, e-mail, Internet, toll-free, fax—all of them that we could find.

A few important notes: The resort's **area code** is listed in the fact box and at the bottom of each even-numbered page. We don't list the local area code for every number in the chapter because you probably will use local numbers most often while you're at the resort (in the case of restaurants, for instance). Some of the fax numbers we list are for the ski area; others are for the central reservations office; some resorts don't have public fax numbers. In almost every instance, the Internet address we list is the officially sanctioned one maintained by the resort.

The **base and summit altitudes** are important for those with altitude-related medical difficulties or for sea-level dwellers who plan to hit the slopes the same day they arrive; **vertical drop, skiable acreage** and **number and types of lifts** provide a good idea of the resort's size.

Our terrain stats reflect *lift-served* terrain. Examples: Breckenridge, Colorado, lists its vertical as 3,398 feet; we list it at 2,546. If you want that maximum vertical, you must hike the extra 852 feet to the in-bounds summit. Grand Targhee has two mountains totaling 3,000 acres, but 1,000 of that acreage is reserved for snowcat skiing and snowboarding. Exceptions like these are explained where they occur.

Uphill lift capacity is the number of riders the lift system can carry each hour. **Bed base** is the approximate number of people who can be accommodated overnight near the resort. If the uphill capacity is much bigger than the bed base, the result is usually shorter lift lines. (Resorts with great uphill capacity/bed base ratios may still have long weekend lines if they are near major cities—we try to identify these.)

We tell you how close the **nearest lodging** is, if the resort has **child care** and the youngest age accepted, and if there are any restrictions on **snowboarding.** The **lift ticket** price in the fact box tells the per-day range of the adult lift ticket. The lower price usually is the per-day cost of the longest adult multiday ticket, or it is the midweek price. The higher price is the weekend walk-up-to-the-window cost. Ticket prices in the stat box are intended as an approximation; look in the chapter for more details.

Finally, **we rate the slopes** (based on five ability levels), the **dining**, the **nightlife** and the **other activities**. One star means it's poor, two is okay, three is good, four is very good and five is outstanding. Ratings are quite subjective, but they are a general consensus of the *Ski America and Canada* staff. We are simply trying to point you in the right direction.

Following the fact box is a detailed description of the mountain. **Mountain layout—Skiing** describes various sections of the mountain best for skiers at each of five ability levels. **Mountain layout—Snowboarding** tells riders where to go, where the flats are and whether the terrain parks and features are any fun. **Mountain rating** is a summary of the mountain's best and worst features, such as whether slopes may be too tough for the beginner or too mild for the expert.

Cross-country and snowshoeing information will tell you which resorts have Nordic trails, as well as significant cross-country and backcountry skiing opportunities nearby, and snowshoe rental and tour information.

The **Lessons** section details instructional programs for adults, including any special programs and recreational racing. The term "never-ever package" refers to a package with half-day or full-day first-time lesson, a lift ticket (often just for the beginner lift) and use of rental equipment. Some resorts charge more for first-time snowboarders than for skiers. Though it might appear that resorts are either cashing in on the trendy sport or discriminating against boarders, they tell us that the higher price is because fewer people sign up for first-time snowboard group lessons, and snowboard rental equipment takes a greater beating.

Child care covers non-skiing nursery and day-care programs, either at the resort or nearby, as well as the skiing and snowboarding lesson programs available for children.

Lift tickets are listed for adults, children, teens and seniors. We've organized them in a chart with one-day, three-day and five-day prices, followed by "Who skis free" and "Who skis at a discount" listed in paragraph form. Where prices are from last season, assume an increase of a couple of dollars. Be aware that resorts have various terms for children's lift tickets—"junior," "youth" and "young adult" are common.

Under **Accommodations** we list both the most luxurious places and many of the budget lodges, including features such as slopeside location, pools and spas, health clubs and intra-resort transportation. We also suggest lodging that is particularly suited to families, and our favorite B&Bs and inns.

Dining always includes the gourmet restaurants, but we don't leave out affordable places where a hungry family or a snowboarder on a budget can chow down and relax. We have compiled these suggestions from dozens of interviews with locals and tourists, plus our own dining experiences.

Après-ski/nightlife describes places to go when the lifts close, and where to find entertainment later in the evening. We tell you which bars are loud, which are quiet, what kind of music they play and whether they have live music.

Other activities covers off-slope activities—such as dogsledding, snowmobiling, ice skating, sleigh rides, shopping, fitness clubs and spas.

Getting there and getting around tells you how to get to the resort by air and car (and sometimes by train or bus), and whether a car is optional or necessary at the resort.

Types of accommodations

A **hotel** is relatively large, with 25 rooms or more, and comes without meals. If hotel rates include any meals, that is noted.

A **mountain inn** usually has fewer rooms than a hotel. Many have packages that include breakfast and dinner.

A **bed & breakfast (B&B)** tends to be even smaller, with just a few rooms. Most B&Bs have private baths now, so if guests must share a bath, we say so. Breakfast is included and some B&Bs also offer dinner.

Motels don't have the amenities of a hotel or the ambiance of a B&B, and often are further from the slopes. Motels are good for families and budget-minded skiers.

Condominiums have become the most affordable group lodging at North American ski resorts. They usually have a central check-in facility. Most condominiums have daily maid service for everything but the kitchen.

When you call the resort's central reservations number, ask for suggestions. Most of the staff have been on lodging tours and can make honest recommendations based on your needs. We use $$$ signs rather than listing the prices for restaurants and accommodations. In the Canadian chapters, we note that prices are in Canadian currency, so take into account the exchange rate. Many high-end accommodations and restaurants in Canada may actually be affordable for budget-conscious visitors from the U.S., so at least consider them.

Where you find $$$ signs, refer to this legend (also found on the bottom of pages in each chapter):

Dining: $$$-Entrees $20+; $$-$10-20; $-less than $10.

Accommodations: (double room) $$$$-$200+; $$$-$141-$200; $$-$81-$140; $-$80 and less.

High and low season

North American mountain resorts have several pricing seasons. The highest prices are during the Christmas-New Year holidays in late December. Regular season usually runs all of February and March, but at some resorts March is high season. Value Season is in January after New Year at some resorts. Low Season is usually the first couple of weeks in December, and April until closing. These vary from resort to resort, so ask for more information when you call. The most noticeable change is in the cost of accommodations, but some resorts also vary the prices of lift tickets, especially in pre-season and in spring.

Regional resorts

Throughout the book you'll find coverage of regional resorts too. These resorts are best for weekend or short midweek visits by skiers and snowboarders who live in that region. When a regional resort can be a side trip from a destination resort, we have included the description within that chapter. Regional resorts that are not near a large destination resort are in separate mini-chapters throughout the book.

These ski areas all have the following common features, *unless otherwise noted:*
• lodging within a 20-mile radius (Note: Some of the phone numbers listed for lodging are reservations services; others just provide information about lodging in the area. If no phone number is listed for lodging, call the ski area.)
• a day lodge with food service
• adult and child ski and snowboard lessons (children usually start at age 4)
• equipment rentals

We list toll-free phone numbers where available, plus the resort's recorded information line and Web site address. If you can't get a live voice from the info line, try the ski area's office number. (The toll-free numbers may not be applicable nationwide, since these resorts draw visitors primarily from the nearest urban areas.) Where we say, "None found," for Web site, that means we couldn't find an official site from the resort as of summer 2002.

Where two or more ski areas are close enough to be explored on the same weekend trip, they are presented together, but with separate contact information. Such ski areas usually are owned by different companies and do not have interchangeable lift tickets unless specifically noted.

Ability levels

These are the terms we use in the "Mountain layout—Skiing" and other sections:
● **Never-evers** are just what the name implies. We apply the term to novices during their first couple of days on skis or a snowboard.

●● **Beginners** can turn and stop (more or less) when they choose, but still rely on snowplow turns if on skis and sideslipping if on a snowboard. This group feels most comfortable on wide, fairly flat terrain.

■ **Intermediates** generally head for blue trails and parallel ski or link snowboard turns (more or less) on the smooth stuff. They return to survival technique on expert trails, and struggle in heavy powder and crud.

◆ **Advanced** skiers and boarders can descend virtually any trail with carved turns, but are still intimidated by deep powder, crud and super steeps. Advanced terrain by our definition includes moguls and glade skiing.

◆◆ **Experts** favor chutes, tight trees on steep slopes, deep-powder bowls and off-piste exploration. True experts are few and far between.

Banff, Canada
Sunshine Village
Banff@Norquay

Banff Region Facts
Dining:★★★★
Apres-ski/nightlife:★★★★
Other activities:★★★★★

Internet: www.sblls.com (skiing)
www.banfflakelouise.com (tourism bureau)
www.canadianrockies.net/Banff (townsite)
Bed Base: 10,000 in Banff

While flying into Calgary during the day provides awe-inspiring views of the Canadian Rocky Mountains, perhaps the best surprise is to arrive late at night, when everything is enveloped in pitch black, and make the hour-and-a-half-long drive to Banff. That way, the next morning when you draw back the curtains, the massive craggy mountains are suddenly *right* there, in your face. What a wake-up call!

Banff is home to three resorts—Sunshine Village, Ski Banff @ Norquay and Lake Louise (which we detail in a separate chapter). The three mountains provide very different ski experiences, just one of the reasons Banff makes a fabulous ski trip. For those who have never skied out West, it's easy to be overwhelmed by the massive amount of terrain and the steep craggy peaks. You can plan your vacation accordingly to start at the smallest of the resorts and work up to the larger and more difficult ones: Spend your first day at Ski Banff @ Norquay, the next at Sunshine Village, then head to Lake Louise. We highly recommend you also take a side trip to Marmot Basin, some three hours away in Jasper National Park. After a week of skiing and riding these Alberta resorts, you'll return to your favorite mountain ready to conquer parts where you previously feared to go.

The pristine beauty of Banff National Park is one of the reasons people are drawn to the region's three ski resorts. There is a true sense of being swallowed up by the wilderness—embraced by Mother Nature and then gently released to be part of her bountiful gifts here. Wildlife is plentiful, sightings of elk herds in town are common. Mule deer and bighorn sheep live in the Bow Valley, and sometimes bears and wolves can be seen along less-traveled roads.

From the castle-like Fairmont Banff Springs Hotel, one gazes down a densely wooded valley framed by towering mountain walls and dissected by a shimmering river. To see this scene is to understand the spell which must have overcome the builders of the Canadian Pacific Railway in the late 1800s.

The completion of the coast-to-coast railway in 1885 made one of the most picturesque and remote pockets in the Rocky Mountains suddenly accessible. This virgin landscape—formerly known only to Native Americans, fur traders and explorers—was now open to everyday travelers and tourists. That same year, Canada established its first national park, Banff. Later, four other national parks were created nearby: Yoho, Jasper, Kootenay and Glacier, which explains why much of the region's rugged beauty remains essentially unspoiled. The scenery is still as magnificent as it was to the train travelers of the late 1800s with snow-capped mountain ridges, cliff faces pocked by glaciers, mountain lakes and hot springs.

Sunshine Village Facts

Summit elevation:	**8,954 feet**
Vertical drop:	**3,514 feet**
Base elevation:	**5,440 feet**

Address: Box 1510, Banff, Alberta, Canada T0L 0C0

☎ **Area code:** 403

Ski area phone: 762-6500

Snow report: 760-7669

ⓘ **Toll-free reservations:** (877) 542-2633

Fax: 762-6513

Internet: www.skibanff.com

Number of lifts: 12–1 high-speed 8-passenger gondola, 4 high-speed quads, 2 quads, 1 triple chair, 2 double chairs, 2 surface lifts

Snowmaking: None

Skiable acreage: 3,168

Uphill capacity: 19,400 per hour

Snowboarding: Yes

Nearest lodging: Slopeside, hotel

Resort child care: Yes, 19 months and older

Adult ticket, per day: $56.28-$63.13 (02/03, Cdn$ with GST)

Expert:★★★★
Advanced:★★★★
Intermediate:★★★★
Beginner:★★★★
Never-ever:★★★★

Ski Banff@Norquay Facts

Summit elevation:	**7,000 feet**
Vertical drop:	**1,650 feet**
Base elevation:	**5,350 feet**

Address: P.O. Box 219, Suite 7000, Banff, Alberta, Canada T0L 0C0

☎ **Area code:** 403

ⓘ **Ski area phone:** 762-4421

Snow report: 760-7704

Fax: 762-8133

E-mail: info@banffnorquay.com

Internet: www.banffnorquay.com

Number of lifts: 5–1 high-speed quad, 2 quad chairs, 1 double chair, 1 surface lift

Snowmaking: 90 percent

Skiable Acreage: 190 acres

Uphill capacity: 7,000 per hour

Snowboarding: Yes

Nearest lodging: Base of access road–ski-in only

Resort child care: Yes, 19 months and older

Adult ticket, per day: $49 (02/03, Cdn$ with GST)

Expert:★★★★
Advanced:★★★★
Intermediate:★★★
Beginner:★★
Never-ever:★★

Tri-Area Lift Passes (2002/03 in Cdn$, with GST)

The Banff/Lake Louise Region has an interchangeable lift ticket. It allows unlimited skiing at Sunshine, Ski Banff @ Norquay and Lake Louise and a free shuttle between Banff/Lake Louise hotels and the ski areas. It is available for those skiing at least three days. It also includes a free night-skiing ticket (Fridays only) when used at Ski Banff @ Norquay to make up the price difference. It's easy and convenient.

	Adults	Children (6–12)	Seniors (65+)
Three days	$186	$64	$163.50
Five days	$310	$107	$272.50
Seven days	$434	$150	$381.50

Contrast this with the beautifully designed, compact, yet very cosmopolitan townsite of Banff (that's the word locals use instead of "town"), filled with excellent restaurants, night-clubs, shops and lodging. The atmosphere is a uniquely Canadian blend of quaint and rustic, set amid some of the most rugged scenery in the Rockies—sort of like a good Canadian whiskey sipped smooth but with enough bite to remind you of the point of the exercise.

Because summer is the high season in the park, crowds diminish in winter and lodging prices are rock bottom. The temperature can be numbingly cold, or pleasantly warm if a Chinook wind blows. Unlike the Canadian resorts closer to the Pacific Ocean, ski areas in Banff receive a dry, fluffy powder that is the best thing this side of Utah.

And speaking of dry, fluffy powder that's the best thing this side of Utah… As much as we hate to say it, you won't catch first tracks at Sunshine Village and Lake Louise if you rely on the shuttlebuses—unless you wake up *really* early, in time for the first one of the morning (it's appropriately called the "Powder Express"). They make a lot of stops along the way before they head out to the resorts.

Sunshine Village

Sunshine Village has long been known for its seemingly endless gondola ride that carries you almost 1,650 vertical feet from the parking lot—along the walls of a valley and box canyon—to the village base area and the rest of the lifts. Now a high-speed, eight-passenger gondola whisks you along that same route in just about 13 minutes, instead of the previous 20 (you'll get to Goat's Eye station in about 6 minutes). The number of people that are moved out of the base area is almost doubled, which means shorter lift lines too. Even more good news: The gondola loads and unloads at ground level out of the parking lot, eliminating the need for those pesky metal stairs.

On the 13-minute ride to the rest of the lifts, you have plenty of time to survey the slopes where the real thrill rides begin. Much of the skiing on Sunshine's three peaks is wide-open, bowl-type skiing, but the bottom half of the slopes are covered in evergreens for those who like their runs cut through trees.

Though a restaurant and rental shop are near the parking lot at the gondola base, the real "base area" for Sunshine is at the top of the gondola at 7,082 feet, where you will find a mountain village with a lodge, rental shop, general store, restaurant and the only slopeside lodging in the national parks. (A clarification: The base-elevation stat we list is for the gon-dola base; this book uses the term "base area" to mean the greatest concentration of shops and services.) From this point a half dozen lifts take off in all directions. Most people never head all the way down until the end of the day, and some not until the end of their vacation.

Sunshine has the longest ski season in the region, sometimes extending even into June, because it gets up to three times the snowfall that the other Banff ski areas get. If the weather is clear, the views across and down the canyon are nearly as breathtaking as the runs.

New for 2002/03: The Wawa quad chair replaces the Wawa T-bar. Snowboarders will rejoice at this news, since some of the best riding terrain is here and T-bars are quite simply a pain on boards.

Mountain layout—Skiing

The 3-mile run at the end of the day on Banff Avenue—from the Village down to the parking lot—is a long, luscious trip for beginners, but it will seem tame for many intermediates. Advanced skiers can play on drops to the left, but they're short and eventually rejoin the trail. An alternative way down is Canyon

Trail, which starts out intermediate and turns into a single-black diamond. You catch it near the base of the Jackrabbit Quad.

◆◆ **Expert** ◆ **Advanced:** There's plenty of terrain to explore. If you can't stand the thought of even a 13-minute gondola ride, plus another lift ride before being able to hit the slopes, do what we did. Get off at the Goat's Eye station and board the Goat's Eye Express, which whisks you to the top of 9,200-foot Goat's Eye Mountain and 1,900 vertical feet of black and double-black routes. There are even a couple of excellent blue cruisers thrown into the mix. The skiing at the top is steep and wide-open until you crest a ridge into the glades, at which point the runs are cut fairly wide through trees with plenty of pitch. The glades here are lots of fun, make sure to dip in and out of them at will. Experts wanting to test their mettle can try Hell's Kitchen, a tree shot that's only a few shoulders wide at some points and eventually comes out directly under the Goat's Eye Express Quad. Any struggles on this gut-sucker will be viewed by the masses.

When you're ready to explore the rest of the resort, from the bottom of Goat's Eye Express, follow the signs down a short dip to the Wolverine Express, ski Miss Gratz to the Tee Pee Town chair and head up 8,954-foot Lookout Mountain. Advanced skiers searching for some untracked powder should follow the run under the Tee Pee Town chair. When you hit the ridge, look to a traverse to your right that takes you to The Shoulder, a hard-to-find open slope known primarily to locals. There are some nice short glades here too.

The runs under the Angel Express Quad—especially Ecstasy—have good pitch. At the top, the skiing is wide-open and above treeline, with spectacular views. Those in search of the steep-and-deep will not be disappointed, as the run splits into multiple fingers towards the midway point, some of which represent short but quite steep chutes. You'll also find some delightful but short tree shots where Angel Flight, World Cup Downhill and Ecstasy converge, just above the base of Angel Express.

Heading right at the top of the Angel Express will take you into a fairly steep bowl. Pick your poison, and shoot down to the Continental Divide High-Speed Quad. This lift takes you a soaring 1,450 feet to the almost-summit of Lookout Mountain. At the top you cross the Continental Divide from Alberta to British Columbia. These descents also are wide-open, with moguls on North Divide and powder and open skiing in the Bye Bye Bowl, which is convex instead of concave. Make sure to carry your speed to get out of the bowl.

From the top of the Continental Divide Quad, skiers can climb a short distance for some truly extreme skiing on the Northface of Lookout Mountain, in the chutes of Delirium Dive. Three rules are strictly enforced at the control gate to Delirium Dive: 1) All skiers/riders must wear an avalanche transceiver; 2) All skiers/riders must carry a rescue shovel, and 3) You must ski or ride with a partner. Ask about renting transceivers and shovels at the ski area. Also, helmets are recommended. After cresting the knoll of Lookout Mountain, you are rewarded with a gut-churning entrance into the chutes. Be forewarned: The entrance is remarkably steep, though fairly wide. But after the first 30 or 40 yards, Delirium opens up into one of the finest and least-skied bowls in the Rockies. Instead of dropping in off the cornice, you can climb backwards down a metal stairway but friends told us it was scarier than just sucking it up and "diving in."

You'll also find interesting terrain to the left off the Standish Double Chair, and into the Paris Basin and Birdcage off the new Wawa quad.

■ **Intermediate:** There's terrain from every lift for intermediates; however, be sure you are confident at this ability level if you try the runs on Goat's Eye or the peak of Lookout

Mountain. (Think twice if the weather's socked in, too. Lack of visibility can be nerve-wracking and downright dangerous.) We had a blast playing on the blues off the Strawberry Triple on Mt. Standish. The grade's just right on Boutry's Bowl for those learning to ski powder. Carry your speed and cut through the woods to get back to the chair.

If you're ready to try a few blacks, you'll find some short ones off the Wolverine Express and the JackRabbit Quad, both down-mountain from the other lifts. You can enjoy this area any time of the day, then either ride the gondola to the top from its midstation or take Miss Gratz to the Tee Pee Town chair. Most people play here in the afternoon on their way back.

●● **Beginner:** The Strawberry Triple Chair and the Wolverine Express high-speed quad have gentle wide slopes good for those still perfecting their technique.

● **Never-ever:** Never-evers learn near the base village, where a moving carpet pulls them to the top of a short gentle slope that is off to one side.

Mountain layout—Snowboarding

Mt. Standish is a huge hit with riders. The Dell Valley is a natural halfpipe near the Strawberry Triple Chair. The triangle formed by the new Wawa quad and the Standish Chair is a natural terrain park with lots of air, natural hits, a quarterpipe, lips and drops. The boardercross is on Birdcage and the SilverBullet Halfpipe is on Strawberry Face.

If you like to hike for your turns, there are plenty of choices. You'll find lots of awesome cliffs, chutes and gullies, plus wide-open bowls. Start off with hiking up from the tops of Standish Chair, Wawa quad and Goat's Eye Express. The marked trails in these areas are also favorites with snowboarders.

Sunshine Village has one serious flat on Lookout Mountain when you're coming out of Bye Bye Bowl or South Divide. You need to *really* carry your speed, and even then, you'll probably have to hoof up the last section, which is actually a little hill that then drops you back into the main area so you can work your way to the lifts. Perhaps this is why so many riders avoid the top part of Lookout Mountain. Other flats and runouts you should be aware of (you'll be fine as long as you're ready for them): The beginning of Banff Avenue as you head out of the Village back toward the base, and the bottom section of Sunshine Coast, where all the runs on Goat's Eye dump you on the way back to the lift.

Mountain rating

Sunshine Village has a much-deserved reputation as a cruiser's mountain. Intermediates and advanced skiers and riders will find the most challenge, though Goat's Eye and Delirium Dive now up the ante for experts. This is a well-balanced mountain with fun for all levels, making it a good choice for families and groups of mixed abilities. There are some flats that make it difficult for snowboarders, but you can avoid most of them and still have enough mountain to play on. Many riders come here for the hike-to terrain.

Lessons (2001/02 in Cdn$, without GST)

Group lessons: Daily Workshops are limited to eight people and are available to all ability levels. A full day costs $50 during the value season, $60 powder season. Half day (afternoon only) costs $35 value season, $42 powder season. Multi-day discounts are available.

Never-ever package: A half-day lesson, rentals and lift ticket is $72. A three-day package costs $172 and includes coupons for discounted lift tickets for the remainder of the season, as well as discounts at local restaurants, shops and businesses.

Private lessons: $153 for two hours during the value season (up to five people), $180 powder season. A full day is $339 value season, $399 powder season.

Special programs: Sunshine Village encourages the traditional Ski Week, a week-long stay at the slopeside Sunshine Inn, by providing packages including classes with the same instructor. Groups can be divided by ability level or by family, and include evening activities. Call for prices, which vary by season and size of room.

Sunshine Village participates in Club Ski and Club Snowboard, a three-day program featuring lessons with the same instructor and group, skiing one day each at three resorts (see *Lessons* in the Lake Louise chapter for details).

Child care (2001/02 in Cdn$, without GST)

Ages: 19 months to 6 years.

Costs: Full day with lunch is $39 during value season, $45 powder season. Half day is $22 value season, $26 powder season with multi-day discounts.

Reservations: Recommended; call 762-6560.

Children's lessons: Ages 3–6 can get a combo ski-and-play program. A full day with lunch costs $66 during the value season, $77 powder season; half day is $39 value season, $47 powder season. Equipment is included. Kids Kampus is for kids ages 6–12 just starting or well on their way. The price for a full day with lunch is $57 value season, $67 powder season; half day is $35 value season, $42 powder season. Sunshine Village participates in Club Junior, a three-day program featuring lessons with the same instructor and group, skiing one day each at three resorts (see *Child Care* in the Lake Louise chapter for details).

Lift tickets (2002/03 in Cdn$, with GST)

	Adult	Child (6-12)
One day	$63.13	$21.40
Three of four days	$175.48 ($58.49/day)	$64.20 ($21.40 /day)
Five of seven days	$281.41 ($56.28/day)	$107 ($21.40/day)

Who skis free: Children ages 5 and younger.

Who skis at a discount: Students ages 13–25 and those 65 and older ski one day for $50.29. Students need ID to qualify for the discount.

Note: Check out the Tri-Area Pass if you're staying in Banff. It is valid at Sunshine Village, Ski Banff@Norquay and Lake Louise, and includes bus rides from hotels to the ski areas. The bus ride alone is about $15 round-trip between Banff and Sunshine Village, so the Tri-Area Pass can be a good deal even if you use it at Sunshine most of the time.

Ski Banff@Norquay

This small, but challenging, ski area is just a 10-minute drive from Banff and boasts some of the best grooming in Western Canada. It also has some of the gnarliest bump runs we've ever seen. There are virtually no lift lines here, so you can really rack up the vertical. The winding mountain road that takes you up to the base lodge can be fairly intimidating, but the views are incredible as you climb above the townsite of Banff. Be sure to look out for elk, we saw dozens of them.

The Cascade Lodge at the base was built in 1996 after the previous lodge burned down. The beautiful log lodge includes an excellent restaurant, a bar, three large stone fireplaces and the other usual services.

Mountain layout—Skiing

◆◆ **Expert** ◆ **Advanced:** The view of Banff and the Bow Valley from the North American chair is fabulous. This is the lift that takes you to those ribbons of bumps tumbling down the mountainside. It's an old slow chair that rarely has a line. Be positively sure you want to be here. This is very tough stuff, with no blue or green ways down. That said, we *must* tell you that these are quite possibly the most fun bump runs in all of skidom. And they are *long!* The bumps can get so big, folks of short stature can barely see over them. By the way, look closely at the tea house at the top of the lift—it's built to have avalanches roll right over the top of it.

Lone Pine is the name of that double-black mogul belt that plunges down a 35-percent gradient. We didn't tell the kids how steep it was until after they got down to the bottom and wanted to try it again. That just made them doubly sure they had to do it again. There's a daily contest (when the lift is open) called Club 35,000 to see who can make the most consecutive runs in eight hours on this 1,360-foot-long, skeleton-jarring wall. It takes 26 runs to make the club—many have done it, which says a lot for local physical fitness.

Another appeal for the adventure seeker is a chute called Valley of the Ten, a narrow drainage perfect for thrills. To get to it, skiers at the top of North American chair drop off (correct terminology) to the left into a drop-out (accurate again) called Gun Run, the steepest thing on the mountain. The easiest way down from this chair is Memorial Bowl, and it's still a tough black with monster moguls.

Off the Pathfinder Express, some chutes drop you off into a gully that feeds you back to the lifts. Black Magic and Ka-Poof are screaming cruisers. Like to earn your turns? Look up after you get off the lift, any lift, choose your medicine and start hiking. Just don't go alone and make sure someone knows where you've headed.

■ **Intermediate:** The terrain off the Pathfinder Express Quad, unseen from the base area, is mainly groomed intermediate. The intermediate runs here are pretty steep by most standards, so they're not for the timid, but excellent grooming makes them truly delightful. The mellower terrain is found off the Spirit quad. Start out on Hoodoo and work your way up to the tougher trails. Intermediates wanting to stay in the sun all day have a challenge. At midday none of the Pathfinder trails gets sun except the front two runs, Black Magic and Ka-Poof, which are both blacks.

● **Beginner:** One magic carpet and a short quad chair serve four runs at the base. Adult beginners may get bored after a few runs. There's a big jump from beginner terrain to intermediate terrain here.

Mountain layout—Snowboarding

Ski Banff @ Norquay is a big supporter of snowboarding. The terrain park has a halfpipe, quarterpipe, tabletops, gap jumps and more. The park is groomed at least five nights a week, so you'll get the best riding experience they can give you. The park is conveniently located near the base and served by the Cascade Quad Chair; a reduced-rate Cascade lift ticket is available (see *Lift Tickets*).

Many snowboarders hate moguls, and if you're one of them, you won't find much black terrain unless you hike for it. The exceptions are Black Magic and Ka-Poof, off the Pathfinder Express. However, if you're like our staffer's stepson, you consider moguls to be a challenge that will only improve your riding skills—and give you some true bragging rights. In that case, make a beeline for the bumps off the North American double chair.

The intermediate trails here are groomed to perfection, meaning lots of fun for riders who like to carve arcs or just let it rip. Some of the trails are rolling rides with occasional lips for catching air. You'll find some fun natural hits around the mountain if you look for them. Bruno's Gully is a must-try if it's open.

Mountain rating

Intermediates to experts will find plenty of challenge here, especially since even the blues are far more difficult than those found at most resorts. Excellent grooming on the intermediate runs makes them fun cruisers. If you're a mogul masher or want to improve your bump technique, this is the place to do it. Beginners are better off at Sunshine Village.

Lessons [2002/03 in Cdn$, with GST]

Group lessons: $35 for two hours for skiing or snowboarding.
Never-ever package: $49 for a two-hour group lesson, lift ticket on the Cascade chair and rental equipment for skiers or snowboarders. Additional two-hour lesson in the afternoon, $20.

Private lessons: $70 per hour, each additional person $15.

Special programs: Ski Banff @ Norquay participates in Club Ski and Club Snowboard, a three-day program of lessons with the same instructor and group, skiing one day each at three resorts (see *Lessons* in the Lake Louise chapter for details).

Child care [2002/03 in Cdn$, with GST]

Ages: 19 months to 6 years.
Cost: Full day, without lunch, is $30. Half day, either morning or afternoon, is $19. Add a ski lesson, and costs are $38 and $30, respectively. Lunch is $6.

Reservations: Recommended; call 760-7709.

Children's lessons: Full day is $45; two hours, $30. Lunch is extra. A child's beginner package (lift, two-hour lesson and rentals) is $49.

Lift tickets [2002/03 in Cdn$, with GST]

	Adult	Child (6-12)
One day	$49	$16
Noon–4 p.m.	$37	$14
Two hours	$26	$10

Who skis free: Children 5 and younger ski free when an adult buys a lift ticket.

Who skis at a discount: Students ages 13–24 with student ID and seniors 55 and older ski for $38. Ski Banff @ Norquay has the region's only night skiing, on Fridays, $24 for adults, $12 for children, $22 for seniors and students with ID. If you only want to use the terrain park, a ticket for the Cascade lift costs $33 for adults, $12 for children, $26 for seniors and students with ID.

Although Ski Banff @ Norquay also sells multiday tickets, we've given you the ticket prices we think destination visitors are most likely to use. The area sells hourly tickets for two to five hours, ranging in price from $26 to $43 for adults (discounts for kids, students and seniors). Our recommendation: Use the Tri-Area Lift Pass at Lake Louise and Sunshine Village, and buy a two- or three-hour ticket here. If you want to ski here again after two hours (and you may—it's a fun place, yet small), *then* use a day on your Tri-Area Pass.

Cross-country and snowshoeing—Banff area

There are some lovely, easy loops **along the Bow River.** Take Banff Avenue to the end of Spray Avenue, or turn left and cross the river. Trails wind through the whole area. **Parks Canada** puts out a very informative booklet on the extensive Nordic skiing and snowshoeing in Banff National Park; you can get a copy for a small fee at the Banff Information Center, 224 Banff Ave., 9 a.m. to 5 p.m.

Fairmont Banff Springs Golf Course Clubhouse offers ski and skate rentals, plus group and private lessons. Maps and information on trails are available at the Clubhouse.

Several sports shops rent snowshoes, ask your lodging concierge. **White Mountain Adventures** (678-4099) is just one of many guide outfits that offers naturalist-guided snowshoe treks, guided backcountry tours and cross-country skiing tours.

Accommodations

Banff has accommodations to meet every taste and every budget. Rooms can be found for as little as $50 (Cdn$), and even the premier locations are within most budgets. In addition to the 7 percent GST, Alberta also has a 5 percent lodging tax, tacking on 12 percent to your cost. **Banff/Lake Louise Central Reservations** (800-661-1676) books lodging in Banff, Lake Louise and Jasper. **Ski Banff-Lake Louise-Sunshine Reservations** (877-754-7080) books ski packages including the tri-area lift tickets and lodging at more than 30 Banff and Lake Louise properties. Packages are customized and can include Club Ski, Club Snowboard and Club Junior lessons, rentals, air and other activities. Also visit online at www.skibig3.com.

The Sunshine Inn (762-6500; 800-661-1676; $$–$$$), at 7,200 feet in the center of Sunshine's base village, is the only slopeside lodging in Banff National Park. It's reached by riding the gondola up from the parking lot. All nightly rates include lift tickets; the hotel also runs a Ski Week program. Rooms are neat and simple. There's a giant outdoor hot tub where you and 19 others can relax while watching skiers and riders on Lookout Mountain. You'll also have access to a dry sauna, massage and chiropractic services, a family and game room, and an exercise room.

Ski Banff @ Norquay now owns the cozy, spiffed-up, 1960s-era **Norquay's Timberline Inn** (762-2281; www.banfftimberline.com; $–$$$$) at the bottom of its access road. Technically it's Banff's only ski-in hotel. You can ski in along a 1.5-kilometer trail, but you'll need the inn's shuttle to take you to the lifts. The shuttle also will run guests into town in the evening. Rates include Norquay lift tickets. You'll enjoy a good meal here at The Big Horn Steakhouse.

Other lodging is in Banff. We strongly recommend the experience of staying at **The Fairmont Banff Springs Hotel** (800-441-1414 in the U.S. and Canada, 762-2211; $$$–$$$$), the wine-colored, Scottish-influenced castle perched on a small hill, a short walk from downtown. You have seen this classic, rundle-rock monolith in many photos with its pointed, green-copper roofs rising from the nine-story walls, framed by evergreens and craggy peaks. Its public areas are expansive, designed for turn-of-the-century mingling—we're talking a ballroom for 16,000. The hotel has a magnificent, full-service spa (available at an additional fee) with private mineral pool and waterfall pools, saunas, steam rooms and whirlpools as well as a fitness room, salons and treatment areas. There are also indoor and outdoor pools available free to all guests as well as shops and restaurants and scheduled activities, such as dog-sledding and snowshoeing with guides. Rates during the winter are a bargain compared to the summer. Ask about the Ski with Breakfast package, including lodging, lift tix, ski shuttles, valet parking and gratuities for two.

"An enclave of civility" is how the **Rimrock Resort Hotel** (800-661-1587; 762-3356; $$$$) describes itself, and we agree. It's posh, sophisticated, elegant and refined, with a full-service spa and fitness center, an excellent restaurant and views to match. It is one of only five Canadian members of the Leading Hotels of the World, a group of luxury hotels.

Banff Park Lodge and Conference Center (800-661-9266; 762-4433; $$$–$$$$), which hosts many cultural activities, is an expanse of cedar buildings in a wooded area two blocks from downtown.

Families will most definitely want to stay at the **Douglas Fir Resort and Chalets** (800-661-9267; 762-5591; Calgary direct, 264-2563; $$–$$$$). There are condo-style units with wood-burning fireplaces and full kitchens, two- and three-bedroom chalets, and a few suites. We nearly had to drag the kids off the two indoor waterslides here because they couldn't get enough of them. We're not talking little-dinky kiddy slides, we're talking huge, winding, fast waterslides like you would normally find at an outdoor water park. So we were forced to sit in the steam room, or the hot tub, or the wade pool at the bottom of the slides, watching them whoop it up. And a few times we even played on the waterslides ourselves. The waterslide area is open to the public for a cost, but it's free for hotel guests. In a separate area, for guests only, you'll find an indoor swimming pool, hot tub and saunas. There are also a coin laundry and a convenience store on site.

The Mount Royal Hotel (800-267-3035 Western Canada only; 762-3331; $$–$$$$) has a great location in downtown Banff, an excellent choice for those who enjoy nightlife. It gets a fair amount of street noise from Banff Avenue but has an exceptionally good restaurant.

The Inns of Banff (800-661-1272; 762-4581; $$–$$$$), a modern, multi-level lodge with balconies in most rooms, is a 15-minute walk from downtown. **High Country Inn** (800-661-1244; 762-2236; $$–$$$) on Banff Avenue, two blocks from downtown, is one of the least expensive and has a pool and an Italian/Swiss Restaurant.

Banff International Hostel (762-4122; $) on Tunnel Mountain Road recently added a 66-bed wing with two- and four-bed rooms with private bathrooms. Showers are shared. Facilities include a laundry, kitchen and cafe.

If your flight home is early in the morning, you can't beat the **Delta Calgary Airport Hotel** (291-2600 or 800-268-1133; $$$). Roll out of bed, then walk out the front door of the hotel and into the terminal. It also has a pool and fitness center, lounge and two restaurants. The food is good, and the service is excellent.

Dining: $$$–Entrees $20+; $$–$10-20; $–less than $10. (Cdn$)
Accommodations: (double room) $$$$–$200+; $$$–$141-$200; $$–$81-$140; $–$80 and less. (Cdn$)

Dining

For those staying at Sunshine Village, the **Eagle's Nest Dining Room** ($$) in the Sunshine Inn offers fine dining with lobster and filet mignon. **The Chimney Corner Lounge** ($-$$), the inn's fireplace lounge, serves a very good sit-down lunch. Try the barbecued beef and a local-brewed ale. Ask to sit in the sunroom so you can watch the skiers and riders on Lookout Mountain. The **cafeteria** has the best cafeteria food and selection for a ski area in this region. The **Creekside Restaurant** ($) at the base of the gondola serves a hearty breakfast, or choose à la carte. Like a flavored cappuccino? If you ask, they'll make one for you. Take time to wander around the restaurant to look at pictures from Sunshine's past, during the early glamorous days of skiing, as well as Native American relics and antique outdoor winter gear.

On-mountain at Ski Banff @ Norquay, the food is tasty and affordable in the **Lone Pine Pub** ($), upstairs in the main lodge with gorgeous views. Try the lemon pepper salmon burger, the Alberta wild mushroom and bison stew, or the chicken souvlaki wrapped in a pita. The children's menu (ages 12 and younger) is $5.50 for your choice of pb&j, grilled cheese, chicken fingers, cheese burger or hot dog.

The Big Horn Steak House (762-2281; $$) in Norquay's Timberline Inn offers a cozy atmosphere with a spectacular view of the Valley and The Fairmont Banff Springs Hotel. The menu has a varied selection of pastas, fish and top-grade Alberta beef.

In the townsite of Banff, diners have a tremendous variety and number of restaurants from which to choose. You will find almost every variety of ethnic food, as well as the familiar steak-and-seafood restaurants. Restaurants here, especially those on Banff Avenue, often are often on the second floor above the shops. Sometimes the entrances are not obvious.

The Fairmont Banff Springs Hotel alone has 11 restaurants. **The Samurai** (762-6860; $$–$$$) is the place for Japanese cuisine. **Castello Ristorante** (762-6860; $$) specializes in Italian dinners. The expansive buffet at the **Bow Valley Grill** (762-2211, Ext. 6841; $$–$$$) is a steal at $20 Cdn$, per person. Choose from a wide selection of salads, soups, side dishes and entrees as well as stir-fry and pasta stations. A dessert buffet is available for $5 more. An à la carte menu is also available, but the best value is the buffet. **Waldhaus** (762-6860; $$) serves fondue and other German, Austrian and Swiss fare at long tables that seat a dozen people. **Grapes** (762-2211, Ext. 6660; $$) is the 26-seat wine bar, but you can get light meals here too. **Solace** (762-1772; $$), at the hotel spa, creates healthy, low-fat fare.

Le Beaujolais (on Banff Avenue at Buffalo Street, 762-2712; $$$) receives high praise for its French cuisine. Meals can be ordered à la carte, but the restaurant specializes in fixed-price three- or five-course meals. You are likely to see diners in coats and ties, though neither is required. **The Bistro** (on the corner of Wolf and Bear streets, 762-8900; $$) is owned by the same restaurateurs but is considerably more casual and cozy. It serves a variety of pastas and salads, as well as meat and poultry. Open for lunch and dinner.

Chef Werner Zullig from Ticino has teamed up with Swiss Chef Mario Thorn to create Canadian-themed fine dining at **The Pines** (537 Banff Ave., 760-6690; $$$) in Rundlestone Lodge. Creative contemporary food combined with beautiful presentation—such as a baked rack of venison with lemon pepper pears, sweet and sour red cabbage and blueberry spaetzli—is served in an atmosphere of rustic elegance. Don't miss the opportunity to eat at one of Banff's finest restaurants.

The dining room at **Buffalo Mountain Lodge** (Tunnel Mountain Road, 762-2400; $$$) offers relaxed elegance with hand-hewn beam construction and a massive fieldstone fireplace. Rocky Mountain Cuisine is their specialty, with a variety of wild game and fish. The wine list was awarded Wine Spectator's "Award of Excellence" several years in a row.

For gourmet Italian, you can try **Giorgio's Trattoria** (219 Banff Ave. 762-5114; $$), which serves Northern Italian pastas and pizzas, or **Guido's** (116 Banff Ave. above McDonald's, 762-4002; $$) for American Italian food, such as spaghetti, lasagna and chicken parmigiana. **Ticino Swiss-Italian Restaurant** (415 Banff Ave., 762-3848; $$–$$$) specializes in dishes from the Italian part of Switzerland. Chef Werner Zullig also owns The Pines.

Bumper's The Beef House (603 Banff Ave., 762-2622; $$–$$$), with a cozy log interior, has been serving Alberta beef since 1975. We had melt-in-your-mouth prime rib (which comes in four cuts). Watch out, the horseradish sauce is very hot! Use it sparingly unless you like smoke coming out of your ears. The chicken cafoosalum has a very tasty maple sugar-lime sauce. The meal comes with a good salad bar; try the mango jalapeño salad dressing or the creamy cuke. If you save room for dessert, order a large nut sundae and serve three people. There's a good kids' menu, plus they will take most adult choices and make a smaller portion for children 12 and under.

The popular **Coyotes Deli & Grill** (206 Caribou St., 762-3963; $$-$$$) specializes in tasty Southwestern meals, including vegetarian and pasta dishes. Try the smoked chicken burrito or the roasted vegetable and shaved asiago pizza. Open for breakfast, lunch and dinner. Dinner reservations are recommended and if you're 15 minutes late, you lose it. **Grizzly House** (207 Banff Ave., 762-4055; $$–$$$) specializes in fondue and steaks as well as beef and wild game. **Earl's** (229 Banff Ave. at Wolf Street, 762-4414; $$) gets rave reviews for moderately priced Canadian beefsteak, fresh salmon, pasta and thin-crust pizza. **St. James Gate Olde Irish Pub** (205 Wolf St., 762-9355; $-$$) specializes in hearty Irish pub food that warms the heart on a cold winter day.

Well, we can vouch for it. **Aardvark Pizza & Sub** (304 Caribou St., 762-5500; $-$$), "the locals' choice in homemade pizza for over a decade," makes a great thick-crust pizza. We thought the kids were going to pass out with delight. The buffalo wings are mighty tasty too and they come in mild, medium, hot or suicide (mild is an accurate description). Open 11 a.m.-4 a.m. Delivery is free and there's a money-back guarantee if you're not satisfied.

One of the most fun places to eat breakfast, lunch or an informal supper is **Joe Btfsplk's Diner** (221 Banff Ave. 762-5529; $). Set in a 1950s-style diner decor complete with jukebox and Elvis posters, this restaurant serves huge portions.

For gourmet coffee, the best hot chocolate in town, delicious pastries and darn good chicken sandwiches too, visit **Evelyn's Coffee Bar** (9 Town Central Mall on Banff Ave.; $) and it's sister shop **Evelyn's Too** (229 Bear St.; $). **Fine Grind** (Banff Ave.; $) and **Jump Start Coffee and Sandwich Place** on Buffalo Street (206 Buffalo St., near the post office; $) also serve gourmet coffees and light snacks. There's no Starbuck's in Banff (yet) but **Second Cup** (Cascade Plaza Mall at 317 Banff Ave.; $) serves coffees, pastries and atmosphere that are anything but second rate. Enjoy stuffed chairs and a cozy ambiance.

Après-ski/nightlife

Après-ski is more quiet than rip-roaring in Banff, but things really start hopping at night. Younger crowds probably will enjoy Banff nightspots, while older skiers might be happier at The Fairmont Banff Springs' many bars and lounges. The Happy Bus shuttles skiers to nightspots around Banff until midnight for $1, or you can walk between most lodging and town.

Après-ski, head to **The Paddock** at The Mt. Royal Hotel. Crowds also gather at **The Rose and Crown**, an English-style pub with draught ale, a fireplace, pool table, darts and live entertainment. **St. James Gate Olde Irish Pub,** built in Dublin and assembled in Banff, is a traditional Irish pub with 33 draught beers and more than 65 single malt scotches. In The Fairmont Banff Springs, the **Rundle Lounge** has quiet music for hotel guests. At the **Waldhaus** by The Fairmont Banff Springs Golf Course, Happy Hans and Lauren, on accordion and trumpet, get everybody singing. **Tommy's Neighbourhood Pub** on Banff Ave. is popular with the locals.

At night, **Bumper's Loft Lounge** has a casual crowd, with live entertainment and ski movies. **Wild Bill's Legendary Saloon** on Banff Avenue has Country & Western bands and a huge dance floor. Locals flock to **Barbary Coast** on Banff Avenue for what is repeatedly hailed as the best live music, usually along the rock/blues lines. **Magpie & Stump** serves up great nachos and some of Banff's best après-ski. **Outabounds** on Banff Avenue (but the entrance is on Caribou Street), with DJ dancing and occasional live bands, attracts 20-somethings. **The Aurora,** in the basement of the Clocktower Mall, features a lounge, cigar bar and dance floor with DJs and bands. This is the dance bar where everyone goes after every place else in town closes. Finish off your night on the lower level at 110 Banff Ave.

Other activities

Banff has so much to do, we can only begin to do it justice. We can't imagine anyone coming here and not finding the time to explore the natural beauty of the region and view the abundant wildlife. Just a few of the ways to do that: Go **dogsledding** (Howling Dog Tours, 678-9588) or **ice fishing** (Banff Fishing Unlimited, 762-4936); take a **sleigh ride** (Warner Guiding and Outfitting, 762-4551); or take an introductory course in **ice climbing** or **ski mountaineering** (Yamnuska; 678-4164).

We took the **Johnston Canyon Icewalk** (White Mountain Adventures, 678-4099) and were very impressed with our guide. She knew many interesting things about the canyon's history, wildlife and habitat, and she was a delightful conversationalist. At the end of the canyon, you might be lucky enough to watch ice climbers work their way up the frozen waterfall. You should be in good physical shape, since you are hiking along the canyon on paths that go up, down and around natural formations.

One of the most famous **heli-skiing** companies, Canadian Mountain Holidays, is head-quartered here (762-7100). Plus RK Heli-Ski does day heli-ski trips from Banff (762-3771). You also can go **helicopter sightseeing** with Alpine Helicopters (678-4802) to view the magnificent mountain peaks. On a clear day, take the **Sulphur Mountain Gondola** (762-2523) for a beautiful vista of the Bow Valley.

If you aren't staying at the Douglas Fir Resort & Chalets (762-5591), you can still use their **two giant indoor waterslides, kiddy pool, hot tub, steam room, fitness room, arcade and pool tables** (see *Accommodations*). This is a great way to meet other families and for your kids to make new friends on vacation. Cost is $7.50 Cdn$ per person for non-guests of the hotel; kids 5 and younger swim free.

The **Banff Upper Hot Springs** (762-1515) is a wonderful way to wind down after a day on the slopes. Natural hot mineral waters fill a huge outdoor pool, and you're surrounded by beautiful mountain scenery. $5 for adults, $4 for children and seniors. Winter hours are 10 a.m.-10 p.m., Friday and Saturday until 11 p.m. Restaurant and gift shop on site. There's also a full-service spa here (760-2500 for spa reservations).

Museums of note: Banff Park Museum for the story of early tourism and wildlife management, and a taxidermy collection of animals indigenous to the Park; Cave & Basin National Historic Site, where the hot springs were first discovered; Whyte Museum of the Canadian Rockies, for historic and contemporary art and historic homes; the Buffalo Nations Luxton Museum, for Plains Indians history; and the Natural History Museum for local geology.

In the townsite, **shopping** is almost an athletic activity, with hundreds of shops lining Banff Avenue and its side streets. Most shops are clustered in little malls where you can enter the store from the inside on crummy days, or from the outside in good weather. Worth a drop-in: The Hudson's Bay Company, a department store famed for its blankets and Canada's oldest company, founded in 1670; and Roots Canada, for fine leather-and-cloth backpacks and handbags, and casual clothing.

For non-kitschy Canadian souvenirs: Orca Canada or Great Northern Trading Company (clothing, jewelry, knickknacks), Rocks and Gems (inexpensive jewelry made from native Canadian gemstones), A Taste of the Rockies (smoked salmon, jams and honeys) and Canada House (Canadian artists and artisans).

The Fairmont Banff Springs Hotel has 18 specialty and boutique shops, featuring designer jewelry, gourmet kitchen accessories, toys and clothing. Our favorite in the hotel is The Canadian Pacific Store, with items that reflect the bygone elegance of luxury train travel.

Getting there and getting around

By air: Calgary Airport is served by major airlines, including Air Canada. Rocky Mountain Sky Shuttle (888-762-8754; 762-5200), Brewster Transportation (762-6767) Laidlaw Transportation (762-9102) and Banff Airporter (762-3330) will get you from the airport to Banff.

By car: Banff is 85 miles west of Calgary on the Trans-Canada Highway, an hour-and-a-half drive. Ski Banff @ Norquay is on Norquay Road, one exit past the Banff townsite. The Sunshine Village exit is 5 miles west of Banff; it's 5 more miles to the gondola base parking area. Free shuttles pick up skiers at 11 Banff hotels and the bus depot.

Getting around: It is possible to ski Banff and Lake Louise without a rental car by using free shuttlebuses offered with the Tri-Area Lift Ticket to the ski areas. The Happy Bus (evenings only, $1 a ride) takes you within the town and region. Taxis are available too, but that can add up quickly. For spectacular sightseeing and exploring, it's best to have a car.

Lake Louise Ski Area

Banff Region, Canada

Summit elevation: 8,650 feet
Vertical drop: 3,250 feet
Base elevation: 5,400 feet

Address: P.O. Box 5, Lake Louise
Alberta, Canada T0L 1E0
✆ **Area code:** 403
Ski area phone: 522-3555
Snow report: 762-4766 (Banff)
ⓘ **Toll-free reservations:** (800) 258-7669
Fax: 522-2095
E-mail: vertical@skilouise.com
Internet: www.skilouise.com
Expert:★★★★
Advanced:★★★★
Intermediate:★★★★
Beginner:★★★★
Never-ever:★★★★

Number and types of lifts: 12—4 high-speed
quads, 1 quad, 1 triple, 2 doubles, 4 surface lifts
Skiable acreage: 4,200
Snowmaking: 40 percent
Uphill capacity: 16,400 per hour
Snowboarding: Yes
Bed base: 2,500 within 10 minutes
Nearest lodging: About 2 miles away
Resort child care: Yes, 3 weeks and older
Adult ticket, per day: $55-$59 (2001/02; CdnS)

Dining:★★★
Apres-ski/nightlife:★★
Other activities: ★★★★★ (includes region)

Lake Louise is Canada's second-largest ski area, behind Whistler Blackcomb in British Columbia, and is the third resort in Banff National Park. It's difficult to say what makes it more memorable: its colossal size with incredible terrain diversity or the truly jaw-dropping scenery. One visit is usually all it takes for Lake Louise to make virtually *everyone's* top 10 list of mountain resorts. Lake Louise is a great place to come for a taste of truly steep terrain. Warm-up on Lake Louise's Front Side and then tackle the Back Bowls.

The 36,000-square-foot Lodge of the Ten Peaks, and the corresponding remodeling of the original base lodge, has transformed the mountain's facilities. This massive, split-beam log building is one of the most handsome in the Rockies: Think of a log cabin built by Paul Bunyan. The lodge is constructed of some 2,500 fir, pine and spruce logs, most of them thinned from the Ptarmigan slope to open glade skiing and riding.

More and more U.S. skiers are discovering this resort and the phenomenal value that Canada offers the skier. The British have long known about Lake Louise. More British ski here than any other North American resort.

Mountain layout—Skiing

Lake Louise is comprised of four mountain faces that create three distinct areas: the Front Face, the Back Bowls and the Larch Area. The Lake Louise trail map has an excellent synopsis of where different ability levels should head, so be sure to grab one. If you want sun all day and want to ski the whole area, go to the Back Bowls in the morning, Larch midday and end up on the Front Face. Take a free tour by the Ski Friends, a volunteer group, daily starting at Whiskyjack Lodge.

◆◆ **Expert** ◆ **Advanced:** On the Front Side, expert and advanced skiers can give the Men's Downhill or Ladies' Downhill a try to get an idea of what the big boys and girls ski when Lake Louise hosts World Cup races in early December. Plenty of runs directly below the Eagle Chair, Top of the World Express and especially the Summit Platter have excellent pitch and grade, as evidenced by the liberal smattering of black diamonds on the trail map. Grizzly Bowl, just off the Olympic Chair, has three or four different fall lines, trees and bumps all in one descent. It's a great last run of the day as you return from the back side.

The Summit Platter can become an expert challenge all by itself. The Platter used to be a T-bar until the folks at Lake Louise decided the steepness demanded concentration, not conversation. Whatever you do, don't skip Brown Shirt, it holds freshies for a week. It's totally worth working your way to skier's left a bit, toward the area's boundary. Be fore-warned that while the top entrances to Shoulder Roll, Ridge Run and Whitehorn look rela-tively mild, things get steep very fast once you crest a ridge in the middle of the run. At that point, however, it's too late to turn back. Bonzai! The resort's steepest chutes, the Whitehorn 2 gullies, are off this lift too; they're not for the weak of heart and helmets are recommended.

After Whitehorn 2, probably the next-most-hair-raising area of the mountain is Diamond Mine, accessed off the Paradise Chair (you can't get here from the Summit Platter). The special attractions here include cornices and some of the steepest chutes in the area. Cornice-hoppers should go to the headwalls at the ER3 and ER7 gullies. Parachutes optional. You'll find some sweet, and often untouched, single-diamond terrain if you drop off Saddleback just before or after the intersection with Pika Connector.

You will also want to sample the double- and single-black diamonds under the Ptarmi-gan Chair. These tend to be steep, long and full of moguls. Bark-eaters should aim for the Fall Line Glades, a slew of glades to the right of Ptarmigan Chair. Awesome!

In the Larch area, there's great tree skiing directly under the lift between Larch and Bobcat runs. From the top of the Larch Chair, you'll see that some powder freaks have hiked up the 8,900-foot summit to leave tracks down Elevator Shaft, between two rock outcroppings. The chute is within the ski area boundaries.

For a more modest thrill in a less traveled area, exit left off Larch Chair, then stay right and high on a gladed traverse until you find a deep powder bowl under Elevator Shaft. Called Rock Garden, it's a hidden playground of loops, swoops, moguls and Cadillac-sized rocks. You'll find bump thrills on Lynx.

■ **Intermediate:** On the Front Face, don't miss Meadowlark or Wapta, reached by the Eagle Chair; or Homerun and Gully, reached from Top of the World. The Front Face has a good web of intermediate trails served by Olympic, Glacier and Friendly Giant. Though lore holds that intermediates shouldn't take the Summit lift except to cross to the other side, don't believe it. There are some great Front Face drops down Skyline to Sunset Terrace and then back to the lifts. This run gives intermediates plenty of opportunities to dip into the ungroomed stuff and come back to safety.

Intermediates can reach the Back Bowls via the Top of the World quad or the Summit Platter, which will take you a little higher on the back side to a run called Boomerang, an immensely fun cruiser that seems to go on forever.

If the weather is socked in, however, skip Boomerang. The Larch Area has the best intermediate skiing, access by a high-speed quad. Wolverine, Larch and Bobcat are all long cruisers. And there are tons of trees in the Larch area that are perfect for any intermediate. Lynx has a black-diamond moniker, but can be handled by most intermediates. It's a gas.

●● **Beginner** ● **Never-ever:** Those with a little experience can ride the Friendly Giant quad chair and head down Wiwaxy, a 2.5-mile cruiser. Next step is Eagle Chair to try Deer Run and Eagle Meadows. If you're getting pretty confident and would like to try the Back Bowls, ride the Eagle Chair and take Pika down the back. You also can descend from the Top of the World quad on Saddleback, a cat track that can be a bit intimidating, especially if the snow's iffy. Definitely don't try Saddleback on a low-visibility day, there are no trees to guide you, and you must negotiate a couple of narrow spots. Beginners have a couple of nice runs in the Larch area, Marmot and Lookout. First-timers enrolled in lessons will start on the Sunny T-Bar, which serves an excellent beginner area separated from everything else.

 ## Mountain layout—Snowboarding

Lake Louise gets huge kudos for its terrain park and halfpipe. The resort has built what it claims is the largest terrain park in North America—the Jungle. It features 2,000 feet of vertical drop with tabletops, big air jumps, halfpipes and a superpipe.

The Summit Platter is a Poma lift that's an expert challenge all by itself for snowboarders (and on windy or icy days, yikes!). If you can get over the trials and tribulations of riding the Platter—and you *really* should—there are some great hikes off the top to your left. Want guaranteed freshies? Head to the Back Bowls and stay far left to Brown Shirt, which holds snow for at least a week after a dump. It's worth it to work your way over to it. While you're over there, hike to Upper Boomerang, North Cornice and Wild Gully. The runout from the Back Bowls is kind of a drag, but it does have some pitch to it so just carry your speed and you'll be fine. For trees, head to Ptarmigan Chair and the Fall Line Glades, a slew of sweet tree runs that hold snow when you can't find it anywhere else. Off Larch Chair, hike in whichever direction draws you, you can't go wrong.

Carvers will find fresh cord on groomed runs for ripping arcs. Try Meadowlark, Home Run and Gully on the Front Side, and Larch and Bobcat in the Larch Area. There's nice beginner terrain on the Front Side and in the Larch Area. First-timers enrolled in lessons will start on the Sunny T-Bar, which serves an excellent beginner area separated from the rest of the runs. Too bad it's a T-Bar, a nightmare for snowboarders.

Mountain rating

All abilities have terrain suited to their skill level from all lifts except the Summit Platter. This makes it nice for families and groups of varying levels who want to ride together on the lifts. This is an excellent mountain for skiers and riders who want to improve to the next level. You'll need at least a week to explore the mountain and discover all the fun stashes.

 ## Cross-country and snowshoeing

The Fairmont Chateau Lake Louise (522-3511) has about 150 km. of groomed trails and access to hundreds of miles of backcountry trails, with stunning views of the lake and mountains. The ungroomed, well-marked trail to Skoki Lodge, a rustic log cabin (meaning no electricity, no plumbing, wood-burning stove), begins just above Temple Lodge at the ski area and heads up the valley and over Boulder Pass, 7 miles one way. If you're not up for skiing so far into the wilderness, follow the gentle Shoreline Trail starting in front of the Fairmont Chateau Lake Louise, an easy mile and a half one way. Skiing *on* Lake Louise is not recommended.

A complex 20-km. network called **Pipestone Loops** starts 4 miles west of the Lake Louise Overpass on the Trans-Canada Highway. Although all are marked beginner, some are suitable for the intermediate. About 25 miles from Lake Louise, just over the border into British Columbia, is **Emerald Lake Lodge** (343-6321 or 800-663-6336). It has a 40-km. network of groomed trails with views of the Presidential Range, lodging in comfortable cabins and activities such as skating, snowshoeing and a games room. The lodge has a shuttle to the Lake Louise ski area.

Before setting out on any of the trails, check trail conditions at a park warden's office. Be aware that trail classification is done by healthy Canadians in good shape.

Lessons [2001/02; Cdn$ with GST]

Group lessons: $32 for 1.75 hours for skiers or snowboarders.

Never-ever package: $42 includes a 1.75-hour lesson, equipment rental and beginner lift ticket for skiers or snowboarders.

Private lessons: For skiers and snowboarders, $69 per hour, reduced to $49 if taken after 3 p.m.; extra skiers/snowboarders, $16 each.

Special programs: Lake Louise has a lot of special clinics, some two hours long, others several days long. Clinics cover bumps, freeride and freeskiing, style and technique, women's camps and more. The Club Ski program and Club Snowboard program operates at Lake Louise, Sunshine Village and Ski Banff@Norquay. Groups of similar interest and expertise ski or ride together with the same instructor for four hours a day at each of the three areas, then dine at an optional closing-night dinner with prizes. The program starts Mondays and Thursdays, and one benefit is lift-line priority. The three-day program costs $169 (price includes GST, but not lift tickets or rentals).

Racing: There is a dual-slalom NASTAR course on Wiwaxy that is $5 for two runs.

Child care [2001/02; Cdn$ with GST]

Ages: 3 weeks to 6 years. Toddlers have their own play area.

Costs: Babies' care (younger than 19 months) is $25 per day or $4 per hour. Toddler care (19 months–3 years) is $4 per hour. Day care for kids ages 3–6 costs $3.50 per hour, with three-hour minimums. Hot lunch included.

Reservations: Infants younger than 19 months require reservations. Reservations are recommended for other ages. Call 522-3555.

Children's lessons: The Kinderski program, ages 3–4, provides supervised day care, one ski lesson and indoor and outdoor play at the beginning and end of the day. Cost is $36, or $46 for two one-hour lessons. In the Kids Ski program, children ages 5–12 are guided around the mountain with instruction along the way, $52 for a full day. The program includes a lift ticket. Optional lunch is $7. Children's snowboard lessons are for ages 7–12. The cost is $49 full day, lift ticket included. Rentals are an extra $11.

Lift tickets [2001/02; Cdn$ with GST]

	Adult	Child (6-12)
One day	$59	$15
Three days	$165 ($55/day)	$45 ($15/day)
Five days	$275 ($55/day)	$75 ($15/day)

Who skis free: Children younger than 6.

Who skis at a discount: Students ages 13–24 with student ID and ages 65 or older pay $47 per day. Skiers and boarders interested in visiting other Banff ski areas should buy the Tri-Area Pass (see Banff Region chapter for details).

 ## Accommodations

Banff/Lake Louise Central Reservations (800-661-1676) books lodging and ski packages in Banff, Lake Louise and Jasper. **Resorts of the Rockies** (800-258-7669), which owns Lake Louise, books ski packages and lodging for these Western Canada resorts: Lake Louise, Nakiska, Fortress, Wintergreen, Fernie and Kimberley. You also can book online at www.skilouise.com.

The **Fairmont Chateau Lake Louise** (800-441-1414; 522-3511; $$$–$$$$) nests on the shore of Lake Louise, with the spectacular Victoria Glacier in the distance. This hotel dates back to a log chalet built in 1890. It has nearly 500 guestrooms, restaurants, shops, Nordic ski center, masseuse and free ski shuttles.

The **Post Hotel** (800-661-1586; 522-3989; $$$–$$$$) is a cozy, beautifully furnished, 93-room log lodge with great views on all sides and fireplaces in 38 of the rooms, two of which are lovely riverside cabins with heated slate floors. It's personal and quiet, with the warmth and elegance provided by Swiss innkeepers. The buffet breakfast is a board of tasty delights. There is a free ski shuttle. **Lake Louise Inn** (800-661-9237; 522-3791; $$–$$$$) is a simply decorated hotel that's good for families. Rooms range in size from economy double (2 double beds) to superior lofts that sleep six. Amenities include heated indoor pool, whirlpool, steam room and arcade room.

Deer Lodge (800-661-1595; 522-3747; $$–$$$) is the Fairmont Chateau's antithesis, though they are located quite close to each other. Deer Lodge has no television, for example, but it has a great rooftop hot tub. It's old and rustic, but well kept up.

The **Canadian Alpine Centre & International Hostel** (522-2200; $), on Village Road, is a very modern facility with two-, four- and six-bed rooms with private bathrooms and showers, laundry, kitchen and cafe. Nightly bed rates start at less than $20.

Dining

For breakfast on the mountain, the **Northface Restaurant** ($) in the Whiskeyjack Lodge serves a yummy and affordable breakfast buffet (however, beverages are extra, which took us by surprise). On-mountain lunch options are the **Powder Keg** ($$) with nachos, sandwiches and pizza; the **Sitzmark** ($$), with more substantial fare like burgers and salads; the **Northface Dining Room**, with very affordable hot and cold luncheon buffets; and **Sawyer's Nook Restaurant** ($$) in Temple Lodge, known for its prime rib buffet.

By far, the most enjoyable time we've ever had dining on a mountain is at the **Lake Louise Torchlight Dinner & Ski,** held at the mid-mountain Whitehorn Lodge on Mondays and Fridays (522-3555; reservations required). Tables seat eight, which means everyone has to meet everyone else, because you're reaching across each other to grab appetizers of chicken-fried steak strips, mushrooms in pastry, and fried corn tortillas stuffed with spiced jalapeño cream cheese. Some couples are dancing while the band members leap around the room, jumping up on tables and falling to their knees as they sing the blues. Unfortunately, the fun has to end sometime. But not before you strap on a headlamp and follow a guide carrying a torchlight down the mountain, where buses take you back to your lodging. Cost is $49 per adult, $25 per child (Cdn$).

On Saturday evenings, the **Brewster Cowboy's Barbecue & Dance Barn** (800-691-5085; 762-5454) near the Fairmont Chateau provides hearty cowboy food and Western entertainment from mid-December to early April. It includes a sleigh ride to the barn.

For dinner in the **Fairmont Chateau Lake Louise** (522-3511 for reservations at all its restaurants), the most elegant dining room is the **Edelweiss** ($$$), serving such entrées as salmon and duckling. The **Walliser Stube Wine Bar** ($$–$$$) specializes in Swiss cuisine such as raclette and fondue. The **Poppy Room** is a family restaurant, the only one open for breakfast in winter, aside from the 24-hour deli. **Glacier Saloon** ($$) has steak sandwiches, finger food and salads.

The **Post Hotel** (522-3989; $$$) is recognized as serving the finest Continental cuisine in Lake Louise. For a special occasion, this is a wonderful place. **Deer Lodge** (522-3747; $$$) has homemade breads as well as innovative specials and pastries. **Lake Louise Station** (522-2600; $$–$$$) is a restored railway station with views of the mountains and freight trains that rumble past. The menu is quite extensive, with pastas, lamb, Alberta steaks and fresh salmon, among other dishes. Couples might like a table in the Killarney car, which was the private railroad car of a Canadian Railroad president.

Lake Louise Inn (522-3791) has three dining locations: The **Timberwolf** for pizza and pasta, the **hotel dining room** for lunch and dinner, and the **Explorer's Lounge**.

Après-ski/nightlife

The **Sitzmark Lounge** is the après-ski spot at the mountain. It's in the Whiskeyjack Lodge and has live entertainment on weekends. On sunny spring days, hang out on the deck of the **Glacier Gazebo** near the base lifts.

Après-ski and nightlife in town center in the hotels. At the Fairmont Chateau Lake Louise, The **Glacier Saloon** has a lively atmosphere and dancing, while the **Walliser Stube** is serene. Quiet conversation is possible at the **Saddleback Lounge** in the Lake Louise Inn and the Post Hotel's **Outpost**.

Other activities

The Banff/Lake Louise area has many opportunities for other winter sports such as **skating, ice fishing** and **ice climbing,** as well as **sightseeing, hot springs** and **museums;** see the Banff chapter for phone numbers.

Getting there and getting around

By air: Calgary Airport is served by major airlines, including Air Canada. Rocky Mountain Sky Shuttle (888-762-8754; 762-5200), Brewster Transportation (762-6700) or Laidlaw Transportation (762-9102) will get you from the airport to Banff or Lake Louise.

By car: Lake Louise Village is 115 miles west of Calgary and 36 miles from Banff.

Getting around: Bus service is available from the airport to most hotels. The Lake Louise shuttlebus is free and operates from most hotels to the resort. Buy the Tri-Area ski pass and bus transportation is included. We really recommend a car for extensive sightseeing.

Dining: $$$-Entrees $20+; $$-$10-20; $-less than $10. (Cdn $)
Accommodations: (double room) $$$$-$200+; $$$-$141-$200; $$-$81-$140; $-$80 and less.(Cdn $)

Marmot Basin

Jasper, Alberta
Canada

Summit elevation: 8,534 feet
Vertical drop: 2,944 feet
Base elevation: 5,590 feet

Address: P.O. Box 1300
Jasper, AB, Canada TOE 1E0
✆ **Area code:** 780
Snow report: 488-5909 (Edmonton)
Ski area phone: 852-3816 **Fax:** 852-3533
ⓘ **Toll-free reservations:** (877) 902-9455 and
(800) 473-8135
E-mail: info@skimarmot.com
Internet: www.skimarmot.com (resort)
www.jaspercanadianrockies.com (tourism bureau)

Expert:★★★★
Advanced:★★★★
Intermediate:★★★
Beginner:★★★ **Never-ever:**★★★

Number and types of lifts: 8–1 high-speed
quad, 1 quad, 1 triple chair, 3 double chairs,
2 surface lifts
Skiable acreage: 1,500 acres
Snowmaking: 1 percent
Uphill capacity: 11,931 skiers per hour
Snowboarding: Yes
Bed base: 5,500
Nearest lodging: About 11 miles away in Jasper
Resort child care: Yes, 19 months and older
Adult ticket, per day: $47-$52 (02/03 Cdn$
with GST)
Dining:★★★
Apr s-ski/nightlife:★★★
Other activities:★★★★

Far into the northland and separated from the hustle of Banff by a three-hour drive, Jasper is far enough north, and far enough from a major airport (Edmonton: four hours), that people aren't here by mistake or on a whim. They come for the scenery, the remoteness, the wonder of a herd of elk outside their hotel and the call of Canadian geese swooping over Lac Beauvert in the spring while the ski area still has winter snow.

The largest of the Canadian Rockies National Parks, Jasper has 4,200 square miles studded with lakes, dotted with wildlife, threaded by cross-country trails, and embroidered with spectacular drives such as the Icefields Parkway. Overloaded with tourists in the summer, it's delightfully uncrowded in the winter. It's an understatement to say you won't want to forget your camera for this vacation.

The townsite of Jasper (local-speak for "town") sprang up from a tent city in 1911, when the Grand Trunk Pacific Railway was laying steel up the Athabasca River Valley toward Yellowhead Pass, and its growth was rather helter-skelter. Hugging the Athabasca River and nestled against the train station, the town is relatively simple and nondescript, consisting of clapboard cottages, a steepled Lutheran church, stone houses and lodgings with no single architectural scheme. Here you'll find a friendly, relaxed and homey atmosphere. The townsite and its winter resort, Marmot Basin, are far less slick than the Banff resorts—the Alta to Deer Valley or the Mad River Glen to Stowe Mountain Resort.

Marmot Basin's base lodge, Caribou Chalet, is a beautiful 32,000-square-foot building that blends in with its surroundings. It houses a number of services including tickets, the ski and snowboard school, dinning and restaurant facilities, the Marmot Shop, the nursery, guest services and the rental and repair shop.

Marmot's big news is the development of Eagle Ridge, previously accessed only by hiking to earn your turns, and now serviced by a quad chair. Eagle Ridge has two faces: Eagle East and Chalet Slope. The 20 runs off the ridge include expert, advanced and intermediate terrain, as well as one novice trail that winds its way down the mountain, adding a total of about 148 acres. Phase 2 is underway for 2002/03, during which trees are being selectively removed from the already existing glade skiing to create more skiable terrain and more line choices. The resort is also expanding its terrain park, nearly doubling it in size and adding new terrain features and a boardercross course.

Mountain layout—Skiing

The area's one high-speed quad, Eagle Express, serves as the primary chair to the upper-mountain lifts. It can get somewhat crowded at times, so don't come back to the base during peak loading times, such as mornings before 9:30. Instead, try Caribou Chair on the lower mountain, far to the right, where there's rarely a wait. It has terrain for all abilities and also will get you to the upper-mountain lifts. You can purchase lift tickets here on the weekend. If you want to learn about the local history while you explore the mountain, join a mountain host for a complimentary tour.

◆◆ **Expert** ◆ **Advanced:** Marmot has tree-lined runs toward the bottom and wide-open bowls up top. Generally, the higher you go, the tougher the skiing gets. The Knob Chair takes you to the highest lift-served terrain. From the top of that lift, the hardiest hike the last 600 feet up to Marmot Peak. (Our vertical-foot and summit stats reflect the *lift-served* terrain, while those advertised by the area include this hike.) It's all Alpine bowls up here.

Experts will want to drop into the fine powder in outrageously large Dupres Bowl, with Dupres Chute dividing it from Charlie's Bowl, which is even steeper and stays untracked longer. Charlie's Bowl, with its 50+-degree entrance that mellows out to perhaps 42 degrees, should be a double-black diamond. It's where the true experts test their mettle. You can enter below the steepest part or hike up to enter off a cornice (when patrol opens that access point). We watched several hot skiers, including a patroller, take the fast way down Charlie's Bowl on their stomachs, sides and backs. Incidentally, Charlie's Bowl is named after Charlie Dupres, who died in an avalanche here many years ago. Needless to say, many opt for the "easier" Dupres Chutes and Bowl.

Another good choice for bowls and untracked powder is to stay high and to the right of The Knob (facing down the mountain). Experts have several different playgrounds all to themselves here—including McCready's Choice and Thunder Bowl.

Definitely head for the newly lift-served Eagle Ridge. Chalet Slope is a vast area of glades that are some of the most challenging and grin inducing we've ever skied. Powder lasts the longest here. The chutes, bowl and glades on Eagle East are an experience like no other at Marmot, with warning signs to sober you. Once you drop off the back side, you have no idea you're still at the resort, it's a true backcountry experience. Explore to your heart's content...or until your legs beg for a break. Keep an eye out for the boundary signs that funnel you back toward the trails, it's a long hike out otherwise.

There's also excellent glade skiing off the Triple Chair and Kiefer T-bar, both of which serve Caribou Ridge. Off to the right, facing downhill, you'll have an absolute blast in the trees in a black area misnamed Milk Run. Further down the mountain, drop into any woods that look tempting, especially those off green-circle Old Road.

Directly below the Eagle Express, Tranquilizer Chair and Triple Chair you'll find some super bump runs. Then go to the right of Knob Chair to hammer the most challenging bumps.

■ **Intermediate:** Every lift has an intermediate way down, even The Knob. Punch Bowl and Paradise are especially delightful runs. The Knob Traverse takes you high on the mountain where you'll have incredible views.

On blustery days, stay low on the mountain, where trees provide shelter from winds that sometimes block visibility on the naked summit. The intermediate runs on Chalet Slope off Eagle Ridge, which also hold snow longest, are excellent choices.

●● **Beginner** ● **Never-ever:** The three lifts at the base serve most of the lower-level terrain. Beginners have expansive mountain access, with 1,100 vertical feet on Eagle Express after you master terrain from the School House T-bar. You can even head up to Caribou Ridge for an above-treeline thrill where a wide trail, Basin Run, takes you safely back to the lower slopes. A novice run on Chalet Slope off Eagle Ridge provides gorgeous views from the top before you wind down the mountain.

 ## Mountain layout—Snowboarding

This season look for a new and expanded terrain park on Marmot Run in the upper area of the mountain. The park will nearly double in size, have more features (including tabletops, hips and spines), new rails, a permanent sound system and boardercross. There's also a nice natural pipe on Marmot Run.

But most riders come here for the freeriding. Off the Knob Chair, you can hike another 600 feet to catch freshies in Upper Basin or choose Peak Run to scoot over to the gully off High Traverse or Thunder Bowl. Whatever you do, don't skip Charlie's Bowl, which should really be designated a double-black diamond. Our staffer's teenaged stepson couldn't get enough of this bowl—there are so many lines to choose from, it's possible to literally spend all day here. Dupres Chutes are quite the challenge too.

You'll also want to test yourself on Eagle Ridge. Chalet Slope is a vast area of glades that will keep you challenged—and grinning. Powder lasts the longest over here too. The chutes, bowl and glades on Eagle East are an experience like no other at Marmot, with warning signs to sober you. In Eagle East you'll feel like you've left the resort behind. It's a true backcountry experience with heart-thumping terrain. The drop-ins to this area can be intimidating and often require traverses to get you where you want to go, just suck it up. Pay attention to boundary signs funneling you back to the trails or you'll have a long hike out.

Like to ride the trees? There's excellent glade riding off the Triple Chair on Caribou Ridge. Off to the right, facing downhill, you'll have an absolute blast in the trees in a black area misnamed Milk Run. Caribou Knoll is a real hoot too. Further down the mountain, drop into any woods that look tempting, especially those off green-circle Old Road.

Intermediates have great choices all over the mountain. There's very nice beginner terrain at the base of the mountain, though it's served by a T-bar, which can be a nightmare for snowboarders. After you feel comfortable on your board, you can head higher up the mountain via the chairs.

Mountain rating

Skiers and boarders of different levels can ride the same lifts, which makes Marmot great for family and group vacations. The terrain is fairly evenly divided between ability levels, with appropriate challenge, so everyone will enjoy themselves. If you're looking to improve your skills, Marmot is a perfect choice.

Cross-country and snowshoeing

This is prime ski touring and snowshoeing country, the scenery is guaranteed to delight and enthrall you. For a complete winter trail listing and guide, stop by Jasper National Parks Information Center or call 852-6176.

Jasper Park Lodge trails, about 19 km., are unparalleled for beauty and variety. The gentle, groomed and easily accessible trails wind around lake shores, Alpine meadows and forests. The easiest is Cavell, a 5 km. loop with the elk. The perimeter loop samples a little of everything the Jasper Park Lodge trails offer.

Near Jasper Townsite, a good beginner trail is **Whistlers Campground Loop,** 4.5 km., which is level and lit for night skiing. **Pyramid Bench Trail** is 4.7 km., rated intermediate and overlooks the Athabasca River Valley. **Patricia Lake Circle,** 5.9 km. and rated intermediate (recommendation is to follow the trail clockwise), provides stunning views of Mt. Edith Cavell, the region's dramatically sloped peak. Most lodges have trail maps.

For **guided cross-country skiing, backcountry and snowshoeing tours,** contact Edge Control, 852-4945; Beyond the Beaten Path, 852-5650; Overlander Trekking & Tours, 852-4056 (snowshoe tours only); or Alpine Art, 852-3709. Ask about rentals and/or instruction.

A full day's ski over Maccarib Pass from the Marmot Basin Road on the north shore of Amethyst Lake leads to Tonquin Valley Lodge, hearty home-cooked meals and welcome beds. Contact **Tonquin Valley Ski Tours,** Box 550, Jasper, Alberta T0L 1E0; 852-3909.

Lessons [2002/03, Cdn$ with GST]

Group lessons: For all abilities, $30 for two hours, ski or snowboard (early bird, $25).

Never-ever package: Includes lift pass, two-hour lesson and ski or snowboard equipment for $59.

Private lessons: $59 an hour, with multi-hour discounts.

Special programs: Choose from moguls, carving, technical improvement, snowboard freestyle camps, and powder; meet at 1:30 p.m. daily, $39. Ski Improvement Weeks (Monday to Friday or Friday to Tuesday) include five two-hour sessions, video, a fun race and a Jasper Night Out; cost is $120. New for 2002/03, the Outer Limits Mountain Experience program offers guided tours and instruction for strong intermediates and advanced skiers and riders who want a taste of adventure in Eagle East; $45.

Child care [2002/03, Cdn$ with GST]

Ages: 19 months through 6 years.

Cost: All-day care is $35. Hourly rate is $6; extra child in family, $5/hour.

Reservations: Call 852-3816.

Children's lessons: Ages 4-5, 90-minute lesson in morning or afternoon, $27 includes rentals (five kids per instructor). For ages 6-12, there are several options. A full-day program, ski or snowboard, costs $65 (includes lunch). A two-hour group lesson, ski or snowboard, costs $24. Learn-to-ski or snowboard lessons are $65. One-hour private lessons are $59. Kids 13 and older do not have full-day programs: two-hour group lessons, specialty ski clinics and half-day snowboard freestyle camps cost $30; learn-to-ski or snowboard, including two-hour lesson, rentals and ticket, costs $54; a one-hour private costs $59; Ski & Snowboard Weeks (Monday to Friday or Friday to Tuesday) include five two-hour sessions, video, a fun race and a Jasper Night Out for $96, or full day with lunch for $260.

Lift tickets (2002/03, Cdn$ with GST)

	Adult	Junior (6-12)
One day	$52	$20
Three days	$152 ($50+/day)	$60 ($20/day)
Five days	$252 ($50+/day)	$100 ($20/day)

Who skis free: Children 5 and younger.

Who skis at a discount: Youth/student prices (ages 13–25) are $42 for one day, with multi-day discounts; college-age students must be full time and present a valid student ID. Seniors ages 65 and older pay $37 for one day, with multi-day discounts. Early season rates are lower. During the Jasper in January winter festival, everyone 13 and older pays $37 per day, $20 for juniors.

Accommodations

The resort does not have any mountainside lodging—you'll stay in or around Jasper townsite. As one friendly desk clerk told us, with perhaps the exception of the Fairmont Jasper Park Lodge, rates are often negotiable in winter—Jasper's quiet season. Ask about specials, discounts, AAA/CAA rates, etc. For example, he quoted us a rack rate of $236 for one room, but with a little prodding, that can come down as low as $127. Many of the lodges listed have ski packages, so be sure to ask.

Jasper Tourism and Commerce (Box 98, Jasper, Alberta, T0E 1E0; call 780-852-3858) will send a ski vacation planner that includes rates. Central reservations at (877) 902-9455 has a wide selection of accommodations, activities and tours, transportation and ski packages. This number is good for most all of the Canadian Rockies. For the Jasper area in particular, call **Jasper Central Reservations** at (800) 473-8135. The number is manned October through April. The rest of the year it's an answering machine, but calls are returned.

Although the **Fairmont Jasper Park Lodge** (852-3301 or 800-441-1414; $$–$$$$) is one of The Fairmont Hotels, don't expect a chateau. Set on 900 acres a few miles from the townsite, it's a grouping of traditional log cabins from the 1920s and new cedar chalets with spacious modern suites, all elegantly rustic. The lodging buildings are linked by pathways along Lac Beauvert to the main building, which is built like a hunting lodge and houses all the restaurants, night spots and shops. The lodge suggests all the best qualities you'd expect from someone's wilderness summer camp, combined with the amenities you expect from a fine resort. We found delightful staff and enchanting rooms with beds that gave us one of the best night's sleep we've ever had. Jasper's best restaurant is here (see *Dining*).

Pyramid Lake Resort (888-852-4900; $$–$$$) began its life as a local fishing village and now has skating and cross-country trails at your doorstep. The resort's wilderness setting is stunning, ideal for backcountry skiing fans and others who prefer quiet, remote places. Most of the modern chalet-style accommodations have lovely lake views, private whirlpools, kitchenettes and fireplaces. A spectacular restaurant opened in 2002 (see *Dining*) and new cabins will open for the 2002/03 season.

The upscale **Chateau Jasper** (852-5644; 800-661-9323; $$–$$$$), formerly Royal Canadian Lodge—Jasper, is about a 15-minute walk from "downtown" Jasper and has an indoor pool and whirlpool, Sorrentino's Bistro Bar (see *Dining*), and heated underground parking. The Chateau offers a shuttle to town and back.

In town, **Jasper Inn** (852-4461; 800-661-1933; $–$$$$) has spacious standard rooms, studios, suites, loft units and one- to two-bedroom condo-style units. There's an indoor pool, steam room, sauna, Jacuzzi and coin laundry. Very good restaurant on premises (see *Dining*). The renovated **Sawridge Hotel & Conference Center Jasper** (852-5111; 800-661-6427; $$-$$$$) offers deluxe standard rooms to luxury parlor suites that reflect a Canadian Native American flair. As you enter the lobby, your attention is drawn down the stairs to the three-story fireplace and a sky-lit atrium. Indoor pool, outdoor hot tubs, Finnish sauna and a full-service spa.

The **Astoria** (852-3351; 800-661-7343; $$) is a small hotel with charmingly renovated guestrooms. **Whistlers Inn** (852-3361; 800-282-9919; $$) has nice standards, deluxes and suites. Enjoy steam room, rooftop hot tub, two restaurants, pub and a gift shop.

Marmot Lodge (852-4471; 888-852-7737; $-$$$) has rooms with kitchens and fireplaces. Indoor pool, sauna and whirlpool located on the premises. No charge for children under age 12. **The Athabasca Hotel** (852-3386; 887-542-8422; $-$$), one of Jasper's original lodgings, is close to the bus and VIA RAIL station.

If you fly into or out of Edmonton, stay at the **Fantasyland Hotel** (800-661-6454; 444-3000; $$$-$$$$). Every floor is decorated in a theme such as Hollywood, Canadian Pacific Railway, Roman, and so forth. It adjoins the West Edmonton Mall—part shopping center, part amusement park, it covers 48 city blocks and has an indoor water park and roller coaster.

Dining

On the mountain, Marmot Basin has four places to eat. Upstairs in the Caribou Chalet, the **Caribou Café** ($-$$) has sit-down service, run by the Fairmont Jasper Park Lodge, with excellent sandwiches, burgers and salads. Ask to sit by the windows, views are spectacular. There's also a **cafeteria** ($) in the base lodge. **Paradise Chalet** at mid-mountain has a café and lounge ($), as well as a nice outdoor deck. On busy days, eat lunch before 11:45 or after 1:15. **Eagle Chalet** ($-$$) at mid-mountain is a cozy rustic restaurant with a fireplace to warm you. Or sit on its big outdoor deck that allows you to watch skiers and riders in the bowls as you eat a hearty meal. There's a shooter bar too.

Surprisingly, this little secluded town has some excellent restaurants and an incredible variety as well.

At the lakeview **Edith Cavell Dining Room** (852-6052; $$$) in the Fairmont Jasper Park Lodge the dress is resort casual, the setting is china on white linen, the service is attentive and the food is the best in the area. The menu includes game specialties; be sure to save room for dessert. For breakfast, **The Meadows** ($-$$) serves wholesome food in a country setting; we recommend the mouthwatering breakfast buffet. Lunch is available her too.

The Pines (852-4900; $$-$$$) at Pyramid Lake Resort opened winter 2002. A huge stone fireplace, soaring ceilings and views over Pyramid Lake set the stage. The menu includes appetizers such as Rocky Mountain mushroom bisque and entrées such as rack of lamb and smoked chicken and shrimp carbonnara (delicious!). Portions are huge.

In town, **The Inn Restaurant** (852-4461; $$) at Jasper Inn offers a cozy, casual atmosphere. The creative menu includes such appetizers as citrus-marinated chicken brochettes with mushroom pierogies topped with mango sour cream, and pernod-soaked scallops served over a spring roll-wrapped potato triangle with wilted baby spinach and wasabi crème.

Andy's Bistro (852-4559; $$), new and very popular, especially with locals, has a friendly, intimate setting downtown. The moderate menu emphasizes Swiss and Canadian cuisine. **Walter's Dining Room** (852-5111; $$) in the Sawridge Hotel specializes in tasty Canadian and continental dishes. Check out the stuffed wildlife as you dine. Save room for dessert. **Tonquin Prime Rib Village** (852-4966; $$) serves steaks, prime rib, barbecued ribs and

Dining: $$$-Entrees $20+; $$-$10-20; $-less than $10 (CdnS).
Accommodations: (double room) $$$$-$200+; $$$-$141-$200; $$-$81-$140; $-$80 and less (CdnS).

seafood. It has a bar and a beautiful view. Make reservations. **Fiddle River Seafood Company** (852-3032; $$–$$$) gets raves for fresh fish cooking. **Embers Steakhouse** (852-4471; $$) serves light and healthy cuisine (beef, local fish) in a casually elegant restaurant. **Sorrentino's Bistro Bar** (852-5644; $$$) in the Chateau Jasper features Italian fare.

Families should try **L&W Restaurant** (852-4114; $$), with an atrium setting and remarkably broad menu. Very good Greek cuisine; also choose from steaks, seafood, pasta and pizza. Kids' menu with prices from $5-$7 Cdn$. The **Whistle Stop Bar** (852-3361; $) at Whistlers Inn serves a bar menu. The **Something Else Restaurant** (852-3233; $$) is also good for families.

The area's best sushi is served at **Oka Sushi** (852-3301; $$) in the Fairmont Jasper Park Lodge, but also popular is **Denjiro** (852-3780; $$), with Japanese entrées and a sushi bar. **Miss Italia** (852-4002; $$) is the spot for Italian cooking.

Mountain Foods Cafe (852-4050; $) is an affordable sit-down or take-out restaurant/deli. For pizza by the slice, head to the local's favorite, **Truffles and Trout** (852-9676; $). Pizza and other Italian dishes are served at **Jasper Pizza Place** (852-3225; $).

The **Soft Rock Café** ($), with Internet service, serves the area's best breakfast, all day. Don't miss **Papa George's Restaurant** (852-3351; $–$$) in the Astoria Hotel on the main drag. It has a rich, lengthy history in Jasper and serves some of the best Italian food in the Rockies. **Bear Paw's Bakery** (852-3233; $) sells freshly baked goods daily.

Coco's Café (852-4550; $), on Patricia Street, is a locals' favorite with awesome little dishes, pastries and Jasper's best coffee. They cater to vegans, vegetarians and carnivores.

 ## Après-ski/nightlife

Jasper is not known for rocking nightlife, but it's not dead, either. The **Atha-B Club** in Athabasca Hotel has the liveliest dancing in town. The hotel also has **O'Shea's**, an Irish pub. **Whistle Stop** at Whistlers Inn is a good pub-type nightspot with darts, pool and big-screen sports. **De'd Dog Pub** in the Astoria Hotel is a locals' hangout that draws folks of mixed ages; light food is available. **Fireside Lounge** in Marmot Lodge has nightly entertainment. **Pete's** attracts a younger crowd with disco and occasional live music. **Downstream** is a no-smoking bar with good chicken wings.

At Fairmont Jasper Park Lodge, the **Emerald Lounge** has hearty après-ski snacks, and **Tent City Sports Lounge** recalls the history of the lodge and has lively entertainment.

Other activities

We know part of the reason visitors come to Jasper National Park is to enjoy the pristine wilderness and wildlife. There are a variety of ways to do this. Here are just a few:

Jasper in January is the area's annual winter festival. Lift tickets drop considerably, as do lodging rates. Activities include demo days, a mountain-to-valley relay race, ice and snow sculpting, canyon crawls, snowshoeing, tobogganing, chili cook-off, taste of the town food sampler, ice rescue demonstrations and more. Whew—let's just say it's a lot of fun! And don't overlook the **Jasper Music and Wine Festival** in April. You can still enjoy spring skiing at Marmot, lots of wine-tasting, fabulous food and great evening concerts.

One of the most unusual—and unforgettable—adventures is a **Canyon Icewalk,** a guided tour through Maligne Canyon. You'll hike a little over a mile through a 6- to 20-foot-wide gorge on the frozen river past ice caves and frozen waterfalls. You'll need to be in reasonable physical shape to crawl up some head-high waterfalls and squeeze through narrow spots. A night crawl, wearing headlamps to guide you, is a true other-world experience. Tours last two to three hours and are available after the river's frozen enough to walk on, usually from December through March. Winter boots and crampon-like soles provided. Call Overlander Trekking & Tours, 852-4056. Cost is about $35 per person. Tours also provided by Beyond the Beaten Path, 852-5650, or Jasper Adventure Center at 852-5595.

Ice skating on a lake and sleigh rides are available at Fairmont Jasper Park Lodge. Go dogsledding with Overlander Trekking & Tours, 852-4056. Heliskiing in Valemount, British Columbia, 56 miles away along a scenic drive, is available mid-February to mid-April. Overlander Trekking & Tours, 852-4056. Also Robson HeliMagic, 566-4700. Snowfarmers (250-566-9161) in Valemont has, get this...snowmobile-serviced skiing and riding. Maximum six guests, $250 Cdn$ per person. Snowfarmers also provides snowmobile touring.

Jasper Activity Centre (852-3381) on Pyramid Lake Road has swimming, curling, squash, racquetball and skating. Minor league hockey games on Saturdays and Sundays.

Sightseeing companies run bus tours to the more scenic vistas, including the Icefields Parkway. Call Brewster Transportation, 852-3332, or Jasper Adventure Center, 852-5595. Plan to take one day to drive along the Icefields Parkway (Hwy. 93)—you won't be sorry.

Wildlife spotting is a must-do: You're very likely to see mule deer, bighorn sheep, mountain goats and elk; if you're lucky, you'll also see moose, caribou, wolves and coyotes.

The exhibits at Jasper-Yellowhead Museum and Archives (852-3013) highlight Jasper's history and human heritage, such as the early explorers, the fur trade, the railway and skiing.

The sports shop at Marmot Basin has some very nice logo clothing, as well as the usual snowsports-related necessities. Downtown Jasper has some great specialty shops like Freewheel, Gravity Gear and Jungle Wear, along with the usual touristy merchandise shops. We found the best selection of merchandise for quality, selection and price at the stores at the Fairmont Jasper Park Lodge. The downside is that most of these shops are only open 10 a.m.-5 p.m., prime skiing hours.

You can also go to the movies. Also, Arts Jasper (852-3964) presents arts performances—dance, theatre and music. Make sure to pick up a free winter guide for a complete overview of activities and attractions in Jasper.

Getting there and getting around

By air: Edmonton has the closest airport. Air Canada and Canadian Airlines have the most frequent flights from most North American cities, but Delta, American, Alaska and Northwest also fly here. If you don't rent a car, Greyhound operates daily service from Edmonton and Vancouver; call 421-4211.

By car: From Edmonton, Jasper is 225 miles west on Hwy. 16. The ski area is 12 miles south of Jasper via Hwy. 93, 93A and Marmot Basin Road. Jasper is about 170 miles north of Banff.

By train: VIA RAIL operates service to Jasper from Edmonton and Vancouver on its newly restored '50s-style art deco train, the Canadian. U.S. travel agents have more information. Ask about the Snow Train to Jasper.

Getting around: A car is best here. The ski area is a few miles from the town and lodging. Brewster Transportation operates the Banff-Jasper shuttlebus and the Marmot Basin shuttle into the townsite; call 852-3332.

Fernie Alpine Resort

British Columbia

Summit elevation:	**6,316 feet**
Vertical drop:	**2,816 feet**
Base elevation:	**3,505 feet**

Address: 5339 Fernie Ski Hill Rd., Fernie, British Columbia, Canada V0B 1M6

Area code: 250

Ski area phone: 423-4655

Snow report: 423-3555 or (800) 258-7669 x1

Toll-free reservations: (800) 258-7669

Fax: 423-6644

E-mail: info@skifernie.com

Internet: www.skifernie.com

Expert:★★★★★
Advanced:★★★★★
Intermediate:★★★
Beginner:★★
Never-ever:★

Number and types of lifts: 10—2 high-speed quads, 2 quads, 2 triples, 4 surface lifts

Skiable acreage: 2,504 acres

Snowmaking: 5 percent (125 acres)

Uphill capacity: 13,716 per hour

Snowboarding: Yes

Bed base: 4,299 (mountain); 2,247 (town)

Nearest lodging: Slopeside, ski-in/ski-out

Resort child care: Yes, newborn

Adult ticket, per day: $52-$56 (01/02 Cdn$ with GST)

Dining:★★★
Apr s-ski/nightlife: ★★
Other activities:★★★

Perhaps you've heard the fervent whispers about Fernie already: You'll find some of the steepest terrain you'll ever see in-bounds, and what's out-of-bounds is free for the taking too. The snow is unbelievable—deep and light and almost magical. The terrain seems unlimited—if you see it, and can get to it, you can ski it. There are no crowds, so you have the mountain practically to yourself. Of course, all this tantalizing lore is shared with the necessary forewarning, "I'm only telling you this because I *know* you'll keep it to yourself."

Fernie is not for the faint of heart. While every bowl has some groomed terrain, most terrain is left the way Mother Nature made it—and that's the way Fernie's fans want it to be. Fernie has some of the steepest in-bounds terrain you'll find at any resort in North America. If you suddenly come upon avalanche warning signs, pay close attention. One section can be marked green to go, while just a few hundred feet farther, you'll find danger signs telling you to steer clear. About 60 professional patrollers, all trained in avalanche safety and explosives, keep Fernie under watchful eye.

Fernie, tucked into the craggy Lizard Range of the Canadian Rockies, is several hours from civilization and caters to a casual crowd that comes here for one thing and one thing only: the allure of the mountain. It can easily be lumped in with other resorts known to worship the zen of skiing: Red Mountain, Alta, Snowbird, Crested Butte, Jay Peak. In fact, it is reminiscent of Red Mountain and Rossland, only a bit more grown up. Much of the mountainside village is new and includes lodging, restaurants, apres-ski bars, coffee shops and a grocery store.

The turn-of-the-century coal mining town of Fernie is just 3 miles away. The main street, 2nd Avenue, is actually parallel to the road you'll travel on comin into town. Fernie burned down twice during the early 1900s and when it was rebuilt in 1910 builders were required by code to use brick and stone. The result is a colorful blend of shops, restaurants, clubs and bars.

Fernie is ripe with legends, including the powder-making Griz, honored with an annual winter carnival, and the curse-bearing Ghostrider, who appears in the shadows of Mount Hosmer. Ask any local; they love to share their history.

Mountain layout—Skiing

Fernie consists of five seemingly limitless bowls of pure delight that dump you into gut-wrenching steeps and chutes, gnarly trees, gentle glades and thrilling trails. All have terrain for all abilities, it's really a matter of taking the time to totally explore each and deciding on your favorite. It's easy to spend all day exploring one bowl. If you can see it, you can ski it—and sometimes you can't see it till you work your way *to* it! Obviously, the more adventurous you are, the more you'll want to take a traverse to its end. There's nothing more exciting than deciding whether to duck down or keep going in search of the goods. It's a good idea to take a complimentary mountain tour on your first day so you can become familiar with how to travel the mountain; meet at the carousel in front of Guest Services at 9:30 a.m. and 1 p.m.

◆◆ **Expert** ◆ **Advanced:** What can we say? It doesn't get better than this! Explore to your heart's content. Some traverses cross very steep terrain and if you're prone to vertigo, be prepared, but it's worth getting over it. I'm sure we don't have to tell you that the best goods don't have names, but we'll start you off with some suggestions. Find the "idiot's traverse" in Timber Bowl and head to some *swe-e-eet* trees off Diamond Back and in Anaconda Glades and Gotta Go, or head to Cedar Bowl and jump into King Fir and Cedar Ridge. Bootleg Glades have a sphincter-tightening drop-in, but you'll enjoy the goods once you overcome it. Surprize got its name after an avalanche etched it into the mountain.

After a powder dump, take the Lizard Traverse at least halfway across before dropping into wide-open floatable powder. Siberia Bowl has some great powder stashes too. On clear days after a powder dump, follow the "leaping lemmings" line out of Currie Bowl and up to Polar Peak. And days after deep snow, when much of the mountain is skied off, don't despair, you'll still find powder in the trees off Decline, leading into Easter Bowl and Lizard Bowl. Skip the chutes off the ridge between Currie and Lizard bowls if there hasn't been a fresh snowfall—otherwise they are guaranteed death slides. Check with the ski patrol before going into the out-of-bounds Fish Bowl, while we were there two rescues were necessary.

■ **Intermediate:** If you're an intermediate who loves long cruisers, you'll get bored rather quickly. But if you're ready to test your skills and move to the ungroomed and trees, this is the mountain for you. All of the bowls have very nice intermediate terrain, just search for what you want: small bumps, ungroomed, semi-steep or trees. It's easy to dip in and out off the groomed trails as you gain confidence. You'll have great fun on Currie Powder and Currie Glades, wandering farther afield as you get more adventurous. The trees in Timber Bowl and Currie Bowl are fabulous ego-boosters. Dancer, Cascade and Bow in Lizard Bowl are wide-open slopes perfect for learning powder.

●● **Beginners** ● **Never-ever:** While Fernie has excellent beginner terrain that's nicely separated from other ability levels, it's still adventurous by most standards. Your best bet is to join a ski week group, where instructors can help you overcome any trepidation you may have. The word on the street is that if you learn to ski here, you'll advance more rapidly than at most other resorts. This is a very challenging mountain.

Mountain layout—Snowboarding

While Fernie has a meticulously groomed halfpipe and terrain park, served by the Deer Chair, most riders come here for the natural terrain. Snowboarders will find Fernie a challenge simply because of all the traverses. To access the best-kept secrets, you'll have to follow some harrowing traverses that are lo-o-ong excursions. However, the snowboarders we talked to all said the great terrain is worth every bit of the agony it requires to get to it. Your best bet is to explore each bowl thoroughly before moving on to the next one so as to minimize some of the traversing (such as to get back from the Haul Back T-bar). You definitely want to avoid the very long run-out at the bottom of Falling Star, where you'll end up walking out—most riders only use it when they return from hiking in the backcountry on this side of the mountain.

Mountain rating

This is a mountain for those seeking adventure. If you're a powder hound, it's worth paying extra to join the First Tracks program—you'll ski freshies while others have to wait in line for the lifts to open. Experts and advanced skiers will be ecstatic here. Intermediates who want to push the envelope will find new levels of thrills here, but lower intermediates and those looking for cruisers will be bummed. Most beginners and never-evers should join a ski week program so they aren't overly intimidated by the mountain.

Cross-country and snowshoeing

Fernie Alpine Resort has 10 km. of trails in a figure-eight loop, good for both skating and classic. Trail usage is free; lessons and rentals available. Guided cross-country tours are available. Cost is $27 for two hours, $37 for three hours; rentals included. You also can cross-country ski at the **Fernie Golf & Country Club;** trails are beginner to intermediate.

Guided snowshoe tours with a naturalist are a great aerobic workout, plus you'll be entertained with local legends and lore. Did you know that Fernie burned down twice and you can see exactly where those fires stopped on the mountain by looking at the tree growth? Cost is $27 for two hours, $37 for three hours; snowshoes and poles included. Book through Guest Services.

The network of **mountain biking trails** found throughout Fernie are reported to be excellent for snowshoeing. Pick up a copy of the trail guide at local retailers.

Lessons [2002/03, Cdn$ with tax]

Group Lessons: Skiers up to level 6 and snowboarders up to intermediate level pay $30 for a half-day lesson; multiday discounts are available. Ski levels 7-9 and snowboard levels intermediate-advanced choose from specialty clinics focusing on style and technique, powder and crud, beginner bumps, and experts only, for $41.

Never-ever package: The package, which includes a beginner lift pass, rentals and half-day group lesson (skiing, telemarking or snowboarding), costs $54. Fernie has an excellent learn-to-ski or -snowboard week package that we recommend to help never-evers feel comfortable with this adventurous mountain: Three-day programs start on Monday or Thursday and include rentals, full lift pass and Ski Week lessons (*see Special Programs* below) for $296; youth (13-17) pay $263.

Private Lessons: Skiing, snowboarding or telemarking (three people max) cost $62 for 1 hour; $107 for 2 hours; $163 for 3 hours; each additional person per hour, $24. Group privates, for up to three people, are half day (3 hours), $193; full day (6 hours), $375; early bird or late day (1.5 hours), $77.

Special Programs: Ultimate Edge Ski & Snowboard Weeks will help you rise to the challenge of the mountain and are highly recommended. This three- or six-day program gives you the same instructor every day and includes a Nastar race, video analysis and après-ski reception. For ages 13 and up. Three-day weeks run Mon. to Wed. or Thurs. to Sat., $153; six days run Mon. to Sat., $274.

Ask about Weekend Workshops, offered on certain dates and focusing on certain skills, for ski levels 7-9 and snowboard levels intermediate-advanced.

First Tracks is an early-start program (7:45 a.m.) with lift line priority only available on days that have fresh powder, $53.50 (lift ticket extra). Book the night before. Skiers and riders who are intermediates or better can hire a mountain guide for the day and get lift line priority too (minimum of two people per guide, ages 6 and up). Cost is $80 per person. Mountain Guides and First Tracks combined, $114.

Child care (2002/03, Cdn$ with tax)

Ages: Newborn-6 years of age.

Costs: A full day is $56; half day, $28. Hourly rates, $7/hour. Ask about discounts for multiple children. Free snacks are provided; lunch is available by request for $4. Kids 3-4 years old can take a one-hour group lesson, booked through day care, for $15.

Reservations: Required, at least 24 hours in advance. Resort Kids Daycare is a safe, licensed facility for children. Day care is nut free, so do not send nut products with your child. Bring health insurance information, a small recent photograph, indoor shoes, allergy information and snacks, lunch and drinks. All children's food, drinks and clothing must be labeled.

Other Options: Kids Activity Night is a supervised evening of activities (6-8 p.m.) for ages 6-12. Register for specific activities—such as meeting the sled dogs or horses that pull sleighs—or join for a whole week of fun (arts and crafts, brain teaser games, writing and starring in your own movie). Activities vary nightly. Child must be registered with daycare by 4:30 p.m. that day, $15 per child.

Children's Lessons: Full-day programs (skiing and snowboarding) for ages 5-12 cost $43; half day is $27; multiday rates available. Supervised lunch, $15. Kids 13 and up take adult lessons. The never-ever package, which includes a beginner lift pass, rentals and half-day group lesson, costs $42. Fernie has an excellent learn-to-ski or –snowboard week package that we recommend to help young never-evers feel comfortable with this adventurous mountain: Three-day programs start on Monday or Thursday and include rentals, full lift pass and Ski Week lessons (*see below*), $139.

Ski Week is five days of 4-hour lessons for ages 8–14. Meets Mon. to Fri., 10:30 a.m.–3:30 p.m.; cost is $161, supervised lunch is $15 per day. Ultimate Edge Ski & Snowboard Weeks will help kids ages 5–12 rise to the challenge of the mountain and are highly recommended. This three- or six-day program gives kids the same instructor every day and includes a Nastar race, video analysis and après-ski reception. Three-day weeks run Mon.-Wed. or Thurs. to Sat., cost is $109; six days run Mon. to Sat., $163.

Lift tickets (2002/03, Cdn$ without tax)

	Adult	Child (6-12)
One day	$56	$15
Three days	$156 ($52/day)	$45 ($15/day)
Five days	$260 ($52/day)	$75 ($15/day)

Who skis free: Ages 5 and younger.

Who skis at a discount: Youth (13-17) and seniors (65 and up) pay $45 per day; three days or more cost $40 per day. Students (18-24) who are full-time students with ID pay youth prices. The Mighty Moose lift is $15 for all ages.

Accommodations

Fernie Alpine Resort Central Reservations (800-258-7669 or 403-209-3321) creates custom packages including lodging, lift tickets, flights and car rentals. Most of the mountain village accommodations are newly built, providing state-of-the-art amenities and luxuries.

The magnificent riverstone-and-log **Lizard Creek Lodge** (423-2057 or 877-228-1948; $$$-$$$$), steps away from the Elk Quad chairlift but secluded off to one side of the mountain, does a marvelous job of blending luxury with rustic splendor. Each unit has a fully equipped kitchen, fireplace and balcony. Outdoor heated pool, spa, fitness center, gourmet dining, underground parking.

Cornerstone Lodge (423-4655 or 800-258-7669; $$-$$$$)is smack in the middle of the slopeside village and near the Deer Chair. All rooms are comfortably furnished deluxe suites with gas fireplace, fully equipped kitchen, washer and dryer, and balcony. Warm colors throughout. Indoor hot tub, exercise room, underground parking.

Snow Creek Lodge (800-667-9911; $$-$$$$) is where you'll find studios and one- and two-bedroom suites built with stone and logs. Units have decks, full kitchen and gas fireplace. Guests have a heated outdoor swimming pool, two whirlpools and a fitness room.

We didn't have time to check out the various **townhouse** and **chalet** options that also are available, but be sure to inquire about them if you'd rather stay in lodging of this kind.

Griz Inn (423-9221 or 800-661-0118; $$-$$$$), built in 1982 as the second on-hill accommodation, has simply decorated studios and two-bedroom lofts. For the price, we recommend some of the more recently built lodgings.

If you're on a budget but want to be on the mountain, stay at the older but comfortable **Wolf's Den Lodge** (423-4655 or 800-258-7669; $$), where standard hotel rooms have coffee makers and small refrigerators.

In town:

If you really enjoy nightlife and dining out, stay in town instead of at the mountain.

The upscale **Best Western Fernie Mountain Lodge** (423-5500; $$-$$$) has deluxe guest rooms and some themed Jacuzzi suites. Indoor pool, hot tubs, fitness center, common laundry facilities, restaurant and lounge. You can choose from standard hotel and junior studio rooms at the stone-and-log **Park Place Lodge** (423-6871 or 888-381-7275; $$). Some rooms have kitchenettes and mini-refrigerators. Indoor pool and indoor hot tub.

Riverside Mountain Hotel & Chalets (877-423-5600; $-$$$$) is a resort with a range of accommodations, from value-priced hotel rooms to luxury chalets. **Cedar Lodge** (423-

4622 or 800-977-2977; $-$$) is an older property with prices to reflect it; microwave and fridge in rooms. **Three Sisters Motel** (423-4438 or 877-326-8888; $-$$) is a basic motel.

Choose from two hostels, **SameSun Hostel** (423-4492 or 877-56-CARVE; $), part of a chain that also packages guided tours, and **The Raging Elk Hostel** (423-6811; $). Seasoned hostelers told us SameSun has nicer beds but can be noisy, while Raging Elk is less polished but has a separate common area for people who party or just want to stay up late.

Dining

For such a remote and tiny town, you'll find a remarkable choice of good dining, both on the mountain and in town. We suspect that as Fernie becomes a bigger blip on the radar screen, more skilled chefs will find their way here.

On the mountain:

You'd be missing out on a special gourmet experience if you don't eat at **Lizard Creek Lodge** (423-2057; $$$; reservations recommended). Ask to be seated near the grand riverstone fireplace. The Chilean sea bass and filet mignon were both superb. Make sure to try one of the local Okanagan Valley wines to compliment your meal. The fondue lunch, served in the lounge, is said to be excellent.

Gabriella's Restaurant (423-7388; $) serves heaping plates of pasta and sandwiches on focaccia. **Kelsey's Restaurant** (423-2444; $-$$), in Cornerstone Lodge, is a chain pub-style restaurant with a rustic interior and a broad menu.

We rarely say this, but avoid the **Powderhorn Grill** (423-4656; $$) in the Griz Inn, you'll be sorely disappointed and it won't be a cheap lesson either. Locals tell us this is common knowledge, we just wish someone had shared it with us *before* we ate there.

The Mean Bean (423-2440; $), in Cornerstone Lodge, is the place to go for Starbucks coffee and pastries, as well as light lunches. **The Grizzly Bar** ($) lays out a mean salad bar, plus you'll find a basic bar menu for lunch. Downstairs is the **cafeteria.** For a quick energy fix, check out **Spuds "eh,"** a meals-on-wheels food truck that drops anchor in front of the ticket window and serves handcut fries. We prefer spuds with gravy poutine, yum!

In town:

The most delightful culinary surprise we had was at **The Curry Bowl** (423-2695; $$). The owners say they specialize in "enlightened Asian cuisine" and we say, "that's an under-statement." Their Vietnamese summer rolls are a fabulous—and perfect—blend of chicken and shrimp wrapped in rice paper with cucumbers, red peppers, bean sprouts and fresh mint served with a sweet chili sauce. Absolutely to die for! For entrees, which top out at $12.95, you must try either the Mango Shrimp Curry—shrimp and mango in a fusion of sweet Thai coconut milk and spicy Indian Vindaloo sauce—or the Green Coconut Curry—creamy coconut milk with traditional spices in green-chili-based Thai curry with pumpkin, green beans, peppers and chicken. Creative desserts top off the culinary experience. Whatever your drink preference—beer, martinis, scotch, cognac, port, sherry, BC wines, loose-leaf teas—they have it. They don't take reservations, so get there early; otherwise, expect at least an hour wait (it *is* worth the wait).

The Wood Bistro and Tapas Bar (423-7749; $$) is another gourmet experience in town with a lively jazz-and-blues-influenced ambiance. They serve only BC wines with their creative menu. The fois gras filled Alberta beef tenderloin gets raves from locals.

For a rare dining environment, go to **The Old Elevator** (423-7115; $$-$$$; reservations recommended), a grain feed store and grain elevator built in 1908 that have been lovingly refurbished. Music of the '20s, big band and swing add to the step-back-in-time impression, and stained glass windows add mystery to the mountain views. Continental menu includes steak, veal, seafood, chicken and creative pastas. We enjoyed the chicken Kotopola, a chicken breast with pistachio nuts and Vermouth Buerre Blanc.

Locals recommend "Pasta Tuesdays" at **Boston Pizza** (423-2634; $-$$) in the Best Western Fernie Mountain Lodge, where you'll get heaping plates of pasta for $6.25-$8.75 Cdn$. **The Pub Bar & Grill** (423-6871; $) in the Park Place Lodge is the place for pub grub. Choose from three Chinese restaurants with take-out; locals tell us the best is **Ginger Beef** (423-4611; $).

Relax with a cup of gourmet coffee, cappuccino or espresso at **Cappuccino Corner** on 2nd Avenue. We can't help but rave about the black raspberry mocha. Homemade soups and baked goods round out the choices. Board games and six computers with Internet access make this more than a coffee shop.

 ## Après-ski/nightlife

Crowds start gathering at **The Grizzly Bar** even before the lifts shut down, and it revs up to a loud hum with tall tales of the day's skiing and riding; live music and dancing on weekends. **Kelsey's** is the other on-mountain destination for a lively crowd. A more sedate crowd heads to the **Lizard Creek Lodge Lounge,** where you can be swallowed up by leather chairs and couches while you watch night fall over the mountain or watch the big-screen TV. Appetizers and a menu are available here.

In town, **The Pub Bar & Grill** in the Park Place Lodge has "wing nights" on Tuesdays, drawing a lively and hungry crowd. Play pool, foosball, pub-pong or watch your favorite sports on scattered TV screens here. **Eldorado Lounge** is the town's most aerobic night-club, with a dance floor that's hopping every night but Sunday. Dance to live music and DJs or play pool at **The Northern.**

For those who want a quieter evening, there's a **movie theater.**

 ## Other activities

You can book a slew of activities through the resort's Guest Services (423-4655): **horse-drawn sleigh rides, torchlight run & BBQ, snowmobiling tours, wildlife viewing, ice fishing, backcountry tours,** and **dogsledding.** If you only participate in one non-skiing activity, shell out the bucks to mush your own dogsled with Snow Valley Mushers. You'll have a thrilling adventure with Cat and Eric, who spend the first 20 minutes or so teaching you how to guide your dog team. They do an excellent job pairing you with the best dogs for your temperament. If you feel panicky the first 5 or 10 minutes while you get used to your sled and team, and trying to remember all the commands, don't worry. Once your adrenaline starts pumping you'll have the time of your life. Trips range from two hours to multi-day with overnight camping.

Choose from three **cat-skiing** operations: You probably won't be able to book a stay at the highly respected Island Lake Lodge (888- 422-8754) because they only allow 36 guests per tour, but it's worth a try! Powder Cowboy Cat-Skiing Tours (423-3700 or 888- 422-8754) is now owned by Island Lake Lodge and has its own Bull River Ranch, with terrain. Fernie Wilderness Adventures (423-6704) takes you to terrain that's great for first-time cat-skiers.

This is one small town that believes in staying healthy in mind, body and spirit. Un-wind after a hard day on the slopes at the **Spa at Lizard Creek Lodge** (423-2057), with treatments including aromatherapy, hydrotherapy and massages. You'll also find a hair salon and esthetician here. In town, choose from **Fernie Mountain Massage Therapy Clinic** (423-5522), **Hydrotherapy Spa & Massage Therapy Clinic** (423-7667), **Jade River Healing Center Chinese Medicine Clinic** (423-7667) and **Fernie Chiropractic** (423-4800). It's also comforting to know the town has a **hospital** (423-4453).

If you're interested in learning about Fernie's history, pick up a copy of the **Heritage Walking Tour** booklet from the Fenie Information Center in town. You'll also find enough **shops** along 2nd Avenue to spend an afternoon browsing. There are several alpine sports stores, all worth checking out. If you're looking for unique gifts, we recommend Stephanie's Glass & Art Studio for custom-made stained glass and work by local artists, Ghostrider Trading Co. for handcrafted items by local artisans and mountain-lifestyle clothing, and Carosella Artworks for home décor and jewelry (they have a shop in the mountain village too). Pick up a copy of the *Fernie Guide* for other activity suggestions.

Getting there and getting around

By air: Most people fly into Calgary International Airport because it's served by most major airlines. It's about a three-hour drive to Fernie, though weather can affect travel time. Cranbrook Airport, served by Canadian Regional and Air BC, is an hour away. You also can fly into Glacier International Airport in Kalispell, Mont., which is about two hours away.

If you use the Rocky Mountain Sky Shuttle (888-762-8754 in U.S. and Canada, or 403-762-5200) from Calgary, make sure to ask your driver for local lore and wild tales of living in the rugged British Columbia wilderness. We found both our drivers to be Fernie locals who were very entertaining. Round-trip service only, reservations required, prices are in Cdn$ and include GST: adults, $120; seniors (65+) and youth (12-15), $114; kids (4-11), $60; infants (child seats available), $30.

By car: If you drive, be watchful for moose, deer, elk and bighorn sheep, which often wander into the road. From Calgary: South on Provincial Highway 2 to Crowsnest Highway 3, west on 3 until you reach the town of Fernie. If the weather is nice, you can take a slightly shorter more scenic route: south on 2 to Highway 7, west on 7 to town of Black Diamond, south on 22, west on 3.

From Kalispell, go north on Highway 93 through the United States-Canada border. Continue on 93 to its end, at the junction of Crowsnest Highway 3, then go east on 3. After passing Morrissey, look for the turnoff to Fernie Alpine Resort on your left.

Getting around: Kootenay Taxi runs a ski shuttle between the mountain and town; a schedule is available from the resort Guest Services counter and local accommodations. A one-way trip costs $3; four one-way rides, $10; a Frequent Rider Card (10 rides), $25 (fees are in Cdn$). We found the shuttle schedule to be somewhat inconvenient and ended up calling for a taxi (423-4408) to return to the mountain each time (about $18 Cdn one way with tip). If you plan to do any kind of exploring, rent a car.

Kicking Horse Mountain Resort

British Columbia, Canada

Summit elevation: 8.033 feet
Vertical drop: 4,131 feet
Base elevation: 3,902 feet

Address: Kicking Horse Mountain Resort, 1500 Kicking Horse Trail, Box 839, Golden, BC, Canada V0A 1H0
✆ **Area code:** 250
Ski Area Phone: 439-5400
Snow report: 439-5400
ⓘ **Toll-free reservations:** (866) SKI-KICK (866-754-5425) (North America)
Fax: 439-5401
E-mail: guestservices@kickinghorseresort.com
Internet: www.kickinghorseresort.com
Expert: ★★★★★
Advanced: ★★★★★
Intermediate: ★★★
Beginner: ★★   **Never-ever:** ★

Number and types of lifts: 4–1 8-person gondola, 2 quads, 1 double
Skiable acreage: 2,300
Snowmaking: No
Uphill capacity: 14,000 per hour
Snowboarding: Yes
Bed base: 1,100 in Golden; 66 slopeside
Nearest lodging: Slopeside, ski-in/ski-out
Resort child care: No; can arrange babysitting
Adult ticket, per day: $47.95-$49.75 (02/03 Cdn$ without GST)

Dining: ★★★ (resort) ★ (region)
Apres-ski/nightlife: ★★ (resort) ★ (region)
Other activities: ★★

Kicking Horse Mountain Resort in interior British Columbia is a jeweled crown in the making—a true work in progress. It's on Highway 1, just 48 miles west of Lake Louise between Kootenay and Glacier national parks in the town of Golden. The once locally owned day hill is undergoing a huge infusion of money from its new owners, the Netherlands-based construction giant Ballast Nedam International, a company that traditionally builds dams and bridges. The 2001/02 season marked the second year of its $300-million, 10-year development.

Originally run by local volunteers and known as Whitetooth, Ballast Nedam renamed this potentially world-class ski area Kicking Horse Mountain Resort and transformed the site, adding two new lifts including a bottom-to-top gondola, two lodges, its first slopeside lodging and other amenities. Their goal is to make this resort one of the largest ski areas in North America by the year 2005. The name Kicking Horse has its origins in a near-fatal accident suffered in an 1858 expedition to discover a route through the mountains for the railroad. In an effort to retrieve a recalcitrant pack horse, Sir James Hector was kicked so severely that he was thought dead and almost buried by his guides. When he later discovered the desired pass through the mountains, the nearby river and pass were named in his honor.

The resort has a 4,131-foot vertical drop, second in Canada only to Whistler Blackcomb. When their skiable acreage increases from 2,300 to 4,005 in 2005, Kicking Horse will join the ranks of Vail, Squaw Valley and Whistler Blackcomb with more than 4,000 acres of lift-accessed terrain. A recent announcement of an additional $18.5-million investment promises visitors in the 2002/03 season another new quad (to the 8,033-foot summit of a second peak), expanded terrain, shorter lift lines, and increased beverage and dining facilities. This new kid on the block has extreme potential and its new owners have the vision to make it happen.

Golden is a logger's village in the throes of a failing timber industry that just happens to sit at the foot of a developing ski hill with a very bright future. The influx of outside private and local provincial money promises to change Golden's fortunes forever. What Mother Nature has provided in her "eagle eye" views from the top of the ski area combined with its natural ski terrain make it hard for skiers and riders to resist. Cross a one-lane bridge over Kicking Horse River on a new road built to the resort and travel about 8 miles above the little town of Golden. The resort is situated amongst three mountain ranges—the Purcells, the Selkirks and the Canadian Rockies. Six National Parks surround the resort—Banff, Glacier, Kootenay, Yoho, Mt. Revelstoke and Jasper. On a clear day, the views are stunning.

The mountain gets an average annual snowfall of 23 feet. Brochures label it "The Champagne of Powders," but when we skied there in early March, the powder was a bit thick and heavy, making it very technical. At this stage of development, grooming is spotty with only three machines, especially if the resort gets a heavy dump. But there are plans to rectify the grooming situation.

 ## Mountain layout—Skiing

Kicking Horse is probably the most significant new resort in Canada. For the 20 years prior to the Golden Eagle Express lift, heli-skiing was the main way to enjoy the 4,000 vertical feet from the top. Stairway to Heaven is this season's new fixed-grip quad, rising 1,188 vertical feet from the bottom of Crystal Bowl to the resort's top elevation of 8,033 feet. The lift will add at least 20 new runs, experts only, on 150 acres and gets you to the top in about 10 minutes.

◆◆ **Expert** ◆ **Advanced:** Experts and advanced skiers, this is your mountain. Even without riding the Golden Eagle Express Gondola to the 7,705-foot top of the main peak, there are black-diamond runs to the bottom. The Pioneer double chair, at the head of the parking lot, gets you to all the serious lower-mountain runs. A good warm-up, which you can take at your own speed, is Race Place. It's the longest of the lower runs and is normally groomed. Porcupine and Grizzly Paw also are good single-blacks off the Pioneer chair. Bumpsters will want to drop into Pioneer right under the lift.

Now that you've skied what there is to see, head up-mountain on the gondola. We've heard rumors that it's rarely open, and we asked the mountain specifically about this. They told us that like any high-elevation lift, extreme weather conditions can close it. They also showed us the computer printout for the lift last season: It was closed once—for two days in a row—due to avalanche danger, once it closed 45 minutes early because of winds over 60 km/hour, and once it closed for 45 minutes for maintenance but reopened and stayed running for an extra 45 minutes. So, there you have it, the rumor is quashed.

A good choice for bowls and untracked powder…well, there are actually two: turn either right or left as you get off the gondola and drop into whichever bowl beckons. These were heli-ski runs with steep headwalls before the gondola was built. To the left is Bowl Over, reached by the super-fun Flying Dutchman. Bowl Over is a powder "blue sort of run" till you hit treeline at the beginning of Liberty. Here you have a choice: go right onto black-diamond Liberty (and then choose among more blacks like Terminator and Double Header), or stay blue and keep left onto Knee Deep. To the right of the gondola is Crystal Bowl. Think Twice is the run you want for the upper part, but it quickly joins the green-circle It's a Ten, already in progress from the top. From It's a Ten, at about treeline, you can pull over to the left and get on the new Stairway to Heaven quad. If you stay on Ten, it's 10 km. to the bottom, but there are plenty of chances to drop down some short black diamonds.

■ **Intermediate:** Intermediate skiers were not ignored when the runs were cut. They're all over the mountain and can be reached by any of the lifts. A favorite starts as Sluiceway from the top of the gondola. It veers left as you get off the lift, follows a gentle ridge for a moment and then descends into Bowl Over. Continuing past treeline, the run becomes Knee Deep, aiming back toward the gondola and then veering sharply right as Terminator. It eventually doubles back and joins It's a Ten. As you glide along the Ten track, there is a choice of four blue runs to the bottom, plus a few blacks if you're feeling adventurous and a few greens if you're getting tired.

●● **Beginner** ● **Never-ever:** There is a beginner way down from all of the lifts, except possibly Stairway to Heaven. It serves what used to be heli-ski terrain, and as of press time not all of the runs had been cut. Confident beginners, however, after some warm-up runs from the Catamount quad chair, can take the gondola to the top and ski down the longest run on the mountain—the 10-km.-long It's a Ten.

Never-evers will *NOT* want to do that. Instead, stay on the Catamount quad, it serves all your runs. You can get on the gentler part of It's a Ten from the top of Catamount, or simply go down Big Ben. All the terrain under Catamount is gentle.

Mountain layout—Snowboarding

As yet, there are no terrain parks or pipes for you warpsters, but who needs 'em when most of Kicking Horse has above-alpine heli-skiing-quality snow for the price of a lift pass? The jump-offs into the three bowls are gut-sucking enough for skilled riders, and there are a lot of steep shots off the ridges. Make sure to ride the new Stairway to Heaven for access to the black-diamond My Blue Heaven area.

Intermediates too have great choices all over the mountain. The mid-bowls are comprised of blue and green runs, and a ride out and down Terminator will peg your fun meter for sure. Like to ride the trees? The steeps are above where the gondola makes a slight turn to the left, but below the woods are bigger and thicker.

Beginners will be comfortable in the Catamount lift region, where there are several green runs mixed with blues.

Mountain rating

Kicking Horse, long appreciated as a fine heli-ski mountain, has the roughness and steeps that hardy skiers and riders enjoy. This is especially true above treeline. Fulfillment of ambitious plans by the owners is rather quickly turning it into a ski hill the whole family can enjoy. There is plenty of terrain for all abilities, but always know there is a tougher run somewhere to test your improving skills.

Cross-country and snowshoeing

Cross-country equipment and snowshoes can be rented from the **Kicking Horse Mountain Resort Rental Shop. The Dawn Mountain Nordic Ski Trails** has 14 km. of classic track-set trails, including 1.5 km. of skating track. There are beginner loop trails, plus intermediate and expert trails. A trailside warming hut sits 1 km. into the course. Use of trails is free of charge; lessons will be available beginning this season, but prices were not set at press time.

Lessons (2002/03; Cdn$ without GST)

Group lessons: Half-day lessons cost $35 (without rentals or ticket). A full-day session with rentals and lift ticket costs $110.

Never-ever packages: First-timers pay $94 for a full-day session with rentals and lift ticket. Half-day lessons and sessions without rentals are considerably less. The Learn to Ski/Ride Week, all inclusive, includes three half-day lessons and is $260.

Private lessons: Packages range from $60 for one hour (without rentals and ticket) to $350 for a full day with rentals and ticket. Additional people start at $50 for just one hour (without rentals and ticket).

Specialty programs: The Learn to Ski/Snowboard Mini Week Package includes three half-day sessions for $260 with lifts and rentals; call for more information.

Child care: (2002/03; Cdn$ without GST)

Kicking Horse's future plans include a child-care facility but they don't have one yet. They will, by arrangement, provide a day care/babysitting service for resort guests, much like an in-room babysitting service.

Children's lessons: Kicking Horse offers full-day group lessons for tots (3-5), $25; children (6-12) and youth (13-18), $30. Price does not include lift or rentals.

Lift tickets (2002/03; Cdn$ without GST)

	Adult	Child (6-12)
One day	$49.75	$21.75
Three days	$145.25 ($48.42/day)	$63.25 ($21.08/day)
Five days	$239.75 ($47.95/day)	$104.75 ($29.15/day)

Who skis free: Kids up to age 5.

Who skis at a discount: Youth (13-18) and seniors (65+) pay $39.75; three days, $116.25; five days, $190.75.

Sightseeing Riders: For $17.75, you can ride the gondola up and down for lunch or dinner and savor the food and the spectacular views.

Accommodations

Kicking Horse Mountain Resort has a toll-free reservations number for most area properties, 1 (866) SKI-KICK (754-5425).

Whispering Pines (344-7188; $$-$$$) is currently one of two on-mountain options at Kicking Horse Mountain Resort. The luxurious townhouses provide ski-in/ski-out lodging just a few minutes' away from the day lodge and near the gondola. All units have kitchens, fireplaces, washers and dryers, and maid service.

There is another option for staying (literally) on-mountain: the exclusive $1,500 per room, per night "Winter Getaway" at **Eagle's Eye Suites** (866-754-5425; $$$$). Just upstairs above the Eagle's Eye Restaurant at 7,705 feet, two two-person suites with private balconies overlook the Columbia Valley and three mountain ranges. Amenities include pretty much anything you'd expect for that price, including your own 24-hour valet/concierge service, personalized dining menus, lift tickets, guaranteed first tracks, private ski instructor, champagne, gift basket and other take-aways. The most exclusive part of this package is the VIP gondola cabin with leather seats, CD player and wine bucket for those 12-minute rides up and/or down the mountain.

Dining: $$$-Entrees $20+; $$-$10-20; $-less than $10 (Cdn$).

Accommodations: (double room) $$$$-$200+; $$$-$141-$200; $$-$81-$140; $-$80 and less. (Cdn$)

Most people stay 15 minutes down the hill in Golden, which offers comfortable chains and a number of private facilities, altogether about 25 simple, comfortable inns and B&Bs. Many Golden properties have shuttle service available to the ski area as needed. There is a small charge, $4-$5.

The Prestige Inn (866-754-5425; $$$$) is a four-and-half-star hotel with kitchenettes, fridge, computer link-up and other high-end amenities including an indoor pool and hot tub. **Best Western Mountainview Inn** (866-754-5425; $-$$) includes an indoor pool, coin laundry room and extra-large, family-sized rooms. **Ramada Inn** (439-1888; 866-754-5425; 800-593-0511; $$-$$$) is the newest hotel in Golden. It has an indoor pool, whirlpool, business center with Internet access, Jacuzzi and kitchenette suites. Complimentary continental breakfast is included. At last check, all these chains provide shuttles to the ski area.

Hillside Lodge & Chalets (344-7281; $$), owned and operated by the Baier family, is a B&B located about 15 minutes west of Golden, just north of Highway 1 on the Blaeberry River. They feature new guest rooms with private baths and sumptuous breakfasts. Sonja and Hubert Baier also serve dinner. Five chalets each have twin or queen beds, private baths, hand-crafted furnishings, wood stoves, and fridges. Coffee and tea are provided.

Goldenwood Lodge (344-7685; $), just outside Golden, is about a 40-minute drive from the ski area in the winter. It has separate cottages with kitchens, as well as rooms in the lodge with a breakfast package. One group house sleeps nine, with a kitchen and two washrooms, for a very reasonable price.

Church-en-Taller Lodge B&B (344-7325; 866-344-8184; $$) is five minutes south of Golden. Guest rooms have private baths, plus you'll get breakfast, a sauna hut and breathtaking views. **Cedar House Café & Restaurant** (344-4679; $$), just 15 minutes from the ski hill, rents a cabin that sleeps four and includes laundry, kitchen and TV. It's also a great gathering place for friends and family for good appetizers, meat main courses and an interesting selection of vegetarian options.

Alpine Meadows Lodge (344-5863; $) is on a scenic benchland just outside Golden and near the ski resort. It was popular with heli-ski packages before the lift to the top of Kicking Horse was installed. **Sisters & Beans Guesthouse** (344-2443; $) in Golden has four guest rooms behind its restaurant (see *Dining*). The **Golden Kicking Horse Hostel** (344-5071; $) has beds for $20 per night, full kitchen facilities, free parking, other amenities and no curfew.

Dining

Hands down, the most spectacular and elegant dining at Kicking Horse is at **Eagle's Eye Restaurant** (866-754-5425; $$$), just a gondola ride up to the 7,705-foot summit. Billed as "Canada's Most Elevated Dining Experience," it's actually the highest restaurant in Canada. Ambitious entrees run the gamut from a vegetarian portobello mushroom to a seafood tower, duck, venison, lamb, salmon and wild caribou. Chef Shaben also creates such sumptuous starters like gravlax, mussels, buffalo carpaccio and venison pate that you could just bliss out ordering off the first half of the menu. His wine selection is quite varied and features many BC labels. Lots of interesting salads are also available for those rabbits in your group. It's open for lunch every day, for dinner on Friday and Saturday only. The Cascadian architecture and the views are both spectacular. Be sure to take a tour of the two upstairs suites if the management will allow (see *Accommodations*).

New this season is a 750-square-foot **dining facility,** unnamed at press time, at the base of the new Stairway to Heaven lift in Crystal Bowl. You have to take the gondola and ski down Crystal Bowl to get to it. The only other feeding option on the mountain so far is the cafeteria at the base **Day Lodge** ($), where you can get made-to-order omelets for breakfast, and soups, salads, sandwiches and burgers for lunch.

Off the mountain, **Cedar House Café & Restaurant** (344-4679; $$-$$$) is a great spot for comfort food. Lots of choices on the menu are homemade so you can't go wrong with soups, pastas and sauces. They also feature a vegetarian menu alongside the obligatory Alberta beef, pork, salmon and lamb. **Kicking Horse Grill** (344-2330; $-$$), owned by two Dutch cousins, is in an old log cabin in Golden. The grill, open nightly, features a combo of Thai and Scandinavian fare. **Sisters and Beans** (344-2443; $-$$), also in Golden, specializes in healthy soups, vegetarian Thai curries, pastas and the odd meat dish. Open nightly for dinner, Thursday through Saturday for lunch.

 ## Apres-ski/nightlife

Après-ski is at the base **Day Lodge**, every afternoon. On Fridays and Saturdays, end up at the **Eagle's Eye** ($$-$$$) at the summit for drinks and starters. If you don't stay for dinner, you can download. It stays open until the last person leaves.

For some raucous nightlife, head into Golden to **The Lodge.** Locals refer to it as a "peeler" bar and tell us that "fresh meat" Mondays are the rowdiest since that's opening night on the circuit for the new "peeler" of the week (if you don't know what a "peeler" is, think "better than a wet T-shirt contest").

Other spots in Golden include the **Mad Trapper** with a pub atmosphere and **Packers,** the local dance bar. Otherwise, downtown Golden hasn't grown into its après-ski or shopping britches. Yet.

 ## Other activities

To pre-book winter activities, including **snowmobiling, dogsledding** and **sleigh rides,** call Golden Guides, 866-SKI-KICK (754-5425). Also check out www.go2rockies.net for **all area attractions.**

Getting there and getting around

By air: Calgary International Airport is your gateway to Kicking Horse Resort, which is about three hours west along the Trans Canada Highway in Golden, B.C. The airport is served by all major airlines. There is daily shuttle service from the Calgary Airport into the Greyhound depot in Calgary, $12 one way. You can catch a shuttle from there to Golden that is $81 round trip. Call 888-438-2992 for details and schedules.

By car: If you rent a car at the airport, life gets much easier. From Calgary, take the Trans Canada Highway and travel west, past Banff and Lake Louise to Golden, about a 2.5-hour drive. Follow signs to Golden Town Centre.

Getting around: There are usually shuttles from Golden accommodations to the ski hill for $4-$5. A taxi ride one way from the town of Golden to the resort will cost you $25 Cdn. Be sure to have the correct Cdn$ fare or you'll be charged a lot more in American dollars—the cabbies don't seem to have a handle on the exchange thing yet. If you have your own car, the resort recently paved the curvy road from Golden to the Day Lodge. Note the one-lane bridge over Kicking Horse River, just barely wide enough for a motor coach, so your SUV shouldn't have a scrape-through.

Dining: $$$-Entrees $20+; $$-$10-20; $-less than $10 (Cdn$).
Accommodations: (double room) $$$$-$200+; $$$-$141-$200; $$-$81-$140; $-$80 and less. (Cdn$)

Panorama Mountain Resort

British Columbia, Canada

Summit elevation: 7,800 feet
Vertical drop: 4,000 feet
Base elevation: 3,800 feet

Address: Panorama Mountain Village, Panorama, B.C., Canada VOA 1T0
✆ **Area code:** 250
Ski area phone: 342-6941
Snow report: 342-6941
ⓘ **Toll-free reservations:**
(800) 663-2929 (North America)
Fax: 342-3395
E-mail: paninfo@panoramaresort.com
Internet: www.panoramaresort.com
Expert:★★★
Advanced:★★★
Intermediate:★★★★
Beginner:★★★ **Never-ever:**★★★

Number and types of lifts: 9-1 8-person village gondola, 1 high-speed quad, 1 triple, 2 doubles, 4 surface lifts
Skiable acreage: 2,847 **Snowmaking:** 40 percent
Uphill capacity: 7,000+ per hour
Snowboarding: Yes
Bed base: 2,000 at the base
Nearest lodging: slopeside, ski-in/ski-out
Resort child care: Yes, 19 months and older
Adult ticket, per day: $44-$52 (2002/03 CdnS, without GST)
Dining:★★★ (resort), ★★ (region)
Apres-ski/nightlife:★★★ (resort), ★★ (region)
Other activities:★★★

Panorama Mountain Resort is two hours south of Banff on the west side of the Continental Divide that separates Alberta from British Columbia. Just think about the massive snowfall from clouds trying to rise over the Divide. Yum. British Columbians figure they get the best of the winter deal.

Since purchased by Intrawest Corporation in 1993, the village, known as Panorama Mountain Village, is fast becoming one of the Canadian Rockies' premier winter vacation destinations. With the addition of ski terrain, high-speed lifts, restaurants, giant slopeside hot pools, accommodations and a village gondola, life is looking pretty good here in the Rockies.

With almost 3,000 patrolled acres, including bowls, the backcountry terrain in Taynton Bowl, the Extreme Zone, terrain parks and the FIS-regulation halfpipe, Panorama is definitely on the Canadian ski map. Panorama is known for its high percentage of intermediate, advanced and expert runs and, since everything is below treeline, it has an abundance of glade skiing. One of the lifts travels nearly a mile from the base area. Continue up the Horizon chair nearly another mile to get to most of the black-diamond runs. Two T-bar rides will get you to the very top, where a new summit hut café allows you to enjoy the "view of a 1,000 peaks." Oddly, Panorama seems to have more snowbladers than anywhere else we've ever been. First-time visitors can learn their way around with a free guide service.

Mountain layout—Skiing

The addition of the 700 acres of "Outback" in Taynton Bowl has upped the fun meter here, and it was already almost off the scale. The bowl used to be strictly heli-skiing terrain, providing a backcountry experience for the intermediate and advanced skier, with loads of wide-open and naturally gladed runs. The main chutes are more than 1,700 vertical feet. Access to Taynton Bowl is off the Summit lift. Other good expansions have included Millennium run (fall-line run between the top of the Horizon Chair and the Sunbird Chair), the Extreme Zone and the Sun Bowl. Experts will enjoy the Glades Summit, Schober's Glades, Hideaway and the double-black-diamond Extreme Dream Zone. Intermediates favor the Alive glades and Sunbowl. The beginner area, with a platter and a chair, is in the lowlands, away from the hubbub.

Mountain layout—Snowboarding

The Showzone Terrain Park has an FIS-regulation halfpipe, and the mountain offers night riding to piped-in DMX music. But while most riders give the manmade stuff a thumbs up, they really come here for the natural terrain. This resort rocks for intermediate, advanced and expert riders. Check out the 700 acres of backcountry terrain in the "Outback": You'll find chutes, glades and wide-open runs here. The only bummer for riders is T-bars take you to the summit, which can literally be a drag if you're not adept on them while on a board.

Cross-country and snowshoeing

The **Greywolf Nordic Centre** (342-6941 ext. 3840) offers 20.5 km. of groomed cross-country trails for classic and skating, plus 6.6 km for classic only. The Nordic clubhouse (the Greywolf Golf Course Clubhouse in another season) has rental equipment, waxing service, lessons and refreshments, plus changing rooms, lockers and showers. Trail fees are $10 adults, $7 teens, $6 juniors. The Hale Hut warming cabin, on the Delphine Loop, has bathrooms and a firepit with firewood for those who need to take a break.

Lessons [2002/03 Cdn$, without GST]

The Bilodeau School of Skiing and Snowboarding is highly regarded.

Group lessons: Powder, Bumps and Stumps is a one-day clinic (four hours) for intermediate and advanced skiers that teaches route selection and advanced skills. Cost is $69. Free Skiing Mountain Clinics are for intermediate to advanced skiers who want to gain skill and confidence as all-mountain skiers. These 1-hour clinics meet at 1:15 p.m. and cost $39. The Free Ride Clinic is for novice to intermediate snowboarders who are ready for long, cruising slopes, trees and powder. It includes skill development and guiding with an expert pro. The Half Pipe Clinic teaches halfpipe tricks, jumping and hits. Both clinics are 1 1/2 hours; cost is $39.

Never-ever package: First-time skiers can take a MagicTrax Group Lesson with specially trained MagicTrax instructors and "shortcut" shaped skis. A two-hour lesson costs $39; includes gear rentals. First Run Snowboard (or Second Run for novices) is a four-hour group introduction to snowboarding; cost is $69.

Private lessons: One-hour lessons cost $79, 1 1/2 hours cost $99.

Special programs: Confidence Club for skiers is a three-day group clinic designed to help you master the blue runs. Cost is $149 for 10 hours of instruction.

Child care [2002/03 Cdn$, without GST]

Ages: 19 months through 5 years old.
Costs: $40 for all day (9 a.m. to 4:30 p.m.); $25 half day. Lunch is an additional $5.

Reservations: Call 342-6941 ext. 3260. Telus Mobility call-in stations are on the mountain for parents to check in on their wee ones. Babysitters are available by arrangement.

Children's Lessons: There are extensive lesson offerings for children. Register in advance with the ski school for all children's lessons, 888-SOS-7799 or 342-6941. The Snowbirds program is an introduction to skiing for kids 3-5 years old. Lessons are at 9:15 a.m. or 3:15 p.m. and cost $29; most children spend rest of day in child care. The all-day Adventure Club (10:30 a.m. to 3 p.m.) is for skiers ages 5-13 and costs $69, includes lunch, the snowboard program is for kids 8-13.

First-time skiers ages 14 and older can take a MagicTrax Group Lesson with MagicTrax instructors and "shortcut" shaped skis. A two-hour lesson costs $39; includes gear rentals. First Run Snowboard for kids 8 and older teaches the basic skills of sliding, turning on an easy slope and lift riding. The four-hour lesson starts at 10 a.m. and costs $69. The Free Ride Clinic for kids 8 years and older is for novice to intermediate snowboarders who are ready for long, cruising slopes, trees and powder. It includes skill development and guiding with an expert pro. The Freestyle and Half Pipe Clinic for kids 8 years and older teaches halfpipe tricks, jumping and hits. Both clinics meet for 1 1/2 hours; cost is $39.

Lift tickets (2002/03 Cdn$, without GST)

	Adult	Junior (7-12)
One day	$52	$25
Three days	$134 ($44+/day)	$64 ($21+/day)
Five days	$219 ($43+/day)	$99 ($19+/day)

Who skis free: No one.

Who skis at a discount: Teens (13-18) pay $40; three days, $99; five days, $165. Seniors 65 and older pay teen prices. Children ages 6 and younger pay $9 per day. Full-time students ages 19-25 with ID get 10 percent off adult rates.

Accommodations

Panorama has more than 400 slopeside condos and townhomes, plus a 102-unit hotel. All lodging is packaged with lift tickets. The best deal is $179 (Cdn$) per person for three nights and four days of skiing. Call 800-663-2929 for all slopeside lodging reservations, or book online at www.skipanorama.com.

Ski Tip Lodge, Tamarack Lodge, Panorama Springs Condo/Hotel, Taynton Lodge, Riverbend Townhomes and Hearthstone Townhomes ($$–$$$) are studio to three-bedroom condos and townhomes with a full kitchen, fireplace and VCR. All were built as Intrawest's signature lodging in the heart of the upper village around the slopeside hot pools.

Horsethief Lodge and Toby Creek Lodge ($$) are family-style studio condos with one to three bedrooms, some with lofts, in the lower village. Units have a full kitchen, fireplace, VCR and underground parking. New Village Gondola and Toby chair provide easy ski and upper village access.

The Pine Inn ($–$$), at the base of the ski lifts and close to Greywolf Golf course, is designed for budget-oriented guests. Rooms have full bath, television and coffeemaker.

The Elkhorn Cabin Bed & Breakfast (888-767-7799; $$$$) sits on Panorama Mountain overlooking Toby Creek valley and across to Mount Nelson. It's rustic, romantic and very comfortable. The package includes a fireplace, bed quilts, big pillows, washbasin, soap and towels, plus dinner and breakfast prepared in advance. Price per couple is $239 plus tax (Cdn$); for second couple add $139 plus tax (Cdn$).

 ## Dining

With eight restaurants in the village, plus more down-mountain in Invermere, the dining options are plentiful, though we only had the opportunity to sample two. The **Starbird Steakhouse ($–$$),** behind the quad chair and gondola, serves good hearty breakfasts; light fare, sandwiches and pizza for lunch; and pasta, seafood, oven-baked pizza, beef and pork for dinner. The **Toby Creek Dining Room ($$–$$$)**, underneath the grocery store, serves tasty seafood, Alberta beef, wild game and very imaginative pastas.

 ## Après-ski/nightlife

Outdoor hot tubs are available, plus the **Panorama Springs** giant slopeside hot pools. Inside fun is available at the **Jackpine Pub**, **Kicking Horse Bar & Grill**, **Heli-Plex Bar & Grill** (try the jumbo heli wings and the heli soup!) and the **Glacier Nite Club**.

 ## Other activities

In Ski Tip Lodge, the Mountain Adventure Centre (342-6941 ext. 3440) is a complete information and booking service for activities and events, including hot springs tours; dinner shuttle to Invermere restaurants; day trips to Lake Louise, Kimberley and the new Kicking Horse Mountain Resort; games arcade; sleigh rides; snowmobile tours; massage therapist and more.

Adjacent to the ski area is **R.K. Heli-Ski Panorama Inc.** (342-3889 or 1-800-661-6060), offering one-day heli-skiing packages from $599 (2001/02 prices). The company has 2,000 square kilometers of runs that include glaciers and glades, all between 5,500 and 11,000 feet of elevation.

The nearby town of Invermere on the Lake has **shopping** and **working art studios.** Taxi and shuttle service are available. Toby Creek Adventures (342-5047 or 888-357-4449) offers **guided snowmobile tours,** specializing in hourly and multiday guided tours in the Columbia Valley between Fairmont Hot Springs and Radium Hot Springs.

Getting there and getting around

By air: Calgary International Airport is the gateway to Panorama. The airport is 185 miles from Panorama and is served by all major airlines. There is daily shuttle service from both Calgary International Airport and Banff. Transfers must be pre-booked with accommodations. Cranbrook Airport, 75 miles north of Panorama, is served by regional air carriers.

By car: From Calgary, take TransCanada Highway 1 west through Banff to the Highway 93 junction with Kootenay Parkway (about 12 miles past Banff). Take Highway 93 south to Radium, BC (63 miles). From Radium, drive south about 8 miles on Highway 95 to the town of Invermere, then continue 11 miles from Invermere directly to Panorama Mountain Village.

Getting around: While a car is certainly not needed at Panorama, the reality is that most visitors arrive by car, and they're handy for getting into Invermere on your own schedule.

Dining: $$$-Entrees $20+; $$-$10-20; $-less than $10.
Accommodations: (double room) $$$$-$200+; $$$-$141-$200; $$-$81-$140; $-$80 and less.

Aspen Area

Colorado

Aspen Mountain
Buttermilk
Highlands

Address: Aspen Skiing Company,
P.O. Box 1248, Aspen, CO 81612
Area code: 970
✆ **Ski area phone:** 925-1220
or (800) 525-6200
Snow report: 925-1221 or 888-ASPEN-SNO (277-3676)
Toll-free reservations: (800) 262-7736 or 925-9000
Fax: 925-9008
E-mail: info@stayaspen.com (reservations)
or info@aspensnowmass.com (ski info)

Bed Base: 9,000
Nearest lodging: Slopeside, hotels, condos
Resort child care: See Child Care section
Adult ticket, per day: $51-$68 (02/03 prices)
Internet: www.aspensnowmass.com (ski area)
www.aspenalive.com or www.aspen.com (activities)
www.aspen4u.com or stayaspensnowmass.com (lodging)
Dining: ★ ★ ★ ★ ★
Apres-ski/nightlife: ★ ★ ★ ★ ★
Other activities: ★ ★ ★ ★

Ask a crowd of non-skiing Americans to name a ski resort, and you can bet a bundle that Aspen will be one of those they name, though they will probably know more about the rich and famous who frequent the resort than about its equally notable skiing. With four mountains within a 12-mile radius (one of those, Snowmass, is detailed in its own chapter), offering 39 lifts, 270 trails and more than 5,900 skiable acres, a trip to Aspen just for the skiing would be well worth it. But Aspen has much more.

Aspen fits a niche unique among North American ski resorts. Sure, other resorts attract wealth, but Aspen's wealth glitters and sparkles with a "look-this-way" flamboyance. Here, the well-to-do seem to want everyone else to know it. You'll see the newest ski and city fashions on beautiful women as they pass turn-of-the-century brick façades. Private jets wait for their owners on the airport tarmac. Paparazzi aim their lenses at every celebrity in town so that supermarket tabloids can keep their pages filled.

Don't head to Aspen purely to observe celebrities, however. You may not find any. They are most common during the Christmas-New Year holidays and March's sunshine days, but are difficult to spot when in ski clothes. If you want to mix with the upscale crowd, stay close to the Aspen Mountain gondola base, where the fanciest hotels and shops are clustered. You'll find a mixed crowd here, which combines expensive and reasonably priced restaurants and bars. Beyond downtown, the outward signs of wealth disappear.

If all your information about Aspen comes from *People* magazine, you probably think you can't afford to ski there. True, lift tickets are among the priciest in America, but it's a little-known fact that lodging and restaurants have a huge price range, starting out with inexpensive dorm accommodations and topping out at stratospheric luxury suites.

Aspen also draws skiers and snowboarders who could care less about the off-mountain scene. They come for the slopes, which have received rave reviews for decades. The region has four separate ski areas, all operated by Aspen Skiing Company (ASC). Aspen Mountain challenges intermediate through expert skiers and snowboarders. Buttermilk is the perfect beginner and cruising mountain, plus it's home to the 2003 ESPN Winter X Games and the Crazy T'rain Park, one of the longest in the country. Highlands is the most varied for its size, with terrain for experts and beginners, cruisers and bumpers. Snowmass, larger than the other three combined, is several miles down the road. Though it is one of the four Aspen Skiing Company areas and included in the lift ticket, it has its own lodging, restaurants and shops, and is covered in the next chapter.

If you're determined to see celebrities at Aspen, three sightings are guaranteed on Aspen Mountain. Look for shrines for Elvis Presley, Marilyn Monroe and Jerry Garcia. The Elvis shrine is in a grove of trees just below Back of Bell 3. Marilyn's shrine is on a cat-track above the Elvis shrine and Jerry is memorialized in a grove of spruce trees to skiers' right on Ruthie's Run after you unload from the FIS chair. Ask an Aspen ambassador for directions and be sure to take your camera. For a little romance, check out the Valentine's shrine between Walsh's and Hyrup's on Aspen Mountain where you'll find a secluded "porch swing" to canoodle between runs.

This season at Aspen Highlands marks the opening of *all* of Highland Bowl. New terrain on the north facing aspect includes 16 new runs, adding 10 miles of trails and increasing acreage here by a whopping 46 percent. Most of it is primarily north facing and gladed, meaning dry powder and mid-winter conditions even in the spring.

Mountain layout—Skiing

Aspen's four mountains are close to each other, but not interconnected. A free shuttle runs from base to base. This chapter covers Aspen Mountain, Highlands and Buttermilk. ASC runs a very efficient equipment transfer program between its four mountains. For $5, you hand over your skis, poles or snowboard to an attendant in the base area at the end of the day, tell him/her where you are skiing the next day, and your equipment will be waiting for you at that base area the next morning. It works very well.

Fabulous freebies on Aspen Mountain: "First Tracks" on the first run of the day down empty, freshly groomed slopes. Early birds with lift tickets can sign up for the 8 a.m. gondola at the concierge desk the day before. First Tracks is on a first-come basis, so get there early. Another is the Mountain Tour led every day at 10:30 a.m. and 1:30 p.m. by ASC Ambassadors, a good way to get familiar with the mountain.

◆◆ **Expert:** Highlands is the best-balanced mountain of the three with slopes for every level, and it's the locals' favorite. No need for fur-trimmed outfits here, you can be comfortable if you appear for lunch at mid-mountain in jeans and gaiters. The vertical rise is one of the highest in Colorado. Highlands has three high-speed quads that dramatically cut the time needed to reach the summit and have changed the skiing in the mountain.

From the top of Loge Peak, the run back to the base is an uneven series of steeps, catwalks and gentle runouts. This mountain has some fantastic long cruises. The ridge, knifing directly to the summit, has thrilling pitches down both sides. Other than a few short blacks, such as Suzy Q and Limelight, the terrain makes a pronounced jump from intermediate to double-diamond expert.

Experts should head for the steeps at the top of Loge Peak in the Steeplechase (sunny in the morning) and Olympic Bowl (sunny in the afternoon) areas. These are very steep with no bail-out areas, so be sure you want to be here. Both areas have long cat trails back to the lifts.

Some of Colorado's steepest slopes stand above Loge Peak in Highland Bowl, opened to the public in 1997. You can reach the tops of the 40- to 45-degree slopes by hiking up the ridge for 20-60 minutes; or, if you happen to be at Loge Meadow between 11 a.m. and 1 p.m.,

Aspen Mountain Facts

Summit elevation: **11,212 feet**

Base elevation: **7,945 feet**

Vertical drop: **3,267 feet**

Number of lifts: 8–1 gondola, 1 high-speed quad, 1 high-speed double, 2 quads, 3 doubles

Snowmaking: 31 percent **Skiable acreage:** 673 acres

Uphill capacity: 10,775 per hour **Snowboarding:** Yes

Expert:★★★★ Advanced:★★★★★

Intermediate:★★★★

Buttermilk Facts

Summit elevation: **9,900 feet**

Vertical drop: **2,030 feet**

Base elevation: **7,870 feet**

Number of lifts: 7–1 high-speed quad, 5 doubles, 1 surface lift

Snowmaking: 26 percent **Skiable acreage:** 415 acres

Uphill capacity: 7,500 per hour **Snowboarding:** Yes

Expert:★ Advanced:★★ Intermediate:★★★★

Beginner:★★★★★ Never-ever:★★★★★

Highlands Facts

Summit elevation: **11,675 feet**

Vertical drop: **3,635 feet**

Base elevation: **8,040 feet**

Number of lifts: 4–3 high-speed quads, 1 triple

Snowmaking: 15 percent **Skiable acreage:** 720 acres

Uphill capacity: 5,400 per hour **Snowboarding:** Yes

Expert:★★★★ Advanced:★★★★★ Intermediate:★★★★

Beginner:★★★ Never-ever:★★

---

hop on a snowcat for a ride to the first access gate. This season you'll find 16 new runs here, mostly gladed, so check 'em out.

Also check out the lower mountain. The Thunderbowl chair will take you from the base to the top of Bob's Glades or Upper Stein, or you can drop into double-black territory at several points along blue-square Golden Horn.

The basic guideline for Aspen Mountain is that the intermediate terrain is on the top knob around the summit and in the gullies between the ridges. The expert stuff drops from the ridges into the gullies. Of the blacks, take your pick and be sure you're up to it. These runs are very black. For bumps and trees, Bell Mountain right under the gondola is a good choice. Watch for the ski patrol to open Walsh's after a storm. It can be powder heaven, a run you can brag about all week. Guided "Powder Tours" are offered on the back side of Aspen Mountain; call (800) 525-6200 for information.

♦ **Advanced:** If you consider yourself a very confident advanced skier, read the expert section. If you feel you have recently reached advanced status, read the intermediate section. In our experience, there's a big jump from intermediate to expert terrain at **Highlands** and **Aspen Mountain. Buttermilk's** advanced terrain is really more advanced-intermediate.

■ **Intermediate:** If you'd like to say you skied a black run on **Aspen Mountain**, Upper Little Percy or Red's Run are occasionally groomed. The ticket office or the on-mountain Concierge Center at the summit has a grooming report (available at all the mountains).

Unsure if you can handle the terrain? If you can ski blues at other areas, do this: Ride the gondola to the top and ski the gentlest terrain, at the summit—runs such as Dipsy Doodle, Pussyfoot and Silver Bell. Keep riding the Ajax Express and Gentlemen's Ridge lifts. If any of those blue runs presents a challenge, ride back down in the gondola. The alternative to riding down is Copper Bowl or Spar Gulch, two narrow gullies that get packed late in the day as skiers funnel into them toward the base. Both runs join at Kleenex Corner, a sharp, narrow turn, then dump into Little Nell, a steep blue just above the gondola base. It's known as "Little Hell" because at day's end, it's crowded, usually a little slick and/or moguled, and smack in view of everyone.

The blue cruisers—led by North american—in sight of Bonnie's outdoor deck are a delight. If you're a confident intermediate, don't pass up skiing at Aspen Mountain.

At **Buttermilk,** intermediates with confident turns will have fun on Jacob's Ladder and Bear, which drop from the Cliff House to the main area, but the real playground is under the Tiehack chair. Much of this area is colored black on the trail map, but don't get too excited—it's just the toughest stuff on *this* mountain. You'll discover good upper-intermediate trails that make inspiring cruisers. In one day you can ride the Upper Tiehack chair a dozen times, taking a different cruise on each 1,500 vertical-foot run. Javelin is the best of the lot—a couple of tree islands to keep you awake and a lot of good dips and rolls. Smile in the evening when you overhear others scoffing about what a waste Buttermilk is for real skiers, and savor memories of 15,000 feet of vertical in just one afternoon.

At **Highlands,** intermediates will want to take these lifts: Cloud Nine, Olympic and Loge Peak. (The easiest of the intermediates are off Cloud Nine.) Don't miss Golden Horn and Thunderbowl on the lower mountain, very wide cruisers.

●● **Beginner: Aspen Mountain** may be the only mountain in America that has no designated green-circle runs. Don't try it if you're at this level.

Buttermilk is all that Aspen Mountain isn't. Beginners can experience top-to-bottom runs as soon as they master snowplows. The beginner terrain concentrates under the Buttermilk West chair. Tom's Thumb, Red's Rover, Larkspur, Westward Ho and Blue Grouse will keep beginners improving. The Homestead Road turns back to the Savio chair and lazily winds its way to the Main Buttermilk area.

At **Highlands**, beginners are best served by the trails from the Exhibition chair—Prospector, Nugget, Exhibition, Red Onion and Apple Strudel.

● **Never-ever:** Take your first few lessons at **Buttermilk**. Of Aspen's four mountains, this is by far the best for a first day on skis or a snowboard.

Mountain layout—Snowboarding

At 673 acres, **Aspen Mountain** is not even one-fourth the size of Snowmass, but every acre is infinitely rideable. The mountain scenery is sublime—better, even, than Telluride or Crested Butte. This ain't a mountain for jibbers, bonkers or terrain park pilots—it's for expert riders who respect and even revere a pristine alpine playground. There are no beginner trails and scant few true intermediate runs. But if you have good skills, the mountain is replete with bumps, steeps, natural halfpipes and terrain features perfect for riders.

Aspen Mountain is comprised of three distinct ridges. To the west is Ruthie's, site of spine-tingling steeps and Aztec, the world-class downhill racing course. In the middle is Bell's Ridge (actually a separate mountain), offering mostly bumps and glades. And to the east is Gentleman's Ridge, which has easy groomers as well as the uncompromising steeps of Walsh's Gulch. For a long cruiser that forms a wild natural halfpipe, there's Spar Gulch, which cuts a steep "V" down the heart of the mountain to the patio of The Little Nell.

If you measure the quality of your riding by the perfection of the "esses" and the depth of the trenches you leave behind, Buttermilk is the place for you. Buttermilk has numerous constant-pitch, top-to-bottom fall line, groomed runs ideal for laying out one perfect carve after another.

Buttermilk's biggest asset is its undeserved reputation as a "beginner" mountain. This ensures all the egos go to Aspen Mountain or Highlands, leaving Buttermilk largely deserted. Midweek you and your buddies will often have entire trails to yourself. Buttermilk's solitude allows you to focus on improving your technique rather than constantly dodging skiers.

Buttermilk Mountain consists of the Main Buttermilk area, West Buttermilk and Tiehack. West Buttermilk is served by a rather slow double chairlift serving beginner terrain, but don't skip this area entirely. Larkspur can be one of the most fun carving runs on the mountain, allowing you to make one perfect carve after another, going into the trees on either side if you don't keep your turns tight. Carve Larkspur non-stop, top to bottom, and we guarantee you'll be high-fiving your buddies.

The mountain gets interesting over on Racer's Edge and Javelin, accessed from the Upper Tiehack lift. They'd probably be rated blues on other mountains, but they're labeled black diamonds here. These runs get groomed, meaning no moguls, but they're steep enough to force even advanced riders to concentrate on working their edges. Cutting down from Tiehack Parkway are the Ptarmigan and Timber Doodle Glades. Here's where intermediate boarders can learn to ride in the trees. The terrain is steep enough not to stall out, yet the trees are spaced far enough apart to learn. On a powder day you don't want to miss this area.

The new wild side of "The Milk" is the top-to-bottom Drop Zone terrain park designed by pro rider Jim Mangan. Nearly 2 miles long, it features 30 rails and the only 15-foot superpipe in the four Aspen mountains. It's geared towards intermediate and expert riders. At the bottom of the Drop Zone a gigantic kicker allows boarders with huge, and we're talking huge, air skills to put on a show for everyone at the base area. Hopefully, there's an ambulance standing by.

There also are a lot of runs at Buttermilk with gully-like sides that riders of all ages can swoop up and down, such as Bear. Riding at Buttermilk feels so much like playing you'll find yourself with a perpetual smile.

Buttermilk is home for the Pure Carve Expression Session. Last year the Expression Session brought over 100 carvers together. It's not a competition—there's no prize money—just a collection of individuals who know why snowboards have edges and how to have fun using them. The third annual Pure Carve Expression Session is slated for January. Also of note, a group of serious carvers meets at Buttermilk at 8:30 on Friday mornings, gaining first-tracks on all the groomers. And since Buttermilk is popular with snowshoers, there's a constant procession to the top of the mountain, making an excellent audience for showing off your carving skills.

Highlands attracts riders who are interested in riding blacks and double-blacks. While the resort's quick to point out they actually have more green and blue terrain than black, if intermediate cruisers or a great terrain park is what you're looking for, you'll be happier at Snowmass or Buttermilk. Highlands is where advanced and expert riders go to go steep on big powder days. At the peak, the snowcat- and hiking-accessed 12,500-foot Highlands Bowl gives riders with the legs—and the lungs—the ultimate in deep powder turns. This season you'll find 16 new runs here, mostly gladed, so check 'em out. A free snowcat ride from the top of Loge Peak takes riders to the first access gate and cuts off the first 20 minutes of hiking to Highlands Bowl. You have to hike the rest of the way along a ridgeline that can give you a new perspective on "Into Thin Air." Don't ask for a map of the Highlands Bowl at the base area. They won't give you one. Once you've warmed up your thighs, just past the snowcat drop off, you can pick up your souvenir copy at the 'Rooster's Roost.'

Get ready for a spectacular descent, one hundred or more turns in champagne powder up to your waist—or higher. Your best bet is to do the Highlands Bowl your first time with a guide who has ridden it several times before. Towards the bottom of the bowl, snowboarders need to stay high and rider's left to pick up the section of "Grand Traverse" where the least amount of cursing flats will be required. The "Grand Traverse" back from the Y-Zones and Steeplechase area can be a handful for riders, making you sorely wish you had poles. An icy curve marked with several signs admonishing you to slow down is followed by a slight uphill that will force those who do to unbuckle and skate. The catwalk itself is no wider than your average snowboard in many places, making skating, especially for goofy-footers, difficult.

Other Highland steeps include runs in the Olympic Bowl, which tend to be intense, but short. Dropping into runs like Deception, Aces & Eights, and Why treats you to serious steeps, trees, catwalk launches and powder stashes. And moguls.

Groomers suitable for carving include Thunderbowl and Golden Horn, on the lower part of the mountain. The Thunderbowl triple chair runs from the base of the mountain to the top of Golden Horn, making it easy to rack up vertical. Intermediate riders will want to ride the Cloud Nine, Olympic and Loge Peak lifts. The easiest intermediate runs are off Cloud Nine. Some of the most fun runs are directly beneath the lifts.

Highlands doesn't have a halfpipe or terrain park; however, Prospector Trail is known locally as Grommets Gulch and is a natural halfpipe. In summary, Highlands isn't for poseurs.

Mountain rating

Everyone gets something at Aspen. Beginners will have the most fun at Buttermilk. Intermediates probably will have a more varied day at Highlands, but the longest runs sweep down Aspen Mountain, and it's hard to beat the exhilarating cruising on Buttermilk. Experts have a tossup between Highlands and Aspen Mountain. Our advice to snowboarders: Carvers, riders learning trees and terrain park tricksters should head to Buttermilk, seekers of the pow and steeps will want to beeline it to Aspen Mountain or Highlands.

Cross-country and snowshoeing

Aspen/Snowmass has the most extensive free Nordic trail system in America, more than 65 km. of groomed trails called "Aspen's fifth mountain." The

Aspen Nordic Council's free system is accessible from Aspen or Snowmass and includes easy golf-course skiing as well as more difficult trails rising up to Snowmass.

In addition to the free trails provided by Aspen's Nordic Council, **Ashcroft Ski Touring Unlimited** (925-1971) has 42 km. of groomed and set trails, and backcountry skiers can use summer hiking trails. Trail fees are $15 per day, and lessons and rentals are available.

Hut systems connect Aspen with Vail on the Tenth Mountain Trail and with Crested Butte over the Pearl Pass. Guides are available and recommended. Call Tenth Mountain Trail Association for more information, 925-5775.

Other centers are the **Aspen Cross Country Center** (544-9246) on the Aspen Golf Course off Hwy. 82; **Ute Mountaineer** (925-2849); **Braun Hut System** (925-6618), which has information on trails to Crested Butte; and **Snowmass Cross Country Center** (923-3148).

Snowshoeing is quite popular in town, so ask about those programs at any of the cross-country centers mentioned here. In conjunction with the Aspen Center for Environmental Studies (ACES), **Aspen Skiing Company** has naturalist-guided tours for $49 each day (including lift rides, equipment and snack) on Aspen Mountain and Snowmass. Call 925-1220 or ACES at 925-5756 for reservations. You also can snowshoe up Aspen Mountain or Buttermilk at certain times and on certain runs. The lift ride down is free. Ask an Aspen Skiing Company concierge about this.

 ## Lessons (2002/03 prices)

For brochures and information, or to make reservations for ski and snowboard school programs, call 925-1220 or (877) AT-ASPEN (282-7736), or visit the Web site.

Group lessons: Adult small group lessons cost $105 a day. They are offered at all the mountains, and are limited to an average of four per class for all levels. Unlimited extensions are $90 per day.

Never-ever package: Three-day first-time ski/snowboard packages (including lessons, lift tickets, rentals, and use of ski/snowboard simulator) run $327 and are offered at Buttermilk and Snowmass. One-day programs are $115. Unlimited extensions of the three-day program are $90 per day.

Private lessons: $317 for a half day for one to five people; $1,540 for five half days; and $2,150 for five full days. Other discounts are available. Reservations are required. Lessons are offered in several languages, include ski storage, lift line privileges, and demo discounts. Offered every day on every mountain.

Special programs: Numerous, including clinics and/or ski and snowboard weeks for women, bumps, powder, off-piste, disabled skiers, video analysis, equipment assessment, shaped skis, and many more.

Racing: NASTAR is offered for adults, $6 for two runs or $10 for a day, and for children ages 12 and younger, $4. Courses are located at Silver Dip Swing at Aspen Mountain (daily), Nugget at Highlands (Wed.-Sun.) and Cabin Trail at Snowmass (Monday, Wednesday, Friday, Saturday). Weekly passes are available for $20.

 ## Child care (2002/03)

Ages: 8 weeks to 4 years.
Costs: $95 for a full day; $399 for five full days.

Reservations: Recommended. Child care in Aspen is offered by Kids' Club in the Yellow Brick Building, 315 Garmisch St. Call 925-3136. The state-licensed program offers indoor and outdoor (non-skiing) activities.

Other options: Also try **Aimee's Angels** (923-2809) for child-care needs. **Baby's Away** (800-948-9030; 920-1699) rents and will deliver baby needs to your lodge, such as crib, stroller, car seat and toys. Reservations are recommended for all of these services. Children from 5th through 12th grade can mingle with local kids in the afternoons at the **Aspen Youth Center** (hotline with weekly activities information, 925-7091) in downtown Aspen. The center has games, ping-pong, pool tables, movies and a dance room. The center does special programs depending on the season. Admission is free.

Children's lessons: Aspen Skiing Company has a completely different program for young children at each mountain (except for Aspen Mountain, where only adult lessons are taught). The programs at Snowmass are detailed in that chapter. Ages 7–12 skiing and ages 8-12 snowboarding pay $69 per day at Buttermilk (920-0935) or Aspen Highlands (544-3025). These programs include instruction and lunch, but rentals are extra. All kids 12 and younger *must* wear helmets while in ski and snowboard school. This mandate, the first of its kind by any ski resort, was issued in the spring of 2002. Helmets can be rented for $5 a day.

Lift tickets (2002/03 prices)

	Adult	Youth (13-17)
Four days (out of 10)	$256 ($64/day)	$196 ($49/day)
Five days (out of 10)	$320 ($64/day)	$245 ($49/day)
Six days (out of 10)	$384 ($64/day)	$294 ($49/day)

Who skis free: Ages 6 and younger.

Who skis at a discount: Children (7–12) pay $39 per day for multiday tickets of four to seven days. Ages 65 to 69 pay $59 for multiday tickets of four to seven days. Those 70 years and older get unlimited skiing or riding with The Silver Pass for $149 all season long. The best ticket prices are found by ordering tickets before Dec. 1, 2002, or by making a seven-day advance purchase. A six-day ticket purchased before Dec. 1 costs $307 ($51+ per day); a seven-day ticket purchased seven days in advance costs $404 ($57+ per day). In addition, you'll save 20 percent off ski and snowboard rentals if you purchase your ticket before Dec. 1, 2002, with a minimum five-day rental.

Note: The four Aspen-area mountains are far from other ski resorts and metropolitan areas. Consequently, just about all the visitors ski for more than one day, which is why we don't list the single-day price. All tickets are valid at all four mountains.

Accommodations

Accommodations in Aspen range from luxurious and pricey to modest and inexpensive. **StayAspenSnowmass,** (800) 262-7736 or 925-9000, can reserve nearly all properties listed here. Multiday lift-and-lodging packages are the best deal. You also can log on to www.stayaspensnowmass.com and check out the "Virtual Hostel" for last-minute, discounted lodging packages.

Hotel Jerome (800-331-7213 or 920-1000; $$$$) and The **Sardy House** (920-2525 or 800-321-3457; $$$$), both on East Main Street, reflect Aspen's glory days. The Sardy House is a Victorian home, elegantly transformed into an intimate Bed and Breakfast. A modern addition has been tacked onto the rear, but try to get one of the original rooms. The Jerome—

on the National Register of Historic Places—is a grand old hotel restored to more elegance than the silver barons ever knew. Even if you don't stay there, this Aspen landmark is worth a walk-through to view the antiques and old photos on the walls.

The **Little Nell** (920-4600 or 888-843-6355; $$$$) is just steps from the Silver Queen Gondola at the base of Aspen Mountain. It has received the highest rating (five on a 1–5 scale) from several rating services, such as AAA and Mobil. All rooms have fireplaces, sofas, over-sized beds with comforters, and marble bathrooms. There is a spa and a heated outdoor pool.

The **St. Regis, Aspen** (920-3300 or 800-241-3333; $$$$) is richly appointed, with a tasteful decor that brings to mind an exclusive hunting club. It has a fitness center and various ski packages, and its restaurants are top-flight. Though the red brick building is just a few years old, it looks like it belongs to historic Aspen.

The **Residence** (920-6532; $$$$) has world-class European suites in an historic down-town landmark building. Also luxurious are the newly renovated Aspen Club Lodge, now called the **Sky Hotel** (925-6760 or 800-882-2582) and the delightful award-winning **Hotel Lenado** (925-6246 or 800-321-3457; $$$$). The latter, another property of the Sardy House owners, may be small, but it's huge in amenities, personality and service. A delicious hot breakfast is included in the room price, which drops into the $$$ category during shoulder seasons. Look for the funky-colored building on South Aspen St.

The **Snowflake Inn** (925-3221 or 800-247-2069; $$$), a block from the transportation center on East Hyman Avenue is clean, roomy and is walking distance from the Ajax gondola, the buses to the other areas, and the downtown area. And it has a very friendly staff, laundry facilities, a heated pool and spa, and a free continental breakfast and après-ski snacks. What more does one need?

One of our readers tells us **Hotel Durant** (925-8500; $$-$$$$) is one of his favorite "little hotels." Beautifully renovated in 1996, it's just two blocks from downtown and one-and-a-half blocks from lift A-1. The lounge fireplace and outdoor Jacuzzi provide great ways to relax after a day on the slope.

Our favorite place in Aspen, a lodge of a kind that's disappearing all too fast, is **The Mountain Chalet** (925-7797 or 800-321-7813; $-$$$). This place is just plain friendly to everyone, including families. If you can't stand a 3-year-old crawling over a lounge chair in the lobby or families howling over a game of Monopoly, then don't stay here. Rates are reasonable and include a hearty breakfast served family-style. It's a few blocks from Aspen Mountain's Silver Queen gondola, and across the street from the transportation center (ide-ally situated, in other words). Call early for rooms, because folks reserve space here well in advance. Package deals for lodging, lift tickets and full breakfast are as low as $60 per person per day in a dorm bunk or a four-person room; about $130 per person per night for two to a room. To get these prices, call the chalet directly.

Other places that treat guests very well are the **Mountain House Lodge** (920-3440; $$), the **Hotel Aspen** (925-3441 or 800-527-7369; $$) and the **Molly Gibson Lodge** (925-3434 or 800-356-6559; $$).

Also try **Skier's Chalet** (920-2037; $-$$) across from the Shadow Mountain Lift (for-merly Lift 1-A) with a heated outdoor pool, the **Limelight** (925-3025 or 800-433-0832; $$), and the **St. Moritz Lodge** (925-3220; $), a hostel only five blocks from the center of town.

You can still find inexpensive rooms at the **Christmas Inn** (925-3822; $$), **Innsbruck Inn** (925-2980; $$), and budget champion **Tyrolean Lodge** (925-4595 or 800-321-7025; $).

The **Heatherbed Lodge** (925-7077; 800-356-6782) is a good place to stay near High-lands. Rates are about $120 per night and include a full breakfast.

Several management companies rent condominiums. For luxury, three-bedroom unit, condos right on the slopes, try **Mountain Queen Condominiums** (925-6366). The **Gant** (925-5000 or 800-345-1471) is another choice in condo lodging.

Coates, Reid and Waldron, 720 East Hyman Ave. (925-1400 or 800-222-7736), is the largest management company in the area, with condos and homes. Chateau Eau Claire and Chateau Roaring Fork are two of their popular units. Shadow Mountain is not so luxurious, but has a ski-in/ski-out location.

Condominiums directly on the slopes are the **Fasching Haus** (925-2260), **Fifth Avenue** (925-7397; through Aspen Lodging Co.) and **Durant Condominiums** (925-7910). They also are available through Aspen Central Reservations, (800-262-7736).

The Ritz Carlton Club dominates the lodging at the new village in Aspen Highlands, so unless you are a member of this exclusive timeshare, don't look for a place to stay there.

Dining

Let's start with *the* place to eat breakfast, **The Wienerstube** (a.k.a. "the Stube") at 633 E. Hyman and Spring. Come here for Eggs Benny, omelettes, Austrian sausages and homemade Viennese pastries. **Main Street Bakery Cafe,** 201 E. Main St., has homemade baked goods, granola, fruit, eggs and great coffee for reasonable prices. Another recommended breakfast spot is the contemporary cafe, **Poppycock's**, 609 E. Cooper. For the best coffee in town, head to **Bagel Bites**, Aspen's only bagel shop at 300 Puppy Smith St.; or **Ink! Coffee** inside the D&E Snowboard Shop in the Aspen Mountain Building. The **World Link Café,** 520 E. Hyman, serves gourmet coffee along with DSL high-speed Internet access, a wine bar, breakfast bagels and muffins. **The Pretzelmaker** moved into the space below **New York Pizza** at 411 E. Hyman. A New York family recipe yields 12 flavors of pretzels, as well as frozen yogurt, soups, smoothies and coffee. Stays open late for night clubbers.

Aspen has enjoyed an unparalleled culinary revolution that has bypassed sole meunière for a more exotic "beach party" shellfish. Exotic ingredients and ethnic foods are definitely trendy. Over the past few years, we've seen black trumpets and white truffles, edible nasturtiums and a veal dish called "@*#?&!." Aspen is a place where you can enjoy the fine restaurants thoroughly, knowing that the next day you'll ski off those calories. But be careful—most menu items are separately priced and the bill can add up!

If cost is what you're worried about, many restaurants in Aspen have a "bar" menu. These "bar" menus are the locals' secrets to eating well and they aren't your usual hot wings and nachos, but culinary delights between $8-$15, such as roast sirloin steak with gourmet mashed potatoes at **Cache Cache**, spinach and ricotta cheese ravioli in a light smoked ricotta and sage sauce at **L'Hostaria** or the Sambal shrimp quesadilla at **Elevation.**

One of Aspen's long-time favorites had a culinary rebirth a few years back. **The Montagna at the Little Nell** (675 E. Durant; 920-6330; $$$) is newly renovated and specializes in contemporary American Alpine cuisine. It was voted tops in Colorado by the readers of *Gourmet* and is a Grand Award recipient, the highest achievement from *Wine Spectator*. Open for breakfast, lunch and dinner, as well as Sunday brunch.

Syzygy (520 E. Hyman Avenue; 925-3700, reservations required; $$$) has a menu that combines French, southwestern, Oriental and Italian cuisines. Don't be put off by the hard-to-pronounce name (Siz-i-je) or the obscure explanation of its meaning on the menu. The atmosphere is intimate yet casual.

Dining: $$$–Entrees $20+; $$–$10-20; $–less than $10.
Accommodations: (double room) $$$$–$200+; $$$–$141-$200; $$–$81-$140; $–$80 and less.

Go to **Piñons** (second floor at 105 S. Mill; 920-2021) to dine in a cozy western ranch decor, with stucco walls, a leather bar and menus and huge brass bowls. All meats and fish are grilled over mesquite and cherry wood. Desserts vary daily.

If you think that at these prices, you should be entertained and have your apartment cleaned for a year, one man will at least do the former. Owner Mead Metcalf has been playing to **The Crystal Palace** sellout crowds each evening at 6 and 9 p.m. for more than four decades (300 East Hyman Avenue; 925-1455; $$, reservations may be necessary several weeks in advance). The Crystal Palace's talented staff not only cranks out a full dinner and bar service, but then belts out a cabaret revue spoofing the media's latest victims. You can choose from perfectly pink beef tenderloin with Madeira sauce, roast duckling, rack of lamb or prime rib. The food doesn't have to be good, but it is.

On the outside chance there's still a platinum card burning a hole in your parka, try **Renaissance** (304 East Hopkins; 925-2402; $$$). Chef-owner Charles Dale (who grew up in the palace in Monaco with Caroline and Albert) claims his is one of three restaurants in the world to have a daily changing degustation or tasting menu (five courses), as well as offering course-by-course, by-the-glass wine pairings. Wine gets special attention at Renaissance. The list has won the *Wine Spectator* Award of Excellence. Reservations recommended.

Cache Cache (lower level of the Mill St. Plaza; 925-3835; $$–$$$) gets a thumbs up from locals for French provincial cuisine, especially their half-price early-bird specials. The polenta nicoise, wild mushroom cannelloni and perfectly grilled yellowtail are favorites. On their bar menu, salads begin at about $3 and all entrees are under $11. Named one of America's best new restaurants is another French bistro, **Rustique** (216 So. Monarch; 920-2555; $$-$$$). A child-friendly menu offers 25 classic French favorites under $14 called "Small Plates," but the Cassoulet Toulousain with Duck Confit and Sausage at $23 will please any hungry parent.

Kenichi (233 E. Hopkins; 920-2212) and **Takah Sushi** (on the Hyman Avenue Mall; 925-8588) are *the* locals' favorite for Pan Asian cuisine and sushi. Always crowded, reservations are a must, especially on Friday and Saturday nights.

Outstanding gourmet Italian restaurants are **Campo de Fiori** (205 E. Mill; 920-7717; $$) and Campo's new cousin (same owner) **Gusto Ristorante** (415 E. Main; 925-8222; $$-$$$). Gusto's contemporary cuisine is refreshingly different than the classic dishes of Campo de Fiori and a tad less expensive. Top-rated **Mezzaluna** (624 Cooper; 925-5332; $$-$$$) is a long-time favorite for Mediterranean. **Caffé Torino** (315 E. Hyman; 429-0799; $$-$$$) is known for authentic country style Italian while **Olives** at the St. Regis (920-7356; $$$) has a broader Mediterranean-inspired menu from award-winning Chef Todd English. Valet parking is complimentary.

Ethnic eateries we like are **Matsuhisa** (303 E. Main; 544-6628; $$$), a classic Japanese place that is part of the Nobu restaurant chain found in the best cities around the world; **Asie** ($$), the new "hottest place in town" for Asian food; and **Blue Maize** (308 S. Hunter; 925-6698, $$) for Southwest and Latin American food. **Mogador** (429-1072; $$$) on the Hyman St. Mall (look closely, the sign is very small), overwhelms you with its Spanish atmosphere and tempts you with North African tastes like the traditional Moroccan dish "B'steeya," artesianal cheeses, a platter of tapas, bowls of Sangria on the bar, and exotic desserts. **Little Ollie's** (downstairs at 308 S. Hunter; 544-9888; $) has healthy Chinese food and offers take-out. **La Cocina** (308 E. Hopkins; 925-9714; $) is popular with locals—they call it "Lah-co."

Enjoy great homestyle Mexican food and low prices (no credit cards accepted). **The Cantina** (corner of Mill and Main; 925-3663; $–$$) is a trendier Mexican alternative.

"New" describes **Elevation** (304 E Hopkins; 544-5166; $$–$$$), named "Best New Restaurant for 2001," it serves New American cuisine and has a new sister, **NXT** (pronounced "next), opened in 2002. NXT on the Cooper Avenue Mall (920-4004; $$) oozes the seductiveness of a nightclub, which it becomes when it stops serving its Pan-Asian cuisine. A DJ spins for late-night dancing.

Restaurants recommended by locals and visitors: **L'Hostaria** (925-9022; $$–$$$) showcases decor and recipes direct from Italy. Their special is a two-pound Chilean sea bass Fed-Exed-in daily and baked with olive oil, herbs, clams and mussels. **The Big Wrap** (544-1700; $) features burrito-like wraps but with a variety of exotic fillings. How about a bistro in a bookstore—**The Explorer Bookseller's** upper level graduates into a smart vegetarian bistro with summa cum laude desserts (221 E. Main; 925-5338; $$).

Boogie's Diner (534 E. Cooper; 925-6610; $) is a real '50s diner with oldies music, blue plate specials and meatloaf (great milkshakes, too). Casual **Little Annie's Eating House** (517 E. Hyman; 925-1098; $$) is still the ribs, chicken, burger and potato pancake champ. Try Annie's daily specials. The **Skier's Chalet Steak House** (710 S. Aspen; 925-3381) has been around since 1951 serving traditional steak, seafood and salad. **The Steak Pit** (corner of Hopkins and Monarch; 925-3459; $$) has also been in business for a time. Since 1960, they've served some of the best steaks in Aspen along with a sumptuous all-you-can-eat salad bar.

For a real adventure, head out to the **Pine Creek Cookhouse** (925-1044; $$$) for a casual evening and solid fare. At an elevation of 9,725 feet, this rustic log cabin is in the midst of towering pines beneath Elk Mountain peaks some 12 miles up Castle Creek Road. It is accessible by a one-and-a-half-mile cross-country trek or by a sleigh drawn by a team of Percherons. Views are outstanding. Reservations are essential (at times two to four weeks in advance), as the logistics of running a kitchen not reached by road in winter is no small matter. The Cookhouse feeds several hundred people each day, and all that food (wild game is its specialty) comes in by snowmobile. Meals are prepared right in front of you in the open kitchen and are served by one of your cross-country guides.

On the mountains:

The crown jewel of Aspen's on-mountain dining is the **Sundeck Restaurant** (429-6971), housed in a magnificent new lodge that replaces the old Sundeck building at the top of the gondola. It's a favorite spot for spectacular views, people-watching and innovative cuisine served from individual food stations. Check out the priceless old ski photos on the walls. The members-only Aspen Mountain Club is also housed there—take a peek!

Bump's (925-4027), at the Buttermilk base area, features foods from a wood-fired rotisserie, brick ovens and a pit smoker, as well as huge salads, pastas and stews. **Ajax Tavern** (920-9333; $$$) at the base of Silver Queen Gondola boasts Tuscan influences in a richly wood-paneled room. Lunch is a hearty selection of Colorado lamb, roasted mussels, pastas, salads and sandwiches with a Napa Valley wine list and outdoor seating for primo people-watching. While not a sit-down restaurant, **Bonnie's,** just above Lift 3 on Aspen Mountain, feeds some 1,500 hungry skiers per day between 9:30 a.m. and 2:30 p.m. Go before noon or after 2 p.m., unless you love lines. The double decks outside are *the* places to be during the day. Owner Bonnie Rayburn's gourmet pizza on freshly made crust is a huge crowd pleaser. Homemade soups, such as the Colorado white-bean chili, are served with large crusty pieces of fresh French bread. Save room for her world-famous apple strudel.

Dining: $$$–Entrees $20+; $$–$10-20; $–less than $10.
Accommodations: (double room) $$$$–$200+; $$$–$141-$200; $$–$81-$140; $–$80 and less.

Other on-mountain options include the **Cliffhouse** atop Buttermilk with a new outdoor deck and serving its famous custom-cooked Mongolian Barbecue. **Cloud Nine,** a European-style bistro with a fixed-price menu, is decorated in early evacuation gear since it shares space with the Aspen Highlands ski patrol. It has killer views of the Maroon Bells. Snowcats can bring you there for evening dining; call 544-3063. **Merry-Go-Round**, mid-mountain at High-lands, serves grilled brats, burgers and Mexican fare, and is the location for the legendary jumping show on Freestyle Fridays.

The Village at Aspen Highlands is shaping up nicely, although it's a bit dark in color for our tastes and the buildings block the mountain view. Retail shops and restaurants will be filling the empty spaces, but for now we liked the all-encompassing **World Link Café,** a coffee-house-bakery-deli-wineshop-apres-ski-Internet café all rolled into one location. Also **Willow Creek** at the Ritz Carlton Club, **Thunderbowl Café** and **Iguana's** are alternatives for lunch and dinner.

 ## Après-ski/nightlife

Slopeside **Ajax Tavern** is a big draw for catching afternoon rays as the lifts start to close. If you don't find what you want there, the crowd spreads out to **The Greenhouse** at the Little Nell Hotel, **Mezzaluna, 39 Degrees** at the Sky Hotel, the **Aspen Club Lodge, Little Annie's, Cooper Street Pier,** the **J-Bar** (Jack Nicholson's hangout at the Jerome), the **Red Onion** and **Grottos.** Après-ski comes in all varieties here, from **The Cantina**, with its very happy hour (have a margarita in the compadre size), to the quiet and genteel **Hotel Jerome Bar.** At Snowmass **The Cirque** or **Zane's** upstairs on The Mall are the places to be; at Aspen Highlands it's **The World Link Café** and **Iguana's** in the new village.

At night, the music and dance beat begin to take over. Earlier in the evening, the high-energy place to find out who's in town is **Mezzaluna**, with its brassy horseshoe-shaped bar. It's a good singles bar and gives you the best in upscale people-watching. **St. Regis's The Whiskey Rocks** has live music in the lounge. **The Little Nell** bar and **Syzygy** have jazz. DJ's rule at **Shooters, Club Chelsea, Elevations,** NXT and **The Lava Room.**

Eric's Bar, Cigar Bar and **Aspen Billiards** all attract singles, and have lots of microbrews on tap (great scotch, too). Another upscale beer spot is **McStorlie's Pub.** A relatively mixed crowd with normal tastes congregate in the **Red Onion** and **Little Annie's.**

Cooper Street Pier is very much a local and college student hangout. For the best "last call," try **Mother Lode.** There are many other night spots in town; pick up a copy of Aspen Magazine's Traveler's Guide for a list, or check local papers, The Aspen Times and The Aspen Daily News, for current happenings.

 ## Other activities

Ice skating is across from the transportation center at Silver Circle Ice Rink (925-6360) and indoors at Aspen Ice Garden (920-5141). For winter **fly-fishing** trips call Aspen Outfitting Co. (925-3406), Oxbow Outfitting Co. (925-1505) or Aspen Sports (925-6332). **Sleigh rides** take place at the T-Lazy-7 Ranch (925-7040). The T-Lazy-7 also leads **snowmobile tours** around the Maroon Bells and through the ghost town of Independence.

The Wheeler Opera House (920-5770) hosts a variety of big-time entertainers through-out the season. **Cooking School of Aspen** offers classes from Aspen's finest chefs for adults and kids (920-1879). **Spas and athletic clubs** offer relaxation after a tough day on the hill. Try the Aspen Club and Spa (925-8900), and the Aspen Athletic Club (925-2531).

Many winter visitors to Aspen never touch the slopes during their stay. The place is a **shopper's paradise,** and even if you can't afford the mostly high-end merchandise, browsing is part of the fun. High on the browsing scale is Boogie's, 534 E. Cooper St. In addition to funky clothes and other stuff, you'll find Elvis Presley's 1955 red Corvette (but not for sale). Les Chefs D'Aspen, on the corner of Cooper and Hunter, sells imported kitchenware plus local gourmet foods and coffee. Clothing stores are abundant and filled with unusual items. Some of our favorites: Hildegard's, 228 Mill St., for unique accessories; Goldies and the Kids, 205 S. Mill, for delightful kids' clothing. We usually stop by Gracy's and Susie's Ltd., both on E. Hopkins, to check out what the wear-it-once crowd has on consignment. Prada took over the Planet Hollywood spot at 312 So. Galena. It's near the Roots store (as in 2002 Olympic berets) with Canadian imports. Don't miss a visit to Explore Booksellers and Bistro, 221 E. Main. It's a legend in Aspen. Owned by the former mayor of Aspen, Bill Stirling, and his wife, Katherine Thalberg, this is the place to pick up your favorite novel or ski guidebook and have dinner too (see *Dining*).

Most of Aspen's 30 **art galleries** are within a four-by-three-block area between Spring and Monarch Streets and Hopkins Ave. and Durant St. Our favorites are Omnibus Gallery for vintage poster art; Galerie Du Bois for Impressionism; Highline Gallery for glass art; Pam Driscol Gallery for life-size bronze sculptures; and Baldwin Gallery for contemporary collections.

This next activity is a good way to segue into our transportation section: **The Ultimate Taxi** is a unique way to tour Aspen. This disco on wheels probably will top your list of Aspen Memorable Experiences. Check it out at www.ultimatetaxi.com or for a ride call 927-9239.

 ## Getting there and getting around

By air: Aspen's Sardy Field, 3 miles from aspen and 8 miles from Snowmass, is served by regular flights from four cities: Denver (United Express), Phoenix (America West), Memphis and Minneapolis/St.Paul (Northwest Jet Airlink) and Los Angeles (United Express). Don't make the mistake our staff has: One year we were booked on the Sunday that ended Christmas vacation, just as some 150 private jets were stacked up waiting to fly out. Some of our staff was able to fly in, but with no luggage; others had to be bused from Denver and Glenwood Springs. It was a mess. The city and the FAA are working on a solution, but if you fly on major holidays, expect delays and carry on emergency supplies.

Eagle County airport, about 70 miles away, is becoming the best-served airport for this resort. It hosts flights from Northwest, American, Continental, United, and Delta. American has daily flights arriving from Dallas/Ft. Worth, Chicago, Newark, San Francisco and Saturday flights from New York and Miami. Continental has daily service from Houston and weekend flights from Newark. Delta flies from Atlanta. Northwest flies from Minneapolis daily with Saturday flights from Detroit. United flies daily from Denver and LA and on weekends from Chicago and New York La Guardia. Colorado Mountain Express (800-525-6363 or 949-4227) takes skiers from Eagle to Aspen.

If you find yourself in Aspen without your gear or outdoor clothing, make sure to ask the airlines for a voucher to rent what you need until they show up with your luggage. All the airlines hand out coupons for equipment in case yours is delayed. These vouchers are accepted at virtually every sports shop in town.

If your luggage gets waylaid, call Lorenzo Semple at **Suit Yourself** (920-0295). He will be at your door with a van full of ski and snowboard clothing for you to rent during your stay. His wide inventory includes one-piece ski suits, jackets and pants, and accessories. He takes airline vouchers.

Regular ground transportation also leaves the Denver International Airport for Aspen, but it's about a five-hour drive on I-70, about 150 miles away. Rental cars are available at both Denver and Eagle County Airport.

By train: Amtrak has service to Glenwood Springs, where skiers can get ground transportation the rest of the way.

Getting around: Aspen has a free bus system, RFTA, with several routes in town and to Glenwood Springs. There also is a separate, free shuttle between the various ski mountains during the day; there is a small fee after 4 p.m. Downtown is enjoyably walkable. Thank goodness a car is unnecessary because parking is a pain.

Nearby resorts

Sunlight Mountain Resort, Glenwood Springs, CO; (800) 445-7931

Internet: www.sunlightmtn.com
4 lifts; 440 acres; 2,010 vertical feet

Not only is this a less pricey ski option if you're headed to nearby Aspen, but Glenwood Springs is the home of the world's largest hot springs pool, two blocks long and kept at a toasty 90 degrees. Most of Ski Sunlight is intermediate terrain, though the double-black-diamond Sunlight Extreme provides steep and gladed challenges for the best of skiers and riders.

Lift tickets (01/02 prices): Adults, $32; Junior (6-13) and Senior (60-69), $20; 70+ and younger than 5, free.

Distance from Denver: About 175 miles west on I-70 and Hwy. 82. The closest airport is Vail/Eagle, about 30 miles east of Sunlight Mountain. Aspen is about 50 miles south. Glenwood Springs is a daily stop on Amtrak's California Zephyr route from San Francisco to Chicago.

Lodging information: Call (800) 445-7931 for a free vacation planner.

Snowmass

Snowmass Village, Colorado

Summit elevation: 12,510 feet
Vertical drop: 4,406 feet
Base elevation: 8,104 feet

Address: Aspen Skiing Company
P.O. Box 1248, Aspen, CO 81612 or
Snowmass Resort Association,
P.O. Box 5566, Snowmass Village, CO 81615
✆ **Area code:** 970
Ski area phone: 925-1220 or
(800) 525-6200
Snow report: 925-1221 or (888-ASPEN-SNO, 277-3676)
ⓘ **Toll-free reservations:** (800) 598-2005
Fax: 920-0771
E-mail: info@aspensnowmass.com
Internet: www.aspensnowmass.com or
www.snowmassvillage.com
Expert:★★★★ **Advanced:**★★★★
Intermediate:★★★★★
Beginner:★★★ **Never-ever:**★★

Number of lifts: 20—7 high-speed quads,
2 triples, 6 doubles, 3 surface lifts, 2 magic carpets
Snowmaking: 6 percent
Skiable acreage: 3,010 acres
Uphill capacity: 27,978 per hour
Bed Base: 6,000 rentable units
Nearest lodging: slopeside, condos
Resort child care: Yes, 6 weeks and older
Snowboarding: Yes, unlimited
Adult ticket, per day: $64 (02/03 prices)

Dining:★★★ (at resort)
★★★★★ (in the region)
Apres-ski/nightlife:★★(at resort)
★★★★★ (in the region)
Other activities:★★★

Though it is lumped into the Aspen experience by geography, Snowmass stands on its own as a winter destination. Snowmass ranks among the top 10 resorts in America in size, and it's the second-largest in Colorado (after Vail). It covers more than 3,010 acres—more than Ajax, Buttermilk and Highlands combined. And thanks to a surface lift to the top of the Cirque (formerly reached by a hike or snowcat), Snowmass lays claim to the longest vertical drop in the United States, 4,406 feet. (Big Sky, MT, has a 4,180-foot vertical; Jackson Hole, WY, 4,139 feet. Now you have your après-ski bar conversation opener.)

Snowmass has long been described as a cruiser's mountain. The Big Burn allows you to activate your autopilot, and the cruise from the top of Elk Camp to Fanny Hill lasts 4 miles. But if you know where to go, you can find jaw-dropping steeps, cornices, chutes and cliffs. Just think left. The Hanging Valley area is to your left as you unload from the High Alpine lift, and the Cirque Headwall and East Wall lay just to the left of the wind-powered Cirque lift at the 12,510-foot summit. On big snow days, you'll want to line up early for the rope-drop into Roberto's or Possible that lead into the Hanging Valley Glades.

Snowmass village seems to stretch forever uphill. Like Keystone or Copper Mountain, this is a purpose-built winter resort. A village mall has shops, restaurants, bars and skier services. Hundreds of condos line the lower part of the resort, and about 95 percent of the lodging is ski-in/ski-out. It doesn't get much more convenient than Snowmass. A note to those staying in a ski-in/ski-out condo: Turn around and "bookmark" you place before you head down to the lift for your first run. We had a heck of a time knowing where to cut off from the ski run to our unit in a sea of brown condos at the end of the day.

A tip for those staying in Aspen and skiing here for a day: Park at the Two Creeks base area, which is closer to Aspen. The Two Creeks quad connects to the Elk Creek high-speed quad lift, getting you to the top of Elk Camp in less than 20 minutes.

A cool freebie is "First Tracks" on Wednesday and Friday at 8 a.m. Simply sign up the day before at the concierge desk and you can be one of the day's first to ski or ride down empty, freshly groomed slopes with a Ski & Snowboard School pro!

 ## Mountain layout—Skiing

◆◆ **Expert:** Get a rush dropping through trees in the Hanging Valley Glades or into the bowl at Hanging Valley Wall—both double-blacks. To get there quickly on powder morns, take Wood Run, Alpine Springs and High Alpine Chairs. The ski school offers guided tours back here.

Another extreme playground is the Cirque, a scooped-out place between Sheer Bliss and High Alpine lifts. This is served by a surface lift, at the top of which you'll find the "Rocky Mountain High" run, named in memory of the late singer John Denver. Don't try this area unless you're comfortable on Hanging Valley Wall. You'll have to be deft of foot on Rock Island and KT Gully. Even more challenging is AMF at the top. A local says it stands for "Adios, My Friend," but we think he gave us the "this-is-a-family-guidebook" version.

◆ **Advanced:** Skiers ready to burn up steep-pitched cruising will think they've found nirvana when they make the first descent into the Campground area. Here is a wonderful long run: To come off the top of Big Burn on Sneaky's, tuck to avoid the uphill stretch at Sam's Knob, cut south around the Knob and head into the blacks of Bear Claw, Slot, Wildcat or Zugspitze to the base of the Campground lift. All offer great cruises and patches of moguls normally of the mellow sand-dune variety.

■ **Intermediate:** In addition to its black runs, Sam's Knob also is a great intermediate area, as are Elk Camp and the Two Creeks area. The Big Burn is legendary cruiser fun. It's an entire side of a mountain that was allegedly set aflame by Ute Indians in the 1880s as a warning to advancing white settlers. The pioneers settled anyway, but the trees never grew back thickly, so the run, dotted by a few spruces, is a mile wide and a mile-and-a-half long. On low visibility days, though, watch out.

If the pitch at Big Burn is not quite to your liking, head over to High Alpine, which is perhaps five degrees steeper. If you ride the surface lift to the Cirque and find it too challenging, ski the intermediate ridge back to the Big Burn.

●● **Beginner:** Beginners have a wide gentle area parallel to the village. Fanny Hill eases down by the mall, Wood Run lift opens another easy glide around the Wood Road side of the village, and further to the left a long straightaway, Funnel, will give beginners the feeling they're really covering terrain.

Beginners who want to see more of the mountain can head up to Sam's Knob and try Finestra with its spectacular views and great menu, enjoy the view and head down a meandering trail bearing the names Max Park, Lunchline and Dawdler, which turns back to Fanny Hill. (Avoid the blue runs on the face of Sam's Knob because they are not for beginners.) The next step up would be Elk Camp, labeled blue but very gentle.

● **Never-ever:** We would give the beginner terrain here a higher rating but for one important fact: Many of the ski-in/ski-out condos are along the green runs, so at the beginning and end of the day, they often are used by skilled skiers and snowboarders in a hurry to get to either the lifts or the hot tub. If you're just starting, we recommend a trip to Buttermilk.

Mountain layout—Snowboarding

Snowmass is huge. There's terrain for riders of all levels—and persuasions. Expert riders should head to the legendary Cirque. From the top of the Cirque lift, adrenaline seekers reach the Headwall, AMF and Gowdy's.

The Campground area's snow can stay untracked days after a big snowfall, delighting advanced riders who continue to discover fresh tree lines and bottomless powder stashes. To access the Campground, head to the top of The Big Burn and stay rider's left to Sneaky's.

Intermediate boarders can get away from crowds on Fanny Hill by heading for Elk Camp, with groomed intermediate slopes and a high-speed quad that lets riders rack up the vertical. From the top of the Elk Camp lift, a short 5- to 10-minute hike takes you to Long Shot, a backcountry-like, ungroomed run that winds 3 miles through the National forest—getting you even further away from the bubbas. Long Shot was recently voted "2nd Favorite Snowboard Run" by readers, mostly locals, of the Aspen Times, right behind The Big Burn.

The Big Burn is a gigantic open area on the mountain, intermediate in pitch, approximately a mile wide by a mile long. A few trees here and there disrupt an otherwise completely open snowfield. On a powder day you can make endless turns, until your thighs also feel the big burn. There's nothing like it at any other ski area in North America. Eventually you'll end up on Dallas Freeway or Wineskin, which will take you back to The Big Burn Lift.

If you get powder so deep that even The Big Burn isn't steep enough, head to the High Alpine lift for steeper terrain. From atop of High Alpine, riders hike 10 minutes to get hang time on Hanging Valley Wall. Alpine Springs and Naked Lady lifts serve a variety of intermediate runs including Lunkerville and Coffee Pot. The Naked Lady offers some fun rollers.

If you think tricks are for kids, Snowmass has two halfpipes and two terrain parks with features suitable for freestylers of all levels. Park designer and pro rider Jim Mangan designed both parks. The Sam's Knob and Coney Glade lifts, both high-speed quads, provide dedicated lift access to Trenchtown, home to a halfpipe and terrain park geared for advanced riders (the Coney Glade lift gives you full view of freestylers in action). There's a booming sound system and the Trenchtown yurt is an upbeat warming hut. The Trenchtown halfpipe is 300 feet long and is cut with a 12-foot Pipe Dragon. The Trenchtown Park, separated by the pipe into upper and lower sections, has a variety of tabletops, spine ramps, rail-slides and fun boxes. There's also a boardercross course on Upper Velvet Falls, directly to rider's left of the Trenchtown halfpipe. Beginner and intermediate snowboarders will want to take the Funnel chairlift to the Funnel halfpipe and terrain park.

Assay Hill is a good spot for learning to snowboard. You'll find it near the Funnel lift, to the left of Fanny Hill, the Snowmass Village Mall and the ticket office.

Mountain rating

This is an intermediate mountain, even though it has pockets of excellent advanced terrain and beginner smoothies. If experts know where to go, they will love it here. Skiers and riders who crave cruising will think they have arrived in heaven. Few competent skiers and riders who have returned from Snowmass have been heard complaining. That's the best recommendation of all.

Cross-country and snowshoeing

Nordic skiing at Snowmass is on the golf course at the **Snowmass Cross Country Center** (800-525-6200 or 923-3148). It offers lessons and rentals, plus its trails connect with the most extensive free Nordic trail system in America, which runs between the towns of Aspen and Snowmass and covers more than 65 km. of groomed trails. For other information on cross-country skiing opportunities, see the Aspen chapter.

Snowshoe tours leave daily at 10 a.m. and 1 p.m. from Two Creeks for a naturalist-led tour of a secluded loop through the woods. Tours including lifts, equipment and a snack are $49 for adults, $29 for ages 8–19 and 65 and older. Call 800-525-6200 or 925-5756.

 ## Lessons (2002/03 prices)

Group lessons: Adult small group lessons cost $105 a day. Limited to an average of four per class for all levels. Unlimited extensions are $90 a day.

Never-ever package: Three-day first-time skier packages, including equipment rental, run $327 and are offered at Snowmass and Buttermilk. One-day programs are $115. Unlimited extensions of the three-day program are $90 per day.

Private lessons: $317 for a half day for one to five people; $1,540 for five half days; and $2,150 for five full days. Other discounts are available. Reservations are required. Lessons are offered in several languages and include ski storage and demo discounts.

Special programs: These are numerous, including bumps, powder, disabled skiers, video analysis, equipment assessment, shaped skis, and many more. Call ASC at (800) 525-6200 and ask for a ski and snowboard school brochure. The Women's Edge is a Monday-Thursday program that runs from January through March and includes video analysis, a picnic, and travel to the other Aspen mountains. Reservations are required; call 877-282-7736.

Snowmass has one other instruction program that we believe is unique among U.S. ski resorts: speed skiing. On Fridays, skiers can pay $5 for three runs down Slot, a black-diamond run in the Sam's Knob area, or $15 for the day. Basic instruction and a helmet are included, and participants can rent specialized skis for an extra fee. You'll get a certificate indicating your speed, often as high as 65 miles per hour.

Racing: NASTAR is offered for $6 for two runs or $10 for the entire day for adults; children pay $4 for two runs or $8 for the entire day. Clinics also are offered.

 ## Child care (2002/03 prices)

Ages: 8 weeks to 3 1/2 years.
Costs: $57 half day, $89 a day with multiday discounts.
Reservations: Required; call 923-0563 or 877-282-7736.

Other options: Little Red School House (923-3756) offers licensed day care for ages 3–5; **Aimee's Angels** (923-2809) has care for ages 12 months–3 years. **Night Hawks** is an evening child-care program (877-282-7736) for ages 3–10; $12/hour for the first child; half that price for additional children in the same family. For other suggestions, see the Aspen chapter.

Children's lessons: We've listed the children's programs at Snowmass here; kids' lessons at Buttermilk and Aspen Highlands are in the Aspen chapter. To make reservations for the following lessons, call 877-282-7736.

Snow Cubs is for ages 8 weeks to 3 1/2 years. Toddlers get daycare, lunch and brief ski lessons. Toilet-trained 3-year-olds take group lessons, while the others must enroll in private lessons. The cost is $89 for a full day, plus $65 if a private lesson is needed. Big Burn Bears is for ages 3 1/2–4 years. They have a segregated learning area and indoor area. The cost is $89 for a full day (all full-day lessons include equipment and lunch); $57 for a half day. One-hour private lessons are $99. Grizzlies is the same price, but for ages 5–6. Bears on Board is a snowboard program for ages 5–7. It costs $159 for a full day, and includes rental equipment, which is extra in the other programs. Ages 7–12 for skiing, and 8–12 for snowboarding, have full-day classes for $69 (with lunch); $52 for half-day.

Teens ages 13–19 can enroll in "Too Cool for School" every day of the season, where groups are formed by age, ability and "personality." The program includes races and mountain picnics with evening activities such as ice skating. The cost is $64 per day, $174 for three days, $320 for five days and $55 for a half day.

Lift tickets (2002/03 prices)

	Adult	Youth (13-17)
Four days (out of 10)	$256 ($64/day)	$196 ($49/day)
Five days (out of 10)	$320 ($64/day)	$245 ($49/day)
Six days (out of 10)	$384 ($64/day)	$294 ($49/day)

Who skis free: Ages 6 and younger.

Who skis at a discount: Children (7–12) pay $39 per day for multiday tickets of four to seven days. Ages 65 to 69 pay $59 for multiday tickets of four to seven days. Those 70 years and older get unlimited skiing or riding with The Silver Pass for $119 all season long. The best ticket prices are found by ordering tickets before Dec. 1, 2002, or by making a seven-day advance purchase. A six-day ticket purchased before Dec. 1 costs $307 ($51+ per day); a seven-day ticket purchased seven days in advance costs $404 ($57+ per day). In addition, you'll save 20 percent off ski and snowboard rentals if you purchase your ticket before Dec. 1, 2002, with a minimum five-day rental.

Note: The four Aspen-area mountains are far from other ski resorts and metropolitan areas. Consequently, just about all the visitors ski for more than one day, which is why we don't list the single-day price. All tickets are valid at all four mountains.

Accommodations

Snowmass has few hotels but thousands of condominiums, many of which are slopeside. Hotel and lodge prices generally start at $150 and up a night (condos about $50 more). For other and reservations, call **Aspen Chamber Resort Association** (800-598-2005) or go to www.stayaspensnowmass.com. That agency uses four price categories: economy, moderate, deluxe and luxury. Economy lodging-lift packages start at less than $100 per person per night, while luxury packages will run more than $200.

Hotel accommodations are relatively limited: **The Snowmass Lodge and Club** ($$$$), below the village, offers condos with health club access and serves as the Nordic center. There are regular shuttles to the slopes. **The Silvertree Hotel** ($$$$) is the other luxury hotel, open since the ski area began in 1967. Less expensive hotel or lodge accommodations include the **Pokolodi Lodge** ($-$$$), **Snowmass Inn** ($-$$$), **Stonebridge** ($-$$$), in the center of the village, **Snowmass Mountain Chalet** ($-$$$), which includes a full breakfast and soup lunch and slopeside convenience or **Wildwood Lodge** ($$-$$$$). We're particularly impressed with the Wildwood Lodge and the Silvertree. Both are comfortable with beautiful rooms, and close to everything in Snowmass.

Our staff stayed at **The Crestwood Condominiums** (www.thecrestwood.com; $$$-$$$$) and found them comfortable, roomy, right next to the slopes and well-designed for groups. In the deluxe category, these condos have fireplaces, a bathroom for every bedroom, laundry facilities, a swimming pool, exercise room and airport shuttle service.

Dining: $$$-Entrees $20+; $$-$10-20; $-less than $10.

Accommodations: (double room) $$$$-$200+; $$$-$141-$200; $$-$81-$140; $-$80 and less.

Snowmass Lodging Company (800-365-0410 or 923-3232) books some of the most upscale condos, including **Woodrun V** ($$$$) and **Chamonix** ($$$$). In the economy category, we like **Willows**, two levels below the village mall. In the moderate category, try **Terracehouse** ($$$-$$$$) or **Lichenhearth** ($$$-$$$$), which are close to Willows. The **Top of the Village** ($$$-$$$$) and the **Timberline** ($$-$$$$) condos are a good five- to 10-minute climb above the village mall. The **Sonnenblick** ($$$$) has only large units, three to five bedrooms in the deluxe price category.

Dining

Snowmass Village claims some of the best restaurants in the area. Known for its dogsledding and kennels, **Krabloonik,** (923-3953; $$$) has an even bigger reputation for its restaurant's wild-game selection and extensive wine list. In a rustic log house at Snowmass, this venue offers panoramic views of Mt. Daly and Capitol Peak.

The Snowmass Club bistro, **Sage** (923-5600; $$$), offers distinctive food with a casual unpretentious atmosphere and at more moderate prices.

Most other eateries are in Snowmass Village Mall (if we don't tell you, that's where you'll find them). The chef at **La Provence** (923-6804), Maurice Couturier, was once the late King of Jordan's chef. It serves southern French fare. **The Magarita Grill** (923-6803), also run by Maurice Couturier, serves southwestern cuisine influenced by Central America. Other top spots are **Il Poggio** (923-4292; $$$) and **The Conservatory** ($$$), in the Silvertree Hotel.

Midrange dining can be found at **The Stonebridge Inn** (923-2420; $$-$$$), **Butch's Lobster Bar** (923-4004; $$$) at the top of the village, **Brothers' Grille** (923-8285; $-$$), which reportedly has the best hamburgers in the valley, and **Mountain Dragon** ($-$$) for Chinese, where appetizers are free during happy hour.

Every restaurant in Snowmass has children's menus, but **The Stew Pot** (923-2263; $-$$) features soups, tasty and unusual stews and sandwiches. The best family place is the **Daly Tavern** (923-3259; $), home of the $8 dinner. Eight choices are served nightly. For soups and sandwiches, try **Paradise Bakery** ($) in Silvertree Plaza. Or go to **S'no Beach Café** ($-$$) featuring "eggs S'noBeach" for breakfast.

Spend a family evening at the **Burlingame Cabin** (923-0575; $$$) or the **Lynn Britt Cabin** (923-0460; prix fixe menu) nestled in aspen groves on Snowmass. At both, a heated snowcat and well-blanketed open-air sleigh transport guests to a cabin with wood stove, western-style meal, bluegrass entertainment and sing-alongs.

For a quick breakfast on the way to the slopes, try **Moondogs Cable Car**. Café D&E serves gourmet coffee from inside D&E Snowboard shop. The afore-mentioned **S'no Beach Café** is where our staff—hearty-breakfast fans that we are—chowed down.

Snowmass Village excels with mountaintop cookery. **Gordon's High Alpine Restaurant** (923-5188, reservations are essential), at the top of Alpine Springs (Lift 8), is the family spot for lunch. You can hike up for breakfast before the lifts open. **Krabloonik** (923-3953), mentioned earlier as a dinner choice, is also open for lunch. It is at the base of Campground off the Dawdler Catwalk.

Another on-mountain option is **Up 4 Pizza** (923-0464; $) at the top of the Big Burn in Snowmass. For quick "power food," head to one of the **yurts** near the snowboard halfpipes and the terrain park, or at the bottom of Assay Hill.

At the Two Creeks base area, chorizo and egg burritos start the day at **Two Creeks Mexican Cafe** ($). Fajitas, taco salad and burritos are typical lunch fare. The **Cirque Café** ($-

$$), slopeside at the Snowmass Village Mall, has a buffet breakfast for a fast exit to the slopes in the morning, and a more leisurely sit-down lunch and dinner service.

Après-ski/nightlife

The **Cirque Café** and the **Brothers' Grille** are the hubs of après-ski. The Cirque Café tends to be more crowded and rowdier. Brothers' has five different draft beers and almost a dozen hot drinks for quick warmups. **Zane's Tavern** is a sports bar with après-ski drink specials. At night Snowmass Village is quiet. The best action in town is at the **Tower**, where Doc Eason performs magic throughout the night.

Other activities

The **Anderson Ranch Arts Center** (923-3181) in Snowmass Village exhibits work by visiting and resident artists during the winter. The center also offers a series of workshops in ceramics, woodworking and photography from January through April. Call for current events.

Krabloonik Kennels in Snowmass Village (923-4342) is known for its daily tours through the Snowmass wilderness area, led by Iditarod-experienced huskies. Morning or afternoon rides include a four-course gourmet lunch at the kennel's restaurant in Snowmass Village. Rides last about two hours and cost about $195 per person; $125 for children aged 3-8.

A **sledding hill** at the Snowmass Cross Country Center (923-3148) is open from 9 a.m. to 5 p.m. daily. Plastic sleds and wooden toboggans can be rented for $5 or $15 per day, respectively. A **tubing hill** at Tube Town, on Assay Hill operated from noon until 8 p.m. daily. Cost is $15 for unlimited runs, and the use of tubes.

For more information about off-slope activities, see "Other Activities" in the Aspen chapter or contact Snowmass Village Resort Association (800-598-2006; 923-2000).

Getting there and getting around

See the Aspen chapter for information on getting to the region. Getting around Snowmass Village is a little more involved than getting around Aspen, so we'd like to share some tips based on our experience (and we still recommend that you use public transportation because of limited parking):

Getting around: The Roaring Fork Valley's (mostly) free bus system, RFTA, will shuttle you between Snowmass and Aspen. At Snowmass Village, you board the RFTA bus at the transportation center at the Snowmass Village Mall. Between 8 a.m. and 4:30 p.m., the RFTA bus is free. After 4:30 p.m., however, the charge is $3 per person, one way, between Aspen and Snowmass Village. (RFTA buses within Aspen are free in the evening.) If you have been skiing at one of the three mountains in Aspen and you relax in the bar afterward, keep a close eye on the clock so the charge doesn't take you by surprise.

Snowmass Village has a separate, free shuttle system with several routes that run throughout the village. To get to Aspen, you ride a Snowmass Village shuttle to the transportation center, then transfer to an RFTA bus. Although the system is very efficient (and you can't beat the price), it takes about an hour to get from a Snowmass Village condo to Aspen, and vice versa. If you expect to make two round trips per day into Aspen (one for skiing and the second for nightlife), stay in Aspen. Otherwise, you will feel as if you spent most of your vacation riding a bus.

Summit County

Colorado

Some winter vacationers aren't satisfied with skiing and riding at just one place. When they return to the office, they want to drop resort names and compare the black-diamond plunges or best family vacations. For these skiers, we suggest Summit County.

Summit County, about a hour-and-a-half drive from downtown Denver, has four well-known ski areas—Breckenridge, Copper Mountain, Keystone and Arapahoe Basin. Each resort—except A-Basin—has its own lodging, shopping and restaurants.

If you plan to do most of your skiing at just one area, stay at that resort, but if you want to experience them all and save some money, then set up your base camp in Dillon, Frisco or Silverthorne, three small towns off I-70 that surround Lake Dillon, a reservoir.

This tri-town area is smack in the center of the ski action. Breckenridge is about 9 miles in one direction, Copper Mountain 5 miles in another, Keystone 7 miles away in a third, and A-Basin just a little farther than Keystone. Having a car is nice, but not really necessary. The reliable Summit Stage, the free bus system subsidized by sales tax revenue, runs between the towns and the ski areas all day and into the night—until 2 a.m.

Summit County deserves its lofty name. It has a base elevation above 9,000 feet. (If you have problems with high altitudes, take note. If you like spring skiing, also take note: High elevations usually mean a longer ski season.) Each of these areas stays open at least until late April most years, and Arapahoe Basin—with its base lodge above 10,000 feet—often stays open until July 4.

Vail Resorts Inc. owns Keystone and Breckenridge. It has an interchangeable lift ticket that includes Vail, Beaver Creek, Keystone and Breckenridge, or you can buy a multi-day ticket for Keystone and Breckenridge alone for a little less. Your Keystone-Breckenridge ticket also is valid at Arapahoe Basin, or you can buy that ticket separately. You'll have to buy a separate ticket to ski at Copper Mountain, which is owned by rival ski-resort corporation Intrawest.

This chapter lists accommodations, dining, nightlife and non-ski activities in the tri-town area of Frisco, Dillon and Silverthorne. You can pick up information and helpful brochures at two Summit County Visitor Information Centers, one in Silverthorne at 246 Rainbow Drive in the Silverthorne Factory Stores and another in Frisco at 916 North Summit Boulevard. Or call the chamber at 800-530-3099 or 262-2051. They'll act as matchmaker for you and your lodging needs. Summit County Chamber's site, www.experiencethesummit.com, is packed with information as well. Some other helpful Web sites are www.summitchamber.org, www.summitnet.com, www.townofdillon.com, www.townoffrisco.com and www.silverthorne.org.

Separate chapters detail skiing, lodging, dining and nightlife at Breckenridge, Copper Mountain and Keystone. For information on skiing at A-Basin, refer to the Keystone chapter.

 ## Accommodations

Frisco: This is our first choice for a home base, for several reasons. One, it is the closest town to Breckenridge and Copper Mountain, and Keystone isn't far away. Two, its downtown area along Main Street has lots of funky shops and restaurants, perfect for a late afternoon or evening stroll. And three, we like friendly mountain inns, and found three good ones.

The **Galena Street Mountain Inn** (800-248-9138 or 668-3224; $$), First Avenue and Galena Street (one block off Main Street), has a light and airy feel to it. Its 14 rooms have private baths, televisions and phones, and all are nicely furnished. A hot tub and sauna are among the amenities. A full breakfast with hot entrée is included, as are après-ski refreshments and home-baked treats. No smoking or pets.

The gurgling of Ten Mile Creek is the wake-up call for guests at **Creekside Inn** (800-668-7320 or 668-5607; $–$$$). Innkeepers Vince and Jill Pierse found this quiet setting at the west end of Main Street the ideal spot to build a quintessential mountain inn with a touch of the Old World. Afternoon snacks, special-diet and early-bird breakfasts, ski storage and wheelchair access are a few of the amenities. The seven guest rooms each have a private bath, and a fireplace in the great room and deck hot tub make this a tempting home away from home. No Smoking, no pets, no children younger than age 12.

Hotel Frisco (800-262-1002 or 668-5009; $–$$$) was completely remodeled a few years ago. The cozy ski lodge, located at 308 Main Street, has 16 nicely decorated rooms, a huge river-rock fireplace in the lobby and an outdoor hot tub.

If you're looking for super-budget lodging, try **Just Bunks** (668-4757; $), a "home-style hostel" that is drug, alcohol and smoke free.

Dillon/Silverthorne: Lodging here is chain hotels and motels, plus loads of condos and chalets.

The **Best Western Ptarmigan Lodge** (800-842-5939 or 468-2341; $$–$$$) in the Dillon town center is one of the best bargains, particularly during the early and late seasons and in January. Another moderately priced motel is the **Dillon Inn** (800-262-0801 or 262-0801; $$–$$$), which has an indoor pool. **The Lodge at Carolina in the Pines** (877-484-3563 or 262-7500; $$–$$$$) is a B&B that overlooks Lake Dillon and has a serene setting.

Off the interstate in Silverthorne are side-by-side chain hotels: **Four Points by Sheraton Hotel** (800-321-3509 or 468-6200; $$–$$$) and **Days Inn** (800-329-7466 or 468-8661; $$–$$$). The Summit Stage stops at their doors, and they are convenient to the Silverthorne and Dillon Factory Stores (see *Other Activities*).

Budget travelers should stay at the **Super 8** motel (800-800-8000; 468-8888; $$–$$$) in Dillon, across from the Summit Place Shopping Center. Three of the best cheap restaurants are in this center. Or, try the **Alpen Hutte Lodge** (468-6336; $–$$), 471 Rainbow Drive. Both the Greyhound bus from Denver and the Summit County shuttle buses stop there, and for about $27, you get a bed in an eight-person dorm room. There are also private rooms that sleep two and private family rooms that sleep four. The lodge has a nice kitchen, is clean and it's walking distance from restaurants (especially the brewery) and shopping.

The towns have many more B&Bs, chain hotels, private homes and condos. For reservations, call **Summit County Central Reservations**, 800-365-6365, or **Reservations for the Summit**, 800-999-9510, or the **Summit Country Chamber,** 800-530-3099 or 668-2051.

Dining

Frisco: Perhaps the best restaurant in Frisco is **The Boatyard Pizzeria and Grill** (668-4728), which just changed its name from Uptown Bistro and expanded its menu, on Main Street. A '90s bistro atmosphere complements an uptown á la carte menu. Main courses include such delights as pumpkin squash ravioli with sage brown butter and garlic-ginger-flavored seared ahi tuna with a spicy mushroom spring roll. Great desserts

Dining: $$$-Entrees $20+; $$-$10-20; $-less than $10.
Accommodations: (double room) $$$$-$200+; $$$-$141-$200; $$-$81-$140; $-$80 and less.

and wood-oven-baked gourmet pizzas and calzones. Make reservations and ask to be seated in the back, away from the front-door draft.

A longtime favorite is the **Blue Spruce Inn** (668-5900; $$$) in a historic log cabin at the corner of Madison and Main. Entrées include such dishes as filet béarnaise, vegetables en croûte, grilled venison and scallops dijonaise. The food is good, though a little sauce-heavy, and the atmosphere and service are excellent. The happy hour menu includes an appetizer buffet. Reservations recommended.

People flock to **Tuscato** (668-3644; $$$) on Main Street, which serves an eclectic collection of excellent Italian cuisine. Locals and visitors alike rave about **Silverheels at the Ore House Restaurant and Tapas Bar** (468-2926; $–$$$) on the corner of 6th and Main. Fine Southwestern fare and a Spanish tapas bar are the specialties here. **Fiesta Jalisco** (668-5043; $$), 450 W. Main, has the most authentic Mexican food in the county. **Barkley's** (668-3694; $$) at 620 Main St. serves good prime rib and Mexican food. **Ti Amo** (668-1993) dishes out creative Italian meals and excellent wines.

Budget eats: Locals recommended **Ge-Jo's** (668-3308), upstairs at 409 Main St., for inexpensive Italian fare and **Szechuan Taste** (668-5685) at 310 Main St. for Chinese food (dine in or take out). Frisco also has many fast-food chain restaurants, most along Summit Boulevard. **Deli Belly's** has giant sandwiches at 275 Main Street in Frisco.

Halfway between Frisco and Breckenridge, in an area called Farmer's Korner, are neighboring restaurants that are quite different. **The Blue River Inn** (547-9928; $) is a no-frills local hangout with great burgers, inexpensive draft beers and a 10-ounce sirloin that is probably still less than $10. **The Swan Mountain Inn** (453-7903; $$$) offers an elegant, nightly four-course meal in a seven-table dining room with a fireplace. The inn also has a weekend brunch.

Dillon & Silverthorne: A good choice for finer dining is **Ristorante Al Lago** (468-6111; $$) in the Dillon town center. It serves Northern Italian meals. **The Old Chicago Restaurant** (468-6200; $–$$) with 110 different beers and great happy hours is at the Four Points by Sheraton Hotel.

For more casual dining in Dillon, try the **Dillon Dam Brewery** (262-7777; $$), which lives up to its slogan, "the best dam brewery in town," and is the only non-smoking restaurant and bar in the county; **Pug Ryan's** (468-2145; $) in the Dillon town center is fantastic for steaks and microbrewed beer; or **Wild Bill's Stone Oven Pizza** (468-2006; $), also in the Dillon town center. Some of the best deli sandwiches we've ever had are at **Gastronome's Gourmet Catering & Deli** (469-0218; $), upstairs from Wild Bill's.

In Silverthorne, you can cook your own meat over an open grill at **The Historic Mint** (468-5247; $$) or enjoy Tex-Mex food at **Old Dillon Inn** (468-2791; $), which was relocated to Silverthorne just before Lake Dillon was created.

Budget diners: the Summit Place Shopping Center on Highway 6 on the Dillon-Silverthorne border has several great restaurants, including **Sunshine Cafe** (468-6663), jammed with locals; and **Nick-N-Willy's** (262-1111) for very good bake-your-own take-out pizza.

Breakfast: The best breakfast in the tri-town area is **Claimjumper** (668-3617), on Summit Boulevard across the street from Wal-Mart in Frisco. Not only does it have an extensive omelet-and-pancake menu, it has breakfast specials that taste great and fill the plate.

A close second is the **Arapahoe Cafe** (468-0873) on Lake Dillon Drive in the Dillon town center, a huge favorite with locals. The cafe building used to stand in the old town of Dillon, but was moved in the 1960s when the reservoir flooded the area. The service is great, the menu names are creative (Arapahuevos Rancheros, Hans and Franz Power Breakfast, etc.) and eavesdropping on the other tables will fill you in on local politics. Both restaurants also have inexpensive lunch and dinner menus.

Definitely in the running for the Best Breakfast title are **Sunshine Cafe** in the Summit Place Shopping Center and **Log Cabin Cafe** (668-3847) on Main Street in Frisco.

For those who prefer a lighter breakfast, head for the **Butterhorn Bakery** (668-3997), 408 W. Main Street in Frisco. Across the street is **Pika Bagel Bakery** (668-0902), and in the Summit Place Shopping Center in Silverthorne is **Blue Moon Baking Company** (468-1472). Also try the **Mountain Lyon Café** (262-6229) on Blue River Parkway in Silverthorne.

 ## Après-ski/nightlife

Mountain resorts and brew pubs seem to go hand in hand. Summit County has five, three of which are in the tri-town area. **Backcountry Brewery** is on the corner of Summit and Main in Frisco, **Pug Ryan's** is in the Dillon Town Center and **The Dillon Dam Brewery** is in Dillon. (The others are in Breckenridge and Keystone; read about them in those chapters.) The current trend is to end a day on the mountain with a freshly drawn Colorado specialty brewski. All three places also serve food and have lively happy hours.

The leading sports bar is **High Mountain Billiards**, an upscale game room with pool tables, dart boards, shuffleboard, chess, checkers, backgammon and sports TV. This no-smoking, richly decorated bar in Frisco serves a mostly over-30 clientele. **Barkley's West** in Frisco varies its entertainment from live music to dance classes to Under 21 nights.

Old Dillon Inn in Silverthorne has live Country & Western music on weekends, and the best margaritas in town. Its 120-year-old bar definitely has authentic Old West atmosphere. The building was pieced together from bits of defunct establishments, and the whole thing was moved in 1961 when the old town of Dillon disappeared under the aforementioned lake.

Another popular choices is the **Pub Down Under**, underneath the Arapahoe Cafe in Dillon. **The Cala Inn** in Summit Cove (between Dillon and Keystone) is a new Scottish/Irish bar with great drink specials and delicious food, including a Guinness Steak Pie.

 ## Child care

Services of the Summit, Inc. (668-0255) in Frisco has professional babysitters ages 18–65 who are insured, bonded and child-care trained. They will come to your hotel or condo anywhere in the county. **Baby's Away** (800-979-9030) rents and will deliver baby needs to your lodge, such as crib, stroller, car seat and toys.

Other activities

Companies that offer **snowmobiling** and/or **sleigh and dogsled rides** are Tiger Run Tours, 453-2231; Good Times Tours, 453-7604; and Two Below Zero Dinner Sleigh Rides, 453-1520. In the Dillon/Silverthorne area, call Eagles Nest Equestrian Center, 468-0677.

Summit Activities Center offers an activity concierge service at 888-230-2844.

Cross-country skiing is available at the Frisco Nordic Center on Highway 9 about one mile out of town toward Breckenridge. Trail passes are $10, with discounts for those aged 55 and older or 12 and younger. Rentals and instruction are available. Call 668-0866.

Pack an extra suitcase for **shopping.** Better yet, buy a bag at one of the luggage stores in the **Silverthorne and Dillon Factory Stores.** Then start filling it with bargains at nearly 80 brand-name stores. This is probably the largest factory outlet center in Western ski country. Among the stores are Anne Klein, Liz Claiborne, Jones New York, Levi, Nike, Bass Shoes, American Tourister and Samsonite.

Collectibles and antiques lovers will go nuts at **Junk-Tique,** 313 Main St. in Frisco. It has an excellent inventory of collectible housewares, clothing and furniture. The store also stocks some new jewelry and knickknack items. Kids will love the huge black locomotive that is the centerpiece of the store. Cigar lovers can stop by **Antler's Liquor Store** in Frisco, which has what the owner claims is the largest humidor room in Colorado.

Getting there and getting around

By air and car: Frisco, Dillon and Silverthorne are just off I-70, about 75 miles west of downtown Denver and 90 miles from Denver International Airport. Resort Express vans transport from Denver International Airport, 800-334-7433 or 468-7600. The airport is about two hours away.

Getting around: Frisco is laid out nicely for walking along Main Street. The Summit Stage is a free bus system that links the towns with each other and the ski areas until 2 a.m. Summit Taxi (468-2266) provides transportation to the entire community.

A car is an option here; most distances are too far for walking, but the Summit Stage is reliable. Call 668-0999 for route info, or pick up a route map and schedule from the Summit Country Chamber of Commerce, the two Summit County Visitor Information Centers or various stores. Note that the bus takes about an hour to get from one resort to another. If you really enjoy nightlife and want to do extensive exploration of the restaurants and bars, we recommend a car. There are several car rental agencies in Summit County.

Nearby resorts

Loveland Ski Area, Georgetown, CO; (800) 736-3754 or (303) 571-5580

Internet: www.skiloveland.com

11 lifts; 1,365 acres; 2,410 vertical feet

One of our Colorado-based contributors keeps the daily snow report on her e-mail update, the Loveland Cam on her browser, and is ready to jump into her car at a moment's notice and drive an hour to some of the best big-mountain skiing in the state. The snow is reliably deep (the base at 10,600 feet means this is *real* high in the mountains) from mid-October through mid-May.

You see the area as you approach the Eisenhower Tunnel along I-70 west from Denver. It looms into the distance right up to the Continental Divide, and spreads out on both sides of the interstate. A ski area in two parts, Loveland Basin and Loveland Valley are connected by a lift and a shuttle service. Loveland Valley, on the left as you approach the tunnel, is great for beginners, intermediates and anyone who wants to hide from the stiff winds that sometimes plague Loveland Basin. The Basin is a real stash, jammed with enough expert and advanced terrain to challenge the best and stuffed with intermediate runs and long cruisers, most of which you can't see from I-70. By the way—snowboarding accounts for more than 25-percent of lift ticket sales—the highest ratio of any Colorado area.

Experts can get high here—The Ridge, with its 400 acres of wild terrain, tops out at 13,010 feet, and is an above-timberline alpine garden of glades, chutes and bowls. A few seasons ago the area opened Chair 9, the highest four-passenger chair lift in the world, so you no longer have to hike up to get the goodies. **Advanced** skiers should head for Chair 1 for bumps and chutes. Avalanche Bowl is a nasty short and sweet drop and Busy Gully demands tight turns right under the chair. Chairs 4 and 8 access the far right, a mix of wilderness-type bowls at the top, narrowing into tree bashing in the East and West Ropes and at Fail Safe. **Intermediates and beginners** can handle everything else, particularly Chairs 2, 4 and 6. Snowboarders enjoy their own terrain park.

Child care starts at 12 months. Loveland offers a 3 Class Pass, where beginner skiers and riders (kids and adults) receive a free season pass after taking three lessons. Women in Motion clinics focus on ski and snowboard techniques and industry developments. Telemark Clinics are scheduled throughout the season.

Lift tickets (01/02): Adults, $42; children (6-14) $17; ages 5 and younger ski free. Lower rates early and late season. The Flex Ticket, valid any four consecutive hours during the day, is offered during the regular season only for $32.

Distance from Denver: 56 miles west via I-70 (about 80 miles from Denver airport).

Lodging information: (800) 225-LOVE (5683). Lodging can be found in Georgetown or Dillon, both within 15 miles.

Breckenridge

Colorado

Summit elevation: 12,146 feet
Vertical drop: 2,546 feet (lift-served)
Base elevation: 9,600 feet

Address: Box 1058
Breckenridge, CO 80424
☎ **Area code:** 970
Ski area phone: 453-5000 or
(800) 427-8308
Snow report: 453-6118
ⓘ **Toll-free reservations:**
(888) 533-9884;
UK: (800) 289-7491
Toll-free foreign fax numbers:
UK: 0800-96-0055
Brazil: 000811-715-5559
Germany: 0130-82-7807
Netherlands: 06-022-6653
Fax: 453-7238
E-mail: breckguest@vailresorts.com (ski area)
cenres@gobreck.com (lodging)
Internet: www.breckenridge.com (ski area)
or www.gobreck.com (visitors' bureau)

Expert:★★★★
Advanced:★★★★★
Intermediate:★★★★
Beginner:★★★★
Never-ever:★★★★
Number and types of lifts: 27—2 six-pack chair,
6 high-speed quads, 1 triple, 6 doubles and 12
surface lifts
Skiable acreage: 2,208 acres
Snowmaking: 27 percent (516 acres)
Uphill capacity: 36,880 per hour
Snowboarding: Yes
Bed base: 25,000+
Nearest lodging: Slopeside
Resort child care: Yes, 2 months and older
Adult ticket, per day: $59-$61 (02/03 prices)

Dining:★★★
Apres-ski/nightlife:★★★★
Other activities:★★★

Breckenridge has become one of the snowsports industry's giants, attracting more than a million visits each season. A good number are Front Range skiers and riders, those who live in Denver and its suburbs. Another large portion is destination visitors from the U.S. And a third fast-growing group is visitors from Great Britain, Mexico and other countries.

The town of Breckenridge has a split personality, but it's been that way from the beginning. It was named for a man who became a Confederate brigadier general, but its streets are named after past Presidents—Washington, Lincoln, Jefferson and Adams. The Victorian buildings lining the streets witnessed wild revelry during gold and silver booms and the discovery of Colorado's largest gold nugget—the 13-pound "Tom's Baby" in 1887—but they also stood silent over windswept, vacant streets when Breckenridge nearly joined the list of Colorado ghost towns after WWII.

Though the closest Breckenridge comes to being a ghost town these days is the mud season in May, it still displays its inherited division. Modern architecture around the base area is a contrast to the Victorian downtown, which houses hundreds of boutiques, scores of pubs and dozens of restaurants packed into brightly-colored, restored 19th-century buildings in Colorado's largest historic district.

You'll find your fellow skiers and snowboarders are a mixed bag. Though the general atmosphere is still more down-to-earth than at some other Colorado resorts, Breckenridge also attracts society's upper crust. New shops and restaurants tend to cater to the upscale crowd; now, with Vail's ownership, this trend probably will continue. Restaurant and ski-area workers remain as friendly as ever, and long-time Breckenridge locals still retain much of the devil-may-care attitude of their 19th-century predecessors, which helps balance out any stuffiness that the tourists may bring with them. For now, the Breckenridge crowd is not as free-spending as that of Aspen or Vail, nor as laid back as Crested Butte. It's middle-of-the-road and comfortable with plenty of great skiing.

New for 2002/03, the Peak 8 SuperConnect high-speed quad replaces and extends the old Chair 4 to just a few hundred yards above the base of the Beaver Run Chair on Peak 9, thereby simplifying the transfer of skiers between mountains. While guests will not be able to access the chair from the base area, a quick ride up the Beaver Run Super Chair or Quicksilver Super-Six accesses the new lift and whisks riders to Peak 8, terminating near the Vista Haus restaurant. A mid-station loading point allows skiers to board the lift where Chair 4 previously began. Also a new high-speed, six-passenger chair will provide access to 165 additional acres (seven trails) of much-needed intermediate terrain on Peak 7, as well as the Peak 7 glades.

Mountain layout—Skiing

Breckenridge encompasses four interconnected mountains covering 2,208 acres. Skiers can load lifts from four base areas: the Quicksilver Super-Six high-speed double-loading chair from The Village at the bottom of Peak 9; the Super Chair at Beaver Run, also on Peak 9; the Colorado and Rocky Mountain Super Chairs at Peak 8 (this was the original ski area that opened in 1961); and the Snowflake, a double chair off Four O'Clock Road that accesses all peaks. Free shuttles to these lifts run continuously from town. (Note: A close-in pay lot at Peak 8 fills by 9:30 a.m. most days.)

◆◆ **Expert:** Years ago, Breckenridge was known as an excellent beginner and intermediate resort, but the opening of the bowls of Peak 8, the North Face of Peak 9, and Peaks 7 and 10 added hundreds of acres of expert, steep terrain. Today Breckenridge boasts a very high percentage of black-diamond terrain (55 percent overall) and some of the highest inbounds skiing in North America, but still maintains its wide-open, well-groomed runs for beginners and intermediates.

Imperial Bowl, crowning Peak 8, tops out at nearly 13,000 feet, creating a total vertical that's only 2 feet shy of 3,400. If you noticed that our statistics show a much smaller vertical, it's because we list the highest *lift-served* terrain. Imperial Bowl is in bounds but not lift-served. If you want to ski it, you must hike first. Same with the highest bowls on Peak 7: You can ski from the 12,677-foot summit, but only if you hoof it to the top. Locals love it; visitors from sea level often pass up the opportunity to ski some of the best snow in the country (which is another reason why the locals love it). The above-treeline terrain off Peak 7, by the way, is entirely advanced and expert terrain, but the newly cut runs in the trees are pleasantly intermediate and long.

The North Face on the back of Peak 9 is expert territory. Plenty of good skiers have begged for a rest after playing with Tom's Baby and Tom's Mom, and even prayers won't help lower intermediates who accidentally find themselves in Devil's Crotch or Inferno—once you drop down the face from Chair E, there is no escape.

◆ **Advanced:** Peak 10 is evenly split between black and blue runs. In the black-diamond category you'll find Mustang, Dark Rider and Blackhawk boasting monstrous bumps. Cimarron, marked black on the map, often is groomed because of race training that frequently takes place here. The Burn, dropping to skier's left of the high-speed lift, offers limited short-but-sweet tree skiing.

■ **Intermediate:** For the best cruising, head to Peak 10 and alternate between Centennial, Doublejack and Crystal. Runs here are slightly steeper than those on Peak 9. The pairing of a high-speed lift and mostly expert-marked terrain keeps crowds down.

On Peak 9, intermediates should take the Beaver Run or Mercury chair to the summit and ski down Cashier, Bonanza and Upper Columbia. Advanced-intermediates enjoy Sundown, American, Gold King, Peerless and Volunteer, which may be rated black at smaller resorts.

Peak 8 offers great intermediate terrain alongside the high-speed Colorado lift down Springmeier, Crescendo and Four O'Clock; if those feel good, try the black-diamond slopes in this area, such as High Anxiety and Rounders. There also are seven new intermediate trails on Peak 7, served by a new lift, that are quite pleasant and long.

●● **Beginner** ● **Never-ever:** Peak 9 has the best trails for a first time on skis. Also beginners who have had a little experience will like it here (stick to the Quicksilver lift; the Beaver Run lift will take you higher to intermediate terrain).

Mountain layout—Snowboarding

Three words: Freeway Terrain Park. Peak 8's halfpipe and terrain park have become legendary among snowboarders. Breckenridge was the first mountain in the country to get a superpipe and it shows among the locals. On any given day, show up at the park and you'll quickly realize why you're *not* a pro snowboarder.

Breckenridge hosts the Vans Triple Crown snowboarding event the first weekend in December, where world-class riders compete on Freeway's superpipe, which boasts walls higher than 14 feet. New for this season, you'll find the Swinger Terrain Park and Halfpipe on Peak 8. Swinger is designed specifically with smaller features and an introductory halfpipe for beginner freestyle riders. With a world-class terrain park reputation at stake, expect this new park to meet Breckenridge's stringent design standards while providing a safe and fun introduction to freestyle terrain. If you master the beginner park but are not yet ready for Freeway, then head to Peak 9's Gold King terrain park. It has intermediate features and handrails to practice on for just the right progression according to your abilities.

As for steeps and deeps, Breck's got a few secret spots, but they're under tight lip. Most of the locals get their steeps in the enormous backcountry surroundings of Summit County and only use the mountain for the park. Peak 10's got a few high-speed cruisers that will let you open up your board, but all in all, Breck isn't known for it's steeps.

As for beginners, the whole mountain is your canvas. Stay away from the mogul runs and you'll be smiling ear to ear with the most beginner terrain in Summit County at your disposal. Peak 9 has the best terrain for a first snowboard day. Just stay out of the park.

Mountain rating

Breckenridge has many ingredients for the perfect winter vacation: good terrain for all levels, plenty of slopeside lodging and a charming town. It's urban enough to have a good variety of restaurants and shops, yet not so urban that you'll feel as if you never left home. Snowboarders will find that while Breckenridge might not be the steepest mountain out there, what it lacks in natural terrain it more than makes up for in the manmade department.

Cross-country and snowshoeing

The new **Gold Run Nordic Center** (547-7889), off Tiger Run Road at the Breckenridge Golf Course, features 14 km. of beginner to advanced professionally groomed trails and works throughout the winter with the Summit Nordic and Trails Council to create Nordic and snowshoe events. Equipment rentals (including snowshoes), lessons, and guided backcountry tours are available. The **Breckenridge Nordic Ski Center** (453-6855), near Peak 8 base on Ski Hill Road, has 28 km. of double-set trails for all abilities. Trail passes also are valid at the Frisco Nordic Center. Equipment rentals, lessons, and guided backcountry tours are available. You can also rent snowshoes.

Lessons [2002/03 prices]

We provide prices for high season.
Group lessons: $75 for a full day (five hours; high season).
Never-evers: Novice skiers get a full-day lesson with ticket and rentals for $110; snowboarders get the same for $115. Riders can also opt for a full-day class through the Burton Special Method Learning Center, which offers lessons, lunch, ticket and special Burton equipment designed to "fast track" the learning curve for $193; pre-registration required.

Private lessons: $140 per hour; multihour discounts available.

Special programs: Many, including daily programs and multiday programs offered a few times a season. Among the topics are women's clinics, racing, telemark lessons, bumps, Silver Skiing Seminars (50-plus age group), and lessons for disabled skiers.

Women's seminars are offered Jan. 13-15 and Feb. 27-March 2, 2003. This includes lunch, video analysis, a group dinner, wine and cheese party, and a guest speaker. For more information and rates, call 496-7534.

A two-day 50-Plus program takes place in January and February. This program costs $316 and includes lift tickets, instruction, video analysis and a group dinner.

Racing: NASTAR and self-timed courses are set up on Lower American on Peak 9. NASTAR fees are $6 for two runs and $1 for additional runs. The self-timed course is $1 a run. (2001/02 prices)

Child care [2002/03 prices]

Ages: 2 months to 5 years at the Peak 8 Children's Center; ages 3 to 5 years at the Peak 9 center.

Costs: $80 a full day (high season). Parents must provide diapers, formula, change of clothes, and so forth for infants. Child care for 3- to 5-year-olds includes a snow play program to build snowmen, go sledding and do other outdoor activities. Full-day programs include lunch.

Reservations: Required; call (800) 789-7669 well in advance.

Other options: Another possibility for child care and instruction is **Kinderhut** (800-541-8779 or 453-0379), a privately owned children's ski school and licensed day-care center. It accepts children 6 weeks to 6 years.

Children's lessons: Ski instruction for age 3-5 (must be potty trained) with a special ski-school morning program and afternoon care that includes lunch is $101 (high season). Kids this age ride the lifts for free; rentals are extra. Kids this age ride the lifts for free; rentals are extra. Reservations required for ages 3–5; call 888-LRN-2SKI (576-2754). Children 6–12 (skiing) and 7–12 (snowboarding) have their own classes. Full day with lift, lesson and lunch is $101; half day with lift and lesson is $86. Rentals are extra. Ages 13 and older take adult lessons. Riders ages 7–12 can also opt for a full-day class through the Burton Special Method Learning Center, which offers lessons, lunch, ticket and special Burton equipment designed to "fast track" the learning curve for $179; pre-registration required.

Lift tickets (2002/03 prices)

	Adult	Child (5-12)
One day	$61	$27
Three days	$183 ($61/day)	$81 ($27/day)
Five of six days	$305 ($61/day)	$108 ($27/day)

Who skis free: Ages 4 and younger.

Who skis at a discount: Ages 65–69 pay $42 per day, ages 70+ pay $31. Vail Resorts has a handful of different discounted prices based on time of the year, time of a skiers first visit, ski packages, Internet sales, supermarket sales, pre-purchasing and groups.

Interchangeability: Multiple-day lift tickets of three or more days purchased at Keystone or Breckenridge also are valid at sister resorts Vail and Beaver Creek (one day of a three-day lift ticket purchased at Keystone or Breckenridge is valid at Vail or Beaver Creek; two days of a four-day or five-day lift ticket; three days of a six-day or seven-day ticket). All lift tickets purchased at Keystone or Breckenridge also are valid at nearby Arapahoe Basin.

Accommodations

Breckenridge boasts extensive ski-in/ski-out lodging, and an assortment of condos, B&Bs and private chalets, both in town and in the woods. Most lodging is moderately priced, but luxury and dorm rooms are available for those on both ends of the affordability spectrum. Early December, January and April-May are the most affordable times. Breckenridge's lifts have kept running into May some years, but one caveat: Many of the town's shops and restaurants start closing down at the end of April. Some restaurants that do stay open offer two-for-one meals.

Breckenridge Central Reservations, (888) 533-9884, handles 98 percent of the resort's lodging and can help you find the best property, and best price, for your needs. Online reservations are available at www.gobreck.com.

Four wonderful upscale condo lodges are new to the Breckenridge lodging scene. **Grand Timber Lodge** (877-453-4440; www.grandtimber.com), **Valdoro Mountain Lodge** (800-Hiltons or 800-445-8667; 547-2947; www.valdoro.com), **The Hyatt at Main Street Station** (800-233-1234; www.hyatt.com) and **Mountain Thunder Lodge** (888-268-8376; mtnthunderlodge.com; a Vail Resorts property) are all within steps of lifts, and/or bus stops and all lead the resort into a new dimension of luxury lodging.

The Village at Breckenridge (800-800-7829; 453-2000; $$$–$$$$) surrounds the Peak 9 base area and is located next to the Quicksilver Super-Six chair (a double-loading six-person chair). Try to get into Plaza 1, 2 or 3, which are the most spacious units. The three-bedroom units here are giant. Many amenities are available: on-site health club facilities, indoor/outdoor pools, hot tubs, racquetball, steam, sauna and exercise room.

Beaver Run Resort and Conference Center (reservations and information: 800-525-2253; 453-6000; $$$–$$$$). This complex is slopeside on Peak 9. It has restaurants, outdoor hot tubs, indoor/outdoor swimming pools, a giant indoor miniature golf course and a great game room for kids. The Kinderhut child-care center, in the hotel, will take children from the ages of 1 to 3; kids 3 to 6 can take ski lessons.

Vail Resorts poured $4 million into remodeling each guest room, the entire lobby and pool/spa area at **The Great Divide Lodge** (800-321-8444; 453-4500). But they kept one of its best amenities—it's only 50 yards from the slopes.

The River Mountain Lodge (800-325-2342; UK direct 0800-897-497; local 453-4121; $239–$299 for a two-bedroom unit in January and February) is a group of studio to four-bedroom suites in the heart of town, only steps away from Main Street. The ski bus stops across the street. This is one of the town's most reasonable accommodations.

Distinctive inns have found an audience with guests who appreciate the genteel side of Breckenridge. Four such places—specifically built as B&Bs—are within walking distance of town, on the ski bus route, wheelchair accessible and are no smoking and no pets.

The Wellington Inn (800-655-7557 or 453-9464; $$–$$$$) at 200 N. Main St. captures Victorian romance in its four spacious and beautifully decorated rooms. All have outside decks and bathrooms with spa-jet tubs. Poirrer's, a Cajun restaurant on the main floor, serves lunch and dinner during the summer months and dinner during the winter. One drawback: Its Main Street location is not for light sleepers.

Hunt Placer Inn (800-472-1430 or 453-7573; $$–$$$$) is a B&B off Ski Hill Road near Peak 8 named for the gold mining claim on the property. The decor in its eight rooms (all with balconies, three with fireplaces) evokes various times and places in history.

Little Mountain Lodge (800-468-7707 or 453-1969; $$$–$$$$) is anything but little. This white-washed log home has an intimate staying-at-a-friend's-home feeling. Innkeepers Lynn and Truman Esmond add nice touches, such as placing a silver tray of coffee and tea at each guest-room door (there are 10) a half hour before breakfast.

Allaire Timbers Inn (800-624-4904 outside Colorado; 453-7530; $$$–$$$$) at 9511 Hwy. 9/South Main St. has great views. Hosts Jack and Kathy Gumph are very hospitable. Each of the eight guestrooms and two suites—all named after Colorado mountain passes—have private decks.

Several 19th-century homes in town have been converted into B&Bs, some of which are: **Evans House** (453-5509; request the Colorado Room; $$–$$$), **The Williams House** (453-2975; 800-795-2975; $$-$$$), **Fireside Inn** (453-6456; $–$$$$) and **Ridge Street Inn** (800-452-4680 or 453-4680; $$). The Fireside Inn also has gender-segregated dorm rooms for $20–$30 per night, with two sets of bunk beds per room and shared baths. A *Ski America & Canada* reader stayed there recently and found the accommodations plain but comfortable, and his roommates were "very pleasant and lotsa fun to go brewpubbing with."

The Lodge and Spa at Breckenridge (800-736-1607; 453-9300) underwent an extensive remodeling for its inclusion in the distinguished Small Luxury Hotels of the World by spring of 1998. The hotel—which perches on a cliff at 10,200 feet with a magnificent view of the Breckenridge mountain range—houses Summit County's only full-service spa. The **Casey House,** next to the Lodge and Spa, is a private home that offers the comforts and privacy of a mansion with five bedrooms and all the amenities of the Lodge and Spa available to guests.

 Dining

In recent years, Breckenridge has gradually emerged from the dining doldrums. With the increase in upscale homes and vacationers from overseas, we expect the trend to continue.

Dining: $$$-Entrees $20+; $$-$10-20; $-less than $10.

Accommodations: (double room) $$$$-$200+; $$$-$141-$200; $$-$81-$140; $-$80 and less.

For now, **Pierre's Riverwalk Cafe** (453-0989), 137 S. Main, stands alone in the field of excellent and expensive restaurants (entrées $18-$29). Owner/chef Pierre Luc prepares French dishes with a California twist, consisting mostly of fish and game delicacies such as ostrich, pheasant and rabbit. Desserts are deliciously French.

The **Top of the World Restaurant** (453-9300) is back. It never really left, but under new management, the name has returned and the menu is even better—with everything from Chilean sea bass to bacon-wrapped tenderloin. They also have a lounge menu with a flare added to typical bar food and they serve breakfast as well. It's in the Lodge and Spa at Breckenridge.

Cafe Alpine (453-8218), 103 E. Adams St., has an eclectic mix of entrées, such as Italian arugula chicken, Moroccan lamb, Memphis rubbed pork and Colorado trout. This Victorian-home-turned-restaurant also serves excellent tapas at their Tapas Bar while you watch the chefs prepare your meal. Prices are reasonable.

The Swiss Haven (453-6969), 325 S. Main, has melt-in-your-mouth cheese fondues, raclette, Fondue Chinois, and four types of rösti (a potato dish). Plan to spend the evening and linger over a cappuccino-and-kirsch (or two). As in Europe, they won't bring the bill until you ask for it, which can be pricey ($20+) if you order soup, salad and the homemade apple tart.

The St. Bernard Inn (453-2572), 103 S. Main, is in one of the original historic buildings. They specialize in modern Northern Italian cuisine featuring veal, pork, beef, fresh seafood, chicken and vegetarian offerings. They also make fresh baked bread, homemade pastas, dressings, soups and desserts. The wine list has won the coveted Wine Spectator "Award of Excellence" for years.

The Hearthstone (453-7028), 130 S. Ridge Street, is in a stunning blue-and-white Victorian house that has undergone many facelifts over the years. The Old World ambiance, moderately priced selection of meat, chicken and seafood and the killer desserts make this a very popular spot with locals and visitors.

Carnivores should check out the **Steak & Rib** (453-0063), 208 N. Main Street, where New Zealand rack of lamb and West Indian baby back ribs are served in an intimate, rustic atmosphere. Don't miss the tasty Breckenridge Mudslides mixed in the Caribbean-themed bar downstairs.

Other mid-priced recommendations on Main Street: **The Briar Rose** (453-9948); **Blue River Bistro** (453-6974); **The Whale's Tail** (453-2221) for seafood; and **Quandry Grill** in Main Street Station.

For traditional Mexican and unforgettable margaritas, head for **Mi Casa** (453-2071) on Park Ave or **Fiesta Jalisco**. Other ethnic dining options are **Poirrier's** for Cajun, in the Wellington Inn (453-1877); **Red Orchid** for Chinese (453-1881); **Maori's Asian & Pacific Cuisine** (547-5980) in Main Street Station at the South end of town; and **Sushi Breck** for Japanese (453-8338).

Some suggestions for good cheap eats (less than $10):

Beer lovers should try the **Breckenridge Brewery** (453-1550), 600 S. Main St. The menu has mostly burgers, sandwiches and other brewhouse food, and the atmosphere is noisy; however, the micro-brewed beer is excellent. Or try **Rasta Pasta** (453-7467) for whimsical Jamaican-flavored pasta; **Angel's Hollow** (453-8585) for a big-as-your-head burrito and great burgers; **Giampietro Pizzeria & Pasta** (453-3838) for Italian; and **Breckenridge Barbeque** (453-7313). **Fatty's Pizzeria** (453-9802), a town favorite since 1975, was remodeled this summer and is set to open in October 2002 with another level and new dining area. **Downstairs at Eric's,** 109 Main Street, expanded into the space across the hall that used to be known as The Underworld, naming it **Eric's II** and serving the same family-style menu so you should find plenty of seating. If you don't mind eating in a parking lot, **Windy City Pizza** (453-5570), next to City Market, has great deep-dish pizzas, a specialty. They also deliver.

Breakfast: The hands-down winner is **The Prospector** (453-6858) at 130 S. Main Street. The Huevos Rancheros will test your facial sweat glands. A pancake's width behind is **Columbine Café** (547-4474), 109 S. Main St., for its generous omelets and specialty coffees. For lighter fare and gourmet coffee, try **Clint's Bakery & Coffeehouse** (453-2990), 131 S. Main St., or **Sweet Paradise Bakery**, 161 E. Adams St. And don't forget, **Blue Moose**, 340 S. Main.

Après-ski/nightlife

Breckenridge's liveliest après-ski bars are **Tiffany's** in Beaver Run, the **Breckenridge Brewery** for a great beer, **Park Avenue Pub** in the Village, and **Mi Casa**, with thirst-quenching margaritas by the liter. Tiffany's rocks until the wee hours, but after dinner most of the action moves into town.

If you're having trouble adjusting to the altitude, head over to the **O2 Lounge** (453-6262), 500 S. Main St., where you can enjoy an herbal martini and oxygen-enriched air for increments of 10-, 20- and 30-minutes.

Downstairs at Eric's, 109 Main St., expanded into the space across the hall that used to be known as The Underworld, naming it **Eric's II**. Here you'll find a rowdy crowd on TV sports nights.

Sherpa and Yeti's on Main Street is fairly new but has become the hot spot for live music and dancing, with a variety of bands playing blues, jazz, funk and reggae, plus local musicians' nights, all in an unfinished-sheet-rock atmosphere. This places really rocks, so if you packed your dancin' shoes, head here.

For a non-dancing, quieter time, try the **St. Bernard** on Main Street; a cozy bar in the back is often packed with business-class locals; or **The Breckenridge Brewery & Pub,** that has live music specials and Ladies Night on Mondays, but in our experience, the atmosphere is pleasantly tame for chatting.

Salt Creek, 110 E. Lincoln, is the only Country & Western place in town, and a guaranteed good time. **The Dredge**, which is a replica of the dredge boats that churned the Blue River for gold in the early 1900s, has a classy bar.

The old **Gold Pan**, 103 N. Main Street, is the oldest continuously operating bar west of the Mississippi and was one of the wildest places in the Wild West, with a miner or two known to be thrown through the saloon doors. A long, century-old, mahogany bar presides over a now worn, dimly lit room with a pinball machine tucked into the back corner and a couple of well-utilized pool tables frequented by a crowd of truckers, pool sharks sporting earrings, and the temporarily unemployed.

A slightly more mature clientele gathers at the **Big Easy Lounge** below Poirrier's at the Wellington Inn for brandy next to a roaring fire. If you don't mind the smoke, **Cecelia's Cigar Bar** makes great martinis. It recently expanded to add a dance floor and space for a DJ. A new attraction to the nightclub scene is the **Liquid Lounge**, near Cecelia's. You'll get great drinks and there's usually a DJ spinning tunes on the weekends. The old **Brown Hotel** (453-0084), 208 S. Ridge, is an historic site that's heavy on atmosphere and light on the wallet. With a collection of games such as pool, foosball and even chess, there's plenty to do into the wee hours. **The Crown**, 215 S. Main St., has cozy couches which are perfect for intimate, late-night, drinks, desserts or coffee.

Nightlife ends with a visit to **Charlie Dog's** (547-0350), off Main St. at 111 Ski Hill Rd. When every other restaurant in town is closed, you can still satisfy your late night cravings with a Chicago Dog or a sub.

Other activities

Exploring the old town of Breckenridge is great fun, either with a formal **historical tour** (435-9022) or on your own armed with a free guidesheet.

Good Times Adventure Tours (453-7604) in nearby Frisco offers thrilling dogsled tours and snowmobile rides. Unlike other alpine sports operations, Good Times is very hands-on, letting customers run their own dogsled team or take their own snowmobile for a spin. Guides are professional and friendly and prices are reasonable.

Breckenridge Nordic Ski Center (453-6855) near Peak 8 base on Ski Hill Road, has evening **horse-drawn sleigh rides** (with dinner). The Breckenridge Recreation Center (547-3125) on Airport Road north of town offers an array of indoor activities for non-ski days, such as **swimming, tennis, racquetball, wall climbing, exercise machines** and **basketball.**

Downtown has scores of **boutiques.** Some of our favorites on Main Street: Breckenridge Hat Company, Alpen Collections, Tom Girl, September Body & Home, Soap & Water, Wildflower, and Goods, all for clothing and accessories. Also the Main Street Station Mall if full of fabulous shops. Check out Hamlet's Book Shoppe if you're in the mood for a good read. Browse The Quiet Moose, 326 S. Main, even if you aren't furnishing a mountain home. Peek inside Creatures Great & Small if you're an animal lover. Breckenridge isn't quite an art community like Aspen, but more and more collectors are discovering its **galleries,** six of them fine art. We recommend The Copper Fox; Paint Horse Gallery (western); Skilled Hands for handcrafted goods by Colorado artisans; Breckenridge Fine Art Gallery; and the Highlands Gallery.

Breckenridge has bloomed as a destination for **weddings,** both summer and winter. For a wedding and honeymoon guide, call 888-789-SNOW (7669) for weddings at the ski resort or the **Breckenridge Resort Chamber** at 877-864-0868 for more information on weddings in and around town. Also check the **Summit County** chapter for other activities.

Getting there and getting around

By air: Breckenridge is about 100 miles west of Denver International Airport. Resort Express has regular vans connecting the resort with the airport. Telephone: 468-7600 or (800) 334-7433.

By car: From Denver, take I-70 to Exit 203, then south on Highway 9.

Getting around: Nearly everything is within walking distance and buses cruise the streets regularly. The Breckenridge Free Ride provides bus service throughout Breckenridge and some outlying areas. The Summit Stage provides free transportation between Dillon, Silverthorne, Keystone, Frisco, Breckenridge and Copper Mountain. Call 668-0999 for route information. Keystone and Breckenridge also operate a free inter-resort shuttle, the Ski KAB Express (496-4200), at varying times according to demand.

Copper Mountain

Colorado

Summit: 12,313 feet
Vertical: 2,601 feet
Base: 9,712 feet

Address: P.O. Box 3001,
Copper Mountain, CO 80443
☎ **Area code:** 970
Ski area phone: 968-2882
ⓘ **Toll-free information:** (800) 458-8386
Toll-free reservations: (888) 263-5302
Reservations outside U.S.: 968-2882
Fax: 968-3256
E-mail: contactcenter@coppercolorado.com
Internet: www.coppercolorado.com

Expert: ★ ★ ★ ★
Advanced: ★ ★ ★ ★
Intermediate: ★ ★ ★ ★
Beginner: ★ ★ ★ ★
Never-ever: ★ ★ ★ ★

Lifts: 23–1 high-speed 6-passenger
chair, 4 high-speed quads, 5 triples,
5 doubles, 8 surface lifts
Skiable Acreage: 2,450 acres
Snowmaking: 16 percent
Uphill capacity: 32,088 per hour
Snowboarding: Yes
Bed base: 3,300
Nearest lodging: Walking distance, condos
Child care: Yes, 6 weeks and older
Adult ticket, per day: $49-$57 (2001/02)

Dining: ★ ★ ★
Apres-ski/nightlife: ★ ★
Other activities: ★ ★

If ski resorts were people, Copper Mountain Resort would be the person who's easiest to figure out. He's straightforward, honest and organized, with a touch of wildness. His closet's neat and his attitude is contemporary. He knows where he's going—"the man with a plan." Copper's trail system works the way his brain does: logical, organized and laid out for maximum return on minimum effort.

Copper was lauded by the United States Forest Service as the "most nearly perfect ski mountain in the United States"—a commentary on the area's natural terrain features. As you face the mountain, the beginner slopes meander off on the right; the intermediate trails flow right down the center; and advanced runs drop off to the left. The most difficult stuff—chutes, cornices and double-diamond slits—beckons from the summit, where several lifts serve the wild child behind the man with the plan.

The base consists of corresponding areas: Union Creek for starters, The Village at Copper for most of the rest of us, and East Village for the adrenaline hogs. An efficient shuttle system connects the multiple personalities, and the map to the door couldn't be more straightforward: drive I-70 west from Denver, and you're at the door.

Copper's layout makes for a convenient vacation. Just as Mr. Obvious doesn't waste time or let things get too complicated, you won't waste precious minutes consulting the trail map or riding endless lifts to find your type of terrain.

The area is named after an old copper mine whose remnants remain in the Copper Bowl area (in summer the mine tailings are distinct). But, rather than attempt to honor days of old, Copper Mountain is a paean to modern-day master planning. Born in 1972, the base area has grown from a dowdy conglomeration of buildings with no focus or ambiance into adulthood at the hands of resort developer Intrawest. Now in its sixth year of intensive re-development, the recent improvements reflect commitment to an extensive plan to invest $500 million into Copper over a 10-year period. They're more than halfway to the finish line, and prospering.

The first phase began in 1998 in East Village with the construction of Copper Station, a day lodge and conference center, and Copper Springs Lodge, with 108 lodging units. At the same time the west side of the resort saw the Union Creek Base Lodge transformed into a dining, rental and retail area that connects via walkway to the Schoolhouse at Union Creek, a one-stop-shopping home for all beginner ski and snowboard school operations, especially convenient for families, with improved rental facilities, retail shops and restaurant. Phase II of the development plan, now complete, includes five buildings in The New Village at Copper—Copper One Lodge, Tucker Mountain Lodge, The Mill Club, Taylor's Crossing, and Passage Point. Shops, restaurants, decks, open plazas for year-round festivities, a new Westlake Market and brand-new lodging accommodations sit just steps away from the slopes. Copper's nightlife and restaurants are booming. JJ's (formerly Molly B's) leads the pack of a half-dozen restaurants and bars that are determined to set new standards of après-ski excellence.

Copper has come a long way toward enticing both families and dedicated singles to its village and ski hill—and it only took 30 years! Everything is gnarly, but we especially enjoy the hikes to the glades and chutes on Tucker and the bumps down the West Ridge.

Mountain layout—Skiing

If you use lifts as meeting places, pay attention to the American *Eagle* and American *Flyer* chairs. If you're meeting someone at the top of one of those chairs, be very specific: They start in the same general area but unload on different peaks.

◆◆ **Expert:** Copper's mountain range tops out at 12,313 (Union Peak), 12,337 (Tucker Mountain) and 12,441 (Copper Peak), and there lie the double-diamond runs that slink through chutes, down steep ridges and into the woods. They are legitimate: Consequences of falling are real—whether in powder, bumps or crud. Resolution Bowl's steeps are short and swift; Spaulding bumps up nicely before it drops into glades. Extra added attraction: A no-charge (as in "free") 10-person snowcat makes laps to the top of Tucker Wednesdays through Sundays on a first-come, first-served basis (weather permitting).

◆ **Advanced:** The Super Bee six-person, high-speed chair accesses all terrain on the East Village side, including the relentless bumps on Far East, Too Much and Triple Treat under the Alpine lift. You can slide down any of three short but sweet runs that parallel the Excelerator quad. Brennan's Grin will bring a smile to any serious bump skier's face.

Traverse to the right off Super Bee to Storm King surface lift, the crown of Copper Peak and some of its toughest skiing. In Enchanted Forest to skier's left and Spaulding Bowl to skier's right, if you lose a ski here, you'd better have an uphill friend. If you survive Spaulding, choose from worthy expert runs to the bottom of Resolution Lift where there's seldom a wait.

The consistently good snow in Union Bowl under Sierra lift gets even better when you hike to the top of the cirque. Not always so with Copper Bowl on the backside of Union Peak. Its slopes are south-facing, so ask around before you dive in. It could be ugly or divine.

■ **Intermediate:** Exit to the right of the American Flyer quad and try the American Flyer, I-Beam and Windsong runs under the Timberline Express lift. Better yet, take the American Eagle quad chair from Village Center and dart down any of the runs under this lift.

Intermediates can take the Super Bee to ride up Storm King, a surface lift, for the 360-degree view of the Colorado universe. Snap your pictures, then avoid the black diamonds and ski the blue runs down beside the lift. Off the Excelerator lift, you'll have the best intermediate runs of the resort at your feet. We learned of an event held recently that challenged skiers to log twice the vertical of Everest (that is, 66,000 feet) by doing laps off the Super Bee chair using either Collage or Andy's Encore. A friend hit 70,000 verts by 1:30 in the afternoon on these worthy intermediate highways that offer good grade without the heavy moguls or tight funnels that can turn a blue run black (and an unwary intermediate black and blue).

●● **Beginner:** Hop on the high-speed American Flyer or High Point lifts in the Union Creek area. Nearly the whole side of the mountain consists of sweeping runs lined by trees, perfect for the advanced beginner and lower intermediate.

For a long run to the bottom, beginners should bear left when getting off the high-speed American Flyer and take Coppertone for an easy cruise. From the High Point lift, head right down Woodwinds to the Timberline Express quad chair, ride to the top and ski the sweeping Soliloquy to Roundabout connection to the bottom.

● **Never-ever:** The Kokomo lift, at the far right border of the resort, serves a super gentle, isolated area. When you have these runs conquered, the next step is the nearby Lumberjack lift, another chair with only beginner runs beneath it. Copper Mountain is a never-ever's dream mountain. One of the top 100 ski instructors in the country calls this a ski instructor's perfect hill because the beginner's terrain is naturally separated from the gonzo's terrain on the other side. There are plans to move the beginner's terrain to the top of the Kokomo lift and put in a gondola to access this area.

Mountain layout—Snowboarding

Summit County's best-kept secret, Copper is a favorite of Colorado boarders. Arrayed across the face of Copper Peak are more than 125 trails that progress from easy to thrilling to terrifying. This natural segregation of trails keeps rank beginners out of the way of overconfident intermediates and impatient experts.

For the showoff, there is a well-designed and maintained 400-foot-long superpipe on Loverly at the end of the terrain park, which includes a series of tabletops, spines and kickers of varying sizes and degrees of difficulty.

For those who dig solitude, there are the famed Copper Bowls, which feature treacherous steeps and plenty of fresh pow. Copper Bowl is a true backcountry experience that is now lift-served. Then there's the Spaulding Bowl at the top of the Storm King Poma ground lift—provided you can deal with a Poma. The chutes here funnel down to the quad-exhausting bumps of Resolution Bowl (or "Rezo," as locals refer to it). Three runs, and you'll be heading for the new Indian Motorcycle Café for a beer to chase away the lactic acid. Extra added attraction: A no-charge (as in "free") 10-person snowcat makes laps to the top of Tucker Wednesdays through Sundays on a first-come, first-served basis (weather permitting).

Mountain rating

The terrain keeps various skill levels separated naturally so that no one needs to feel intimidated or slowed down by fellow skiers or snowboarders. With the opening of Copper's upper bowls, this mountain is a contender, easy to navigate and long on choice.

Cross-country and snowshoeing

Head to the trails of the **White River National Forest** to play on 25 km. of groomed trails on your own. **Copper Mountain Cross-Country Center** is no more. However, you can still book overnight tours to Janet's Cabin, part of the 10th Mountain Division system and a gentle ski tour with a four-course progressive meal; various women's clinics; the Backcountry Telemark Series and other telemark camps through the **activities center**: 968-2882 ext. 4INFO (83222). The same network of trails can also be explored on snowshoes.

Lessons (2002/03 prices)

Group lessons: $55 for a half day.

Never-ever package: Half-day ski lesson, lift ticket and rentals cost $87; snowboarders, cost is $91.

Private lessons: For one person, $229 for two hours; $279 for half day (three hours); $399 for full day (six hours); $169 for a 90-minute bonus private on weekends and certain holidays.

Special programs: Woman's Wednesdays and Testosterone Tuesdays (men's specific workshops) highlight the list.

Child care (2002/03 prices)

Ages: 6 weeks to 4 years.

Costs: Full day with lunch costs $70; half day is $60 (morning only). Parents should provide diapers, a change of clothing, a blanket and a favorite toy. In-room babysitting services require 24-hour advance reservations or cancellations, and cost about $10 per hour, plus $1 for each additional child. Fun tip: In the "Belly Button" programs, the kids make chocolate chip cookies to give to mom and dad when they return at the end of the ski day. Yum.

Reservations: Required; call 968-2318, Ext. 38101; or (800) 458-8386. Copper Mountain long has received high marks for its children's care and learning programs.

Other options: Kids' Night Out, a "kids only" night filled with fun and games, videos and pizza for children up to age 10. Participation is free to parents who spend $30 or more while shopping or dining at Copper Mountain. Copper also offers **evening babysitting** in a guest's accommodations. **Baby's Away** (800-479-4030) rents and will deliver baby needs to your lodge, such as crib, stroller, car seat and toys.

Children's lessons: Full day (lunch, rentals, lesson, lifts), $99; without rentals, $93. Ages are 3–13 for skiing, 7–13 for snowboarding.

Lift tickets (2001/02 prices)

	Adult	Child (6-13)
One day	$57	$25
Three days	$156 ($52/day)	$75 ($25/day)
Five days	$245 ($49/day)	$125 ($25/day)

Who skis free: Ages 5 and younger, 70 and older ski free. Children stay free (some restrictions apply). Children 13 and younger ski free at certain times. There is a Seniors Ski Free program for those 62 and older when they stay at Copper Mountain at certain times.

Who skis at a discount: Skiers aged 60–69 pay $41 per day.

Note: Discounted Copper lift tickets are sold at hundreds of ski shops, grocery stores and convenience stores in Denver and the rest of the Front Range. Call the resort to find out where to buy these tickets.

Accommodations

Copper has been adding and renovating its accommodations rapidly, so most lodging is or seems brand new. Lodging through **Copper Mountain Reservations** (888-263-5302 or www.coppercolorado.com) includes hotels, condos and homes just steps from the slopes. Hotel rooms go for $123-$369 per night; one-bedrooms, $154-$360; two-bedrooms, $225-$369; three-bedrooms, $357-$593; and four-bedrooms, $369-$689. All guests who book their vacation through CMR can use the Copper Mountain Racquet and Athletic Club, which has an indoor pool, tennis, racquetball, massage facilities, weight room, spas, saunas and steam rooms (massages and racquetball are extra).

The five buildings in **The New Village at Copper** include everything from studios to three-bedroom condos. Some units have jetted soaker tubs, gourmet kitchens and gas fireplaces; select buildings also provide outdoor spas, ski lockers and bike storage, and are steps away from the lifts. The **Copper Springs Lodge,** a classic mountain lodge in East Village, has 108 units.

As with all ski areas that manage property, Copper offers lift/lodging packages that can save considerably, especially in early and late season. For example, from Nov. 1 through just before Christmas, deluxe studio units start at $119 per person, and again from April 6 through closing, when the area is blessed with some of the best snow of the season. Last-minute lodging discounts are available all season at www.coppersavers.com.

If you book accommodations and lift ticket package through the new Copper Reservations (800-458-8396), you get the "Bee Line Advantage." This includes (at no additional cost) exclusive priority lift access through a dedicated line at base areas (you get to "cut" lift lines); 15-minute early access to the mountain via the American Eagle lift; VIP line at rental shops, 8-11 a.m.; and ski tunes guaranteed by 7:30 a.m. the next day. Since you'll probably be staying at one of these properties anyway, this is a great way to save time and line frustrations all 'round.

Two other companies book accommodations: **Carbonate Property Management** (800-526-7737) and **Copper Vacations** (800-525-3887).

Dining

Just as the new village has spiffed up its act, so has the food scene. **JJ's Rocky Mountain Tavern** (formerly Molly B's) in East Village's Copper Station day lodge is the no-contest winner for both après-ski and later in the evening. Named after J.J. Astor, husband of the Titanic's "Unsinkable" Molly Brown, a Colorado legend, it's reminiscent of an 1800s tavern and serves casual American fare; lunch, dinner and bar menus available.

Endo's Adrenaline Café in the Mountain Plaza building enjoys a strong following for great salads, burgers and fries. **Jack's Slopeside Grill** at Copper One Lodge, a giant food court serving a wide variety of food from 7 a.m. to 6 p.m., also draws crowds. **Camp Hale Coffee** is there when you need it, serving bean brews and pastries at wake-up call and throughout the day.

Dining: $$$-Entrees $20+; $$-$10-20; $-less than $10.

In the Foxpine Inn, the **Double Diamond Bar and Grill** ($–$$) serves up the best burgers and soup around, and does a great job with pasta and its specialty, Colorado beef. A tip: Owner Dave Luthi hosts Friday Night Fish Frys all year long for only $5.95. He may even offer to take you for a personal ride on his snowmobile, so stay strong. The place is usually jumping on Fridays.

Restaurants near the Center Village include **Salsa Mountain Cantina** ($) for Mexican and **Imperial Palace** ($–$$) for Taiwanese and Szechwan Chinese. One local who used to live in Asia raves about the authentic deep-fried chicken wings and the great service at this family-owned eatery.

At **Creekside Pizza**, you can get single slices or the whole thing; their new management is doing a bang-up job.

Dinner sleigh rides (968-2232; reservations required) cost about $60 for adults; $35 for children aged 5-12. A horse-drawn sleigh takes diners to a heated miner's tent for a gourmet meal.

Après-ski/nightlife

The old days are gone: Copper used to die at the end of the ski day. At 4:00, the base area was a ghost town as people retired to their condos. Things have changed. Under Intrawest's savvy eye, new spots that merit attention join old favorites. **JJ's** (formerly Molly B's) with its live entertainment and bar menu, is without question the hottest spot here. Moe Dixon, a longtime favorite entertainer, always gets people dancing on the tables. Recently, in fact, the owners had to reinforce the bar top, thanks to the hordes who refused to remove their ski boots when dancing on the bar. Ban dancing? *NEVER!*

A popular hangout is **Endo's Adrenaline Café** in the Mountain Plaza building, promising rocking music delivered by D.J.s and drink specials in a sport-oriented atmosphere. Endo's also features an oxygen bar where you can catch your breath while recalling highlights of your day. **Jack's Slopeside** at Copper One Lodge, with live entertainment five nights a week, headlines Jolly Dimas. The **Indian Motorcycle Café** brings the term "unique" to Copper. This retail store, bar and restaurant is premised on the trendy 1901 Indian Motorcycles. Consider the flat screen TV, the red felt pool tables, chairs as soft as your leather jacket, and live music piped in from the only other Indian café—in Ontario—and you have something brand new in the west. The food is actually quite upscale and creative, including Fussy Chicken, Lamb Wellington, lots of steak and unusual appetizers. And don't miss the Ally McBeal "wannabe" bathrooms: Men's on the right, women's on the left, with a common frosted glass wall between featuring small see-thru slits to either side. Rumor has it that the men's needs more than one pissoir. (We don't know yet about this one...)

Other activities

Other activities in and around the resort include **ice skating, tubing, sleigh rides, snowmobiling, dogsled rides** and **hot air balloon floats**.

Copper Mountain Racquet and Athletic Club (968-2318 ext. 27201) has a lap pool, sauna, steam room, Jacuzzis and two indoor tennis courts. Spa services and massages are available.

Opportunities abound in the **shops** at Copper Station, West Village and The New Village at Copper. Upper-end souvenirs, logo clothing and sports gear fill most of them. All American Goods sells USA- and Colorado-made products; 9600' specializes in outdoor clothing; and

Rocky Mountain Chocolate Factory makes you-know-what. Also browse through the new boutique shops on West Lake at Copper One Lodge.

For more activities see the Summit County or Vail chapters. Copper is about 20 miles from Vail and about 10 miles from the tri-town area of Dillon, Frisco and Silverthorne.

Getting there and getting around

By air: Copper Mountain is 90 miles west of Denver International Airport on I-70. **Resort Express** runs vans between the airport and your lodge, with many daily departures. You can make arrangements when you reserve lodging, or call Resort Express at 468-7600 or (800) 334-7433.

By car: Right off I-70 at Exit 195. You can see many of the trails from the freeway.

Getting around: Copper Mountain's updated, fairly new fleet of buses enhances an already superb (and free) shuttle service, running constantly between 8:00 a.m. and 11:00 p.m. Walking is also easy between the outlying condos and the village center. Free Summit Stage buses serve three nearby ski areas—Breckenridge, Keystone and Arapahoe Basin—as well as the towns of Dillon, Silverthorne and Frisco. Warning: The buses make lots of stops, and it can take up to an hour-and-a-half to make it down the road to the next resort. If you plan to head over to Vail or to the other Summit County areas frequently, you'll probably want a car, otherwise you don't need one. If you are not staying at Copper, one warning about parking: All parking lots charge about $10 per day, except the outlying Alpine lot near the highway, which is free.

Keystone

Colorado

Summit elevation: 11,980 feet
Vertical drop: 2,680 feet
Base elevation: 9,300 feet

Address: Box 38, Keystone, CO 80435
☎ Area code: 970
Ski area phone: 496-2316 or (800) 427-8308
Snow report: 496-4111 or (800) 427-8308
ⓘ Toll-free reservations: (800) 427-8308
Toll-free foreign numbers:
UK (fax): 0800-89-6868
Germany (fax): 0130 82 0958
Netherlands (fax) 060 22 3972
Mexico (fax) 95-800-936-5633
Brazil: (fax) 000811-712-0553
Fax: 496-4105
E-mail: keystoneinfo@vailresorts.com
Internet: www.keystoneresort.com
Bed base: 8,000
Nearest lodging: Slopeside, ski-in/ski-out
Resort child care: Yes, 2 months and older
Adult ticket, per day: $50–$59 (01/02 prices)

Number and types of lifts: 24–2 gondolas, 1 high-speed six-person chair, 5 high-speed quads, 1 quad, 1 triple, 5 doubles, 5 surface lifts, 4 magic carpets
Skiable acreage: 1,861 acres
Snowmaking: 49 percent
Uphill capacity: 32,175 skiers per hour
Snowboarding: Yes

Expert: ★★★★
Advanced: ★★★★
Intermediate: ★★★★★
Beginner: ★★★★★
Never-ever: ★★★

Dining: ★★★★★
Apres-ski/nightlife: ★★
Other activities: ★★★

Many winter vacationers associate Colorado skiing with 19th-century Victorian mining-town charm. You won't find that here, because Keystone was built to be a smoothly humming resort with buses shuttling to every corner, foot-of-the-mountain child care, one of the Rockies' largest snowmaking systems and one-number central reservations. The resort is perfect for families, couples or small groups of friends.

Keystone is a superb intermediate playground, but it has good terrain at either end of the ability scale, too. It has one of the nation's best summit-to-base beginner runs (Schoolmarm), and advanced skiing on North Peak and The Outback (known for bump runs, bowls and trees).

Keystone belongs to Vail Resorts, Inc., which has made many improvements in the past few seasons. The resort's largest new base area is River Run, a village that includes boutiques, coffee shops, restaurants and condominiums at the base of the River Run Gondola.

Mountain layout—Skiing

Unlike other areas that have peaks side by side, Keystone has three peaks one behind another. In front is Keystone Mountain, with beginner and intermediate terrain, and some new expert glades on its backside. In the middle is North Peak, and finally, the Outback. Other than one snaking green-circle trail, these latter peaks have just blue and black terrain. This unusual arrangement lends an exploratory quality to the day. As you get farther from the base area, the skiing feels a little wilder, a little more off-piste.

◆◆ **Expert:** Head to the farthest peak, the Outback. The 889-acre Outback is a mix of open-bowl skiing, natural chutes and tree-lined glades. The quartet of Timberwolf, Bushwacker, Badger and The Grizz are visible from North Peak and allow tree fans to pick how tight they want their forest to be. Two black-diamond bowls are accessible by a short uphill hike from the top of the Outback Express high-speed quad. (This in-bounds terrain tops out at 12,200 feet, giving Keystone a 2,900-foot vertical descent, slightly more than is listed in the stat box, where we list lift-served terrain.)

◆ **Advanced:** North Peak, the middle mountain, also has good advanced terrain, though it is generally tamer. From the top of Keystone Mountain, advanced skiers can reach the North Peak base down Mineshaft or Diamond Back. North Peak is a great spot for working on technique and steeps. Star Fire, rated blue, is a superb steep, groomed run, and a good warmup for this area. Black diamonds that plunge off this run are Ambush, Powder Cap or Bullet. On the other side of the lift, Cat Dancer and Geronimo offer a challenge, and experts can break their own tracks through the trees directly beneath the Santiago Express, a high-speed quad that serves this area.

On Keystone Mountain, there's only one section that develops pitch—Go Devil and The Last Hoot, which drop down the far-right edge of the area as you look at the trail map.

■ **Intermediate:** This level has the run of the three mountains, with appropriate terrain on each. Keystone Mountain has runs such as Paymaster, the Wild Irishman, Frenchman and Flying Dutchman that play with God-given terrain. The twists and natural steps on these cruisers represent trails at their best—they obviously did not have their character bulldozed out of them. Snowmaking covers 100 percent of the trails on Keystone Mountain, and the slope grooming ranks among the best in the country. The Mountain House base area has three chair lifts taking skiers up the mountain, and the other base area, River Run, is the lower station of the River Run Gondola. The gondola serves the night-skiing area until 8 p.m. The resort says it's the largest single-mountain night ski operation in the United States, covering 17 runs and 235 acres of terrain.

Intermediates also can head to North Peak down Mozart, a wide blue run. Its width is essential, because it's the main pathway to the two rear peaks. On North Peak, Prospector and Last Alamo are the easiest of the blues, with Star Fire a good test for the Outback. If you think Star Fire is fun, not scary, head down Anticipation or Spillway to the Outback and play on the intermediate runs under the Outback Express chair. The advanced-intermediate glades to the far right of the map—Wolverine, Wildfire and Pika—are not as tough as the glades of the Black Forest, but also not a spot for timid intermediates.

●● **Beginner:** Stay on Keystone Mountain. Trails cutting across the mountain are principally for beginners. You can take most of them traversing from the top of the Peru Chair, or take Schoolmarm along the ridge and drop down Silver Spoon or Last Chance. You can—and you should—ride the Outpost gondola to the gorgeous Outpost Lodge on North Peak. There, you can try Fox Trot, a gentle trail. If you're up for a blue, head down on Prospector and Mozart for the ride to the Keystone Mountain summit; otherwise, ride the Outpost gondola back to Keystone Mountain.

● **Never-ever:** Keystone has a learning center at the top of the Diamond Back trail on Keystone Mountain, with two learning runs and a triple chairlift. Discovery Learning Area at the base of Keystone Mountain is serviced by a chairlift, a magic carpet and a T-bar. Keystone Mountain also has plenty of gentle terrain to practice on.

Mountain layout—Snowboarding

Ahhh…Keystone, the red-headed stepchild of Summit County. One of the last great holdouts to snowboarding, Keystone opened its doors to boarders only a few years ago, but like the father who wasn't there during his children's upbringing, is now showering boarders with presents.

That's right, Keystone has been progressively dropping down the cash to get snowboarders to go there, and so far it's been working. With a fine terrain park and halfpipe, various events, and the only legal night riding in Summit County, Keystone's been actively recruiting riders from its sister mountain Breckenridge. This season Keystone has committed to offering riders at least one hit from their opening day until they close for the season.

Experts are after one thing—that's powder—so head to the farthest peak, the Outback. The 889-acre Outback is a mix of open-bowl riding, natural chutes and tree-lined glades. The quartet of Timberwolf, Bushwacker, Badger and The Grizz are visible from North Peak and allow tree fans to pick how tight they want their forest to be. Two black-diamond bowls are accessible by a short uphill hike from the top of the Outback Express high-speed quad. (This in-bounds terrain tops out at 12,200 feet, giving Keystone a 2,900-foot vertical descent, slightly more than is listed in the stat box, where we list lift-served terrain.)

Other than the Outback, Keystone's steeps are mainly moguled, a major drawback for many advanced snowboarders. However, Keystone has been getting rather creative with its snowboard parks. This season Keystone vows it'll have the *best* intermediate and beginner parks, so we'll have to wait and see what the designers have up their sleeves. On the down-side, the resort still does not have a superpipe, which really puts a damper on its forward progress with advanced riders.

Keystone is perfect for budding park riders and halfpipe tricksters. The Area 51 halfpipe at its highest is around 9 to 10 feet (while Breckenridge's superpipe ranges in the 14-foot area) so it's much easier to learn in and less crowded. About 80 percent of the tabletops in the park are intermediate-friendly and there's an abundance of rails to conquer. However, this is where you'll spend most of your time, there aren't a ton of cruisers at Keystone, and the ones that are here are rather crowded. Remember, this is a mountain that's only been snowboarder-friendly for a short time, but they're learning.

Beginners should stay on the trails cutting across Keystone Mountain. Start from the top of the Peru Chair, or take Schoolmarm along the ridge and drop down Silver Spoon or Last Chance. Or ride the Outpost gondola to the gorgeous Outpost Lodge on North Peak. There, you can try Fox Trot, a gentle trail. If you're up for a blue, head down on Prospector and Mozart for the ride to the Keystone Mountain summit; otherwise, ride the Outpost gondola back to Keystone Mountain.

Keystone Mountain also has plenty of gentle terrain to practice on. There's a learning center at the top of the Diamond Back trail on Keystone Mountain, with two learning runs and a triple chairlift. There's another learning center at the base of the mountain in the Mountain House neighborhood/base area.

Mountain rating

These mountains divide easily into categories, with some exceptions as noted above. Keystone has great beginner and cruising terrain. North Peak is for advanced skiers with expert tendencies. The Outback is for upper intermediates and experts. For snowboarders, Keystone's got some great potential. Hidden nuggets of fun exist throughout the mountain, but you've got to remember the resort's still pretty new to the game. Our guess is that we'll continue to see a lot of big changes over the next few seasons, and Keystone will eventually turn into a heavyweight contender.

Cross-country and snowshoeing

Keystone has an extensive cross-country touring area, with 18 km. of groomed trails around the resort, and an additional 57 km. of ungroomed backcountry skiing trails to ghost mining towns in the Montezuma area and around the region. The **Cross Country Center** (496-4275) is now at the River Course clubhouse off Hwy. 6. Lessons and rentals are available. Cross-country activities include moonlight tours and ecology tours. Snowshoe rentals also are available.

Lessons (2001/02 prices)

Group lessons: Meet daily at 10:30 a.m. and 1:30 p.m. for a 2.5-hour session, $45 ($99 with lifts and rentals). Other options: An intermediate instruction, called "Parallel Breakthrough," costs $45 for 2.5 hours ($94 with lifts and rentals). An equivalent intermediate snowboarding session costs $92 with lifts and rentals. Advanced skiers can take "Mountain Masters" for a full day for $65 ($119 with lift and rentals). Advanced riders can take a half-day semi-private for $65 ($114 with lift and rentals).

Never-ever package: A 2.5-hour lesson, lift ticket and equipment rental is $74 for skiing. An adult snowboard lesson-lift-rental package is $114 (lesson is five hours).

Private lessons: $150 for 90 minutes, $185 for two hours, $265 for three hours, and $400 for six hours. Each additional skier pays $30.

Special programs: Clinics are held for women skiers, upper-intermediate to advanced skiers who want to cross over to snowboarding, snowboarders who want to learn halfpipe freestyle jumps, and more. Call for prices and details.

A two-day series of ski and snowboard programs guarantee you'll "graduate" from class or you can return for a free lesson; $85 for lessons only, lesson-lift-rental packages available. "Guarantee to Green" is for beginner skiers, "Guarantee to Parallel" is for intermediate skiers, plus there's "Guarantee to Moguls." For snowboarders, there's "Get on Board" for beginners and "Get on the Mountain" for intermediates.

The Mahre Training Centers are held here exclusively. These are three- and five-day sessions conducted in part by either Phil or Steve Mahre, Olympic medal winners. The skiing, for all levels, teaches fundamentals. Evening classroom sessions review on-slope activities and techniques, and one of the Mahre brothers is available to answer questions. Both include six hours of instruction daily, video, races and time for fun. Lodging and lifts are not included. The Mahre courses run in December and January. Call for details and prices.

Racing: Nastar racing, clinics and a self-timed course are on Keystone Mountain.

Child care (2001/02 prices)

Ages: 2 months and older. (Keystone doesn't specify an upper age limit, but most kids older than 6 or 7 want to be on the mountain.)

Costs: Child care is $75 for a full day and $60 for a half day. Both include lunch. Children ages 3 and older get outdoor snow play as part of the fun.

Reservations: Required; call 496-4181 or (800) 255-3715.

Other options: Baby's Away (800-979-9030) rents and will deliver baby needs to your lodge, such as crib, stroller, car seat and toys.

Children's lessons: 3-year-olds can take a learn-to-ski program that includes lesson, rentals, lunch and crafts, $80 for a full day, $70 half day. Reservations are required, call (800) 255-3715. The programs for ages 4–14 include rental equipment, lift ticket, lesson and lunch for a full-day rate of $92. Snowboarding lessons start at age 8. Keystone puts a big emphasis on families and children's lessons. It has parts of the mountain that are designated Children Only, and they try to keep classes small, usually no more than five students.

 ## Lift tickets (2001/02 prices)

	Adult	Child (5-12)
One day	$59	$27
Three days	$156 ($52/day)	$72 ($24/day)
Five of six days	$250 ($50/day)	$120 ($24/day)

Note: These prices valid from December 22, 2001 to April 6, 2002.
Who skis free: Ages 4 and younger.
Who skis at a discount: Ages 65–69 pay $42 per day; 70+ pay $31 per day. Vail Resorts has a handful of different discounted prices based on time of the year, time of a skiers first visit, ski packages, Internet sales, supermarket sales, pre-purchasing and groups. Keystone also has one of the largest night-skiing operations in the country. If you buy a full-day ticket, night skiing is included. Night-skiing-only prices are available.
Interchangeability: Multiple-day lift tickets of three or more days purchased at Keystone or Breckenridge also are valid at sister resorts Vail and Beaver Creek (one day of a three-day lift ticket purchased at Keystone or Breckenridge is valid at Vail or Beaver Creek; two days of a four-day or five-day lift ticket; three days of a six-day or seven-day ticket). All lift tickets purchased at Keystone or Breckenridge also are valid at nearby Arapahoe Basin.

Nearby resorts

Arapahoe Basin,   Arapahoe Basin, CO; 888-ARAPAHO (272-7246)

Internet: www.arapahoebasin.com
5 lifts; 490 acres; 2,270 vertical feet

A-Basin, as the locals call it, has the highest skiable terrain in North America, with a summit of 13,050 feet. The upper half of the mountain serves two above-timberline bowls. On a clear day, you have amazing views from the top of the Continental Divide. This is the closest thing Colorado has to skiing and riding the high Alps.

Dozens of expert runs drop from the top of the Pallavicini Lift. The "Pali" side of A-Basin is for the strong, hardy skier or snowboarder who braves bumps, weather and super-steep terrain to push his or her envelope of experience. On the other side of the mountain, the entire east wall has chutes, gullies and steeps regularly searched out by experts. When all is said and done, the heart of A-Basin for experts is Pali, a steep stamped in nature.

For all its gnarly reputation, A-Basin has excellent beginner terrain. Sixty percent of the terrain is rated beginner and intermediate. Never-evers start on their own lift, Molly Hogan, and the flat, nearly separate terrain beneath it. You can buy a ticket to use only this lift for $5. Wrangler is a very wide flat trail on the far-left side of the map. Chisholm and Sundance are the next steps up the ability ladder. All three wind down from the top of the Exhibition chair lift. Intermediates can test themselves from the top of either the Lenawee quad (which accesses more terrain than the previous double chair) or Norway chairs and enjoy above-timberline bowl skiing. Thanks to its elevation, A-Basin doesn't hit its stride until late January when the east wall opens with sufficient snow cover. It's skiable until June, sometimes into early July. A-Basin is known for its spring skiing and "beach" scene with barbeques and volleyball games along the slope.

Here's our advice for **snowboarders**: For those of you stuck on the idea of perpetually heading to Mexico for spring break, it's time to rethink your plans. There's nothing like A-Basin's spring corn snow, with a frequent overnight dose of powder. The riding here is *au natural,* with no manmade features, and no reason to regret this fact. The terrain varies from cornice jumps off of the Norway Lift to sweeping beginner and intermediate runs. With a quick hike, the East Wall delivers treeless powder runs with an intermittent jump or two. Bigger air hits can be found in the Rock Garden off of the Pallavicini Lift, along with some rowdy, tree-lined chutes. On the lower part of the mountain, North Fork's natural berms and bumps are also worth a diversion. There are no treacherous runouts to avoid, as every trail winds nicely back to the base. What really sets A-Basin apart, however, is its relaxed, no-frills attitude—oh, and it's unbelievably sunny base lodge deck.

Lift tickets (2002/03 prices): Adults, $46; children, $18. These are the prices mid-January to mid-April. Before and after, prices drop for adults; children's tickets stay the same. One child skis free with a full-price adult lift ticket. Though Vail Resorts doesn't own A-Basin, it has arranged for Keystone/Breckenridge lift tickets to be valid at A-Basin, too.

 ## Accommodations

Keystone Central Reservations (800-427-8308) can book lodging and arrange for air transportation, lift tickets and other needs. Keystone is mostly a condominium community, but it also has two hotels and a quaint bed and breakfast that formerly was a stagecoach stop in the 1800s. Room or condo rates start at about $120 per night. Kids ages 12 and younger stay free with their parents, provided minimum occupancy is met and maximum occupancy not exceeded. All room reservations include free activities such as night skiing, ice skating, snowshoeing, cross-country skiing, yoga classes and Kids' Night Out.

One hotel is the modern **Keystone Lodge** ($$$), which also houses the main restaurants and conference rooms for business meetings. **The Inn** ($) has 103 rooms within walking distance of Keystone Mountain.

The quaint **Ski Tip Lodge** ($–$$$$), which was a stagecoach stop in the late 1800s, is a near-perfect ski lodge. Rooms are rustic (in the best sense of the word) with true ski history, the dining room elegant and the sitting room warm and inviting. The Ski Tip Lodge rents rooms with breakfast included. Private rooms have baths, and the dorm rooms share one. The rooms are not huge but are comfortable and the food is very good.

Keystone divides its **rental condominiums** into seven "neighborhoods," with each group having a central swimming pool, shops and restaurants, and serviced by excellent shuttlebus access. Generally, the closer the condo group is to the lifts, the nicer it is and the more interior amenities it has.

The newest lodging at Keystone is in the attractive **River Run area**, which is walking distance from the River Run Gondola. The condos are spacious and convenient to the slopes and the best shopping in Keystone. The newest ski-in/ski-out condominiums in River Run are Lone Eagle and The Timbers.

Slopeside condominiums are virtually ski-in/ski-out—they are right across the street from the Keystone Mountain Base Area. The **Chateaux d'Mont** condos are spectacular, luxurious and worth every penny. We strongly recommend trying to get one of these units. Farther from the slopes, **The St. Johns** units have spectacular views and were built with just about every amenity. We also highly recommend the **Pines** condominiums.

Keystone platinum collection of lodging properties continues to define luxury. When guests stay at one of these upscale condos or townhomes, they receive free ski check, welcome gifts, fresh flowers, a complimentary bottle of wine, personal concierge and daily newspapers. Be sure to ask about it if you're in the mood for pampering.

Dining

Keystone is quietly gaining a reputation for fine dining, thanks to the Colorado Mountain College Culinary Institute based there. Qualified students apprentice for three years in the resort's restaurants under world-renowned chefs before receiving degrees in culinary arts from the American Culinary Federation. So, lucky Keystone visitors get to sample the fruits of their labors. Keystone has three dining experiences not to be missed—**The Keystone Ranch** ($$$), the **Ski Tip Lodge** ($$–$$$) and the **Alpenglow Stube** ($$$), the latter perched at 11,444 feet on North Peak and considered the highest gourmet restaurant in the country.

All are sophisticated gourmet restaurants in charming settings, perfect for romantic dinners or groups of adults (and not at all suitable for noisy young children). The chefs at each have a friendly rivalry, which helps to keep the standards high. Save room for dessert and appetizers. All require reservations, which you can make before leaving home by calling the activities/dining toll-free number, (800) 354-4386 (354-4FUN). If you're staying at a resort property, dial extension 4FUN (4386). If you're staying elsewhere in Summit County, call 496-4386. Use these numbers for all the restaurants we list here.

The **Alpenglow Stube** in The Outpost features rough-hewn timbers, massive fireplaces, vaulted ceilings and expansive windows. The Alpenglow Stube serves what we rate as the best mountain dinner available in the U.S.A. The adventure begins two valleys away with a ride on two separate gondolas suspended over the lighted slopes of Keystone Mountain. The restaurant, a large but cozy room that looks as if Martha Stewart's Swiss cousin was the decorator, features a six- to eight-course menu (for a fixed price of about $80 per person or a $95 degustation menu) of such non-traditional skiing fare as wood-grilled salmon, grilled wild game and slow-roasted duck. Figure about another $40 a bottle for wine. Patrons can sit at a counter with a view of chefs preparing the meal on open grills. Everything from the setting to cuisine is perfect—even more amazing considering that every bit of fresh food on your plate was transported via gondola or snowcat.

The **Keystone Ranch** ($$$) is a restored log ranch house, built in the 1930s as a wedding present to Bernardine Smith and Howard Reynolds. Reportedly, the only completely original part of the house is the fireplace, yet you feel as if you're dining at the home of an intimate friend. American regional cuisine is prepared with Rocky Mountain indigenous ingredients—such as piñon-encrusted lamb or elk with wild mushrooms.

The **Ski Tip Lodge** ($$$) exudes a homey, rustic flavor. It was an 1800s stagecoach stop turned private residence for Arapahoe Basin and Keystone founders Max and Edna Dercum. The restaurant follows its country inn theme with an elegant but down-home menu. It serves a prix-fixe, four-course meal for adults and a three-course meal for children 12 and younger.

The famous Ski Tip Coffee, fortified with Irish cream, chocolate liqueur and Grand Marnier, restores your body heat after a chilling day on the slopes.

You say your kids want to ride the gondolas for dinner, too? Take the family to **Der Fondue Chessel** ($–$$), also at The Outpost at the top of North Peak. Enjoy fondue, raclette and wine with music by a Bavarian band.

We like the Keystone Lodge's **Garden Room** ($$) overlooking the lake much better now that it's been refurbished to a more elegant contemporary setting. It's fun to watch the tableside preparations of the chef's specialties.

Keystone Village and River Run have several restaurants for more casual dining. In Keystone Village, try **The Bighorn** ($$) in Keystone Lodge or **RazzBerrys** ($$) in the Keystone Inn, which serves grilled items and pastas. The entertainment at **Out of Bounds Restaurant and Sports Bar** ($) begins with reading its unique menu with specialties such as Tree Hugger Linguine and Belt Buster Pub Steak. (We won't spoil the fun and tell you what they are.) Bring the kids. This place is really fun. For truly casual dining, we got a tasty individual-sized pizza and a draught beer sitting at the bar in the **Snake River Saloon.** Across Hwy. 6 in the Mountain View Plaza is **Mi Casa** (262-9185), which serves the same high-quality Mexican dishes as its sister restaurant in Breckenridge.

At River Run, try **Kickapoo Tavern** ($) for appetizers or light fare. **The Great Northern Tavern** ($$), an elegant 1930s-style watering hole, features everything from pistachio encrusted walleye fillet to venison stew. **Paisano's** (pronounced pie-zano's; 468-0808, $$) features casual country-Italian dining. You can get a wide variety of pasta; also pizza for eating in or take-out.

 ## Après-ski/nightlife

Keystone's nightlife is limited, at least in the categories of leaning on a bar, knocking back a few brews and dancing.

The best bet for hanging out and meeting the other nightlife denizens is **Out of Bounds** with two bars and 29 television sets including one 60-incher with non-stop sports. The **Snake River Saloon**, one of Keystone's older establishments, rocks on weekends with live music for dancing.

For immediate après-ski activity, try the **Last Lift Bar** in the Mountain House at Keystone Mountain base or the **Snake River Saloon. Tenderfoot Lounge,** in Keystone Lodge, has piano entertainment and a 15-foot fireplace. **Gassy Thompson's Smokehouse Grill**, home of the generously spiked hot chocolate drink called the Jackwacker, serves up the best après-ski specials, at least in terms of price.

At River Run, **Kickapoo Tavern** draws a crowd on its patio on sunny days, and inside on snowy ones. Don't miss the Kickapoo Mountain Joy Juice, a surprisingly potent blend of rums and fruit juices. **The Great Northern** is Keystone's only brewery and chophouse, and its handcrafted brews make it a favorite après scene in River Run. The **Inxpot** brews specialty teas, gourmet coffees and offers a full-service bar.

A "don't miss" is the **Goat**—the true locals' hang out. The Goat recently opened a dining room and more upscale/sleek bar adjacent to the old, smoky dive that locals seem to still prefer. At the original Goat, catch a game of foosball, grab a Pabst Blue Ribbon and soak up the local scene. Warning: The décor is something you'd find in the basement of a fraternity house or at a garage sale in the 1970s.

Razzberry's is also a great place to relax. With live jazz music throughout the season and some of the valley's best martinis, this is the place to unwind after a day on the slopes.

Dining: $$$–Entrees $20+; $$–$10-20; $–less than $10.
Accommodations: (double room) $$$$–$200+; $$$–$141-$200; $$–$81-$140; $–$80 and less.

Other activities

All non-skiing activities are booked by calling the **Adventure Center** at 800-354-4FUN. **Discovery Tubing Hill** is a lighted tubing hill and is fun for the whole family.

Four different outfits lead **snowmobile tours**, which include guide, helmets, warm suits and boots. Keystone Lodge has a good **athletic club** across the street with two indoor tennis courts and a fitness center connected to the lodge featuring massages, a steam room, outdoor heated pool, cardio and weight rooms, and a hot tub. **Dinner Sleigh Rides** to the Soda Creek Homestead (800-354-4386) include a dinner with all the fixin's.

Ice skating in the middle of Keystone Village is open every day and night. The outdoor lake, reportedly the largest Zamboni-maintained outdoor skating lake in North America, is smoothed twice a day. Fees are about $6 for adults, $5 for ages 13-17, $4 for children 5–12, and $1 for 4 and younger, not including skate rental.

You'll find a few of the standard souvenir and T-shirt **shops** in Keystone Village, but nothing memorable. River Run has some very good shops, mostly selling upscale costume jewelry, Native American pottery and crafts, and elegant clothing. Nearby good shopping is in Breckenridge or the Silverthorne Factory Stores.

Getting there and getting around

By air: Keystone is 90 miles from Denver International Airport via I-70.

Transportation between the airport and the resort can be booked with the central reservations number, (800) 427-8308. Several ground transportation companies provide connections from the airport to the resort. Ask when you book your trip, or check in with one of the companies when you arrive in Denver.

By car: Take I-70 west from Denver, through the Eisenhower Tunnel, to Dillon at Exit 205. Head east for six miles on Hwy. 6.

Getting around: Within Keystone an excellent free shuttle system runs continuously from 7:30 a.m., passing every 15 minutes. In the evenings the shuttles run every 20 minutes until midnight on weeknights, and until 2 a.m. on Fridays and Saturdays. Bartenders and hotel doormen will call the shuttle to ensure pickup in the evenings and late at night, 496-4200. If you are staying and skiing mostly at Keystone, you won't need a car.

The Summit Stage provides free transportation between Dillon, Silverthorne, Frisco, Breckenridge and Copper Mountain. Call 668-0999 for route information. Keystone and Breckenridge also operate a free inter-resort shuttle, the Ski KAB Express, at varying times according to demand. To check the schedule, call 496-4200. From Keystone you can catch a shuttle to Vail/Beaver Creek by making a reservation at the above number.

Beaver Creek

Colorado

Summit elevation: 11,440 feet
Vertical drop: 4,040 feet
Base elevation: 7,400 feet

Address: P.O. Box 7
Vail, CO 81658
✆ **Area code:** 970
Ski area phone: 476-5601 or (800) 427-8308
Snow report: (800) 427-8308
ⓘ **Toll-free reservations:** (800) 427-8308
(see Vail chapter for foreign toll-free numbers)
Fax: 496-4980
E-mail: bcinfo@vailresorts.com
Internet: www.beavercreek.com
Expert:★★★
Advanced:★★★★
Intermediate:★★★★
Beginner:★★★★ **Never-ever:**★★★

Number and types of lifts:
13–6 high-speed quads, 3 triples, 4 doubles
Skiable Acreage: 1,625 acres
Snowmaking: 43 percent
Uphill capacity: 24,739 per hour
Snowboarding: Yes, unlimited
Bed Base: 3,341 in resort, 4,000 in Avon
Nearest lodging: Slopeside, hotels
Resort child care: Yes, 2 months and older
Adult ticket, per day: $60-$65 (01/02)

Dining:★★★★
Apres-ski/nightlife:★
Other activities:★★

Beaver Creek over the past few years has become a village. What started out as a series of seemingly random hotels and condominiums has been knit together with a series of walkways and trails to create a true village atmosphere with a European flair. The concrete and stone complex of condominiums, hotels and shops now has a real soul and can rightfully take its place as one of the top luxury resorts in the country.

The central complex is pedestrian only, and shops and restaurants are scattered throughout. The Vilar Center for the Arts features top entertainment, and forms the focus of the development along with the Black Family Ice Rink. Four sets of escalators whisk skiers and snowboarders from the shuttle drop-off point to the Centennial Express lift. More upscale than big sister Vail, the Beaver Creek experience is carefully scripted to appeal to the A-list guests and wannabes it draws. At the same time, those of more modest means won't feel out of place here anymore.

Those with a taste for being pampered are plopped squarely in the lap of luxury—at a price. Beaver Creek's unofficial motto used to be, "If you aren't worth a million dollars, don't even bother coming here." That pretentiousness is slowly wearing off as the resort comes of age, but evidence of its ambitious youth remains. No one will ask for a copy of last year's tax return to verify your earnings, of course. Yet it's clear that this isn't a place for penny-pinchers, or even the budget-conscious. The art galleries, gift shops and outfitters feature prices that are fitting for visitors with six-figure incomes.

Beaver Creek is nowhere near the celebrity magnet that Aspen and Vail are. It attracts much the same type of visitor as Deer Valley in Utah: The Fortune 500 crowd is right at home here and many of the condominiums are corporate-owned. The corporate owners have worked hard to create an exclusive air, with prices as upscale as its visitors. If you can afford it, the experience is enjoyable with all the bells and whistles.

But you don't *have* to go broke to truly enjoy the Beaver Creek experience, just don't stay in the village. Surprisingly, the regular resort amenities such as après-ski and dining are all very affordable and staying in a nearby town such as Avon, with a good shuttle system, makes this a resort for Everyman. It's fair to say that Beaver Creek is now in the same class as Deer Valley.

The rich and famous as well as the common folk will find very good skiing and snowboarding for all ability levels here. Visitors can ski or snowboard between Beaver Creek, Arrowhead and Bachelor Gulch. If you do this, be aware of the time it involves so you don't get stuck at Arrowhead after the lift closes when your car or lodge is at Beaver Creek (or vice versa). Complimentary Resort Transportation shuttles make the loop, but not as frequently as you might like.

Mountain layout—Skiing

If there's one characteristic that sets Beaver Creek apart from other mountain resorts, it's the extent to which its slopes are groomed. An enthusiastic fleet of snowcats patrols the mountainside 20 out of every 24 hours, looking for an opportunity to plow over a chunk of ice or a patch of powder. To ski at Beaver Creek is "to ski on corduroy." If you're an expert or advanced skier, don't let this scare you away. Beaver Creek leaves your terrain alone, so you'll find plenty of challenge. Other distinguishing features: a conspicuous absence of lift lines and copious snowmaking abilities.

◆◆ **Expert** ◆ **Advanced:** When Beaver Creek opened in 1980, its first runs were mostly beginner and intermediate. Some still think of it—mistakenly—as a cruiser mountain. Not so: Advanced skiers and experts should spend at least a day here, maybe more. Our advice is to choose a Saturday or Sunday, when the lines can climb over the 15–20-minute barrier at Vail, yet be nonexistent here.

What's surprising is the amount of truly tough stuff. The Birds of Prey runs rival anything Vail offers—all long, steep and mogul-studded. If you want to feel like a world-class racer, the downhill course, one of the most difficult in the world, is groomed as often as possible for a long and super-fast double-diamond cruiser. While somewhat shorter, Ripsaw and Cataract in Rose Bowl, and Loco in Larkspur Bowl, are equally challenging. Grouse Mountain is strictly for black-diamond types, no matter what the trail map may suggest. Only in spring, when slushier snow slows skiers down, should such runs as Screech Owl, Falcon Park and Royal Elk Glades be attempted by thrill-seeking advanced skiers.

■ **Intermediate:** Beaver Creek is an excellent resort for intermediates at every level. For those intermediates bordering on advanced, the runs under the Centennial Express lift are long and have a moderately steep pitch—enough to be exciting, but not the kind to scare you out of your bindings. If you can catch these runs after a grooming, the black-diamond-designated sections are definitely within the abilities of upper-intermediates. Centennial, the main run in this area, is not the best choice for a warm-up if the resort hasn't had snow in a while. It's in the shade early in the morning, and everyone uses it, so the surface can get skied off and a bit slick (but it's a super run under good conditions). Harrier, to the skier's left of Centennial, is a locals' favorite where you'll often find yourself skiing solo. Don't miss Harrier when it's been groomed. Another great intermediate route from Centennial Express is Redtail to the Larkspur Lift, then descend down Larkspur Bowl.

Early in the morning, the runs under the Strawberry Park lift are in the sun. We recommend Pitchfork for your warm-up, and a couple of the runs in the Bachelor Gulch area for a follow-up. Bachelor Gulch's runs are shorter and gentler than the ones above Beaver Creek

Village—perfect for those in the middle of the intermediate ability range. Arrowhead is another good choice for intermediates, though its southerly exposure means thin snow at the tail end of dry spells. (By the way, Arrowhead's one black-diamond run, Real McCoy, is not that tough—unless the moguls have had a chance to build.)

If you're on the lower end of the intermediate scale, try the runs at the top of the Birds of Prey Express, explained further in the beginner section. Trails to avoid unless you have lots of confidence (or it's a soft-snow spring day) are the blue trails on Grouse Mountain.

●● **Beginner:** The easiest runs are at the top, accessed by the Centennial Express and Birds of Prey Express lifts. Once you reach the top, head over to Red Buffalo, Mystic Island and the other runs in the Slow Zone. Ride the Drink of Water lift again and again, because this area has no intermediate or expert runs where faster skiers will zip past you at high speeds. Flattops, Piney and Powell, to the other side of the Birds of Prey lift, are wide and gentle. A bonus is you get to see the same magnificent summit view that everyone else does. You get back to Beaver Creek Village on a long, clearly marked beginner run (it's really a catwalk) called Cinch. One thing beginners should watch out for: Beaver Creek has sudden shifts from beginner to expert terrain. The trails are well-marked, but when you're moving fast and trying to concentrate, the signs can fly by. The Arrowhead section also is good for beginners, with a winding run called Piece O' Cake.

● **Never-ever:** Beaver Creek's learning area is at the base, served by two lifts.

 ## Mountain layout—Snowboarding

Riding at "The Beav" is an experience all its own. With so much grooming and round the clock snowmaking, the runs can have a consistency that's sometimes almost too perfect. Don't worry, natural deep powder can still be found almost all season—just look in the woods. The woods are Beaver Creek's No. 1 asset to snowboarders. Powder lines, world-class log slides that will make any skateboarder envious and cliff lines abound, making The Beav one of the favorites among Colorado locals in the know. Be sure to check the trail map for snowboard gladed zones.

◆◆ **Expert** ◆ **Advanced:** Beaver Creek has gotten a bad reputation as being too ritzy to be a serious mountain for riding. Some still think of it as a cruiser mountain, but ask any local and they'll claim an allegiance to the mountain for life. The Beav's got everything…and more…the best part is that while Vail's getting tracked up on a Saturday, most of The Beav's lines will remain untracked for days, so make it a point to head here instead.

What's surprising is the amount of expert riding here. Beaver Creek has an abundance of backcountry access gates that are perfect for any experienced rider. The best feature is that all the backcountry-accessible terrain funnels back to the lifts. So, in essence, you can ride up the lift with your family, run a line filled with drops and powder face shots while they're on a cruiser, and meet them back at the lift.

About 80 percent of the goods at Beaver Creek can be found off Centennial and Birds of Prey. It's actually kind of funny, because the best beginner areas are at the top of the Birds of Prey lift, but it's also the access for Bald Spot, a favorite among powder hounds and locals.

Insider tip: If you want logging, ask around, check the woods, but beware: Log slides are a favorite with the locals at The Beav and they take their locations very seriously.

■ **Intermediate:** Intermediates should let it rip down one of America's best unheralded cruisers, Centennial, which dips and turns down the lower half of the mountain. Centennial will bring you right to the Moonshine Terrain Park, which has definitely stepped up to the plate in the past few years. Now sporting a superpipe, a yurt with foosball, cable TV and beverages, every type of rail imaginable and some nice-sized tabletops, Moonshine Terrain

Park is great for everyone. From the expert who's working on his backside Rodeos, to the advanced-beginner in the pipe learning how to do frontside airs, it's the ideal park to perfect your style and to get away from the crowds that some of the other mountains draw.

All of the runs under the Strawberry Park lift, and just about every run under the Centennial Express, are great for intermediates. Bachelor Gulch and Arrowhead also offer solid intermediate riding, with just the right pitch and pockets for first-time powder hounds. Beginner park riders head to Zoom Room off the Birds of Prey lift.

●● **Beginner/Never-ever:** Stay away from Cinch! It's a beginner's nightmare: Intermediate and advanced riders should have no problem maintaining their speed on this catwalk, but to the first-time rider, it's literally a speed death-sentence.

The best place for the never-ever is the Haymeadow lift right at the base. It has the perfect pitch for learning to ride. Once you master the Haymeadow lift, move on to the easy carving family runs off Latigo. Remember: Just don't learn to jump on these runs, because ski patrol will not hesitate to pull your pass for airing in a family area.

Mountain rating

There's a bit of everything for everyone. Birds of Prey and Grouse Mountain are the spots for aggressive, bump-hungry experts. Intermediates have long cruising runs that are expertly groomed. Beginners can ski at the summit and see the view, a rare treat. Beaver Creak is a diamond in the rough for snowboarders. It may come off at first as being too glitzy and glamorous, but it has a reputation among riders for being the real deal once you get under its fur coat. That's one feature that a lot of high-profile resorts only wish they could claim.

Cross-country and snowshoeing

For a truly different Nordic experience at an Alpine ski area, head to the **McCoy Park Cross-Country, Telemark and Snowshoe Center** at the top of the Strawberry Park Express Lift. Instead of skiing on the flats (usually a golf course) at the base of a ski area, you'll be on a 32-km. system at the summit, 9,840 feet, with spectacular views in every direction. Groomed and tracked for both skating and diagonal skate skiing, the trail system has one advanced (and exciting) loop, the Wild Side trail, but is basically beginner and intermediate. An ungroomed single track for snowshoers is called the Upper Atlas Traverse. Skiers and snowshoers can take one of several trails to the base, download on the Strawberry Park Express Lift or take the very gradual Home Comfort trail (6 km.) all the way down—fun with new snow to slow you down but speedy if there isn't.

Adult fees are $19 for an all-day pass, $12 for a half day beginning at noon; $9 and $6, respectively, for children and seniors. Half-day track tours and half-day lessons for adults are $42 during regular season; $45 during peak season. The park also has snowshoe rentals and tours that include rental equipment. The full-day tour gourmet lunch tour costs $77.

For more information on Nordic activities, call the Beaver Creek Cross-Country, Telemark and Snowshoe Center at 845-5313.

Lessons (2001/02 prices)

Lessons meet at the base area near the Centennial Express lift and at Spruce Saddle Lodge atop the Centennial Express lift. Instruction is available in nearly 30 languages. Call the Beaver Creek Ski and Snowboard School at 970-845-5300 or send a fax to 845-5321. The prices we list are for peak season, which is when most skiers are on the mountain.

Group lessons: A day-long group is $100.

Never-ever package: Lesson and lifts for a half day costs $94; a full day costs $130 (with rentals, $156). A great deal, available only during the value season (opening day through Dec. 13, 2001 and April 7, 2002, through closing), is the First Time Series (for ages 15 and older), which offers three consecutive full days of lessons for the price of one day: $145 for lessons, lifts and rental. Skiers and snowboarders who complete the program will be given a coupon good for three more lessons for the price of one at the next ability level. The same offer is available Jan. 15-Feb. 12, 2002, for $155.

Private lessons: $250 for two hours, $330 for a half-day afternoon, $360 for a half-day morning, and $485 for a full day (for one to six people). One-hour lessons, when available, are $130. Call the Private Lesson Concierge at (800) 354-5630.

Racing: Two NASTAR courses and a coin-op course are next to the Centennial run.

Child care [2001/02 prices]

Ages: 2 months to 5 years.

Cost: $76 per day during value season; $82 regular; $89 high season.

Reservations: Required; call 845-5325 or fax 845-5327. Hours are 8 a.m. to 4:30 p.m. Free pagers are available.

Note: With one main base area, Beaver Creek is a good place to bring kids. The ski school and child-care center are right in the base village, although the Small World Play School is a bit hard to find. After crossing the Covered Bridge that leads into the village, turn left and walk down the stairs until you see the sign to your right. The Children's Ski and Snowboard School is located in Village Hall.

Other options: The **Park Hyatt** (949-1234) offers programs for children, as well as babysitting, days and evenings. **Baby's Away** (800-369-9030; 926-5256) rents and delivers baby needs, such as crib, stroller, car seat and toys.

Children's lessons: Ski lessons are offered for kids 3 years (toilet-trained) to 14 years; snowboarding lessons are for ages 6-14. Cost is $87 per day off-peak; $99 peak. Prices include lesson, lift and lunch. Classes are divided by age and ability. Register at 8 a.m. or pre-register the day before. Reservations are not required. Call 845-5464 for information.

Skiing with your kids: Like Vail, Beaver Creek is sprinkled with Kids Adventure Zones. Kids can search out such haunts as the Tombstone Territory or the Hibernating Bear Cave. Most are located off Cinch near the top of the Centennial Lift.

Lift tickets [2001/02 prices]

	Adult	Child (5-12)
One day	$65	$39
Three days	$186 ($62/day)	$108 ($36/day)
Five of six days	$300 ($60/day)	$180 ($36/day)

Note: These prices valid from December 22, 2001 to April 6, 2002.

Who skis free: Ages 4 and younger.

Who skis at a discount: Ages 65–69 pay $57 per day, seniors 70+ pay $28. Vail Resorts has a handful of different discounted prices based on time of the year, time of a skier's first visit, ski packages, Internet sales, supermarket sales, pre-purchasing and groups.

A great deal is Vail's Perfect 10, which allows vacationers to ski 10 days at Vail or its sister resorts Beaver Creek, Breckenridge and Keystone, as well as Arapahoe Basin, for less than $32 a day throughout the 2001/02 season. The multi-day lift ticket program rewards guests who ski early and often. Early, because it must be used at least once before Jan. 31, 2002 and often, because it includes up to 10 days of skiing and snowboarding that can be used consecutively or non-consecutively throughout the season. An adult Perfect 10 sells for $319, and a child (ages 5-12) Perfect 10 is $159. Valid all season with the exception of Dec. 21, 2001 through Jan. 5, 2002. Additional restrictions apply. The Perfect 10 is available at any Vail, Beaver Creek, Keystone or Breckenridge ticket window during the season or by visiting www.vail.com or www.snow.com.

Interchangeability: All lift tickets purchased at Vail or Beaver Creek also are valid at sister resorts Keystone and Breckenridge, as well as at nearby Arapahoe Basin. Only multiday tickets of three or more days purchased at Keystone or Breckenridge are valid at Vail and Beaver Creek (one day of a three-day lift ticket purchased at Keystone or Breckenridge is valid at Vail or Beaver Creek; two days of a four-day or five-day lift ticket; three days of a six-day or seven-day ticket). All lift tickets purchased at Keystone or Breckenridge also are valid at nearby Arapahoe Basin.

Accommodations

Beaver Creek lodging is expensive. It's tough to find a room for less than $200 per night, unless you want to vacation pre-Christmas or in April.

Consistently rated among the top hotels in the world, the ski-in/ski-out **Park Hyatt Beaver Creek Resort & Spa** (949-1234; $$$$) just underwent an $8.1-million room renovation and the addition of a 20,000-square-foot Allegria spa. All rooms have free Internet access and wireless keyboards with flat screens. Ski Ambassador Cory Carlson gives lessons and tours (fee), and Storyteller Frank Doll, a third-generation Vail Valley resident, weaves tales fireside. There's a heated outdoor pool, whirlpools, fitness rooms, concierge and ski attendant services. The six restaurants and lounges address all styles of dining.

Chateau Residence Club (949-1616, fax 845-7710; $$$$) offers private luxury hillside condos with all the amenities of a hotel: concierge, daily maid service, a great restaurant and lounge, etc. It echoes the castle-like elegance of the Banff Springs Hotel with suites starting at $750 per night with a three-night minimum. The staff is warm and welcoming no matter whether you're wearing a floor-length mink or fleece vest.

The **Ritz-Carlton, Bachelor Gulch** (800-241-3333 or 748-6200; $$$$), slated to open in November 2002, is inspired by the grand national park lodges of Yellowstone, Grand Teton and Yosemite promises seclusion, luxury and excellence. All guestrooms have separate showers and marble bathtubs; Frette linens and feather beds with duvets and goosedown and non-allergenic foam pillows; three telephones, including one cordless, with private voice mail; television with Internet access; DVD players and other high-end amenities. Twice-daily maid service and evening-turndown, valet, ski-valet, concierge, and a technology butler are among the services. Also available are a full-service and fully equipped 21,000-square-foot spa, outdoor heated pool, Ritz Kids program and ski and snowboard services.

The **Inn at Beaver Creek** (800-859-8242; $$-$$$$), ski-in/ski-out lodging on a far smaller scale than the Park Hyatt, has 37 rooms and eight suites with a free hot gourmet breakfast. Cocktails, cappuccinos and a light menu are offered après-ski. Guests also have a sauna and steam room.

The **Beaver Creek Lodge** (800-525-7280; 845-9800; $$-$$$$) is the only all-suite resort in the Vail Valley. The 71 units have living rooms, fireplaces, and TVs with VCRs. Once guests find the lobby to check in, the rest is easy.

The **Centennial Lodge** (800-845-7060; $$$$) claims to have the best prices on the mountain, but doesn't provide full hotel service. It has underground parking and a pool. This lodge has some condos and three hotel rooms. Both the Centennial Lodge and **Creekside Lodge** (949-7071; $$$$) are in the village. **The Poste Montane** (800-497-9238 or 845-7500; $$-$$$$) is located directly in Beaver Creek Resort Village as is **St. James Place** (800-859-8242 or 845-9300; $$$$). **The Pines Lodge** (800-859-8242; $$$$) is a condo-hotel near the Strawberry Park lift. Guests can enjoy a Jacuzzi, heated outdoor pool, fitness room and massage therapy. **The Borders Lodge** (800 846-0233; 926-2300; $$-$$$$) is a comfortable ski-in/ski-out condominium complex next to Chair 14, within easy walk of the village. Its condos range in size from one- to three-bedrooms and the list of facilities includes two outdoor hot tubs and year-round pool.

Many corporate- or privately owned condominiums are available for weekly rentals. Note that restrictions are more severe than for a hotel reservation. Hefty cancellation fees apply, so read the fine print before booking.

Elkhorn Lodge (888-833-5018; 845-2270; $$$$) has studios and one- to four-bedroom condos and penthouses with ski-in/ski-out convenience adjacent to the Elkhorn Lift (Chair 14). Amenities include fully equipped kitchens, fireplaces, balconies, spa tubs in the bathrooms, two outdoor hot tubs and a fitness area.

The Charter (800-525-6660 or 949-6660; $$-$$$$), which bills itself as having "all of the conveniences of a condominium with all of the luxuries of a world-class hotel," gives guests more of the typical Beaver Creek amenities—wonderful wood-paneled interiors, European decor, fireplaces and stunning mountain views. One- through five-bedroom units are available. Three restaurants offer menus to suit anyone's tastes.

If your budget won't support accommodations inside Beaver Creek's gates, head to the nearby town of Avon for the valley's best condo deals at the **Christie Lodge** (800-551-4320 or 949-7700; $$-$$$$). Or, you can stay in the town of Edwards, about 5 miles from Beaver Creek. One possibility there is **The Inn at Riverwalk** (888-926-0606 or 926-0606; $$-$$$). VailNet (www.vail.net) has a very good lodging search feature that will suggest lodging according to location, amenities and price.

Dining

Beaver Creek is infatuated with the term "gourmet." Everything, right down to the garden-variety burger, is designated gourmet. Plus, these Colorado chefs do love their spices. The dishes we tried featured gratuitous amounts of onions, garlic and exotic flavors.

Splendido at The Chateau (845-8808; $$$) is very popular for locals, especially for special occasions. Many regulars come for the piano player, Taylor Kundolf, but chef David Walford has a huge following for his succulent game and international finesse with offerings such as roasted Maine sea scallops and fried sweetbreads. The wine cellar is vast. It's one of the most elegant yet accessible properties in Vail/Beaver Creek.

Mirabelle (949-7728), a longtime local favorite at the bottom of the resort access road in an old farmhouse, serves well-prepared Belgian-influenced nouvelle cuisine.

SaddleRidge (845-5450; $$-$$$) is decorated with impressive Western antiques and artifacts the likes of which might only be found in a museum. It's open for dinner with a game-dominated a la carte menu. After dessert take a look at the saddle with Buffalo Bill's sketch impressed into the leather. The image is his own handiwork.

Dining: $$$-Entrees $20+; $$-$10-20; $-less than $10.
Accommodations: (double room) $$$$-$200+; $$$-$141-$200; $$-$81-$140; $-$80 and less.

The **Golden Eagle** (949-1940; $$) is a less costly, though not less exotic, place to dine. With entrées such as medallions of Australian kangaroo and roast loin of elk on the menu, guests can take a culinary world tour without leaving their seats. Decorations are Bavarian and desert Southwest, exactly the unlikely mix you'd expect from a restaurant that serves a blue corn elk quesadilla and other odd but tasty treats.

The French-fusion menu in the slopeside **Patina** restaurant (949-1234; $$–$$$) in the Park Hyatt Beaver Creek uses indigenous Colorado ingredients. For (relatively) inexpensive meals, head to the **Cafe**, also in the Park Hyatt, for baked goods, soups, salad bar and sandwiches. A new exclusive, gourmet restaurant in the Park Hyatt is planned to open this winter.

The **Grouse Mountain Grill** (949-0600; $$$), adjacent to the Pines Lodge, serves Rocky Mountain cuisine, featuring such dishes as Colorado Lamb and pretzel-crusted pork chops.

By Beaver Creek standards, **traMonti** (949-5552, $$-$$$) is one of the more inexpensive places to eat, with meat entrees between $20 and $30, and pastas less than that. Located in the Charter at Beaver Creek Hotel, traMonti serves pastas and risottos, and Northern Italian-prepared veal, steak, chicken and seafood. The restaurant is cozy, with upholstered highback chairs and white linen tablecloths, and has an outstanding view of the mountain through oversized windows. Reservations are advised.

In Market Square, follow your nose to **Toscanini** (845-5590; $$-$$$), a busy Italian restaurant overlooking the outdoor ice rink and featuring excellent seafood and pasta dishes. Special children's menu selections are available.

The Swiss Stubli (748-8618; $$-$$$) in Beaver Creek Plaza's Poste Montane Building has a comfortable, cozy atmosphere combined with the authenticity of genuine Swiss cuisine from Swiss chefs. It is perfect for both an intimate dinner for two and group get-togethers. Owners Christel and Roby Kuster, also native Swiss, recommend either the wiener schnitzel, veal bratwurst or rostizza lugano for lunch. Also try the veal Zurich style for dinner. Reservations are highly recommended. Open in the winter season from 3–9:30 p.m. (unofficially 10 p.m.) and in the summer season from 11:30 a.m.

In Avon try **The Vista Brasserie** (949-3366; $$) and **Cassidy's** (949-9449; $). **Masato's Sushi Bar** (949-0330; $$-$$$), in the Chapel Square complex, has great sushi chefs and reasonably priced Japanese food. **Ti Amo** (845-8153; $$-$$$) is Avon's best for good-value Italian. Or try the town of Edwards, just west of Avon. In the Riverwalk Center, **Zino** (926-0444; $$) is the "in" place to be (same owners as Vail's Sweet Basil). Try the roasted mussels served in an iron skillet before diving into entrees that include pasta, risotto, and creative meat and fish dishes. The **Gore Range Brewery**, another hang-out, has outrageous salads, wood-fired thin-crust pizza, and peel-and-eat shrimp. There's also a very hip sushi restaurant called **Sato's** (926-7684).

Beaver Creek has a wonderfully memorable dining experience, a night at **Beano's Cabin** (949-9090, book early; $$$). Groups are bundled onto a 40-person sleigh and pulled up the mountain under the stars by a snowcat. The cabin (a bit of a misnomer, since the building is fairly large) is upscale-rustic on the outside and elegant inside, with a roaring stone-hearth fire, log beams and well-prepared cuisine. The five-course meal concludes with remarkable desserts. The cost is per person, including the sleigh ride but not the wine, tax or gratuity. Equally delightful is **Allie's Cabin** (949-9090, book early; $$$), a pine cabin with cathedral ceilings, river-rock fireplace and a romantic atmosphere. It's named for Allie Townsend, Beaver Creek's first female resident in the late 1800s. It's now open to the public for dinner. A snowcat-drawn sleigh takes diners to the cabin, where you'll indulge in a five-course steakhouse meal. The cost is per person, including the sleigh ride but not the wine, tax or gratuity.

Few people seem to eat breakfast in Beaver Creek, or else they grab a bite in their condos or hotel restaurants. The village doesn't have a lot of choices for your first meal of the day. **Patina** ($$) at the Park Hyatt has full breakfast buffet, featuring omelets made-to-order. You can get eggs, pancakes and waffles at **McCoy's**, a cafeteria set-up at the base of the mountain. **On The Fly,** a tiny take-out place near the covered bridge and main bus stop, has egg wraps (scrambled eggs in tortillas) that are pretty tasty, but seating is limited to two small tables. For muffin-and-coffee breakfast fans, **Starbucks** is located one level down from the Centennial Express lift. **Beaver Creek Chophouse** in the Beaver Creek Lodge serves an American continental breakfast. **Pacific Ranch** in the Charter Lodge dishes out hot breakfasts daily.

Après-ski/nightlife

Asked what nightlife was worth a look, one worker first told us, "There isn't anything," then after a bit of thinking, amended her response to, "Well, there are some meeting places." The first place to stop on the way back to town from the Larkspur Bowl is **Red Tail Camp,** where revelers gather to begin après-ski. In the spring, the deck is packed and Sundays mean live entertainment al fresco.

The Coyote Cafe would surely qualify as a meeting place, particularly among locals such as the Beaver Creek Ski Patrol, at the end of the day. This Mexican cantina/watering hole caters to locals, and with well drink and draught beer specials at the end of the day, its prices are reasonable. Bartenders can whip up a margarita to get you in the après-ski mood, and the staff is intentionally informal—in contrast with the rest of Beaver Creek. Don't plan on staying out late—it closes at 11 p.m. (as late as 1 a.m. on hopping nights). Some exciting news this season: Coyote Café is now non-smoking! No more stinky ski clothes the next morning. If you're young and looking for après-ski, this is it.

McCoy's is the place to go for live après-ski entertainment as soon as you leave the slopes. Also try the **Dusty Boot Saloon,** where you'll find mondo 46-ounce margaritas and a comprehensive tequila list. **Blue Moose Pizzeria** has great pizza and a fun atmosphere, and the lowest prices in Beaver Creek Village.

The Park Hyatt's **Antlers** bar, which stays open until 2 a.m., features entertainment from local musicians. At night, when the stars are out, it's a dazzling display for tired skiers and snowboarders.

Other activities

The **Vilar Center for the Arts** (888-920-2787 or 845-8497) is a 528-seat performing arts center snugged under the ice rink in Beaver Creek. It's modeled after a turn-of-the-century theater in Munich and presents world-class entertainment four to six nights a week. The year-round outdoor **Black Family Ice Rink** is in the heart of Beaver Creek. Ice skating exhibitions are held here in the winter every Monday night.

If you need to restore mind and body (like those sore skiing legs), visit one of Beaver Creek's **spas.** Treat yourself to an afternoon at the Allegria Spa (748-7500) at the Park Hyatt Beaver Creek Resort, where the Feng Shui design encourages relaxation. It has 20 treatment rooms, a quiet Sanctuary room, private whirlpool tubs in the locker rooms and the usuals. Splurge on the 75-minute Barefoot Massage ($150), also known as Ashiatsu, that encom-

Dining: $$$-Entrees $20+; $$-$10-20; $-less than $10.
Accommodations: (double room) $$$$-$200+; $$$-$141-$200; $$-$81-$140; $-$80 and less.

passes massage, hot stones and foot pressure. Other treatments include a variety of massages, scrubs, facials, water therapies, hot oil wraps, hair services, manicures and pedicures and Feng Shui inspired rituals for balance, peace and energy. Fitness facilities include cardio equipment, free weights, a pool and group and private classes.

Every Thursday night, level-five and above skiers are invited to join in on **BMW Thursday Night Lights,** a ski-down with glow sticks followed by a huge fireworks show. Register at the Chidren's Ski and Snowboard School. The resort concierge (845-9090) can make reservations for other activities, such as **dogsledding, snowmobiling, snowshoeing, fly fishing, ice fishing,** and **sleigh rides.**

Beautiful **boutiques** line the pedestrian walkway in the heart of the resort. A special stop on your list should be The Golden Bear, just to the west of the skating rink in Beaver Creek. It's owned by local women whose logo is the golden bear (it's Vail's logo too), which you can find in all forms of jewelry and art. Great stylish clothes and other special gifts tempt the wallet. The Golden Beaver, in the Beaver Creek Lodge, sells golden beaver jewelry, Beaver Creek's insignia.

 # Getting there and getting around

By air: Flights land at the Vail/Eagle County airport, about 35 miles west of Vail, and the Denver International Airport, 110 miles east. Eagle County airport is served by American, Northwest, Delta, America West and United.

Ground transportation between Denver and Vail is frequent and convenient. The trip to Vail takes about two-and-a-half hours. Contact Colorado Mountain Express at (800) 424-6363; Vail Valley Taxi (476-8294); or Airport Transportation Service (476-7576). Though flights into Denver may be a bit less expensive than Eagle, also consider the cost of round-trip ground transportation, where per person rates from Denver are about double those from Eagle.

By car: Beaver Creek and Vail are right on I-70, 100 miles west of Denver and 140 miles east of Grand Junction. Beaver Creek is 10 miles west of Vail and just 3 miles south of Avon.

Getting around: Beaver Creek is very self-contained. There is a complimentary shuttle that takes you anywhere within Beaver Creek between 6 a.m. and 2 a.m. daily. The shuttle is like a taxi, so ask your concierge or restaurant hostess to call (949-1938), and allow 10-15 minutes for pickup. Shuttles between Beaver Creek and Vail cost $3. If you plan to commute frequently between Vail and Beaver Creek, or if you are staying in one of the outlying towns such as Edwards or Minturn, you may want to rent a car. If you're not staying at Beaver Creek lodging, you can park in two different locations. In the village, at the base of the mountain, there are two lots that charge to park. Two free parking lots are located just outside the entrance to Beaver Creek, a free shuttle takes you the 2 miles to the base of the mountain. Allow extra time for this.

Here's something that's pretty tough to pass up: BMW's Complimentary Mountain Driving Tour operates out of the Pines Lodge. All Beaver Creek guests are invited to reserve a BMW for a test drive or for an entire evening. Call the Pines Lodge at 845-7900.

Crested Butte

Colorado

Summit elevation:	**11,875 feet**
Vertical drop:	**2,775 feet**
Base elevation:	**9,100 feet**

Address: P.O. Box 5700
Mt. Crested Butte, CO 81225
☎ **Area code:** 970
Ski area phone: 349-2333
Snow report: (888) 442-2333
ⓘ **Toll-free reservations:** (800) 544-8448
Toll-free foreign numbers:
U.K.: 0800 894085
Germany: 0800-101-0808
Mexico: 95-800-417-2772, ext. 2286
Australia: 0014-800-127-665, ext. 2286
Fax: 349-2397
E-mail: info@cbmr.com
Internet: www.CrestedButteResort.com (ski resort)
crestedbuttechamber.com (chamber of commerce)
Expert:★★★★★
Advanced:★★★★★ **Intermediate:**★★★★
Beginner:★★★ **Never-ever:**★★★★

Number of lifts: 14—3 high-speed quads,
3 triples, 3 doubles, 5 surface lifts
Snowmaking: 37 percent (300 acres)
Skiable acreage: 1,058 acres
Uphill capacity: 18,160 per hour
Snowboarding: Yes
Bed Base: 5,750
Nearest lodging: Slopeside
Resort child care: Yes, 6 months and older
Adult ticket, per day: $21-55 (02/03)

Dining:★★★★★
Apres-ski/nightlife:★★★★
Other activities:★★★

Great skiing and snowboarding for all abilities—especially for advanced and expert levels—and down-home western friendliness make Crested Butte one of our favorite resorts. Many Colorado resorts cater to the well-to-do celebrity or CEO visitor, and that's fine, but this is one place you can come if you want to avoid that scene. Crested Butte has a laid-back attitude and the locals have a way of looking at the better side of life. It may be a bit harder to get here compared to the Colorado resorts spread along the interstate highway, but it's worth the trouble if you really want to get away from it all.

The town is Colorado's largest National Historic District, with charm impossible to convey in words. More than 40 historic structures are tucked in and around the town. A walk down Elk Avenue, the main street, takes you past the old post office, built in 1900, and The Forest Queen, reputed to have once been a brothel. Buildings have been lovingly restored, and others have been built to look as though they've been there for 100 years. While other resorts try to fabricate images of the Wild West, Crested Butte is the real thing. In contrast, the resort, about 3 miles away, is surrounded by modern condominiums and hotels: the Sheraton Crested Butte Resort, various smaller lodges, and the all-inclusive, hassle-free Club Med family village.

Crested Butte has made a major commitment to snowmaking, which has ensured excellent coverage for early-season skiing; plus the resort has one of the highest average snowfalls of any ski town in Colorado. Crested Butte, with its world-renown steeps and gnarly terrain, has been home to the U.S. Extreme Freeskiing Championships for the last 12 years and the U.S. Extreme Boarderfest for the last nine years. Also of interest, Crested Butte was the pioneering resort in the rediscovery and popularization of telemarking. It has long had more of these skiers per capita than any other big-time ski resort. The U.S. Telemark Championships are held here each February. Plus, in late March hundreds of free-heel skiers scramble up the North Face and drop 1,200 vertical feet through deep snow to compete in the Al Johnson Memorial Uphill/Downhill Race. Johnson used to deliver mail on Nordic skis to 1880s mining camps. It's also home to the Elk Mountain Grand Traverse, a grueling telemark two-person team event from Crested Butte to Aspen beginning at midnight.

Mountain layout—Skiing

Guest services leads free "base to the face" tours meeting daily at 10 a.m. introducing the mountain to new visitors. All ability levels are welcome.

◆◆ **Expert:** The Crested Butte skier likes the terrain just as nature left it. You'll notice that named trails cover only about half the terrain. Looking at a trail map, on the left is a huge area called the Extreme Limits with a series of double diamonds punctuating the mountainside, and on the far right is another grouping of double diamonds hard against the area boundary. Both areas are tough, offering what experts claim is Colorado's best extreme terrain, comparable to Utah steeps. If you want to ski this terrain, plan to arrive mid-January or later, or you might find it closed.

A couple of random notes: The resort has free mountain tours for all levels, and tours on the North Face, part of their extensive expert terrain, for $20 per person. Our stats reflect lift-served terrain—you can hike to the 12,162-foot level for a 3,062-foot vertical descent. (Also, our base elevation is at the point of the lowest lift, East River. The base area where the facilities are is about 200 feet higher.)

◆ **Advanced:** Crested Butte's single blacks are long, bumpy and fun. Most are found under the Silver Queen and Twister lifts, but don't miss the Double-Top Glades served by the East River Lift.

■ **Intermediate:** Those in search of long cruising runs should go up Keystone or Silver Queen, and head down Treasury, Ruby Chief, Forest Queen, Bushwacker, Gallowich and variations of the same. Runs under the Paradise and Teocalli lifts are the best cruisers on the mountain—long and fast. The Paradise Bowl at the top of the Paradise lift gives intermediates a taste of powder on good days.

Advanced-intermediates can manage most of the runs down from the Silver Queen high-speed quad. Twister and Crystal both have good bail-out routes about halfway down.

●● **Beginner:** Crested Butte has extensive green-circle terrain, served by the Keystone lift. However, this is not stuff you want to attempt with the skiing ability you learned from a book on the plane. Houston probably is the most gentle of the greens, but we'd color the rest turquoise—greens leaning into blues.

● **Never-ever:** Head to the Peachtree lift, take a couple of lessons and practice for a day or two before attempting the Keystone lift. When you're ready for Keystone, get off at the second stop and try Houston.

Mountain layout—Snowboarding

Advanced and expert riders can tackle true "extreme" terrain that includes 50-degree slopes, cliffs, chutes and untrammeled pow in any of five bowls that make up "Extreme Limits." These areas (often closed 'til mid season, awaiting deep snow conditions) are not for the weak or faint hearted; if you can't confidently negotiate the steepest double-blacks at other Colorado resorts, you don't belong in this lightly patrolled backcountry terrain that could justifiably be marked "triple-black diamond."

That said, the Headwall (just off the High Lift lift) is a good place to do a reality check: If this 40-degree steep and narrow chute gives you the heebie-jeebies, better stay on the groomed and patrolled runs within view of the Treasury, Teocalli and Paradise lifts.

Crested Butte's well-deserved reputation for extreme terrain masks the fact that this mountain is well suited to beginners and intermediates too. Intermediates get their kicks in the Paradise Bowl, with its smattering of variably pitched slopes, easy glades, and mild, rolling mogul fields. The main Keystone Lift, which departs from the busy base area, accesses 145 acres of freeway-width beginner terrain.

The halfpipe and terrain park are on Bushwacker, under the Teocalli Lift, with easy shots into the trees. The park features a 370-foot halfpipe with 12.4-foot-high walls, a triple air, five rails and three tabletops. The halfpipe has nice vertical with smooth transitions—perfect for both the beginner and for going big. Not only that but the park annually hosts the now legendary Subaru U.S. Extreme Boarderfest Competition's Triple Air Event.

Mountain rating

Crested Butte has terrain for every level of skier and rider. It needs it, because there are no alternatives in the near vicinity, with the notable exception of 2,200 acres of snowcat powder skiing at nearby Irwin Lodge, the largest such operation in North America.

Cross-country and snowshoeing

Crested Butte is linked with one of the most extensive cross-country networks in Colorado. The **Crested Butte Nordic Center** (349-1707) is located at the edge of town, on 2nd Street between Sopris and Whiterock Streets. There are about 70 km. of Nordic tracks, which begin a few yards from the Nordic Center. The center also has an outdoor rink and sledding hill for après-Nordic activity. There are more than 100 miles of backcountry trails. Group lessons, half-day and all-day tours are scheduled several times each week, but private lessons and special tours must be requested two days in advance. Snowshoe activities are offered. Snowshoe and cross-country rentals are available. There are also hut-to-hut cross-country and snowshoe trips.

Snowshoe tours at the mountain resort (349-2211 or 800-444-9236) depart from the Ski and Snowboard School at 9:45 a.m. and 1:15 p.m. daily. You'll ride the Keystone lift up the mountain, then make an easy loop that offers spectacular views. Tour takes about two-and-a-half hours and includes a snack break. The price of $45 includes Atlas snowshoe rentals, lifts, guides and snacks. Moonlight tours are offered Dec. 19, 2002, and Jan. 18 and Feb. 16, 2003.

Lessons (2002/03 prices)

Registration and reservations for all programs are at the ski school desk in the Gothic Center, 349-2252 or 800-444-9236. This year, 20 of Crested Butte's professional instructors received the first-ever "New Skiers Retention Accreditation" from the Rocky Mountain Division of the PSIA. The skills acquired through this certification enable instructors to deliver the best first-time lesson possible.

Group lessons: Adult group lessons are $60 for a 2.5-hour lesson.

Never-ever package: A three-hour novice lesson with lift ticket is $75.

Private lessons: $180 for two hours. Multihour and multiperson discounts available.

Special programs: Many, including workshops for extreme skiing and boarding plus clinics for seniors, halfpipe tricks, bumps, telemark, shaped skis, powder, and turning fundamentals; $75 for 2.5 hours. There's a four-person maximum for these clinics.

Kim Reichhelm, a renowned extreme ski champion and former U.S. Ski Team member, teaches several multiday women's workshops here. We know Kim personally and can vouch for her ability to improve women's technique and confidence without scaring them to smithereens. These Women's Ski Adventures will be offered by the resort, Jan. 22-27, 2003, and through Club Med, Feb. 23–27, 2003. The program includes clinics with video analysis, daily off-slope fun, gift bags, product demos, welcome and award dinners, breakfasts and lunches, lift tickets, lodging and more. Call (888) 444-8151.

Beginning daily at 9:45 a.m., North Face tours for extreme skiers guide you through some of Crested Butte's most challenging terrain. $20 per person.

Racing: NASTAR races cost $6 for two runs and $1 for each additional run. Race workshops are offered. Register at the ski and snowboard school desk. NASTAR races are offered daily from 10 a.m.–3 p.m. (weather permitting) on Smith Hill and Canaan.

Child care [2002/03 prices]

Ages: 6 months to 7 years.

Costs: $70 for a full day, or $12 per hour. It includes crafts, games and other activities, but no ski lessons, and toddlers have separate programs from the older children.

Reservations: Strongly recommended; registration and information are in the Kid's Ski & Snowboard World in the Whetstone Building at the base of the Silver Queen Lift; 349-2259 or (800) 600-7349.

Children's lessons: Programs for ages 3–7 include ski rental and supervised day care after the lesson; $85 for a full day (with lunch) or $75 for half-day (no lunch). More experienced kids have classes separate from beginners. For ages 8–12, half-day lessons in skiing and snowboarding are $75 (no lunch); a full day is $85 (includes lunch). These prices do not include lift tickets or rental equipment. The all-day Rip Session is for ages 8–15, Level 8 and 9 skiers and snowboarders; cost is $150. Race workshops are offered for children. Register at the ski and snowboard school desk.

Lift tickets [2002/03 prices]

	Adult	Child (5–16)
One day	$55	Pay their age (see below)
Three days	$165 ($55/day)	
Five days	$235 ($47/day)	

Who skis free: Ages 4 and younger and 70 and older always ski free.

Who skis at a discount: Ages 65-69 ski for half the adult price at the ticket window. Children ages 5–16 pay their age per day for a lift ticket. This program has no blackout periods, nor any limits to the number of days or number of children, but proof of age may be required. Purchasing a multiday lodging package is the best way to go: With a lodging package, lift tickets start as low as $26 per day for three days of skiing, $21 per day for six days.

Irwin Lodge

Irwin Lodge at Lake Irwin, 12 miles west of Crested Butte, is Colorado's most exclusive and remote ski area. It stretches over 2,200 acres with an overall 2,100-foot vertical drop, but you won't find a chair lift or a snowmaking gun anywhere, and only 40 or so skiers and snowboarders can use the area at a time. Irwin Lodge specializes in snowcat skiing.

The 22-room lodge was built in 1974 by an eccentric millionaire. The only way in is by snowmobile, snowcat or cross-country skis. There are no phones (the only contact with the outside world is two-way radio), no network television, and one massive wooden lodge, perched on a ridge. Its isolation creates a special magic. A new group of owners took it over in 1997 and bought new snowcats, renovated the lodge's interior and bought new rental equipment— fat powder skis, cross-country skis, snowboards, snowshoes and avalanche locating beacon transceivers, a precaution supplied to all guests and guides.

Mornings begin with breakfast, then snowcats make their first climb to the ridge loaded with skiers and snowboarders, and cross-country skiers take off on organized tours. Skiing is available for every level of ability. We don't recommend this for a first-time ski experience, but we do recommend it for a first time in powder. Two groomed slopes serve the needs of intermediates. There are plenty of untracked, steep slopes for those with more experience.

Skiing normally starts at 9 a.m. and continues until 4 p.m. From noon to 1 p.m. everything stops for the lunch buffet while guests dine and the snowcats are serviced. Irwin also offers snowmobiling, guided cross-country skiing, ice fishing and snowshoeing.

Packages combine lodging, three gourmet meals, activities and transportation from Crested Butte. Last season, per-person, per-day in February costs were $480 for single occupancy, $430 double, or $405 triple or quad. Rates are for three days, from Sunday through Wednesday; and four days, from Wednesday through Sunday, only. Savings in January or March are about $100 per person, and there's a 5-percent savings for stays of seven days or longer.

Contact Irwin Lodge, PO Box 457, Crested Butte, CO 81224; 349-9800 or (888) 464-7946 (888-GO-IRWIN); fax, 349-9801.

 ## Accommodations

Most of the accommodations are clustered around the ski area in Mt. Crested Butte. The historic town has a handful of lodges and quaint B&Bs, but they aren't as convenient to the slopes. However, they are less expensive and closer to the nightlife; and offer a taste of more rustic Western atmosphere. A free bus service takes you right to the slopes every 15 minutes, so the primary inconvenience of in-town lodging is the short bus ride.

Crested Butte Vacations (800-544-8448) can take care of everything from your plane tickets to lodging, lift tickets and lessons with one phone call. It also offers some of the best packages available. Before you make any arrangements, call and ask for the best deal.

The Sheraton Crested Butte Resort ($$$–$$$$), 200 yards from the lifts in the heart of the base village, is the only full-service hotel other than Club Med. It has 248 oversized rooms, including 106 suites. You'll find an indoor/outdoor swimming pool, hot tub, fitness room, concierge, room service, gift shop and business center here.

Club Med (1-800-CLUBMED; $$$–$$$$), offers Club Med's only North American ski village and it's dedicated to families. Club Med is all-inclusive with rooms, meals, beer and wine, lessons and entertainment included at one price. It's rated as Club Med's top village in guest satisfaction worldwide.

Dining: $$$-Entrees $20+; $$-$10-20; $-less than $10.
Accommodations: (double room) $$$$-$200+; $$$-$141-$200; $$-$81-$140; $-$80 and less.

The Plaza ($$$$), only 80 yards from the Silver Queen superchair, features one of the most luxurious and roomy condominium units in Mt. Crested Butte. There are two hot tubs, a sauna and covered parking. They give excellent value and are especially popular with groups because special functions can be arranged. There's also a great pizza joint and pub here, The Firehouse Grill. Kid's World is just 50 yards away.

The newly constructed **Treasury Point** ($$$$) features luxury four-bedroom townhomes with three-and-a-half baths. They are spacious and beautifully furnished, and include a garage and a complex with an outdoor hot tub.

The Villas ($$$$), the newest and most luxurious townhouses in Mt. Crested Butte, are 225 yards from the lifts (just across the street). The three- and four-bedroom units are tastefully decorated, and have private balconies and fabulous views of Mt. Crested Butte.

The Buttes ($$$–$$$$) are well-appointed condos close to the lifts. Rooms range in size from studios to three bedrooms. **The Gateway** ($$$–$$$$), across from the Peachtree lift and about a two-minute stroll from the Silver Queen, may be the best luxury of any condo on the slopes when you trade price for space and amenities.

Wood Creek and **Mountain Edge** ($$–$$$$) are convenient to the lifts, and the **Columbine** is a more moderate ski-in/ski-out property. These three, together with nine others within shuttlebus distance of the lifts, are managed by several agencies, so it's best to book through Crested Butte Vacations (800-544-8448).

The Crested Butte Club (349-6655; $$–$$$$) on Second St. in town, is the upscale, old-world elegance champion of the area. Though the lifts are a bit far, this place is worth the inconvenience. Seven suites have been individually furnished with Victorian furnishings including double sinks and a copper-and-brass tub, as well as beautiful four-poster or canopied beds and a fireplace. The amenities include the fitness club, with heated swimming pool, two steam baths, three hot tubs, weight room, and massage and weight trainer. This is a No-Smoking property.

The Claim Jumper (349-6471; $$–$$$), 704 Whiterock St., is a historic log-home bed-and-breakfast and the class act in town. It's filled with a collection of memorable antiques. Bedrooms have themes and are furnished with brass or old iron beds. There are only five rooms, four with private bath. Room rates include a full breakfast. Children are not encouraged. The Claim Jumper can arrange catered weddings and special-occasion receptions.

The Christiana Guesthaus (800-824-7899; 349-5326; $–$$), 621 Maroon Ave., is only a block from the ski shuttle and a five-minute walk from downtown. This has a mountain inn atmosphere and most of the guests manage to get to know one another. The rooms are small, but guests spend a good deal of time in the hotel's living rooms so this doesn't really matter. Let the owners know if you need quiet, because some rooms get quite a bit of traffic from the owner's family and folk using the washers and dryers.

The Forest Queen (349-5336; $), corner of Elk and 2nd, is inexpensive for a double with bath. **The Elk Mountain Lodge** (349-7533; $$–$$$), around the corner from the Forest Queen on 2nd Street, has simple but comfortable rooms, all with private bath. Ask for Room 20 on the third floor with lots of space, a balcony and a great view.

Other B&Bs in town (which we have not inspected) are **Elizabeth Anne** (349-0147; 703 Maroon Ave.); **Purple Mountain Lodge** (349-5888; 714 Gothic Ave.) and the **Last Resort** (349-0445; 213 3rd St.).

PR Property Management (349-6281), at 214 6th Street, has rentals in homes as well many special condominiums. For something out of the ordinary, check with them for help.

Dining

Crested Butte is blessed with more excellent, affordable restaurants than any other resort in the West. One writer noted that the fine dining per capita is highest here of any resort in Colorado. You can dine on gourmet French cuisine in an intimate setting, or chow down on platters of family-style fried chicken and steaks.

The **WoodStone Grille** (349-8030; $$$) at the Crested Butte Sheraton Resort is open for breakfast, lunch and dinner. It has well-prepared contemporary cuisine.

For excellent fondue, raclette and other Swiss fare, head to the **Swiss Chalet** (349-5917; $$–$$$) across the street from the Sheraton. It is open only for dinner.

The **Timberline Restaurant** (349-9831; $$$), at 201 Elk Ave., mixes a trendy bar downstairs with Mediterranean decor upstairs. Chef Tim Egelhoff combines seasonal products to create a Café French Cuisine, whose roots are classic French, with a pinch of California and a dash of the Rockies. The menu changes often. Open nightly from 5–10 p.m.

Near the four-way stop at 435 Sixth St. is **The Buffalo Grille** (349-9699; $$–$$$), specializing in buffalo and beef steaks, free range and organic entrées served with a Western flair. Make reservations—the place is tiny, but filled with atmosphere and one not to miss.

Le Bosquet (349-5808; $$$) is in the Majestic Plaza at Sixth and Bellview. Signature dishes include Colorado rack of lamb, hazelnut chicken, and salmon with ginger glaze. This is possibly Crested Butte's finest in formal French cuisine. There's also a bistro menu at its bar.

Soupçon Restaurant (349-5448; $$$) is hidden in the alley behind Kochevar's Bar. This log cabin started at half its current size in 1916 as a private residence to the Kochevars. This place is as romantic as it gets. Current owners Maura and Mac Bailey have created an innovative French cuisine, with menu items posted daily on a chalkboard. Reserve two to three days ahead for one of two seatings, 6 p.m. and 8:15 p.m.

The **Idle Spur Steakhouse and Crested Butte Brewery** (349-5026; $$–$$$) is always crowded and noisy. It offers the finest hand-cut steaks in town plus burgers (including vegetable and elk—sounds better than it is), Mexican entrées and a selection of fresh fish, all reasonably priced. Award-winning beers are brewed in-house from the White Buffalo Peace Ale to the full-bodied Rodeo Stout. Brewery tours 2–5 p.m. daily during happy hour. Film and television star Tom Skerritt is the co-owner, so you might just see him here while you're tossing back some brews and chowing down.

The **Powerhouse Bar Y Grill** ($$–$$$), next to the Old Town Hall bus stop (130 Elk Ave.), is known for its unique Mexican specialties like cabrito, grilled trout, fajitas, tamales and tacos. Sip from dozens of types of Tequilas. Prices are quite reasonable and portions are huge. Be prepared to wait for up to an hour—they don't take reservations.

For hard-to-beat group and family dining, head to **The Slogar** (349-5765; $$). It used to be the first bar the miners hit when returning from the mines and is decorated in old bordello decor. Slogar's offers a skillet-fried chicken dinner with mashed potatoes, biscuits, creamed corn, ice cream and even some other extras for a flat price. It also offers a family-style steak dinner. Reservations recommended.

For other substantial meals, head down Elk Ave. to **Donita's Cantina** (349-6674; $$), where the margaritas are giant and strong, and Mexican food comes in heaping portions. Be early or be ready to wait. No reservations. For a quick meal, try **The Last Steep** ($–$$), very popular with locals. **The Gourmet Noodle** (349-7401; $–$$) has many pasta dishes prepared fresh daily, espresso and cappuccino and tempting desserts, such as peanut butter pie and chocolate mousse.

Dining: $$$-Entrees $20+; $$-$10-20; $-less than $10.
Accommodations: (double room) $$$$-$200+; $$$-$141-$200; $$-$81-$140; $-$80 and less.

The best breakfast is under debate by members of our staff. Some say it's the **Paradise Cafe.** Others swear by the **Forest Queen.** Paradise Cafe hasn't been around quite as long as Forest Queen, where the atmosphere is authentic turn-of-the-century. Both are downtown and both serve hearty, traditional breakfasts (and lunch and dinner). New to the mix is the **Ruby Mountain Bakery,** across the street from the Paradise Café, which is more for the pastry-and-muffin crowd and can get very crowded.

For breakfast on the mountain, head to **The Avalanche** in the Treasury Center. Or make reservations for a **First Tracks Breakfast** (349-2378), where you'll meet at 8:15 a.m. at the Keystone Lift for first tracks on the mountain and an all-you-can-eat breakfast buffet.

For a good lunch, try **Bubba's on the Mountain** at the base of the Paradise lift or **The Avalanche** in the base area. **Camp 4 Coffee** is the locals' favorite hangout and serves the "Best Coffee in Town" with tasty breakfast items to go. You can sit on the world's largest bench if you'd like…or not.

Crested Butte has several outdoor dining experiences, such as the **Twister Fondue Party,** every Sunday, Wednesday and Friday when at 4:30 p.m., diners board the Keystone Lift for a three-course on-mountain fondue dinner, followed by a gentle ski to the base by torchlight. **Paradise Sleigh Ride Dinners** are every Tuesday, Thursday and Saturday via snowcat-drawn sleigh. Call 349-2211 or 349-2378 for either of those.

 ## Après-ski/nightlife

Here nightlife means wandering from bar to bar. The immediate après-ski action is centered in **Rafters** at the base of the lifts or **The Avalanche.** Then it begins to move downtown to the **Wooden Nickel,** with some wild drinks, and **The El Dorado,** known around town as "The Eldo" and, according to one local, has a "smokin' dance floor." **Talk of the Town** is a smoky locals' place with video games, shuffle-board and pool tables. **Kochevar's** is another local favorite where Butch Cassidy and the Sundance Kid used to saddle up to the bar. **The Crested Butte Brewery/Idle Spur** is a microbrewery with live music and dancing on weekends. Cover charges are $5 to $10, depending on the talent.

Rafters has dancing and good singles action most nights in Mt. Crested Butte, and it's within stumbling distance of most of the lodging. Those staying in town can take an inexpensive town taxi service if they miss the last bus of the night.

The **Princess Wine Bar** at 218 Elk Ave. is the place to finish your night on the town. Serving a limited menu of appetizers, there are a few tempting desserts to enjoy with cappuccino or a fine dessert wine. With no doubt the best selection of quality wines by the glass, the Princess also carries a full list of cognacs, ports and single malts. Come relax by the fire. Open daily from 10 a.m. to "whenever."

 ## Other activities

Crested Butte has several winter activities to choose from. These include **snowmobiling, dog sledding, ice skating, sledding, winter horseback riding** with Fantasy Ranch, and **sleigh rides** (with and without dinners) through Just Horsin' Around. Call the Crested Butte Chamber of Commerce at 349-6438 for brochures and information. For resort activities, call 349-2211.

There are loads of great **shops and boutiques** at the resort and especially in town. Among them: Diamond Tanita Art Gallery, for jewelry, glass, ceramics, paper, forged iron and other functional art pieces; Cookworks, Inc., a gourmet kitchen shop; The Book Store, with local maps, Western art and collectibles; and the Milky Way for unique women's apparel and lacey things. The Alpineer has outdoor gear for mountaineering, biking, hiking and backpacking, plus guide services and rentals are available here.

Getting there and getting around

By air: Despite its seemingly isolated location, Crested Butte is quite convenient to reach. The nearest airport is Gunnison, 30 miles from the resort. Continental has new jet service from Houston, United Express offers four daily commuter flights year round, and United offers daily jet service in addition to the commuters during the winter months. American offers non-stop daily flights from Dallas into Montrose Airport (two hours from the resort).

Alpine Express (641-5074 or 800-822-4844) meets every arriving flight and takes you directly to your hotel or condo for about $41 round-trip ($26 for children 12 and under). For reservations, call Crested Butte Vacations or directly to the company.

By car: Crested Butte is at the end of Hwy. 135, about 30 miles north of Gunnison. It's about 230 miles from Denver via Hwys. 285, 50 and 135. Hertz, Budget and Avis operate at the Gunnison Airport.

Getting around: No need for a car. Crested Butte's free town-resort shuttle, running every 15 minutes, is reliable and fun to ride, thanks to some free-spirited and friendly drivers. Town taxi for after-hours travel is available at 349-5543.

Nearby resorts

Monarch, Monarch, CO; (888) 996-7669, (719) 539-3573

Internet: www.skimonarch.com
5 lifts; 670 acres; 1,170 vertical feet

Monarch, located on the Continental Divide, is known for powder and more powder. It gets about 350 inches of snow a year, but only about 170,000 skier visits (many Colorado destination resorts get that in just a couple of weeks). That means a lot more untracked snow to play in. Monarch installed a fixed-grip quad two seasons ago, its first chair larger than a double. The resort caters to families, and has groomed beginner and intermediate terrain for those who don't like the steep and deep. Experts can opt for snowcat skiing and riding on more than 900 acres of expert backcountry terrain. This area is fairly isolated and without many off-slope activities. Child care starts at 2 months.

Lift tickets (02/03 prices): Adults, $39; Adult Holiday, $41; Children (7–12), $17; Seniors (62–69), $26. Children 6 and younger & seniors 70 and older ski free. Snowcat skiing/riding, $200 per person.

Distance from Denver: About 160 miles southwest via Hwys. 285 and 50. **Distance from Gunnison** (closest airport): About 35 miles east on Hwy. 50.

Lodging information: (800) 332-3668. Monarch has an overnight lodge 3 miles away; other lodging is in Salida, 18 miles east.

Purgatory at Durango Mountain Resort

Colorado

Summit elevation: 10,822 feet
Vertical drop: 2,029 feet
Base elevation: 8,793 feet

Address: One Skier Place, Durango, CO 81301
☎ **Area code:** 970
Ski area phone/Snow report: 247-9000
ⓘ **Toll-free reservations:** (800) 525-0892
E-mail: info@durangomountain.com
Internet:
www.durangomountainresort.com (ski area)
or www.durango.com (town)
Expert: ★
Advanced: ★★★
Intermediate: ★★★★★
Beginner: ★★★★★
Never-ever: ★★★★★

Number of lifts: 11–1 high-speed six-pack,
1 high-speed quad, 4 triples, 3 doubles,
2 surface lifts
Snowmaking: 34 percent
Skiable acreage: 1,200 acres
Uphill capacity: 15,600 per hour
Snowboarding: Yes
Bed base: 3,120 near resort; 7,000 in Durango
Nearest lodging: Slopeside
Resort child care: Yes, 2 months and older
Adult ticket, per day: $53 (02/03)
Dining: ★★★ **Apres-ski/nightlife:** ★★★
Other activities: ★★★

Purgatory at Durango Mountain Resort is a hidden gem. It's tucked away in Southwest Colorado, closer to Albuquerque than it is to Denver. It doesn't have the movie stars you'll find in Aspen or Telluride, nor does it draw the crowds you'll encounter at resorts west of Denver. What it offers is more bluebird days than any other resort in Colorado, plus snow that's usually good, and often great. And it's uncrowded. You'll seldom wait in lift lines.

Durango draws heavily from New Mexico, Arizona and Texas. Skiers wearing jeans and cowboy hats, whooping and hollering their way down beginner runs aren't uncommon. The preponderance of intermediate skiers means Purgatory's advanced trails are uncrowded and boarders will love the mountain's many terraced runs.

Durango's historic downtown is full of great restaurants, brew pubs and galleries. If you and your group can't have fun in Durango, well, you'd better just stay home. Inexpensive motels line Main Avenue, and rates for a single can dip as low as $29 a night during the ski season. Families, students, and others on a budget can enjoy a very low-cost ski vacation here.

Purgatory Mountain receives an average of 260 inches of snow per year. Early-season snowmaking efforts here focus on covering a few runs well rather than a large area. The best snow conditions are typically in February and March.

Mountain layout–Skiing

Thousands of years ago glaciers scraped out the Animas Valley, leaving terraced mountainsides. The terraces mean several of Purgatory Mountain's runs plunge downward for a bit, then level off, then plunge, then level off—all the way to the bottom, no matter what ability level you are. The effect is like a roller coaster ride. The roller coaster effect lures those who love to catch air (yes, there are warnings all over the place, but who can resist?). We counted, and you'll get about 10 to 15 turns in before the pancake, keeping terror to a minimum and forgiving the less athletic among us.

◆◆ **Expert:** The toughest trail on the mountain is Bull Run, a double-black route that starts off rather gently beneath Dante's restaurant, next to Lift #5 (Grizzly). Once you're on the lower part of it, there's no getting off. It has a tough pitch as well as funnels and moguls. Bottom's Chute is a nasty surprise on your way to Lift #8 (Legends). Adventure skiers can try the powder stashes between Peace and Boogie. On the front side of the mountain, tree fans will like the aspens between Pandemonium and Lower Hades.

◆ **Advanced:** From the top of Lift #1 (Purgatory Village Express), what starts out as Paradise soon turns into Pandemonium, a black diamond that gets steeper and bumpier the further you go. Upper Hades also starts out mild, but turns hellacious once you drop over the headwall. Styx can be heavenly after a fresh snowstorm. The short traverse to Styx from Lift #1's top station means you'll encounter fewer skiers than ever on this utterly fabulous run.

On the back side of the mountain, Snag, perhaps the most terraced run on the mountain, leads skiers to challenging chutes all leading back to Lift #3 (Hermosa Park). Bump fans should also consider Wapiti, a black run under Lift #5 (Grizzly) that grows igloo-sized bumps. Lift #8 (Legends) in the far back is the home of most of the black-diamond terrain. Poet's Glade and Paul's Park offer nice glade skiing, Elliott's has a nice sustained pitch.

■ **Intermediate:** Intermediates seem to prefer the terrain served by Lift #3 (Hermosa Park Express). Regularly groomed runs include Peace, Boogie, Where, Zinfandel, and Airmail. On days with fresh snow Harris Hill can provide a fun cut-off. Want to ratchet it up a notch? From the top of Lift #3 continue down Legends toward Dead Spike. Dead Spike is frequently split groomed, with good intermediate "starter bumps" on the ungroomed side. Still not challenged enough? Continue further down Legends to the mid-loading station on Lift #8 (Legends). From the top of this lift, check out either Sally's Run or Chet's.

●● **Beginner:** After graduating from the bunny hill, beginning skiers should head for Lift #4 (Twilight). It serves terrain ideally suited for beginners and families with small children. You won't be endangered by a lot of advanced, fast skiers in this area. The easiest trail is Pinkerton Toll Road, a winding cat track. Divinity and Angel's Tread are wide runs. Columbine winds through several stands of trees, giving beginners the feeling of being deep in the woods. If this terrain is simply too easy, you may want to cut over from the top of Lift #4 over to Lift #3 (Hermosa Park) via Salvation, where you'll find groomed intermediate terrain.

● **Never-ever:** First-timers have their own learning area, Columbine Station, with its own lifts, ticket office and restaurant. It's directly across from the lower parking lots. After a couple of lessons on the terrain under the Columbine Lift, beginners can ride the Lift #7 (Graduate) back to the base area. The "Family Ski Zone" under Lift #4 (Twilight) would be the logical place for beginners to head next rather than taking Lift#1 (Purgatory Village Express) to the top of the mountain. A catwalk down to the Columbine beginner area takes intermediate and advanced skiers back to their cars in the two lower lots at the end of the day, and this year an added route on the other side (south) of Lift #7 will make it easy for beginners to get back to Columbine. Both trails will cross a new overpass over Sheol Street.

 ## Mountain layout—Snowboarding

The signature run is Snag, an exciting roller-coaster ride of steep, moderate, steep, moderate steps—all the way down! Advanced riders can catch air off each of the steps. Intermediates use the flats above each headwall to catch their breath. Rider-constructed hits can often be found here and beneath Lift #8 (Legends).

On days with freshies, locals head for Lift #8. Powder hounds can head into the trees on Poet's Glade or Paul's Park. From Lift #5 (Grizzly), a delightful powder stash can often be found hidden away on Cathedral Tree Way (rider's left off Bull Run). On the front side try Styx—you'll most likely find waist-deep powder. Upper Hades transitions into Lower Hades, a major steep mogul field that, when covered with a foot or more of fresh powder, can be an absolutely amazing ride, along with Pandemonium and Catharsis.

Paradise offers wide-open corduroy for laying out sick carves. Sa's Psyche is equally good carving country. Pitchfork Terrain Park has a 450-foot halfpipe that transitions to a 15-foot quarterpipe, plus jibbing rails, a rainbow rail, two street rails, a balance beam and "The Serpentine," a 45-foot rail with kink to curve to kink to curve. There's also a 50-foot Big Air competition jump. Adjacent is Limbo, the slopestyle area, with back-to-back tables, multiple hits, line combinations and a "Hollywood Hit," visible from the lift, strictly for hot dogs.

You'll find way-too-flat traverses connecting the front and back side. Getting to the back side requires carrying a lot of speed on Hermosa Parkway. Reaching the maze at the bottom of Lift #3 (Hermosa Park) without having to unstrap and skate requires executing a kamikaze-style run. To return from the back side, avoid the much-too-flat BD&M Expressway. Instead, zigzag: Take Path to Peace, ride Lift #3 back up the mountain, Silver Tip it to either black-diamond Cool It or blue-square The Bank, then continue on past the bottom of Lift#2 (Engineer) to Demon. The right side of Demon is a gully that provides a natural halfpipe but be extremely careful of beginners finding their way home on Demon after lunch.

Beginners should take Lift #1 (Purgatory Village Express) and head for Sa's Psyche, beneath Lift #2 (Engineer). It's nicely groomed, gentle-pitched terrain, with only one flat spot. Snowboarders generally avoid Lift #4 (Twilight) because of lack of suitable terrain.

Mountain rating

Despite the mountain's name, this is Intermediate Paradise—such are the variety and plenitude of trails. Intermediates enjoy endless options for whoop-de-doing at high speeds. There are occasional frustrating flats—some folks call the resort "traversatory"—but for the most part you'll find plenty of fun. The Columbine area is devoted strictly to neophytes, with everything from a magic carpet to the Graduate triple when you're ready for the main mountain. Advanced skiers and riders will have a great time, too, taking laps off the Legends Lift. Only experts looking for extremes will be disappointed.

Cross-country and snowshoeing

The **Nordic Center** (247-6000 Ext. 114 or 385-2114), maintained by the Durango Nordic Ski Club, is just north of the Alpine ski area across Highway 550. There are 16 km. of groomed trails for classic and skate skiing. Nordic skiers find the same undulating terrain as alpine skiers do. The center offers clinics, races, group and private lessons, rentals, children's programs, daytime and moonlight tours. Daily trail fees are $8 for adults and $4 for children 12 and younger and seniors 65 and older. Rentals are $10 for adults, $6 for children and seniors. As part of Purgatory's Total Adventure Ticket™, one Alpine ski day can be exchanged for the Nordic package.

Lessons (2001/02 prices)

Group lessons: $30 for a 2_-hour lesson. A three-lesson booklet is $79 (half-day lessons, use 'em when you want). Hint: Afternoon sessions tend to have far fewer students so you can receive much more personalized instruction.

Never-ever package: Called First Things First, it offers first-time skiers and snowboarders half-day group lessons for $30; $60 includes lift ticket and rentals. This is a guaranteed lesson. For people who have been on skis or a snowboard before who might not be ready to "go up the hill," a Second Things Second program is offered at the same rate.

Private lessons: $140 for two hours during peak hours (9 a.m.-1 p.m.); $110 for three hours during off peak hours (1- 4 p.m.). A full-day private lesson is $300. For a lesson with Purgatory's top snowboard instructor, ask for Nancy Vogel.

Special programs: Throughout the season, the resort offers clinics for snowboarding, racing, telemark skiing and mogul techniques. Call ahead for details, or check with the Resort Concierge desk. Clinics and daily events are announced on the daily snow report and posted with the list of groomed trails throughout the resort and on shuttles.

The Adaptive Sports Association (385-2163, Nov.-April; www.asadurango.org.) runs one of the nation's leading adaptive skiing programs here. Programs include lift ticket, adaptive equipment and lessons for the visually, physically or mentally impaired.

Racing: NASTAR racing occurs daily at the Paradise Events Arena. Runs are $2 or skiers can opt for self-timed race training gates.

 ## Child care (2001/02 prices)

Ages: 2 months to 3 years.
Costs: $75 for a full day with lunch and $60 for half day. Toddlers (ages 2-3) get outdoor snow play, arts and crafts, games, movies and story time.

Reservations: Required; call 385-2144 or (800) 525-0892.

Note: The day-care staff also can recommend a babysitter who can watch your kids while you enjoy a night out. If you're not sure whether to put your child in day care or lessons, Durango Mountain's Kids Central, located on the second floor of the Village Center, will help assess your child's abilities and interests, then escort him or her to the appropriate spot.

Children's lessons: Ski lessons are available for kids 3-12 years old, snowboarding lessons are for kids 8-12. Full-day programs, including lift ticket and lunch, cost $75; half day with ticket, $60. Rentals are an additional $10. The program for ages 3-4 includes lunch, indoor activity, and an introduction-to-ski lesson with special skis that attach to snowboots (included in cost); ages 4-5 get the same only using full Alpine equipment (rental is additional $7). Reservations required for kids ages 3-5 (800-525-0892 or 385-2144).

Lift tickets (2002/03 prices)

	Adult	Child (6-12)
One day	$52	$25
Three day	$156 ($52 per day)	$75 ($25 per day)
Five day	$235 ($47 per day)	$100 ($20 per day)

Who skis free: Ages 5 and younger and 70 and older.

Who skis at a discount: Ages 62–69 ski for $35. Skiers who book packages through Durango Mountain Resort receive discounted lift tickets.

Note: There are early/late season discounts. Holiday day tickets cost $55 for adults and $27 for children. The resort offers a Total Adventure Ticket™: Guests purchasing a four-day or more ticket can apply credit for a day of downhill skiing against a day of cross-country skiing or one of several vacation activities in southwest Colorado (examples include the Durango & Silverton Narrow Gauge Railroad train, a soak and massage at Trimble Hot Springs, or a sleigh ride). Call for details.

Accommodations

Durango Mountain Resort has three primary lodging areas. The condos at the base area are the most expensive. A limited number of resort hotels and condos within 10 miles of the ski area are slightly less. Motels in Durango can cost as little as $29 per night, but are 25 miles away. Except on holidays, motel reservations are seldom needed in town. Resort lodging can be booked at **Durango Central Reservations,** (800) 525-0892, or the **Durango Chamber of Commerce** (800) 525-8855. Online, check lodgings at www.durango.org or check **Vacation Rentals by Owner** www.vrbo.com.

Base-area lodging is available at the **Purgatory Village Condominium Hotel** (385-2100), **Best Western Lodge at Durango Mountain** (247-9669), which accepts pets, and the following condo complexes: **Angelhaus** (247-8090), **Brimstone** (259-1066), **East Rim** (385-2100), **Edelweiss, Graysill, Sitzmark** and **Twilight View**. Condos have full-service units (kitchens, fireplaces, common-area hot tubs and laundry facilities) and cost about $115 for a studio to $595 for larger suites. Hotel costs are about $105–$285.

Several other complexes are within 10 miles of the ski area. The prices at **Cascade Village, Needles, Silver Pick** and **Sheraton Tamarron Resort** range from $115–$445. Most of the outlying condo complexes offer free shuttles to and from the ski area.

In-town lodging can be found at the **Hampton Inn** (247-2600), the **Doubletree** (259-6580), which accepts pets, and the **Marriott Residence Inn** (259-6200). A plethora of older, less-expensive motels line North Main Ave. such as **Day's End** (259-3311). The **Spanish Trails Inn** (247-4173) offers kitchenettes. For fans of funky (but clean) little motels, consider the **Wapiti Lodge** (247-3961), which is walking distance to downtown.

Five historic lodging properties are worth mentioning. **The Strater Hotel** (800-247-4431; $$$) and the **General Palmer Hotel** (800-523-3358; $$–$$$) are hotels that date back over 100 years. The Strater has a great Victorian-style hot tub area that would be the envy of many larger, more sophisticated properties and its Diamond Belle Saloon is a classic that's now non-smoking. **The Leland House Bed & Breakfast** and **The Rochester Hotel** (800-664-1920 for both; $$–$$$ for both), on East Second Ave., are historic lodges owned by the same family, located in the heart of the downtown historic district. The Rochester has two dog-friendly rooms. The Leland House has a Durango history theme, with the rooms named after local historic figures. The Rochester Hotel has a Hollywood theme, with each room named for a film shot at least in part in Durango. "Butch Cassidy and the Sundance Kid," "Around The World in 80 Days" and "City Slickers" were all filmed here. **Jarvis Suites** (800-824-1024, 259-6190; $$–$$$) at 10th and Main are newly redecorated with a killer view of the action on Main St. Built in 1888, the hotel is on the National Register of Historic Places.

Two B&B's located between Durango and the ski area bear mention: the **Apple Orchard Inn** (247-0751; $$), located on CR203 near Trimble Hot Springs, and **Country Sunshine** (247-2853; $$) near where CR250 runs into 550N. Staying at either would drastically reduce the amount of driving you do.

Dining

There are several options at the base area. **Purgy's Pub** serves burgers, barbecue and pizza in a bar atmosphere. After a full morning of skiing you'll savor the hearty homemade soups and stews at the **Mountain Market Deli,** a local's favorite lunch spot. There's also the upscale **Joey's Italian Café**. The **Columbine Station** at the base of the beginner hill has lunch items and local brews along with "kid food."

Dante's, at the midway station of Lift #5 (Grizzly), serves lunch. Upstairs, **Café de los Pinos** has gourmet lunches with great views of the slopes and a nice bar. **The Powderhouse Restaurant** beneath Lift #2 (Hermosa Park) serves lunch fare along Italian themes.

For fresh fish and local game, try the **Cascade Grill** (259-3500; $$$), 2 miles north of the resort that offers elegant dining in a rustic setting. The new **Hamilton Chop House** (259-6636), north of the resort entrance, is excellent. **The Sow's Ear** (247-3527), at the SilverPick lodge, is famed for its large hand-cut steaks.

You'll find restaurants of almost every persuasion downtown. Most don't require, or accept, reservations. Entrées typically run $15–25 at the finer restaurants.

Seasons (382-9790, $$$), 764 Main Ave., features rotisserie-roasted dinners (sea bass, trout, chicken, lamb) and fine wines by the glass. Try the garlic mashed potatoes.

Ken & Sue's Place (259-2616, $$), 937 Main Ave., a locals' favorite, serves Continental fare with a homey twist. Start with the field green salad with apples and gorgonzola, then order the pistachio-encrusted grouper served with a rum sauce on a bed of yams.

Ariano's (247-8146, $$-$$$), 150 East College Dr., serves northern Italian cuisine. Swanky **Randy's** (247-9083, $$-$$$), next door at 152 East College Dr., serves just about the nicest prime rib in town. Make reservations for a curtained booth for a romantic dinner.

The Ore House (247-5707, $$-$$$), 147 College Dr., is an Old West steak house, rustic and casual. **The Red Snapper** (259-3417, $$-$$$), 144 East 9th St., has fresh seafood, by far the nicest salad bar in town, along with an exotic saltwater-aquarium decor.

The Cyprus Café (385-6884, $$), 725 E. Second, offers delicious Mediterranean dishes at reasonable prices. Their lamb dishes are to die for. **Francisco's Restaurante Y Cantina** (247-4098, $$), 619 Main Ave., has a Southwestern menu. Hidden-away **Gazpacho** (259-9494, $$), 431 E. Second Ave., has authentic (read: spicy!) New Mexican cuisine. **Tequilas** (259-7655, $$), 948 Main, where the waiters pretend not to speak English, is the new local's favorite and serves the best margaritas, made with fresh-squeezed limes. Ask for an Especial.

Olde Tymer's Cafe (259-2990, $-$$), 1000 Main Ave., is tops for a good hamburger. Monday is burger night, Friday is the taco special. They recently went non-smoking. **Christina's Grille and Bar** (382-3844, $$), 3416 (North) Main Ave., offers very reasonably priced continental cuisine. The parking lot is always full, telling you something!

Carver's Bakery and Brew Pub (259-2545, $$), 1022 Main Ave., is the best place in Durango for breakfast; muffins and bagels are baked fresh daily. Carver's has a nice children's menu—their meals are served on a Frisbee they get to keep. **College Drive Café** (247-5322) bakes the best homemade cinnamon rolls (closed Monday/Tuesday). If you prefer the eggs-and-bacon-type breakfast, head for the **Durango Diner** (247-9889), 957 Main Ave. Sunday brunch at the **Doubletree Hotel** ($$) is outstanding and a good choice for visitors departing on Sunday, since the hotel is between the ski area and the airport. Or start the day off at the **Steamin' Bean** (385-7901, $) on Main Street, a great hangout for coffee, chess and chai.

 ## Après-ski/nightlife

Throngs congregate at **Purgy's Pub** after the lifts close. It sometimes has a band. **Shakers Martini Bar** on the 2nd floor at Purgy's, features top shelf liquors and good eats. In general, however, après-ski is found in town, not on mountain.

Most ski areas have a "locals" spot, and here it's the **Schoolhouse Cafe**, a small and friendly hangout located 2 miles south of the resort. It's across the road from the Needles Country Store on U.S. Hwy. 550. This is where the lift ops, ski patrollers and other insiders fill up on beer and calzones the size of footballs. The music rocks, and the pool table is free.

Dining: $$$-Entrees $20+; $$-$10-20; $-less than $10.
Accommodations: (double room) $$$$-$200+; $$$-$141-$200; $$-$81-$140; $-$80 and less.

A wa-aay popular après-ski spot that's available on trade with your Total Adventure Ticket™ is **Trimble Hot Springs**, 8 miles north of Durango on the way back from the ski area. Mineral springs bubble into two outdoor therapy pools, one heated to 90 degrees and the other to 105. A heated outdoor 50-meter pool awaits swimmers. Call ahead (247-0111).

If you really want to party, go to downtown Durango—it's either jumping or mildly hopping. Spring Break packs 'em in and the bars schedule lots of entertainment.

Carver's Bakery and Brew Pub offers beers brewed on-site along with a dinner menu. **Steamworks**, a brew pub on the corner of 8th Street and East Second Ave., pours award-winning beer and serves moderately priced food. **Lady Falconburgh's Barley Exchange** has 20 microbrews on tap and more than 80 different bottled beers. It attracts large groups of students from nearby Fort Lewis College. Their Philly Cheese Steak is excellent. **El Rancho** is Durango's old standby. Stop and have at least one drink there, along with a bowl of free popcorn. "The Ranch" has served liquid refreshment since the days when Jack Dempsey fought his first fight there, although historians now say the fight actually occurred across the street. A mural on the side of the old Central Hotel depicts Dempsey's first TKO.

Durango has quite a variety of musical entertainment. Flyers posted around town will tell you who's playing where. The **Wild Horse Saloon** at College St. and Second Ave. has dancing and live music. **Solid Muldoon's** is a dance and pool-shoot spot for the college crowd, but worth a visit for the decor. **Coloradaponga's** is a smokey pool hall. **Scoot'n Blues** dishes up soul, jazz, and, of course, blues, blues, blues. Over at the **Diamond Belle Saloon** in the Strater Hotel, a ragtime piano player plunks out hit tunes from the Gay '90s—1890s, that is. The Diamond Belle recently went non-smoking, and their waitresses wear vintage-era costumes that are worth the price of a drink to see! A new favorite is **The Office** at the Strater, where the three-martini après-ski is *de rigueur*. Check out the $11,000 chandelier.

 # Other activities

The resort has a **tubing** hill. **Star Safaris,** a real family affair, takes you on a ride to the Powderhouse for nighttime stargazing with Colorado's largest privately owned telescope.

Durango has two **snowcat operations**. The **San Juan Ski Company** (259-9671; www.sanjuanski.com; closed Tuesdays) takes skiers and boarders to 35,000 acres of powder for about $175 (including lunch, guide included, age 12+). Reservations strongly recommended. **El Diablo** (877-241-9643, 385-7288; www.snowcat-powder.com), provides tours in the San Juan Mountains. Cost is about $125 including lunch.

One of America's finest national parks is nearby, **Mesa Verde.** Anasazi Indian (Ancestral Puebloans) cliff dwellings dating back more than 800 years have been preserved here. Plan an early start for a day trip to Mesa Verde; it's about an hour west of Durango but over a mountain pass.

Take the **Durango & Silverton Narrow Gauge Railroad** (www.durangotrain.com). Durango was founded in 1880 by the Denver and Rio Grande Railroad when they extended their line to Silverton in order to haul ore. Today, the train hauls tourists. Daily in winter, it goes halfway to Silverton then returns to Durango, a five-hour round trip. The winter fare is about $45 for adults, $22 for children ages 5-11. Warm clothing is highly recommended. If you purchase a Total Adventure Ticket, you can exchange a day of skiing for the train ride. New this year, the train leaves at noon and arrives back in Durango at 5 p.m.

Visit the **Railroad Museum**. There are memorabilia, locomotives, a galloping goose, handcars and putt-putts. Admission is $5. There are several other museums in Durango to consider. The **Animas Museum** (259-2402), 31st St. & W. 2nd Ave., has exhibits on local history and Indian cultures. Winter hours are Wed.-Sat., 10 a.m.-4 p.m. **Children's Museum of Durango** (259-9234), in the Durango Arts Center, has hands-on exhibits for kids ages 2-11. Open Wed.-Sun. **Grand Motorcar & Piano Collection** (247-1250), 586 Animas View Dr., displays a variety of antique and classic automobiles and grand pianos. Call for hours.

The **Sky Ute Lodge and Casino** offers basic gambling and some 380 Vegas-style slots.

Durango's **shops** smack of shabby chic, Old West and unique custom designs. The **art galleries** are first rate, and clothing and knick-knack shops stock great finds. Among our favorites: New West Galleries on Main between 7th and 8th, and Toh Atin Gallery, 145 W. 9th Street, for Southwestern art; and The Bookcase, 601 E. Second Ave., offers a fine inventory of used and collector books. The O'Farrell Hat Company, on Main offers what are acknowledged as the world's finest cowboy hats. You'll have to dig deep in your pocketbook to put one of their hats on your head, though. Real deep.

 ## Getting there and getting around

By air: The Durango-La Plata County Airport is 40 miles south of Durango Mountain Resort and about 15 miles from downtown Durango.

By car: The resort is 25 miles from Durango. There are no major mountain passes from the south or west. In summary, Durango is an easy, 4-hour drive from Albuquerque. It is a 6-8+ hour drive from Denver in the winter over numerous mountain passes, which frequently close when it snows. Chains or 4WD are occasionally required heading from Durango to the resort during and immediately after major snowstorms; however, 99 percent of the time a front-wheel drive vehicle is all that's needed.

If you don't need lessons or rentals, the bunny hill offers the fastest access onto the mountain. Either get off the shuttle at the bunny hill or park your car in one of the two lower lots. Purchase your lift tickets here, and at the end of the day, ski back to your car. From the bunny hill ride Lift #7 (The Graduate) directly to Lift #1 (Purgatory Village Express). To access the upper parking lots requires either chains or 4WD, and you'll do a lot more schlepping in ski boots and waiting in line at the base village than if you park low.

Getting around: Visitors have several ground transportation options: (1) Rent a car. If possible, request a front-wheel-drive vehicle. (2) Some of the larger hotels offer shuttle service to and from the slopes. Others offer free or low-cost airport shuttles. Some lodges on the north end of town offer free nightlife shuttles for guests. (3) **Mountain TranSport** shuttles between town and the slopes, nine round trips 6 a.m. to 10 p.m. (4) **Durango Transportation** (259-4818) provides on-call taxi service and airport pick-ups. Round-trip fare from the airport to the mountain resort is $60 per person. From the airport to the town of Durango, the fare is $15 per person, one-way. (5) The **Durango Trolley**, a red minibus decorated to resemble an antique trolley, provides in-town service up and down Main Ave. year round, every 30 minutes for 50¢ from 7 a.m. to 7 p.m. (6) **The Buzz Bus** takes intoxicated patrons home when the bars close. It only costs $2. (7) More than a few locals simply **hitchhike** from this point rather than waiting for the bus.

Downtown Durango is delightfully walkable. Here's something to know when trying to find a Durango street address: Nearly all of Durango's streets have numbered names. The streets parallel to Main are "Avenues" and the numbers usually are spelled out (Second Avenue, for example). The streets that intersect Main all are "Streets" and the number is seldom spelled out. Most tourists hang out on Main between 5th and 11th, and occasionally venture onto Second Avenue. 6th Street is better known as "College Drive."

Nearby resorts

Wolf Creek Ski Area, Pagosa Springs, CO; 970-264-5639
Internet: www.wolfcreekski.com
6 lifts, 1600 acres, 1600 vertical feet

Wolf Creek is the "non-resort" where skiers and riders go to drown themselves in fresh powder, explore the trees and launch off cliffs. Most of the time, you're not on a marked trail and fresh tracks can be found days after storms. This isn't a destination resort with endless groomers, cute shops and activities for non-skiers. It's a gateway to the backcountry.

Because of the tremendous amounts of snow, avalanche control is a big issue. There are gates to access the ridgeline between Treasure Chair and Boundary Bowl, the Waterfall area, Montezuma Bowl, the Knife Ridge Chutes and Horseshoe Bowls. For 2001/02, Wolf Creek is looking into installing a natural gas cannon in Horseshoe Bowl to reduce the amount of explosives required to clear chutes. Unlike bigger resorts, Wolf Creek doesn't go out of its way to dynamite every rock, pull every stump, or remove every downed tree, all of which actually improve the stability of the snow pack. They just let the snow bury it all.

The facilities at the base of family-owned Wolf Creek are limited: the ticket office, a cafeteria and bar, a restaurant, restrooms, a tiny ski shop and an even tinier rental shop. But Wolf Creek has a wonderful feel to it. In the cafeteria you'll enjoy homemade soups served from crockpots, and fresh egg salad sandwiches rather than frozen production-line, hockey-puck burgers. On sunny days the patio is popular, and brown-bagging is welcome.

Holy Moses, visible from the lift, only begins to give advanced skiers and riders a taste of what's available. For an even bigger taste, try black-diamonds Prospector and Glory Hole. The Waterfall area is served by the new Alberta Lift (formerly served by snowcat). To access the gates leading here, ride Treasure Chair, then follow Navajo Trail or shortcut down lower Glory Hole. Stay slightly skier's right to get to Alberta Lift, which serves only expert terrain off Knife Ridge. The only other way to reach the intermediate Burn Area farther down the bowl is Park Avenue, an intermediate run that's available as an escape route. A bit of hiking will take extreme skiers and riders over to Horseshoe Bowl, the resort's eastern-most bowl.

Advanced-intermediates should head for Silver Streak, Treasure, Alberta and Tranquility off Treasure Chair. Lower-level intermediates will enjoy trails like Charisma, Powder Puff and Windjammer off Bonanza chair. Snowboarders: Don't bother looking for a halfpipe and terrain park, you won't find one. Take advantage of the natural terrain features instead. Beginners should stick to Dickey Chair and either Bunny Hop or Kelly Boyce trails. Never-evers have a magic carpet and beginner's lift in front of the lodge.

We suggest you stay in either South Fork or, preferably, Pagosa Springs. As in Pagosa Hot Springs. Once you get past the slight sulfur smell, Pagosa's 11 different pools, all at different temperatures, are about the finest apres-ski experience there is. They're on the river, suitable for an icy plunge to make your skin tingle. Pagosa Springs has an old-world charm that's hard to describe. And it's inexpensive compared to destination resorts.

Lift tickets (2001/02): Adults, $42; children younger than 12 and seniors 65 and older, $25.
Driving distances: From Durango, 72 miles east on Highway 160; from Pagosa Springs, 23 miles; from South Fork, 18 miles. You'll need a 4WD vehicle to get to the mountain.
Lodging information: The resort does not have lodging and it doesn't handle lodging reservations, but you'll find a complete listing of nearby accommodations on the resort Web site. Other resources: Pagosa Springs Chamber, 800-252-2204 or www.pagosaspringschamber.com; South Fork Business Association, 800-571-0881 or www.southfork.org/lodging.

Steamboat

Colorado

Summit elevation:	**10,568 feet**
Vertical drop:	**3,668 feet**
Base elevation:	**6,900 feet**

Address: 2305 Mt. Werner Circle
Steamboat Springs, CO 80487
✆ **Area code:** 970
Ski area phone: 879-6111
Snow report: 879-7300
ⓘ **Toll-free reservations:** (800) 922-2722
Fax: 879-4757
E-mail: info@steamboat-ski.com
Internet: www.steamboat.com
Expert:★★★
Advanced:★★★★
Intermediate:★★★★★
Beginner:★★
Never-ever:★★

Number and types of lifts: 20–1 gondola,
4 high-speed quads, 1 quad, 6 triples,
6 doubles, 2 surface lifts
Skiable acreage: 2,939 acres
Snowmaking: 15 percent
Uphill capacity: 36,195 per hour
Snowboarding: Yes
Bed base: 18,306
Nearest lodging: Slopeside
Resort child care: Yes, 6 months and older
Adult ticket, per day: $59-$64 (2002/03)
Dining:★★★★
Apres-ski/nightlife:★★★
Other activities:★★★★★

Steamboat's ad campaign would have you believe that horses outnumber the cars in its parking lot, that cowboy hats and sheepskin jackets are the preferred ski wear and that you trip over Lone Star longnecks on the dance floors. In reality, this is a big, sleek, modern ski area with more microbrews and gourmet coffees than spittoons. It had more than 1 million skier/rider visits last season.

Steamboat Mountain Village, the cluster of condos, shops and restaurants next to the mountain, is unpretentiously upscale. Boutiques offer elegant high-priced goods intermixed with T-shirt shops; gourmet restaurants are within steps of ribs-and-hamburger eateries. An occasional socialite swathed in fur passes, but right behind her will be someone wearing a 15-year-old ski parka. Everyone looks right at home.

In the village, the only cowboy hats you're likely to see grace the heads of Steamboat's resident celebrity, Billy Kidd, and the ticket punchers in the gondola building. Venture into downtown Steamboat Springs, though, and you may see cowboys sauntering down Lincoln Avenue. Northwest Colorado still has cattle ranches, so they'll probably be the real thing.

The downtown area—about five minutes by car and 15 minutes by a free shuttlebus from the village—squeezes into its dozen blocks a hodgepodge of old Victorian buildings, 1950s storefronts and a gas station or hardware store here and there. Good restaurants and nightlife hideouts are at the village, downtown, and on the highway linking the two. The bus runs between slopes and town every 20 minutes, making it easy to enjoy the village, town and everything in between.

Steamboat is also a great place for non-skiers. In addition to great shopping, it has activities that go beyond the usual sleigh rides and snowmobile tours (see *Other Activities*). There's even a Starbucks in the Sheraton.

Mountain layout—Skiing

◆◆ **Expert** ◆ **Advanced:** There are a handful of double-diamond stashes here, but they're short and totally do-able. Expert descents here mean trees, bumps in trees, and short and sweet bump runs. The runs from the Sundown Express chair are tree skiing and riding developed to an art—all have been expertly thinned, both by humans and Mother Nature. Some trees are only about 10 feet apart, so stay alert. Such trails—natural slalom courses where the poles aren't spring-loaded—produce gallons of adrenaline even for the best skiers.

Other tough areas are off The Ridge to the north of Storm Peak. After a short hike along Over Easy, the double-diamond challenges are provided by Chutes 1, 2 and 3, No Name Chutes, the Christmas Tree Bowl, and other descents. The top of Morningside lift opens up expert skiing, but the runs are frustratingly short and end up in a long runout to the lift.

Morningside Park consists of 179 acres of intermediate and advanced terrain on the backside of Storm Peak. The 260 acres that make up Pioneer Ridge, off the Pony Express lift below the mid-mountain chairs, have gained a local fan club with long, winding and pinball-machine-style runs. It's fun because Steamboat shied away from the straight-down cut and went with the terrain angles here. It's black-diamond territory, but easy black diamond.

In Steamboat, glades abound: Don't be shy about ducking into places like the space between Concentration and Vagabond or the "Twisticane" trees between Twister and Hurricane. Once you start looking, you'll see that the entire mountain is one big skiable forest.

■ **Intermediate:** Among the great cruisers are the blue trails from the Sunshine Chair (locals call this area "Wally World"), Sunset and Rainbow off the Four Points lift and Vagabond and Heavenly Daze off Thunderhead Express. The Sunshine Chair blues also have spots where beginning tree skiers can practice. If crowds build in any of those areas, take laps on the intermediate runs reached by the Bashor and Christie chairs, which often are deserted.

Longhorn, off Pioneer Ridge, is a locals' favorite with unparalleled views of the Yampa Valley. Skiers and riders can duck in and out of the lodgepole pines that border both sides of this run as they cruise off the Pony Express lift to the base of the Storm Peak Express lift.

Though the terrain has steep spots and the moguls get pretty high, the trails are generally wide, allowing room for mistakes and recoveries. Westside, a trail below Rendezvous Saddle, is steep but usually groomed. It's a good starting point for intermediates who wonder if they can handle the other black runs. If you're learning to do moguls, head for Concentration or Surprise. Often half of these runs are groomed, while the other half is left to build bumps.

●● **Beginner:** With the exception of some gentle terrain served by the Bashor and the two Christie chairs, most of the green trails above the base area are cat trails. Wally World's gentle runs often attract classes, though, and you have to forgive skiers and riders who can't turn and stop. Many of the green runs feel narrow at times. Some intersect higher-ability runs where bombers sometimes use the intersection as a launching pad for the next section, and a few have slightly intimidating drop-offs on the downhill side. If beginners are part of your group, encourage them to enroll in a clinic so they will have a pleasant experience.

● **Never-ever:** A successful first-time experience—especially for adults—depends on two things: great instruction and suitable, uncrowded terrain. In the past, we've said Steamboat rates highly on the former, but not on the latter. However, the resort has re-shaped the learn-to-ski terrain and improved the grade of the slope and fall line. The new terrain, at the base of the mountain and separated from other traffic, lets novices totally concentrate on the fun. The Filly moving carpet in the Preview Area is double last year's length.

Mountain layout—Snowboarding

Steamboat's renowned light-as-champagne powder, which seems to fall in well-timed weekly accumulations, makes this a tree-boarders paradise. Shadows, with its steady pitch and widely spaced aspen trees, is arguably the most perfect tree run in Colorado. And the new Pioneer Ridge expansion, below Storm Peak, invites exploration, although the long run-out makes a little hiking likely. When the pow blows out (*as if*) ride "The Bashor Terrain Park," Steamboat's terrain park, or enter The Twilight Zone, a difficult glade run studded with moguls. If you're lucky, you might run into Banana George Blair, Steamboat's 80-something snowboard ambassador and barefoot water skier extraordinaire. Always clad in yellow, Banana was extreme before the term was coined, and he's cooler than you, so share the love. Another local, Sherman Popper, invented the Snurfer in 1965 and is considered the "Grandfather of Snowboarding." He rides about a day per year for each year of his age, currently 74.

Mavericks Superpipe was a big hit last season. It's currently the longest superpipe (measuring 675 feet long, 50 feet wide and 15 feet high) on the continent, according to the resort, and this season celebrates the installation of a mega music system and increased snowmaking so the pipe can open in December. The mountain also has two terrain parks and a quarter-pipe.

For beginning snowboarders, there's a new moving carpet in the expanded learning area. The resort re-shaped the learning terrain last season, improving the grade of the slope and fall line. The learning area, at the base of the mountain and separated from other traffic, lets novices totally concentrate on the fun.

Mountain rating

Excellent tree skiing for experts, nice mogul runs for advanced, great cruisers for intermediates. Improvements to the learning area make it better for beginners and never-evers now.

Cross-country and snowshoeing

The **Steamboat Ski Touring Center** (879-8180) at 2000 Clubhouse Drive has about 30 km. of groomed set tracks winding along Fish Creek and the surrounding countryside. The touring center has group and private instruction, rentals and backcountry guided tours. Snowshoeing also is available on 8 km. of trails.

Steamboat offers on-mountain snowshoe tours that meet each Monday through Saturday from the top of the Gondola and are guided by the Mountain Ambassadors. Bring your own shoes or rent from Steamboat Ski Rentals (879-6111).

Track skiing is available at **Howelsen Hill** in downtown Steamboat Springs (879-8499) and at **Vista Verde** (879-3858; 800-526-7433), **High Meadows Ranch** (736-8416; 800-457-4453) and **Home Ranch** (879-1780), all guest ranches 18–25 miles from Steamboat Springs. The latter trio cater to overnight guests, but day visitors also are welcome. Vista Verde's 30-km. system is especially good for beginners—most of the terrain is quite gentle. High Meadows grooms about 12 km., with additional trails groomed as needed. Home Ranch has 40 km. of groomed track, and it offers cross-country, backcountry and telemarking.

For a real thrill, take a tour to **Rabbit Ears Pass** (guided tours available through Steamboat Touring Center and Ski Haus, 879-0385); you'll be skiing on the Continental Divide. The marked backcountry ski trails range from 1.7 to 7 miles, from relatively gentle slopes to steep and gnarly, but on a clear day you can see forever. Call or visit the **U.S. Forest Service** (29587 W. US 40 in Steamboat Springs, 879-1722) to get current ski conditions and safety tips. Other popular backcountry areas are **Buffalo Pass, Pearl Lake State Park, Stagecoach State Recreation Area** and **Steamboat Lake State Park.**

Lessons (2002/03 prices)

Group lessons: Lessons cost $53 for a half-day and $68 for all day.
Never-ever package: All-day lesson, lift and rental package for skiers and snowboarders costs $86; a three-day package costs $195. Half-day lesson, lift and rental package costs $81. The resort allows novices to repeat the first lesson at no charge until they've learned to descend from the Preview lift in a controlled manner.

Private lessons: $150 for one hour, $225 for two, $235 for a half-day/afternoon, $275 for a half-day/morning, $430 for all day. Reservations required; call (800) 299-5017.

Special programs: First Tracks, Bumps, and Parks & Pipe clinics last from 1.5 to three hours and cost $35–53. Women's programs are offered as one-day (Jan. 4, Feb. 1 and March 1) for $110, or three-day (Dec. 17-20, Jan. 14-16, Feb. 11-13 and March 11-13) for $330.

Racing: Steamboat is the home to 54 Olympic and world medalists, so it's a natural for racing and competition programs. Steamboat has a course open most days from 10:30 a.m. to 12:30 p.m. for $5, with each additional run $1. A dual "pro race" format course also is available 9:30 a.m. to 3:30 p.m. at $1 per run. Both courses are in the Bashor area.

Steamboat also has the Billy Kidd Performance Center, which offers two- and three-day camps for adults who are at least of intermediate ability. The camps refine technique in the bumps, through race gates and on tough terrain. Two-day camps (Thursday/Friday) and three-day camps (Monday-Wednesday) are $199 per day.

Child care (2002/03 prices)

Ages: 6 months to kindergarten (usually age 5).
Costs: $81 all day (lunch included) or $61 half day. Multiday discounts are available. Parents must provide lunch for kids younger than 18 months.

Reservations: Required for all care programs, and must be prepaid. Cancellations must be 24 hours in advance to avoid being charged. Call the Kids' Vacation Center, 879-6111 or (800) 299-5017.

Note: Steamboat's children's programs have been very highly rated over the years by various magazines. The resort offers numerous, supervised evening programs for children and teens, cost is $36 per child. Call or visit the Web site for details.

Other options: Baby's Away (800-978-9030; 879-2354) rents and will deliver baby needs to your lodge, such as crib, stroller, car seat and toys.

Children's lessons: Ages 2–5 can opt for a one-hour private lesson and all-day child care for $181, including lunch. Ages 3–5 who want more time on snow can take all-day clinics that have two to four hours on snow plus playtime for $81, including lunch. Ages 6–15 pay $80 for an all-day lesson (including lunch), or $53 for a 2.5-hour afternoon lesson. Classes are grouped according to age and ability. Ages 13–17 who are at the intermediate level or higher can join the "Steamboat Teens" program offered each day Dec. 21, 2002, to Jan. 5, 2003, and again from Feb. 14 to April 6, 2003. The cost is $80 per day, with lunch; multiday discounts available. Children and teens also have a Ski and Snowboard Week program for $375. Their lessons are all day and lunches are included. Kids stay with the same instructor the entire week. Lift tickets are extra for all programs listed here. Steamboat also has the Billy Kidd Performance Center, which offers two- and three-day camps for teens and kids who are at least of intermediate ability. The camps refine technique in the bumps, through race gates and on tough terrain; $199 per day.

Lift tickets (2002/03 prices)

	Adult	Child (6 to 12)
One day	$64	$39
Three days	$186 ($62/day)	$117 ($39/day)
Five days	$295 ($59/day)	$195 ($39/day)

Who skis free: Children 5 and younger. One child up to age 12 skis free the same number of days as his or her parent when the parent buys a five-day or longer lift ticket. Two kids, two parents, both kids ski free. Three kids, two parents, the third kid buys a ticket at $39 a day. No blackout periods, even during Christmas. Children must bring proof of age.

Who skis at a discount: Teens 13–18 ride lifts for $57 a day for up to four days; five or more days, teens pay $52 per day; ID required. Ages 65–69 pay $40 per day; ID required. Ages 70 and older pay $20; ID required. Early- and late-season prices are less for adults, children and teens.

Accommodations

In general, staying in Steamboat Mountain Village is more expensive than in town. Condos outnumber hotel and motel rooms. Rates vary throughout the season. Before mid-December and after March 31 are cheapest; January comes next, and Christmas and Presidents' Weekend are most expensive.

Steamboat Central Reservations (800-922-2722 or 879-0740; fax, 879-4757; www.steamboat.com) will match your needs and desires. Let the reservationist know the price range, location and room requirements (quiet location, good for families, laundry or other special amenities).

The Sheraton Steamboat Resort and Conference Center (800-848-8878, 800-848-8877 in Colorado, 879-2220; $$-$$$), a luxury full-service hotel, sits 60 feet from the Steamboat Gondola. Rooms were recently renovated, with more to come, plus its Morningside tower condominiums opened a few seasons ago. You'll find two- to four-bedroom units.

The newly built $80-million **Steamboat Grand Resort Hotel and Conference Center** (877-269-2628 or 871-5500, fax 871-5501; $$$-$$$$) is across from Gondola Square. There are studios to three bedrooms and penthouses, all Western-themed. Rooms have VCRs, pay movies and CD players. There is on-site childcare with activities, a heated pool and a spa.

Nearly all the other lodging at the ski area is in condominiums—hundreds of them surrounding the base. **Torian Plum** (879-8811 or 800-228-2458; $$$-$$$$) has spotless rooms and facilities, an extremely helpful staff, the ski area out one door and the top bars and restaurants out the other. Torian Plum's sister properties, **Bronze Tree** and **Trappeur's Crossing,** have similar prices. Bronze Tree has two- and three-bedroom units. Trappeur's Crossing is about two blocks from the lifts, but offers a free private shuttle from 7 a.m. to 11 p.m. **Timberline** at Trappeur's Crossing and **Creekside** at Torian Plum (800-228-2458 or 879-8811, fax 879-8485) have mountain-facing views and the ski-in/ski-out at Creekside.

Generally, prices are based on how close the property is to the lifts. Among those in the expensive category are the **Best Western Ptarmigan Inn** (800-538-7519 or 879-1730; $$$) at the base of the Gondola, **Storm Meadows Townhomes** (800-262-5150 or 879-5151; $$$), **Norwegian Log Condominiums** (800-525-2622 or 879-3700; $$$) and **Thunderhead Lodge and Condominiums** (800-525-5502 or 879-9000; $$$).

Others in this price category are **Timber Run Condominiums** (800-525-5502 or 879-7000; $$$) with three outdoor hot tubs of varying sizes; **the Harbor Hotel** in downtown Steamboat (800-543-8888, 800-334-1012 in Colorado, 879-1522; $$$) that includes a free bus pass; **The Lodge at Steamboat** (800-525-5502 or 879-6000; $$$); and **The Ranch at Steamboat** (800-525-2002 or 879-3000; $$$), with great views of the ski hill and the valley.

Economy lodging includes **Alpiner Lodge** (800-538-7519 or 879-1430; $$) downtown, **Shadow Run Condominiums** (800-525-2622 or 879-3700; $$) 500 yards from lifts, and **Alpine Meadows Townhomes** (800-525-2622 or 879-3700; $$), just a bit further.

The Steamboat Bed and Breakfast (879-5724; $$$), just a few years old, is at 442 Pine St. This B&B has rooms filled with antiques. Rates include breakfast. No children or pets allowed. **Caroline's Bed and Breakfast** (870-1696; $$), 838 Merritt St., is another good choice for those who like B&Bs.

Travelers who enjoy remote rural elegance will be delighted by a stay at **The Home Ranch** (879-1780; $$$$) in the town of Clark, a 40-minute drive up the Elk River Valley north of Steamboat. This is one of a handful of Relais et Chateaux properties in the U.S. Eight wooden cabins are nestled in the aspens of the Elk River Valley, with views of Hahn's Peak. Each is distinctly decorated and has a hot tub on the porch and a wood stove inside. The main lodge also has six guestrooms, and is where everyone is served three gourmet meals per day. Rates include lift tickets and a shuttle to the ski area, though many people will be happy exploring the cross-country and snowshoe trails at the ranch.

Between town and the mountain is the pleasant **Iron Horse Inn** (879-6505, fax 879-6129; $$) offering recently renovated suites with kitchenettes (small but functional) and a two-story building of clean and comfortable hotel rooms.

Some chain motels have shown up in the last couple of years. They're generally scattered in a row along Hwy. 40 just before the turnoff to the mountain. The newest is the **Fairfield Inn & Suites** (870-9000, fax 870-9191; $$). Sixty-five no-frills rooms are located a half-mile from Gondola Square on the free bus route. You'll find the 20-year-old **Holiday Inn Hotel & Suites** (824-4000; $$), as well as the newer **Inn at Steamboat** (879-2600, fax 879-9270; $$), **Bunkhouse Lodge** (871-9121, fax 871-9072; $$), and the **Super 8 Motel** (879-5230, fax 879-3341; $$). Of course you can decide to say in the world-famous **Rabbit Ears Motel** (800-828-7702 or 879-1150, fax 870-0483; $$) on Lincoln Ave. right downtown.

Another option out of town is **Strawberry Park Hot Springs Cabins** (879-0342; $), about 10 miles north of Steamboat at the hot mineral springs. Covered wagons and cabins are both available for overnight stays. Lodging price includes a hot springs pass. Also on the road to the hot springs, 6 miles from the ski area, are the **Steamboat Log Cabins** (879-1060; $$) at Perry-Mansfield, complete with kitchens and woodburning stoves.

 Dining

Steamboat has a great variety of restaurants. The area has more than 70 restaurants, including one or more Cajun, Chinese, French, Italian, and Scandinavian. Look for the Steamboat Dining Guide—it has menus and prices.

Set off in the gondola on a journey into the stars to **Hazie's** (879-6111; reservations required for dinner, available Thursdays through Saturdays; $$$) at the top of Thunderhead. Hazie's serves a special continental dinner, with unbeatable views. You can also have lunch (reservations recommended) daily from 11:30 a.m. to 2:30 p.m., featuring an assortment of soups and salads, entrées and burgers.

For elegant dining, it's hard to beat **The Cabin** (871-5550; $$$), on the lobby level of the Steamboat Grand. It features contemporary Colorado cuisine for breakfast and dinner, specializing in steaks and chops. The Cabin recently was awarded the 2002 *Wine Spectator* "Award of Excellence" for its wine list.

Ragnar's (879-6111; reservations for lunch suggested; $$–$$$) at Rendezvous Saddle halfway down the High Noon ski run features Scandinavian and continental cuisine. Start with the baked Camembert tivoli or gravlax with mustard dill sauce. Or, perhaps, try the excellent Norwegian salad with proscuitto. Entrées include daily specials. Three nights a week (Thursday through Saturday), Ragnar's offers a fixed-price Scandinavian menu at $69 (2001/02 price) for adults. This evening also starts at Gondola Square, but once off the Gondola at the top of Thunderhead, you climb into a sleigh to continue your journey to Rendezvous Saddle. Reservations are required at night.

Western BBQ Nights (871-5150; reservations required; $$$), Thursday through Saturday, feature live country-western entertainment, dancing, an all-you-can-eat buffet and a full cash bar, all on the third floor of the Thunderhead Building.

For Steamboat's pinnacle of French dining, try **L'Apogee** (911 Lincoln Avenue, 879-1919; $$$). While the food cannot be too highly praised, it is the wine list that is truly impressive. There are more than 500 wines, ranging from $12 to $1,000 a bottle, all maintained in three temperature-controlled cellars.

This crew also services the more casual **Harwig's Grill** (same address, no reservations; $–$$). Here, the menu reflects a passion for Southeast Asian flavors. Accompanying the selection of appetizers and entrées is a list of 60 very affordable wines. Open daily from 5 p.m.

Another fine-dining choice is **Antares** (57-1/2 Eighth St., 879-9939; $$$). Not coincidentally, all the principals are alums from L'Apogee. Serving new American cuisine, this restaurant—named for a star in the Scorpio constellation—is housed in the historic Rehder building, built in the early 1900s. Open daily 5:30 p.m. to 10:30 p.m.

For more than Mex, **La Montaña,** (2500 Village Drive, 879-5800; $$–$$$) goes way beyond tacos and fajitas. Their irresistible guacamole sauce is the house special.

Chef Michael Fragola (formerly of La Montaña) has started his own fine-dining restaurant, the **Cottonwood Grill** (701 Yampa Aveune, 879-2229; $$-$$$). Downtown on the Yampa River, Fragola features vibrant Pacific Rim Cuisine blending American and Asian flavors.

The **Steamboat Smokehouse** (912 Lincoln Ave.; $–$$) has a no-credit card, no-reservations, no-nonsense atmosphere, with some of Colorado's best Texas-style hickory-smoked barbecued anything—you name it—brisket, sausage, turkey, chicken, ham and more. We love that we can toss our peanut shells on the floor and the beer mugs are iced.

A popular seafood restaurant is the **Steamboat Yacht Club** (811 Yampa Ave., 879-4774; $$). The dining room overlooking the river is perfect for watching night skiing or Wednesday night ski jumping on Howelsen Hill. Its menu is designed to mix and match fish, cooking techniques and sauces to suit your tastes. The Yacht Club also serves meat and poultry, and is one of the best restaurants for the price in town.

The **Rendezvous Saddle** building, halfway down the High Noon ski run, has a two-level contemporary food court and large ground level deck where you can get BBQ. **Stoker Bar** (871-5150; $-$$), on the first floor of the Thunderhead Building (at the top of the Gondola), has full-service lunch of soups, chile, sandwiches, micro beers and specialty drinks. The **Bear River Bar & Grill** (formerly known as Buddy's Run), at the base across from the Gondola bay entrance, has very quickly gotten very popular.

Dining: $$$-Entrees $20+; $$-$10-20; $-less than $10.
Accommodations: (double room) $$$$-$200+; $$$-$141-$200; $$-$81-$140; $-$80 and less.

Dos Amigos (879-4270; $$) serves Tex-Mex food and sandwiches and is part of the infamous "Steamboat Triangle" après-ski circuit along with **Tugboat Grill & Pub** ($-$$) and **Slopeside** ($$). **Grubstake** (879-4448; $) serves hamburgers and steak sandwiches. **Café Diva** (871-0508; $$) is a wine bar in the Torian Plum Plaza that serves meals.

Swiss Haven (871-1761; $$) serves all kinds of fondues, raclette and traditional Alpine fare. You'll find it downtown next to the Harbor Hotel. **Old West Steakhouse** (879-1441; $$) is somewhat expensive, but has packed the crowds in for years with its generous portions of steak and seafood. You easily could make a meal out of the appetizers.

Giovanni's (879-4141; $$) has not only Brooklyn-style Italian fare, but also what may be the largest collection of Brooklyn memorabilia this side of the borough. For more moderate Italian, head to **Riggio's** (879-9010; $$) on Lincoln. Seafood and veal are especially good, and be sure to leave room for their homemade desserts.

Ore House at the Pine Grove (879-1441; $$) is a Steamboat tradition serving steaks, seafood, elk and buffalo for more than a quarter-century. **Yama-Chans** (879-8862; $$) is Steamboat's first Japanese restaurant and sushi bar. It's always doing a booming business. **The Cantina** (879-0826; $$), Steamboat's original Mexican food restaurant, has a fun bar and a decent restaurant. **Cugino's** (879-5805; $) makes a fine pizza.

If you're in town for breakfast or lunch, try the **Creekside Café and Grill** (879-4925; $). Homemade soup, sandwiches and salads are served along with soothing classical music. For some quiet-time and a light lunch (sandwiches, homemade pasta salads and soups) head to **Off The Beaten Path** bookstore and coffeehouse (879-6830; $).

Good breakfast spots are **Winona's**, where the lines form early and often, or **The Shack Café**, both downtown, or **The Tugboat Grill & Pub** at the base area. Also try **Market on the Mountain**, in the same complex as La Montaña, for homemade muffins, cinnamon rolls and bagels for breakfast and deli sandwiches; or **Mocha Molly's**, serving muffins, bagels and designer coffees at both the ski area base and in town. Avid skiers can board the gondola at 8:15 a.m. and have breakfast at **The Early Bird Breakfast Buffet** at the top of the gondola until the slopes open. Biscuits and gravy are a specialty, with other high-fuel fare also served, cafeteria-style.

Après-ski/nightlife

Dos Amigos, as already noted, is one leg of the "Steamboat Triangle." Have margaritas here, then head for **Slopeside** and **The Tugboat Grill & Pub** for beer or mixed drinks. **Chaps**, in the Steamboat Grand, is a Western-themed bar and grill with live entertainment most evenings throughout the winter. **The Bear River Comedy Club** (871-5150) features comedians from Comedy Works in Denver on Friday and Saturday nights; an appetizer buffet is served. Doors open at 7:45 p.m., the show starts at 8:30 p.m. Downtown, the **Old Town Pub** and **The Steamboat Yacht Club** have great-après ski.

A quieter après-ski on the mountain can be found at **Three Saddles** in the Sheraton. Three Saddles, the former HB's, had a makeover a few years ago and is a wide-open, great-view kind of place now.

Steamboat has a single brew pub—the **Steamboat Brewery & Tavern** downtown. **Dos Amigos, Levels, Slopeside, The Bear** and the **Tugboat Grill & Pub** bring in the bands and the crowds. Downtown, the lively spots include **The Tap House**, the **Steamboat Smokehouse** and **The Old Town Pub**. You might also check out **The Cellar Lounge** (formerly Murphy's) for good times late at night.

Other activities

Steamboat has so much to do off the mountain, it's tempting to skip the skiing. Here is a mere sampling:

Soak in the natural thermal waters at **Strawberry Park Hot Springs** (879-0342), about 10 miles north of the ski area. Admission to the hot springs is $5 weekdays to 5 p.m., $3 for ages 3-12; after 5 p.m. on weekends adults pay $10; a tour (transportation and admission) is $30. Unless you have four-wheel drive, spend the extra for the tour—the road to the springs is narrow, slick, steep and winding, and parking is extremely limited. It's open from 10 a.m. to 10 p.m. during the week and stays open a little later on weekends. Helpful info: After dark, many bathers go without suits (unless it's a moonlit night, you won't see much), and Wednesdays are often designated as "clothing optional" days/nights. The only place to change is an unheated teepee, so wear your swimsuit under your clothes. Many people bring a plastic bag to store their clothes; otherwise steam from the pools combined with the cold air may freeze them. Water shoes will protect your feet from the rocky entry. Beverages are OK as long as they aren't in a glass container.

Families might prefer the **Steamboat Health and Recreation Center** (879-1828) downtown, with workout rooms and hot springs pools, and a water slide that kids enjoy.

Learn to drive on slick roads at the **Bridgestone Winter Driving School** (879-6104 or 800-WHY-SKID). Half-day ($145), full-day ($275) and multiday lessons on a specially constructed course are a unique experience, one that could save your life. Three of our contributors have taken the course, and all give it their highest recommendation.

Other activities include weekend **theater** from the Steamboat Community Players (879-3254), **dogsled rides** (879-4662), **backcountry snowcat skiing/riding** (879-5188), **ice skating** at Howelsen Ice Arena (879-0341), **ice climbing** (879-4857), **indoor climbing** (879-5421), **indoor tennis** (879-8400), guided **snowshoe hiking** with a gourmet lunch, **snomobile touring, tubing, horseback riding** and **hot-air balloons** (several businesses offer these last two activities, ask when you get into town), and far too many more to list.

You can make reservations for activities through **Steamboat Central Reservations** (879-0740 or 800-922-2722), or **Windwalker Premier Tours** (879-8065; 800-748-1642).

Shopping opportunities are many and varied, both in the village and downtown. Steamboat's **movie theaters** are downtown and at the mountain. Other resort services include **grocery delivery** to your unit before your arrival. **The Sports Stalker** (879-0371) at Gondola Square rents ski clothes, mainly courtesy of the airline that lost your luggage.

Getting there and getting around

By air: Yampa Valley Airport at Hayden, 22 miles away, handles jets. American, Continental, United and Northwest have direct or nonstop flights from more than 100 North American cities. Three transportation companies provide service from the airport and from Denver International Airport—Alpine Taxi/Limo, 879-2800; Western Coach 4x4 Limo, 870-0771, and Mountain Luxury Limousine, 879-0077. Avis, Budget and Hertz have cars available at the Yampa Valley Airport.

By car: Steamboat is 157 miles northwest of Denver. Take I-70 west through the Eisenhower Tunnel to exit 205 at Silverthorne (allow extra time if you want to stop at the factory outlet malls), north on Hwy. 9 to Kremmling, then west on Hwy. 40 to the resort.

Getting around: A car is optional. Steamboat has an excellent free bus system between town and ski area running every 20 minutes. Call 879-5585 for information.

Dining: $$$-Entrees $20+; $$-$10-20; $-less than $10.
Accommodations: (double room) $$$$-$200+; $$$-$141-$200; $$-$81-$140; $-$80 and less.

Telluride

Colorado

Summit elevation:	**12,260 feet**
Vertical drop:	**3,535 feet**
Base elevation:	**8,725 feet**

Address: 565 Mountain Village Boulevard, Telluride, CO 81435
✆ Area code: 970
Ski area phone: 728-6900
Snow report: 728-7425
ⓘ Toll-free reservations: (866) 287-5016
Fax: 728-6228
E-mail: skitelluride@telski.com
Internet:: www.tellurideskiresort.com (ski area)
www.telluride.com (visitors guide)

Number and types of lifts: 16–2 gondolas, 7 high-speed quads, 2 triples, 2 doubles, 2 surface lifts, 1 magic carpet
Skiable Acreage: 1,700 acres
Snowmaking: 15 percent
Uphill capacity: 20,286 per hour
Snowboarding: Yes
Bed base: 5,300
Nearest lodging: Slopeside
Resort child care: Yes, 2 months and older
Adult ticket, per day: $51-$65 (02/03)

Expert:★★★★★
Advanced:★★★★★
Intermediate:★★★★
Beginner:★★★★★
Never-ever:★★★★★

Dining:★★★★
Apres-ski/nightlife:★★★
Other activities:★★★

When Butch Cassidy robbed the Bank of Telluride more than 100 years ago during the town's celebrated mining heyday, he left the best treasure behind.

But then, it would be difficult to fit the town of Telluride and its slopes into a pair of saddle bags. Nestled in a box canyon 8,725 feet high in the jagged San Juan Mountains of southwestern Colorado, the town of Telluride is a neat pattern of streets eight blocks wide and 12 blocks long, miniaturized by massive 14,000-foot peaks tumbling into neighborhoods. On a sunny day, when those white-capped peaks and red-brick buildings pop out from the bluest sky you've ever seen, there are few places on earth more beautiful.

Telluride is in a delightful time warp—a nostalgic blend of the Old West captured in Victorian buildings you'd swear were a movie set, and all the civilized pleasures of a modern resort. When skiing replaced the mining industry in the early 1970s, it saved the tiny community from becoming a ghost town. It also paved the way for preservation of the entire town— a National Historic District—and the orderly development of a world-class ski resort.

Telluride also has a different face, built up on the mountain. This hamlet, called Mountain Village, offers excellent access to the mountain, but is quite different in look and feel. Mountain Village is a master-planned community anchored by what is considered the area's most luxurious hotel, The Wyndham Peaks at Telluride.

A 2.5-mile gondola links the town of Telluride with Mountain Village. This free "gondola transportation system"—as the resort calls it—operates seven days a week from 7 a.m. to midnight and makes commuting between the two towns for shopping or dining a snap. It also is used as a lift to the slopes, but you need a lift ticket to ski.

Though Telluride's early reputation was a place dedicated to steeps, it has added terrain that has transformed it into one of the nation's best learning slopes. Last season the resort installed three new high-speed lifts in Prospect Bowl, adding 733 acres of above-treeline thrills and world-class views along with glades, bowls and trails. The new expansion unites Prospect Bowl and the Gold Hill area with the rest of the mountain and nearly doubles the resort's lift-served terrain.

 ## Mountain layout—Skiing

◆◆ **Expert:** Start with what put Telluride on the skiers' map—The Plunge and Spiral Stairs. This duo is as challenging a combination of steep bumps as you can find anywhere. The left half of The Plunge is now normally groomed. If you manage to get down without too many bruises or sore spots, you can savor a sense of accomplishment. Mammoth is an alternate trail but not any easier.

Another good area for experts is the 450 acres of glade and above-timberline skiing in the Gold Hill area. These double-diamond runs are now lift-served to the 12,260-foot mark, which makes Telluride's legal vertical drop 3,535 feet. If it's a clear day after a powder dump, take a nanosecond to admire the view from the summit before you plunge in. It is magnificent. And, of course, you'll want to check out the new lift-served areas of Prospect Bowl.

◆ **Advanced:** Telluride uses a winch cat to "split-groom" (meaning half is smooth and half is left to build bumps) some of the runs on the front face. The Plunge is normally split-groomed, creating one of the steepest and most daringly exciting snow highways we've seen. Bushwacker's normally monstrous bumps were merely huge, thanks to a grooming a few days earlier. While some highly accomplished skiers may mourn this development, the face still has plenty of terrain that mere advanced skiers won't touch, and at least now there are enough bodies riding Chair 9 to justify the electric bill.

■ **Intermediate:** Telluride used to have little to offer intermediates, but the addition of Prospect Bowl thankfully addresses this. See Forever is a long glide down the mountain—nearly 3 miles top to bottom. True intermediate terrain is under Lift 5 (Palmyra) and Lift 4 (Misty Maiden), but the Telluride Face with its occasional grooming is now acceptable for strong intermediates looking to rise to the next level.

The most fun for an intermediate would be repeated trips up Lift 4, and down Peek-a-Boo, Humboldt Draw, Pick and Gad and Tomboy. The black-diamond runs off Lift 6 are short and you can assess from the chair whether you can handle them. If not, just head toward See Forever. The new Prospect Lift in Prospect Bowl adds terrain that is ideal for intermediates, including open bowls and gladed runs.

Just learning moguls? Head for the top of Lifts 4 for split-grooming and Lift 5, where you can practice, practice, practice before trying out The Face.

●● **Beginner:** Lift 10 is a perfect spot to develop confidence because the runs are long and very gentle, and no high-ability speed demons come here. With the addition of Ute Park—the new beginner training area in Prospect Bowl—Telluride is one of the top spots on the continent for this ability level.

For those looking to improve: Telluride divides its runs into six categories instead of three or four. One green circle is easiest, then double greens, then single blues, then double blues, single black and double black. This allows an easier progression for those still developing their skills.

● **Never-ever:** The Meadows, served by a Chondola (a hybrid high-speed quad with gondola cars also on the cable), is as close to a perfect novice area as you will find.

Mountain layout—Snowboarding

Telluride's Air Garden Terrain Park has more than 11 acres and 480 vertical feet of berms, banks, spines, rails, mailboxes, quarterpipes, tombstones and tabletops. Get there by riding Lift 4 or the Gondola. The Launch Pad hangout is at the top of the halfpipe and offers riders a crankin' stereo system and excellent views of the park while taking a break. If you want, you can skip the manmade and head to Lift 9. East and West Drains form two natural halfpipes that are 2,000-feet and 4,000-feet long respectively. In addition, there's a 1,200-foot natural quarterpipe on Bushwhacker. Lift 9 provides more vertical than any other lift on the mountain, serving runs including The Plunge, a sick run visible from town.

For big powder days intermediate boarders will enjoy short and steep runs off Lift 5 including Dew Drop (look for hits), Ophir Loop and Silver Tip. Avoid Cake Walk when you're done riding this lift. Instead, ride it back to the top then stay rider's right and pick up Lift 6. You can then ride See Forever back to Mountain Village or the Gondola. For advanced gladed areas, Lift 6 is your best bet. Check out the trees between Alais Alley and Silver Glade. Too-flat runs for snowboarders to avoid include Bridges and Galloping Goose.

For riders addicted to bowl skiing and deep powder, Gold Hill offers the ultimate in big-board freeriding. Say *adios* to the 10- to 20-minute hike accessing Little Rose—it's now lift served. And so is the vast terrain in Prospect Bowl.

Mountain rating

Telluride is a rite of passage for experts. It's a chance to test oneself against consistent steeps and monstrous bumps. Telluride makes a serious effort to groom formerly expert slopes to make them advanced, and advanced slopes to put them within reach of intermediates trying to graduate to the advanced level. If you are an intermediate whose trademark trails are long, mellow cruising terrain, head elsewhere. For never-evers and beginners, there are few better places to be introduced to snow sports.

Cross-country and snowshoeing

Here again the spectacular scenery makes cross-country a joy to experience. For high-mesa cross-country skiing this area is difficult to beat. The **Telluride Nordic Center** (728-1144) offers a 30-km. network of groomed trails around town and the ski area.

Lessons are also available; group lessons meet daily at 11 a.m. at the center. If you'd like to ski the intermediate and advanced groomed trails at the top of Lift 10, buy a $20 ticket at the downhill ski area ticket windows. Adult and children's group lessons are priced at about $30; $38 with rentals. Full-day backcountry tours cost approximately $65. Equipment rentals—skis, boots and poles—for a full day are about $14 for adults and $9 for children.

Guided tours wind through the San Juan Mountains and a five-hut, 68-mile network of intermediate and advanced trails. Huts are approximately 6 miles apart and each is equipped with padded bunks, propane cooking appliances and a big potbelly stove. The same rates apply to all programs: about $22 per person cabin fee and $25 a day for provisions, which covers breakfast, lunch and dinner. Guides are available for groups, held to a maximum of eight skiers. Call the **San Juan Hut System** for rates: 728-6935.

Nearby is the **San Juan Guest Ranch** (626-5360; 800-331-3015), which accommodates overnight visitors. Day visitors also may use the trails. Usually, at least 12 km. are groomed, but sometimes additional kilometers are groomed if guests' needs warrant it. The ranch also offers ice climbing, backcountry touring and avalanche awareness training.

 ## Lessons (2002/03 prices)

Telluride's school has a good reputation. A successful learning experience requires two things: good instruction and appropriate terrain. Telluride has both. Clinics operate out of the Mountain Village Activity Center, a one-stop facility that has lift tickets, lessons, full-service rental shop, overnight equipment storage, children's ski school and child care. A computer system links Telluride Sports' six rental shops and stores client information permanently so future rentals can be paperwork-free and equipment can be returned to any shop.

Group lessons: All-day group lessons cost $80; two-hour morning clinics are $40.

Never-ever package: $95 for skiers or snowboarders, includes a full day of lessons, lifts and rentals. Nordic and telemark are offered only on certain days; call for specifics.

Private lessons: $180 for early bird or late riser; $300 half day; $490 full day.

Special programs: Many, including a highly acclaimed Women's Week program that offers lifts, races, video analysis, seminars, parties and more. A five-day session is $575. Call for dates; reservations required. Adaptive and telemark clinics also available; call for details and cost.

Racing: NASTAR two-hour clinics cost $40 or run the course for $3 per run or $9 for five runs. The course is near the Smuggler Express lift. A self-timed course is $1 per run.

 ## Child care (2001/02 prices)

Ages: 2 months to 3 years.

Costs: $70 for a full day with lunch, $60 for a half day.

Reservations: Required; call 728-7531 or (800) 801-4832 at least 24 hours in advance. Children's ski and day-care programs are in the Village Nursery and Children's Center in the Mountain Village Activity Center. The activity center's most unique design is the glass kiosk atop the nursery's central playroom, which allows parents to peer down at their little ones without being seen.

Children's lessons: The Children's Ski & Snowboard School teaches kids ages 3–12 (snowboard lessons are offered for kids 6–12). Lessons, lift and lunch are $90 a full day, with multiday discounts. With lessons, rentals cost an additional $15. Half-day lessons are available. A one-hour, one-on-one lesson is $60 available from 8:45–9:45 a.m. A supervised program called Adventure Club is available before and after ski school programs; it's free for those enrolled in ski school.

 ## Lift Tickets (2002/03 prices)

	Adult	Child (6-12)
One day	$65	$36
Three days	$195 ($65/day)	$108 ($36/day)
Five days	$299 ($59+/day)	$180 ($36/day)

Who skis free: Ages 5 and younger.

Who skis at a discount: Seniors ages 65–69 ski for $46. Ages 70 and older pay $31. Before Dec. 23, tickets are $51 for adults, $29 for kids, $36 for seniors 65–69, and $23 for ages 70+.

Accommodations

In Telluride you can stay down in the historic town or in the Mountain Village. We start with some of our favorite spots in town; lodging in the mountain village is listed at the end of this section. Some lodging prices include lift tickets. For more information on these and other places to stay, call **Telluride Central Reservations,** (888) 783-0257.

The **Franklin Manor** (888-728-3351; $$$–$$$$) specializes in romantic getaways. Named for artist Richard Franklin, the manor showcases his neo-classical works in a gallery and all five uniquely decorated bedrooms. **The San Sophia Bed & Breakfast** (800-537-4781; $$$–$$$$) is near the gondola and Lift 8. This cozy B&B is considered one of Telluride's best, with exceptional service.

A luxury spot to stay is **The Hotel Columbia** (800-201-9505 or 728-0660; $$$–$$$$) right at the Telluride base of the new gondola. The hotel was built to look historic, but with the space and amenities of modern hotel rooms, such as fireplaces, big beds, a rooftop hot tub and luxurious bathrooms. The hotel has an office for guests' use, equipped with fax, copier and computer.

The historic **New Sheridan Hotel** (800-200-1891 or 728-4351; $–$$$$) is a step back in time. It's on Colorado Avenue close to everything, with a shuttle stop for the resort outside the front door. **The Johnstone Inn** (728-3316 or 800-752-1901; $$–$$$$) is a B&B with eight small quaint rooms with private bath and a full breakfast every morning. **Bear Creek Bed & Breakfast** (728-6681 or 800-338-7064; $–$$$), in a brick building on Colorado Avenue, has 10 rooms with private bath and TV, roof deck, sauna and steam room.

The Ice House Lodge (800-544-3436 or 728-6300; $$$–$$$$), a block from the gondola, has 6-foot tubs, comforters, balconies, custom furniture, a continental breakfast and après-ski goodies. **The Camel's Garden** (888-772-2635 or 728-9300; $$$$) was opened in 1998 in the gondola plaza. In stark contrast to the town's prevalent Victorian theme, this contemporary luxury property has underground parking and a small conference space.

The elegant and intimate **Hotel Telluride** (866-468-3501 or 369-1188; $$$–$$$$), on the western edge of town, opened in September 2001. Prepare to be pampered here, from the featherbed and down comforter for a peaceful night's sleep to the granite countertops and Italian tile in the bathrooms. A full-service spa is on the premises, as well as a bistro.

The **Manitou Bed & Breakfast** ($$$) is decorated with country fabrics and antiques. It is near the gondola and is a two-minute walk from the town center. Each room has a double bed. **The Riverside Condos** are perhaps the nicest in town and near the base of the gondola. **The Manitou Riverhouse** is just as close to the lifts, but be ready for lots of stairs if you rent here. Around the Coonskin Base check into **Viking Lodge, Etta Place** and **Cimarron Lodge,** where you can almost literally fall out of bed and onto the lifts. More moderately priced units are **West Willow** and **Coronet Creek.** All the properties in this paragraph (and others not listed) are managed by **ResortQuest at Telluride,** (800) 538-7754 (LETS-SKI). The central check-in desk can get backed up at times—if you are traveling with young children, or need to get into your condo right away for other reasons, discuss that with the reservations agent at the time of booking.

In the Mountain Village

The most luxurious property is **The Wyndham Peaks at Telluride** (800-789-2220 or 728-6800; $$$$). This ski-in/ski-out resort hotel boasts one of the largest full-service spas in the country. Rates include daily spa access.

The highly praised **Inn at Lost Creek** (888-601-5678 or 728-5678; www.innatlostcreek.com; $$$$) is a beautifully rustic, yet classic, slopeside lodge with 32 uniquely decorated rooms that include fireplaces, jetted tubs and steam showers, plus two roof-top hot tubs, topnotch guest service and the 9545 restaurant. The great room, crafted of native stone and weathered timber, is warmly inviting. Choose from studios to two-bedroom suites. **Aspen Ridge Condominiums** (800-324-6388; 728-4217) is another of the Mountain Village's newest luxury properties, offering three-bedroom condos with saunas, steam showers, hot tubs and fireplaces.

Mountain Village has many **condos,** some of which start at $200 per night (double that for the ones closest to the lifts) and top out around $800. Call **ResortQuest Telluride** (800-538-7754) for more information.

Telluride has a **Regional Lodging Program** with seven neighboring towns. If you stay in one of these spots, you can get discount lift tickets throughout the season, saving up to 41 percent. The towns, their distance from Telluride and the numbers to call are: Cortez/Dolores/Rico/Mancos, four towns 25–70 miles away, (800) 253-1616; Montrose, 65 miles, (800) 348-3495; Ouray, 47 miles, (800) 228-1876; and Ridgeway, 37 miles, (800) 754-3103. Durango, which is nearer to Durango Mountain Resort, also is part of this program, (800) 228-1876. Durango is 125 miles from Telluride and just 25 miles from Durango Mountain Resort. If you want to do both resorts on one trip, it might be worth a call to this program.

Dining

Telluride has about 30 restaurants in town and the Mountain Village. There are several fine restaurants. **La Marmotte** (728-6232; $$–$$$) near the Ice House Lodge serves French cuisine. **221 S. Oak** (it's both the name and address; 728-9507; $$–$$$) is in a Victorian house with regional American dishes that vary in response to the freshest products available. **Appaloosa** (728-6800; $$–$$$) at Wyndham Peaks serves gourmet Southwestern fare.

The Cosmopolitan (728-1292; $$), in the Hotel Columbia at the gondola base, serves eclectic American fare. **Rustico** (728-4046; $$), on Telluride's main street, is run by Italian natives and has good food at good prices. In addition to pasta, it has homemade foccacia and a tiramisu worth the fat grams. **Campagna** (435 W. Pacific, 728-6190; $$) serves Italian specialties.

The timber-and-stone **Allred's** (728-7474), at the top of the gondola and 10,535 feet above sea level, gives you staggering views of the 13,000-foot peaks that frame Telluride and the twinkling lights of the historic town 1,800 feet below. The menu features regional American dishes with international overtones that change each night, along with a special tasting menu for guests who wish to pair a selection of fine wines with several signature dishes.

Other on-mountain spots are **Gorrono Ranch**, mid-mountain on Misty Maiden, a rustic barn-like spot that offers American favorites and barbecue on a sunny deck; **Giuseppe's**, at the top of Lift 9, with quick Italian fare in a cozy setting; and **Big Billie's**, at the base of lifts 1 and 10, with southwestern and barbecue items and is ideal for families.

In the Mountain Village, **Legends** at Wyndham Peaks (728-6800) is open for breakfast and lunch only. Get pizza at **Pizza Chalet** (728-7499).

Back to town for more casual and moderate dining: **Leimgruber's** (728-4663) serves German cooking and beer imported from Munich. It's a hot spot when the lifts close, too. **The Floradora** (728-3888) claims the best burgers. **Excelsior Cafe** (728-4250) has good-value North Italian cuisine. For pizza, head to **Roma Bar and Grill** (728-3669). **Sofio's** (728-

Dining: $$$–Entrees $20+; $$–$10-20; $–less than $10.
Accommodations: (double room) $$$$–$200+; $$$–$141-$200; $$–$81-$140; $–$80 and less.

4882) serves good Mexican cuisine but be prepared for a wait. It's worth it—have a margarita. For a more holistic evening, take a dip in the Orvis Hotsprings, followed by dinner at **Bon Ton** in Ouray. Call Telluride Express, 728-6000, at least 24 hours ahead if you need a ride.

Coffee houses have hit Telluride, and visitors have several to choose from: **The Steaming Bean, Maggie's, Between the Covers** and **Coffee Cowboy.** All are on Colorado Avenue. **Skiers Union,** located at the bottom of Lift 4, has great juices and coffee. **Wildflour** is a gourmet bakery in Camel's Garden by the gondola, and **Baked in Telluride** is a 20-year-old bakery in a century-old warehouse. The locals call it by its acronym, BIT, and it's great for deli sandwiches, pizza and inexpensive dinners, washed down by its own brews.

Plan one evening for a magical sleigh ride dinner at **Skyline Guest Ranch,** even if you aren't staying there. Call (888) 754-1126 far in advance for reservations and information.

Après ski/nightlife

For immediate après-ski, stop at **Leimgruber's Bierstube** near the Coonskin Lift (Lift 7) for a selection of great German beer, oom-pah-pah music and a sure shot at meeting folks. The new **Limeleaf** in the old Swede Finn Hall on Pacific Street is another locals' favorite. **Eagle's Bar and Grille** on Colorado Avenue has a huge bar, a No Smoking policy and great happy-hour prices.

For live music go to the **Fly Me to the Moon Saloon** with entertainment Thursday through Saturday. **The Last Dollar Saloon** has the best selection of imported beer in Telluride, plus pool tables and dart boards. It's a bit of a manly-man beer bar—not many women hang out. The old Victorian **New Sheridan Bar** is one of the "must sees" in Telluride to experience the essence of the Old West.

Other activities

The mountain offers **snowbiking** daily. A lift ticket is required; one session includes a lesson and boot and bike rental. You can go on **sleigh rides** at Skyline Guest Ranch (888-754-1126); **horseback riding** with Roudy, Telluride Horseback (728-9611); **hot-air ballooning** with San Juan Balloon Adventures (626-5495); and **snowmobile tours** with Telluride Outside (728-3895). There's a pond in Mountain Village for **ice skating**. It isn't every town that has a colorful past like Telluride's, so the **Historic Walking Tour** (835-5050) is well worth the time.

Helitrax (728-8377, 866-435-4754) provides helicopter skiing for powderhounds. **Telluride Outside** (728-3895, 800-831-6230) is a good source for almost any outdoor winter activity.

Non-skiers and those who need a break might enjoy stretching their creative muscles at the **Ah Haa School for the Arts** (728-3886), which offers weekly and daily classes on painting, silk dyeing and more.

Telluride has great **shopping.** Some of our favorites, all on Colorado Avenue: Lizard Head Mining Co., for its extraordinary custom-made jewelry; At Home in Telluride, with distinctive housewares; and Picaya, with some nice and inexpensive jewelry and clothing. A nice souvenir is Kornbluh candles, locally made beeswax candles with an unusual scent, or a hat from Horny Toad Activewear, a national outdoor clothing company headquartered here. If you decide you'd like a Nordic wool-and-felt hat like a lot of locals wear, call Kim Chapin-Richard, a member of the ski patrol and hat maker, 728-3443. She'll need a few days' notice.

Getting there and getting around

By air: Telluride has a small, weather-plagued airport 5 miles from town, served by United Express from Denver and America West Express from Phoenix. Montrose, 65 miles away, is where most visitors arrive, either by plan or by a weather diversion from Telluride. Continental has daily nonstop jet service to Montrose from Houston, and nonstop service from Newark on Saturdays. American Airlines offers daily nonstop jet service to Montrose from Dallas/Forth Worth and Chicago. United has daily jet service from Denver and often, from other cities as well.

If you fly into the Telluride airport, no matter what the weather, pack a carry-on with enough essentials to get you through 24 hours. These small planes fill with people, then add as much luggage as they can safely transport. This is a sound policy, but it also means that your bags may be delayed. If you arrive without your bags, check with your airline to see if it will provide a voucher for rental clothing and gear at local sporting goods stores. Ways around the problem: 1) Fly to Montrose. The drive is farther, but you'll have your bags with you. 2) Send your bags early via UPS or Federal Express to Mail Boxes Etc. in Telluride. That business will arrange for your bags to be delivered to your lodging (inbound and outbound). Allow 10 business days for shipping. Call 728-8111 for complete details.

Ground transport is provided by Telluride Express (728-6000), Mountain Limo (728-9606) and Alpine Luxury Limo (728-8750). Call 24 hours in advance for Montrose airport pickups.

By car: Telluride is 335 miles from Denver via I-70 west, and Hwys. 50, 550, 62 and 145. From the southwest, it is 125 miles from Durango via Hwys. 160, 184 and 145. From the Montrose airport head south on Hwy. 550 to Ridgway, then take Hwys. 62 and 145 to Placerville and Telluride.

Getting around: A car is unnecessary. The town is just 12 blocks long—you can walk anywhere. If you have them, bring boots with at least an ankle-high cuff. During warm spells, the snow melt on the side streets can get quite deep. A free bus service runs in town, and the free gondola makes the commute between town and the Mountain Village a snap. Call Dial-A-Ride (728-8888) when you get to the base of the gondola in Mountain Village, and a van will ferry you without charge to destinations in the Mountain Village.

Vail

Colorado

Summit elevation: 11,570 feet
Vertical drop: 3,450 feet
Base elevation: 8,120 feet

Address: P.O. Box 7
Vail, CO 81658
✆ **Area code:** 970
Ski area phone: 845-2500
Snow report: 476-4888 or (800) 404-3535
ⓘ **Toll-free reservations:** (800) 404-3535
Toll-free foreign numbers:
U.K. (fax): 0800-891-675
New Zealand (fax): 0800-44-0415
Australia (fax): 0014-800-128-088
Mexico (fax): 95-800-010-1028
Brazil (fax): 000811-515-5557
Fax: 845-2609
E-mail: vailinfo@vailresorts.com
Internet: www.vail.com (resort)
www.snow.com (corporate)
web.vailalways.com (Vail Valley)

Expert:★★★★ **Advanced:**★★★★★
Intermediate:★★★★★
Beginner:★★★ **Never-ever:**★★★
Number and types of lifts: 33–
14 high-speed quads, 1 12-person gondola,
1 quad chair, 3 triple chairs,
5 double chairs, 9 surface lifts
Skiable acreage: 5,289 acres
Snowmaking: 10 percent
Uphill capacity: 51,781 per hour
Snowboarding: Yes
Bed base: 41,305 within 10 miles
Nearest lodging: Slopeside, condos & hotels
Resort child care: Yes, 2 months and older
Adult ticket, per day: $60–$65 (01/02 prices)
Dining:★★★★★
Apres-ski/nightlife:★★★★★
Other activities:★★★★

Vail turns 40 this year. It opened on Dec. 15, 1962, boasting one gondola, two chairs, eight ski instructors and a $5 lift ticket. Today Vail is a *complete* area, lacking none of the essential ingredients that form the magical stew of a world-class winter resort. Vail was conceived as a transplanted Austrian village with condominium convenience, raucous nightlife and quiet lounges, fine dining and pizzeria snacking. Its off-slope activities are unsurpassed—shopping, skating, movies, museums, sleigh riding and so much more—everything money can buy. Bring lots of money—temptations abound, and bargains are few.

But village and expenses aside, there is above all The Mountain. Vail Mountain is a single, stoop-shouldered behemoth. Though it does not have ultra-steeps or deeps, what it does have is three distinct mountain experiences: There's a huge front face of long and very smooth cruisers, an enormous back-bowl experience of wide-open adventure unlike anything this side of the Atlantic, and now the Blue Sky Basin expansion providing lift access to a backcountry experience.

Vail's network of 14 high-speed quads is also the largest in the country. Combined, the mountain and its system of 33 lifts let you do more skiing and less backtracking than almost any other resort you can name. This is truly a skier's mountain.

As important as it is, skiing and riding only constitute part of the total winter-vacation experience. A true world-class resort has to have amenities and atmosphere, and Vail is one of a kind in both areas. You'll find city conveniences such as 24-hour pharmacies (which you don't appreciate until you need medication in a more rural resort), but you won't find the typical Colorado mining-town atmosphere because Vail never was a mining town. Forty years ago, it was pasture. Developers who saw the potential of the mountain built a village styled after an Austrian ski town. Vail seems to have transplanted most of the good from the Austrian experience and eliminated a lot of the bad. Heck, they actually did a pretty good job.

Vail is what we call "urban skiing." This city-town just doesn't feel rural. It bustles with traffic—and people—jams in peak periods. You won't see too many stars at night in the village—too many streetlights. But for many of the urban guests, Vail is just rural enough to let them feel they are getting away from it all. They find the well-lit streets comforting. They want the amenities of big-city life and they don't mind paying for it. Vail is their kind of place.

Vail Mountain lays claim to the biggest single ski mountain in North America. Fortunately, it is segmented: You can concentrate on separate bowls and faces for a morning or afternoon, always having the choice of a new path down the mountain. And none of these runs seems intimidating, although there is plenty of challenge for every level of skier.

The Lionshead area makes up the western end of the front side of Vail and is a good place to start if you're staying on that side of the village. The main access is the Eagle Bahn Gondola (lift 19), but three more chair lifts also serve the trails here. Chair 8, directly parallel to the gondola, is rarely crowded—that's where the ski school and locals start off to dodge the occasional hordes.

At Blue Sky Basin, skiers and snowboarders will find an experience unlike anything else at Vail—from the rustic character of the buildings to the views, the snow, and the challenging glade skiing and steeps. When some of the trails are groomed, low-intermediates can ski this remote area, which is peaceful and secluded. If they are not groomed, you need to be a strong intermediate who can handle powder and dance through some trees. It's really quite exciting. The two main areas of Blue Sky Basin were named for Vail founders Pete Seibert and Earl Eaton (Pete's Bowl and Earl's Bowl). The basin is to the south of Vail Mountain's Back Bowls, on the south side of Two Elk Creek.

 ## Mountain layout—Skiing

If you're skiing with a group, arrange a meeting place in case you get separated. This is one big big mountain. After about a week here, you'll still be discovering new pitches and trails. BTW—locals call the lifts by their numbers rather than their names. If you want to play with them, do the same.

Another suggestion: If you're staying at the Vail Cascade Resort & Spa, take Cascade Way back to the hotel at the end of the day. This run is really a hoot and is reminiscent of skiing in the Alps as it curves, twists and ducks under bridges. Look for it skier's left near the bottom of Simba.

◆◆ **Expert** ◆ **Advanced:** While expert and advanced terrain is a relatively small proportion of Vail's total offerings, we give it thumbs up because of the "sheer volume" quotient. That is, advanced and above can comfortably spend a week working out kinks in trees and bumps, and if you luck into a powder day, doing laps on Genghis Kahn alone will test your mettle. Overall, nothing should scare the bejeebers out of you, but you *will* have to sweat.

On the front side, as you face the hill, check out the double-black diamonds named Blue Ox, Highline and Rogers Run. Don't let the double-diamonds fool you—this is advanced terrain, but nothing that's dangerous. The straight-down-the-lift, waist-high, mogul-masher Highline is the stiffest test of the three, its challenge upgraded by the fact that it spills right under Chair 10 (Highline lift) where other talented skiers are free with their vocal evaluations of your work. Nearby Prima, off Chair 11, is tougher still, and the best skiers like to make the Prima-Pronto run their endurance test. Pronto drops right down to Chair 11 (Northwoods Express) and gets its share of oglers in line. The Prima Cornice can get you sucking air at the top, but it needs plenty of snow to open. The only authentic gut-suckers on the front face are the tops of South and North Rim off the Northwoods lift, leading to a tight but nice Gandy Dancer, and even those are short and sweet.

Under the Vista Bahn, when there's enough snow, The Chutes beckon. It's a bit of work to get to them, and the payoff is short, straight timber bashing. Lionshead has only three very short sections of advanced terrain. Simba's short, steep stretch at the bottom often bumps up, as does Minnie's Mile, a short run that pops out onto the cruiser Born Free, and Lower Ledges.

Solid skiers, of course, will also want to explore Vail's famous Back Bowls. Stretching 7 miles across, they provide more than 2,734 acres of choose-your-own-path skiing. On a sunny day, these bowls are about as good as skiing gets. Just about any skier will tell you there is no other place to be on a powder day. Skiers who have skied Vail for years say they now ski the front side only when they come down at the end of the day. The bowls also are an excellent way to escape crowds.

You'll certainly want to try the steeps and glades in Blue Sky Basin for a taste of lift-served backcountry skiing. The secret in Blue Sky Basin is that it's north facing, so the snow stays better here longer and there's a lot more of it. The Skyline Express Lift runs from the bottom of Tea Cup Bowl up the ridge between Pete's Bowl and Earl's Bowl, providing the main access to terrain in the area. Earl's Express Lift (Chair 38) is in the western part of Earl's Bowl and runs up the east face, where skiers and riders can access acres of gladed terrain.

■ **Intermediate:** These folks will run out of vacation time before they run out of trails to explore. Few other mountains offer an intermediate expansive terrain and seemingly countless trails. Especially worthy cruising areas include the long ride down the mountain under and to the right of the Eagle Bahn Gondola, almost any of the runs bordering the Avanti express chair, the Northwoods run, and the relatively short but sweet trio down to Game Creek Bowl. Our vote for best run on the mountain, and one available to advanced-intermediates (though parts are rated black), is the top-to-bottom swath named Riva Ridge.

Lionshead is all about intermediate skiing. The trails tend to roll from Eagle's Nest down to the valley like ribbon candy—each trail has a steeper section followed by an easier stretch, and steep is a relative term. Simba is a long swooping run, good anytime, and often chosen as the last run. But beware, it can resemble a freeway of skiers "heading to the barn" for après-ski. Born Free is another classic intermediate run that leaves from Eagle's Nest and loops lazily to the valley floor.

Confident intermediates also can enjoy the Back Bowls, but stick close to groomed trails in China Bowl and Tea Cup Bowl. (Poppy Fields in China Bowl often is groomed during the day, too.) If you get tired or frustrated with the natural conditions, you can bail out easily.

In Blue Sky Basin, when some of the trails are groomed, low intermediates can ski this remote area, which is peaceful and secluded. If they are not groomed, you need to be a strong intermediate who can handle powder and some trees. Pete's Express Lift (Chair 39) runs up the eastern-most point of Blue Sky Basin in Pete's Bowl to access more than 125 acres of intermediate terrain.

●● **Beginner:** Best areas are at Golden Peak and Eagle's Nest, and a group of short green runs under the Sourdough Lift on the top left of the trail map. Unfortunately, Vail doesn't have a large area of concentrated green runs. Most lifts on the front face have one or designated trails, a bunch of blue trails and one or two blacks. Take a trail map and pay attention to the signs.

Vail is one of the few resorts with beginner terrain at the top of the mountain. Take the Eagle Bahn Gondola to Eagle's Ridge. A group of short green runs are served by a chair lift to skier's right (east) of the gondola, and beginners can do laps on this chair. The best part is beginners are the only ones using the chair. Beginners can follow a series of cat tracks with names like Cub's Way and Bwana Loop that crisscross the mountain. On the trail map, they are denoted with dotted green lines.

A series of crisscrossing cat tracks, some of which are named Cub's Way, Gitalong and Skid Road, allow beginners to work their way down the mountain. If cat tracks make you nervous, Vail's trail map marks them with dotted lines. However, it's tough to avoid them here, unless you stay in the Eagle's Nest area and ride that gondola back down.

● **Never-ever:** There are small learning areas in the Golden Peak base area and the top of the Eagle Bahn Gondola at Eagle's Nest. From Eagle's Nest, never-evers can return to the valley via the gondola.

Mountain layout—Snowboarding

If you're with a big group, set up a meeting place and make sure to give at least a 15-minute meeting window, this mountain is huge. A good meeting place is at the top of the Vista Bahn, or any of the Mid Vail restaurants because of their location at the middle of the mountain.

◆◆ **Expert ◆ Advanced:** Let's make it easy: If you're going to ride Vail, I mean really *ride* the mountain, it's time to ignore trail names. If you tried to remember every little run at Vail, not only would you go mad, but you'd probably drop a few levels in I.Q. Besides, you're not going to ride runs, you're going to ride chairs. What you want to do here is focus on the kind of terrain you want to ride, then stick to the chair that accesses it. By the way, riding the trees is the most direct way to avoid taking catwalks and multiple lifts.

On the front side, experts are going to want to spend time at the Northwoods lift. On a powder day this is a great place—rocks, steep lines and cliff gaps abound—but once it's tracked, leave. Head rider's right of the Vista Bahn (on a good snow day), or to The Riva Bahn and Vail's world-class terrain park and superpipe. Advanced riders who prefer trees enjoy Sheer Terror Glade, Riva Glade, Hairbag Alley, and Bird Baths. All are tight trees where snowboarders rule, but you'll see the occasional skier drop in. On Lionshead, you'll get a kick out of Cheetah Gully, a gladed run just to the west (snowboarder's left) of the gondola.

The back side of the mountain is where Vail really shines. A good place to start is at the top of Game Creek Express, where you can access the Cornice through a short five-minute walk. Drop in off the cornice, then head down to the motocross jumps, which are exactly that, three giant windlips form natural tabletops that are perfect for throwing down new tricks.

Make sure you check out Blue Sky Basin, it's not to be missed. You'll find an experience unlike anything else at Vail—from the rustic character of the buildings to the views, the snow, and the challenging glades and steeps. This area is different from the rest of Vail in terms of terrain—in layman's terms, if it's a powder day get back here as soon as you can! This is lift-accessed backcountry riding like nothing you've ever found at Vail. Blue Sky Basin is a rider's paradise—and since it's very remote, you won't have to ride a sequence of chairs once you get here.

Insider Tip: For experienced backcountry riders *only*, find a local to guide you, get your Pieps and shovel, and check out East Vail for some of the best resort-accessed backcountry in Colorado. There are five backcountry access gates at Vail. As we repeatedly warn throughout this book, do not go into the backcountry without a knowledgeable guide. People die out there!

■ **Intermediate:** Again, there are just too many runs to go into specifics, especially since this mountain was really designed for intermediates. The Avanti Chair and the gondola will be equal to heaven for you. Everything can be found here: Long high-speed cruisers, woods runs, gaps, kickers, logs and even hot dog stands.

●● **Beginner/Never-ever:** Gold Peak is it. Not only do you get to learn on variable pitches and cruise on a high-speed quad, but also Vail was nice enough to put their immense terrain park right next to the beginner runs. Sometimes seeing the best riders in the world destroying the park right next to you can be humiliating for never-evers, but it can also inspire a beginner to greatness. Vail makes sure that beginners absolutely know what they are getting involved in when they first start out.

Insider tip: Vail has an excellent beginner's instruction program. It's highly recommended that beginners take lessons, not only for the valuable skills they can pick up, but also for the guide service that the instructors provide on the mountain.

Mountain rating

Vail is one of the best winter resorts in the world for all but the extreme fringes of the ability chart. Super experts will miss the extreme terrain of a Snowbird, Jackson Hole or Squaw Valley, and frankly, Vail is a little overwhelming for a first-timer's adventure. But for ability levels 2-9 (on a scale 1-10), Vail offers everything you can dream of.

Cross-country and snowshoeing

Two cross-country centers serve Nordic skiers and snowshoers, one at **Golden Peak** and one at the **Vail Golf Course.** Both offer lessons, tours and rentals. Call 845-5313. Last season Vail beefed up its Cross-Country and Snowshoe Adventure Center at Golden Peak. Here guided tours and instruction are available through the Vail Cross-Country Ski School, where instructors specialize in cross-country skiing, telemark skiing, snowshoeing and skate skiing. Guests can book snowshoeing tours, telemark lessons and cross-country ski lessons and tours.

Lessons (2001/02 prices)

The ski school has offices and meeting places at Vail Village near the base of the Vista Bahn Express, at Lionshead next to the gondola, at Golden Peak next to Chairs 6 and 12, at Mid-Vail next to Chairs 3 and 4, and at Eagle's Nest at the top of the gondola. Private lessons meet at Vail Village. Lessons are taught in more than 30 languages. Call the ski school at 476-3239. The prices we list are for peak season, which is when most skiers are on the mountain.

Skiers and riders watch a video that displays nine levels of skills the school uses to form classes, then place themselves accordingly in classes ranging from never-evers to advanced.

Group lessons: $90 for a full day. Vail offers a wide variety of lesson-lift-and/or-rental packages too detailed for us to list here.

Never-ever package: Full day lesson and beginner lift cost $120; with rentals, $150. A great deal, available only during the value season (opening day through Dec. 13, 2001 and April 7, 2002 through closing), is the First Time Series (for ages 15 and older), which offers three consecutive full days of lessons for the price of one day: $135 for lessons, lifts and rentals. Skiers and snowboarders who complete the program will be given a coupon good for three more lessons for the price of one at the next ability level. The same offer is available Jan. 15-Feb. 12, 2002, for $145.

Private lessons: One to six people cost $130 per hour, $250 for two hours, $330 for a half day afternoon, $360 for a half day morning, and $485 for the day.

Special workshops: Focus on specific skills or snow conditions, such as parallel skiing or bumps. Most are afternoon three-hour sessions for around $76.

A free Ski Tips program meets at 11 a.m. daily at Mid-Vail. The session gives you a chance to ski down a gentle slope alongside an instructor who will provide a critique and suggestions on which lesson program will offer the best benefits.

Kenny's Double Diamond Ski Shop in Vail hosts one of the best women's ski programs in the country. Owner Heidi Friedman brings equipment guru Jeannie Thoren to Vail in December and January to teach women the importance of properly fitted equipment. Participants demo the latest brands that Thoren modifies and custom-fits to each woman's specific bio-mechanics. Then they go skiing—better than ever. We know Jeannie well, and can heartily recommend this program. Call (800) 466-2704 or 926-5936 for more information.

Pepi's Wedel Weeks were created in the European tradition, which allows skiers to start off the ski season with an inexpensive lesson package. These are held for three weeks only, in November and early December. It's a seven-day program with breakfast, lessons every morning and afternoon, races, a welcome reception, an evening party, a fashion show and a farewell dinner. Call (800) 445-8245.

We've had first-hand experience at the "Her Turn" Adventure Workshops for Women, and strongly recommend them. Scheduled over weekends, you'll arrive on Thursday, and ski or snowboard on Friday, Saturday, and half-day Sunday with other women of like ability. Breakthroughs are common in the supportive small-group atmosphere. Program includes demo alpine skis and boards, video feedback, on-mountain lunch, après social, discussion sessions and goodie bag. Call (800) 475-4543 for cost and reservations.

The Telemark Workshop Series is also a personal fave. Scheduled on weekends, they focus solely on the on-snow experience for a single day, and come in unisex, kids, and women-only varieties. Call for prices.

Racing: Vail has quite a recreational racing complex near the bottom of the Avanti Express lift with two NASTAR courses, two coin-operated courses, two courses reserved for groups, a course for teaching clinics and a Sybervision area. A surface lift serves the courses.

Child Care (2001/02 prices)

Ages: 2 months to 6 years.

Costs: Supervised playroom and non-skiing programs, $79 peak season.

Reservations: Required; call 479-3285 or fax to 479-3290. Small World Play School is run by the ski school and is in the Golden Peak base area. Small World Play School is open 8 a.m. to 4:30 p.m. Free pagers are available. Of note, Vail's child-care programs are state of the art.

Other options: For **babysitters** call 476-7400. **Baby's Away** (800-369-9030; 926-5256) rents and delivers baby needs, such as crib, stroller, car seat and toys to your lodge.

Lessons: Classes are divided by age and ability. Children ages 3 years (toilet-trained) to 6 years can sign up for lessons in the Mini Mice, Mogul Mice or SuperStars programs. Children ages 6-14 can spend their day on the mountain or be entertained with videos and have supervised meeting rooms. Ski lessons are offered for kids 3-14; snowboarding lessons are for ages 6-14. Cost is $94 peak season. Prices include lesson, lift and lunch. Register at 8:30 a.m. or pre-register the day before. Reservations are not required. Call 479-3239 for information. Children's Ski and Snowboard Centers are located at both Lionshead and at Golden Peak. Both centers offer "one-stop shopping" for lessons and rentals. You can reach either facility via the town bus.

Skiing with your kids: The resort is sprinkled with Kids Adventure Zones, like Thunder Cat Cave, Fort Whippersnapper and Chaos Canyon. Here children enter a magical land and follow in the tracks of the little Indians Gitchee and Gumee, as they accompany Jackrabbit Joe and Sourdough Pete on a quest to find the treasure of the Lost Silver Mine. Your little ones can hunt for these zones on the trail map. Once they find them, they can dive through tunnels, into trees and over bumps. Kids even have their own restaurant at Mid-Vail called Chaos Canyon Kids' Café.

Lift tickets (2001/02 prices)

	Adult	Child (5-12)
One day	$65	$39
Three days	$186 ($62/day)	$108 ($36/day)
Five of six days	$300 ($60/day)	$180 ($36/day)

Note: These prices valid from December 22, 2001 to April 6, 2002.

Who skis free: Ages 4 and younger.

Who skis at a discount: Ages 65–69 pay $57 per day; ages 70+ pay $28 per day. Vail Resorts has a handful of different discounted prices based on time of the year, time of a skiers first visit, ski packages, Internet sales, supermarket sales, pre-purchasing and groups.

A great deal is Vail's Perfect 10, which allows vacationers to ski 10 days at Vail or its sister resorts Beaver Creek, Breckenridge and Keystone, as well as Arapahoe Basin, for less than $32 a day throughout the 2001/02 season. The multi-day lift ticket program rewards guests who ski early and often. Early, because it must be used at least once before Jan. 31, 2002 and often, because it includes up to 10 days of skiing and snowboarding that can be used consecutively or non-consecutively throughout the season. An adult Perfect 10 sells for $319, and a child (ages 5-12) Perfect 10 is $159. Valid all season with the exception of Dec. 21, 2001 through Jan. 5, 2002. Additional restrictions apply. The Perfect 10 is available at any Vail, Beaver Creek, Keystone or Breckenridge ticket window during the season or by visiting www.vail.com or www.snow.com.

Interchangeability: All lift tickets purchased at Vail or Beaver Creek also are valid at sister resorts Keystone and Breckenridge, as well as at nearby Arapahoe Basin. Only multiday tickets of three or more days purchased at Keystone or Breckenridge are also valid at Vail and Beaver Creek (one day of a three-day lift ticket purchased at Keystone or Breckenridge is valid at Vail or Beaver Creek; two days of a four-day or five-day lift ticket; three days of a six-day or seven-day ticket). All lift tickets purchased at Keystone or Breckenridge also are valid at nearby Arapahoe Basin.

Accommodations

Vail's lodging choices are so vast we can't even begin to list them here. Before you call Central Reservations, know your price range, what amenities you need and which ones you want, how close you'd like to be to the lifts and how close you'll settle for if you find nothing in your budget within that distance. Prices dip from 25 to 40 percent before Christmas and in April. But if you come at that time, be sure the bus system is in full operation or that you're within walking distance of necessities; otherwise rent a car.

Vail's premier properties are clustered in Vail Village at the base of the Vista Bahn Express. Selecting the best place in town is a virtual toss-up between four hotels.

The Lodge at Vail (476-5011 or 800-331-5634; $$$$) is the original hotel around which they built the rest of the resort. It is only steps away from the lifts, ski school and main street action. The Lodge serves a great buffet breakfast. **Gasthof Gramshammer** (476-5626; $$$$) is at the crossroads of Vail Village. Our favorite and the most economical within this group of hotels is the **Christiania** (476-5641 or 800-530-3999; $$$$). **Sonnenalp Resort** (476-5656 or 800-654-8312; $$$$) is a group of buildings that exude Alpine warmth and charm. The spa is the place to head for sore muscle relief.

At the Lionshead end of town, the **Marriott's Mountain Resort at Vail** (476-4444 or 800-648-0720; $$$–$$$$) is top of the line and has an excellent location only three minutes' walk from the gondola. **Lion Square Lodge** (476-2281; $$$–$$$$) is steps from the Eagle Bahn Gondola and Born Free Express lift.

The slopeside **Vail Cascade Resort & Spa** (800-420-2424 or 476-7111; $$$$) lodges guests in rooms, suites and condominiums. The multi-award-winning property includes the Aria Spa & Club, the Vail Valley's largest fitness facility, as well as two ski shops, two movie theaters and its own chair lift accessing Vail's slopes. There's free shuttle service to Vail Village and Lionshead, and ski valet service. The Chap's Grill & Chophouse specializes in steaks and grilled food as well as Colorado specialties.

Condominiums are plentiful in the Vail region. The most reasonable for those who want to be on the shuttlebus route are **in Lionshead,** clustered around the gondola, and in East Vail at **Vail Racquet Club** (476-4840 or 800-428-4840; $$-$$$).

The **Vailglo Lodge** (476-5506; $$-$$$), in Lionshead, is a 34-room Best Western hotel that operates like an elegant B&B. It has easy access to the slopes and town. For other relatively more affordable lodging, try **Antlers** (476-2471; $$-$$$$) in Lionshead; **Manor Vail** (476-5000 or 800-950-8245; $$-$$$$) in Gold Peak; the **Chateau Vail** (476-5631; $$$-$$$$); and **Vail Village Inn** (476-5622; $$-$$$$). A recommended B&B is the **Black Bear Inn** (476-1304; $$-$$$) in West Vail.

Dining

Eating out in Vail is as much of a tradition as skiing the Back Bowls. Always make reservations. Walk-ins have a slim chance of being seated. More than 150 bars and restaurants offer the spectrum of options from pizza to fine gourmet dining.

In the expensive category, **La Tour** (476-4403; $$$) and **The Left Bank** (476-3696; $$-$$$), both French, have long been considered Vail's best. Another standby, **Sweet Basil** (476-0125; $$-$$$), is consistently good with creative dishes. **The Tyrolean Inn** (476-2204; $$$), one of Vail's oldest and best-known restaurants just east of the village (and the Transportation Center), serves exotic game dishes like wild game pasta jambalaya in a classic Austrian set-

Dining: $$$-Entrees $20+; $$-$10-20; $-less than $10.
Accommodations: (double room) $$$$-$200+; $$$-$141-$200; $$-$81-$140; $-$80 and less.

ting. **Terra Bistro** (476-6836; $$-$$$) is just down the road from the Tyrolean on the east end of the Vail Mountain Lodge. Although difficult to find (the sign is very small), this upscale, eclectic restaurant specializing in "fusion cuisine" is a local favorite. **Chap's Grill and Chophouse** (476-7014; $$-$$$), in the Vail Cascade Resort & Spa, serves some of the best steaks, wild game and seafood in the Vail area. We like **Lancelot** (476-5828; $$-$$$) for prime rib, **Montauk** (476-2601; $$$) for seafood, **Alpenrose** (476-3194; $$$) for German and its wonderful breads and pastries, and **Wildflower** (476-5011; $$-$$$) in The Lodge for contemporary American and an excellent wine list.

Less expensive but just as scrumptious is the legendary **Pepi's** (476-5626; $$) for the best goulash and white veal bratwursts; and **Campo de Fiore** (476-8994; $$), with fine Italian fare, an extensive wine list and a friendly staff. **Cucina Rustica** (476-5011; $$-$$$) serves Tuscan-style Italian in The Lodge. **Blu's** (476-3113; $) fixes great classics, and if you're willing to drive west to a local's favorite in Eagle Vail, **Ti Amo** (845-8153; $$-$$$) won't disappoint. **The Gore Creek Grille** (476-2828; $$) offers creative seafood, meat and fowl specialties. Its bar claims the town's longest martini menu.

Those on a budget should try **Pazzo's** (476-9026; $), which offers pasta and create-your-own-pizza. **Bart and Yeti's** (476-2754; $$) in Lionshead is great for lunch or light dinner.

On the mountain, we recommend lunch at the **Two Elk Restaurant** (479-4560; $-$$) above China Bowl. It was re-built after being burned to the ground in an arson fire. Go early or late, because finding a seat at prime time is tough. Or try the lunch at **Larkspur** (479-8050; $$-$$$) in the Golden Peak base lodge. This restaurant is also one of our top choices for dinner. **Mid-Vail's food court** has moderate (for Vail) prices—$10 buys a huge potato with toppings, a local beer and a piece of fruit, for example. Or try the Lunch For Less meal deal for $7.95 including a bowl of pasta, salad and a drink. For an inexpensive lunch, try the **Clark Market Deli** (476-1199; $) in Vail Village. Hungry, and frugal, skiers enjoy sandwiches, tofu, tabouli, Santa Fe rice and beans, and other tasty treats in a small seating area facing the front slopes of Vail.

The **Game Creek Club** (479-4275; $$$) is extremely exclusive with only 350 members (Ross Perot, Charles Schwab and so on), and it's members-only for lunch. However, they do let non-members in for dinner, and it is just a snowcat ride from the top of the Eagle Bahn. For about $85 per person, sans alcohol and gratuity but including the transportation, you get a six-course gourmet meal—a choice of game, seafood, veal, steak and lamb—and a gorgeous view of the valley below. Make your reservation to coincide with sunset. Another memorable dining experience is **Beano's Cabin** (949-9090; $$-$$$) at Beaver Creek Resort. See the Beaver Creek chapter for details.

For breakfast, the best deal in town is at **D.J. MacAdams** ($) in Lionshead's Concert Hall Plaza, a tiny diner where you'll watch cooks make heaping plates of omelettes, scrambletts (like an omelette only using scrambled eggs) and blintzes. Wash it down with a fruit smoothie. It's open 24 hours, except Mondays (reopening at 7 a.m. Tuesday). If you're looking for a buffet breakfast (continental or hot) in a fine-dining atmosphere, head to **Chap's Grill** ($$) in the Vail Cascade Resort & Spa or the **Mountain Grille Restaurant** ($$) at the Marriott's Mountain Resort at Vail. You can also get a la carte items at both.

Down Valley

Visitors with a car should drive west to exit 171 and turn off at old town Minturn where the **Minturn Country Club** ($$$) lets you grill your own meat or fish steak. Just across the street, the area's best Mexican food is dished out at the raucous **Saloon** (827-5954; $–$$)—a favorite of World Cup racers—or **Chili Willy's** (827-5887; $–$$). Stop by **Bonjour Bakery** (827-5539; $) for loaves of to-die-for bread, but call for winter hours before you make the trip. The **Turntable Restaurant** (827-4268; $–$$) wins accolades for its green chili.

Further down valley, past the Beaver Creek exit about 4 miles, keep an eye out for **The Grille at Singletree** (926-3528; $$–$$$) on your right. You'll find a lovely high-end Continental cuisine restaurant where you can dress up and enjoy the fabulous sunsets behind the New York mountain range. Lots of rock and an intimate atmosphere.

At the Edwards exit, left off the highway, check out the valley's oldest restaurant and bar, **The Gashouse** (926-3613; $–$$). Seafood, homemade soups, steaks, wild game and award-winning chili are served in a rustic 50-year-old log cabin. Après is good for lobster tails, little neck clams and jumbo lump crab cakes. At the Edwards Riverwalk center, drop into **Zino** (926-0444; $–$$) for antipasti, salads, pizza and pasta. The grilled yellow fin tuna is a lip-smacker. The best sports bar and grill could be **Paddy's** (949-6093; $–$$) on Highway 6. The house specialty prime rib is big and fat.

At Edwards Plaza II, look for **Asia** (926-8862; $–$$). There's Chinese, Thai, Japanese and Vietnamese cuisine all over the place. Personal and family dinners at $29-$33 per person seem pricey, but your dollar buys more food than a human should be allowed to eat at one sitting. The margaritas at **Fiesta's Café & Cantina** (926-2121; $–$$) are yummy (20 tequilas to choose from) and the family-style meals are user-friendly. Chicken enchiladas in white jalapeno sauce are the house specialty.

At **Markos** (926-7003; $) in the Edwards Business Plaza, you'll find pastas, pizzas and Caesar salads at rock bottom prices.

Après-ski/nightlife

Après-ski is centered in the Village or in Lionshead. **The Red Lion** has a deck, live music and great nachos. In the Village, try **Sarah's** in the Christiania for squeezebox music with Helmut Fricker on Tuesdays and Fridays; and **Vendetta's**, a locals' favorite. **Mickey's** at the Lodge at Vail has the top piano bar. Several restaurants have house entertainers who are long-time career musicians. In Lionshead, **Sundance Saloon** fills up with locals and probably has the best drink prices in town, especially at happy hour in the late afternoon.

In Lionshead, Oktoberfest happens daily at **Katlenberg Castle**, the latest brewhouse of the 700-year-old royal brewing family of Prince Luitpold of Bavaria. Its massive dining room, built in the likeness of an authentic Bavarian castle, serves traditional German food, but we preferred the sun-splashed porch for end-of-the-day relaxing. Three specialty beers on tap and oom-pah-pah music create post-slope fun fit for a (Bavarian) king.

For later nightlife, **Club Chelsea** on Bridge Street caters to the over-30 crowd with three rooms—a DJ dance area, a piano bar and a sealed-off cigar bar—while a few doors away, **Nick's** attracts a young crowd with loud rock'n'roll. **The Club** normally offers acoustic guitar music. **8150** has live alternative music. On weekends the **Sundance Saloon** in Lionshead has music.

Other activities

Adventure Ridge at Eagle's Nest is an on-mountain activity center, open from 2 p.m. to 10 p.m. Families and adrenaline junkies enjoy this addition in the Eagle's Nest area at the top of the gondola. It includes an ice-skating rink, kids' snowmobile track, a lift-served tubing hill, ski-biking, thrill sledding and other activities. If you haven't tried ski-biking, do so. It is a hoot to go careening down the mountain at night with a light strapped to your head; just be prepared for exhausted legs (and don't do it the night you arrive if you tend to suffer at high altitude). Something we didn't try, but we think sounds, well, thrilling, is thrill sledding. You'll sled headfirst down the mountain at night from Adventure Ridge to the bottom of the Eagle Bahn gondola. Sleds have a hand-activated hydraulic brake system and four independently suspended skis. Headlamps and clear goggles are provided; helmets are available (must be at least 14 years old). Some activities require reservations, so call in advance. A restaurant serves very affordable family dinners. The gondola cabins are heated and lighted.

Vail has a number of **athletic clubs** and **spas.** The Aria Spa & Club (spa 479-5942, club 476-7400) at the Vail Cascade Resort has 14 treatment rooms including a couple's spa suite. Treatments include massages, wraps, soaks, facials and manicures and pedicures. The athletic facilities—the best in Vail—include a pool; 48 pieces of cardio equipment; free weights; indoor running track; and basketball, volleyball, racquetball and squash courts. The Spa at Vail Mountain Lodge (476-7960) has fitness facilities and the only climbing wall in the Valley. The Vail Racquet Club (476-3267) in East Vail has indoor tennis, squash and racquetball courts, swimming pool and weight room.

Take a ride on the Vail Golf Course with **Steve Jones Sleigh Rides** (476-8057). The **Colorado Ski Museum** in the Vail Transportation Center traces the history of skiing in the state. Admission is free. Vail also has several **movie theaters,** an indoor **ice-skating rink,** several **hot-air balloon companies** and many other things to do. Call the Vail Activity Desk at 476-9090 for the complete list.

Vail's unique **boutiques and shops,** mostly upscale, can keep your credit card active for days. Late March is the best time to find bargains in ski wear and winter clothes.

Getting there and getting around

By air: Flights land at the Vail/Eagle County airport, about 35 miles west of Vail, and the Denver International Airport, 110 miles east. Eagle County airport is served by American, Northwest, Delta, Continental, America West and United.

Ground transportation between Denver and Vail is frequent and convenient with Vail Valley Transport at (800) 882-8872; Colorado Mountain Express at (800) 525-6363; Airlink Shuttle at (800) 554-8245; or Vail Valley Taxi (Eagle airport only) at 476-8294. Though flights into Denver may be a bit less expensive than Eagle, also consider the cost of ground transportation, which is about $60 per person round trip from Eagle and about $115 from Denver.

By car: Vail is off I-70, 100 miles west of Denver and 140 miles east of Grand Junction.

Getting around: Most parts of Vail are very self-contained, and the free, reliable bus service runs throughout town from East to West Vail. Visitors and locals ride the bus, because parking is very limited and expensive. Shuttles to Beaver Creek cost $3 one way and depart from the Transportation Center above the parking structure in Vail Village.

During most times of the season, you won't need (or want) a car if your lodging is in Vail Village or Lionshead. Be sure to ask when you make your lodging reservations how close you are to the free bus service. The buses go where cars are not allowed, so the bus often will get you closer to your destination than if you drive. If you come in early or late season (early December or April), be sure to ask the person making your reservations whether the bus schedule will be cut back during your visit. If so, rent a car.

Winter Park
Colorado

Summit elevation: 12,060 feet
Vertical drop: 3,060 feet
Base elevation: 9,000 feet

Address: P.O. Box 36, Winter Park, CO 80482
☎ **Area code:** 970
Ski area phone: 726-5514
Denver line: (303) 892-0961
ⓘ **Toll-free reservations:** (800) 729-5813; (970) 726-5587 outside the U.S. and Canada
Fax: (970) 726-5993
E-mail: wpinfo@mail.skiwinterpark.com
Internet: www.skiwinterpark.com (ski area), www.ridewinterpark (snowboarding) or www.winterpark-info.com (town)
Expert:★★★★ **Advanced:**★★★★
Intermediate:★★★★
Beginner:★★★★
Never-ever:★★★★★

Number of lifts: 22–8 high-speed quads; 4 triple chairs, 7 double chairs, 3 magic carpets
Snowmaking: 15 percent
Skiable acreage: 2,886
Uphill capacity: 34,910 per hour
Snowboarding: Yes, unlimited
Bed Base: 12,500
Nearest lodging: Slopeside
Resort child care: Yes, 2 months and older
Adult ticket, per day: $41-$58 (02/03 prices)

Dining:★★★
Apres-ski/nightlife:★★
Other activities:★★

In the early 1900s, when the Moffat Tunnel through the Rockies was completed, Denverites began to ride the train here. The shacks first built for the tunnel construction crews made perfect warming huts for hardy skiers who climbed the mountains and schussed down on 7-foot boards. The ski area now is part of the Denver public parks system, which explains its name. Today Winter Park ranks as one of the largest ski areas in Colorado.

This is a great mountain with a wonderfully easy-going atmosphere. The ski area and most of the lodging are tucked into the woods off the main highway, which retains this town's rural feel. Winter Park also has several traditional mountain inns—the kind with large common rooms where people can read, talk or play board games. They are tough to find these days. We like them, and you'll find descriptions in the Accommodations section.

But, the times are changing. Completion of the Zephyr Mountain Lodge, with shops and a restaurant on the ground floor and condos above, has moved upscale slopeside lodging to Winter Park. These condos are available for nightly rentals. Winter Park is still charmingly funky, affordable and low-key, with lodging designed with families in mind, plus one of Colorado's most respected ski schools. The children's and disabled-skier programs are among the biggest, most advanced and most respected in the nation.

Although Winter Park maintains a great family reputation, it is a surprisingly good destination for singles. The town benefits from having only a few, but good, nightlife centers. Meaning that you get to meet most of the other skiers in town if that's what you want; and the mountain inn lodging gives singles a great opportunity to meet other vacationers over dinner and drinks, or while enjoying the hot tubs. If you're looking for a solid good time without the fanfare, Winter Park presents you with one of the best opportunities.

Mountain layout—Skiing

Completely interconnected by lifts, the mountain has separate base areas— Mary Jane and Winter Park. The "Winter Park side" refers to the portion of the resort to the trail-map right of the Zephyr Express chair lift.

◆◆ **Expert:** Visitors who have read about Winter Park arrive expecting a good intermediate resort with plenty of lower-intermediate and beginner trails. Yes, that's all here—what is surprising is the amount of expert terrain. Vasquez Cirque has nearly 700 acres of steep chutes and gladed powder stashes accessed by a hike along the ridge from the Timberline chair lift.

Mary Jane is where you'll find the famous bumps and super-steeps. Try the chutes accessible only through controlled gates: Hole in the Wall, Awe Chute, Baldy's Chute, Jeff's Chute and Runaway, all reached by the Challenger or Summit Express chair lifts.

◆ **Advanced:** For advanced skiers, the most popular lift on the Winter Park side is the Zephyr Express. It provides access to Mary Jane (via Outhouse), or the advanced runs on the Winter Park side—Bradley's Bash, Balch, Mulligan's Mile and Hughes. From the top of Zephyr, bump fanatics can bop down Outhouse and end up at the base of Mary Jane.

At Mary Jane, head for the black runs off the Iron Horse chair. If you're still standing, you're ready for the runs off the Challenger chair—all black diamond, all ungroomed with monstrous moguls, and all tough as a bag of nails.

■ **Intermediate:** Parsenn Bowl has more than 200 acres of open space. If you can hit Parsenn on a good day, you're in for a treat. The upper part is wide open and medium-steep, while the gladed bottom is a delight, especially if you're just learning to ski between trees. Though rated blue and blue-black on the trail map, wind and weather conditions can make the bowl a workout. Winds occasionally close the Timberline lift, which provides the only access.

Vasquez Ridge on the Winter Park side has an excellent collection of cruising runs. (The only drawback to Vasquez Ridge is a long runout down the Big Valley trail; the Buckaroo trail lets you avoid it.) To change mountains, green-circle Gunbarrel takes skiers to the High Lonesome Express quad and the Mary Jane area.

The Sunnyside lift on the Mary Jane side has excellent runs for intermediates. If you can handle these with no trouble, try Sleeper, one of Winter Park's "blue-black" runs.

●● **Beginner:** The Winter Park base area serves most of the beginner trails. Beginners can ride to the top of the mountain to Sunspot and then ski down March Hare, or they can ski all the way back to the base using the Cranmer Cutoff to Parkway. When these become easy, try Cranmer, Jabberwocky and White Rabbit.

● **Never-ever:** Winter Park is one of the best ski areas in the nation for novices. Groswold's Discovery Park is 25 acres of gentle, protected learning terrain for beginners, served by a double, triple and a high-speed chair lift, which slows down for loading and unloading. Three "magic carpets," gently sloped ramp escalators at the base of the resort, allow children *and* adults to make repeated runs without getting on and off a chair lift.

Mountain layout—Snowboarding

While Mary Jane is famous for its bumps, it also boasts smooth glades and chutes off of the Summit Express and Challenger lifts. Catch them on a powder day and you'll feel like a hero. Overall, the Mary Jane terrain is ideal for experts and advanced-intermediates, plus it's easy to negotiate with no flat runouts.

This year the terrain park will be on upper Allan Phipps and will include rails, a teeter totter and a rainbow rail (these features will be set up on opening day on one of the resort's lower trails, then will be moved to Allan Phipps as soon as conditions permit). You'll also find jumps and hips and, below Cranmer Cutoff, two distinct lines will let you choose to continue on traditional terrain park features such as tables and spines, or take The Rolls boardercross course with crescents, compression rolls, spines and a chicane. The halfpipe will be moved to just above Snoasis mid-mountain restaurant and to rider's right of lower Allan Phipps, so riders exiting The Rolls can complete their run in the halfpipe.

While the Winter Park side is better suited for beginners, it can be a challenge for riders simply because it is riddled with flats and runouts. To minimize walking, the Zephyr Express lift is the safest bet. Once you figure out how to get there, the Pioneer Express lift also offers some interesting intermediate terrain. On the way back to the Winter Park base, just be sure to take Parkway Trail to avoid Turnpike at *ALL COSTS*—it's long and flatter than Kansas.

Mountain rating

Winter Park is one of the few mountain resorts that can truly serve the needs of all ability and interest levels. Very few mountains have both the nearly flat, isolated terrain that never-evers need, and the precipitous plunges that experts adore. Winter Park is lucky enough to have both, plus plenty at every stage in between. Riders should be aware that there are some flats on the lower-ability-level terrain that can be frustrating.

 # Cross-country and snowshoeing

Devil's Thumb Cross-Country Center (726-8231) has great views of the mountains and 105 km. of trails groomed for both skating and gliding. National-level competitors race and train here. The center is near Tabernash on County Road 83. Trail fees are $13 a day for adults and $8 for children and seniors; those ages 6 and younger ski free. Private lessons are $30 an hour; group lessons are $15 for a two-hour session. A learn-to-ski package is $30 with rentals and trail fee; children and seniors, $23. You'll also find 20 km. of marked, groomed snowshoe trails. The adult trail fee is $13 all day or $9 half day. Rentals cost $12 all day, $8 half day. Guided snowshoe tours cost $30 per hour.

Snow Mountain Ranch (887-2152; www.ymcarockies.org), 8 miles west of Winter Park on Highway 40, offers 100 km. of groomed trails through a variety of terrain—open, wooded, hilly and flat. There is a lighted 3-km. loop for night skiing. The staff includes national-level coaches and racers. Ski lessons, rentals, lodging, dining and child care are available. Trail fees are less than $10 per day. This is also a YMCA with inexpensive dorm and cabin lodging.

Nearby **Arapahoe National Forest** has more than 600 km. of Nordic and snowshoeing trails, and the **Fraser Experimental Forest Ranger Station** is the take-off point for marked trails suitable for all skiing levels of skiers, with no trail fees, but also no facilities.

Redfeather on-mountain snowshoe tours are offered several times daily from the base of **Winter Park Resort**. The two-hour guided tour includes a chairlift ride to the tour's starting point, rental snowshoes, and information about native plants and animals. Cost is $25.

Winter Park and the Fraser Valley's extensive mountain biking trails are used in winter for snowshoeing. The trails are easy to follow and often packed down by snowmobile riders. The **Winter Park/Fraser Chamber of Commerce** has maps and information.

 # Lessons (2002/03 prices)

The Ski & Snowboard School desks are at the Balcony House at the Winter Park base and for privates only at the Mary Jane Center. Teaching is Winter Park's forte, so a large variety of clinics and lessons are offered.

Group lessons: $40, 2.5 hours, for intermediate and higher; $30 for beginner levels. Quick Tips Learning Lane is a 15-minute session for advanced beginners to experts for $5. This program is located at the Winter Park Video Arena above the Snoasis restaurant.

Private lessons: $120 for 90 minutes (for one or two people). A First Tracks private lesson gets you on the mountain 30 minutes before the lifts open to the public—lesson goes from 8-9:30 a.m., cost is $85. Last Tracks is from 2:30-4 p.m., cost is $85.

Special programs: Many. An example: The Family Private lesson allows a up to six family members to learn together, even if they have different abilities. The instructor tailors the lesson to meet their needs. Cost is $275 for three hours and $445 for six hours.

Winter Park's National Sports Center for the Disabled, the world's leader in disabled ski instruction, has a full-time race-training program for disabled skiers. Instruction is available for all levels, and the race program is open to advanced intermediates or above.

The resort also has special multiday clinics at various times during the season.

Racing: NASTAR, daily on the Cranmer Trail above Snoasis Restaurant. It costs $5 for the first run; $1 for each additional run. Drop-ins are welcome in the Masters (25 and older) race-training program.

Child care [2002/03 prices]

Ages: 2 months to 5 years.
Costs: Including lunch, $75 a day; $60 half day. Parents can rent beepers for $5 per day. Half day does not include lunch.

Reservations: Advanced reservations are required for day care; reservations for lessons are strongly recommended, especially on weekends. Reservation forms are required and may be obtained from Winter Park Central Reservations or the Winter Park Children's Center. A $5 non-refundable fee is charged. Call 726-1551, or make your child-care reservations when you book your lodging. Winter Park sometimes hits capacity in its daycare program.

Note: Winter Park has always been a leader in creative children's ski programs. Its multistory Children's Center handles more than 600 children on some days and does it very well. The center is open from 8 a.m. to 4 p.m.

Children's lessons: Tots aged 3 and 4 have a full-day program for $90 with rentals and lunch. All-day programs for older children, including lifts and lunch, cost $80 without rentals; $90 with rentals; $5 discounts for each additional day. Snowboard lessons start with third-graders (in American schools, that's usually age 7) to age 14 through the Children's Center. Snowboard and boots rental is $20 per day.

Lift tickets [2002/03 prices]

	Adult	Child (6-13)
One day	$58	$18
Three days	$144 ($48/day)	$54 ($18/day)
Five days	$220 ($44/day)	$72 ($18/day)

Who skis free: Kids 5 and younger; seniors 70 and older.

Who skis at a discount: Ages 62–69 ski for $34. Disabled skiers ski for about half of the adult one-day price. Winter Park also offers early- and late-season discounts, and has discounts through Denver businesses. Half-day tickets are offered for mornings or afternoons. Beginner lift tickets on the Galloping Goose lift at Mary Jane cost $5 per day. Try to ski here at least two consecutive days. The per-day cost drops significantly for a two-day or longer ticket.

Accommodations

Winter Park Central Reservations can book 150 different lodging properties, plus air transportation, lift tickets and special activities. Call (800) 729-5813. This resort has a group of mountain inns unique in Colorado. They are like small bed & breakfasts but many include dinner, as well. They all serve meals family-style so guests get a chance to meet one another easily. Most inns have transportation to and from the slopes. The food is usually fantastic and plentiful, and the inn owners go out of their way to please their guests. These inns are perfect for solo travelers who want to meet others. In fact, Central Reservations can book a four-night package for solos that includes mountain inn lodging with its meals, three days of lift tickets, and a Ski & Snowboard School workshop to improve your skills while meeting others of similar slope abilities. Prices begin at $600.

There are several mountain inns in Winter Park. Perhaps the most upscale is the **Gasthaus Eichler** (726-5133 or 800-543-3899; $–$$$). The inn is very European and the rooms are well decorated with down comforters on the beds. Each bathroom is equipped with a jetted tub. It's perfect if you want quiet elegant lodging in the center of town within walking distance of restaurants and nightlife. Prices include breakfast and a massive dinner.

Arapahoe Ski Lodge (726-8222 or 800-754-0094; $–$$$), also downtown, is a No-Smoking mountain inn that feels like home. The rooms have private baths. It features a large spa and indoor swimming pool. Prices include dinner, breakfast and transport to the slopes.

The Woodspur Lodge (726-8417 or 800-626-6562; $–$$$) has a massive living room with a fireplace, soaring roof and plenty of space. This central area makes a perfect meeting place for the guests. The rooms here are of two types—newly restored and old style. Ask for one of the updated rooms if you are staying as a couple and one of the older rooms for larger groups. The lodge is served by local buses as well as lodge vans that shuttle skiers to the area and the town. Rates include breakfast and dinner.

The Timber House Ski Lodge (726-5477 or 800-843-3502; $–$$$) is tucked into the woods at the edge of the area. A private trail lets you ski directly back to the lodge. You'll meet other guests in the giant living room with its stone fireplace, at family-style meals, or soaking in the outdoor hot tub. Rates include breakfast and dinner.

The other mountain inns and B&Bs are outside of town toward Tabernash.

The Wild Horse Inn (800-729-5813; $$–$$$) is the most elegant of the local B&B's and is built with large pine logs. The seven rooms each have a private bath and private balcony. The living room is large and comfortably furnished with leather chairs and couches. Special attractions include a hot tub, an on-site masseuse, and endless freshly baked cookies.

Whistle Stop Bed & Breakfast (726-8767 or 800-729-5813; $–$$) is a casual B&B located just a block from the train station in Fraser. Two of the rooms have private baths and two have shared baths. Each guest room is located on a different level of the inn for increased privacy. The hearty breakfasts have become one of their top enticements.

The Outpost Inn (726-5346 or 800-430-4538; $–$$$), a B&B, is comfortable and homey. Vans shuttle skiers to and from the ski area. A spa attached to the building becomes a social center in the evenings. A maximum of 20 guests at a time stay at the inn. Rates include breakfast, but no dinner.

Winter Park also has many condo complexes. The most luxurious is the **Zephyr Mountain Lodge** (726-8400 or 877-754-8400; $$$–$$$$), a new slopeside condo-style hotel at the Winter Park base, featuring retail and restaurants on the ground floor with one-, two- and three-bedroom units on the upper floors. The **Iron Horse Resort Retreat** (726-8851 or 800-

Dining: $$$-Entrees $20+; $$-$10-20; $-less than $10.
Accommodations: (double room) $$$$-$200+; $$$-$141-$200; $$-$81-$140; $-$80 and less.

621-8190; $$-$$$$) has a swimming pool and a fitness center. Iron Horse is about 2 miles outside of the town center near the base of the slopes, but has excellent shuttle service if you want nightlife.

Winter Park Mountain Lodge (726-4211 or 866-726-5473; $-$$$), across from the ski resort, is part hotel, part ski lodge. It was remodeled and enlarged in 1999 and is an attractive and affordable choice for those who want to be close to the slopes. It has an indoor pool, hot tubs, brew pub and game room, and also has cable TV and phones in each room.

The Vintage (726-8801 or 800-472-7017; $$-$$$$) is also slightly out of the center of town but right next to the ski area. It features a restaurant, fitness room, swimming pool and good shuttle service into the town. The owner admires Winston Churchill and has Churchillian memorabilia throughout the hotel. The beautiful wooden bar came from a London pub. One of the finer properties in Winter Park, the Vintage has studios and suites available.

For condos in town, try either the **Snowblaze** (726-5701; $$$-$$$$) or **Crestview Place** (726-9421; $$$-$$$$). Both are across the street from Cooper Creek Square. Snowblaze has a modest athletic club with racquetball court, swimming pool and fitness center included in the price of the condo. Studio units normally come with a Murphy bed, and two- and three-bedroom units have baths for each bedroom, private saunas and fireplaces. Crestview Place does not have an athletic club or private saunas, but has fireplaces and full kitchens.

One of the most popularly priced condominiums is the **Hi Country Haus** (726-9421; $$$-$$$$). These condos are spread out in a dozen buildings and share a recreation center with four hot tubs, sauna and heated swimming pool. They are within walking distance of town and are on the shuttlebus routes.

A couple of inexpensive places to stay a few miles from town are especially good for Nordic skiers. **Devil's Thumb Ranch** (726-5632 or 800-933-4339; $-$$) is a rustic retreat at a cross-country area in Fraser and offers some of the best dining in the Fraser Valley at the Ranch House Restaurant. Also try the **Snow Mountain Ranch** (970-887-2152; Denver line, 303-443-4743), which has Nordic trails, plus dorm facilities and cabins. It's owned by YMCA of the Rockies, and it conducts year-round recreational programs.

Dining

Winter Park isn't packed with high-priced restaurants; instead, the emphasis has always been on good solid cooking. Recently, local bistros have gotten away from homestyle, stodgy cooking and are leaning toward new, innovative cuisine.

For fine food *and* a great view, head to the **Lodge at Sunspot** (726-5514; $$$$; reservations required) for dinner. The Zephyr Express converts to a gondola for a comfortable ride to this spectacular mountain restaurant. In the Dining Room, a five-course menu is $59 (without alcohol and gratuity) on Friday and Saturday nights during ski season. A family buffet featuring carved prime rib, turkey and ham for $39 is served in the Provisioner. A twilight snowmobile tour with dinner at Snoasis mid-mountain restaurant is also available.

The **Gasthaus Eichler** (726-5133; $$-$$$) in the center of Winter Park has an Austrian/German-influenced menu. Locals all rave about **The Shed** (726-9912; $$) on Hwy. 40, which has one of the most imaginative menus with an emphasis on Southwestern cuisine; and **Fontenot's Cajun Cafe** (726-4021; $$), with fresh fish dishes prepared New Orleans style.

The **Ranch House Restaurant at Devil's Thumb** (726-5633; $$$) has quickly rocketed to the top of the "must" dining experiences in Winter Park. Tenderloin steaks, rack of lamb, and fresh seafood entrees are expertly prepared in this rustic dining room that looks up to the Continental Divide.

The **Divide Grill** (726-4900; $$–$$$) in the Cooper Creek Square serves fresh fish, game and steaks as well as Northern Italian dishes and has a good salad bar. **Deno's** (726-5332), a locals' favorite, has pasta dishes as well as chicken, steak and shrimp selections. **Smokin' Moe's** (726-4600; $$), in Cooper Creek Square, has established itself as *the* place to load up on spicy barbecued ribs, hot links, chicken and "Okie baloney." **Wildcreek Restaurant** (726-1111; $$–$$$) is a fairly new entry, serving American food—beef, game, poultry, pasta, seafood and classic western fare (like buffalo wings)—with a Continental flare. Also new is the **Base Camp Bakery & Café** (726-5530; $–$$), a tiny place that makes excellent breakfasts, baked goods, and nice sandwiches, salads and desserts for lunch.

For family fare try **The Last Waltz** (726-4877; $$), which serves three excellent "good old fashioned home cooked" meals daily, American and Mexican, in a friendly atmosphere.

In Fraser, **DeAntonio's** (726-9999; $) makes good pizza and take-out food. **Randi's Irish Saloon** (726-1172; $–$$$) in downtown Winter Park was voted by locals as the best family restaurant of 2001 with plenty of traditional pub food served at lunch and dinner.

The recently renovated and renamed **Marvin's Hideaway Park** (726-1081; $$–$$$) has two dining options: The Point is family-friendly fare with items such as peanut butter and honey presented as a California sushi roll. Meanwhile, upstairs in the main dining room, the menu features stuffed trout, buffalo, roast chicken and stuffed pork chops prepared by chef Marvin Bronstein, who was named one of America's top 50 by *Gourmet.*

Hernando's Pizza & Pasta Pub (726-5409; $–$$), with its central fireplace, is highly recommended by locals, but is often crowded—you can opt for free delivery though. Great thin-crust pizza and unusual combinations are their specialty. It's especially popular with families. Also try the **Winter Park Pub** (726-4929; $$), downtown on Hwy. 40, which offers traditional pub fare, 15 beers on tap, and "Mystery Beer Night." There are a lot of 20-somethings here.

The best eggs-and-bacon breakfast in town is found at **The Kitchen** (726-9940; $), but only if you aren't pressed for time. **Carver's Bakery & Café** (725-8202; $–$$) behind Cooper Creek Square serves hearty breakfasts, amazing cinnamon roles and superb sandwiches.

On the slopes, the best lunch is in the smallish, cozy **Club Car** (726-1442; $) restaurant at the Mary Jane base area. Save room for dessert—particularly the mud pie. The **Lodge at Sunspot** (726-1446; $–$$) atop the mountain is a spectacular setting for a gourmet lunch.

Condo dwellers and others who want to gather their own provisions will find a large **Safeway** supermarket (726-9484) in Fraser; it can be reached by the free shuttlebus.

 ## Après-ski/nightlife

For après-ski, the **Derailer Bar** in the West Portal of the Winter Park Base area is the place to be. **The Shed,** in downtown Winter Park, has happy hour deals on margaritas and appetizers, and is popular with locals and visitors alike. **The Pub** is best described as "hardcore local," while **La Taqueria,** a Mexican spot, is a good happy hour locale with two-for-one drinks and $1 tacos from 4–6 p.m.

For sports events, go to **Deno's Mountain Bistro** with half-a-dozen TVs, plus more than 100 types of beer and 200 wines. **Kickapoo's** is a tavern/restaurant on the ground level of Zephyr Mountain Lodge at the base of the slopes, with two outdoor decks for drinks and dining on sunny days.

The dancing nightlife centers in these spots: **Wildcreek Restaurant** has pool tables as well as live music—this place really moves after 10 p.m. **Randi's Irish Saloon** also features live music that draws the dancing crowd after dinner.

Dining: $$$–Entrees $20+; $$–$10–20; $–less than $10.

Accommodations: (double room) $$$$–$200+; $$$–$141–$200; $$–$81–$140; $–$80 and less.

For a quiet drink without the loud music, head to **Winston's** in the Vintage Hotel or **Eichler's**. **The Iron Horse** sometimes has a guitar player in the bar, and a Comedy Club every other Wednesday. **Higher Grounds** is an excellent martini bar.

Diehards using public transportation, take note: After midnight, the free shuttle service is finished, but **Home James** (726-5060) has taxi service available until 2 a.m.

Other activities

Devil's Thumb Outfitters (726-1099) and Dashing Through the Snow (726-5376) have old-fashioned **sleigh rides** with a stop for refreshments around a roaring campfire. Devil's Thumb Ranch (726-8231) has **winter horseback riding, sleigh rides** (including a dinner ride) and **ice skating**.

Grand Adventures (726-9247 or 800-726-9257), with **dogsled rides** pulled by spirited Siberian huskies, go through miles of spectacular backcountry. Dog Sled Rides of Winter Park (726-8326) is another option.

Trailblazer (726-8452 or 800-669-0134) or Grand Adventures (726-9247 or 800-726-9257) offer **snowmobile tours**. They run about $35 for one hour, with multi-hour discounts. The resort offers an evening dinner tour where riders go up the ski runs. **Snoscoots** are scaled-down snowmobiles that drivers ages 9 and older can operate around a marked, flat track next to the highway between Winter Park and Fraser. For **snow tubing,** go to the Fraser Valley Tubing Hill (726-5954). Cost is $12 per hour after 6 p.m. and $11 per hour before 6 p.m.

The Base Camp 9000 Indoor Climbing Wall is a newly installed, 750 square-foot, state-of-the-art apparatus located in the base area's West Portal Station building.

There are a few **shops,** especially for sports equipment and clothing.

Getting there and around

By air: Denver International Airport is a hub for several major airlines. Home James vans take skiers from the airport to Winter Park. The fare each way is about $41. Reserve through central reservations, or contact the van lines directly. Home James: 726-5060 in Colorado; or (800) 729-5813.

By car: Winter Park is 85 miles northwest of Denver International Airport on Hwy. 40. Take I-70 west to Exit 232, then head toward Winter Park and Fraser on Hwy. 40.

By train: Amtrak's California Zephyr, which runs between Chicago and San Francisco, makes a stop in Fraser, only a few miles from the ski area. Special packages make the trains very affordable. Call Winter Park Central Reservations for details at (800) 729-5813. Call Amtrak for information and train-only reservations: (800) 872-7245 (USA-RAIL).

The Ski Train is an unusual treat. This train leaves Denver's Union Station every Saturday and Sunday from mid-December to April, and adds a Friday departure from mid- February to early April. It also adds special trips on a holiday schedule. Operating for more than 60 years, it brings 750 passengers from Denver directly to the Winter Park base area, chugging along 56 miles and climbing 4,000 feet. The train snakes through 28 tunnels and across canyons, ravines, and ice-crusted rivers. The scenery is as gripping as any in the Swiss and Austrian Alps. Round-trip rates are about $65 club and $40 coach. For Ski Train information and reservations, call (303) 296-4754.

Getting around: Rent a car for any extensive restaurant or bar hopping. If you plan to stick close to your lodging at night and your lodge transports you to the slopes, you won't need a car. The Smart Shuttle runs between all bars and lodging on Friday and Saturday from 10:30 p.m. to 2 a.m. No need to book first, just wait for the shuttle at the bar's entrance.

Nearby resorts

SolVista Golf and Ski Ranch, Granby, CO;
(970) 887-3384; (888) 283-7458
Internet: www.solvista.com
5 lifts; 287 acres; 1,000 vertical feet

SolVista caters to families and is well suited for them, with ski-in/ski-out condos, gentle terrain, one central base lodge and many off-slope activities (be aware that they do not have child care). SolVista's ski area is comprised of two separate interconnected mountains. East Mountain is primarily for beginners and intermediates, while West Mountain's terrain is mainly intermediate and advanced with limited beginner access. Bear Bahn Park is a separate learn-to-ski park. All lifts radiate from a central base lodge making it easy for families and groups to ski together. Groups can rent SolVista for private night-skiing parties. The resort also has 40 km. of groomed Nordic track adjacent to the base lodge.

Lift tickets (2001/02 prices): Adults, $37-39; Juniors (6-12), $15-18; Seniors (61-69), $23-25; 70+ and younger than 6, free.

Distance from Denver: About 80 miles west via I-70 and Hwy. 40. It's 15 miles north of Winter Park.

Lodging information: SolVista Reservation and Travel (888-283-7458; 887-3384) is the booking agency for more than 20 properties that include condominiums, family-style mountain inns, hotels, bed and breakfasts, motels, and property management companies.

Berthoud Pass, Winter Park, CO;
(970) 726 0287; (800) 754-2378.
Internet: www.berthoudpass.com
No lifts; snowcat and hike-to-ski programs only

Just 15 miles from Winter Park, Berthoud Pass is Colorado's oldest ski area—it started operations in 1937, but folks have been skiing here since the late 1800s. Closed in 1992, it reopened for the 1997/98 season with lift operations, but switched to backcountry skiing in 2001. Its 1,700 acres of prime backcountry terrain is strictly for strong intermediate to expert skiers and riders.

Snowcat Tours: Full-day, guided snowcat tours are based on ability levels and include continental breakfast, powder ski demos, guide service and instruction, lunch, and afternoon refreshments; $185 per person; $1,700 for the whole cat (seats 12 people); advanced reservations required.

Hike-to-Ski Tours: All-day guided tours with skiers and riders trekking uphill the old-fashioned way; $100 per person (groups of 2 or more); $150 per person for a private tour; advanced reservations required.

Distance from Denver: About 50 miles via I-70 and Hwy. 40.

Lodging Information: Lodging is in Winter Park; Winter Park Central Reservations (800) 729-5813.

Sun Valley

Idaho

Summit elevation:	9,150 feet
Vertical drop:	3,400 feet
Base:	5,750 feet

Address: Sun Valley Resort,
1 Sun Valley Rd., Box 10, Sun Valley, ID 83353
Area code: 208
Toll-free reservations: (800) 786-8259
(for Sun Valley properties)
or (800) 634-3347 (Central Reservations)
Snow report: (800) 635-4150
Fax: 726-4533 or 622-3700
E-mail: ski@sunvalley.com (general info) or
reservations@visitsunvalley.com
Internet: www.sunvalley.com or
www.visitsunvalley.com
Expert:★★★★ **Advanced:**★★★★★
Intermediate:★★★★★
Beginner:★★★ **Never-ever:**★★★

Number of lifts: 19–7 high-speed quads,
4 triple chairs, 5 doubles, 3 surface lift
Snowmaking: 60 percent
Skiable acreage: 2,054 acres
Uphill capacity: 28,180 per hour
Snowboarding: Yes
Bed Base: 6,000
Nearest lodging: Walking distance, condos
Resort child care: Yes, 6 months to 6 years
Adult ticket, per day: $63 (2002/03 price)

Dining:★★★★★
Apres-ski/nightlife:★★★★
Other activities:★★★★

Sun Valley may provide America's perfect ski vacation. It has a European accent mixed with the Wild West. It is isolated, yet comfortable; rough in texture, but also refined; Austrian in tone, cowboy in spirit.

Ageless would be the one word to describe Sun Valley Village, America's first ski resort, built in 1936 by Union Pacific tycoon Averell Harriman. It exudes restrained elegance with the traditional Sun Valley Lodge, village, steeple, horse-drawn sleighs and steaming pools. In contrast, the town of Ketchum is all-American West, a flash of red brick, a slab of prime rib, a rustic cluster of small restaurants, shops, homes, condos and lodges. It's the town of Ketchum that actually curls around the broad-shouldered evergreen rise of Bald Mountain, known as Baldy to locals. Each snow ribbon dropping from the summit into the valley leads to the streets of Ketchum.

This is Hemingway country. When he wasn't hobnobbing with the glitterati of the day, he wrote most of *For Whom The Bell Tolls* in the Sun Valley Lodge, where photos show Hollywood celebrities who first made the place famous. Sun Valley has developed many famous winter-sport athletes: the late Gretchen Fraser, who was the first American Olympic ski champion in 1948; Christin Cooper, a 1984 silver Olympic medalist; Picabo Street, who won a silver at the 1994 Olympics and a gold in the 1998 Olympics; and Muffy Davis, 2002 three-time Paralympic silver medalist and overall World Cup Champion. The Sun Valley Company keeps the skiing as up-to-date as any in America: The resort has a large computerized snowmaking system and seven high-speed quads, including one that rises a whopping 3,144 vertical feet in 10 minutes. Its three lodges—Seattle Ridge, Warm Springs and River Run—have won raves from skiers and architectural awards from the ski industry.

And yet, it is the celebration of its history that makes Sun Valley stand out from the rest of America's ski areas. If you enjoy history, you must stay at the Sun Valley Lodge, a beautifully kept-up property with a pronounced mid-20th-century feel. The elegance of a bygone era is in the details: uniformed doormen; a formal dining room; a large second-floor "drawing room" with the piano in the center, overstuffed chairs and sofas in the middle, and fireplaces at either end; and an immense "hot tub" swimming pool that dates to the early days of the resort. Then there are the continual showings on the lodge's in-room televisions of "Sun Valley Serenade," a 1941 movie starring Sonja Henie and John Payne that is as corny as can be when you see it at home, but is lots of fun when you see it in Sun Valley, especially when you later try to track down the exact filming locations on the mountain and in the lodge.

America's oldest ski resort has managed to age gracefully without losing any of the magic it had in its youth. Sun Valley's magic is in its fresh powder and vacation ambiance. It's the American version of the European ski week.

Mountain layout—Skiing

The main drawback to Sun Valley is the split in the ski areas. Bald Mountain (called "Baldy") is best suited for intermediate and advanced skiers, while beginners and never-evers should stick to Dollar/Elkhorn.

◆◆ **Expert** ◆ **Advanced:** Baldy's terrain is best known for its long runs with a consistent pitch that keeps skiers concentrating on turns from top to bottom, rather than dozing off on a flat or bailing out on a cliff or wall. Mile-long ridge runs lead to a clutch of advanced and intermediate bowls.

Limelight is a long, excellent bump run for skiers with strong knees and elastic spinal columns. Of the other black-diamond descents, the Exhibition plunge is one of the best known. Fire Trail, on the ski area boundary, is a darting, tree-covered descent for those who can make quick, flowing turns. The Seattle Ridge trail with hypnotic views curves around the bowls. The bowl area below is a joy. The downhill skier's right is a little easier, skier's left a little tougher, and you can catch the sun throughout the day. There are sections where you can do 50-yard-wide turns, but there is no easy terrain where you can relax your quads. The only flats are on top.

■ **Intermediate:** Baldy is good for this level, too. Trails are not apt to be quite so wide as at other Rocky Mountain resorts, but they're a lot wider than the ones in New England, and these trails are—for the most part—long, very long.

The best warm-ups are either the Upper and Lower College runs leading to the River Run area, or the Warm Springs run. Both descend from the top and head to the base (College takes a little jog and joins with River Run near the bottom). Warm Springs is labeled blue-square, while College is labeled green. Frankly, we didn't observe that much of a difference. Both are long, moderately steep, very well groomed and loads of fun. Other good spots are Cozy, Hemingway and Greyhawk in the Warm Springs area, often less crowded because the trail map shows a black-diamond entry (there's an intermediate cat-track entrance a little farther down that isn't as obvious on the map), as well as the Seattle Ridge runs, marked green but definitely intermediate level.

If you want to follow the sun, start your day in the River Run area, then shift to the runs dropping off Seattle Ridge and finish up cruising the Warm Springs face.

●● **Beginner:** Do not be fooled by the green-circle markings on the Baldy trail map. Beginners should not ski Baldy. The runs are seriously underrated for difficulty. Yes, yes, we're well aware that the green-blue-black ratings system reflects the relative difficulty of the trails at each individual resort. Sun Valley followed the rules and marked the "easiest" runs on Baldy with green circles. Compared to other resorts, however, these runs are blue—royal blue. If you are at all tentative about your skills, start out on Dollar. However, this means you'll be isolated for lunch and après-ski from family and friends who are skiing Baldy. When you feel you're ready for Baldy, try the Upper and Lower College run first.

● **Never-ever:** Skiing parents can enroll their children in ski school at the River Run Lodge and Skier Services building at the base of the River Run trail on Baldy. The ski school will transport children enrolled in novice lessons to Dollar. Adult never-evers should head directly to Dollar. The terrain here is perfect for learning and good for intermediates perfecting technique or starting out in powder. Skiing on the Dollar side of this mountain is shorter and more limited than on the Elkhorn face, which offers a small bowl with greater pitch and more challenging runs.

Mountain layout—Snowboarding

Baldy's terrain is best known for its long runs with a consistent pitch, great for turning perfect arcs. Be prepared for the mile-long ridge runs that lead to several advanced and intermediate bowls, but don't avoid them or you'll miss out on some prime terrain. If you're an intermediate planning to sample the Warm Springs terrain, just be aware that the intermediate entrance is a cat track. Novices and beginners will want to head to Dollar. Pay close attention to the advice we've given in the skiing section above.

Mountain rating

If your group is solid intermediate to expert, you will thoroughly enjoy skiing and riding together on Baldy. If your group is entirely never-ever to intermediate, you also will enjoy skiing or riding together on Dollar. When the intermediates are ready for Baldy, the lower-level skiers and riders may be ready for a day off to explore town. Mixed-ability groups may not be so thrilled, unless they truly don't mind being separated.

Cross-country and snowshoeing

The Sun Valley/Ketchum area has about 210 km. of trails overall. The closest facilities are at the **Sun Valley Nordic Center** (622-2250 or 622-2251), within walking distance of the Sun Valley Lodge, where 40 km. of cross-country ski trails are groomed and marked for difficulty. They range from easy two-way trails on the golf course to isolated forest escapes; 2 km. are dog friendly. There is a half-track width for children as well as a terrain garden. The daily trail fee is $12, with discounts for half-day, children and seniors. Group and private lessons are available. There is also an Atlas snowshoe center, along with 6 km. of free designated snowshoe trails. Snowshoe rental is $15 a day or $12 for a half day.

The Blaine County Recreation District grooms the **North Valley Trails**, which have more than 100 km. of groomed trails in the Sawtooth National Recreation Area supported by set trail fees or donations. More than 30 km. are dog friendly. The largest center is **Galena Lodge** (726-4010; grooming report, 726-6662) with 56 km. of trails, a full restaurant and a ski shop. It also has a 15-km. snowshoe trail and snowshoe rentals. A popular event is dinner, followed by moonlit skiing. Rentals and lessons are available, and every Thursday you can full-moon ski with a ranger and learn about natural history or wildlife. These tours are free with a trail pass. Galena is 24 miles north of Ketchum on Hwy. 75.

Wood River Trails features 30 km. of trails stretching north of Ketchum to Hailey and Bellevue. **Lake Creek** has 15.5 km. of trails, and three other areas have less than 10 km. each. The **Boulder Mountain Trail** stretches 30 km. from the Sawtooth National Recreation Area headquarters 8 miles north of Ketchum to Easley Hot Springs and Galena, and is groomed all winter, snow conditions permitting.

Avalanche and snow reports are available 24 hours a day from the Ketchum Ranger District at 788-1200, ext. 8027. North Valley Trails maintains a **grooming hotline,** 726-6662.

For backcountry tours through the largest wilderness area outside Alaska, contact either **Sun Valley Trekking** (788-9585) or **Sawtooth Mountain Guides** (774-3324). Both feature hut-to-hut skiing and the opportunity to stay in yurts as well.

Lessons (2002/03 prices)

Call the Sun Valley Ski School (622-2248 or 622-2231) for more information on any of these programs.

Group lessons: $44 for two hours, with multiday discounts, for skiing and snowboarding.

Never-ever package: None. Never-evers will need to sign up for lessons, rent equipment and buy lift tickets separately.

Private lessons: $93 per person for one hour. Discounts are available for multiple hours (cheaper in the afternoon). All-day private costs $425 per person.

Special programs: Racing clinics run three hours per day for $65. A multiday women's clinic for upper intermediates is held several times each season—call for exact dates.

Child care (2002/03 prices)

Ages: Sun Valley's Playschool in the Sun Valley Village offers care for kids 6 months to 6 years, but the upper age limit is not strictly enforced, should you have a 7-year-old who doesn't ski or ride.

Costs: Ages 6 months–2 years, $90 full day, $64 for a half day. Toddlers in diapers: $68 all day, $54 half day. Toilet-trained and older: $58.50 full day, $48.50 half day.

Reservations: Required, and priority is given to guests in Sun Valley resort hotels and condos. Call 622-2288.

Other options: Super Sitters (788-5080) has screened sitters trained in CPR and first aid who do in-room babysitting. **Baby's Away** (800-327-9030; 726-0199) rents and will deliver baby needs to your lodge, such as crib, stroller, car seat and toys.

Children's lessons: A four-hour ski session, including lunch, is $85 for kids 4-12 years old; snowboard lessons are for kids 7-12. Tiny Tracks is a ski lesson, from noon to 1 p.m., for kids 3-4 years old; cost is $45. Discounts are available for multiple days in all children's programs.

Lift tickets (2002/03 prices)

	Adult	Child (Up to 12)
One day	$63	$36
Three of four days	$186 ($62/day)	$105 ($35/day)
Five of six days	$306 ($61+/day)	$170 ($34/day)

These are prices for tickets at Baldy.

Who skis free: Children 15 and younger ski and stay free when they are with a parent (one child per parent) in a Sun Valley Resort hotel or condo or any participating property in Ketchum, Elkhorn or Warm Springs. Blackout periods for this offer are the Christmas/New Year holiday, most of February and half of March; call 622-2231 for specific dates.

Who skis at a discount: Ages 65 and older pay $43 per day. Prices for those who ski only at Dollar/Elkhorn are: adult $25, child $20. Sun Valley lowers ticket prices in early and late season.

 ## Accommodations

For **information or reservations** for Sun Valley and Ketchum, call (800) 634-3347.

The **Sun Valley Lodge & Sun Valley Resort** (800-786-8259, spells SUN-VALY; $$–$$$$) is the heart of the resort, though it is not slopeside. You can relax on terraces and in grand sitting rooms beneath coppery chandeliers. Gleaming outside is a skating rink once ruled by ice queen Sonja Henie. The village is a 3,800-acre Alpine enclave of pedestrian walkways, wall paintings, snow sculptures and spruce foliage. Because the Lodge was built well before the time of group tourism, each room is unique: pricing depends on room size and added factors such as view and balcony. **The Sun Valley Inn** (800-786-8259, spells SUN-VALY; $$–$$$$), about a hundred yards from the Lodge, is a bit less expensive but shares most amenities. Condos and suites are available; ask about packages.

Knob Hill Inn (800-526-8010 or 726-8010; $$$–$$$$), recently accepted into the exclusive Relais et Chateaux group, is one of the Ketchum area's most luxurious. The building is so Austrian you feel as if you've stepped out of your car into the Tyrol.

Pennay's at River Run (800-736-7503 or 726-9086; $$$–$$$$) is a cluster of family-perfect condos within walking distance of River Run lifts. There is a big outdoor hot tub, and units have VCRs.

Best Western Tyrolean Lodge (800-333-7912 or 726-5336; $–$$), only 400 yards from the River Run lift, has an Alpine atmosphere with wood-paneled ceilings and downy comforters dressing the beds. A champagne continental breakfast is served.

Best Western Kentwood Lodge (800-805-1001 or 726-4114; $$) with an indoor pool is in the middle of town, convenient to everything.

Clarion Inn (800-262-4833 or 726-5900; $$–$$$$) is a hotel with a large outdoor Jacuzzi and continental breakfasts. Rooms are open to outdoor walkways and the decor is simple.

Christophe CondoHotel (800-521-2515 or 726-5601; $–$$$$) has roomy condos with underground parking and heated pool. A fire truck races guests back and forth to the lifts.

Tamarack Lodge (800-521-5379 or 726-3344; $$) is smack in the middle of town with a hot tub and indoor pool. Good for families, the lodge is equipped with microwaves, refrigerators and coffee makers. It doesn't get any more convenient than this for nightlife and dining. Rooms with fireplaces cost more.

Povey Pensione (128 W. Bullion St., Hailey; 800-370-4682 or 788-4682; $) is a 108-year-old residence maintaining the original character of its builder—John Povey, a British carpenter—who built and lived in the house when Hailey was a mining town. Pastel wall coverings and antique furnishings give the three bedrooms an Old West character. This Pensione is about 13 miles south of Ketchum and Sun Valley. Children under 12 are not allowed.

Ski View Lodge (726-3441; $) near downtown Ketchum has eight rustic cabins with open space in front of them and woodland and Bald Mountain views behind. The cabins have kitchens and phones, pets are welcome and there is a senior citizen discount. Rates drop 40 percent during slow seasons.

Lift Tower Lodge (800-462-8646 or 726-5163; $) gets its name from a section of an old ski lift. All rooms have two beds, a refrigerator, TV and phone, and the lodge has a Jacuzzi. Complimentary breakfasts include bagels, coffee and orange juice. The free bus stops in front. During value season the price of a room can be halved.

If you have a large group and need to rent a private home, call **Base Mountain Properties** (800-521-2515, 726-5601; www.basemountain.com) or **Premier Resorts** (800-635-4444, 727-4000). They have rentals near the lifts, downtown Ketchum, out at Elkhorn Village near the Dollar Mountain lifts, and homes that offer privacy and isolation.

Dining

On the mountain: The **Warm Springs, Seattle Ridge** and **River Run day lodges** have excellent restaurants. Skiers can settle down to a lunch of prime rib, salmon, stone-fired pizza and many other delights, all while enjoying panoramic views. The deck at Seattle Ridge is gorgeous. Deli and gourmet cafeteria-style clusters are the latest in on-mountain dining, and Sun Valley has these, too.

In Sun Valley Village: The **Sun Valley Lodge Dining Room** has old-time elegance and is the only spot in the area with live music and dinner dancing. Specialties include Steak Diane, Chateaubriand Béarnaise Bouquetière, and fresh Idaho trout or poached salmon.

The **Ram** attached to the Sun Valley Inn serves basic fare ranging from pasta to chops and steaks. **Gretchen's** in the Lodge has a fine dinner menu, and serves breakfast and lunch. The **Konditorei** has an Austrian flavor and excellent lunches, such as hearty soups served in a bread bowl next to a mountain of fruit.

In Ketchum: Sun Valley has some of the best restaurants in any ski resort in America. Anyone with fine dining on his or her mind will not be disappointed. The region's real gourmet action takes place here. The price ranges we give here are a rough guide.

These restaurants all vie for "best of Ketchum." **Michel's Christiania** (726-3388; $$$) run by Michel Rudigoz, serves fine French cuisine. **Felix** (726-1166; $$$), which has moved to 380 1st Ave. North, has a continental menu in a very Austrian setting. **Evergreen Bistro** (726-3888; $$$) has an elegant setting of wood, crystal and glass and quite possibly the town's best wine list. **Chandler's** (726-1776; $$$) serves gourmet meals in a series of tiny rooms. Ask to be seated near the fireplace if you are with a group; couples should ask for the small alcove off the main fireplace room. The three-course "prix fixe" meal is one of Ketchum's best bargains.

The **Sawtooth Club** (726-5233; $$) has a long bar with couches in front of a fireplace and small dining rooms tucked above and behind the bar. The food is good and reasonable.

The **Pioneer Saloon** (726-3139; $$), a local hangout going back into Ketchum history, is known for its prime rib and baked potatoes. **Ketchum Grill** (726-4660; $$) has a daring, innovative menu with flavor mixtures that will keep your tastebuds tingling. **China Pepper** (726-0959) is the place to head for spicy Thai and Chinese food, as well as sushi. They get rave reviews from visitors.

Sushi on Second (726-5181; $$) also has Japanese fare. Locals say **Globus** (726-1301; $$) has good Chinese/Thai food. **Panda Chinese Restaurant** (726-3591; $) serves Chinese meals from several regions. **Smoky Mountain Pizza** (622-5625; $) has great, very affordable Italian fare and massive salads.

Dining: $$$-Entrees $20+; $$-$10-20; $-less than $10.
Accommodations: (double room) $$$$-$200+; $$$-$141-$200; $$-$81-$140; $-$80 and less.

Warm Springs Ranch Restaurant (726-2609; $$) serves a wide-ranging menu including children's specials, and mountain trout swim in pools near the cozy cabin.

The spots for excellent and inexpensive Mexican food are **Mama Inez** (726-4213; $), at the start of Warm Springs Road near downtown Ketchum, or **Desperado's** (726-3068; $), just behind the visitor's center on Fourth Street. **Grumpy's** (no phone, we're told; $) is the locals' favorite for great burgers and beer; it's across the street from Mama Inez (and next door to a laundromat, in case you need to wash a few clothes).

Breakfast is important to most skiers. At the Sun Valley Lodge **Gretchen's** (622-2144; $) has plentiful fare with moderate prices and **Konditorei** (622-2235; $) in the Sun Valley Village has good breakfasts. The **Lodge Dining Room** (726-2150; $) serves an excellent Sunday brunch. The best breakfasts, however, are downtown in Ketchum. The **Kneadery** (726-9462; $) on Leadville Street has a cozy woodsy atmosphere. It's open for lunch as well.

Directly across the street from the Warm Springs Lodge at the base of Baldy is a Ketchum institution, **Irving's Red Hot** stand, where you can get great hotdogs. "The Works" (a dog smothered in fixings and chips) for only $2 is a lunch bargain that can't be beat.

One evening dining adventure that should not be missed is the horse-drawn sleigh ride dinner at **Trail Creek Cabin**. The cozy rough-hewn cabin dates from 1937 and can be reached by sleigh, car or cross-country skis. For the sleigh ride, make reservations 72 hours in advance, but you can always check for open space; call 622-2135. The sleigh ride costs $17. Dinners are approximately $16–$24. **Galena Lodge** (726-4010) also offers moonlight dinners in the warmth of a rustic lodge.

Après-ski/nightlife

The **Boiler Room** at Sun Valley has the Mike Murphy comedy show every afternoon at 5 p.m. for a moderate cover charge. Check the schedule for "Sun Valley Serenade" and Warren Miller movies at the **Opera House** in Sun Valley starting at 5 p.m. And the **Duchin Room** in the Lodge has music starting at 4 p.m. On Thursdays, head to **River Run Lodge** for jazz. If you are staying in Warm Springs, wander over to **Apples** for good après-ski crowds.

At the western-bar-themed **Whiskey Jacques,** patrons can listen to live music and dance inside an authentic log building. **The Pioneer Saloon** is famous for its steaks, prime rib, and decorations (mounted elk and moose). The saloon gets very crowded very early on weekends.

Another popular spot is **The Casino**, so named because there used to be slot machines where the tables now stand (gambling is now illegal in this part of the country). It's something of a departure from the more intense nightclubs in the area, with the dance floor replaced by pool tables.

For more sedate and elegant night action try the **Duchin Room** at the Lodge, which features the Joe Foss Trio until 1 a.m. **The Sun Valley Wine Company** has a wine cellar, reportedly the largest wine selection in Idaho, and offers a light lunch and dinner menu. It is above the Ketchum state liquor store on Leadville Street. Choose a bottle of wine from its large inventory, then enjoy it in a quiet, conversation-oriented environment next to a fireplace.

Remember—if you are staying in Sun Valley or Warm Springs and plan on partying in Ketchum, the KART bus system stops running at midnight, but A-1 Taxi (726-9351) and Bald Mountain Taxis (726-2650) are available until closing.

Other activities

Snowmobiling is available through Mulligan Adventure Center (726-9137). The Sun Valley Athletic Club (726-3664) with daily and weekly rates is open to visitors with **child care, massage, aerobics, weights and swimming.** Also try High Altitude Fitness (726-1956). **Ice skating** is available year-round on the Sun Valley Resort outdoor rink.

Sun Valley Heli-Ski (622-3108) offers **backcountry ski adventures** for all levels of skiers. **Soaring** or **winter glider rides** are available through Sun Valley Soaring (726-3054). **Ice fishing/fly fishing** is offered by Silver Creek Outfitters (726-5282) and Lost River Outfitters (726-1706).

Shopping opportunities are extensive. The Sun Valley Village is full of boutiques and shops offering everything from Bogner and jewels to handmade chocolates. A few shops worth highlighting: The Toy Store, for unique and educational toys from around the globe; Barry J. Peterson Jewelers, for Limoges collectors' boxes, Lesäl ceramics and unique jewelry; The Country Cousin for low-priced accessories and gifts; and T. D. Bambino, where you can have fleece clothing custom-made. You can pick up some great bargains on secondhand items at the Gold Mine Thrift Shop, 331 Walnut Ave. Because this supports the The Community Library in Ketchum, residents give their (sometimes barely) used clothing and sporting goods to this store. By the way, the **library** is a gem. It has an amazing regional history section.

Sun Valley Center For Arts and Humanities has performances and showings during the ski season. Call 726-9491 for a schedule or the Chamber of Commerce, 726-3423. **Art galleries** are another center of Ketchum and Sun Valley's cultural life. Sun Valley's Art Gallery in the Village and twelve galleries in Ketchum are members of the Sun Valley Art Gallery Association (726-2602). They provide a beautiful brochure with a map and offer guided evening gallery walks about a dozen times during the year.

Getting there and getting around

By air: The closest airport is Friedman Memorial, 12 miles south in Hailey, served by Horizon Air (with daily non-stop flights from Los Angeles) and Delta's SkyWest Airlines. Weather sometimes closes it, and it cannot handle big jets. Most guests arrive by jet at Twin Falls, about 90 minutes away, or Boise, about 155 miles and 2.5 hours away.

Several properties provide transportation, or you can use one of the following companies, most of which will pick you up in Hailey, Twin Falls or Boise: Sun Valley Stages (800) 574-8661; Teton Stage Lines 529-8036; or Sun Valley Express (800) 622-8267 or 342-7795.

By car: Sun Valley/Ketchum is 82 miles north of Twin Falls on Hwy. 75, and 152 miles from Boise.

Getting around: You don't really need a car if you're staying in Sun Valley Village or near the KART bus routes, which link Sun Valley, Ketchum and Baldy, running about every 20 minutes. For schedule information, call 726-7140.

Idaho regional resorts

Idaho

Bogus Basin, Boise ID; (208) 332-5100; (800) 367-4397

Internet: www.bogusbasin.com

8 lifts; 2,600 skiable acres; 1,800 vertical feet

Bogus Basin, 16 miles from Boise, is much more than a day hill you might expect so close to a city. Like Colorado's Winter Park, Bogus is a big, community-owned, full-service destination resort. The mountain also has two restaurants, Nordic skiing and the 70-unit, mid-mountain Pioneer Inn. Child care starts at 6 months.

Bogus has night skiing every day until 10 p.m. on 1,500 vertical feet. That's the most extensive night skiing in the Northwest. It also has 360-degree skiing around its highest peak. The Superior Lift services 7,590-foot Shafer Butte on the front side and the Pine Creek lift serves the back side. Don't miss the back side. It's like the front on steroids.

And the name? Legend says that "fool's gold"—iron pyrite—was mined there and marketed to gullible city folks as the real thing. Real gold also was mined in the area, however, and all the ski runs are named after legitimate mines.

Lift tickets (01/02 prices): Adults, $37; children (7–11), $10; ages 6 and younger and ages 70 and older ski free.

Distance from Boise: About 16 miles north. Coming east or west on I-84, take the City Center Connector to River Street exit, then 15th Street to Hill Road to Bogus Basin Road.

Lodging information: The number for the on-site Pioneer Inn is (800) 367-4397. In Boise, the Grove Hotel (a Westcoast 5-star hotel) is central to downtown: (800) 426-0670.

Brundage Mountain, McCall, ID; (800) 888-7544, (208) 634-7462

Internet: www.brundage.com

6 lifts; 1,300 acres; 1,800 foot vertical

Brundage is definitely one of those underrated resorts. Payette Lake, which Brundage overlooks, is beautiful and sparsely populated, with many outdoor activities including good intermediate downhill skiing. From the top of the mountain, you can see the Salmon River Mountains, Payette Lakes, Oregon's Eagle Cap Wilderness and the Seven Devils towering over Hells Canyon, America's deepest river gorge. The skiing is pleasant and uncrowded, with occasional challenging drops, but mostly cruisers.

Brundage has a reputation for some of the lightest powder in the Pacific Northwest, and the mountain offers guided skiing via snowcat in a permit area of over 19,000 acres in the Payette National Forest. Child care starts at 6 weeks.

Lift tickets (01/02): Adults, $34; junior (13-18) and senior (65+), $27; children (7–12), $18; younger than 7, free.

Distance from Boise: About 100 miles north via Hwy. 55. The drive is quite scenic.

Lodging information: (888) 844-3246.

Silver Mountain, Kellogg, ID; (208) 783-1111

Internet: wwwsilvermt.com

7 lifts; 1,500 acres; 2,200 vertical feet

Silver Mountain's original name was Jackass Ski Bowl. The name honored the discoverer of the metal that brought riches to the valley more than a century ago. Local legend says a donkey got away from its owner, scampered up a hill, and was standing on a rock with a silvery glint when the owner caught up with it. Bunker Hill Mine, which also took lead, zinc and copper from the hillsides, ran the ski area for employee recreation and changed the name to Silverhorn. But in the early 1980s silver prices plunged and Bunker Hill closed.

The town decided to build a four-season resort, serviced by an aerial gondola to take skiers from the valley floor to the slopes. Silver Mountain began ski operations in 1990. The gondola, which the ski area claims is the longest in the world, descends low over the houses and yards of the town of Wardner before climbing to Silver's "base area," called Mountain Haus, at 5,700 feet. (A hefty portion of Silver's terrain is below the Mountain Haus, which gives the area its 2,200-foot vertical drop.) The gondola is the only way in and out. Silver has two connected peaks, Kellogg and Wardner. The gondola deposits skiers and snowboarders at Mountain Haus on the Kellogg side. From here they can fan out in several directions.

Silver has a lot of serious terrain, including monster glade skiing. For advanced skiers, the run rating always depends on snow conditions. On fresh powder days, take Silver Belt to Rendezvous on the Kellogg side. For great thrills on the Wardner side, cut down anywhere from the early section of the Wardner Peak Traverse. The best skiing on powder days is off the slopes between the tops of Chairs 4 and 2.

Experts love Silver Mountain. They can take the Wardner Peak Traverse to an inspirational knob with a stupendous view of the Silver Valley below. Some nice black-diamond runs go back down to the Shaft and Chair 4.

Silver Belt, from the triple Chair 2, is a wide and terrific intermediate warmup run. At the Junction you can turn down Saddle Back for a bumpier ride, or take a hard left on the Cross Over Run to the Midway load station on Chair 4 for a ride to Wardner Peak. From the top there are several trails back to Midway. Only advanced skiers pass Midway and keep going down through the Shaft to the Chair 4 base.

As good as Silver is for experts, it also offers a lot for beginners. Chairs 1, 2, 3, and 5 at the Mountain Haus base area all serve beginner terrain. Below the lodge, Ross Run is a wide beginner favorite, allowing crossover to Noahs and back again, ending on Dawdler with a choice to return to Chair 5 or Chair 3.

Note: Most skiers ski the Kellogg side, so to avoid even a mirage of crowds, ski the Wardner side. Lift lines are rarely a problem, but the gondola queue can back up for downloading at closing time (remember, you can't ski to the gondola base). To avoid morning clog, ride up a half hour early for breakfast at Mountain Haus.

Silver has some nice surprises. One is the free ski wax, right by the free ski check at Mountain Haus. Another is the guarantee: If snow conditions don't please you, return your lift ticket to the gondola base within an hour and a half and get a pass for another day.

Lift tickets (02/03): Adults, $35; college/senior (18-23/62+), $27; junior (7-17), $25. Night skiing costs $10 per evening for everyone.

Distance from Coeur d'Alene: 30 miles. **Lodging information:** (800) 204-6428. The best lodging is at the Coeur d'Alene Resort; packages available, call (800) 688-5253. The most affordable place to stay is at the base of the gondola in Kellogg.

Schweitzer Mountain, Sandpoint, ID; (208) 263-9555

Internet: www.schweitzer.com

8 lifts; 2,500 skiable acres; 2,400 vertical feet

Schweitzer is one of Idaho's largest ski areas, but it's still very uncrowded. One skier per acre (2, 500 acres) is a good-sized crowd here. Its acreage is second biggest in Idaho (Bogus Basin is slightly larger), and its vertical drop is second only to Sun Valley's 3,400.

Schweitzer has one slopeside hotel and a bunch of condos. A European-style village with shops, restaurants and lodging is planned for the future. White Pine Lodge, with one- to three-bedroom condos, plus 6,000 square feet of commercial space, is under construction; it's supposed to be ready for the 2001/02 season. Many visitors stay in Sandpoint, 11 miles away on the shore of beautiful Lake Pend Oreille. This is the sort of place that people visit, then try to figure a way to move there.

Schweitzer gets plenty of snow from its position in the Selkirks. When the storms come from the north, the snow is dry and fluffy, but more often it is wet and dense. It's drier than the Cascade Concrete that falls on Washington and Oregon areas, but still wet enough to have earned the local term, Panhandle Premix. When the skies are clear, the vistas are outstanding: From the top of Schweitzer, skiers can look east into Montana's Cabinet Range and north to the Canadian Selkirks. The view of big Lake Pend Oreille is memorable. Stella The Six-Pack Chair, a high-speed six passenger lift, replaced Chair 5 for the 2000/01 season. It carries skiers and riders to the ridge of the new Northwest Territory, what the resort calls "the land of dreams and adventure" encompassing the lift and an additional 150 acres of gladed and groomed terrain.

Schweitzer's runs and chutes are steepest at the top of its two broad ski bowls, North and South. The bowls are separated by the Great Divide run, a long wide ridge that gives you a continuous option to drop into either bowl. Chutes await advanced skiers in the South Bowl, reached by either Chair 1 or The Great Escape Quad. They're lettered A Chute, B Chute, and so forth. Upper Stiles and the adjacent Headwall Chutes are gonzo favorites. There is some double-black skiing from the rim of South Bowl, but most experts will head up the Great Escape and turn right to North Bowl. Patient trekkers will be rewarded with the Siberia Chutes. Intermediate skiers can wend their way down from the South Bowl summit, but are advised to unload midway on the Snow Ghost chair heading toward the summit of North Bowl. The runs under the Timber Cruiser chair, Cathedral Aisle and Zip Down, are intermediate favorites.

Beginners won't be able to get to the top, but can get a view by unloading midway up Chair One and heading down Gypsy. The Enchanted Forest and Happy Trails are perfect for children. Both run the length of the Musical Chairs chair, which goes right by the windows of the 40,000-square-foot Headquarters Day Lodge. The Enchanted Forest, with kid-high, widely-spaced mounds that children can go over or around, is barred to adults and jealous snowboarders. Schweitzer has a wonderful learning area, served by a separate chair and completely isolated from other traffic. Better yet, it is below the base area, so that never-evers can start out skiing, rather than sidestepping up the hill or riding a lift.

Lift tickets (01/02): Adult, $40; seniors, $35; junior (7-17), $30; 6 and younger free.

Distance from Coeur d'Alene: 50 miles. **Lodging information:** (800) 831-8810. We suggest you stay on the mountain at the Selkirk Lodge or ask about the new White Pines Lodge. In Sandpoint lodging is inexpensive (many rooms less than $100 a night) and fairly basic, ranging in size from the four-room lakeside Coit House B&B (208-265-4035) to the 60 rooms of the Lakeside Inn (800-543-8126) and Super 8 Motel (800-800-8000).

Big Mountain

Montana

Summit elevation: 7,000 feet
Vertical drop: 2,500 feet
Base elevation: 4,500 feet

Address: P.O. Box 1400
Whitefish, MT 59937
☎ Area code: 406
Ski area phone: 862-1900; (800) 858-4152
Snow report: 862-7669
ⓘ **Toll-free reservations:** (800) 858-4157
or (800) 858-3930
E-mail: bigmtn@bigmtn.com
Internet: www.bigmtn.com
or www.skiwhitefish.com (resort)
www.stayatbigmountain.com (lodging)
www.whitefishchamber.org (Chamber of Commerce)

Expert:★★★★　**Advanced:**★★★★
Intermediate:★★★★★
Beginner:★★　**Never-ever:**★★★★

Number and types of lifts: 11–2 high-speed quads, 1 quad, 5 triples, 1 double, 2 surface lifts
Skiable acreage: 3,020 acres
Snowmaking: 5 percent
Uphill capacity: 13,800 per hour
Snowboarding: Yes
Bed base: 1,600 on mountain
Nearest lodging: Slopeside, hotels and condos
Resort child care: Yes, infants and older
Adult ticket, per day: $47 (2002/03 prices)

Dining:★★★
Apres-ski/nightlife:★★★
Other activities:★★★

True ski-resort discoveries are getting harder to find. If you live in a state or province along the U.S.-Canadian border west of the Great Lakes, you probably already know about Big Mountain with skiing that stretches on forever. You probably don't want to tell anyone in the rest of the country about it. We understand, and of course we'll keep your secret.

The town or Whitefish is not the folksy, rustic place that we discovered more than a decade ago. It seems that lots of other people have discovered it as well. However, most visitors come in the summer months, which makes winter off season and uncrowded.

If you are a skier who wants lots of terrain to explore and a no-fluff, off-slope atmosphere, you should head for this aptly named ski resort tucked into the far northwest corner of Montana. This is an area popular with Seattle, Calgary, west coast and northern midwest skiers. Many hop on Amtrak's Empire Builder, which on its run between Seattle and Chicago dumps a load of eager skiers in the town of Whitefish within sight of Big Mountain's trails.

Though sometimes the resort and the community business leaders long to see their name in the various annual listings of top ski resorts (acreage-wise, it ranks in the top 10, maybe even the top five, depending on how you count), most other times, they'd rather just keep it the Northwest's little secret as long as they can. Many folks here are expatriates from other ski areas that were once as laid-back and unpretentious as Big Mountain is now.

If you were here a dozen years ago, you won't believe the town now. The mouse races are gone and everything is getting dolled up and fancy (at least in the view of old timers still meeting in the mornings for breakfast and skiers who remember it the way it was).

Everything is clean and comfortable, but you won't find concierges or valet parking. This is a down-home place where a fur coat still would look out of place except on a grizzly-bearded mountain man.

The ski area is 8 miles from the town of Whitefish, up a winding road that can be a bit scary in bad weather. At the ski area base is a cluster of hotels and condo properties and a few restaurants and bars. In Whitefish there are more hotels, the best restaurants, shopping and the biggest variety of nightlife.

The weather here is a mix of the Rockies and Pacific Northwest maritime, called "inland maritime." It creates spectacular "snow ghosts," trees encased in many layers of frost and snow, at the summit. It also produces plenty of fantastic light powder, but without the sunshine you'll find in the southern Rockies. If you forget your sunscreen, you'll probably survive, but don't forget your goggles. Pack your sunglasses too—sunny days do occur, and when they do, the skiing is spectacular. You'll want those sunglasses to see the seemingly endless view of the mountains of Glacier National Park as well as the Flathead Valley and the huge lake that dominates it.

Expanded beginner terrain last season included a triple chair that replaced the "Platter" lift on the lower west mountain just above Big Mountain Village. Beginner skiers now enjoy enhanced lift access to Question Mark and Hope Slope.

Mountain layout–Skiing

Big Mountain's ski school offers free tours of the mountain, open to intermediates and above, at 10 a.m. and 1 p.m. The main access to Big Mountain is the Glacier Chaser that moves skiers up 2,200 feet to the summit.

◆◆ **Expert** ◆ **Advanced:** If you can see it, you can ski it! Within the boundaries are 3,000 acres of sprawling terrain; another 1,000 acres is in the U.S. Forest Service permit area.

Ski straight ahead when you get off the Glacier Chaser chair and you'll drop down the north slope, a mostly intermediate series of runs alternating with tree-studded steeps. Make a U-turn when getting off the chair to reach the Good Medicine area with its wide, well-groomed intermediate trails, surrounded by fields of powder and thousands of trees beckoning to advanced and expert skiers. Here, skiers can choose how tight they want their trees, and they have plenty of opportunities to bail out onto the groomed trails.

Locals also can direct skiers to Movie Land, which starts with dense trees and then opens for great steep tree skiing before ending on Russ's Street. The Bigfoot T-bar provides access to north-facing expert terrain that includes gladed powder runs through a big timber forest.

For big-air fans, Big Mountain has a cornice next to the Summit House. Runs from this cornice, and almost all skiing to the left of the high-speed quad, end up on Russ's Street.

■ **Intermediate:** Go straight off The Glacier Chaser for the groomed runs under Chair 7, or make a U-turn to reach Toni Matt, The Big Ravine or MoeMentum (named for Olympic downhill champ Tommy Moe), all perfect for power cruising with wide GS turns. Toni Matt, Inspiration and the Big Ravine provide top-to-bottom cruising.

Lower-intermediates should make a few runs off Chair 2 or the T-bar before they try The Glacier Chaser. Chair 2's runs are equivalent in pitch to the blue runs off the front of the summit, but much shorter. This lower-mountain area is also lighted for night skiing. The Bigfoot T-bar, going into its second winter, accesses three new low-intermediate trails covering about 20 acres that have been cut on the southern exposure above Russ's Street and the Evan's Heaven area. When you're ready to try the summit runs, try the ones down the North

Slope first. The toughest part will be the upper part of MoeMentum, which can build formidable moguls by afternoon.

●● **Beginner:** Chair 3 is the best bet for beginners, though they may be frustrated at not being able to ski from the summit. There's a green trail from the summit called Russ's Street, but it has a few intermediate pitches. Look for the expanded beginner terrain, which we haven't had the chance to ski yet, and a new triple chair that replaces the "Platter" lift on the lower west mountain just above the village.

● **Never-ever:** Never-evers have an excellent learning area, separate from other skiers, on the gentle trails under Chair 6 (which costs nothing to ride, by the way).

Mountain layout—Snowboarding

From the top of Glacier Chaser, the hardest choice is deciding on which wide-open, rolling, impeccably groomed trail you should lay out a string of razor sharp, horizontal-flying Euro carves. A hint: There's no wrong answer, but just be sure to keep your speed on the cat track at the bottom. After a few warm-ups, duck into the trees almost anywhere across the mountain for some smooth powder turns, or head to the expansive out-of-bounds areas.

It's no wonder why Big Mountain is consistently rated highly by snowboard magazines, as it makes an honorable attempt to cater to riders. It sponsors its own snowboard team and has a handful of seasonal events. It also has a terrain park on Silvertail that serves up tabletops, hits, gap jumps, rails, boxes and berms.

Mountain rating

Big Mountain's generous out-of-bounds policy and the abundance of tree skiing make this a delight for expert and advanced skiers. Intermediates will like the resort's superb grooming and long cruisers. The learning area is one of the best. The recent expansion of lower-intermediate trails and beginner terrain is a welcome addition. There's now plenty to keep skiers and boarders of all abilities happy for four or more days...or a lifetime!

Cross-country and snowshoeing

Big Mountain Nordic Center (862-2900) is adjacent to the Outpost Lodge (bottom of Chair 6) and has 15 km. of groomed trails for classic and skate skiing. There is no trail fee for children 6 and younger. Downhill ski pass holders can use the cross-country trails for free. All others pay $5. Trail passes, maps and rentals are available at the Outpost Lodge or the Big Mountain Sports in the base village.

Grouse Mountain Lodge (862-3000) in Whitefish has 15 km. of groomed cross-country trails and night skiing with 2.4 km. lighted. The **Izaak Walton Inn** (888-5700), 62 miles east on Highway 2 (also an Amtrak flag stop), has 30 km. of groomed trails as well as guides who take skiers into the Glacier National Park wilderness. Guides for groups of two to four or more cost $60–$95 per person.

Glacier National Park provides a natural cross-country paradise. Here the unplowed park roads and trails provide kilometer after kilometer of ungroomed passages. Check with the communications center (888-5441) or the park rangers for weather and snow conditions.

Lessons (2002/03 prices)

Group lessons: Half day, $30; full day, $48.

Never-ever package: Lower-mountain lift ticket and two-hour lesson for skiing or snowboarding is $30. Rentals cost extra.

Private lessons: One or two people, half day costs $155 ($50 for each additional person); full day costs $300 ($50 for each additional person). One-hour Quick Tips costs $72 (as available).

Special programs: Big Mountain has design-your-own clinics for groups of up to 11; plus afternoon lessons for bumps, steeps and powder for $30. Ask about them if you're interested. Telemark and Nordic lessons are by appointment only, $75 each for one or two people. Women's workshops and advanced skiing seminars are taught at select times. Call the ski school at 862-2909 for dates and prices.

Racing: A NASTAR course is open off Chair 3 Thursdays through Sundays 11 a.m.–2 p.m. Cost is $5 for two runs and $1 for each additional run.

Child care (2002/03 prices)

Ages: Newborns to 12 years.

Costs: Full day, 14 months and older, $45.50 including lunch. Full day for infants younger than 14 months is $65 ($35 for half day), not including lunch. The day-care facility is open three nights a week until 10 p.m. for babysitting at $7.50 per hour for 14 months and older. The facility has room for just three infants at a time, so reserve far in advance. Discounts available for families with multiple children.

Reservations: Required for infants and recommended for toddlers, 862-1999.

Children's lessons: For skiers ages 3–4, and snowboarders ages 4–7, private lessons are required. Cost is $45 for a 45-minute lesson. Ages 5–6 have a one-hour lesson that costs $18. Rentals and lift tickets are extra in both cases. Full day for older children includes four hours of lessons (two sessions) for $48; half-day, $30. Lift tickets, rental gear and lunch are optional, but not included in the price. Learn to Ski (ages 7-14) and Learn to Snowboard (8-14) is a half-day lesson, limited lift ticket and rentals; skiers pay $42, snowboarders pay $46. Reservations are recommended for all children's lessons.

Lift tickets (2002/03 prices)

	Adult	Junior (7-18)
One day	$47	$34
Three days	$138 ($46/day)	$99 ($33/day)
Five days	$220 ($44/day)	$155 ($31/day)

Who skis free: Children ages 6 and younger. Night skiing costs $14, but is free with a day or multiday ticket. Chair 6 is free each day for skiing and snowboarding.

Who skis at a discount: Skiers 62 and older and college students pay $39, with no multiday discounts. A ticket for lower-mountain lifts only is $26, and can be upgraded to a full-mountain pass by paying the difference. If you have a season pass or frequent skier card at *any North American resort,* you pay just $39 (no blackout dates). All skiers and riders pay just $25 between Nov. 28 and Dec. 20, 2002. Between April 1 and April 13, 2003, lift tickets are just $20.

Note: Day and multiday ticket holders may ride the Glacier Chaser to the Summit House for dinner without charge on select nights. The Glacier Chaser turns into a gondola for night riding. Other passengers headed for the summit at night pay $9.

Nearby resorts

Blacktail Mountain, a fairly new area in northern Montana, offers panoramic views of Glacier National Park and Flathead Lake. The parking lot is at the top of the mountain so you get to ski before you ever board a lift. If the facilities seem familiar, it's because Blacktail's three lifts were bought used from Crystal Mountain, WA; Steamboat Springs, CO; and Calgary's Olympic Park.

Blacktail Mountain offers three lifts, 24 runs on 200 acres with a vertical drop of about 1,500 feet. Lift tickets (2002/03 prices) are $27 for adults; $18 for students ages 13–18; $12 for children ages 8–12; free for ages 7 and younger and 70 and older. The 17,000-square-foot lodge at the "base" area houses everything—the ski shop, ski school, bar and restaurant all are located in the three-story building. Day care is available. The ski area is in Lakeside, about 45 minutes south of Kalispell, which itself is about half an hour from Whitefish. Phone: 406-844-0999; Internet: www.blacktailmountain.com.

Accommodations—on mountain

All accommodations, both in town and on-mountain, can be reserved by calling **Big Mountain Reservations** at (800) 858-4152 or the **Whitefish Chamber** at (877) 862-3548. Lower rates are available before Christmas, in January and in April; higher rates apply during the Christmas/New Year and Presidents' Day.

The **Alpinglow Inn** (800-SKI-6760; $$) lies at the center of the village. This lodging has beautiful views from the restaurant and is perhaps the most convenient location for skiers. Sauna, two outdoor hot tubs overlooking the valley, laundry facilities and gift shop on site. The American plan includes lodging, lifts and meals, and the Alpinglow is the only one on the mountain to offer such an all-inclusive plan that lets you know your vacation costs before you leave home.

The **Kandahar Lodge** (862-6098; $$–$$$$) at Big Mountain looks like a mountain lodge should—log decor, spacious public areas and a soaring stone fireplace. The rooms are large and the food outstanding. A free shuttle takes guests to the base area and at the end of the day skiers and riders can glide right to the door.

The **Edelweiss** (800-858-3930; $$–$$$$) is centrally located in the base area and has studios as well as one- and two-bedroom condos. Complimentary ski waxing and bottle of wine offered to guests.

The **Hibernation House** (800-858-4152; $$) is touted as the "friendliest lodge on the mountain." It is the least expensive and has rooms with queen beds, twin bunks and private baths. There is a large indoor Jacuzzi, laundry and a clean and inviting lobby. Breakfast is included in the cost.

Kintla Lodge (800-888-5439 or 862-1960; $$$–$$$$) at the base of the mountain features outdoor hot tubs, sauna and underground parking. It is Big Mountain's newest facility and features all the luxuries of home in every unit.

Dining: $$$-Entrees $20+; $$-$10-20; $-less than $10.
Accommodations: (double room) $$$$-$200+; $$$-$141-$200; $$-$81-$140; $-$80 and less.

Accommodations—in Whitefish

Eight miles away in Whitefish is a variety of lodging. Many properties offer ski packages, which include lift tickets, and free transportation to and from the mountain. Be sure to ask when you make your reservation.

The biggest and most convenient hotel is the **Grouse Mountain Lodge** (800-321-8822; $$-$$$). It has an indoor pool, two restaurants and a spacious bar. A free guest shuttle takes guests to the mountain every morning as well as downtown for those who don't want to walk the short distance. Cross-country skiing on the golf course is right out the back door. **The Pine Lodge** (800-305-7463; $-$$$) boasts an indoor-outdoor pool with connecting swim channel, hot tub and free continental breakfast. **The Best Western-Rocky Mountain Lodge** (800-862-2569; $-$$$) includes a continental breakfast in its rates and features an outdoor pool and spa.

On the B&B side, the **Garden Wall Inn** (888-530-1700; $$-$$$) is on the free S.N.O.W. bus route and within walking distance of downtown. It's an impeccably restored 1920's house-turned-inn featuring five guestrooms furnished with antiques. A three-course gourmet breakfast is included. **Good Medicine Lodge** (800-860-5488; $-$$) is built of cedar timbers and has a rustic informal atmosphere and **Hidden Moose Lodge** (888-733-6667; $$-$$$) is another that is highly recommended.

For rock-bottom prices, try the clean and comfortable **Cheap Sleep Motel** (406-862-5515 or 800-862-3711; $), which is further from town; or the European-like hostel, the **Bunk House Traveler's Inn and Hostel** ($) in town.

Dining

The **Summit House** (862-1971; $$$) hosts four Moonlight Dine & Ski evenings throughout the winter. The high-speed Glacier Chaser quad chairs are replaced by gondola cars to whisk evening diners up the mountain. Lunch and breakfast items served daily.

For a special evening (and probably the best meal on the mountain) in the base village, try **Café Kandahar** (862-6098; $$-$$$), where chef Andrew Topel serves fine French Provincial fare in an intimate setting. The restaurant has an extensive wine list.

At the base of the ski area is **The Hellroaring Saloon** (862-6364; $$). This 50-year-old, log-decor building served as the original base lodge. All food on the menu is homemade. It serves lunch and dinner. **Moguls Village Pub** (862-1980; $$) is at the base of Chair 2 and serves breakfast, lunch and dinner.

The **Alpinglow Restaurant** (862-6966; $$) has the best view of the Flathead Valley. **Horsepower Adventures** (862-2900) offers a 30-minute sleigh ride and a chuckwagon dinner in the livery stable. Family-style dinners, live music and cowboy tales top off the evening.

The bulk of restaurants are in Whitefish and offer a surprising variety. The finest dining in the area is at the **Whitefish Lake Restaurant** (862-5285; $$-$$$) in a historic log building built in the 1930s by the WPA at the golf course. Its known for its excellent steaks and prime rib. **The Grill** and the more upscale **Wine Room** (862-3000; $$-$$$) are in the Grouse Mountain Lodge. On Central Avenue, there is the New Orleans-influenced **Tupelo** ($-$$$, 862-6136), which always has fresh fish on the menu. For topnotch sushi and inventive Asian dishes, head to the **Wasabi Sushi Bar & Ginger Grill** (863-9283; $-$$$).

For local color (and a special après-ski), try **Truby's** (862-4979; $-$$) for wood-fired pizza and great steaks. The Southwest menu at **Serrano's** (862-5600; $-$$) is good and even better is that they start serving early, right when skier's get off the hill, and offer pitchers of Margaritas.

The **Quickie Sandwich Shop** ($-$$) offers East Coast subs and great sandwiches and in the Satsang Yoga Center, you'll find organic vegetarian food at the **Moonbowl Kitchen** ($-$$). Locals and tourists sip espresso at the **Montana Coffee Traders** or eat in "the Buff," at the **Buffalo Café** (862-2833; $), a local gathering place. At the latter spot, try the Buffalo Pie—layers of hashbrowns, ham, cheese, and poached eggs. It's open for lunch as well. **Baker Street Bistro** (862-6383; $), on the road out of town to the mountain, is an excellent breakfast spot with homemade bagels.

Après-ski/nightlife

The **Hellroaring Saloon** serves some of the best après-ski nachos anywhere. Best deal: If you buy a Hellroaring baseball cap you get your second beer free every day you wear it to the bar. Also on the mountain, **Moguls Village Pub** has entertainment nightly. The **'Stube** offers free beer every Wednesday at 5:30 p.m. to celebrate the Frabert Award, presented each week to the employee or visitor who commits the biggest goof-up.

It's worth a visit to the **Palace Bar** on Central Avenue in Whitefish just to see its turn-of-the-century carved mahogany bar. Microbrew fans can head for the tasting room at the **Great Northern Bar & Grille** on Central Ave. They have live music from Thursday to Saturday and acoustic, open-mike on Tuesday. Locals come for the burgers and wide selection of microbrewery beers and stay for the music and general debauchery. For free beer, stop by the **Great Northern Brewery,** home of Buckin' Horse Beer, with a friendly tasting room open to the public.

Another top spot is **Dire Wolf**, which is a favorite hangout for Big Mountain's boarders and teleskiers. It's just outside town on the road down from the ski area.

Having all the Central Avenue bars lined up makes it easy to check out the scene and decide where you want to set up camp. Choose from the no-smoking **Truby's; Casey's,** located in the oldest building in town; and the sports bar (high school sports, that is) **Bulldog Saloon.** For a more mellow time, head to the adult lounge at the **Grill** in the Grouse Mountain Lodge.

For later night carousing, try the **Remington** or the **Palace Bar**, both on Central Avenue. The latter features a turn-of-the-century carved mahogany bar. For a no-glitz, real cowboy evening—complete with live foot-stomping music and longneck beer bottles—head to the **Blue Moon Nite Club** in Columbia Falls at the intersections of Hwys. 2 and 40.

Other activities

Adrenaline junkies should try **snow cycles,** similar to full-suspension mountain bikes but with skis on the bike and mini-skis on your feet. A real blast! Lift-accessed **snow tubing** is offered in the "Snow Toy" area along with a **snow maze, snow carts** and a **sledding** hill. **Snowcat skiing and riding** is offered in backcountry areas outside the resort's eastern boundary. Snowcat tours are four hours and cost $60 per person (that's on top of the regular lift ticket) with four or more people; call 862-2909 for information.

Near the resort, Horsepower Adventures (862-2900) has **sleigh rides** and **chuckwagon dinners.** Downtown in Whitefish, sleigh rides leave the Grouse Mountain Lodge (862-3000)

Dining: $$$-Entrees $20+; $$-$10-20; $-less than $10.
Accommodations: (double room) $$$$-$200+; $$$-$141-$200; $$-$81-$140; $-$80 and less.

for a 20-minute ride to a camp near Lost Coon Lake. **Snowmobiling** is a favorite pastime of Montanans, so a variety of guide services are available. Canyon Creek Cat House (800-933-5133) is in nearby Columbia Falls, with more than 200 miles of groomed trails. Contact the Flathead Convention and Visitors Association at (800) 543-3105 for additional guide services. Also guided snowmobile tours into the backcountry of the Whitefish Range are available from Big Mountain's summit (862-1900).

Shopping is limited at the base area although there are a variety of specialty shops along the Kintla shopping pavilion. Whitefish's Central Avenue has many **art galleries** and stores that stock Western clothing, jewelry and crafts. Montana Coffee Traders, on Hwy. 93 south of town, has many Montana food gift items, such as huckleberry syrup.

Big Mountain has a terrific **Guest Services and Information** center in the base village where you can find out more about other activities. Call 862-2900.

Getting there and getting around

By air: Glacier Park International Airport is in Kalispell, 19 miles south of the resort, served by Delta, Horizon/Alaska Air and Northwest airlines. Call Flathead Glacier Transportation (892-3390) for ground transportation or check with your hotel for guest shuttle availability.

By car: Big Mountain is 8 miles from the town of Whitefish at the junction of Hwys. 2 and 93.

By train: Amtrak's Empire Builder stops in Whitefish daily from Seattle and Portland to the west and from Chicago and Minneapolis to the east. Kids ride free. Call (800) USA-RAIL (872-7245) for information.

Getting around: If you stay and play at the mountain, you won't need a car. The S.N.O.W. bus makes free daily runs between Whitefish and the mountain. Party animals staying up on the mountain need to pay attention. The last SNOW Bus run back up the mountain is at 11:27 p.m. Wednesday through Saturday and even earlier on other evenings. If you miss the bus home, most lodges have free shuttle service available for guests and taxi service also is available. A car is essential if you plan to explore.

Big Sky
Montana

Summit elevation: 11,150 feet
Vertical drop: 4,180 feet
Base elevation: 6,970 feet

Address: P.O. Box 160001
Big Sky, MT 59716
Area code: 406
Ski area phone (Hotel guest calls and switchboard): 995-5000
Snow report: 995-5900
ⓘ **Toll-free reservations:** (800) 548-4486
Fax: 995-5001
Internet: www.bigskyresort.com

Expert:★★★★★
Advanced:★★★★
Intermediate:★★★★
Beginner:★★
Never-ever:★★

Number and types of lifts: 18–1 aerial tram, 1 four-passenger gondola, 3 high-speed quads, 1 quad, 4 triples, 4 doubles and 4 surface lifts
Acreage: 3,600 skiable acres
Snowmaking: 10 percent of trails
Uphill capacity: 18,000 per hour
Snowboarding: Yes, unlimited
Bed base: 4,250
Nearest lodging: Slopeside, hotel
Resort child care: Yes, infants and older
Adult ticket, per day: $56-$58 (02/03)

Dining:★★★ **Apres-ski/nightlife:**★★
Other activities:★★

From the moment you land at Bozeman's Gallatin Field, which feels more like a private rancher's massive lodge than an airport, you know you're in for a different kind of vacation. Here you can expect lots of friendly employees in cowboy hats holding open doors for you, a genuine laid-back atmosphere, spectacular scenery and plenty of challenging terrain.

Big Sky, with its impressive Matterhorn-shaped peak scraping the heavens at 11,166 feet, is a serious skier's mountain near the summit, yet it has excellent cruisers closer to the base. In fact, the intermediate cruisers are such a delight that experts who wear themselves out on the tougher terrain will still have plenty to grin about as they swoop down the lower mountain, and adjacent Andesite Mountain, with friends and family.

An aerial tram with two 15-passenger cars whisks you up to the 11,150-foot mark on Lone Peak, giving you a stomach-in-your-throat close-up of the craggy mountain just before coming in for a landing. If you get to the top and find that the chutes, couloirs and steeps are over your head, no problem—admire the views of the nearby Spanish Peaks Wilderness area and ride back down. Only 15 people per tram, so you'll have a marvelous feeling of privacy as you descend, either in the capsule or while attempting the steeps beneath it.

Big Sky is a true destination resort, far from large urban areas, yet just an hour from the nearest jet airport. It has a very European feel. Ski school director Hans Schernthaner is from Austria, and each year he brings in English-speaking Europeans to teach. And lift tickets work just like the computerized systems in the Alps.

Mountain layout—Skiing

◆◆ **Expert** ◆ **Advanced:** The runs from the Lone Peak summit have become the test of who is an expert and who wants to be. Every run from the top is rated double-black diamond, and justifiably so. Fortunately, if you decide once you're on top that you're in over your head, you can ride the tram back down.

On a clear day, you'll get your first close-up view of the peak when you get off Gondola One. "Breathtaking" is an over-used word, but there is none other to describe the magnificence of Lone Peak and the immense bowl beneath it. Above-treeline slopes beckon advanced skiers and snowboarders for untouched powder. You'll find steep pitches and wide-open terrain on the bowl's South Face.

The more adventurous can register with the ski patrol and test their skills in A-Z Chutes, the Pinnacles and Big Couloir, which are all out of bounds. (The latter run is 42-degrees steep and half-a-mile long). Out-of-bounds skiing is permitted, but only with the right equipment—a transceiver, a shovel and a partner.

Want a really long run that will leave you weak in the knees? A fun mix of terrain from the summit is the steeps of Lenin to wide-open (and steep) Liberty Bowl to Dakota Gully to the delightful trees of Bavarian Forest.

Experts also should head to the vast area on Lone Mountain's north side, where many locals ski. The Challenger chair climbs 1,750 steep vertical feet to open, hair-raising, in-bounds terrain—some of the toughest in-bounds skiing in the country. If you don't like riding chairs without safety bars, height makes this a super-scary ride. Even scarier: Steep, long pitches drop down Big Rock Tongue, north-facing bowls greet skiers in Nashville Basin and trees pepper narrow chutes on Little Tree and Zucchini Patch.

Bump enthusiasts may be a little disappointed. Not enough traffic to build big bumps here, except maybe in the spring. On our last visit, we found the biggest moguls on Bad Dog, Moonlight and Midnight off the Challenger chair, in The Bowl off the Lone Peak Triple and on Upper Africa on Andesite Mountain.

■ **Intermediate:** Big Sky has two mountains that connect at the base, Lone Peak and Andesite. The blue-rated trails on both have a wide range in pitch and grooming. Some are kind and rolling, but others—such as the blues in the Shedhorn area—lean toward black. Not all the blue trails are groomed, and some have cat-track runouts or are simply too short.

On Lone Mountain, fine-tune your technique on the groomed cruisers under Gondola One and under the Swift Current high-speed quad, such as Calamity Jane, Huntley Hollow and Lobo. If you want to try some bowl skiing, head to Upper Morningstar. Also try the terrain off the Iron Horse Quad. For advanced-intermediates, trails off the Shedhorn lift are south-facing and get plenty of sun at times when the lower mountain is in the shade. Upper Sunlight to Sunlight is absolutely delightful. Views are of the backcountry and you'll feel a world away.

On Andesite, skis run fast and long on Big Horn, Elk Park Ridge, Elk Park Meadows and Ambush. Fine-tune your techniques on the manicured slopes of Tippy's Tumble or Silver Knife. During the spring, make sure to hit the trails off the Thunder Wolf quad early in the day, before the sun has turned them into heavy mashed potatoes.

●● **Beginner:** The south side of Andesite Mountain is great for beginners because of the wide, gentle slopes and because it gets a lot of sun. You can enjoy runs such as Sacajawea, El Dorado and Ponderosa from the Southern Comfort triple chair. Fewer hot shots ski on Andesite, a comfort if you get unnerved when someone passes by closely at high speed. On the way back to the base village, the winding Pacifier lets you admire awesome views.

On Lone Mountain, gentle rollers such as Mr. K, White Wing and Lone Wolf are reached via the gondola or the Explorer Lift. Mr. K gets high traffic as the lifts close down for the day, but it's nice and wide. If you're with people who are more accomplished than you, convince them to take a few runs on Mr. K and Lone Wolf, they'll enjoy it too.

● **Never-ever:** Though not physically isolated from the rest of the terrain, the learning area, at Lone Mountain's base, is away from high traffic until the end of the day. A magic carpet transports beginners up the slope to learn their first turns (the magic carpet replaced the surface tow and Poma). For the youngest ones, a smaller magic carpet and merry-go-round are in a fenced off area in the base area used by the children's ski school.

 ## Mountain layout—Snowboarding

Big Sky has a nice halfpipe and terrain park on Andesite, by Ambush Meadows, reached by taking the Ramcharger quad and turning left. On Lone Mountain, there's a natural halfpipe on Lower Morningstar and another on Lower Buffalo Jump.

For some ridge riding and above-treeline faces, continue up from those chairs via the adjacent Lone Peak Triple and the Lone Peak Tram to the top of Lone Mountain at 11,150 feet (if you want to reach the 11,166 foot summit, you'll have to hike it, enjoy the view and hike back down). Under the Lone Peak Tram, you'll find some serious descents. The most extreme—and narrow—run on the mountain is Big Couloir, just to the right of the tram. If it's even open, watch some others pick their way down before you decide to try it. If you do, you are required to check in with the patrol and have a partner, beacon and shovel.

The South Face isn't as steep as the chutes under the tram, but you'll still find yourself leaning into the mountain when you're "taking a breather." Death slides are not uncommon here, so stay on the ball. If you like catching air time with the locals, there's often a group building jumps on Screaming Left, at the bottom of Liberty Bowl. If you prefer the woods, Bavarian Forest is a great romp. After the woods and runs below the face, try to stay central to avoid most of Cow Flats and Hippy Highway. End up as close to the Shedhorn lift as you can and try to avoid Middle Road when working your way back to the mountain village.

This mountain's great for laying out arcs too. Pick any groomer to your left off the Swift Current Express and Gondola One.

Mountain rating

Big Sky is excellent for most skiers and snowboarders; however, it doesn't have vast beginner terrain. The black-diamond runs here are solid black, so be careful not to get in over your head. If you don't like a combination of heights and chairs without safety bars, you may want to avoid the Lone Peak Triple and the Challenger lift (Shedhorn doesn't have safety bars but it's lower to the ground). Big Sky gets high marks for no lift lines, magnificent scenery and grooming that isn't overdone. This is a great mountain for groups with members of varying abilities, the lower-level trails are actually lots of fun for more accomplished skiers and riders too. Don't forget to bring your camera.

 ## Cross-country and snowshoeing

Nationally acclaimed **Lone Mountain Guest Ranch** (995-4644; 800-514-4644) offers 75 km. of international-caliber Nordic skiing for all levels, with groomed and skating lanes. The trail system winds through open meadows and forested canyons.

Lone Mountain Ranch teams with **Alpenguide Tours of West Yellowstone** to offer a variety of backcountry skiing, including snowcat tours into the interior of Yellowstone,

America's most beloved national park, to view its winter wonders. Tours also are available into the Spanish Peaks.

Deluxe, cozy cabins with fireplace and full bath can be rented for a week, with all meals, trail pass and evening programs for $1,250–$2,500, based on the group and cabin size. The Ranch has a Nordic shop with apparel, equipment and mementos. Trail pass is $10 for adults; children ages 12 and younger ski free. Half-day tickets are available, as are lessons.

You can rent **snowshoes** from the Lone Mountain Guest Ranch, Grizzly Outfitters (995-2939) and Big Sky Ski Rental (995-5841) in the Mountain Village Plaza's Snowcrest building for about $15 per day. Big Sky has a marked and separated snowshoe trail up a portion of Lone Mountain called Moose Tracks.

Lessons (2002/03 prices)

Group lessons: Half day, $38 for ski or snowboard lesson, with discounts for multiple half-day sessions.

Never-ever package: Half-day lesson with beginner lift ticket and rentals, $63. Those who wish to ski the whole day can upgrade to beginner chair ticket for additional $25.

Private lessons: Two hours (1-3 guests) costs $190 in morning, $175 in afternoon, with multiple-hour discounts. A private one-hour telemark lesson is $80. Guide services (1-3 guests) are $220 for half-day afternoon, $240 for half-day morning; $390 for a full day.

Special programs: Advanced clinics concentrate on Lone Peak's steeps and tackle moguls, powder or other conditions du jour, $40.

Racing: Check in with the ski school daily for details.

Child care (2002/03 prices)

Ages: 6 months and older.

Costs: $80 for a full day, ages 6-16 months; and $70 for a full day, $50 for a half day for 17 months–8 years.

Reservations: Call 995-2335. Hours are 8:30 a.m. to 4:30 p.m. Immunizations records are required. Reservations are required for all child care services and parents will need to bring some things, so call ahead. The bright, airy facility is at slopeside Snowcrest Lodge.

Children's lessons: Ages 3–4 can take a 45-minute introduction to skiing in the afternoon, $31 (day care and rentals extra). Mini Camp, ages 4–6, $99 includes lessons, activities and lunch. Ski Camp, ages 6–14, $94 includes lessons, activities and lunch. Prices do not include lift ticket and rentals for kids 11 and older. For information on lessons, call 995-5743.

Lift tickets (2002/03 prices)

	Adult	Juniors (11-17)
One day	$58	$46
Three days	$168 ($56/day)	$138 ($46/day)
Five days	$270 ($54/day)	$230 ($46/day)

Who skis free: Two children (up to age 10) ski free per paying adult.

Who skis at a discount: 70 and older ski for half price. College students with ID can ride lifts at the junior rate.

Accommodations

Big Sky is divided into four areas—the Mountain Village, Moonlight Basin Ranch, the Meadow Village and the Canyon. The farther you are from the lifts, the less you generally pay. A free shuttle system runs between the areas during the winter. A good starting point is **Big Sky Central Reservations**, (800) 548-4486.

In the Mountain Village:

At the center of the Mountain Village are the new **Summit at Big Sky** ($$$$), the **Shoshone Condominium Hotel** ($$$$) and **Huntley Lodge** ($$$–$$$$). The Summit is a ski-in/ski-out condo-hotel. The Shoshone is a luxury ski-in/ski-out condo-hotel with kitchens, fireplaces and jetted tubs, plus a lap pool, health club and more. The Huntley has an outdoor pool, Jacuzzis, sauna, workout room and more.

Mountain Village has many condo complexes, some of which are only a few years old. **Lone Moose Meadows** ($$$$) is one of the newer slopeside complexes. If you want luxury, try **Snowcrest, Beaverhead and Arrowhead Condominiums** with two to four bedrooms ($$$$). You'll find two- and three-bedroom units at **Skycrest** ($$$$), which also has underground parking, or try the more moderately priced **Stillwater** ($$–$$$$).

The slopeside **Mountain Inn** (1-800-HOLIDAY; $$$–$$$$), part of the Holiday Inn Express chain, opened last season. It has 90 suites that sleep up to six people, continental breakfast, pool, two hot tubs and exercise room.

Condo and home rental agencies with Mountain Village and Meadow Village properties include **ResortQuest of Big Sky** (800-548-4488; 995-4800) and **Big Sky Chalet Rentals** (800-845-4428; 995-2665).

In Moonlight Basin Ranch (a mile from Mountain Village, on north face of Lone Mtn.):

The new and very upscale **Moonlight Lodge and Spa** (800-845-4428; 995-2665; $$$$) has four ski-in/ski-out penthouse suites, and is home base to the two- and three-bedroom **Saddle Ridge Townhomes** and two-bedroom log cabins in **Cowboy Heaven.** Restaurant, bar, full-service spa and outdoor rink at the lodge. Everything you need and more.

In the Meadow Village (6 miles away):

River Rock Lodge (800-548-4488; 995-4800; $$–$$$$) is a "boutique-style European hotel" built of stone and log with beautiful interior decor. Rates include continental breakfast.

East West Resorts (800-845-4428; 995-2665) manages several condo complexes here, including **Hidden Village** ($$$$), units set in the forest with in-house Jacuzzis and garage, and **Park** ($$$–$$$$), with head-on views of Lone Peak. **ResortQuest of Big Sky** (800-548-4488; 995-4800) has many condos on the cross-country trail system.

In the Canyon (3 miles from the Meadow Village, in the beautiful Gallatin River Canyon, 9 miles from the lifts, serviced by the shuttle):

Buck's T-4 Lodge (800-822-4484; 995-4111; $$$–$$$$), a Best Western hotel, with two pool-size outdoor Jacuzzis, a large stone fireplace and a restaurant that specializes in wild game (see *Dining*). Lodging/lift packages (with continental breakfast) are priced *per room,* with lower rates for single guests—rare and welcome in a world that penalizes solo travelers.

The Rainbow Ranch Lodge (800-937-4132; 995-4132; $$–$$$) is on the Gallatin River. A luxurious lodge with a western-ranch style, it has 12 rooms with private baths, and an excellent bar and restaurant. Ski packages are available.

The Comfort Inn (800-228-5150; 995-2333; $–$$) is new and clean, though it has little charm. Budget accommodations include the **Corral Motel** (995-4249; $) and the **Cinnamon Lodge** (995-4253; $). The latter has RV hookups for $15–$20.

Dining

In the Mountain Village:

The best dining on the mountain is found at **Peaks** (995-8000; $$–$$$) in the Summit. The menu is new western cuisine, the atmosphere is casual, yet elegant. **Huntley Lodge** (995-5783; $$–$$$) is fine dining in a rustic setting. The breakfast buffet is excellent and the mountain views are hard to beat. We weren't impressed with dinner, but the Chocolate Bomb dessert was simply yummy. The restaurant has one of Montana's largest wine selections. In the Mountain Mall, **Dante's Inferno** (995-3999) has tableside slope views and Italian cuisine, and **M.R. Hummers** (995-4560) is known for its baby back ribs. **Black Bear Bar 'n' Grill** (995-2845) is a casual spot for breakfast or dinner. Other lunch spots: **Mountain Top** for pizza, **Scissorbills Bar and Grill** at the base of Silverknife ski run, or **The Dug Out**, on Andesite Mountain, which has super barbecue and seats about 30 good friends.

In Moonlight Basin Ranch:

The Timbers (995-7777; $$$) at Moonlight Lodge is a new slopeside restaurant on the Moonlight Basin side of the resort, on the north face of Lone Mountain. The food is average, but the rustic lodge atmosphere with stuffed mountain goats clambering up the 37-foot stone fireplace is magnificent. Lunch is served here also; on warm days, eat on the large deck.

In the Meadow Village:

Most of the restaurants we liked best are located here. Intimate candlelight and linen service await you at **First Place** (995-4244), featuring American and Continental cuisine and famous desserts. **Edelweiss** (995-4665) has excellent Austrian and German food. **Rocco's** (995-4200) has Mexican and Italian food with a full bar. **Gallatin Gourmet Deli** (995-2314) is a great choice for a casual but very tasty lunch or dinner. For breakfast, try the **Huckleberry Cafe** (995-3130), which has the best reputation in town, or the **Blue Moon Bakery** (995-2305), also great for lunch.

Lone Mountain Ranch Dining Room (995-2782; $$–$$$) serves excellent meals in a quiet, smoke-free environment in rustic elegance. Sleigh-ride dinners are offered here; call ahead as space is limited. There's Guinness on tap and terrific pesto pizza at **Uncle Milkies Pizza and Subs** (995-2900). **Allgoods Bar and Grill** (995-2750) serves hickory-smoked ribs, chicken, pork, homemade stews and burgers. It also has a pool table, darts and poker.

In the Gallatin Canyon:

Buck's T-4 Restaurant (995-4111; $$$) is the area's oldest and most popular dining establishment. Its specialties are wild game, Montana beef, veal and seafood. There's an extensive wine list and an original rustic bar built in 1946. If you're staying at the mountain or the meadow, ride the free shuttle. **The Rainbow Ranch Lodge** (995-4132; $$–$$$) may be the best restaurant in the area, with elegant dining overlooking the Gallatin River. An imaginative menu focuses on wild game, fresh seafood, vegetarian and terrific salads.

Après-ski/nightlife

First check *The Lone Peak Lookout*, which has entertainment listings.

The hub of night activity is the Mountain Village. Happy hour kicks off in **Chet's Bar** in the Huntley Lodge, with the Crazy Austrian show (just go see it). Chet's also has poker games (legal in Montana). The **Carabiner** in the Summit is a wonderful place to relax with a drink. Mellow live entertainment provides background music you can talk and hear over. Other places to check out in the Mountain Village are **Lolo's, Dante's** and **Roost-**

ers. In Moonlight Basin Ranch, **Timbers** has a great outside deck and ice rink, inside you'll find a beautiful rustic setting. In the Meadow Village, it's quieter, but **Rocco's** and **Allgoods Bar and Grill** are likely to attract crowds at night.

In the canyon, check out the **Buck's T-4** game room, with pool tables, foosball and video games. Locals like the **Corral** and **The Half Moon Saloon**, with darts and pool. Both are roadhouse-style Western bars.

Other activities

Poker is legal gambling in Montana, and nightly games are available. Ask around if this is your kind of fun. Just about all of the other activities are of the outdoor variety.

Snowmobiling in Yellowstone National Park is a major attraction. Most snowmobile shops offer a 10 percent discount with a Big Sky lift ticket and provide bus service from the resort and West Yellowstone. For information, Rendezvous Snowmobile Rentals, (800) 426-7669 or 646-9564; Snowmobile Yellowstone, (800) 221-1151; Yellowstone Adventures, (800) 231-5991 or 646-7735; West Yellowstone, (800) 541-7354 or 646-9695. To snowmobile closer to Big Sky call Canyon Rentals (995-4540) a half a mile south of the Big Sky entrance.

Dogsled rides are offered by Spirit of the North Dog Adventures (995-4644), Lone Mountain Ranch (995-2783) or 320 Ranch (995-4283). **Dinner sleigh rides** are also available.

Winter fishing on the Gallatin River is available through Gallatin Riverguides (995-2290) or East Slope Anglers (995-4369), who have licenses, equipment rentals and supplies. **Yellowstone National Park** is a big attraction, and yes, it's open in winter. The drive south along Hwy. 191 follows the Gallatin River, where much of the movie, "A River Runs Through It," was filmed. A 7:30 a.m. bus runs daily from Big Sky to West Yellowstone, where snow coaches pick up riders and go into the park to see Old Faithful. Riders are back at Big Sky in time for dinner. For more information on the area and all its recreation choices, call the West Yellowstone Chamber of Commerce at 646-7701 or www.westyellowstonechamber.com.

There are several **full-service spas** on the mountain: Solace Spa at Big Sky (995-5803), in the Huntley/Shoshone complex, and The Moonlight Spa (995-7704) in the Moonlight Lodge.

The Huntley Lodge shows free **movies** in the amphitheater at night. If you have the opportunity to attend an **avalanche search and rescue demo** by the ski patrol and their dogs, don't miss it. It's fascinating, and someday these dogs just might save your life.

The Mountain Mall has **shops and boutiques**. Plum Logo has Montana-made gifts and Big Sky T-shirts and souvenirs. The Lone Spur in the Shoshone Condo complex is a good spot for high-quality western clothing, jewelry and gifts. In the Meadow Village, shop at Grizzly Outfitters, Willow Boutique and By Word of Mouth (great wine selection and prices). Moose Rack Books has new, out-of-print and rare books in two locations, one at the mountain and another in the canyon. If you're into taste-testing local yummies, look for anything made with huckleberries.

Getting there and getting around

By air: Several airlines serve Bozeman Gallatin Field Airport, an hour from the resort. The 4X4 Stage shuttles passengers between the airport, the resort and West Yellowstone. Call 388-6404.

By car: The resort is 45 miles south of Bozeman (and 50 miles north of West Yellowstone) on Hwy. 191 along the Gallatin River.

Dining: $$$-Entrees $20+; $$-$10-20; $-less than $10.
Accommodations: (double room) $$$$-$200+; $$$-$141-$200; $$-$81-$140; $-$80 and less.

Getting around: If you stay at the Mountain Village, a car is unnecessary unless you plan to do a lot of sightseeing. A free shuttlebus runs between the Big Sky villages 7 a.m.–11 p.m., starting in mid-December through the winter.

Montana regional resorts

Bridger Bowl, Bozeman, MT; (406) 587-2111
Internet: www.bridgerbowl.com
7 lifts; 1,000 acres; 2,000 vertical feet

Bridger Bowl is a funky, friendly ski area that offers some of the best steeps, narrows and radical chutes in Montana. Its non-profit status means it can offer some great skiing and riding at a low price. Experts can enjoy the upper mountain and hike the perilous Ridge and Fingers. Skiing and riding the Ridge and Fingers requires expert ability, an avalanche transceiver, shovel, partner and knowledge of the terrain. Those of a lower ability level and families can ski groomed intermediate and beginner cruisers on the lower mountain.

The lift system adequately handles weekend traffic from the nearby Montana State University town of Bozeman. Child care starts at 18 months.

Distance from Bozeman: About 16 miles north by Hwy. 86.

Lodging information: Bridger Bowl Vacations, (800) 223-9609.

Red Lodge Mountain Resort, Red Lodge, MT; (406) 446-2610 or (800) 444-8977
Internet: www.redlodgemountain.com
8 lifts; 1,600 acres; 2,400 vertical feet

Tucked in a valley in the Beartooth Mountain Range lies the quaint old mining town of Red Lodge. Red Lodge Mountain's Grizzly Peak, located 4 miles west of town, caters to families and skiers and riders who are intermediates and above. The mountain recently added 700 acres of terrain in the Cole Creek area, two high-speed quads and snowmaking. There's a terrain park with tabletops, rail slides, spines, a quarterpipe and more; at least every two weeks features are upgraded or changed. Affordable lodging/lift packages can be arranged.

Distance from Billings: About 65 miles west on I-90 and south on Hwy. 212 (no passes).

Lodging information: (800) 444-8977.

Montana Snowbowl, Missoula, MT; (406) 549-9777
Internet: www.montanasnowbowl.com
4 lifts; 950 skiable acres; 2,600 vertical feet

This virtually unknown Montana hangout has been called The Un-resort—untamed, ungroomed, unpretentious and undiscovered. It also had a reputation of being unforgiving and not easily mastered by the faint of heart. Beginners and intermediates may find much of the terrain beyond their abilities. This unusual area is a local favorite and attracts the college crowd from the University of Montana.

Distance from Missoula: About 12 miles.

Lodging information: Gelandesprung Lodge is a slopeside, European-style lodge with shared and private baths, hot tub and kitchen; (800) 728-2695 or (406) 549-9777. The resort's Web site has a listing of nearby lodging. Missoula Chamber of Commerce, (406) 543-6623.

Ski Apache

Ruidoso, New Mexico

Summit elevation: 11,500 feet
Vertical drop: 1,900 feet
Base elevation: 9,600 feet

Address: P.O. Box 220
Ruidoso, NM 88355
☎ **Area code:** 505
Ski area phone: 336-4356
Snow report: 257-9001
ⓘ **Toll-free reservations:**
(800) 253-2255 (Ruidoso Chamber)
Fax: 336-8327
Internet: www.skiapache.com (resort)
or www.ruidoso.net (town information)
Expert:★★
Advanced:★★★★
Intermediate:★★★
Beginner:★
Never-ever:★★

Number and types of lifts: 11—1 gondola,
2 quads, 5 triples, 1 doubles, 2 surface lifts
Skiable acreage: 750 acres
Snowmaking: 35 percent
Uphill capacity: 16,500 per hour
Snowboarding: Yes
Bed Base: 2,200+ in Ruidoso; 4,000 in Ruidoso area
Nearest lodging: 12 miles away in Ruidoso
Resort child care: See child care
Adult ticket, per day: $42-$45 (02/03)

Dining:★ (on mountain) ★★★ (in Ruidoso)
Apres-ski/nightlife:★★★
Other activities:★★★

Ski Apache, where trails cruise through the pines of the Mescalero Apache Indian reservation, sits at the end of a dramatic access road high above the cowboy town of Ruidoso in south-central New Mexico. This is the southernmost major destination ski area in North America, only 120 miles north of the Mexican border.

The region with the town and the resort occupies an oasis of pine-covered mountains surrounded by the sprawling New Mexican desert. From the Lookout Snack Bar, at the top of the gondola, the panorama is one of the most expansive to be found at any ski resort in North America. The view takes in the White Sands National Monument, the site of the first atom bomb explosion, the forest where Smokey Bear was rescued and the Old West towns where Billy The Kid roamed.

Trail names echo the Apache heritage—Geronimo, Screaming Eagle, Chino and Ambush. Skiers from Texas, Germans from nearby Holloman Air Force Base, and Mexican visitors all mix with the Mescalero Indians who make the resort work. You'll find no condo developments and no ski-in/ski-out hotels at the ski area—this is a pure ski resort. The elevation between 9,600 and 11,500 feet guarantees snow and the location in southern New Mexico tempers the weather and favors plenty of sunny days.

Twelve miles from the snowfields of Ski Apache and about 3,000 feet below the sacred Sierra Blanca peak, the town of Ruidoso spreads along a valley floor surrounded by gentle pines. This town is mainly a summer resort with the focus on Ruidoso Downs—home of quarter-horse racing, five golf courses and a full May-to-October program of music and cultural events. This makes winter the bargain time for most B&Bs, motels and hotels.

Mountain layout—Skiing

Bounded by two ridges, Ski Apache is divided roughly in half by a third ridge that runs parallel to the boundary ridges. The area's gondola runs along the center ridge from the base to the summit. At the top of the area on trail-map left, expansive Apache Bowl has wide-open skiing from 11,500 feet with about 650 feet of vertical. Most of the rest of the slopes are off the center ridge, which has a long intermediate trail running along the crest with expert and intermediate trails dropping to trail-map right. The rest of the skiing is near the bottom of the left boundary ridge. Again, a blue cruiser snakes along the crest and black-diamond pitches fall toward the base area.

◆◆ **Expert** ◆ **Advanced:** Experts may want to head elsewhere for extreme terrain and glades, but for advanced skiers there are plenty of steep pitches. Apache Bowl and The Face (which drops into the bowl from the center ridge) offer great powder skiing when the conditions cooperate. Those who want to stay in the bowl can upload using a triple chair that allows them to stay right in the bowl without working their way back down to the base.

■ **Intermediate:** This is a great resort for intermediates looking to improve. The blues are mellow and the blacks reach some excellent pitches. For cruising, stick to the ridges, or take your first runs on Ambush, Chino or Meadows, to the right as you unload from the gondola. For showoff time, take a few zips along Capitan, the blue-square run that drops right to the base area—it is a joy. For bumps head to The Terrible and Incredible. Plan to be challenged.

●● **Beginner:** Beginners have their own area served by Chair 7. Those shifting from beginner to intermediate should try Lower Deep Freeze, Snowpark and Smokey Bear.

● **Never-ever:** The learning area is off Chairs 3 and 5 at the base. This area is fenced off so those taking first-time lessons are not subjected to more advanced skiers and snowboarders zipping through their classes.

Mountain layout—Snowboarding

Apache Bowl is a favorite spot when powder falls or is blown over the ridge. Do laps off the lift that exclusively serves the bowl, then toss in some variety by riding up The Face and dropping off the ridge trails. The terrain forms natural halfpipes known locally as "the fingers" in the center of Apache Bowl. Yee-haw, as the Texans would say! The area has an excellent snowboard rental program with more than 150 boards from Burton and Gnu.

Mountain rating

This is an intermediate's playground, but advanced levels won't be disappointed. Beginners will be pushed for all they're worth—the shift from mellow terrain to more significant steeps is a big one. Sometimes it's hard to tell the blues from blacks. They're both tough.

Cross-country and snowshoeing

There is no cross-country skiing and snowshoeing at this resort.

Lessons (2002/03 prices)

Group lessons: Adult ski and snowboard lessons start daily at 10:30 a.m. and 2 p.m. Cost is $30 for a morning or afternoon session and an additional $15 for a full day.

Never-ever package: A full-day skiing or snowboarding lesson and ticket for the beginner lift is $45; a half day is $31 (add a couple of bucks during peak days). Two-day programs including lifts costs $113 for adults ($120 peak days).

Private lessons: $58 for one hour; $35 for each additional person.

Racing: Ski Apache has NASTAR races on Smokey Bear on Saturdays and Sundays.

Child care (2002/03)

Ski Apache does not offer child care for non-skiing children younger than 4; however, day care is available through **Tender Tots** (257-5784), Kidz World (630-8089) and the Ruidoso Christian School (378-4628) in Ruidoso.

Children's lessons: Kiddie Korral takes 4- to 6-year-olds in an all-day instruction program including lunch and snow play. Cost is $87 with rentals; $76 without rentals (peak rates are $4 more). Ski and snowboard lessons for children ages 7 and older start daily at 10:30 a.m. and 2 p.m. Cost is $31 for a morning or afternoon session and an additional $14 for a full day (lift ticket not included). First-time skiers and snowboarders ages 7 and older can take an all-day lesson for $45, including a free lift ticket. The best buy for first-timers is two days of lessons, lift tickets and rentals. For kids ages 12 and under, it's $114 for skiers, $133 for snowboarders; for kids 13 and older, it's $132 for skiers, $149 for snowboarders. Reservations are recommended for the Kiddie Korral program, call 336-4356 ext. 211.

Lift tickets (2002/03 prices)

	Adult	Child (12 and younger)
One day	$45	$29
Three days	$126 ($42/day)	$81 ($27/day)

Who skis free: Members of the Mescalero Apache Tribe.

Who skis at a discount: Half-day prices during regular season are $31 for adults and $20 for kids.

Note: Just 13 days are classified as "peak season," when half-day prices are $34 for adults and $22 for kids. These days are Dec. 26–31, 2002, and Jan. 18-19, Feb. 15-16 and March 10–12, 2003.

Accommodations

The Inn of the Mountain Gods (257-5141; 800-545-9011; $$) is set on a lake in the midst of the Mescalero Apache Indian Reservation, operated by the tribe. Rooms are basic motel with upscale touches.

For luxury amidst beautiful art, head to the **Hurd Gallery & Guest Homes** (800-658-6912; 653-4331; $$$$) in San Patricio near the junction of Rtes. 70 and 380, about 30 miles from Ruidoso. Spectacular lodging starts at $200 a night.

Hawthorn Suites (258-5500; 800-527-1133; $$) is Ruidoso's newest upscale choice in lodging. Adjacent to the Links Golf Course, it features all suites with an indoor pool, spa, massage, a fitness room and a free hot breakfast.

Dining: $$$-Entrees $20+; $$-$10-20; $-less than $10.
Accommodations: (double room) $$$$-$200+; $$$-$141-$200; $$-$81-$140; $-$80 and less.

Best Western Swiss Chalet Inn (258-3333; 800-477-9477; $), perched above town, is one of the last lodges before the turnoff to the resort. Views from the restaurant are beautiful. Enchantment Inn (378-4051; 800-435-0280; $) is a full service hotel. Shadow Mountain Lodge (257-4886; 800-441-4331; $) is designed for couples, with kingsize beds, fireplaces and hot tubs. Holiday Inn Express (257-3736; 800-257-5477, $) includes breakfast. Sitzmark Chalet Motel (257-4140; 800-658-9694; $) offers inexpensive packages including lift tickets.

Casa del Cocinero (336-7815; 800-360-3500) is very intimate with only three rooms—one with private hot tub—and a self-contained casita, or cabin.

Condotel (800-545-9017; 258-5200) offers a large selection of 2–6 bedroom condos, cabins and private homes. Choices can be viewed and booked online at www.ruidosoreservations.com.

Dining

The best meals in town seem to be found at La Lorraine (257-2954; $–$$) for French cuisine; Pasta Cafe (257-6666; $–$$) for beautifully prepared Italian specialties; and The Deck House (257-3496; $–$$) for Mexican and American fare. The Cattle Baron (257-9355; $$) is the place to head for steaks. The Texas Club (258-3325; $–$$) also serves great steaks and all-American fare.

Tinnies Silver Dollar (653-4425; $$) provides dining with a step back in time about 3 miles toward Roswell from the junction of Rtes. 70 and 380, or about 30 miles from Ruidoso. The yesteryear dining rooms are lined with paintings harking back to the Old West or showcasing the Hurd/Wyeth family art. Spanky's (354-2234; $$), in nearby Capitan, serves wonderful gourmet meals that belies it's name. Both are worth the drive.

Cafe Rio (257-7746; $–$$) on downtown's main drag serves a curious Mediterranean mixture (Italian, Portuguese, Greek) of pizza, pasta, soups and seafood in diner-like surroundings. Ahna-Michelle's (258-3333; $$) at the Best Western serves a Friday night, Old Country, German buffet and Saturday night prime rib in a Swiss atmosphere. La Fuente (257-0814) and Casa Blanca (257-2495; $) offer Tex-Mex and margaritas. Farley's (258-5676; $) has a good western family atmosphere with fajitas, burgers and pizzas. Circle J Bar-B-Que (257-4105; $) claims the best "homecooked BBQ." Michelena's Italian Restaurant (257-5753; $–$$) has good pasta and pizza with takeout.

For breakfast, we suggest The Deck House Restaurant (257-3496), Pena's Place (257-4135) and the Log Cabin (258-5029).

Après-ski/nightlife

Ruidoso is a good nightlife town but dancing is limited to two spots downtown. The Western flavor is strong and can't be beat at W.P.S. (Win, Place and Show) where you can dance the two-step and drink beer into the wee hours. This place is a blast.

Across the street from WPS is Quarters, a rock'n'roll and blues bar. Top up-and-coming southwestern talent plays here. It's a world of difference from WPS.

The Inn of the Mountain Gods has that age-old American pastime, gambling. You'll find blackjack tables, roulette wheels and slot machines. The Billy the Kid Casino is next door to the race track and has hundreds of slots, a grand bar and big buffet dinners.

Other activities

The added activities in the Ruidoso area make this far more than simply a ski vacation. Ruidoso has Western history, a fine museum, an extraordinary center for the performing arts and plenty of special events.

The Hubbard Museum of the American West (378-4142) encompasses the Museum of the Horse with horse art and thousands of artifacts from old carriages to wagons.

Spencer Theater for the Performing Arts (www.spencertheater.com; 336-0010; 888-818-7872) is stunning, rising dramatically from the plain. Examples of the ambitious world-class programs are singer Jack Jones, the Jimmy Dorsey Orchestra, and the Russian Ballet.

In nearby Capitan, visit the **Smokey Bear Historical State Park,** where you'll see a display about forest fire prevention and pay a visit to Smokey Bear's grave.

The entire region is dotted with sites linked with **Billy the Kid and Pat Garrett.**

 ## Getting there and getting around

By air: Fly into Albuquerque, about a three-hour drive away; or El Paso, about a two-hour drive. Rent a car for your trip to Ruidoso.

By car: Ski Apache and Ruidoso are approximately halfway between Roswell and Socorro on U.S. Hwy. 70. The resort is 180 miles from Albuquerque and 130 miles from El Paso.

Getting around: You will need a car. A town shuttle takes skiers to the mountain once a day (early morning/late afternoon) or by reservation. Call Shuttle Ruidoso at 877-903-7483 or 336-1683.

Dining: $$$-Entrees $20+; $$-$10-20; $-less than $10.
Accommodations: (double room) $$$$-$200+; $$$-$141-$200; $$-$81-$140; $-$80 and less.

Ski Santa Fe

New Mexico

Summit elevation: 12,000 feet
Vertical drop: 1,650 feet
Base elevation: 10,350 feet

Address: 2209 Brothers Road, #220
Santa Fe, NM 87505
✆ **Area code:** 505
Ski area phone: 982-4429
Snow report: 983-9155
ⓘ **Toll-free reservations:** (877) 737-7366
Within New Mexico: 747-5557
Fax: 986-0645
E-mail: info@skisantafe.com
Internet: www.skisantafe.com
Expert: ★★
Advanced: ★★★
Intermediate: ★★★
Beginner: ★★★★
Never-ever: ★★★

Number and types of lifts: 6—1 high-speed quad, 1 triple, 2 doubles, 2 surface lifts
Acreage: 550
Snowmaking: 50 percent
Uphill capacity: 7,300 skiers per hour
Snowboarding: Yes
Bed base: 5,500 in Santa Fe
Nearest lodging: About 15 miles away
Resort child care: Yes, 3 months and older
Adult ticket, per day: $39–$44 (02/03)

Dining: ★★★★★
Apres-ski/nightlife: ★★
Other activities: ★★★★

At Ski Santa Fe, snow-covered trails curl through towering Ponderosa pines in the Sangre de Cristo mountains, only 16 miles from the city of Santa Fe, the very heart of Southwestern style. When you take the bright sunlight of the high desert, fresh powder snow and a skier-friendly mountain, then add pre-Columbian Indian Pueblos, Spanish architecture, art galleries and top it with a renowned regional cuisine, you have the savory mix that makes up a unique ski vacation.

Santa Fe (elevation 7,000 feet) offers interesting contradictions. It is old and new, high mountains and flat desert, with cool winters that surprise out-of-staters who think of New Mexico as hot and dry. Skiing in this state is unlike anywhere else on the continent. To get a more foreign-feeling ski vacation, you'd need a passport.

Some skiers think Taos Ski Valley is the only New Mexico ski area worth a long plane ride—not so. If your main interest is racking up vertical feet, then by all means head for Taos, but Santa Fe (just an hour north of Albuquerque) is a better destination for those who prefer a balanced ski-and-sightseeing vacation. Santa Fe is one of the most culturally fascinating cities in the United States. It is loaded with great restaurants, superior art galleries, a variety of activities, and the ski area is a lot bigger than most people imagine.

Founded by Spanish conquistadors in 1610, 10 years before the pilgrims landed in Plymouth, Santa Fe is North America's oldest capital city. It is rich in history and culture, but of a different kind from mining-town ski areas.

When the Spanish arrived, the area was already populated with 100,000 Native Americans who spoke nine languages and lived in some 70 multi-storied adobe pueblos, some still inhabited today. For the next 150 years Santa Fe grew as a frontier military base and trading center, where Spanish soldiers and missionaries, Anglo mountain men and Native Americans mixed. In 1846, during the Mexican War, New Mexico was ceded to the United States. Santa Fe, at the end of the Santa Fe Trail, became a frontier town, hosting the likes of Billy the Kid and Kit Carson.

In the early part of this century, Santa Fe took on a new flavor. It became a magnet for men and women of the arts and literature. D.H. Lawrence, Ezra Pound, Willa Cather, Jack London and H.L. Mencken either lived or vacationed here. Artists Edward Hopper and Marsden Hartley spent time here, and Santa Fe was home to Robert Henri, George Bellows, Randall Davey, Georgia O'Keeffe and Aaron Copland. Today this city of 60,000 people is home to one of the world's premier art colonies.

Mountain layout—Skiing

Ski Santa Fe sits 16 miles north of the city. Though the mountain is known as a day-area destination for Santa Fe and Albuquerque skiers, out-of-town visitors will find a surprising amount of terrain. All the mountain amenities such as restaurants, ski rentals, child care, ski school and ticket sales are at the base of the mountain just a few steps from the parking lot.

◆◆ **Expert** ◆ **Advanced:** For the most part, the mountain's expert terrain is to the left of the Tesuque Peak chair. With fresh snow, locals go first to Columbine, Big Rocks and Wizard. These runs all check in as very steep and are for advanced skiers only. Roadrunner is the expert bump run directly under the Tesuque chair. Tequila Sunrise and Easter Bowl have the best glade skiing. On the far side of the mountain, reached by the Santa Fe Super Chief quad, Muerte and Desafio have isolated trail skiing for advanced skiers.

While there are hopes to overcome environmental objections and put in a lift in the Big Tesuque Bowl, for the moment the intrepid ski into this area via Cornice. (Once skiers leave Cornice, they are outside the ski area's permitted boundary.) Big Tesuque skiers find natural powder, bowl skiing and trees. The bowls empty onto the area's entrance road, 3 miles below the base area, leaving you to hitchhike back up. First-timers should go with a local who knows this area: It's genuine backcountry; it's big and people occasionally get lost.

■ **Intermediate:** On a fresh powder day (once a week on average), local intermediates and advanced skiers head straight for the Tesuque Peak triple chair, up to 12,000 feet and the top of the mountain. To the right of the lift (as the trail map reads) is Gayway, a glorious, groomed pitch with several spicy turns that gives new meaning to the term "spectacular scenery." On a clear day, you almost get the feeling of flying, thanks to the 150-mile vista as the trail drops away. Parachute, which parallels Gayway, is a groomed black diamond with a somewhat steeper pitch. On the far side of the mountain, reached by the Santa Fe Super Chief quad, Middle and Lower Broadway have isolated trail skiing for intermediate skiers.

●● **Beginner:** This level will be happiest on the lower part of the mountain, on the wide boulevard of Easy Street. Advanced-beginners will find more challenges and a slightly steeper pitch on Open Slope and Upper and Lower Midland. If you're feeling adventurous, try Lower Burro for an exhilarating, winding trip through the trees on a mild pitch.

● **Never-ever:** Good terrain at the mountain's base served by Pine Flats lift is protected by snowfences. For children, Chipmunk Corner lift provides a tucked-away learning area.

Mountain layout—Snowboarding

Generally speaking, the mountain's expert terrain is to the left of the Tesuque Peak chair. After a dump, locals go first to Columbine, Big Rocks and Wizard—all very steep and for advanced riders only. Tequila Sunrise and Easter Bowl have the best glades. Hike to the Big Tesuque Bowl via Cornice for freshies, bowl skiing and trees (once you leave Cornice, you're outside the ski area's permitted boundary). The bowls empty onto the area's entrance road, 3 miles below the base area, and you have to hitchhike back up. Go with a local who knows this area: It's genuine backcountry, it's big and it's easy to get lost.

On a fresh powder day (about once a week), local intermediates head straight for the Tesuque Peak triple chair and the top of the mountain. To the right of the lift (as the trail map reads) is Gayway, a glorious, groomed pitch with several spicy turns that gives new meaning to the term "spectacular scenery." On a clear day, you almost get the feeling of flying, thanks to the 150-mile vista as the trail drops away.

Beginners will be happiest on the lower part of the mountain, on the wide boulevard of Easy Street. Advanced-beginners will find more challenges and a slightly steeper pitch on Open Slope and Upper and Lower Midland. If you're feeling adventurous, try Lower Burro for an exhilarating, winding trip through the trees on a mild pitch.

Depending on conditions, Santa Fe opens an "alternative terrain" area for snowboarders.

Mountain rating

Many people think Ski Santa Fe is a small, gentle day area. It's not. It has enough terrain to keep a skier of any level happy for two to three days. Its glades are great, though short; and Big Tesuque Bowl, when skiable, is an adventure. Santa Fe has a nice beginner area isolated by snowfences. Combined with Santa Fe's outstanding sightseeing opportunities, this is an excellent destination for skiers who don't want to be on the mountain every day (or all day). One warning: Ski Santa Fe has one of the highest lift-served elevations in the nation—12,000 feet on top, 10,350 feet at the base. If you're susceptible to altitude problems, take note.

Cross-country and snowshoeing

Santa Fe has no groomed or tracked trails. However, there are maintained backcountry trails in the **Santa Fe National Forest. Aspen Vista Road,** 2 miles below the ski area, is a popular and moderately difficult 7-mile trail. **Black Canyon Campground,** 8 miles up the ski road, is a popular area for beginners. Maps and information on conditions in the Santa Fe National Forest are available from the National Forest Service at 988-6940. For ski area information only, call 982-5300.

Lessons (2002/03 prices)

Group lessons: Adult lessons cost $30. A second session on the same day only costs an extra $18.

Never-ever package: Two group lessons, beginner lift and rentals is $58 for skiers, $75 for snowboarders.

Private lessons: $65 per hour; discounts for multiple hours.

Special programs: Among them are a women's program, classes for ages 50 and older, mogul clinics, telemark lessons and powder workshops. Check the ski school, 982-4429.

Racing: Coin-op and NASTAR Thursday through Sunday.

Child care (2002/03 prices)

Ages: 3 months to 3 years.
Costs: All-day program costs $56; $40 half day; $12 per hour. Ages 3 and 4 who are completely toilet-trained can register for Snowplay, a program that is "an introduction to the skiing environment." This program, which includes indoor and outdoor activities, is $62 all day and $46 half day.

Reservations: Required; call 988-9636. Only full-day packages for child care are sold during holiday periods.

Children's lessons: Ages 4–9, all day including lunch and lift ticket, $62 (add $12 for rental equipment). Half-day programs are $46. Four-year-olds have a morning lesson with play activities in the afternoon; others have lessons in both morning and afternoon.

Lift tickets (2002/03 prices)

	Adult	Teen (13-20)	Child (Up to 12)
One day	$44	$36	$32
Three days	$123 ($41/day)	$100 ($33+/day)	$89 ($29+/day)
Five days	$196 ($39+/day)	$160 ($32/day)	$142 ($28+/day)

Who skis free: Skiers age 72 and older and kids shorter than 46 inches in ski boots.

Who skis at a discount: Ages 62–71 pay the child rate. A ticket valid only on the beginner lift is $22.

Accommodations

Ski Santa Fe has no base lodging, but even if it did, you'd want to be in Santa Fe for dining, shopping and the museums. More than 70 hotels, motels, inns, condominiums and B&Bs serve Santa Fe visitors. Winter is low season in this region, but the increase of visitors trying to take advantage of this have actually caused prices to rise from bargain to a moderate level during the past few years. Expect to pay about $75–$110 a day, per person, for a ski-stay package at one of the many hotels on Cerrillos Road and 25 to 50 percent more downtown.

Lift-and-lodging packages are the best deal; call **Santa Fe Central Reservations** (800-776-7669 or 983-8200) or the **Santa Fe Visitors Bureau,** (800) 777-2489 (777-CITY). Downtown is where the best restaurants, shopping and nightlife are concentrated, although we do recommend a few great dining options outside the Plaza area.

Inn at Loretto (800-727-5531; 988-5531; $$$) is Santa Fe's ultimate pueblo-style hotel. It was completely restored in 1998 and provides fabulous rooms only steps from the Plaza. Rooms have traditional New Mexican decor with carved wood furnishings and Native American art. **La Fonda Hotel** (800-523-5002; 982-5511; $$$–$$$$) is the historic place to stay. An inn has been on this site for 300 years (Billy the Kid worked in the kitchen here washing dishes). The current La Fonda incarnation was built in the 1920s. If you don't stay, at least stroll through and take a look—they don't make them like this anymore.

The way they make them now is **The Inn of the Anasazi** (800-688-8100; 988-3030; $$$–$$$$)—the politically correct place to stay. The hotel's restaurants use vegetables grown by local organic farmers. Leftovers are given to a homeless shelter and everything is recycled. The Southwestern decor and furnishings are immaculate. The dining room is very pleasant and the menu selections enjoyable; however, this is also a very expensive place to stay.

Dining: $$$-Entrees $20+; $$-$10-20; $-less than $10.
Accommodations: (double room) $$$$-$200+; $$$-$141-$200; $$-$81-$140; $-$80 and less.

Next door, the **Hotel Plaza Real** (800-279-7325; 988-4900; $$$) has 56 hotel units, 44 are suites with fireplaces. Continental breakfast is included. We also enjoyed the adobe **Inn on the Alameda** (800-506-9206 or 984-2121; $$$), which is handy to Canyon Road and offers a continental breakfast. In a village of adobe cottages, **La Posada de Santa Fe** (800-727-5276; 986-0000; $$–$$$), just restored, is a short walk from the Plaza. On the grounds is the Staab House, a Victorian mansion serving as the restaurant.

Excellent B&Bs are **Adobe Abode** (983-3133; $$$–$$$$), **Alexander's Inn** (986-1431; $$–$$$), the spacious **Dancing Ground of the Sun** (800-645-5673; 986-9797; $–$$$), the **Grant Corner Inn** (983-6678; $$), the intimate **Inn of the Animal Tracks** (988-1546; $$) and the classy **Water Street Inn** (984-1193; $$–$$$). The B&B Association of New Mexico does not have a Web site, but they can be reached at 982-3332.

Other lodging to consider are the **Hotel St. Francis** (800-529-5700; 983-5700; $$), the **Hilton of Santa Fe** (800-336-3676; 988-2811; $$$) and the **Hotel Santa Fe** (800-825-9876; 982-1200; $–$$$). Families should try the **El Rey Inn** (800-521-1349; 982-1931; $$–$$$), **Garrett's Desert Inn** (800-888-2145; 982-1851; $$), the **Campanilla Compound** condominiums (800-828-9700; 988-7585; $$$), and the **Otra Vez** condos (988-2244; $$–$$$). **Eldorado** (800-955-4455; 988-4455; $$–$$$$) is the city's largest hotel with 219 rooms.

The closest lodging to the ski area is **Fort Marcy Hotel Suites** (800-745-9910; $–$$), just off the ski area road. They have 80 condominiums from one to three rooms and are only four blocks from the Plaza.

Many of the chain hotels, such as **Comfort Inn** ($$), **Days Inn** ($), **Holiday Inn** ($$) and **Hampton Inn** ($), have adopted the local adobe architectural style and are a little less expensive. They are conveniently on Cerillos Road, which makes them handy for getting to the ski area, but out of walking range for downtown.

Dining

On the mountain, skiers have two choices. **La Casa Cafeteria** in the base lodge called La Casa Mall, and **Totemoff's Bar and Grill** at the base of the Tesuque Peak Chair. La Casa, with a French chef, offers a variety including a pasta bar and a daily special such as salmon with lemon tarragon. Its breakfast burrito is wicked good, but only for brave palates. Totemoff's features burgers, salads, pasta, cocktails and a sun deck.

Back in the city, Santa Fe cooks and you're in for a treat. Including fast food, Santa Fe has nearly 200 places to strap on the feed bag. From New Mexican cuisine to steaks and seafood, Santa Fe has more food variety than you could consume in a year and far more good restaurants than we have room to recommend.

We recommend the spectacular dining room at La Fonda, **La Plazuela** (992-5511; $$$). Breakfast lets you enjoy the colorful dining room for reasonable prices. We also recommend **The Restaurant at the Inn at Loretto** (984-7915; $$), steps from the Plaza. The food is reasonable and inventive (such as bourbon-glazed veal chop or coriander-grilled sea bass).

Everyone recommends the **Coyote Cafe** (132 W. Water St.; 983-1615; $$$). The main dining room has a fixed-price menu and modern Southwestern cuisine; those in the bar can order à la carte. **Pasqual's** (121 Don Gaspar; 983-9340; $$$) is great for breakfast, but it's good anytime for beautifully presented New Mexican cuisine. Call for dinner reservations or expect to wait a long time. If you want to meet people, ask to be seated at the communal table. **La Casa Sena** (125 East Palace Ave.; 988-9232; $$$) is tastefully Continental. Don't miss the adjacent **Cantina** ($$), where waiters and bartenders sing cabaret between food and drinks.

If you want to nibble tapas instead of dinner, this is the place to do it. **Julian's** (221 Shelby; 988-2355; $$$) is very upscale Italian, recommended by locals. **The Palace** (142 W. Palace Ave.; 982-9891; $$$) is a re-creation of a famous San Francisco eatery. This is Santa Fe's power lunch spot. It has been run for years by a trio of Italian brothers and offers respite from the pervasive Southwestern cooking. They also operate the more informal **Osteria d'Assisi** (58 S. Federal Pl.; 986-5858; $).

Moderately priced restaurants include **Maria's New Mexican Kitchen** (555 W. Cordova Rd.; 983-7929; $), where you'll probably meet the affable owner Al Lucero, who wrote *Maria's Real Margarita Book* featuring history and recipes of the more than 50 "real" margaritas served in the restaurant. Robert Redford, a frequent customer when he's in town, wrote the foreword. The food is wonderful also, especially the posole and green chile stew.

Locals flock to **The Shed** (113 Palace Ave.; 982-9030; $$) and **La Choza** (905 Alarid St.; 982-0909; $$) but watch out for the green chile—it could burn a hole in your ski boots.

The Pink Adobe (406 Old Santa Fe Trail; 983-7712; $$) is Santa Fe's oldest restaurant, a local favorite and sometimes difficult to even get reservations (which are necessary). They specialize in New Mexican and Creole foods. Next door, **The Dragon Room** is a favorite for cocktails. **El Farol** (808 Canyon Rd.; 983-9912; $$$) is the oldest Spanish-food restaurant. Specialties include curry dishes, hot and cold tapas as well as one of the best selections of Spanish wines in the U.S.

For a romantic evening try **Andiamo** (322 Garfield St.; 995-9595; $$). It is a little off the beaten track but serves unique pasta dishes with candlelight ambiance.

Cowgirl Hall of Fame (319 S. Guadalupe; 928-2565; $–$$) is what the name implies with authentic Texas-style barbecue, kid's menu and play area; plus fine dining at the attached **Mustang Grill**. Don't hestitate to join the tourists at **The Ore House** (upstairs at 50 Lincoln Ave.; 983-8687; $$) on the Plaza for free après-ski snacks. On Canyon Road, **Celebrations** (613 Canyon Rd.; 989-8904; $$) is in the heart of gallery row and is jammed at lunchtime. **Tomasita's Cafe** (500 S. Guadalupe; 983-5721; $) is fast food with a twist. Portions are large, service is friendly, and it's a favorite of Santa Fe families, so be prepared to wait. It is inexpensive, and has some of the best New Mexican fare in town.

The Plaza Restaurant (54 Lincoln; 982-1664; $) is a throwback to diner days; regulars swear everything is good and very affordable. **Zia Diner** (326 South Guadalupe; 988-7008; $) is an easy 15-minute walk from the Plaza and features All-American favorites (New Mexican style, of course) such as meat loaf stuffed with piñon nuts, basic pastas and soups. **Atomic Grill** (103 E. Water St.; 820-2866; $) serves wood-fired pizza, pastas and hamburgers together with about 80 bottled beers. There's take-out and delivery too.

The **Telecote Café** (1203 Cerrillos Rd.; 988-1362; $-$$) is the place for breakfast just like Mom used to make if your mother liked using spices.

 ## Après-ski/nightlife

Santa Fe has the usual live bands, bars and places to dance. But it has some unusual off-slope activities as well. To work out the kinks of a fresh powder day, stop at **Ten Thousand Waves** (988-1047, 982-9304) for a relaxing hot tub under the stars. About 3 miles from the Plaza and on the road from the ski area, it's a Japanese-style hot tub resort not to be missed.

For elegant après-ski (you can go in ski clothes), head for **Inn of the Anasazi** or **La Posada**, close to the Plaza. **Swig** (135 West Palace Ave.; 955-0400; $$) is the pick-up spot.

Dining: $$$-Entrees $20+; $$-$10-20; $-less than $10.

Accommodations: (double room) $$$$-$200+; $$$-$141-$200; $$-$81-$140; $-$80 and less.

Serving "global" cuisine and Asian tapas, this spot was designed to intoxicate the senses. A wonderful place to mix dinner with entertainment is at **La Cantina** (988-9232) in the historic Sena Plaza, a stately adobe built as a family home in the 1860s. It features singing waiters and waitresses. For about $20, you can eat, drink and hear an exceptional dinner theater show, belted out between courses. Children are welcome, reservations a must.

The **Catamount Bar & Grill** (125 E. Water St.; 988-7222) is a sports bar teeming with locals and tourists featuring big-screen TV, pool tables and specials like "Jägermeister Night."

Other activities

The **museums** are first rate. A three-day pass for $15 will admit you to five of the best: the Museum of International Folk Art (strong in regional Spanish art), the Palace of the Governors (for local history), the Museum of Indian Arts and Culture, the Museum of Fine Arts, and the Museum Of Spanish Colonial Art (opened in July 2002). All are free on Fridays. The Georgia O'Keeffe Museum has its own entry fees.

You should consider **touring** the eight Indian pueblos near Santa Fe. The San Ildefonso Pueblo, famous for its distinctive pottery style, is the most scenic. Its annual festival to honor its patron saint is in late January. If you have a car, and especially if you are driving north on U.S. Hwy. 84/285 to Taos, be sure and take the Hwy. 503 turnoff at Pojoaque and drive east to Chimayo, site of the Santuario de Chimayo, famous for its dirt thought to have healing powers. At the end of the church parking lot, you'll find Leona's, a funky little walk-up where the tamale pie and burritos are exceptional. On the way to Taos wind through foothills and into mountain Hispanic villages like Truchas and Las Trampas. For woven blankets, stop at Ortega's in Chimayo, where family members still practice a craft brought to New Mexico in the 1600s.

An initial warning: It will be much cheaper to ski all day than venture into Santa Fe's many tempting **shops** and **galleries.** That warning given, more than 200 galleries feature Native American crafts and art, as well as fine art on a par with galleries in New York, Florence or Paris. Every day of the week now, you can find bargains and excellent workmanship when local artisans sell their wares on blankets in front of the 390-year-old Palace of the Governors, a long-standing Santa Fe shopping tradition.

Canyon Road is the world-famous strip of galleries featuring art of all styles. The Waxlander Gallery features pastel still-life works of J. Alex Potter. Our favorite is Nedra Matteucci's Fenn Galleries, 1075 Paseo de Peralta, just south of Canyon Road. The day we visited, we counted four Zuniga sculptures starting at $80,000 each. Don't miss the garden.

For about $10 a day, the 19,000-square-foot **Santa Fe Spa,** 786 N. St. Francis Dr. (984-8727), has state-of-the-art exercise equipment, a heated indoor lap pool, massage staff, free child care and more. Also check out **Fitness Plus,** for women only, at 473-7315.

Call the **Santa Fe Visitors Bureau** (955-6200; 800-777-2489) for more information on these and other activities.

Getting there and getting around

By air: Albuquerque has the nearest major airport, 60 miles away. Private pilots can use the Santa Fe Regional Airport. For shuttles from the airport in Albuquerque to Santa Fe, call 982-4311.

By car: Santa Fe is north of Albuquerque on I-25, an easy hour's drive. The ski area is 16 miles from town on Hwy. 475.

Taos

with Red River and Angel Fire
New Mexico

Summit elevation: 11,819 feet
Vertical drop: 2,612 feet
Base elevation: 9,207 feet

Taos Ski Valley

Address: Box 90,
Taos Ski Valley, NM 87525
☎ **Area code:** 505
Ski area phone: 776-2291
Snow report: 776-2916 **Fax:** 776-8596
ⓘ **Toll-free reservations:** (800) 776-1111;
(800) 821-2437
E-mail: tsv@skitaos.org
Internet: http://skitaos.org/
Expert:★★★★★
Advanced:★★★★★
Intermediate:★★★★
Beginner:★★ **Never-ever:**★

Number of lifts: 12–4 quad chairs,
1 triple chair, 5 double chairs, 2 surface lifts
Percent snowmaking: 46 percent
Uphill capacity: 15,000 per hour
Total acreage: 1,096 acres terrain, 687 acres trails
Snowboarding: No
Bed Base: 3,705 at base and in town
Nearest lodging: slopeside; hotels, condos
Resort child care: Yes, 6 weeks and older
Adult ticket, per day: $45-$49 (02/03 prices)
Dining (Including town)**:**★★★★
Apres-ski/nightlife:★★
Other activities:★★★

Northern New Mexico has some of the best skiing to be found in the United States. Taos has long been legendary for its steeps and deep powder, and nearby Red River and Angel Fire both offer excellent and different ski experiences. Most of the information in this chapter concentrates on Taos, which is a true destination resort, but we'll also give you a flavor of Red River and Angel Fire (see *Nearby Resorts* at end of chapter).

Taos Ski Valley is a little piece of the Alps, founded by a Swiss native and surrounded by hotels and restaurants built by Frenchmen and Austrians. It's near the town of Taos, which is a rich mix of Spanish and Indian cultures, blended over the centuries to produce the Southwestern style. This style, in art, cuisine and architecture, isn't trendy here; it's the way things have always been.

Taos Ski Valley holds another distinction: While many resorts walk a delicate marketing tightrope, touting whatever expert terrain they possess while trying not to scare anyone off, Taos enjoys its tough reputation. It wisely advises visitors to meet the challenge by enrolling in Ski-Better-Week, a package of lessons, accommodations, meals and lift tickets. Just about everybody staying at the mountain enrolls in ski school. If you aren't part of a class, you feel like the kid that didn't get chosen for the baseball team. Après-ski talk centers on Ski-Better-Week anecdotes, leaving independents to sit at the bar with little to add to the discussion.

The town of Taos is 18 miles from Taos Ski Valley. Long a haven for artists, the town has galleries, shops, restaurants and hotels ranging from luxurious to pedestrian.

Mountain layout—Skiing

Taos has something for everyone in the intermediate, advanced and expert levels. Every good skier will be challenged every day.

◆◆ **Expert:** For tree skiers, Taos has a special challenge, the twin runs Castor and Pollux. They hardly look like runs, just steep wooded parts of the mountain, unskiable, where some joker put a sign that looks just like a trail marker. The trees are 2 to 15 feet apart, and advanced classes regularly train here.

Powder skiing lasts on Highline Ridge and Kachina Peak, for two reasons: They are double-black diamonds and Kachina Peak is reachable only after an hour-and-fifteen-minute hike from the top chair at 11,800 feet to the ridge at 12,500 feet. You can, however, ski off Highline Ridge and West Basin Ridge after only a 15-minute hike. Skiers are advised to go with an instructor or a patroller; at the very least, they must check in with the patrol at the top of Chair 6. The ski patrol will give you a rough screening to see if you can handle the double-diamond terrain. In any case you must ski the ridge with a partner.

◆ **Advanced:** An advanced skier won't be disappointed. All of the tree skiing is an effort and the black-diamond trails are as advertised. Hunziker, isolated by a short climb, provides good bumps that narrow about halfway down the trail. Otherwise test yourself on some of the off-trail skiing dropping from the ridges.

■ **Intermediate:** Taos has a lot of terrain at this level. Smooth bowls are found off the Kachina quad chair. Other good intermediate terrain is under Chairs 7 and 8. Anything marked as a blue trail is a blast, with plenty of length for cruising. Some at this level may feel pushed; if you're in that group, go ski the greens for a while and keep your head held high. Better yet, sign up for a class.

●● **Beginner:** Taos has some nice beginner terrain, such as Honeysuckle, which descends the skier's right side of the ridge. Bonanza and Bambi give beginners a way down on the other side of the ridge. The main problem is negotiating either White Feather or Rubezahl when they are crowded with skiers coming back into the village. Despite the slow-down efforts of ski hosts stationed every 20 feet or so, both runs resemble the Hollywood Freeway at rush hour, except that the faster skiers aren't stalled in traffic. They zip around the slower ones, who are gingerly wedging their way home. On busy days it's a mess. Timing is important: Come down early, or better yet, be one of the last to descend.

● **Never-ever:** Only athletic novices should attempt to learn here. Despite the highly regarded ski school, the jump from the tiny learning area to the mountain is enormous. Better learning terrain is at nearby Angel Fire or Red River.

Mountain layout—Snowboarding

Snowboarding is not permitted. Head to Angel Fire or Red River.

Mountain rating

Fifty-one percent of Taos' runs are rated expert, and half of the expert runs are double-black diamonds. True experts will be thrilled with the skiing off Highline Ridge and Kachina as well as the narrow chutes off West Basin Ridge. Intermediates will have a field day with great steep cruising. Beginners will be limited and never-evers terrified.

Rise up to meet Taos' challenge. If you normally ski blue runs at other resorts, you can ski Taos. It may be tough at first, but persist—you'll catch on. Taos can be an extremely rewarding ski experience *because* of its challenge. The runs demand you give it your best.

Lessons (2002/03 prices)

Group lessons: Two hours, morning or afternoon, $40. Some lessons at Taos concentrate on specific skills, such as moguls or telemarking.

Never-ever package: Novice-lift ticket, 4.5-hour lesson and rentals for $65; two days cost $105.

Private lessons: For up to four skiers, costs are $110 for an hour, $165 for two hours, $250 for a half day, and $400 for a full day.

Special programs: Ski Better Weeks are the core of the Taos ski experience, developed by former French Junior Alpine champion and ski school technical director Jean Mayer. Participants are matched for five or six mornings of intensive lessons, and they ski with the same instructor all week. Sixty-five percent of the participants are intermediate or higher. Ski Week costs $180 for five or six days (lift ticket extra). Many lodging properties offer the Ski Better Week as a package with meals and accommodations.

Super Ski Week is an intense course for adults who wish to focus seriously on improving their skills. Skiers are analyzed, videotaped and put through what amounts to a mini ski-racing camp every morning and afternoon for a total of five hours. This is not a program for the timid or late-night party types, but most will find their skills much improved by the end of the week. It's offered at select times. Lessons only cost $460. During regular season, $730 includes lessons, lift tickets, Nastar and apres-ski talks; spring season rate is $700. There are Ski Week programs for women, teens and for ages 50 and older at select times during the season.

Taos Ski Valley also has shorter programs that concentrate on specifics, such as Moguls or Extreme Weekends, designed to aid advanced and expert skiers; and Women's Weekends.

Child care (2002/03 prices)

Ages: Ages 6 weeks to 3 years.

Costs: Full day including lunch and snacks is $63. Toddlers get indoor activities and snow play.

Reservations: Required; call 776-2291. There is one staffer for every two infants.

Children's lessons: The Kinderkäfig children's center is unfortunately an inconvenient distance from the main base area. A full-day program for ages 3–15, including lesson, lunch and afternoon supervised skiing, costs $80 a day. (Ages 3–5 get a program that combines lessons, snow play and indoor activities.) Reservations are recommended; call 776-2291.

Lift tickets (2002/03 prices)

	Adult	Child (Up to 12)
One day	$49	$30
Three days	$135 ($45/day)	$84 ($28/day)
Five days	$225 ($45/day)	$140 ($28/day)

Who skis free: Ages 70 and older. Any child 6 or under skis free when an accompanying adult purchases a lift ticket.

Who skis at a discount: Ages 65–69 ski for $33. Ages 13–17 ski for $39 a single day; $37 multiday. Taos reduces its ticket prices in the early and late seasons; prices are higher during holiday periods.

Cross-country and snowshoeing

Personal fitness trainer Bonnie Golden runs **Taos Fitness Adventures** (751-5977), with guided cross-country skiing and snowshoeing in the winter, plus hiking and custom programs in warmer weather. **Southwest Nordic Center** (758-4761) has cross-country lessons, tours and yurt trips. **Enchanted Forest Cross-Country Ski Area** (754-2374) is 40 miles northeast of Taos by Hwys. 522 and 38. It has 34 km. of backcountry trails, some groomed, and an elevation of 10,300 feet, from which you have great views of the Moreno and Red River valleys. Trail rates are $10 for adults, with discounts for teens, seniors and children. At the Miller's Crossing headquarters in downtown Red River, you can rent equipment (including pulks) and pick up trail maps.

Accommodations

Taos' **Ski-Better-Week** packages include up to seven nights lodging (Saturday to Saturday), six lift tickets and six morning lessons. In some cases, meals are included, too. Prices range from about $586 to about $1,600 per person, double occupancy. If price or specific amenities are concerns, call **Taos Valley Resort Association** (800-776-1111 or 776-2233) or **Taos Central Reservations** (800-821-2437) to book lodging or ski-stay-air packages.

The **Inn at Snakedance** (800-322-9815 or 776-2277; $$$$) has 60 ski-in/ski-out rooms. Amenities include a spa with hot tub, sauna, exercise and massage facility; a glass-walled bar; and a restaurant serving continental cuisine with a Southwest flair. Owners Mary Madden and Dan Ringeisen saved the fireplace from the old Hondo Inn, which used to occupy the space. The Inn offers the Ski-Better-Week packages with an optional meal plan.

The **Bavarian Lodge** (770-0450; $$$$) is about as good as it gets on the mountain when it comes to the German/Austrian good life. The interior art was created by Swiss artist Reto Messmer and the building features Bavarian antiques.

Hotel St. Bernard (776-2251; $$$), managed by Taos ski school technical director Jean Mayer, offers the flavor of a European retreat. The cuisine and ambiance are both legendary and French. This hotel also offers the Ski-Better-Week packages with meals.

Hotel Edelweiss (800-458-8754 or 776-2301; $$–$$$$) is right at the base of the village. The charming hotel has an outdoor hot tub and large sundeck. It offers the Ski Week package, including meals.

The **Austing Haus** (800-748-2932 or 776-2649; $$) is 1.5 miles from the base of Taos Ski Valley and is an unusual structure. It is the tallest timber frame building in the United States and owner Paul Austing is justifiably proud of the 24-unit lodge he helped build himself. The food in the glass dining room is very good.

The **Alpine Village Suites** (800-576-2666; $$–$$$$) is one of the newest accommodations available on the mountain. Most suites have private balconies with streamside or mountainside views.

Between the ski area and town is a bed-and-breakfast inn, the **Salsa del Salto** (776-2422; $$–$$$). Formerly the residence of Hotel St. Bernard owner Jean Mayer, it's now run by Jean's brother, Dadou, a French-trained chef who cooks Salsa del Salto's gourmet breakfasts.

The town of Taos offers a wide range of accommodations. Prices are generally less expensive than staying at Taos Ski Valley. At the northern edge of town, **Quail Ridge Inn** (800-624-4448 or 776-2211; $$–$$$$) is a fully appointed condominium complex at a tennis ranch, including indoor and outdoor courts. Looking much like a pueblo, it exudes the Southwestern atmosphere. The **Fechin Inn** (800-911-2937 or 751-1000; $$–$$$$) is the most luxurious place to stay. The **Historic Taos Inn** (800-826-7466, spells TAOS-INN; $–$$$$) is the cultural center of Taos. The lobby, built around the old town well, is a gathering place for artists. Rooms feature adobe fireplaces, antiques and Taos-style furniture built by local artisans. The **Sagebrush Inn** (800-428-3626 or 758-2254; $$$–$$$$) is an historic inn with a priceless collection of Southwestern art in the lobby and some of the best nightlife in town. At the lower end of the price range are **El Pueblo Lodge** (800-433-9612; $–$$$), **Indian Hills Inn** (800-444-2346; $), and often, rooms in the chain hotels, such as **Holiday Inn** or **Ramada.** The least expensive is the skiers' hostel, **The Abominable Snowmansion** (776-8298; $) in Arroyo Seco, 9 miles from the Village, where the rates are about $25–$60.

We also enjoyed three other B&Bs in Taos, which seems to have an unusual number of fine choices: **Hacienda del Sol** (758-0287; $$), owned by John and Marcine Landon; the **Old Taos Guesthouse** (758-5448; $–$$), owned by Tim and Leslie Reeves (who are fun to ski with); and **Inn on La Loma Plaza** (758-1717; $$–$$$$), owned by Peggy Davis and her husband, Jerry (both former mayors in Vail and Avon, CO). **Alma del Monte** (776-2721; $$), halfway between the hubbub of the plaza and Taos Ski Valley, is managed by Suzanne Head. B&Bs can be booked through the **Taos B&B Association,** (800) 876-7857.

The **Inger Jirby Guest Houses** (758-7333; $$$$), a creation of an artist from Sweden, are eclectically decorated, luxurious and only two blocks from the plaza.

Dining

Because so many properties here offer Ski-Better-Week packages, which include meals, most restaurants are operated by the lodges. The best independent eateries in the village are **Rhoda's Restaurant** (776-2005; $$), serving many New Mexican specialties, and **Tim's Stray Dog Cantina** (776-2894; $$).

The **Bavarian** (770-0450; $$–$$$), at the bottom of the Kachina Lift, may be the best lunch spot in the ski valley. If it is sunny, ask to sit on the deck. They serve wonderful spätzle, wienerschnitzel and strudel.

The **Hondo Restaurant** ($$–$$$) at The Inn at Snakedance is open to non-guests for breakfast, lunch and dinner and features winemaker dinners with California vintners. **Hotel Edelweiss** ($$–$$$) also serves three meals daily to the general public.

On the road into the valley, the **Casa Cordova** (776-2500; $$–$$$) specializes in American and Continental cuisine. **Tim's Chile Connection** (776-8787; $) is known for its chicken chimichanga and Pollo Borracho. **Renegade Cafe** (776-8319; $$) at the Quail Ridge Inn specializes in Mediterranean-style food.

The town of Taos has great variety when it comes to restaurants. **The Trading Post** (758-5089; $$) has a bit of everything—Cajun, New Mexican, Italian, steaks. **Jacquelina's** (751-0399; $$), on S. Santa Fe Road (also known as Paseo del Pueblo Sur), specializes in Southwestern cuisine. The pork loin, marinated in honey and chipotle chili, is outstanding. The menu at the **Apple Tree Restaurant** (758-1900; $$–$$$) lists Southwestern dishes and continental cuisine. On the historic plaza, **The Garden Restaurant** (758-9483; $$-$$$) offers New Mexican as well as American, Italian and French entrées. **Doc Martin's** (758-1977; $$-$$$) in the Taos Inn has Southwestern cuisine.

Michael's Kitchen (758-4178; $) has phenomenally large and excellent breakfasts. Or head to **El Taoseño** (758-4142) for a great breakfast burrito.

Dining: $$$–Entrees $20+; $$–$10-20; $–less than $10.
Accommodations: (double room) $$$$–$200+; $$$–$141-$200; $$–$81-$140; $–$80 and less.

Après-ski/nightlife

When lifts close at Taos Ski Valley, skiers head to the deck of the **Hotel St. Bernard**, the **Martini Tree Bar** at the Resort Center, or to drink German beer at **The Bavarian**. **The Inn at Snakedance** has entertainment nightly. **The Thunderbird** typically has music of all kinds throughout the winter. Not much else happens here.

It's livelier in Taos town, but not wild (unless you hit the Alley Cantina on a good night). The **Alley Cantina** has a live band and wild dancing some nights. Check the schedule, you'll love it. **The Sagebrush Inn** has C&W dances. The Kachina Lodge's **Cabaret Room** has a dance floor and occasional acts such as Arlo Guthrie, and **Ogelvie's Bar and Grill** in Taos Plaza hops. For microbrew fans, **Eske's Brew Pub** off the Taos Plaza is the spot. Be sure to try the unique Green Chili Beer at least once. Skiers and local artists mix at the **Adobe Bar** of the Taos Inn, the living room for artsy locals. Order a margarita and watch the beautiful people. Up at the Taos Pueblo there is gambling at the **Taos Mountain Casino**. The *Taos News* has a weekly entertainment guide.

 ## Other activities

Make a trip to **Boot Doctors** (776-2489) and upgrade your equipment. This shop is one of the premier ski boot fitters in the United States. If it's time to get new gear, have custom boot beds tailored to your foot shape and body balance while you're in town. It will have a profound effect on your skiing.

Taos is quite historic. The **Martinez Hacienda,** built in 1804, is a monument to the Spanish Colonial era in Northern New Mexico. **Kit Carson** is buried in Taos and his home and museum are open to the public. The **Millicent Rogers Museum** has a fantastic collection of Indian jewelry and art. The **Fechin Institute** is worth a visit to see the Russian artist's art and architecture.

Adventure Tours in Taos (758-1167) has **sleigh rides** and **snowmobile tours. Taos Ice Arena** (758-8234) is open Thanksgiving through February. **Fly fishing** tours are offered in winter on the Red River by Los Rios Anglers (758-2798). For **snowmobiling** in Red River call BobCat Pass Adventures (754-2769), Sled Shed (754-6370) or Fast Eddie's (754-3103). Roadrunner Tours (377-6416) offers **horse-drawn sleigh rides** to a sheepherders' tent with a dinner cooked over an open fire.

In Red River there is a unique **Night Sky Adventure** (754-2941) that provides a powerful telescopic universe tour that takes advantage of the altitude and the clear winter skies.

Visit the **Taos Pueblo,** the 700-year-old home of the Tiwa Indians. Visitors are welcome to the pueblo, workshops, ceremonies and sacred dances, except for a four- to six-week period each winter when the pueblo is closed for religious reasons. For exact dates, call the Taos Chamber of Commerce (800-732-TAOS). The pueblo is open from 9 a.m. to 4:30 p.m.

Georgia O'Keeffe and R.C. Gorman have made Taos legendary with art lovers. You'll find about 80 **galleries** are here. Get a list from Taos Chamber of Commerce, 758-3873 or (800) 732-TAOS.

Getting there and getting around

By air: Albuquerque is the nearest major airport, 135 miles south. Rental car agencies are at the airport. For ground transportation, contact Faust's Transportation, 758-3410 in Taos or 843-9042 in Albuquerque; or Pride of Taos, 758-8340.

By car: I-25 north to Santa Fe, then Hwys. 285, 84 and 68 to Taos. Taos Ski Valley is 18 miles farther north on Hwy. 150. For Red River head north on Hwy. 522 and east on Hwy. 38. For Angel Fire go east on Hwy. 64.

Getting around: If you stay in Taos Ski Valley village and have no desire to go into the town of Taos 18 miles away, you won't need a car. If you want to visit the town, or aren't staying at the ski area, you'll need one. In Red River you won't need a car, but you'll need one to get there. The same goes for Angel Fire, where you can park your car and forget it.

Nearby Resorts

Angel Fire Resort, Angel Fire, NM; (505) 377-4207 or (800) 633-7463

Internet: www.angelfireresort.com
5 lifts; 445 skiable acres; 2,077 vertical feet

Angel Fire is a modern, purpose-built resort about a half-hour—22 miles—east of Taos. The accommodations are all very close to the slopes and the mountain has been created for families and mellow skiing with touches of challenge.

This resort is especially good for beginners and intermediates. You have to go out of your way to get into trouble. It's about as good as it gets for families and those who want to take it easy. The resort has added some expert terrain, but it's tucked away where no one will accidentally get into trouble. **Beginners** will want to take Headin' Home from the top of the high-speed Chile Express quad. Stay on the trail or drop down Bodacious and wend your way back to the base area. Beginners can also experience the back bowl by winding down Highway, then dropping off Hallelujah or La Bajada to end up at the base of the Southwest Flyer, another high-speed quad. **Intermediates** will have fun on Fat City, Fire Escape, Mother Lode and Arriba in the back bowl. We recommend staying in the back bowl. On the front side you can cruise down some good intermediate trails such as I-25, Prospector and Jasper's, but all end in a long runout to the base area. **Advanced/Expert** levels will find meager offerings but they can be fun. A cluster of black runs under Lift 6 provides a challenge. To the far skier's right of the back bowl, a series of advanced runs were recently added to Detonator and Nitro.

Angel Fire has snapped up the opportunity to become New Mexico's premier **snowboarding** destination, thanks to Taos' steadfast refusal to allow snowboarding. The recently installed Chile Express high-speed quad whisks boarders to the top of the 10,622-foot mountain in a fraction of the time it took the two triples it replaced. Sound systems pump out great tunes underneath the lifts. Angel Fire has a young feel to it, unlike the conservative, staid atmosphere of some larger resorts.

There are three terrain parks with tabletops, rail slides and spines. One is near the top of the mountain, on Fat City, reached by Lift #3. The second park is off Exhibition near the base of the mountain, served by Lift #2. Angel Fire also has the only halfpipe in New Mexico, on Angel Food. The resort hosts world-famous shovel racing in February, after which the course is transformed for a slopestyle competition held each March.

Beginner boarders will appreciate both Dreamcatcher and Lift #2, servicing Exhibition and Valley. You get what is, in effect, a superb bunny hill with two distinct levels of difficulty. In addition there's beginner terrain at the top of the mountain, on either side of the Nastar race area, that's served by a short lift. The Summit Haus, a yurt-style restaurant with a full-service bar at the peak, adds a nice extra touch. Intermediate and advanced riders will prefer the back side of the mountain, serviced by yet another new, high-speed quad. Hell's Bells is a favorite run amongst advanced boarders. Intermediates will enjoy Fire Escape and Hully Gully, shifting to front-side runs like I-25 and Prospector on days when the sun is hidden and snow is powering down. Unfortunately, front-side runs all end in a long runout to the base area since the new lift eliminated midway loading. Expert are not forgotten—hiking-accessed trails in the Back Basin including Nitro, Detonator and Baa-da-bing offer some of the steepest terrain.

Angel Fire has an excellent **ski school** that focuses on beginner and intermediate skiers and children. Snowboarding instruction is highly rated too. Angel Fire Resort **Day Care** (800-633-7463), housed in a separate building, is open 8 a.m. to 5 p.m. Full-and half-day programs provide activities for children ages 6 weeks through 11 years. Costs range from $55 to $75 for day care and children's lesson programs. Angel Fire resort has recently expanded its children's ski and snowboard school with a 6,000-square-foot building designed specifically for kids.

Adventure Park, at the summit, has a day tubing hill and Nordic Center. Here you'll find 19 km. of **cross-country and snowshoe** trails with beautiful views of New Mexico's highest mountain, Wheeler Peak. Lessons and rentals are available.

Lift tickets (2002/03): Adult, $45; teen (13–17), $36; youth (7–12), $28; multiday discounts apply. Early/late season rates are lower. Ages 6 and younger and 70 and older ski free.

Accommodations: The Angel Fire Resort Hotel (800-633-7463; $$–$$$) has standard and deluxe rooms and suites. The resort has managed **condominiums** ($$-$$$) and has a full program of ski packages. The hotel is slopeside and the condos have a shuttlebus.

Dining/après-ski/nightlife: Dining is a resort affair. There aren't many choices outside of the base area. The top spot is **Aldo's Cafe and Cantina** (377-6401; $$), with southwestern cuisine, right next to the Chile Express lift. **Branding Iron** (337-4201; $) has breakfast and lunch in the resort hotel. **Zebadiah's** (377-8005; $–$$) is off the resort and has a good family restaurant. The **Roasted Clove** (337-0636; $$) cooks flavorful Italian dishes but is difficult to spot. Be sure to ask for directions. For pizza call the **Pizza Stop** (337-6340; $) specializing in freshly made crust and sauces, or **Beverly's** (377-2337; $) in town. **Summit Haus,** at the summit, and **Village Haus,** on the base area deck, both have snacks, grilled items and full-service bars. Angel Fire snoozes in the evenings, but **Village Haus** has live entertainment, 3 p.m.-7 p.m. every weekend. There is also a bit of an après-ski buzz in **Jasper's.**

Other activities: After a long day on the slopes you may wish to recharge with a Leg Anti-Fatigue Treatment at **Sage Skin and Body Care** (377-5959). Roadrunner Tours (377-6416) offers **winter horse rides** and old-fashioned **sleigh rides.** Try your hand at **ice fishing** in nearby Eagle Nest through the Eagle Nest Marina (337-6941). For solitude and meditation visit the **Vietnam Veterans National Memorial** (337-6900), the first memorial built to honor the men and women serving in Vietnam.

Red River Ski Area, Red River, NM; (505) 754-2223 or (800) 331-SNOW

Internet: www.redriverskiarea.com
7 lifts; 290 skiable acres; 1,600 vertical feet

Red River, about an hour drive—37 miles—north of Taos, has no pretensions about Indians or the Spanish. This once was a down-and-dirty goldmining town with saloons and bordellos lining the streets. Today, Red River is one of the prettiest ski towns and most convenient to be found in the U.S. Two main lifts drop right into town and most hotels and condos are within walking distance of them. If you don't want to walk, take the town trolley that makes its rounds every 15 minutes.

This is a fun mountain, a lot of fun. Red Chair and Copper Chair reach the summit from different spots in town. This is not high-speed quad territory; all these lifts are fixed-grip. There's a terrain park for those who like tricks and air. From the highest point, Ski Tip, **begin-**

ners can drop to the other side of the peak to test about a dozen easy runs served by a double chair. Beginners can also ski all the way back to the base area along Cowpoke Cruise, which meanders down the entire 1,600 feet of vertical. **Intermediates** have the entire skier's right of the mountain for fun and games. These trails are the definition of cruiser delights. **Advanced and expert** skiers can head to skier's left from Ski Tip. Here, those seeking challenge will find a mix of trees and black-diamond trails.

Red River claims to be one of the great teaching mountains. It has an excellent ski school that focuses on beginner and intermediate skiers as well as children. Red River's Youth Center and Buckaroo **Child Care** is open from 8 a.m. to 4:30 p.m. Children from 6 months to 4 years are accepted for child care; $30 for half day, $48 for full day. Kids ages 4–10 have lessons and indoor activities, and are grouped in classes according to age and ability. Costs range from $32 to $78.

Lift tickets (2002/03): Adult, $44; teen (13–19), $39; juniors and seniors, $30; multiday discounts are available.

Accommodations: Almost all hotels are relatively close to the lifts and the town. For **lodging information,** call (800) 348-6444 or 754-2366. **Lifts West Condo/Hotel** (800-221-1859 or 754-2778; $–$$) has spacious rooms and a wild second-floor hot tub. For European charm, stay at the **Alpine Lodge** (800-252-2333; $$$) or **Edelweiss** (800-445-6077; $$-$$$), both boasting heated swimming pools. **The Auslander Condominiums** (800-753-2311 or 754-2311; $$), **Black Mountain Lodge** (800-825-2469 or 754-2469; $$), **Copper King Lodge** (800-727-6210 or 754-6210; $–$$), **The Riverside** (800-432-9999 or 754-2252; $) and **Silver Spur Lodge** (800-545-8372 or 754-2378; $–$$) are all almost ski-in/ski-out. Groups and large families can find great deals rentals through **Red River Real Estate** (800-453-3498; $$-$$$$) or **Bandanna Red River Properties** (800-521-4389; $$-$$$$).

Dining/après-ski/nightlife/other activities: Don't come here looking for fancy gourmet fare. This town is focused on good down-home meals with quantity. That said, **Brett's** (654-6136; $$) has an elegant dining room and a menu where everything from seafood to lamb is spiced with gourmet phrases. **Texas Reds Steakhouse and Saloon** (754-2922; $$) is everything a cowboy steakhouse should be. From the newsprint menu to the charbroiled beef, this is a carnivore's paradise. **The Lodge at Red River** (754-6280; $$) has a good family restaurant with plenty of steaks, but you can find trout and shrimp as well. **Timbers** (754-3090; $$) is another western-style steakhouse. For Tex-Mex head to **Sundance** (754-6271; $) or to **Angelina's** (754-2211; $). For N.Y.-style pizza and other Italian meals try **Pappa's** (754-2951; $). For breakfast head to **Colonel Js,** across from the Chamber of Commerce, for an "All U Can Eat" feast, to the **Alpine Lodge** for their breakfast burritos, or to **Shotgun Willie's** for the "Mountain Man Breakfast."

Red River is the nightlife capital of the region. If you want a rocking time, this is the spot to come. The town is normally packed with a young college crowd that loves to dance and sing. Head to the **Motherlode Saloon** for a chance to two-step and hear great live music. The **Mineshaft Theater** has concerts. **The Black Crow Coffeehouse** boasts top C&W and folk acts. **Texas Reds** often has singers in the bar. And the **Bull O'The Woods Saloon** has cowboy karaoke. **The Lonesome Pine Pub** serves eight New Mexico microbrews on tap. **Chubbies Tavern** rocks during après-ski with the college crowd.

Residents of Red River have an excellent sense of humor—and mischief. In January it's **BYOT** (bring your own turkey) for the annual Turkey Toboggan, where competitors race down the slope seated on the frozen beasts. February brings fully costumed **Mardi Gras** celebrations with awards for best and most unique masks. **St. Patrick's Day** is celebrated with a Limerick-style rolling of the stone down main street. This is a good party town.

Utah skiing

and staying in Salt Lake City

If a corporation could build the perfect ski resort, it would have lots of feathery snow overnight and frequent sunny weather during the day, a nearby major airport yet no airplane noise, and a variety of lodging and nightlife to appeal to a broad section of the skiing public. No ski corporation built Salt Lake City, but it certainly fits that description.

Eleven downhill ski areas, three Nordic ski areas and the only North American facility with public ski-jumping instruction and bobsled rides are within an hour's drive of the Salt Lake City International Airport, one of the country's major air hubs. Utah's snow is legendary. It's light, fluffy and abundant. But that's not all. These resorts don't feel the need to be carbon copies of each other. Each of the 11 nearby resorts has a distinct personality. If you think variety is the spice of life, get ready for a well-seasoned feast. Seven of the 11 resorts are detailed in the next three chapters, plus we provide capsule descriptions of two others.

If you still think you can't get a drink in Utah, you're way behind the times. In most places you won't notice any difference between buying a beer here and at home (we explain the liquor laws later in the chapter). But you can't have two drinks in front of you at the same time, and at some tables, only beer and wine are allowed. Salt Lake City claims more microbreweries per capita than any other western metropolitan city. Though we can't verify that claim, we can verify through firsthand experience that the breweries serve a very tasty product. Salt Lake City is unsurpassed in its variety of evening entertainment. Pro basketball, hockey, theater, comedy clubs and high-energy dance clubs are among the options.

Salt Lake City

Salt Lake City is a great spot to stay for several reasons. One, you're centrally located to sample all the major ski areas. Two, hotels are relatively inexpensive, perhaps a result of having more than 17,000 rooms available for nightly use. Three, Salt Lake City has lots of fun stuff to do at night.

The Utah Transit Authority (287-4636) has a very efficient ski bus system serving Brighton and Solitude in Big Cottonwood Canyon and Snowbird and Alta in Little Cottonwood Canyon. The buses are clean, pleasant and inexpensive, and go directly from downtown to the ski areas. This system incorporates the city's TRAX light rail trains and specially equipped ski buses to the ski areas. UTA also has a free fare zone downtown, convenient for sightseeing and evening activities. Lewis Brothers Stages (800-826-5844 or 359-8677) has a SkiExpress service that picks up skiers and snowboarders from downtown hotels and takes them to one of seven ski areas. Many of the hotels include the service in their rates.

The **Salt Lake Convention & Visitors Bureau** can help you plan your stay in the city, call (800) 541-4955 or 521-2822, or visit www.visitsaltlake.com. Once you're in Salt Lake City, there are several Visitor Information Centers. The main location is at the Salt Palace Convention Center, 90 South West Temple (open daily). Others are at the airport (open daily) and I-80 at 7200 West (Wed.-Sun. only). Another source of information is **Ski Utah,** call 534-1779 or go to www.skiutah.com.

Accommodations

Although rates are a little higher downtown than in outlying parts of the city, it is worth the extra few bucks to be close to Salt Lake City's major attractions.

The Grand America Hotel (801-258-6000 or 800-621-4505; $$$-$$$$) is Earl Holding's latest holding (Sun Valley Resort, Snowbasin Ski Resort, Little America). Located in downtown Salt Lake City, the luxury hotel has 377 rooms and 398 suites.

Salt Lake Marriott (531-0800 or 800-345-4754; $$-$$$) is across from the Salt Palace Convention Center and is connected to the Crossroads Plaza shopping mall. **Howard Johnson Express Inn** (521-3450 or 800-541-7639; $-$$) is two blocks from Temple Square.

Doubletree Hotel (801-328-2000; $$-$$$) is a few blocks farther south on West Temple, but it's within stumbling distance of the Zephyr Club (see *Après-ski/nightlife*). Another choice in this area is the recently renovated **Peery Hotel** (521-4300; $$-$$$$), historic, nicely elegant, but subject to street noise.

The **Hotel Monaco** (595-0000; $$-$$$), an upscale boutique hotel, is in an historic renovated bank building. Definitely not a cookie-cutter property, the Monaco will deliver a pet goldfish to your room at your request and serves up free back and neck massages during the complimentary evening wine reception in the lobby. And don't be surprised if you see your favorite rock star or NBA team in the lobby. This is *the* place to stay for those hot groups. The lively Bambara, an award-winning bistro-type restaurant, is just off the lobby (see *Dining*).

Little America Hotel and Towers (363-6781; $-$$) has some of the largest rooms we've seen in a hotel—great for spreading out all the gear that skiers carry. Also recommended are **Embassy Suites Hotel** (359-7800; $-$$) and the **Sheraton Salt Lake City** (532-3344; $$$-$$$$). The **Marriott University Park Hotel** (801-581-1000; $-$$$) is near the University of Utah, farther from downtown but closer to the resorts. It is at a higher elevation than downtown, so it has a dandy view of the city from its glassed-in hot tub.

Also try **Salt Lake City Center Travelodge** (531-7100; $-$$), **Travelodge Temple Square** (533-8200), **Deseret Inn** (532-2900; $) or **Cavanaughs Olympus Hotel** (521-7373; 800-426-0722; $$-$$$$).

Those looking for the coziness of an inn can try **The Brigham Street Inn** (364-4461; $$-$$$), on East South Temple near the university. Three B&Bs in historic buildings are clustered about seven blocks from Temple Square, each with wonderfully decorated rooms: **The Anniversary Inn** (363-4900; 800-324-4152; $$-$$$$), **Anton Boxrud Bed & Breakfast** (363-8035; 800-524-5511; $-$$) and **The Armstrong Mansion B&B** (531-1333; 800-708-1333; $$-$$$$).

The **Salt Lake Convention & Visitors Bureau** offers a free consumer housing service at 800-847-5810 and local reservationists promise to get you the best rate at dozens of Salt Lake hotels.

Dining

Downtown Salt Lake City has many restaurants in nearly every food category you can name, including Peruvian and Thai. It leads the nation in per capita Jell-O consumption, but that must be due to the stay-at-homes—we've never seen Jell-O on a menu here. You may want to dress up a bit (meaning a buttoned shirt and khakis instead of a T-shirt and jeans) for the finer establishments. See our nightlife section for an explanation of "private clubs," which some of these restaurants are.

Dining: $$$-Entrees $20+; $$-$10-20; $-less than $10.
Accommodations: (double room) $$$$-$200+; $$$-$141-$200; $$-$81-$140; $-$80 and less.

We're told **Metropolitan** (173 W. Broadway, 364-3472; $$$), once voted "Salt Lake's Best Restaurant," has world-class gourmet cuisine that rivals some of the best of any other major city. It also serves vegetarian entrees.

Bambara (363-5454, 202 S. Main St.), another of "Salt Lake's Best Restaurants" and voted "Best Contemporary American" in 2001, specializes in fresh, seasonal foods in a nouveau bistro setting next to the lobby of the newly refurbished Hotel Monaco.

Casually elegant Italian dining can be found at **Baci'Trattoria** (134 W. Pierpont Ave., 328-1500; $$). For Asian dining, **Xiao Li** (307 W. 200 South; 328-8688; $$) in the warehouse district has the most interesting atmosphere, but **Pagoda** (26 E St., 355-8155; $–$$) has been around the longest, since 1946. **Mikado** (67 W. 100 South, 328-0929; $$) has fresh fish and sushi, and has been in business for four decades. **The Golden Phoenix** (539-1122) in downtown Salt Lake has been recognized as one of the top Chinese restaurants.

Cafe Pierpont (122 W. Pierpont Ave., 364-1222, $–$$) and **Rio Grande Cafe** (270 S. Rio Grande, at the Amtrak Station, 364-3302; $) are downtown's best bets for Mexican.

Salt Lake's American and steak and seafood restaurants offer a wealth of choices. **New Yorker** (60 W. Market St., 363-0166, $$$) has an elegant atmosphere in the dining room. Its more casual neighbors, **Market Street Grill** (322-4668; $$) and **Oyster Bar** (531-6044; $$), emphasize seafood, but also serve steaks and chicken. (Market Street Grill has great breakfasts, by the way.) Big appetites will love the **Radizio Grill** (220-0500), an authentic Brazilian-style steakhouse. Kids younger than 9 eat free. **Lamb's** (169 S. Main, 364-7166; $$) is Utah's oldest restaurant, dating to 1919, and features fine art photography by Utah artists.

At the base of Little Cottonwood Canyon is **La Caille** (942-1751; $$$), which gets rave reviews for its French cuisine, serving staff and setting, the latter built to look like a French chateau and surrounded by gardens filled with swans, peacocks, rabbits and other animals. Make reservations; this place is *tres chic.* There's a B&B on premises.

These are just a tiny portion of what's available in Salt Lake City. A great resource for finding restaurants—particularly if you like certain kinds of food—is the Web site www.citysearchutah.com, which has a searchable database.

Après-ski/nightlife/other activities

Utah's liquor laws: Baby-boomer skiers remember when getting a glass of wine meant a trip to the state liquor store before going to a restaurant, then paying a setup fee before you could consume your own brown-bagged bottle. Now it's much easier, but here are a few tips:

Restaurants that have liquor licenses (most do) can serve alcohol from noon to midnight "to customers intending to dine." However, you won't find the wine list at the table. Your server will ask if you'd like "a beverage," at which point you can ask for the alcohol menu. Some restaurants are designated as private clubs, which means you'll have to pay a temporary membership fee to get in.

Bars don't exist in Utah, at least not by that name. If you are planning just to drink, not eat, you'll have to do so at a **private club.** Don't be deterred by restaurant or nightclub advertising that has phrasing like this: "A private club for the benefit of its members." You, too, can become a member. Utah residents buy an annual membership costing up to $35 for each club. Visitors pay $5 for a membership, valid for two weeks for the visitor and five guests. Annual members can bring guests, too.

To avoid the charge, ask outside the facility if someone will agree to be your "sponsor." Once you're inside, thank your sponsor and split for separate tables. Legally, you're supposed to leave with your sponsor, but no one watches that closely (and once inside, you can always find a new sponsor). If you lack such audacity, just think of the membership as a cover charge. But don't be shy about asking. Utahans are accustomed to this method of staying within the law; in fact, some single Utahans use "Need a sponsor?" as a handy pickup line.

Taverns may or may not serve food, depending on the establishment. The only alcohol served at taverns is 3.2-percent beer.

After a day of skiing at Alta and before you get back to Salt Lake, check out **River's Restaurant,** on your left at the southeast end of the Salt Lake Valley at the bottom of the mountains, for high-end brew, pub food and great après-ski atmosphere.

For an unusual happy hour, stop by the **Cotton Bottom Inn** (273-9830) at the base of Big and Little Cottonwood Canyons. This is a raucous, sawdust-on-the-floor tavern with great garlicburgers and an earthy crowd. The address is 2820 E. 6200 South, but it's a little hard to find. Ask a local to direct you.

For good blues, try the **Dead Goat Saloon** (Arrow Press Square, 165 S. West Temple). A quieter, pleasant spot is **Green Street** (in Trolley Square), which the career crowd favors.

Salt Lake City has three brew pubs, **Squatter's Pub** (147 W. Broadway; 363-2739), **Desert Edge Brewery at the Pub** (Trolley Square; 521-8917) and **Red Rock Brewing Co.** (254 South 200 West; 521-7446). All brew their own beer and serve excellent pub fare.

If you like movies *and* microbrews, head to **Brewries** (677 South 200 West; 322-3891). This establishment combines second-run (movies that already have been shown but aren't yet in video stores), independent and classic films with a gourmet-pizza-and-beer restaurant. Many people come to eat or drink, then decide whether to hang around for the movies being shown on four screens. You must be 21 years old.

This isn't the typical ski-town nightlife activity, but classical music lovers shouldn't miss the free 8 p.m. Thursday night **rehearsals of the Mormon Tabernacle Choir** at Temple Square. You can drop in and leave as you wish.

One of the top five ski-town dance nightclubs is **Zephyr Club** (301 S. West Temple; 355-5646). It is "Salt Lake City's premier showcase for local and national entertainment."

Club Manhattan (5 E. 400 South; 364-7651) is in the "everything-old-is-new-again" genre, with cocktails, overstuffed chairs and a live piano-and-strings band for swing and ballroom dancing. Enjoy a little cheek-to-cheek dancing. The crowd here dresses up.

Go shopping at **Trolley Square,** shops and boutiques in a restored trolley barn; attend a **Utah Jazz** (355-DUNK) basketball game; or attend theater, symphony, dance or opera performances. Check out your ancestors at the **Family History Center** at the Mormon computer center inside the restored historic Hotel Utah (15 ES Temple St.). Built in 1912, this was every U.S. president's elegant shelter. Be sure to bring a list of family ancestors, names and dates to make your free search worthwhile.

For a more complete list of restaurants, nightlife and other activities, pick up a free copy of *This Week Salt Lake.* This excellent guide tells you what is happening within a two-week period (sports, theater, etc.) and is a handy reference guide to the city's ongoing attractions. Another great guide is *Utah After Dark,* which rates the private clubs and taverns throughout most of the state, and tells which ones have live music, pool tables, sports TV and more.

The Interconnect Adventure Tour

Experienced skiers can ski to five different resorts via backcountry routes on this all-day tour. Six to 14 skiers are led by mountain guides. Traversing and walking are necessary, so you need to be a confident skier and in good condition. The four-area tour (Solitude, Brighton,

Dining: $$$-Entrees $20+; $$-$10-20; $-less than $10.
Accommodations: (double room) $$$$-$200+; $$$-$141-$200; $$-$81-$140; $-$80 and less.

Alta and Snowbird) is offered three days a week, while the five-area tour (those four and Park City) goes the other four days. Each tour costs $150 (2001/02 price), including return transportation and lunch. Reservations are required. Call 534-1907 and have a credit card.

Getting there and getting around

By air: Salt Lake City is one of the country's major airports. Several major airlines fly in here: American, Delta and Continental. But Southwest Airlines provides the most flights at affordable fares with connections to every corner of the country. Fares from Southern California are particularly good, thanks to ongoing competition between Delta and Southwest Airlines.

By train: Amtrak's California Zephyr stops here, arriving at 4 a.m. for eastbound trains and midnight for westbound trains. Call (800) USA-RAIL (872-7245).

Getting around: Rent a car if you want to cover a lot of ground in the evening; otherwise, use public transportation. Getting to the resorts is a snap: several ground transportation companies operate shuttles to the ski areas from Salt Lake City hotels. We have found Lewis Brothers Stages (800-826-5844; 359-8677 in Salt Lake City) to be very reliable. Round-trip from the airport to the Cottonwood Canyon or Park City resorts is about $25 per person; reservations required; minimum of three people. Don't worry too much about the minimum; in our experience, the vans are fairly full during winter.

Lewis Brothers also picks up at downtown hotels. Or take the Utah Transit Authority Ski Bus, $4 each way (exact fare required) to the four Cottonwood Canyon resorts (Alta, Snowbird, Solitude, Brighton). We take the UTA bus whenever we're at a hotel that's near the bus stop. The buses are clean, convenient and best of all, cheap. UTA buses run at night downtown until about 11:30 p.m., but only about once per hour. Call 287-4636 for more info.

Nearby resorts

The next three chapters detail the skiing and amenities at Snowbird, Alta, Solitude and Brighton, and the three Park City resorts. Here is information about three other Utah resorts—two near Salt Lake City and one at the southern part of the state.

Snowbasin, Huntsville, UT; (801) 399-1135

Internet: www.snowbasin.com
9 lifts; 3,200 acres; 2,940 vertical feet

You haven't really lived until you've run the Men's Downhill course at Snowbasin before breakfast. The 2002 Olympic committee chose Snowbasin to host the men's and women's downhill, Super G and Alpine combined races because of its very long runs within sight of the day lodge.

Three lifts, all high-speed quads, rise more than 2,300 vertical feet in one ride (installed for the 2002 Winter Games). All other lifts, except the one serving the beginner slope and the Tram, are triples that rise 1,100 vertical feet or more. That's a lot of skiing from one lift ride. The very top of the downhill course, Allen's Peak, is reached by the Olympic Tram, an 8-passenger gondola that loads just below the top of John Paul Express. Snowbasin is rimmed by jagged peaks. There is a gentle learning area, but the vast majority of the terrain is best suited for intermediate level and higher. Three day lodges ranging in size from 14,000 square feet to 24,000 square feet were built on the mountain for the 2002 Winter Olympics.

Right now, Snowbasin is visited mostly by skiers and boarders who have heard good things from their friends. But now that the world has seen it on television, the secret is out. Snowbasin is owned by the same company that owns the Sun Valley resort in Idaho.

Lift tickets (01/02 prices): Adults, $48; Children (11 and younger), $28; Senior (65+), $36; ages 6 and younger, free. All Olympic day passes will be presold exclusively; contact resort for details.

Distance from Salt Lake City: About 40 miles from the airport north via I-15 to Farmington, north on US 89 to South Weber, east on I-84 to exit 92 and north on UT 167 to Trapper's Loop. The route is very well signed.

Lodging information: Most lodging is in Ogden City, about 17 miles west, or Ogden Valley, about 9 miles west. (800) 554-2741.

Sundance, Sundance, UT; (801) 225-4107; (800) 892-1600

Internet: www.sundanceresort.com

4 lifts; 450 acres; 2,150 vertical feet

Though this ski area has been owned by actor-director Robert Redford for over 30 years, it has never been highly marketed—and that's on purpose. Skiing is not the resort's main event; rather Redford has achieved a balance between outdoor recreation of all kinds, the arts and an intimate environment. Located on the slopes of breathtaking 12,000-foot Mt. Timpanogos, Sundance is regarded as the most beautiful ski area in Utah. To experience the challenging and varied terrain, get there early because the ski area limits lift tickets to 1,200 per day. Locals comprise 80 percent of the skier/snowboard visits. Even when the 105 guestrooms are full there is never a crowd on the mountain. Lodging packages offer many different possibilities like free lift tickets and full breakfasts in the Foundry Grill.

Snowboarding is allowed. The area has a full service Nordic Center featuring 40 km. of groomed cross-country trails and 10 km. of snowshoe trails. You'll also find two excellent restaurants, an eco-friendly gift shop, the historic Owl Bar, and the Sundance Art Shack offering a full schedule of classes, retreats and workshops throughout the year. Guests also enjoy screenings of award-winning films from past and present Sundance Film Festivals. (This annual event, held in larger Park City during late January, celebrates the achievements of independent filmmakers.)

Lift tickets (01/02 prices): Adults, $34 ($28 midweek); Children (12 and younger), $16; Children (5 and younger), free; Seniors (65 and older), $10.

Distance from Salt Lake City: About 50 miles south via I-15, east on Hwy. 52, north on Hwy. 189, then a short hop west on Hwy. 92.

Lodging information: 225-4107or (800) 892-1600.

Alta
Utah

Summit elevation: 10,550 feet
Vertical drop: 2,020 feet
Base elevation: 8,530 feet

Address: P.O. Box 8007
Alta, UT 84092-8007
☏ Area code: 801
Ski area phone: 799-2263
Snow report: 359-1078
ⓘ Reservations: 942-0404
or (888) STAY-ALTA (782-9258)
E-mail: info@alta.com
Internet: www.alta.com
Expert:★★★★★
Advanced:★★★★★
Intermediate:★★★★
Beginner:★★★★ Never-ever:★★★

Skiable Acreage: 2,200
Snowmaking: 3 percent (50 acres)
Number and types of lifts: 12–1 quad,
1 high-speed triple, 2 triples, 4 doubles, 4 surface lifts
Uphill capacity: 11,284 skiers per hour
Snowboarding: Not allowed
Bed Base: 1,136
Nearest lodging: Slopeside, inns
Resort child care: Yes, 2 months and older
Adult ticket, per day: $40 (02/03)
Dining:★★
Apres-ski/nightlife:★
Other activities:★

At the top of Little Cottonwood Canyon lies the ski land where time stands still. Entering Alta is like stepping back into an earlier, less hurried era of skiing. Instead of sky-rise hotels and flashy new condos, visitors find a handful of rustic, comfortable lodges. No giant billboards scream advertising messages, no faux-Swiss ski villages house trendy restaurants and no high-speed quads hurry skiers to the summit. Snowboarders are prohibited from using the lifts, and even the all-day lift-passes costing only $40 are decidedly retro.

How first-time visitors feel about the dichotomy of an absolutely world-class ski area with unsurpassed snow and beauty but no hyper-speed lifts to whisk them up the mountain will prove crucial to how they view Alta. Those who long for a less hurried, more communal skiing experience, then swapping lies and stories around woodsy bars and roaring fires, will find kindred spirits in Alta.

It's not that Alta isn't feeling the pressure created by high-speed expectations or the popularity of snowboarding. Rather, Alta officials have opted for occasional crowds at the bottom of the mountain instead of on the slopes. So during very busy times you may have to wait in line, but the reward of uncrowded slopes is worth its weight in gold. And they choose to keep sacred their world-famous powder for skiers.

"In a sense Alta is old-fashioned, but a lot of people tell us they're tired of the corporate feel of many newer ski resorts," said Bill Levitt, long-time mayor of Alta and owner of the Alta Lodge. "Eighty percent of my customers at Alta Lodge are return customers, and they hunger for skiing as it used to be, with lodging in small inns where people eat together at the same table and share that camaraderie, and where there are a lot of little kids running around. That's our future. We call Alta the Last Resort." Talk about old-fashioned: In his position as mayor, Levitt makes an annual salary of $1. Note: There are no developers on Alta's planning commission.

Alta's low-key attitude is rooted in its history. In half a century of mining, Alta went from obscurity to boom, followed by outrageous scandal when the mines suddenly collapsed in the early 1900s. By the 1930s, when the new Sun Valley was courting glamorous international figures, Alta was born from the simple desire of Salt Lake residents to have a place where they could ski without having to climb uphill. Beginning in 1939 using its old ore tram, Alta has pulled nearly four generations of skiers up to its ridges (some guests at the Alta Lodge have kept returning since the mid-1940s). It still bears a modest name: Alta Ski Area, without the word "resort" anywhere in sight. It's pronounced AL-ta, like the name Al.

Alta provides a fine contrast to its neighbor Snowbird, just a mile down the road in Little Cottonwood Canyon. Where Snowbird with its high-occupancy tram and multistory hotel is high-tech, Alta with its serviceable lifts and multitude of mountain inns is homey. Skiers can purchase an Alta Snowbird ticket for $64 a day and enjoy the two resorts' combined terrain (don't be surprised if snowboarders start converting to skiing *en mass*, snowboarding is still banned at Alta). Snowbird added a second high-speed quad in Mineral Basin, connecting the two resorts. The lift transports skiers to the Sugarloaf saddle area (elevation 10,600 feet), joining Alta's Albion Basin and Snowbird's Mineral Basin. Skiers access the area by beginner and intermediate trails from the Albion Basin side, and by intermediate trails from the Mineral Basin side. In addition, Utah Transit Authority connects the resorts' base areas with an expanded free daily bus service.

Last season, in efforts to improve the skiing experience in the Albion Basin, the Sugarloaf lift was upgraded to a detachable and the Supreme lift was upgraded to a fixed-grip triple (don't worry about crowded slopes, uphill capacity is marginally affected).

The common areas of Alta's lodges provide a great way to meet new buddies. You may find yourself returning the same week each season and seeing the same faces. Skiers seem to forgive Alta for not keeping up with the trends. Of the skiers we know who have been here, the vast majority plan to return. Must be that no-fuss, home-baked warmth.

 Mountain layout—Skiing

The ski area has front and back sides, and two base stations. Wildcat Base is the first one you reach. It has basic facilities—ticket office, restaurants, restrooms and ski patrol. The Albion Base houses the Children's Center, Ski School, restaurant, and retail and rental operations. Albion is where you find the beginner slopes, but it has intermediate and expert terrain at higher elevations. Albion and Wildcat are connected by a long, horizontal, two-way transfer rope tow: Just grab the rope and let it pull you along to the other base.

From the top of Germania Pass the runs down the front side return you to the Wildcat base area; runs down the back return you to Albion, or give access to the Sugarloaf and Supreme lifts. Skiers wishing to cross back into the Germania/Wildcat area have two choices: a traverse from the top of the Sugarloaf lift or at the base on the transfer tow.

To follow the sun, start the morning on Sugarloaf, then move to Germania on the front side at midday, and finish on Supreme.

◆◆ **Expert** ◆ **Advanced:** Powder is what Alta is all about. Not just because it gets a lot, but because, with its terrain of trees and sheltered gullies, it tends to keep it longer. While most skiers are swishing down groomed runs a couple of days after a storm, the Alta cognoscenti are secretly diving into snow pockets in side canyons and upper elevations. Alta, like Snowbird, is a what-you-see, you-can-ski resort, with many ways down that aren't named on the trail map. Be individual. Be creative. That's the spirit of Alta.

Uphill from the Wildcat Ticket Office, Wildcat and Collins lifts serve advanced runs on the right side of the trail map—narrow trails, bump runs and many glades—with intermediate and more advanced runs on the left.

From the left of these two lifts, skiers can get to an entirely different ridge, West Rustler, by taking the Germania lift. That means more steep and deep at Eagle's Nest and High Rustler for experts. The line at Germania may appear daunting on powder days but rarely averages more than 10 minutes, although if there's powder on weekends, it can crank up to 20.

If you head down the back side under the Sugarloaf chair, you'll find expert bowls as far as the eye can see. Swooping down into a gully to the left of the lift as you descend usually gives you powder pockets. A day or two after a storm try Devils' Castle, the steeps under the rocks accessible from Sugarloaf.

To the far left of the trail map, experts can take Supreme lift to Point Supreme, the 10,550-foot summit, and from there have plenty of steep tree skiing to the left in an area near the boundary called Spiney Ridge. Some sections are known as Piney Glades and White Squaw. It's all known as steep, and tremendously popular with Salt Lake skiers. Up here you can ski all day without ever going the same way twice.

Experts in search of a unique Alta experience should reserve the last run of the day for Alf's High Rustler, named after one of the founding fathers of Alta. Getting to the run is adventure enough for some. Ride the Germania lift and take the high traverse. Stay on the traverse as it crosses the ridge toward Greeley Bowl, and keep right on traversing. The height and width of the traverse at this stage are not for the faint of heart. Eventually the traverse spirals around the top mountain knoll to High Rustler, a beautiful, steep run that is little skied, enjoys breathtaking views of the valley, and spills right out into the lodges at the bottom.

■ **Intermediate:** This group can start at either Wildcat or Albion. From Wildcat, stay to the left as you leave the Collins chair, then head down to the base on Meadow or over to Germania, where you'll find Ballroom and Mambo to the right as you leave the chair.

On the Albion side, intermediates also have appropriate terrain under the Sugarloaf and Supreme chairs. Intermediates have wonderful slopes here, plus a few very gentle pitches off to one side in the Albion area that don't get groomed—a super place to take your first powder turns. Where they groom it's good—the intermediate and beginner runs are quite negotiable.

●● **Beginner** ● **Never-evers:** From the Albion base, the Sunnyside lift and Albion lift access gentle terrain, a wide rolling beginner playground. Sunnyside has been upgraded to a bit more advanced-beginner run. Given a choice between Snowbird and Alta, beginners should definitely start here. Kids are very safe here. Not only are the slopes less intimidating, but also the skiers (we're talking fashion and attitude here, not ability). The mile-long beginner run serviced by the Albion and Sunnyside lifts can make a newbie feel like a real skier—and that's what the sport is all about.

Mountain layout—Snowboarding

Snowboarding is not permitted. Head next door to Snowbird.

Mountain rating

Alta is a great place for any level of skier. Teamed with neighboring Snowbird, it's especially hard to beat. Snowbird has the edge in continuous vertical drop—the Snowbird tram opens almost 3,000 feet of continuous expert vertical, versus the maximum expert drop of about 1,000 at Alta. However, Alta is much better for groups of mixed abilities. Alta is one of the few resorts that still bans snowboarding.

Lessons (2001/02 prices)

Bearing the name of Alf Engen, the Norwegian ski jumper who came to Utah in 1930, the ski school is recognized in the industry for its contributions to the development of professional ski instruction. Lower-level ski lessons meet at the base of the Albion lift, while upper skill levels meet below the base of the Germania lift. For all ski school programs, call 359-1078.

Group lessons: Two hours, $35.

Never-ever package: All-day group lessons cost $55; includes the learning tow. Rentals are available.

Private lessons: $130 for two hours. Alta recommends a two-hour lesson as a minimum. Additional persons can join the lesson for $40 each.

Special programs: Afternoon workshops focus on specific skills and are $45 for two-and-a-half hours; meet at the blue and white signs below the base of Germania lift. A telemark workshop is offered Tuesdays, Thursdays and Sundays for $45. Diamond Challenge is a two-and-a-half-hour afternoon workshop for Level 9 (true expert) skiers for $45. The instructor gives pointers, but mostly acts as a guide to Alta's steep powder stashes.

Racing: Alta's race course is at the Sunnyside lift; Friday and Saturday from 11 a.m. to 3 p.m. Pay the $7 fee ($10 for unlimited runs) at the race arena or at the ticket office.

 ## Child care (2001/02 prices)

Ages: 2 months to 12 years.

Cost: All-day infant care by reservation only is $75. All-day child care (3 and older) with lunch is $55. Multiday discounts available.

Reservations: Requested. Alta's child care center is a state-licensed facility owned and operated by Redwood Pre-School, Inc. (742-3042).

Children's lessons: For beginner and intermediate skiers (skill levels 1–6), ages 4–12: All Day Adventure for skill levels 1–2 is $80 (with lunch); for skill levels 3–6, it's $95 (including lunch and lift ticket). Half Day Adventure for levels 1–6 is $35. For advanced and expert skiers (skill levels 7–9), ages 7–teens: All Day Explorer costs $107 (with lunch and lift); Afternoon Explorer costs $45. All children's lessons meet at the Albion base. For ski school programs, call 359-1078.

 ## Lift tickets (2002/03 prices)

	Adult	Child (12 and younger)
One day	$40	$32
Three days	$120 ($40/day)	$96 ($32/day)
Five days	$200 ($40/day)	$160 ($32/day)

Who skis free: Ages 80 and older.

Who skis at a discount: Skiers pay $22 to use the beginner lifts in the Albion area. If you aren't too sure about the conditions, buy a single-ride ticket for any lift for $5. Bonus: All surface lifts are free.

Note: The Alta Snowbird ticket that allows you to access both resorts' terrain costs $64 a day; multi-day Alta Snowbird tickets cost $56/day for 3-4 days, $52/day for 5+ days.

Accommodations

Alta is one of the few ski areas that still has traditional ski lodges where breakfast and dinner are included in the cost. This is perfect to meet new people, particularly if you are traveling alone. Most of these lodges have either dorm rooms or single occupancy rates available. Some of Alta's lodges do not accept all major credit cards; some don't accept any. Some rooms do not have private bath. Rates are lower in value season, which is early December, most of January, and April to closing.

Rustler Lodge (742-2200, 888-532-2582; $$–$$$$) is recently remodeled, and is mid-way between the Albion and Rustler/Wildcat base areas. It has an outdoor pool, saunas and hot tubs. Don't miss the restaurant and bar with picture windows looking right out onto the mountain. Prices include breakfast and dinner. No credit cards are accepted here; pay by personal check, travelers checks or cash.

Alta Peruvian (800-453-8488, reservations only; 742-3000; $–$$$) has similar amenities, features movies each night, and is a short walk from the Wildcat base (or you can take the lodge's free shuttle). The rates include breakfast, lunch, and dinner (food's great, by the way). Dorm rooms, single rooms, double rooms with private bath, one- or two-bedroom suites and multiday discounts also are available. Alta Peruvian accepts credit cards.

The Alta Lodge (800-707-2582, reservations only; 742-3500; $$–$$$) is a 57-room mountain inn with saunas, hot tubs, and several common areas, including a library. By guest preference over the years, the lodge has only one television. Skiers grab a rope tow at the end of the day to get back up a small hill to the lodge. The Alta Lodge has the homey feel of a pair of well-worn slippers, not surprising since many of the guests are repeat customers who return each year and know each other on a first-name basis. Alta Mayor Bill Levitt is the proprietor, and he will be happy to regale guests with tales from Alta's storied past (and present). Our favorite is how a comely ski instructor once caught the eye and changed the life of the East Coast boy who would become mayor of Alta. Breakfast and dinner are included in the price, and the food is excellent. Credit cards and personal checks accepted. The same chef has been in the kitchen for 30 years.

Goldminer's Daughter (800-453-4573, reservations only; 742-2300; $$–$$$), named after a huge mining claim, is closest to the Wildcat lift. Step out your door into the lift line and drop by your room between runs for a hat or neck gaiter. Visa and MasterCard accepted here.

Snowpine Lodge (742-2000; $–$$$) is Alta's oldest and smallest. It was extensively renovated a few years ago, and has an outdoor hot tub, Scandinavian sauna and a warm and homey atmosphere. Visa and MasterCard accepted here.

Two large condominiums, **Hellgate** (742-2020; $$$–$$$$) and **Blackjack** (742-3200; $$$$) are between Alta and Snowbird, with Blackjack better situated for skiing between the two resorts and therefore slightly higher-priced. Both have van service to the ski areas. Studios, one-bedrooms sleeping four, two-bedrooms sleeping six and three-bedrooms are offered. There is no service charge.

Canyon Services (800-862-2888) rents luxurious condos and homes with fully equipped kitchens, washers and dryers and cable TV.

 Dining

At night, most skiers dine in their lodges, since the meals are included in the lodging cost. Those who stay in condos need to make a grocery stop in Salt Lake City, or dine in the lodge restaurants that also are open to the public. For a sit-down lunch on the mountain, head to the **Collins Grill,** upstairs in the Watson Shelter. **Shallow Shaft** (742-2177; $$–$$$), on Alta's main road, is open for dinner only and has salmon, steak, pasta and chicken entrées.

Après-ski/nightlife

Bring your own. There's nothing going on but what visitors cook up—either in their condo or the lodge's common rooms. That said, the best nightime gatherings we found were at the **bar at the Alta Peruvian Lodge**, where guests and locals gather (with a cover charge on weekends) for drinks at a lively bar or around the fire. The dog curled around the couch is the local mascot. The **Sitzmark Bar** at the Alta Lodge is also good for après-ski story swapping. Local lore has it that the bookshelves at the Alta Peruvian have been voted the best nightlife in Alta.

If your ski vacation is not complete without a vigorous night of dancing, stay in Salt Lake City and take the ski bus here during the day. (See the Salt Lake City chapter for details.)

Other activities

Weekends and holidays at 1:30 p.m., 45-minute **guided interpretive ski tours** are given by a Wasatch-Cache National Forest ranger. Meet at the sign at the bottom of Cecret lift. **Heli-skiing** is available in Little Cottonwood Canyon from Wasatch Powderbird Guides, 742-2800 or www.heliskiwasatch.com. A few **shops** in the Little Cottonwood Canyon area have local handicrafts, artwork and books, but skiers don't come to Alta for the shopping. Note, however, that one of our staff writers found a replacement lens for his goggles in the general store at Alta Lodge—no other shops in the region carried them. This place attracts those who like to ski from morning 'til the last lift shuts down. If you must, you can always take a bus or drive down to Salt Lake City for a day of heavy-duty shopping.

Getting there and getting around

By air: Salt Lake City is a major airline hub, so flights are numerous from every corner of the continent. See the Snowbird chapter for ground transportation information. An additional ground transportation option is Alta Ski Shuttle (800-742-3406), which has airport shuttles every 30 minutes between 8 a.m. and 11 p.m. for $40 per person, round trip. The company also will provide transport outside of those hours for $100 per van, one-way, for up to five people, with advance notice.

By train: Amtrak's California Zephyr pulls into Salt Lake City at 4 a.m. for eastbound trains and midnight for westbound trains. Call (800) USA-RAIL (872-7245) or see www.amtrak.com.

By car: Alta is 25 miles southeast of Salt Lake City in Little Cottonwood Canyon on State Hwy. 210. Drive east on I-80, south on I-215, Exit 6 to Wasatch Blvd., then follow the signs to Alta and Snowbird.

Getting around: If you fly in, don't bother renting a car. Ground transportation from the airport or the city is frequent and plentiful. Most of Alta's lodges have free shuttles to get you to the slopes or to visit neighboring restaurants. If you are staying in Salt Lake City, take the Utah Transit Authority bus ($4 from downtown, $1.50 from the bottom of the canyon; exact fare required) or a Lewis Brothers SkiExpress van to Alta (about $20 roundtrip from downtown; 800-826-5844, or 359-8677 from Salt Lake City). A free bus service links Alta and Snowbird.

Dining: $$$-Entrees $20+; $$-$10-20; $-less than $10.
Accommodations: (double room) $$$$-$200+; $$$-$141-$200; $$-$81-$140; $-$80 and less.

Deer Valley

Park City, Utah

Summit elevation:		9,570 feet
Vertical drop:		3,000 feet
Base elevation:		6,570 feet

Address: P.O. Box 1525, Park City, UT 84060
☎ **Area code:** 435
Ski area phone: 649-1000
Snow report: 649-2000 **Fax:** 645-6939
ⓘ **Toll-free reservations:** (800) 558-3337
Internet: www.deervalley.com

Expert: ★★★★
Advanced: ★★★★
Intermediate: ★★★★
Beginner: ★★
Never-ever: ★

Number of lifts: 19–1 gondola, 5 high-speed quads, 3 quads, 8 triples, 2 doubles
Snowmaking: 27 percent
Skiable acreage: 1,750 acres
Uphill capacity: 39,700 per hour
Snowboarding: None
Nearest lodging: Slopeside
Resort child care: Yes, 2 months to 12 years
Adult ticket, per day: $60–$67 (02/03 price)
Dining:★★★★★
Apres-ski/nightlife:★
Other activities:★★

Deer Valley is one of America's most exclusive resorts. Everything is top notch from the manicured snow conditions to the gleaming brass and glass cafeterias. Deer Valley is as upscale as it gets in America, but without the upscale snobbery that seems to infect other expensive places in the country. Here, even the common folk can relax and leave feeling like they have received great value for their dollar.

The resort itself is just a couple miles from the historic town of Park City. Deer Valley is basically a cluster of condominiums and upscale hotels huddled around a spectacular ski area. You can lounge in luxury up on the mountainside or head downtown to have fun in one of America's best ski towns (see Park City chapter).

Deer Valley is renowned for pampering its guests with top-flight gourmet meals, palatial accommodations, attentive service and impeccable slopes. Some of the many amenities include guest service attendants who help get skis off car racks as you pull up to unload, tissues at every lift, restaurants to make a gourmet salivate, a free ski corral service where you can safely leave the best equipment, and grooming crews who comb the snow so pooltable smooth that everyone moves up a notch in ability. Experts who sneer at the daily slope manicure can ditch the main drag. Do not pass "Go" on your way to the chutes and bowls off Empire Canyon or to cop some bumps off the Sultan and Mayflower chairs, and quit your complaining. Deer Valley fills a marvelous niche in the ski world, satisfying those who want to be pampered and are willing to pay a little more for the privilege, as well as those who need some juice along with their eggs and toast.

Park City is the most accessible destination resort of its caliber in the country, just 30 miles from Salt Lake City via a major freeway. Accessibility was one of the key factors that helped Salt Lake City get the 2002 Olympic Winter Games. Olympic preparations at Deer Valley resulted in improvements like the Empire Lodge, a lavish day lodge and restaurant at the bottom of the Empire Express in Empire Canyon. A race course for guests on Silver Hill in the Deer Crest area operates similarly to Race Course on Bald Mountain, with a designated race course, timing and announcement system.

New for 2002/03: A high-speed quad replaces the Ruby quad chairlift, making the ride much speedier. An as-yet-unnamed restaurant owned and operated by Deer Valley, with sit-down service for lunch, apres-ski and dinner, takes over the space previously occupied by McHenry's in the mid-mountain Silver Lake Lodge. Deer Valley also will host the 2003 Freestyle FIS World Championships in late January.

 ## Mountain layout—Skiing

Keep in mind that there are really four mountains here, ranging from Bald Eagle at 8,400 feet to the top of Empire Canyon at 9,570 feet.

◆◆ **Expert:** Request an Experts Only trail map, which points out the toughest runs and several gladed and chute areas. Empire Canyon, topping out at 9,570 feet, is not only the highest point at Deer Valley, but also the gnarliest. The double-diamond Daly Chutes, the Daly Bowl and the Anchor Trees are short, steep and superbly challenging. Single-diamond terrain at Lady Morgan Bowl in Empire adds some nice vertical. The Empire Express accesses the 500 acres of eight chutes and three bowls.

Flagstaff Mountain, with both bump and cruising runs, is easy to navigate and a good rendezvous when several members of your group ski at different ability levels. Experts take a short traverse to the left off the top of this lift to Ontario Bowl's double-diamond tree skiing.

◆ **Advanced:** The Mayflower Lift, to the far left on the trail map, supplies respectable single-diamond terrain on both sides of the lift. Moguls on Morning Star, Fortune Teller, Paradise and Narrow Gauge are a delight. The long trails are bordered by glades—great places to drop into and out of on a whim.

While Mayflower and its neighboring chair Sultan feature ungroomed runs, the bumps rarely grow too big. Orient Express and Stein's Way are advanced cruisers with good pitch, and Perseverance—coupled with the initial steeper sections of Thunderer, Blue Ledge and Grizzly—is good for those entering advanced status.

■ **Intermediate:** Deer Valley offers both intermediate and advanced-intermediate terrain, though we're hard pressed to tell the two apart. If you want to have plenty of company and beautiful scenery, the best runs are Sunset, Birdseye (both on Bald Mountain) and Success (on Bald Eagle Mountain). Areas with the most intermediate runs are served by the Wasatch Express, Sterling and Northside Express chairs. Run after run down trails such as Legal Tender, Wizard, Nabob, Sidewinder and Hawkeye are a blast. The runs under Northside Express are farther from the base, so they're not as crowded as the Wasatch Express area.

The Empire Canyon and Deer Crest areas also have some fun slopes for this level—try the advanced-intermediate bowls Conviction, Solace and Orion in particular. The view of the Jordanelle Reservoir from the Deer Crest area is fabulous; however, the Jordanelle run has one wicked narrow part that may intimidate newly intermediate skiers (and don't even think about taking a beginner down it, assuming it'll be easy to get to the gondola base parking lot). A fun place to test your intermediate tree- and bump-skiing legs is in the unnamed area on Flagstaff off the Ontario trail, or by sneaking through the trees at the top of the Quincy Lift. They're marked, but not named (as of this printing), and are worth a giggle.

Other great areas are Flagstaff Mountain and Bald Eagle Mountain, known as the "lower mountain." Last Chance passes by a lot of spectacular homes, perfect for lookie-loos.

If you are a timid intermediate, stick to Deer Valley's green-circle runs at first. We find the greens here to be a bit turquoise, just a shade easier than the true blues.

●● **Beginner:** Deer Valley's offerings at this level have improved in past years. Best spots are the outside runs on Flagstaff Mountain, Ontario and Mountain Daisy/Banner. If you are a timid beginner, read the Never-Ever advice. If you're a brave soul who just needs some practice, we especially recommend Sunset, a gentle, scenic route that descends from the top of Bald Mountain—but head back to the base before day's end or you'll find yourself in the role of a human slalom pole, being passed at close range by more proficient skiers. There's also the Little Chief Family Ski Area in Empire Canyon, which is one run that hardly seems worth the traverse and chair lift experience to get there.

● **Never-ever:** The novice area is gentle enough, but it's a big step to the next level. Some of Deer Valley's green runs also access trails and runouts that better skiers use to reach the base area. A beginner might feel as though he or she is riding a scooter on a freeway, which can be intimidating in this land of speed and curve.

Mountain layout—Snowboarding

Snowboarding is not allowed. Head for The Canyons or Park City Mountain Resort.

Mountain rating

Deer Valley has built a reputation for pampering at a price, but its slopes include tougher trails than it gets credit for. Expert skiers on our staff were hugely surprised by the challenging terrain and found plenty of reasons to grin. On a scale of one to 10, one being a never-ever and 10 being a top-flight expert, we'd say that Deer Valley is best for levels three through eight (maybe a nine with the Empire Summit terrain). And that's no slam: The vast majority of skiers fit that profile.

Lessons (2002/03 prices)

Semi-private lessons: Semi-private lessons have replaced group lessons. A semi-private (all levels) costs $100; choose from 9 a.m.–12:15 p.m. and 1 p.m.–4 p.m.

Never-ever package: None. Take semi-private or private lessons.

Private lessons: $90 for one hour (for one or two skiers), $310 for three hours, $550 all day; reserve in advance.

Special programs: Women and men have three-day clinics at certain times in the season for $385-$465 (lift ticket extra).

Racing: A race program called Medalist Challenge is held on the Race Course above Silver Lake Lodge, reachable by the Sterling or Wasatch Lifts. The cost is $10 for two runs and the daily chance to earn a medal. About once a week, Deer Valley's Director of Skiing, Stein Eriksen, an Olympic gold medalist and World Champion, runs the course so you can compare your time to his. Heidi Voelker, a U.S. Ski Team veteran, also does this about once a week. A self-timed dual slalom is available too.

Child care (2002/03 prices)

Ages: 2 months to 12 years.

Costs: Full day, with lunch, ages 2–12 years, $82. Full-day infant care, ages 2 months–8 months, including lunch if appropriate, $82. Half day, sold on space-available basis, cannot be reserved in advance. New this season is Toddler Care for ages 9–24 months (child must be at least to crawling stage). Full day, including lunch if appropriate, $82.

Reservations: Recommended at all times but essential during holiday periods. Call 435-6648 or make reservations when you book lodging.

Other options: The Park City Chamber of Commerce can refer visitors to **child-care facilities** or **babysitting services.** Call (800) 453-1360 or locally, 649-6100 or visit www.parkcityinfo.com. **Baby's Away** (800-379-9030; 435-645-8823) rents and will deliver baby needs to your lodge, such as crib, stroller, car seat and toys.

Children's lessons: Full day, ages 7 to 12, is $120 for lessons, lift ticket and lunch. Ages 4 to 6 years old get a full-day program, also for $120. Three-and-a-half-year-olds have a program that is a combination of day care and ski lessons for $125. Advanced registration is recommended for these programs; definitely during holiday periods.

Lift tickets (2002/03 prices)

	Adult	Child (Up to 12)
One day	$67	$36
Three days	$189 ($63/day)	$93 ($31/day)
Five days	$300 ($60/day)	$145 ($29/day)

Who skis free: No one.

Who skis at a discount: Skiers 65 and older ski for $46 for a single day, $126 for three days and $200 for five days.

Note: For seven or eight days between Christmas and New Year's, Deer Valley's multiday discounts are suspended. However, ticket sales are limited, so on holidays the extra few bucks to ski Deer Valley are worth it. You can make advance ticket reservations when you book your lodging, and this is highly recommended during the Christmas period and February, Presidents' Day holiday week.

The Silver Passport gets you on the lifts at Deer Valley, Park City Mountain Resort and The Canyons. You must advance-book at least three nights of lodging to purchase the pass. You can use the pass at one resort each day that it is valid (meaning, you can't ski at Deer Valley in the morning and Park City in the afternoon). Snowboarders may not use Deer Valley's lifts, and the pass is not valid the week between Christmas and New Year. The 2002/03 cost for adults will be $186 for three days ($62/day), $300 for five days ($60/day); children ages 6-12 pay $93 for three days ($31/day), $145 for five days ($29). More information: Deer Valley Central Reservations, (800) 558-3337, Park City Mountain Reservations, (800) 222-7275 or The Canyons Reservations, (888) 226-9667.

Cross-country and snowshoeing

White Pine Touring (615-5858) offers 20 km. of track and skate skiing, plus track, skate and telemark lessons at the Park City golf course and an adjacent dairy farm. Rates are $10 daily for adults; $5 for kids 6-12; younger than 6 and older than 65 ski free. For those who want to get off the flats, half-day snowshoe (Wed. & Sun.) and ski (Tues. and Fri.) tours in the Uinta mountains are also available. When venturing out on your own, stop here for advice and maps of the local mountain bike trails that are accessible (many from downtown Park City) and perfect for snowshoeing.

The Homestead Resort (654-1102; 800-327-7220), 14 miles southeast of Park City in Midway, has 12 km. of skiing at Homestead Golf Course and 18 km. at Wasatch Mountain State Park. Snowshoeing and snowmobiling also are available. Trail fees are $6 for adults and $3 for children. Nearby **Soldier Hollow,** site of the 2002 Olympic cross-country competitions, offers 26 km. of both track and skate skiing for all levels.

Accommodations

At Deer Valley the lodging has a decidedly upscale flavor—and tariffs to match. Even in the value season the least expensive starts at about $200 per night. Accommodations have the same high quality one finds at the resort itself, and much of it is slopeside. If it's in your budget, book it. If not, stay in Park City—only a short ride away on a frequent shuttlebus (see Park City chapter).

Top dog is the **Stein Eriksen Lodge** (800-453-1302 or 649-3700; $$$-$$$$). Think of any luxury or service and you will probably find it here—heated sidewalks between buildings, fireplaces in the rooms, fresh terrycloth robes, floor-to-ceiling windows. A $42-million expansion just added 11 lavish condominiums and a conference center. A new 4,340-square-foot, full-service spa is open for both guests and the public.

After Stein's the places to stay on the mountain are the **Stag Lodge Condominiums** (800-453-3833 or 649-7444; $$$$) and the **Goldener Hirsch Inn** (800-252-3373 or 649-7770; $$$$), with the elegance and service of a top Austrian hotel at midmountain.

The **Pinnacle Condominiums** ($$$$) have spacious and well-appointed interiors, and they aren't too far from the bus stop. Closer to the lifts—actually ski-in/ski-out properties—are the **Pine Inn** ($$$$) and **La Maçonnerie** ($$$$). All units have private spas.

The most economical Deer Valley condos are the **Snow Park** units, where a one-bedroom without hot tub is about $325 in the regular season.

For reservations in Deer Valley, call **Deer Valley Lodging,** which also manages numerous lodges, condominiums and private homes (800-453-3833 or 649-4040), or **Deer Valley Central Reservations** (800-558-3337 or 649-1000).

Dining

Deer Valley's dining mirrors the overall high quality (and cost) of the resort, but the variety of exquisite places to eat may make it difficult to figure out which will be the site for the special evening of your ski vacation. It's easy to get there from Park City—if you don't have a car, take the free Park City Transit buses, which run until 10 p.m. To make advance dinner reservations (recommended) from anywhere in the United States, call (800) 424-3337 (424-DEER).

The multi-level **Mariposa** (645-6715; $$$) at Silver Lake Lodge is the gourmets' top choice. Try either the Chef's Vegetable Tasting or the Mariposa Tasting.

The **Glitretind Restaurant** (649-3700; $$$) at Stein Eriksen Lodge surprisingly offers creative, but very American fare. Glitretind's all-you-can-eat skier's lunch buffet with made-to-order pasta dishes, a carving table, various salads, cold meats and delectable desserts is a not-outrageously-expensive feast. The lodge's smaller, cozier **Valhalla** (645-6455; $$$) sticks with the American, too, but has more "exotic" main dish choices such as elk, buffalo, and pheasant. Generally, the lodge (or Deer Valley for that matter) is not the place to come if you're pinching pennies, but it's well worth the cost.

The **Seafood Buffet** (645-6632; $$$) at Snow Park Lodge, spread out Mondays through Saturdays, is magnificent. Every type of seafood you can think of is here, and it's all you can eat—a real bargain. You won't want to miss the Dungeness crab and tiger shrimp. By the way, there's a gorgeous roast beef for landlubbers. And don't forget to save room for their desserts.

The **Goldener Hirsch Inn** (649-7770; $$$) in Silver Lake Village serves breakfast, lunch and dinner in an Austrian setting. Traditionalists will find weinerschnitzel, handmade bratwurst and raclette cheese; others can enjoy the regional American specialties. The interior is a replica of a restaurant in in Salzburg, while the inn is styled after an Austrian mansion.

Sai-Sommet (645-9909; $$$), pronounced say-so-may, in the Deer Valley Club is open to the public Wednesdays through Sundays. Locals say make reservations early and save room for dessert.

The **Olive Barrel Food Co.** (647-7777; $$$), an Italian trattoria-style restaurant at Silver Lake Lodge, is overpriced in our opinion.

For a great breakfast value, head to the buffet at the **Snow Park Restaurant** and for lunch go to the **Silver Lake Restaurant.** The food is laid out like a magazine photo—great presentation. These cafeteria-style restaurants glisten with shiny brass and sparkling glass. P.S. You gotta have the turkey chili. Then ask someone to direct you to the shop where you can buy the dry ingredients to take home and make your own huge pot of this delicious stuff.

See the Park City chapter for dining in town.

Après-ski/nightlife

Immediate slopeside après-ski is found at **The Lounge,** where the deck in the spring gets packed and there is live entertainment on the weekends. There are bars in the hotels for later on, but the real party animals head downtown to Park City, where music plays and the fun really goes full steam (see Park City chapter).

Other activities

Nearby Park City is packed with other activities to keep you busy after the skis are put away and Salt Lake City is only about a half hour away. See the *Park City chapter* and the *Salt Lake City chapter* for more details.

Sundance Film Festival, in late January, showcases new films from around the world.

Many companies offer **sleigh rides, snowmobile tours** and **hot-air balloon trips.** To reserve any or all of these activities and more, call one central number at ABC Reservations Central, (800) 820-2223 or 649-2223. There is no fee and most adventures provide free shuttle service.

Getting there and getting around

By air: The drive from the Salt Lake City International Airport to Park City takes 45 minutes (36 miles). Ground transportation makes frequent trips from the airport for $34-$46, round-trip (children's fares are $17-$35). Providers include Lewis Brothers Stages, (800) 826-5844 or 649-2256; Park City Transportation, (800) 637-3803 or 649-8567; and All Resort Express (800) 457-9457 or 649-3999. If you arrive without reservations, go to the transportation counter at the airport and you'll ride on the next available van. Call 48 hours in advance for Park City-to-airport reservations.

By car: Park City is 32 miles east of Salt Lake City, by I-80 and Utah Hwy. 224.

Getting around: If you're staying close to the town center or near a stop on the free bus line, you can do without a rental car. The town bus system has five routes with service every 20 minutes, if not more frequently, from 7 a.m. to 1 a.m. If you take a side trip to one of the Cottonwood Canyons ski resorts, Lewis Brothers Stages and Park City Transportation have shuttles for $22-$35 round-trip. Lewis Brothers offers a Canyon Jumper package to Solitude and Snowbird for $49 and $52, respectively, including transportation and lift ticket. Prepay the evening before you wish to ski.

Dining: $$$-Entrees $20+; $$-$10-20; $-less than $10.
Accommodations: (double room) $$$$-$200+; $$$-$141-$200; $$-$81-$140; $-$80 and less.

Park City, Utah

Park City Mountain Resort

The Canyons

ⓘ Toll-free information:
(800) 453-1360 (Park City Chamber)
Fax: 649-0532 (lodging)
Internet: www.parkcityinfo.com (town)
Dining:★★★★
Apres-ski/nightlife:★★★★
Other activities:★★★

Walk outside the No Name Saloon at dusk, just as the lights of Main Street begin to twinkle seductively and the sidewalks fill with après-ski traffic, and you can almost hear the clank of spurs. Squint your eyes and the strolling figures become the miners and cowboys who roamed this same street a hundred years ago, swaggering through 30-odd saloons in what was once one of the country's largest silver mining towns. Soon the vision is gone, and the people are once again modern-day funseekers. Yet the flamboyant atmosphere of the silver rush remains. Park City's mining heritage is quite evident at Park City Mountain Resort, where old mine ruins dot the slopes. The Park City Historical Society has put up signs describing each of the sites, so skiers and boarders can get a sense of history as they enjoy the day.

Park City originally was founded by soldiers who had been sent west to discourage Brigham Young from ending the Utah Territory's association with the Union. Park City boomed during the mining era, then almost became a ghost town during the Depression and World War II. Now Park City can be counted among the world's top winter resorts. This is the most accessible destination resort of its caliber in the country, just 30 miles from Salt Lake City via a major freeway. Accessibility was one of the key factors that helped Salt Lake City get the 2002 Olympic Winter Games.

Park City interchangeable lift ticket

The Silver Passport gets you on the lifts at Deer Valley, Park City Mountain Resort and The Canyons. You must advance-book at least three nights of lodging to purchase the pass. You can use the pass at one resort each day that it is valid (meaning, you can't ski at Deer Valley in the morning and Park City in the afternoon). Snowboarders may not use Deer Valley's lifts, and the pass is not valid the week between Christmas and New Year. The 2002/03 cost for adults will be $186 for three days ($62/day), $300 for five days ($60/day); children ages 6-12 pay $93 for three days ($31/day), $145 for five days ($29). More information: Deer Valley Central Reservations, (800) 558-3337, Park City Mountain Reservations, (800) 222-7275 or The Canyons Reservations, (888) 226-9667.

Park City Mountain Resort

The Town Lift triple chair loads from the lower part of Park City's Main Street to the base of the Bonanza lift partway up the mountain. Even on holidays or peak periods, the Town Lift is often empty, so you may want to take the free shuttle here and avoid the crowds. The Town Bridge that links Park City Mountain Resort to the heart of Park City allows skiers and riders direct on-snow access to the Main Street hub of Park City. This means you can ski or ride straight to Main Street, have a choice of some 200 restaurants and shops to visit during lunch,

Park City Mountain Resort (PCMR) Facts

Summit elevation: 10,000 feet
Vertical drop: 3,100 feet
Base elevation: 6,900 feet

Address: P.O. Box 39, Park City, UT 84060
☎ **Area code:** 435
Ski area phone: 649-8111
Snow report: 647-5449 or (800) 222-7275
ⓘ **Toll-free reservations:**
(800) 222-7275 (Park City Mountain Reservations)
Fax: 649-0532 (lodging)
ⓘ **Toll-free information:** (800) 453-1360 (Park City Chamber)
Internet: www.parkcitymountain.com (resort)
www.parkcityinfo.com (town)

Number of lifts: 14–4 high-speed six-person chairs, 1 high-speed quad, 5 triple chairs, 4 double chairs
Snowmaking: 14 percent
Skiing acreage: 3,300
Uphill capacity: 27,200 per hour
Snowboarding: Yes
Bed base: 12,000
Nearest lodging: Slopeside, condos
Resort child care: None; lessons start at age 3
Adult ticket, per day: $55–$63 (01/02 prices)
Expert:★★★★
Advanced:★★★★
Intermediate:★★★★
Beginner:★★★ **Never-ever:**★★★

and then ride back up the mountain on the Town Lift. If Bonanza has a long line, ski down Sidewinder a tad, catch the Crescent chair, ski down King Con to the Silverlode chair and it'll take you to the Summit area. If Payday has a line, try the Eagle chair (to the far right of the base area) and head down blue-square Temptation to the King Con chair.

Mountain layout—Skiing

◆◆ **Expert:** Start off with a trip to the top of Blueslip Bowl off the Pioneer Lift. Reportedly, when this was the boundary of the ski area, resort workers regularly slipped under the ropes, made tracks down the bowl and then skied back into the resort. The management passed out blue (you're fired) slips to anyone caught floating through this powder bowl. If you can ski Blueslip with confidence, then try Jupiter Bowl and its neighboring bowls—McConkey's, Puma and Scott's.

Jupiter Bowl has every type of steep expert terrain. To reach the Jupiter lift, take the Jupiter access road from the top of the Pioneer or Thaynes lifts. It's a long, flat traverse, so don't lose your speed. To the left as you get off the Jupiter lift are wide-open faces, especially on the West Face, which is the easiest way down (a relative term). The West Face is as far from the Jupiter Lift as you can ski. It can be covered with windblown crust, so you might want to ask about conditions before you board the lift. Narrow gullies and chutes, such as Silver Cliff, 6 Bells and Indicator, drop vertically between tightly packed evergreens. Head to the right as you get off the chair and try Portuguese Gap, a run more akin to having the floor open below you, or traverse to Scott's Bowl, which is just as steep. Main Bowl, closer to the lift, also offers some nice turns as it drops under the chair.

The adventurous (and those with parachutes) will find definite thrills in McConkey's Bowl and Puma Bowl. McConkey's is now served by McConkey's Hi-Speed Six-Pack. Puma still requires a long traverse across a ridge and some hiking from either the Jupiter or McConkey's lifts to reach its steep faces and chutes on the backside of Jupiter Peak.

◆ **Advanced:** If you're looking for steeps or moguls, try the blacks off the Motherlode triple or the neighboring Thaynes double. Glory Hole, Double Jack and the like offer a good challenge. Or, ski the front face on the runs off the Ski Team Lift. Most of the deliciously long trails here are left *au naturel*, but Willy's is on the occasional grooming list. Hit it on the right day, and it's *fun*. For a steep cruiser that is groomed daily, head down nearby Silver Queen.

■ **Intermediate:** Choices are mind-boggling. If you want to start with a worthy cruiser, take Payday from the top of the lift by the same name. The views are spectacular, and at night it becomes one of the longest lighted runs in the Rockies. This run also has a halfpipe.

Probably most popular are the 11 trails served by King Consolidated (called "King Con" by just about everyone). These runs have a steep, wide, smooth pitch. Both intermediates and advanced skiers will enjoy the runs under the Silverlode chair. To avoid crowds, try the four blues under the Pioneer chair. Or, board McConkey's, enjoy the spectacular view, and take the intermediate ridge routes down from the top.

●● **Beginner:** Even those just getting into their snowplow turns can take the Payday and Bonanza chairs to the Summit House and descend a very long, easy, multi-named run. This trail starts as Claim Jumper, shifts to Bonanza, then finishes at the base area as Sidewinder. For an adventure and to see a different part of the mountain, take the Mid-Mountain Run to the Pioneer chair, where you can have lunch and watch experts head down Blueslip Bowl.

The only complaint about the beginner runs here is that everyone else uses them too. The upper parts of the green-circle trails are used as access routes, while the bottoms are the end runs for skiers coming off more advanced terrain. The greens here are wide and gentle, but they wind in and around tougher stuff. If you're just starting out and concerned about getting in above your head, carry a trail map and pay attention to the signage. And head to the bottom well before day's end if you like plenty of room.

● **Never-ever:** At the base area, the Three Kings and First Time lifts service good learning terrain.

 # Mountain layout—Snowboarding

Park City Mountain Resort has some long, nearly flat runs that snowboarders will want to avoid. The two worst ones are Jupiter Access and Thaynes Canyon, both of which are used primarily to reach other parts of the mountain. In particular, Jupiter Access road from the top of the Pioneer or Thaynes lifts is a long, flat traverse, so don't lose your speed. You can avoid the worst traverses with advance planning. However, snowboarders have a bit of an advantage in Park City's hike-to powder bowls, because they get to hike to the best stuff in soft boots.

The best all-around freeriding area is below Home Run between the Claim Jumper and Parley's Park runs. Three lifts can get you there: Silverlode Hi-Speed Six-Pack, Motherlode Lift and Bonanza Hi-Speed Six-Pack. There are some good cuts through the trees, plenty of bumps and some wide smoothies good for kicking up the speed. At the opposite end of the ski area, both the Town Lift and the Payday Hi-Speed Six-Pack deposit you above the huge halfpipe on Payday. You'll also find a superpipe on Eagle, similar to the one used in the 2002 Winter Olympics. Three new terrain parks will spread out the tricksters on Seldom Seen, Claim Jumper and King's Crown. The resort committed more than a million dollars this season to improve the riding experience, including the purchase of terrain park features, a Super Dragon and a Park Bully, and additional snowmaking in the parks and pipes.

Mountain rating

Most reviews of Park City Mountain Resort characterize it as a cruisers' paradise, which is true enough. While it may not have as many steeps as Snowbird or Alta, its bowl skiing and chutes are serious—even on the expert scale. It doesn't have a huge amount of lower-end terrain, but beginners can get high enough to see the views—something they can't do at every resort. In our opinion, it's the most predictable and most uninspired of the three resorts here.

Lessons (2001/02 prices)

Prices below are for peak periods, which covers most of the season.
Group lessons: $70 for three hours.
Never-ever package: $165 for a full day, includes lift ticket and rental equipment (skis and snowboards).

Private lessons: $100 for one hour, $195 for two hours. The VIP Series, which teaches a skier or rider to move to the next skill level, is designed to assure that your learning experience will be glitch-free and effective. Choose from a six-hour private lesson for $495, or a three-hour private lesson for $270.

Racing: NASTAR is on the Blanche trail Wednesday through Saturday. Two runs cost $6; each additional run is $1. Park City Dual Challenge is set up on Clementine nearly every day. The cost is $1 per run; $5 for seven runs.

Child care (2001/02 prices)

The resort does not have non-skiing child care. The Park City Chamber of Commerce can refer visitors to **child-care facilities** or **babysitting services.** Call (800) 453-1360 or locally, 649-6100. **Baby's Away** (800-379-9030; 435-645-8823) rents and will deliver baby needs to your lodge, such as crib and toys.

Children's lessons: Ages 3–12, $115 for a full day including two 90-minute lessons, hot lunch, snack. Children ages 3-5 also have some indoor recreation. Snowboard lessons, for ages 7-12, cost the same. Reservations are required for all programs. Call (800) 227-7275.

Lift tickets (2001/02 prices)

	Adult	Child (Up to 12)
One day	varies day to day*	varies day to day*
Three days	$183 ($61/day)*	$96 ($32/day)*
Five days	$275 ($55/day)*	$140 ($28/day)*

Who skis free: Ages 70 and older and 6 and younger.

Who skis at a discount: Ages 65–69 ski for $32 to $34 (daily variable rate).

*****Notes:** Park City Mountain Resort charges slightly more during holiday periods. It also does not announce its one-day prices until the day you walk up to the window, basing those prices on "market demand." That "demand," a resort spokesperson told us, not only includes factors such as holiday periods, but also weather and snow conditions—a "powder premium," as we termed it. The resort says to expect to pay between $61 and $63 for adults, and between $32 and $34 for kids. The only way to guarantee a price is to buy a three-day or longer multiday ticket. The resort has night skiing and riding from 4–9 p.m. Call for prices.

The Canyons

The first resort you pass on the way into Park City, The Canyons Resort is a few miles away from the historic downtown area, though it is connected by a free shuttle service from many points. Ever since taking over The Canyons, American Skiing Company has transformed the resort. Just about every lift and building has been replaced, rebuilt or otherwise improved. And every year, they open more terrain. The Canyons is now in the top five in the nation in skiable terrain.

The Grand Summit Resort Hotel is the focal point of the base development. It appears as if ASC has finally tossed aside the cookie-cutter design used in their eastern Grand Summit hotels, and the hotel may actually be worthy of the adjective "grand." The circular base village with its arched entrance is warm and inviting, creating a cozy feel to an area that opens up to a humongous amount of terrain and awesome vistas. If you watched the Today show during the 2002 Winter Games, you've seen much of this hotel and the resort because Katie Couric & Matt Lauer made The Canyons their home base.

New for 2002/03, The Canyons is overhauling its terrain park and pipes to take advantage of new technology and design, guaranteeing the resort's standing as one of the best in North America. Not only will it be bigger, it will be even better than it's always been (see Mountain Layout—Snowboarding for details).

 ## Mountain layout—Skiing

Terrain at The Canyons is spread across eight mountain peaks.

◆◆ **Expert** ◆ **Advanced:** Most of The Canyons' terrain is not visible from the base area. What you can't see are chutes and gullies as extreme as any in Utah. Most of the Canyons' real expert terrain is in the trees off the Ninety Nine 90 Express, Tombstone Express and the Super Condor Express. These lifts follow ridges, and the trees and snow drop away on either side. Ninety Nine 90 has heart-stopping chutes off to the right, like Red Pine and Charlie Brown. Peak 5 terrain is touted as intermediate tree skiing, but the trees—lots and lots of trees—make this area more of an expert's playground. The Condor chair takes you to terrain that is very steep, such as the South Side Chutes, or the dense glades of Canis Lupis. You can hike a few hundred feet to the top of Murdock Peak for ungroomed bowl descents. (Our stats reflect lift-served terrain; with the hike, the total vertical is 2,580 feet.)

■ **Intermediate:** There are blue runs from every chair, but sometimes only one or two descents per chair. The best trails for this level are in the center of the resort, under the Saddleback Express (Snow Dancer is quite nice), The Snow Canyon Express (wide paths here) and the lower mountain. The blue runs under the Condor and Tombstone chairs are nice intermediate challenges, especially the double-blues like Cloud 9 (running the length of the Tombstone Express) and Apex Ridge next to the Super Condor Express. Ski Aplande, which takes off from Apex Ridge, a few times and you may feel ready to move on to the black runs like Devil's Friend and Rendezvous Ridge.

●● **Beginner** ● **Never-ever:** Last season The Canyons added seven acres of beginner terrain near the top of the Flight of The Canyons gondola. The area is set aside from skier traffic, and is framed by trees, separating the beginners from any main trails. This year, the resort will continue to work on trails off the High Meadow and Saddleback lifts to accommodate more beginners. There's also beginner terrain in the Dreamscape area. We suggest this level enroll in lessons, in order to have a guide to keep them out of trouble.

Mountain layout—Snowboarding

Way back when The Canyons was ParkWest, it was the first Park City ski area to allow snowboarding. The policy never changed, even though the area's name did a few times. Utah boarders are loyal because of that support, plus they know incredible terrain when they ride it.

The Canyons has six natural halfpipes and one constructed pipe. The naturals are spread throughout the area. Nearest the base area are two that can be reached via the Golden Eagle chair. The higher of the two, The Tube, runs off Broken Arrow next to Grizzly. The lower, The Black Hole, cuts off Super Fury and comes out on Flume, below the Snow Canyon Express. A long narrow creek bed/halfpipe runs next to Spider Monkey. It's a beginner's terror. Perhaps the most well-known natural pipe is adjacent to Upper Boa and called Canis Lupis. Two more natural halfpipes can be reached via Saddleback Express: The first is part of Pine Draw, the beginner/intermediate terrain park, and the second is to rider's left of the trail CIA.

Last season The Canyons moved its award-winning terrain park to the front face of the resort, dedicating one lift, Red Hawk, to the snowboarders and freestyle skiers who frequent the area. Transworld Snowboarding and Freeze Magazine both ranked The Canyons' park the best in Utah, and top 10 in the nation. This season The Canyons will add a state-of-the-art sound system, lighting and 25 new jibs to the park, plus they're doubling the number of hits/jumps to more than 30. There will be a designated beginner area with a children's pipe, along with a 400-foot superpipe with 15-foot walls. Park fanatics also can expect expanded hours and terrain (now totaling 18 acres).

For riding in the trees, Peak 5 is a good option. Also try the steeps and chutes off the Ninety Nine 90 Express chair. A 20-minute hike from the top of Super Condor Express to Murdock Peaks' 9,602-foot summit will get you freshies in Murdock Bowl, The Saddle Chutes or One-Hundred Turns. If you're looking for groomers with lots of space, the runs off Snow Canyon Express will get your board screaming and warm you up for trails off the Super Condor Express.

The Canyons

Summit elevation: 9,990 feet
Vertical drop: 3,190 feet
Base elevation: 6,800 feet

Address: 4000 The Canyons Resort Drive
Park City, UT 84060
✆ **Area code:** 435
Ski area phone: 649-5400
Snow report phone: 615-3456
ⓘ **Toll-free information:** (800) 754-1636
Toll-free reservations: (888) 226-9667 (CANYONS)
Fax: 649-7374
Internet: www.thecanyons.com
E-mail: through Web site

Expert: ★★★★★
Advanced: ★★★★★
Intermediate: ★★★★
Beginner: ★★ **Never-ever:** ★
Number of lifts: 16–1 high-speed cabriolet, 1 gondola, 5 high-speed quads, 4 quads, 2 triples, 1 double, 2 surface lifts
Snowmaking: 4 percent (160 acres)
Skiable Acreage: 3,500 acres
Uphill capacity: 25,700 per hour
Snowboarding: Yes
Bed base: 1,200 slopeside, 12,000 in town
Nearest lodging: Slopeside
Resort child care: Yes, 6 weeks to 4 years
Adult ticket, per day: $50–$62 (02/03)

Mountain rating

The local motto is "If you can see it, you can ski it." Gates to out-of-bounds skiing have serious signs warning of avalanche danger. Lives have been lost in recent years by skiers who didn't heed the warnings. There is so much expert and advanced terrain within bounds at The Canyons that you can literally explore the mountain until you drop from exhaustion and still not get to everything during a weeklong vacation. Experts from the East Coast who prefer tree skiing and riding won't be disappointed—you'll find woods as tight as anything back home. Intermediates have plenty to choose from, and this is a great mountain if you want to improve to the next level. Beginners and never-evers now have increased terrain, though we haven't tried it yet. Hopefully, this rounds out the resort's terrain and ups the options for everyone.

Lessons (2002/03 prices)

Group lessons: Two-hour Perfect Turn clinics are $62; take two clinics in one day, $98. Smaller two-hour group lessons, limited to five people, cost $67; take two in one day, $98.

Never-ever package: Skiing or snowboarding, a three-day package with a four-hour lesson on day one, two-hour lessons on days two and three, equipment rental and limited lift access is $174. Reservations are recommended. A single-day package is $72 for day one, $82 each for days two and three.

Private lessons: $100 per hour (one or two people); $189 for two hours (one or two people) and $199 for two hours (three to five people); all-day lessons are $468 (for one or two people) and $520 (three to five people).

Special programs: Women's Workshop, a three-day program with U.S. Olympian Holly Flanders, is offered several times during the season and costs $368 plus lift ticket.

Child care (2002/03 prices)

Ages: 6 weeks to 4 years.
Costs: Full day for kids 2–4, with lunch, $72; half day, $52 with lunch. For kids, 3 months to 2 years, cost is $80 for a full day and $60 for a half day. Day care is offered 8:30 a.m.–4:30 p.m. No hourly rates available. Parents should supply a change of clothes and snow clothes.

Reservations: Recommended at all times but essential during holiday periods. For advance reservations, call 615-3402. For same-day reservations, call 615-8036. The Day Care Center keeps a list of independent babysitters.

Other options: The Park City Chamber of Commerce can refer visitors to **child-care facilities** or **babysitting services.** Call (800) 453-1360 or locally, 649-6100. **Baby's Away** (800-379-9030; 435-645-8823) rents and will deliver baby needs to your lodge, such as crib, stroller, car seat and toys.

Children's lessons: The most-requested program is a full day that includes lunch, lift ticket and equipment, plus indoor play time for younger children. It costs $115 for Canyon Cats, ages 4–6, skiing only, and $130 for Canyon Carvers, ages 7–12, skiing or riding. Reservations are recommended: 615-3449. Canyon Cubs, ages 2–3, get full day care plus an hour-and-a-half private lesson for $168—reservations are required; call 615-8036.

Lift tickets (2002/03 prices)

	Adult	Child (6-12)
One day	$62	$33
Three days	$168 ($56/day)	$96 ($32/day)
Five days	$250 ($50/day)	$160 ($32/day)

Who skis free: Younger than 6.

Who skis at a discount: Skiers 65 and older ski for children's prices. Check out the American Skiing Company ticket Web site at www.meticket.com for other deals. Early- and late-season prices are lower, peak are higher.

Cross-country and snowshoeing

White Pine Touring (615-5858) offers 20 km. of track and skate skiing, plus track, skate and telemark lessons at the Park City golf course and an adjacent dairy farm. Rates are $10 daily for adults; $5 for kids 6-12; younger than 6 and older than 65 ski free. For those who want to get off the flats, half-day snowshoe (Wed. & Sun.) and ski (Tues. and Fri.) tours in the Uinta mountains are also available. To venture out on your own, this is a good stop for advice and maps of the local mountain bike trails that are accessible (many from downtown Park City) and perfect for snowshoeing.

The **Homestead Resort** (654-1102; 800-327-7220), 14 miles southeast of Park City in Midway, has 12 km. of skiing at Homestead Golf Course and 18 km. at Wasatch Mountain State Park. Snowshoeing and snowmobiling are also available. Trail fees are $6 for adults and $3 for children. Nearby **Soldier Hollow**, site of the 2002 Olympic cross-country competitions, offers 26 km. of both track and skate skiing for all levels.

Accommodations

In and around Park City are bed-and-breakfasts, country inns, chain hotels and condominiums. Park City's lodging is roughly grouped either in the old town surrounding the Resort Center Complex or in the Prospector Square area. A wonderful new part of town is Lower Main (also called South Main), which surrounds the base of the Town Lift. All areas are served by the free shuttlebus system.

Downtown and at the Park City Mountain Resort base:

In old Park City the best is the **Washington School Inn** (800-824-1672 or 649-3800; $$–$$$$). This is a very elegant 15-room (including three suites) country inn built in a former schoolhouse. Each room has a private bath and the name of each room honors a former Park City teacher. Everything is definitely first class. It has a hot tub and steam bath, and is steps away from the center of the old town. If you are on your honeymoon, ask for the Miss Urie Room. Room rates include breakfast and afternoon tea. No children under age 12.

The **Blue Church Lodge & Townhouses** (800-626-5467 or 649-8009; $$–$$$$) are constructed around an old church a block from Main Street. Listed on the National Register of Historic Places, it is a grouping of seven condominiums ranging from one to four bedrooms in the church, with four additional townhouses across the street. A continental breakfast is included, but it doesn't fit the category of B&B in the classic sense. It has indoor and outdoor spas and laundry facilities.

If the key to lodging, as in real estate, is location, location, location, then **Treasure Mountain Inn** (800-344-2460; $$–$$$$) at the top of Main Street is a winner. These are studio and one- and two-bedroom condos with kitchens. Each of the three buildings has a coin-operated laundry, and there is a hot tub in the courtyard. Rooms are quiet, but step outside and you are smack dab in the middle of the nighttime action. Another spot on Main Street is the **1904 Imperial Hotel** (800-669-8824 or 649-1904; $$$), a B&B in a historic old house. All rooms have their own bath, telephone and TV, and most accommodate couples. There's a big hot tub for everyone to use (guests also can reserve private hot-tub time). Lizzie is the hotel's ghost, who turns lights on and off and rings bells to get attention (she never appears in person). Legend is that Lizzie was killed in the Mayflower Room by a jealous lover. The hotel's sister property, **The Old Miners' Lodge** (800-648-8068 or 645-8068; $$–$$$) is two blocks from Main Street on Woodside Avenue. Intermediate skiers can ski to the back door, but it's a long walk down a hefty flight of stairs to get to the Town Lift. The lodge is historic and quiet (it's a member of Select Registry), with rooms that all have private baths but no TV or in-room phones.

The bargain spots are dormitory digs and rooms in the **Chateau Après Lodge**, "A Skier's Ski Lodge" (649-9372; $–$$). Another choice is **Budget Lodging** (649-2526 or 800-522-7669; $$–$$$$), with hotel rooms to four-bedroom. College students should head to **Base Camp Park City** (888-980-7244, $) to save money and be close to all the best nightlife. You'll share bathrooms, a lounge and a kitchenette, but there are private ski lockers. A four-bed room is $140 during the regular winter season, so you and three friends will each pay $35 per night.

The South Main area is the newest hot spot in town. The **Marriott Summit Watch** (647-4100 or 800-223-8245) is smack in the middle of this pedestrian complex with restaurants, shops and the Town Lift right outside the door. A draw is the Marriott's Aquacade, a pool and activities center built under old trestles. Every evening there's something scheduled for kids, such as crafts, movies or an ice skating excursion, ranging in cost from $15 to $30.

Near the Resort Center you'll find another cluster of hotels and condos. The best is the **Silver King Hotel** (800-331-8652 or 649-5500; $$$–$$$$). This condo hotel is about 100 yards from the lifts and at the hub of the transportation system. Some units have private hot tubs. **The Lodge at the Mountain Village** (800-824-5331 or 649-0800; $$$–$$$$) is the second choice for luxury. It literally surrounds the base area lifts for true ski-in/ski-out. Lots of amenities—spas, health club, pool, steamroom and concierge.

Shadow Ridge Resort Hotel & Conference Center (800-451-3031 or 649-4300; $$–$$$$) is the other top property near the lifts. It has a sauna, hot tub and laundry, plus underground parking. Offers hotel rooms to three-bedroom condos. **Snow Flower Condominiums** (800-852-3101 or 649-6400; $$–$$$$) is 100 feet from the beginner area. Each unit has single-person jetted hot tubs and underground parking. Studios to five-bedroom units.

For more economical condos, try the **Edelweiss Haus** (800-245-6417 or 649-9342; $$–$$$$) across the street from the lifts and the Silver King Hotel. Extras are a heated outdoor pool and hot tub. Hotel rooms to two-bedroom condos available.

Other locations in town:

The **Inn at Prospector Square** (888-870-4386 or 649-7100; $$–$$$$) is a group of condos that includes use of its athletic club in the rates. **The Yarrow Resort Hotel** (800-927-7694 or 649-7000; $$–$$$$) is considered good family lodging. Children under 12 stay free and the hotel sits amid shopping, movies and restaurants. It is on the shuttlebus route, about a five-minute ride from Park City's Main Street.

The 199-room **Park City Marriott** (800-754-3279 or 649-2900; $$–$$$$) is an absolutely gorgeous full-service resort hotel. There are refrigerators and coffee makers in every room, plus double phone lines and desks with built-in outlets for those who must combine work with pleasure. The bus stop is right outside the door.

For luxury condos and houses at affordable prices as well as a chance to get some last-minute or off-peak bargains in the entire Park City area, call **Accommodations Unlimited** (800-321-4754 or 649-1128). A friend of ours also recommended **High Mountain Properties** (800-239-6144 or 655-8363; www.highmountainproperties.com) for assistance booking condos, private homes and other lodging.

Accommodations at The Canyons

A few steps from the Flight of The Canyons gondola, **The Grand Summit Resort Hotel** (1-888-CANYONS; $$$$) has luxurious penthouses, one- to three-bedroom suites, studios and hotel rooms. Most of the 360 rooms have balconies, fireplaces, whirlpool tubs and full kitchens. Also offers full-service health club, including a heated outdoor pool with whirlpools, steamroom, sauna and massage. On-site restaurant, bistro and lounges.

The 150-room **Sundial Lodge** (1-888-CANYONS; $$$$) is in the heart of The Canyons Resort Village. The condominium lodge offers guestrooms and one- and two-bedroom condominium-style accommodations with kitchens and jetted tubs. Most condominiums have fireplaces and balconies. Guests have access to a rooftop hot tub and plunge pool.

Dining – Park City Area

Park City's restaurants get better every year—and more expensive. Pick up one of the two free dining-guide magazines to get menus, but be aware that not all the restaurants are listed. Main Street is where you'll find many of the best restaurants in town: The top four are **Grappa, Chimayo, Zoom** and **Riverhorse.**

If you can pay the freight, the Northern Italian menu, wine list and ambiance are outstanding at chef Bill White's **Grappa** (645-0636, $$$). It's in a 100-year-old building, try and get a table by the fireplace. Many locals recommend **Chimayo** (649-6222; $$–$$$), also owned by chef Bill White, for its inventive Southwestern cuisine (don't miss the dark chocolate flan). **Zoom Roadhouse Grill** (649-9108; $$$) is housed in the old train depot. Owned by Robert Redford, whose Sundance Film Festival transforms the town each January, it serves "plain folks food." Finally, the **Riverhorse Café** (649-3536; $$$) is a can't-miss choice for anyone who enjoys Contemporary American food in a low-key, elegant atmosphere.

Lakota (658-3400; $$$) is another restaurant favored by the trend-setting crowd. For Italian, **Mileti's** (649-8211; $$$) is still going strong after 27 years, or try **Cisero's** (649-5044; $$) and **Café Terigo** (645-9555).

Asian restaurants are popular, with **Mikado** (655-7100; $$$) the choice for Japanese, **Bangkok Thai** (649-8424; $$$) for Thai, and **Taste of Saigon** (647-0688; $$) for Vietnamese food. Park City also has four Chinese restaurants. **The Dragon Garden** (655-0101; $) is the spot for a quick and cheap Chinese fix. Many Park City restaurants offer excellent take-out. After a wipe-out day on the slopes and a soak in the hot tub, we devoured a tender Moo Goo Gai Pan and a tasty mixed vegetable dish from **Szechwan** (649-0957; $). Take a free shuttle into town for pick up or have food delivered for an additional 20 percent of the total.

The hot spot is Lower Main. The restaurants here are new, and most lean toward expensive. **Wahso** (615-0300), again owned by the ubiquitous Bill White, is where to go for Asian/European food. **Dynamite Dom's** (615-8457; $$–$$$) and **Prime Steakhouse** (655-9739, $$$) are upscale steakhouses. **Picasso's** (658-3030; $$) is a Spanish Tapas restaurant, **Mul-**

Dining: $$$-Entrees $20+; $$-$10-20; $-less than $10.
Accommodations: (double room) $$$$-$200+; $$$-$141-$200; $$-$81-$140; $-$80 and less.

berry Street (649-0888, $$) bills itself as "American with an Italian flair," and **Mulligan's Pub** (658-0717, $$) has an Irish menu.

Off Main Street, one restaurant that vies for best-in-town honors is **Adolph's** (649-7177; $$$) next to the U.S. Ski and Snowboard Team office on Kearns Blvd. It serves Swiss and American cuisine. Hidden on Park Ave., **Chez Betty** (649-8181, $$$) in the Copperbottom Inn serves excellent American/French cuisine in a formal setting.

Head to **Nacho Mama's** (645-8226; $–$$) for tasty Southwestern/Mexican food and margaritas that go down far too smoothly; **Baja Cantina** (649-4440; $$) at the Resort Center; and the **Irish Camel** (649-6645; $$) on Main Street for good drinks and acceptable Tex-Mex food. The lowest-priced Mexican spot is **El Chubasco** (645-9114; $), in Prospector Square.

The Eating Establishment (649-8284; $) is a locals' cheap-eats favorite, as is the **Park City Pizza Company** (649-1591; $). **Texas Red's Pit Barbeque** (649-7337, $–$$) is the red-meat-eater's choice. **Grub Steak** (649-8060; $$–$$$) gets high marks.

For breakfast, **The Eating Establishment** on Main Street is the leader for hearty-meal fans (the menu includes some trendy selections, such as smoked salmon Eggs Benedict), while **Ziggy's** is the egg-and-pancake choice for those staying at the Park City Mountain Resort base. **Off Main Cafe and Bakery** does omelets and pancakes in the Prospector Square area. For a lighter breakfast, try **Einstein Brothers Bagel Bakery** in the Prospector Square area for a huge variety of bagels and spreads, as well as great coffee, or **Wasatch Bagels** on Kearns Blvd. next to Dan's Grocery Store. For funky local ambiance and a cheap breakfast special ($3.89 for egg, ham and cheese on a bagel), hit **The Main Street Deli**. The **Morning Ray Cafe** or **Mountain Air** are the places to share a java with the locals.

The Canyons has three on-mountain lodges for dining: **Red Pine Lodge,** at the top of the Flight of The Canyons gondola, serves healthy grilled food, pizza and deli sandwiches; **Sun Lodge at Snow Canyon** serves Asian and Mexican dishes; and the award-winning **Lookout Cabin,** at the top of Lookout chairlift, has a table-served luncheon menu of grilled fish, meats and salads (not only is the food wonderful here, the mountain views are spectacular). **Doc's at the Gondola,** in the Grand Summit, is good for lunch and après ski. Also in the base area, **Smokie's Smokehouse** serves family-style BBQ and Cajun fare and has an unobstructed view of the terrain park. **Yurt dining** is available at 5 p.m. daily.

You also should refer to the *Deer Valley chapter* for dining recommendations.

Après-ski/nightlife

Despite rumors of Utah party blahs, Park City has some of the best nightlife of any ski town. For the lowdown on Utah's liquor laws, including the "private club membership" you'll need for most of these places, see the Salt Lake City chapter.

Immediate slopeside après-ski centers are the new bar, **Legends,** in the Legacy Lodge, and **Moose's,** both at Park City Mountain Resort base; and **The Forum** at The Canyons.

According to locals, **O'Shucks** is the place to be on Main Street for the younger folks (skiers and boarders) and **Lakota** is the hot spot for the more mature population. **Harry Os,** half way down Main, is a giant warehouse of a bar, complete with six pool tables, a big-screen TV showing the game, and a boisterous younger crowd who need to be carded to get in. It is *the place* on Saturday nights. **The No Name Saloon,** next door, is your basic bar with pool tables, loud music and louder conversation.

Mother Urban's, named after a famous bordello madam, is a cellar version of a knotty-pine mining shack that sells 55 beers (not bad for Mormon territory) and features live jazz Tuesdays, Thursdays and Fridays. Also try the **Wasatch Brew Pub** at the top of Main Street, where you can watch the brewing process even as you reap its yeasty rewards. **The Spur** on Main Street offers a comfortable, smoke-free setting with live music on weekends. **Mileti's** is casual, cozy and dark, making it a great place for the last drink of the night. **Adolph's**, with piano music, has been recommended for quieter evenings.

When the **Egyptian Theater** has plays, as it does often during the winter, it makes a nice evening's entertainment. **The Eccles Center**, which opened in 1998, houses two live stages and is a year-round focal point for the performing arts in Park City. For weekly arts and entertainment events, call 647-9747 or 655-3114.

 Other activities

Park City offers some rare sports treats: **ski jumping, luge and bobsled** at the Utah Olympic Park (658-4200). The park hosted the 2002 Olympic competition in those events. Yes, you can fly off the end of a ramp just like the Olympians do (you'll be on much smaller ramps, but it will feel like the 120-meter jump, let us assure you). You can take jumping lessons (required rental helmets included), or ride on the Olympic luge/bobsled track in a neophyte-friendly luge "ice rocket" or as a passenger in a four-person bobsled. (They supply the driver and brakeman.) Schedules are different each day, and not every activity is offered every day, so call for specifics and prices. Definitely call in advance for a spot in the bobsled. The 48-second ride of your life, wild and rugged. You won't be disappointed. The park is closed Mondays and Tuesdays. It's worth a tour even if you don't participate in the sports, particularly with the recent opening of its museum celebrating Utah's ski history, from the first jumping competitions to XIX Olympic Winter Games.

Gorgoza, a tubing park owned by Park City Mountain Resort, is off of I-80. Or try the **Legacy Launcher,** a circus-style trampoline where four people are harnessed for safety. Jump, twist, flip and spin through the air till your legs collapse. The resort also has **sleigh rides** and **snowmobile tours** for family activities.

Many companies offer **sleigh rides, snowmobile tours** and **hot-air balloon trips**. For reservations, call one central number at ABC Reservations Central, (800) 820-2223 or 649-2223. There is no fee and most adventures provide free shuttle service.

Stop by the Mormon church's **Family History Center** at 531 Main Street. Computers are available for genealogy checks for anyone free of charge. **The Park City Museum** on Main Street details local history, and is excellent. Admission is by donation, and it is open every day, at varying times.

Park City's calendar has some unusual events. The **World Cup** ski racing tour kicks off each year at Park City Mountain Resort in mid-November. The resort also will host the **Snowboard Grand Prix** (a World Cup event) and the **World Superpipe Championships**. Following the Olympics, Park City's three venues will undoubtedly continue hosting world class events, from those contested at the Utah Olympic Park to skiing and snowboarding. Robert Redford's **Sundance Film Festival** is in late January, showcasing new films from around the world.

Park City has two popular **shopping** areas: Historic Main Street in downtown Park City and a factory outlet center on the edge of town. The outlets include Eddie Bauer, Brooks Brothers, Gap, Nike and Polo among many others. You can jump on a free shuttle or take a cab for $6 round trip per person. Park City's free shuttle bus system now operates in town and out to Kimball Junction/Factory Outlet Mall (including The Canyons Resort). Take an hour or two and walk Main Street to find museums, art galleries and fine and funky shops. A must-see is Silver Junction Mercantile with every nook and cranny crammed full of old stuff, from

Dining: $$$-Entrees $20+; $$-$10-20; $-less than $10.
Accommodations: (double room) $$$$-$200+; $$$-$141-$200; $$-$81-$140; $-$80 and less.

rusty license plates and political buttons to Elvis and Beatles memorabilia. Nativo offers high-end young clothing and avant-garde jewelry. Tiff's owner buys amber directly from Poland which her partner polishes and sets in stunning silver for very reasonable prices. The Pendleton store in the Main Street Mall sells vintage Pendleton clothing at vintage prices.

Don't miss Changing Hands, a consignment shop way off the beaten track in the back of Galleria Mall. Great high-fashion ski clothes during the season and higher end labels for the rest of the inventory. Hard to find, but well worth it. If you are traveling with your pet or had to leave him at home, stop at the Love Your Pet Bakery to bring home a treat.

Getting there and getting around

By air: The drive from the Salt Lake City International Airport to Park City takes 45 minutes (36 miles). Ground transportation makes frequent trips from the airport for $34-$46, round-trip (children's fares are $17-$35). Providers include Lewis Brothers Stages, (800) 826-5844 or 649-2256; Park City Transportation, (800) 637-3803 or 649-8567; and All Resort Express (800) 457-9457 or 649-3999. If you arrive without reservations, go to the transportation counter at the airport and you'll ride on the next available van. Call 48 hours in advance for Park City-to-airport reservations.

By car: Park City is 32 miles east of Salt Lake City, by I-80 and Utah Hwy. 224.

Getting around: If you're staying close to the town center or near a stop on the free bus line, you can do without a rental car. The town bus system has five routes with service every 20 minutes, if not more frequently, from 7 a.m. to 1 a.m. If you take a side trip to one of the Cottonwood Canyons ski resorts, Lewis Brothers Stages and Park City Transportation have shuttles for $22-$35 round-trip. Lewis Brothers offers a Canyon Jumper package to Solitude and Snowbird for $49 and $52, respectively, including transportation and lift ticket. Prepay the evening before you wish to ski.

Snowbird
Utah

Summit elevation: 11,000 feet
Vertical drop: 3,240 feet
Base elevation: 7,760 feet

Address: P.O. Box 929000
Snowbird, UT 84092-9000
☎ **Area code:** 801
Ski area phone: 742-2222
Snow report: 933-2100
ⓘ **Toll-free reservations:**
(800) 453-3000
Fax: 947-8227
Internet: www.snowbird.com
Expert:★★★★★
Advanced:★★★★
Intermediate:★★★★
Beginner:★★★ **Never-ever:**★★★★

Number of lifts: 11—1 aerial tram,
3 high-speed quads, 7 double chairs
Snowmaking: Minimal
Skiable acreage: 2,500-plus
Uphill capacity: 16,800 per hour
Snowboarding: Yes
Bed Base: 1,800+
Nearest lodging: Slopeside, hotel
Resort child care: Yes, 6 weeks and older
Adult ticket, per day: $43-$56 (02/03)
Dining:★★
Apres-ski/nightlife:★
Other activities:★★

Practically every devout skier or snowboarder has a mecca for annual pilgrimages to rekindle the flame and commune once again with the snow spirits. The choices for these meccas are deeply personal. When the winds of November bring the year's first snowfalls, however, many devoted skiers find themselves drawn almost irresistibly up the winding ascent to the brawny splendor of Snowbird Ski & Summer Resort.

The initial allure is the snow, but it is much more than that. Suffice it to say that Utah's little disputed claim to the "greatest snow on earth" is based largely on the slopes and bowls of Little Cottonwood, a canyon whose steep sides and craggy beauty are more reminiscent of the Alps than much of the Rockies. Snowbird itself receives an annual average of 500 inches of light, champagne powder that typically arrives early and stays around long enough for everyone to enjoy 200 days of skiing. Among powder aficionados, Snowbird is spoken of in the hushed tones of the truly reverent.

Snowbird's sleek, modern, high-rise hotel and condo complex that seems to spring out of the mountain's roots—the Iron Blosam Lodge, The Cliff Lodge, the Lodge at Snowbird and the Inn at Snowbird—also speak to the soul of the serious skier. Snowbird has luxurious accommodations and fine dining. The rock-solid but unobtrusive design of the resort takes nothing away from the looming mountains, leaving no doubt that their majestic appeal is what truly draws skiers back year after year.

Governed by strict laws regulating development, Snowbird has not been particularly aggressive in expanding its realm over the years. Recently, however, there have been subtle signs of promising change. A couple of seasons ago, Snowbird started guided snowcat tours on 500 acres in Mineral Basin, south of the Hidden Peak summit on the back side. Two seasons ago, this powder paradise became a reality for all skiers and riders when Snowbird installed a high-speed quad in Mineral Basin. The speedy, four-minute-long Mineral Basin

Express keeps powder hounds in their pleasure while the Basin's 1,429 vertical feet test their stamina. This new terrain includes intermediate, advanced and expert runs in a nearly treeless setting.

Snowbird has been amending its reputation as a destination primarily for the steep-and-deep skiers and powder monkeys. Off the Baby Thunder lift, the resort has a largely protected area that has gentle slopes great for less experienced skiers. Two additional slopes are also being regularly groomed to the corduroy smoothness favored by cruisers. Snowbird is a resort where the whole family can find skiing to suit them. But Snowbird still has the tough stuff that put it on the map.

Now skiers can purchase an Alta Snowbird ticket for $64 a day and enjoy the two re-sorts' combined terrain (don't be surprised if snowboarders start converting to skiing *en mass*, snowboarding is still banned at Alta). Snowbird added a second high-speed quad in Mineral Basin, called Baldy Express, connecting the two resorts. The lift transports skiers to the Sugarloaf saddle area (elevation 10,600 feet), joining Alta's Albion Basin and Snowbird's Mineral Basin. Skiers access the area by beginner and intermediate trails from the Albion Basin side, and by intermediate trails from the Mineral Basin side. In addition, Utah Transit Authority connects the resorts' base areas with an expanded free daily bus service.

Mountain layout—Skiing

With the addition of Mineral Basin, Snowbird is now divided into three distinct areas: Peruvian Gulch, Gad Valley and Mineral Basin. Thanks to a computer overhaul, the Tram now whisks skiers to Hidden Peak in six minutes, where a day at "The Bird" can begin. A good suggestion is warming up in Mineral Basin, where the sun shines and warms early in the day. After a couple runs in the bowls, head over to Gad Valley for a leisurely 3,000-vertical-foot drop down to the Gadzoom high-speed quad. A northeast exposure on the Peruvian Gulch side keeps The Cirque's steep runs good all day, a treat for the late morning or early afternoon once the legs are warmed up but not shot.

◆◆ **Expert:** No gut-wrenching decisions here. The most experienced skiers head for the tram. Hanging across a cirque and rising to the 11,000-foot summit, it brings 125 skiers at a time to Hidden Peak, unseen from the base lodge. When the first tram arrives on powder days there's a dash for the slopes. Skiers and snowboarders hurl their equipment and then themselves over the railings to make the first tracks. After this thrill, things calm down a bit, and you can decide whether to get equipment on quickly and be the first down The Cirque, or wait a bit, let others dash, and then go where they don't.

Drop under the tram into Peruvian Gulch, with intermediate, advanced and expert routes down, or head left into the Little Cloud area. Most tram riders opt for Peruvian because of its zigzag intermediate run, Chip's. Experts can go either way. On the Peruvian side, experts tackle The Cirque, a plunge that drops into almost 3,000 vertical feet of expert slopes. You can choose a run about as steep as you want, some with chutes that hold only enough powder to slow your virtual freefall. Anyone who has dropped down Upper Silver Fox, Great Scott or Upper Cirque deserves to be treated with reverence—they're using up the extra lives they were blessed with. From the tram ridge, Primrose Path is an unrelenting black diamond, nor-mally the choice of those who think twice about tiptoeing around The Cirque. Here at Snow-bird, what you can see, you can ski. So pick your own way.

Should you decide to drop over to the Little Cloud side of Hidden Peak, the skiing is somewhat tamer—by Snowbird standards. You reach the toughest stuff on this side—Gad Chutes, Barry Barry Steep and others—by taking the Cirque Traverse from the tram.

♦ **Advanced:** Before you tackle the tram blacks at the top, take a test run on Chip's on the Peruvian side, or Regulator Johnson or Road to Provo on the Little Cloud side. Regulator Johnson, which is marked black on the map, now has a wide groomed swath down the center. Some of our staff think this descent is easier than Chip's sharp and crowded switchbacks, even though Chip's is rated blue.

Another good spot for advanced skiers is the Gad 2 chair. Gad 2 opens narrower trails through the trees and over megabumps. Gadzooks, Tiger Tail, Black Forest and Organ Grinder are equal challenges.

■ **Intermediate:** Do not board the tram without a test run elsewhere. A good tryout run is Big Emma from the top of Mid-Gad. Big Emma is rated green on the trail map, but its difficulty can vary with conditions. Many a beginner has halted along its upper rim, asking passing skiers and boarders, "Is there an easier way down?" On cold hardpacked days, Big Emma is a challenge even for intermediates.

If you can ski Emma with ease, you have several options for the next test. Any of the blue-square runs off the three Gad chairs will be fun, and if you can handle them, you should be ready to tackle the easiest advanced runs off the tram.

The Baby Thunder area helps to bridge the steepness gap between Snowbird's novice slope and Big Emma. You can also work on technique on the greens under the Wilbere chair.

●● **Beginner:** The Baby Thunder area is great for lower-level skiers. It's gentle and isolated from faster traffic. Terrain between the runs is left ungroomed, great for practicing powder or tree skiing. Because it's a little off to one side, the initial access is a bit tricky to find. Ask a host at the base area to advise you, because directions may vary depending on the day's conditions. We recommend lessons for beginners, if only to have a guide to keep you out of trouble. Baby Thunder also includes a dedicated family area.

If it's a gorgeous day and you'd like to see the view, buy a tram ticket and ride back down. (And don't let any of the hot-shots shame you into skiing down—nothing from the top is easy by beginner standards. Oddly, the Mineral Basin Road run on the back side is an easy green, but there is no easy route down the front side to the base area.)

● **Never-ever:** Chickadee, out the door from the Cliff Lodge, is a near-ideal novice slope. (Our only gripe is the chair lift height is set for children, but we can work around that minor inconvenience.) At the very beginning of the day, skilled skiers use Chickadee to get to the other chairs, but aside from that, novices have it all to themselves.

Mountain layout—Snowboarding

With the addition of Mineral Basin, Snowbird is now divided into three distinct areas: Peruvian Gulch, Gad Valley and Mineral Basin. Thanks to a computer overhaul, the Tram now whisks you to Hidden Peak in six minutes, where a day at "The Bird" can begin. A good suggestion is warming up in Mineral Basin, where the sun shines and warms early in the day. After a couple runs in the bowls, head over to Gad Valley for a leisurely 3,000-vertical-foot drop down to the Gadzoom high-speed quad. A northeast exposure on the Peruvian Gulch side keeps The Cirque's steep runs good all day, a treat for the late morning or early afternoon once the legs are warmed up but not shot.

Many Snowbird riders head straight to the wide-open, sometimes mogul filled Little Cloud Bowl or to the enticing trees off of Gad II. Follow a local for the best lines here, and if possible, take the tram to the Gad lifts to avoid a walk on the cat track. For hardcore riders, nothing beats the runs off either side of the Cirque. While the Cirque Traverse is long and filled with annoying dips, it's worth every bit of pain. The farther down the traverse you go on the Peruvian Gulch side, the easier it gets, though nothing off of here is for the faint of heart. A side note: Avoid the testosterone market on Great Scott Chute—within 100 yards there's others that are harder with better snow and more fluid fall lines. For some solitude, try the 10-minute hike to Baldy Mountain's chutes and powder fields. For air, head to the enormous halfpipe on Big Emma, or any number of cliffs and drop-offs. On most parts of the mountain there are intermittent flats; just anticipate, keep your speed, and you'll get through them. And at the end of the day, take the Traverse to the very end, and join the partyers atop Lone Pine, basking in the day's last rays of sun.

Mountain rating

Experts, you have arrived. A healthy half of Snowbird terrain is for you. These are not public-relations black diamonds, either—they really are tough. You will leave exhilarated or frustrated, depending on whether you attack them or they attack you.

Everyone else, expect to be pushed. Owner Dick Bass, who has climbed the highest mountain on every continent, affirms, "What we gain too easily, we esteem too lightly." Let that be your rallying cry. You will improve, a phenomenon you may not recognize until you ski those home slopes you thought were a challenge. If Snowbird exhausts you or you're here for a week and know all the routes in your comfort zone by heart, go next door to Alta, which has more mellow intermediate and beginner trails.

 ## Lessons (2001/02 prices)

Snowbird Mountain School has four one-stop locations for ski and snowboard school registration and buying lift tickets. Tickets are not included in the lesson price. The offices are on Level 1 of the Cliff Lodge (you'll find two here, Camp Snowbird is for kids' programs), the Plaza Deck of the Snowbird Center and the Cottonwood Room on Level 2 of the Snowbird Center. For more information or reservations, call 933-2170.

Group lessons: $72 for all day; $54 for half-day, afternoon-only classes.

Never-ever package: $59 includes ski or snowboard rentals, half-day lesson and access on the Chickadee lift.

Private lessons: For one to two people, $90 per hour ($80 between 9 and 10 a.m.) with multi-hour discounts; for three to six people, $125 per hour ($100 between 9 and 10 a.m.).

Special programs: Mountain Experience allows advanced or expert skiers to join a guide and launch an assault on the entire mountain for $85 for one day. Other 2.5-hour clinics teach style, bump skiing and snowboarding. A four-day women's camp is offered several times a season, and can be purchased with or without lifts and lodging. Skiing and snowboarding are separate women's seminars. Call for current prices.

Racing: A coin-operated course is open each day, weather permitting. The course is to one side of Big Emma, accessible by the Wilbere or Mid-Gad chairs.

 ## Child care (2001/02 prices)

Ages: 6 weeks to 12 years.

Costs: $80 a day, with lunch, for ages 6 weeks to 3 years, and $70 for ages 3–12. Half-day and multiday discounts are available. Evening babysitting is $13 an hour, a little more for an additional child, but you must be staying in a Snowbird lodge to use this service.

Reservations: Required. Call Camp Snowbird at 933-2256, or reserve when you book your vacation. A non-refundable $25 registration fee is applied toward your final day.

Children's lessons: Full day (lunch and lessons) is $80. Half day for beginner and lower intermediate skiers is $54. Ability levels are separated. Ages 3 and 4 get 90-minute lessons for $55. Two children per instructor makes this very popular, so sign up in advance.

Lift tickets (2002/03 prices)

	Adult	Child (0–12)
One day	$56	Free (see below)
Three days	$141 ($47/day)	
Five days	$215 ($43/day)	

Who skis free: Two children younger than 12 ride the chairs free when an accompanying adult purchases a lift ticket. (Tram access costs $15.) Children of lodging guests ski the entire mountain free, and there's no limit on the number of children as long as they are Snowbird lodging guests.

Who skis at a discount: Ages 65 and older ski for $44. A ticket for the Chickadee chair only is $11.

Note: These are the prices with Tram access. For chairs only, the one-day prices are $47 for adults; $36 for seniors. Don't buy Tram access if you aren't skiing there; you can always upgrade a day's ticket to include the Tram for $9. The Alta Snowbird ticket that allows you to access both resorts' terrain costs $64 a day; multi-day Alta Snowbird tickets cost $56/day for 3-4 days, $52/day for 5+ days.

Accommodations

All lodging at Snowbird is within walking distance of the base lifts, and can be reserved by calling Snowbird Central Reservations (800-453-3000; fax, 947-8227; www.snowbird.com). Winter season is mid-December through early April; value season is before and after those dates. Snowbird also has added a January value season, where rates are between the high and low seasons. Snowbird's season is a long one, lasting well into May most years. Lodging is plentiful in Salt Lake City.

The Cliff Lodge ($$$–$$$$) spreads like an eagle's wings at the base. Inside there's an 11-story atrium, a renowned spa, and a glassed-in rooftop with a heated pool that overlooks the slopes. The pool complex has a trio of hot tubs and an outdoor heated pool, and a nearby fruit-juice bar. Mountain-view rooms have picture windows from the shower that peer into the sleeping area and the view beyond (there's a shower curtain you can pull for modesty). The Cliff Lodge also has luxurious suites. Children younger than 12 stay and ski free with adults. The 27,000-square-foot Cliff Spa, on the top floor of the hotel, has 20 treatment rooms and a variety of treatments for body, face, hair and nails, as well as an exercise facility. Call 933-2225 for the spa, 933-2268 for the salon.

The Lodge at Snowbird ($$–$$$$), **The Inn** ($$–$$$$), and the **Iron Blosam Lodge** ($$–$$$$) are three condominium complexes with similar layouts. Not as elegant or as expensive as the Cliff Lodge, but they are well maintained, roomy and comfortable. Amenities include outdoor swimming pools, indoor hot tubs and saunas. Rates start at $119 for an efficiency or studio during value season, and top out at $519–$769 for a one-bedroom with loft during winter season.

Dining: $$$–Entrees $20+; $$–$10–20; $–less than $10.
Accommodations: (double room) $$$$–$200+; $$$–$141–$200; $$–$81–$140; $–$80 and less.

Dining

The **Aerie** ($$$) on top of the Cliff Lodge is considered one of Utah's best restaurants, for good reason. The decor is elegant and tasteful, the views from the large picture windows spectacular, and the food and house piano player are excellent. The **Keyhole Junction** ($–$$) offers Mexican and Southwestern fare. The **Summit Sushi Bar** ($–$$) on Level 10 of the Cliff Lodge serves fresh hand-rolled sushi. At ground level of the Cliff Lodge's atrium, the **Atrium Restaurant** ($-$$) is fine for quick continental breakfasts, lunches and snacks. At the Iron Blosam Lodge, **Wildflower Ristorante & Lounge** ($$–$$$) serves outstanding Mediterranean cuisine. **The Lodge Bistro** ($$) in the Lodge at Snowbird has a cozy atmosphere with an eclectic bistro menu.

Other restaurants are in the Snowbird Center at the base of the mountain. **The Steak Pit** ($$) serves steak and seafood. There's usually a wait, but it's worth it. The rest of the eateries in the Snowbird Center cater to the ski crowd, serving breakfast and lunch. **The Forklift** has easy access to the slopes yet with a large fireplace that adds atmosphere. For cafeteria service, **The Rendezvous** has the usual, plus a well-stocked salad island. **Pier 49 San Francisco Sourdough Pizza** has pizza with lots of toppings, and **Birdfeeder** has gourmet coffees, including espressos, and light snacks.

Après-ski/nightlife

Snowbird's nightlife is very quiet. For the liveliest après-ski, try **Tram Club**, on the bottom floor of the Snowbird Center, with retro decor and a picture-window view of the tram's huge operating gears. It's your best bet if you want to dance. **Wildflower Lounge** is mellow. In the evening, **The Aerie** has a bar with live jazz several nights a week. **Keyhole Junction** has TVs showing sports events.

Remember: The nightspots are "private clubs" that charge a $5 two-week membership fee. If you are staying at a Snowbird lodge, the membership is included with your accommodations; however, the Tram Club is owned separately and so requires a separate membership. At night, you can take the free Snowbird shuttle to and from the Snowbird Center and the various restaurants and nightspots at the lodges. If you're staying at the Cliff Lodge, you can walk across the Chickadee novice slope to get to the Snowbird Center; however, we recommend the shuttle, which runs until 11 p.m. (sometimes later). The walking route is slippery, and you'll be dodging skiers and others who use that slope at night.

Other activities

Snowbird offers **guided backcountry tours** and **snowshoe tours**. All tours are dependent upon weather conditions, ability level and time availability. Call 933-2147 for more information. During the day, Snowbird operates a tubing hill. **Ice skating** is available during the day and in the evenings. You also can go **night skiing** on the Chickadee novice slope outside the Cliff Lodge.

Little Cottonwood Canyon has no cross-country skiing or snowmobiling, but spectacular **helicopter skiing** is available from Wasatch Powderbird Guides (742-2800, or www.heliskiwasatch.com).

The **Snowbird Canyon Racquet Club,** at the mouth of the canyon, has indoor tennis, racquetball, squash courts, aerobics classes and a complete fitness center. The resort owns it; ask about rates.

Snowbird is not a good place for non-skiers and people who don't love the outdoors unless they plan to spend considerable time at the Cliff Spa (see Accommodations). The only other diversion is **shopping**, and a champion browser will finish off the dozen or so shops in half a day. However, the Salt Lake Valley, where you'll find more extensive shopping, is a short drive away.

An actors' troupe stages a **Murder Mystery Dinner Theatre** once a month from January through March; call the resort for information on that and other entertainment special events.

Getting there and getting around

By air: Salt Lake City is a major airline hub, so flights are numerous. Ground transportation is well organized—Lewis Brothers Stages charges $45 per person, round-trip, between the airport and Snowbird or Alta. Call (800) 826-5844 or head to the Lewis Brothers counter at the airport when you arrive.

By train: Amtrak's California Zephyr stops in Salt Lake City (at 4 a.m. coming from the West Coast, but the fare is cheap. From Chicago, the train arrives at midnight). Call (800) USA-RAIL or consult the Amtrak Web site, www.amtrak.com.

By car: Snowbird is 25 miles southeast of Salt Lake City in Little Cottonwood Canyon. The most direct route from the airport is east on I-80, south on I-215, Exit 6 to Wasatch Blvd., then follow the signs.

Getting around: If you fly in, don't bother renting a car—Snowbird is entirely walkable. If you plan to ski a lot of other Utah areas, stay in Salt Lake City (see Utah Skiing chapter). Utah's new light rail system makes getting to Snowbird quick and easy. Take the light rail from the downtown hotels for $1, for an additional 75 cents a bus will take you to Snowbird's doorstep. A Lewis Brothers SkiExpress van to Snowbird is about $15 roundtrip from downtown (call 359-8677 from Salt Lake City). Lewis Brothers also has the Canyon Jumper between Park City and Snowbird for $20. Bus service links Alta and Snowbird for $1.25. A free Snowbird shuttle will get you to various points within the resort complex.

Solitude Mountain Resort & Brighton

Utah

Big Cottonwood Canyon's two resorts may only be a couple of miles apart, but they look like they're on different continents. Solitude is an emerging master-planned resort. Its blueprints call for a series of upscale, European-style condominiums, shops and restaurants. Brighton, at the canyon's end, continues to court local snowboarders and skiers with no-frills facilities. It has no ambitious blueprints for future development to rival Solitude's (indeed, it's limited by local watershed restrictions).

Although Solitude resisted the snowboard movement for many years, Brighton was one of the first Utah resorts to embrace the sport. Snowboarders remain quite loyal to Brighton as a result. The combination of exciting terrain, lots of snow and low prices adds to Brighton's popularity with snowboarders.

While the two resorts look different, they remain similar in many ways. Ticket prices, at less than $45, are reasonable by Utah standards and a bargain by destination-visitor standards. Both have lots of intermediate slopes and comparable lift capacity, though Solitude has mre diverse expert and advanced terrain.

Solitude has won awards for its trail and lift system. Its full-service hotel—The Inn at Solitude—includes a restaurant and shops. The recent opening of the Powderhorn Lodge added 83 condominiums in an elegant building, with more retail space for skier services, in Solitude's cozy pedestrian village. The luxurious Eagle Springs East is the newest lodging. The legendary A-frame bar, The Thirsty Squirrel has been moved inside the Powderhorn Lodge. Solitude's new appearance is decidedly continental. A model of the new and improved village makes it look as if it were in Switzerland, not the Western United States.

Brighton refurbished many of its aging buildings and built a huge Brighton Center to house lift ticket sales, rental and retail shops and more restrooms and lockers. But it retained its cleanly utilitarian, Western appearance—a cross between log cabin and military barracks, that concerns itself more with substance than style. The Snake Creek Express high-speed quad recently replaced the Snake Creek triple, cutting travel time in half.

Cosmetic changes notwithstanding, both Brighton and Solitude continue to share a mountain ambiance that architecture and marketing can't alter. People come to ski or snowboard, period. Locals still mention both mountains in the same breath, and it will probably be decades before the resorts are thought of as separate—at least by Utahans.

Mountain layout—Skiing

Solitude's lift layout has a logical progression from beginner to expert areas. Skiers and snowboarders easily can progress here by a choice of terrain. If you are a novice, or hovering between two levels, be sure to read the section for the ability level you are now, and the one you want to be.

Solitude Mountain Resort

Expert:★★★★ Advanced:★★★★
Intermediate:★★★★
Beginner:★★★★ Never-ever:★★★★
Number of lifts: 7–1 high-speed quad,
2 triple chairs, 4 double chairs
Snowmaking: 120 acres
Skiable acreage: 1,200
Uphill capacity: 11,200 per hour
Snowboarding: Yes
Bed base: 350; 12,000 in Salt Lake City
Resort child care: None
Nearest lodging: Slopeside, condos & hotel
Adult ticket, per day: $42-$44 (01/02)
Dining:★★★
Apres-ski/nightlife:★
Other activities:★

Summit elevation:	10,035 feet
Vertical drop:	2,047 feet
Base elevation:	7,988 feet

Address: 12000 Big Cottonwood Canyon
Solitude, UT 84121
☎ **Area code:** 801
Ski area phone: 534-1400
Snow report: 536-5777
ⓘ **Toll-free reservations:** (800) 748-4754
Fax: (435) 649-5276
E-mail: info@skisolitude.com
Internet: www.skisolitude.com

◆◆ **Expert:** Experts will like the routes off the Summit Chair. Test yourself first with the routes we describe in the Advanced section. If you think you're ready, head down the Back Door trail to Corner Chute, a steep black diamond clearly visible from the Summit chair. You might instead go into Headwall Forest, where you can pick your own line through the trees, or jump into a couple of long, steep, narrow chutes. You also can head over to Evergreen, rated a single-black diamond, but it looks mighty tough from the lift.

Another option will take you into Honeycomb Canyon, a wonderful playground for high-level skiers and boarders. Woodlawn is a marked run that follows the canyon floor. On the map it's rated black and blue. Check the grooming report before you head in: When groomed, it's a great advanced-intermediate run—otherwise, it's advanced all the way, with some gigantic mogul fields and a short but extremely steep section that looks like it might be a small waterfall in the summer.

The canyon sides are an expert's delight. From the top, traverse until you find a line you like, then go for it. You also can enter Honeycomb Canyon from the Eagle Ridge run in the main part of the ski area, but this entry is strictly double-diamond through trees. Speaking of trees, you'll find others to the left as you exit the Powderhorn chair and head down Milk Run, Middle Slope, Parachute or Cirque.

◆ **Advanced:** The Powderhorn chair has some single-black groomed screamers, such as Diamond Lane. Another lift that this ability level will like is the Summit chair. From its top, you can go one of three ways. The first takes you back down to the Summit chair base on upper-intermediate runs like Dynamite and Liberty. Eventually you'll meet the runs off the Sunrise chair, which head back to the base.

■ **Intermediate:** The Powderhorn and Eagle Express chairs have no green runs, just blue with a few black. If you're at the high end of the intermediate level, you'll like this terrain. If you're new to the intermediate level, try the Sunrise or Apex chairs.

●● **Beginner:** When skiers conquer Link, the next step is the Moonbeam II chair, where Little Dollie, Pokey Pine and Same Street will take them back down gently. Next is either the Apex or Sunrise chairs, where one green trail is surrounded by lots of blue.

● **Never-ever:** Novices start on the Link chair, a slow-moving lift that serves a nearly flat, very wide, isolated run, Easy Street.

Mountain layout–Snowboarding

Although Solitude resisted the snowboard movement for many years, riders are perfectly happy with the runs here. Solitude has more diverse expert and advanced terrain than Brighton. Snowboarders usually try to avoid Woodlawn/Honeycomb return because of the flats toward the bottom—they're just no fun as the terrain becomes travail. For that reason, riders may want to avoid Honeycomb Canyon off to the right of the Summit lift. They're fine runs, all single- or double-black, but it takes a traverse to get to them and then a runout to get to the Eagle Express lift. Any run toward the base from Eagle Ridge, above the Roundhouse, will satisfy. Take the Powder Horn chair to get there. Solitude's best collection of double-blacks is left of the Powder Horn chair—Middle Slope, Parachute and Milk Run.

Mountain rating

Solitude is one of the few resorts in the United States that has excellent terrain for all levels; however, its green slopes tend to be crowded, which some novices will find very intimidating. One disadvantage to the trail layout for some groups: If your group has skiers or riders at the opposite ends of the ability scale, you'll likely spend your day on different parts of the mountain. Intermediates can ride lifts with beginners or experts, choose different trails and meet at the bottom, but not so for beginners and experts. At the same time, beginners may find this comforting, since they don't have to worry about hotshots on their trails.

Cross-country and snowshoeing

Located at 8,700 feet between Solitude and Brighton, the **Solitude Nordic Center's Silver Lake Day Lodge** is a spectacular setting for cross-country skiing and snowshoeing. It has 20 km. of prepared trails for both classic and skating styles, plus ski and snowshoe rentals, lessons (including telemark), light snacks and guided backcountry tours. During full moons, you can do moonlight cross-country skiing. Trail passes cost $10 for ages 11 to 69, and free for older or younger skiers. A half-day pass is $7; a two-day pass is $17. For more information, call 536-5774.

Lessons (2001/02 prices)

Group lessons: $40 for two hours. All-day lessons are $60.
Never-ever package: Rentals, lift ticket and a lesson is $80.
Private lessons: $80 an hour (one to three skiers); $155 (four to six skiers).
  Special programs: For women, snowboarding, Nordic and racing, offered at various times. Call for details, 536-5730.
  Racing: Solitude has an electronically timed, side-by-side dual course on the Main Street trail, open every day, weather permitting, $1.50 per run.

Child care (2001/02 prices)

Solitude does not have any non-skiing child care.
  Children's lessons: Full day with lunch for ages 4-12 is $70; a half-day without lunch is $45. An all-day never-ever kids' package is $80.

Lift tickets (2001/02 prices)

	Adult (11–59)	Child (7–13)
One day	$44	$14
Additional days	see "Note" below	

Who skis free: Ages 6 and younger & 70 and older ski for free, but need to get a ticket at the ticket window.

Who skis at a discount: Seniors (60-69) pay $37. A beginner lift ticket, valid on the Link and Moonbeam II chairs, is $29.

Note: For multiday guests, it costs $44 for the first day and $42 for each additional day. Also, Solitude uses Ski Data Access, an electronic ticketing system that allows skiers to pay by the run, get future discounts or share a ticket with someone else. Basically, Access is geared towards locals who take a few runs a day, parents with young children (Mom and Dad share the ticket so they can switch babysitting duties), and destination guests who only want to ski or ride for a half day. The reuseable card allows you to pay for individual lift rides, sold in increments of 10. Ten rides cost $40. Radio-frequency beams deduct one ride from the card and you can use the remaining lift rides another day. Remember: Help keep ticket costs down be recycling your card when leaving the resort; drop it at any of the convenient locations resort-wide.

 Accommodations

Solitude has beautiful base-area lodging—just enough to be a full-service destination resort without the sprawl or crowds. If you like to be first on the lifts, stay here. All lodging can be booked by calling (800) 748-4754.

The newest slopeside lodging is **Eagle Springs East** ($$$–$$$$), featuring luxurious one- to three-bedroom condominiums with hand-finished furnishings, generous gourmet kitchens, comfortable living areas and balconies. Heated sidewalks surround a large outdoor heated swimming pool with a waterfall, plus a waterslide for kids of all ages. On each side of the pool are 18-person hot tubs. In addition, there's a kids' playroom with board games, a Playstation, foos-ball table, and computers with games. Just down the hall adults can play billiards or relax in the fireside lounge in the Club.

The **Inn at Solitude** ($$$$) has 46 rooms that are spacious, most with two queen beds (though kings and suites are available). All have terry-cloth robes to wear to the pool and spa, hair dryers, mini-refrigerators, TV with VCR (tape rentals are $5 a night), and daily newspaper delivery. Cost includes lift ticket, plus breakfast and dinner at St. Bernard's.

Solitude also has 18 condo units (one to three bedrooms) in a development called **Creekside at Solitude** ($$$–$$$$). The condos are spacious and well-appointed, and share an outdoor rooftop hot tub. Each unit has a private deck and fireplace, full kitchen and TV with VCR. The three-bedroom units have a jetted tub and four bathrooms, so the person sleeping on the living room sofa has a bathroom, too.

Powderhorn Lodge ($$$–$$$$), completed during the summer of 2000, is slopeside with one-, two- and three-bedroom condos. Guests can enjoy an outdoor hot tub, pool table in the lobby and access to Club Solitude, located in Eagle Springs East.

 Dining/après-ski/other activities

Dining: A very popular program is the **Solitude Yurt.** Twenty people cross-country ski or snowshoe to a yurt for a five-course gourmet meal and then ski or snowshoe back (it's a beginner trail both ways and the equipment is included in the cost). Reservations are a must for this, and don't be too disappointed if you can't get in. Salt Lake City residents really enjoy it and hog many of the available spaces. Coffee and water are the only provided beverages, but guests may bring their own corked wine and other beverages. The cost is $80, and no children younger than 8 are allowed. Call 536-5709 for reservations.

St. Bernard's is in the Inn and has a menu that leans toward Swiss and German entrées, such as wild boar stew and wienerschnitzle. The après-ski menu features an excellent cheese fondue, with generous portions of thick, European-style bread and warm cheese. Dinner for two at St. Bernard's will set you back about $100. **Creekside**, which is on the first floor of the Creekside condos, serves breakfast, lunch and dinner with much of the cooking done in the wood-burning oven. Pasta and pizza large enough for two to split are its specialties. Its entrees are less expensive than St. Bernard's—about $45 for two, including drinks.

Solitude's cafeteria, **Last Chance Mining Camp**, is on two levels and can seat about 400 skiers. **Sunshine Grill** is open for lunch and features a lively grill adjacent to the best people-watching on the mountain, affectionately called "the beach." Another place for a quick bite is the **Stone Haus** in the village or the **Thirsty Squirrel,** which serves items such as panini, nachos and pizza.

Après-ski: The "new" **Thirsty Squirrel** opened during the summer of 2001. Resort staff assures us its ambiance is much like its predecessor, right down to the pool table, widescreen TV and local beer sold by the pitcher. There's also a beer bar at the **Last Chance Mining Camp** in the day lodge.

Other activities: The Inn at Solitude has a full-service **health and fitness spa** with a workout room, sauna, facials, massages and more.

Brighton Ski Resort

Mountain layout–Skiing

◆◆ **Expert ◆ Advanced:** Brighton regulars refer to the "Majestic" side, served by the Majestic and other chairs, and the "Millicent" side, served by the Millicent and Evergreen chairs. If avoiding lower-level skiers and boarders is your goal, stay on the Millicent side with fewer greens and blues than Majestic.

But don't miss the Majestic side, either. Experts should try a short but heart-stopping run called Hard Coin off the Snake Creek Express. The trees are so thick you can hardly pick a line, but it's a marked trail. Most of the advanced runs on the Majestic side are under the Great Western quad. From its summit one can see the Great Salt Lake and Mt. Timpanogos, home of the Sundance Ski Resort. For moguls, try Rockin'R under Great Western, or Ziggy under Snake Creek. Clark's Roost and Rein's Run are the toughest in-bounds descents.

■ **Intermediate:** Intermediates have the run of practically the whole area. The Majestic side is more heavily wooded but with gentler pitches, while the Millicent side is a bit steeper, but with fewer trees. The Elk Park Ridge run descends 1,745 feet, summit to base, from the Great Western chair.

●● **Beginner:** Good beginner runs descend from the Majestic chair, and from the Snake Creek Express, which goes to the top of the mountain. Beginners should keep an eye out so they don't get onto an intermediate trail: Greens and blues do a lot of intertwining here.

● **Never-ever:** Brighton has a stellar reputation as the place where Utah skiers learn. The Explorer chair serves a gentle slope apart from general traffic.

Brighton Facts

Summit elevation:	**10,500 feet**	Number of lifts: 7–3 high-speed quads,	

Summit elevation: **10,500 feet**
Vertical drop: **1,745 feet**
Base elevation: **8,755 feet**
Address: Star Route
Brighton, UT 84121
✆ Area code: 801
Ski area phone: 532-4731
Snow report: 532-4731
ⓘ Toll-free information: (800) 873-5512
Internet: www.brightonresort.com
Expert:★★ Advanced:★★★
Intermediate:★★★★
Beginner:★★★★
Never-ever:★★★★

Number of lifts: 7–3 high-speed quads,
1 triple chair, 3 double chairs
Snowmaking: 25 percent
Skiable acreage: 850
Uphill capacity: 11,500+ per hour
Snowboarding: Yes
Bed base: About 50; 12,000 in Salt Lake City
Resort child care: No
Nearest lodging: Walking distance
Adult ticket, per day: $39 (2002/03)

Dining:★★
Apres-ski/nightlife:★
Other Activities: ★

Mountain layout—Snowboarding

Even skilled snowboarders like to avoid runouts because they're tedius and tough to navigate when they flatten out. Thankfully Brighton doesn't have runouts below its excellent riding terrain, so there's no problem. Hotshot riders spend their time on the Millicent side, where you'll find fewer lower-level riders and the most diverse terrain. Expert and advanced riders can go for the Great Western quad, or for the trees off the Snake Creek Express. Clark's Roost and Rein's Run, off Great Western, are the toughest in-bounds descents. Brighton has an open-boundaries policy, which means experts can head into the backcountry as they wish, just don't go alone. The resort also has two halfpipes and a terrain park that attract topnotch tricksters like flies to honey.

Brighton has a stellar reputation as the place where Utah snowboarders learn. The Explorer chair serves a gentle slope apart from general traffic. With Brighton's abundance of beginner and intermediate terrain, it's an excellent mountain for learning to link those turns. Start off the Explorer chair—busy speeders stay elsewhere on the mountain, so you can practice without looking over your shoulder all the time. Head next to the gentle runs off the Majestic chair. Once you have some confidence, go for the top of the Snake Creek Express. You'll be on top of the world. There are some nice green runs from both chairs.

Mountain rating

Good for beginners, excellent for intermediates and very good for advanced skiers and snowboarders. Brighton has a bit of true expert terrain, but it is not nearly as extensive as the other Cottonwood Canyons resorts. We recommend that out-of-state visitors head into the backcountry only if they are with a local guide.

Lift tickets (2002/03 prices)

Ages 11 to 69 pay $39. Brighton does not sell multiday tickets. Twilight tickets are available when lifts are running into the evening. Brighton also has about 200 acres of night skiing every day except Sunday.

Dining: $$$–Entrees $20+; $$–$10-20; $–less than $10.
Accommodations: (double room) $$$$–$200+; $$$–$141-$200; $$–$81-$140; $–$80 and less.

Who skis free: Ages 10 and younger, two children per paying adult with no restrictions or blackout dates.

Who skis at a discount: Ages 70 and older pay $10. A beginner lift pass, good on two lifts, is $25. A single-ride ticket is $8. Night skiing and riding costs $20–$35, depending on the number of hours.

Lessons (2002/03 prices)

Group lessons: $26 for two hours, also offered at night (at night, the lift ticket is included). "The Works" package includes a group lesson, all-day ticket and all-day rentals for $70 for skiers and snowboarders.

Never-ever package: Includes a full day of rentals, beginner lift ticket and a group lesson—$55 for skiing and snowboarding.

Private lessons: $60 per hour, with each additional person $20.

Special programs: Includes clinics for women, Burton Method Center Learn-to-Ride, seniors, telemark, adaptive and advanced technique. Inquire at the ski and snowboard school.

Child Care (2002/03 prices)

Brighton does not have non-skiing child care.

Children's lessons: Ages 4 to 7 get 1.75-hour lessons for $30 without equipment, $40 with equipment. A full day with lunch is $70.

Accommodations

The **Brighton Lodge** (800-873-5512 or 532-4731; $–$$) is small, cozy, has a Jacuzzi and is at the base of the lifts. **Das Alpen Haus** (649-0565; $$–$$$) is a charming B&B near the base of Brighton. Each of the four suites is named for a Swiss ski resort, and the atmosphere is Swiss Alpine. **Mt. Majestic Properties** (888-236-0667) rents a tremendous selection of cabins right on the Brighton Circle with the easiest access to the resort.

Getting there and getting around

By air and train: Salt Lake City is a major transportation hub, so flights are numerous. Amtrak also serves the city.

By car: Solitude and Brighton are about 23 miles southeast of Salt Lake City in Big Cottonwood Canyon on State Hwy. 190. The most direct route from the airport is east on I-80, south on I-215, Exit 6 to Wasatch Blvd., then follow the signs to Solitude and Brighton.

Getting around: You can ride the Utah Transit Authority ski buses for $4 from downtown or $1.50 from the park-and-ride at the canyon's mouth (exact fare is required). Or, take a Lewis Brothers SkiExpress van ($22 roundtrip from downtown; call 359-8677). During the day, UTA buses run between Solitude and Brighton for $1.

If you don't like to eat at the same place twice, or you like nightlife, we recommend staying in Salt Lake City. There is no public transportation at night between Salt Lake City and the canyon.

Grand Targhee

Wyoming

Summit elevation:	11,477 feet
Vertical drop:	3,477 feet
Base elevation:	8,000 feet

Address: P.O. Box SKI, Alta, WY 83422
✆ **Area code:** 307
Ski area phone: 353-2300
Fax: 353-8148
Toll-free snow report:
(800) TARGHEE (827-4433)
ⓘ **Toll-free reservations:**
(800) TARGHEE (827-4433)
E-mail: info@grandtarghee.com
Internet: www.grandtarghee.com
Expert:★★★★★
Advanced:★★★★★
Intermediate:★★★★
Beginner:★★   **Never-ever:**★★

Number of lifts: 5—2 high-speed quads,
1 quad, 1 double, 1 magic carpet
Snowmaking: None
Skiable acreage: 2,000 lift-served acres
Snowboarding: Yes
Bed Base: 432 pillows (96 lodging units)
Nearest lodging: Slopeside, hotel and condos
Resort child care: Yes, 2 months and older
Adult ticket, per day: $46–$49 (02/03)

Dining:★★★
Apres-ski/nightlife:★
Other activities:★

If you like to ski or snowboard in powder but can't afford a heli-trip, Grand Targhee is the next best thing. About 500 inches of snow falls here each winter, and when it does, Targhee's groomers don't exactly work overtime. You gotta love a ski resort that designates beginner, intermediate and advanced *powder* areas on its trail map.

Did we scare away those of you who still flounder in fluff? Don't flip the page yet. This is one of the two best lift-served resorts in America for learning powder skiing (ironically, Alta, UT, is the other; Grand Targhee's address is Alta, WY). The trouble with powder at other resorts is you usually find it only on the steepest slopes, and it's tough to get a feel for loose snow when you're also struggling with the pitch. Grand Targhee leaves powder on some of its gentle rolling terrain, too, so anyone who wants to conquer powder will never have a better chance. If you are an intermediate, rent a pair of fat skis and cut loose. If you really don't want to deal with powder, Targhee grooms a few paths from the top of each lift.

The Sacajawea high-speed quad takes you to 500 acres of terrain on Peaked Mountain that could previously only be reached by snowcat. About a third of this terrain is groomed, the rest is pristine glade skiing and open bowls that are left untouched for freshies. Better yet, on adverse weather days, Peaked Mountain provides protection from the wind and low clouds.

The best part of this powder paradise is you won't have to share their fresh pillowy snow with the masses, because this resort is grandly isolated. Grand Targhee is in Wyoming, but the only way to get here is through Idaho. Its huge bowls of snow are on the western slope of the Tetons, which hug the border between the two states.

Targhee was the name of a local peacekeeping Indian chief who lived in the area more than 100 years ago. (You'll see his portrait painted on one of the buildings.) Grand comes from the 13,770-foot Grand Teton Peak. From here, you can see the peak's less photographed but equally impressive west face.

When Averell Harriman was scouting for his dream resort in the 1930s, he narrowed the search to Targhee and the site that became Sun Valley. Local ranchers and farmers opened Targhee as a ski resort about 30 years ago. Targhee is close to ranch country, and many of its employees herd cattle or grow potatoes in the snowless months. A good number have never lived anywhere else. Though not talkative, they are quite friendly.

No ski area is perfect for everyone, however. If you go stir-crazy without a variety of restaurants and other things to do, we suggest you stay in Jackson and spend one day of your vacation here. But if you'd like to completely unwind, ski during the day, read a good book at night and head home new and invigorated, this is the place.

Mountain layout—Skiing

◆◆ **Expert ◆ Advanced:** Targhee has two mountains: 1,500-acre Fred's Mountain, which is lift-served, and Peaked Mountain, which now has 500 acres of lift-served terrain and another 1,000 acres of snowcat skiing. Experienced powderhounds will want to exercise the latter option. Ten skiers per snowcat, with two guides, head out to enjoy this snowy playground. The longest run is 3.2 miles and covers slightly more than 2,800 vertical.

The lift-served 500 acres on Peaked has glades, bowls and some groomed runs. While we haven't had a chance to check out the new area, we're sure you'll want to take the time to do it.

■ **Intermediate:** As we said earlier, your best bet is to rent fat skis and head to the intermediate or beginner powder areas marked on the trail map. On Fred's Mountain, three chair lifts serve high, broad descents mostly above treeline. Fred's has excellent cruiser runs and good bump slopes. Targhee doesn't have enough skiers per acre to make bumps, so the groomers make their own on the Big Thunder run. Widely spaced and perfectly symmetrical, they are excellent for beginning mogul skiers and those whose knees can't take the pounding of skier-made bumps. There is also tree skiing here and there. The resort grooms about one-third of the runs; the rest is left to accumulate powder. About 80 percent of the lift-served 500 acres on Peaked is for intermediates, including some groomed runs, bowls and glades.

●● **Beginner ● Never-ever:** Targhee has a small area of groomed beginner runs at its base, served by a magic carpet. We used to steer never-evers away from here, suggesting they learn elsewhere. However, the resort has built some fun rollers and other terrain features designed for teaching to make the learning experience more enjoyable.

Mountain layout—Snowboarding

So you want to ride the deep stuff… I mean the really deep stuff, but you can't afford heli gas? No problem, head to Grand Targhee, the thrifty powder hound's choice. Powder, powder, powder…this place is all about powder. Where else can you ride where the grooming policy on a powder day is to plow three lanes down the mountain for people who get stuck to get out?

Targhee has two mountains: 1,500 acres of lift-served terrain on Fred's Mountain, and 500 acres of lift-served and another 1,000 acres of snowcat riding on Peaked Mountain. Experienced powder hounds will want to take advantage of the snowcat riding. Ten riders per snowcat, with two guides, head out to enjoy this snowy playground. The longest run is 3.2 miles and covers slightly more than 2,800 vertical.

If you can't do the snowcat trip, don't fret—it's all good! Check the access gate to Mary's Nipple and you'll be more than happy. Hike up to the top and drop in for some 40-degree madness, or pick from your choice of doable cliffs (10- to 100-foot-plus) off the back side of the mountain. You'll have to hike back in if you opt for the cliffs. The lift-served 500 acres on Peaked has glades, bowls and some groomed runs. While we haven't had a chance to check out the new area, we're sure you'll want to take the time to do it.

Intermediates have 1,200 acres of powder for riding. What else do you want? Targhee has a small area of groomed beginner runs at its base, served by a magic carpet. For first-time snowboarders, Grand Targhee is one of the best places to learn. Where else can you learn how to ride without getting a single bruise?

Mountain rating

Great for intermediates and above. Superb for learning powder skiing or snowboarding. Beginners and first-time skiers have limited terrain. New teaching features have improved the learning experience to make it more fun. It's perfect for first-time snowboarders, partly because loads of snow makes for soft landings and partly because snowboards are made to float. Targhee usually gets double their famous neighbor Jackson Hole's amount in snowfall. And with days where there are maybe 200 people on the mountain, and 2-plus feet of powder, it's worth every dime.

Cross-country and snowshoeing

Grand Targhee Nordic Center has 15 km. of track groomed for touring and skating. The trails wind through varied terrain, offering beautiful vistas of the Greater Yellowstone area as well as meadows and aspen glades. Trail passes are $8 a day; $5 for a senior or child; children 5 and younger ski free.

The ski school teaches telemarking as well as touring and skating techniques. Group lessons are $38 and private lessons $62 an hour.

A snowshoe tour focuses on wildlife, with the guide pointing out tracks and explaining how animals survive the winter. This tour is free; snowshoe rentals are available for $16 for the day.

Lessons (2002/03 prices)

Many instructors have been with the Ski Training Center since its first season in 1969.

Group lessons: 38 for adults, at 10 a.m. and 1 p.m.

Never-ever package: A lift-lesson-equipment package costs $59. If a friend brings a beginner to the Ski School for this package, the friend gets a full-day ticket free of charge.

Private lessons: $62 an hour, $30 for each additional person.

Special programs: The resort has several special clinics such as Extreme Skiing, Women Ski The Tetons, snowboarding and telemark. Call for details and prices.

Child care [2002/03 prices]

Ages: 2 months to 7 years.

Costs: Kids 2 months to 2 years cost $45 per day, $33 per half day. Ages 3 to 5, day care only, is $42 per day, $30 per half day. The program includes two snacks and lunch for the full day, a snack for half day.

Reservations: Required; call (800) TARGHEE (827-4433). Babysitting services are available outside of regular day care; ask at the lodge front desk.

Children's lessons: Ski programs for ages 3–5 are $48 for a half day, $69 for a full day, with lessons, lifts, lunch and day-care activities. Ages 6 and older are $35 for a half-day; $68 for a full day, with lessons and lunch, but not lift ticket.

Lift tickets [2002/03 prices]

	Adult	Child (6-14)
One day	$49	$31
Three days	$141 ($47/day)	$93 ($31/day)
Five days	$230 ($46/day)	$155 ($31/day)

Who skis free: Ages 5 and younger.

Who skis at a discount: Those who ski more than one day at Grand Targhee probably are staying here too. In those cases Targhee's lodging-lift packages are the most economical and practical. On all Targhee lodging packages, children ages 14 and younger stay and ski free, one child per paying adult. Ages 62 and older ski at children's prices.

Note: A full day of snowcat skiing, including lunch, snacks and beverages served in a Snowcat Skiing souvenir mug, is $299, half day is $225. Here's a great deal: Book a three-day or longer package stay from opening (mid-November) through Dec. 24, 2002, and get a free day of snowcat skiing; on a seven-day package, you'll get two days on the cat free.

Accommodations

The village sleeps about 450 people at **two hotel-type lodges and a 32-unit, multistory condo building.** All are within an easy walk to lifts and base facilities. Most units come packaged with lift tickets, though you can rent the rooms and condos without buying lift tickets (though frankly, we have no idea why you'd want to). Nightly rates per room at the lodges run $69 to $181, at the condos $192 to $371.

Packages that include ski tickets and two group lessons are offered for seven nights and six days, five nights and four days, and three nights and three days. Value Season for 2002/03 include November through mid-December, January, and late March through mid-April, where you'll save 30 to 40 percent. If you book a package from opening day to mid-December, not only will you get 30 to 40 percent off, you'll also get the free snowcat skiing described in the Lift Ticket section.

For the hotel and motel rooms, regular season (February and March) packages per person for two people range from $324 to $390 for three days and three nights, $495 to $570 for five nights and four days, and $680 to $795 for seven nights and six days. For the Sioux 2-bedroom condos (there also are loft studio condos that sleep up to four), regular-season packages per person for four people are $440 for three days and three nights, $665 for five nights and four days, and $902 for seven nights and six days. Call (800) 827-4433 (800-TARGHEE) for information.

Dining

There's not much variety in this small village, but there's a lot of quality.
Targhee Steakhouse ($$–$$$) is Targhee's finest restaurant, with entrées such as rack of lamb, whiskey chicken, shrimp scampi and poached salmon. It also serves breakfast and lunch. **Snorkel's** ($) is the spot for great gourmet pizza and pasta with fun and games for the family. Breakfast here features sinful pastries and espressos. **Wild Bill's Grill** ($) in the Rendezvous Lodge has breakfast, pizza, a soup and salad bar, sandwiches and Mexican food. The **Trap Bar** ($) serves a fine Idaho potato with all the trimmings, basic grilled sandwiches, burgers and chicken, plus après-ski snacks.

Après-ski/nightlife/other activities

This is not Targhee's strong point. **Snorkel's** has après-ski with varietal wines by the glass, microbrew beers and upscale appetizers in a relaxed atmosphere.
The **Trap Bar** is livelier, with live music. Otherwise, outdoor activities include a **heated swimming pool** and **hot tubs**, a **tubing park** ($8 per hour) and an **ice skating rink** (rental skates are $5; use of the rink is free). You can take a **sleigh ride** or go **snowmobiling**. **Dinner sleigh rides** cost about $32 for adults and $15 for kids. **Shopping** is limited to one boutique, a small general store, a hard-goods shop, snowboard shop, rental and ski repair shop, and a ski clothing shop. At the **Spa at Grand Targhee**, you can indulge in a massage, herbal or mud wrap, sauna or aromatherapy session. Or settle in to watch **complimentary movies**.

Getting there and getting around

By air: Targhee is served by airports in Jackson, Wyoming, and Idaho Falls, Idaho. Jets fly into both airports and resort shuttles pick up guests by reservation. Five major carriers now serve Jackson Hole with jets: American, United, Northwest, Delta and Continental. There's non-stop daily service from Salt Lake City, Denver, Chicago, Minneapolis and Houston, plus weekend non-stop service from Atlanta and Newark. You can rent cars at either airport.

By car: Targhee is just inside the Wyoming border on the west side of the Tetons, accessible only from Idaho. From Jackson, follow signs to Wilson on Hwy. 22, then go north on Hwy. 33 at Victor, Idaho. Turn east at Driggs (the sign is on the roof of a building), and drive 12 miles to the ski area. About 8 miles from Driggs, you'll start to suspect you're lost, but keep going—you can't make a wrong turn. Coming from Idaho Falls, take Hwy. 20 to Rexburg, and turn east on Hwy. 33 to Driggs. Grand Targhee is 42 miles northwest of Jackson, 87 miles northeast of Idaho Falls and 297 miles north of Salt Lake City.

Getting around: If you are spending your entire vacation at Grand Targhee, don't rent a car—there's nowhere to drive. If you stay in Jackson, we recommend you ride the Targhee Express bus that picks up in Jackson and at Teton Village. It's $61 for round trip and full-day lift pass; call 733-3135. The highway between Jackson and Grand Targhee is steep going over Teton Pass (up to 10-percent grade). We caution against staying at Targhee and driving to Jackson for the nightlife—if you want Jackson's nightlife, stay there.

Dining: $$$–Entrees $20+; $$–$10-20; $–less than $10.
Accommodations: (double room) $$$$–$200+; $$$–$141-$200; $$–$81-$140; $–$80 and less.

Jackson Hole

Wyoming

Summit elevation: 10,450 feet
Vertical drop: 4,139 feet
Base elevation: 6,311 feet

Address: P.O. Box 290
Teton Village, WY 83025
☎ Area code: 307
Ski area phone: 733-2292
Toll-free snow report:
(888) 333-7766 (DEEP-SNO)
ⓘ **Toll-free reservations:**
(800) 443-6931 **Fax:** 733-2660
E-mail: info@jacksonhole.com
Internet: www.jacksonhole.com (resort)
www.jacksonholetraveler.com (region)
Expert:★★★★★ **Advanced:**★★★★★
Intermediate:★★★★
Beginner:★★
Never-ever:★★★★

Number and types of lifts: 10–1 aerial tram, 1
eight-person gondola, 2 high-speed quads, 4
quads, 1 triple, 1 double
Skiable acreage: 2,500 acres
Snowmaking: 11 percent
Uphill capacity: 12,000+ per hour
Snowboarding: Yes, unlimited
Bed base: 10,000 in valley, 2,500 at base
Nearest lodging: Slopeside
Resort child care: Yes, 2 months and older
Adult ticket, per day: $56–$61 (02/03 price)

Dining:★★★
Apres-ski/nightlife:★★★
Other activities:★★★★★

Take your average Western ski resort, put it on steroids, and you're at Jackson Hole. The slopes are steeper, with more than half the runs rating a well-deserved black- or double-black-diamond designation. The runs are longer, including the 4,139 vertical feet covered by its infamous aerial Tram. And the views are more astonishing.

The base area, Teton Village, is almost complete, with only one hotel left to finish constructing. It now offers everything you might need, including a grocery and liquor store. From what must be the cheapest slopeside lodging in the states, at Hostel X, to the posh Snake River Lodge and Spa, to a multitude of condos, you can find lodging that meets your needs and your budget. Add in restaurants serving everything from burgers to sushi to wild game, and a smattering of nightlife, and you could easily spend your vacation right here.

But wait, the town of Jackson, 12 miles down the road, is worth visiting for at least an afternoon or two. Here you'll find a wide range of lodging at off-season rates, a wealth of restaurants, outfitters for snowmobile and dogsledding trips to nearby hot springs or Yellowstone or Grand Teton National Parks, galleries and shops galore and one of the prettiest town squares anywhere, defined by elk antler gateway arches.

Mountain layout—Skiing

No mistake about it. Jackson Hole is a skier's and rider's mountain—not for the feint of heart or the weak of quads. It's steep, often deep, the trees are tight and most skiers would have it no other way. The resort has two mountains: Apres Vous Mountain is best known for its groomed intermediate cruisers as well as the black Saratoga Bowl. Rendezvous Mountain has a handful of groomed runs; most of the blues here would be blacks anywhere else. As you ride the chairs or tram, you'll see skiers and riders hucking themselves off cliffs, snaking clean lines through seemingly impenetrable trees and treating gigunda moguls as mere debris in the trail. You'll also sense an attitude of superiority. Ignore it, or rise to the occasion.

If you've got a group of five or six, hire a guide as few of the mountain's prizes appear on the trail map. For even more thrills, head out-of-bounds, but only with the proper equipment. Remember: The trail map is only a guide to what's available; don't expect to find trails such as Dog Leg or Elephant Tree or areas such as the Liquor Cabinet on it. If you rely on the map, you're going to be frustrated, and your skiing experience will be unfulfilled.

◆◆ **Expert:** Fully half of Jackson Hole's 2,500 acres is marked with one or two black diamonds. It's no wonder the area has a reputation for steep, exciting skiing. Board the big red tram for the 12-minute rise to the top of Rendezvous Mountain. Once at the top, you have two choices. In one direction is the infamous Corbet's Couloir, a narrow, rocky passage that requires a 10- to 20-foot airborne entry. No thanks? Take the "easier" way down, Rendezvous Bowl. Conditions here can vary from mild to intimidating. We've seen waist-high bumps, knee-deep powder, easy gliding, and, Egad! breakable crust and crud. It's not groomed, so be prepared for anything. You can always ride the tram back down or take the guided tour, offered on the hour. Corbet's Cabin, at the Summit, provides a warm, dry place to make your decisions; snacks and restrooms are available.

Below the bowl, drop into Cheyenne Bowl or Cheyenne Woods, hit the bumps on Bivouac, and find your way into the Liquor Cabinet. Or continue down Rendezvous Trail until you see the access for the Hobacks. The Hobacks deliver steep, continuous fall-line skiing to the mountain's base. For the most part, if you can see it, you can ski it; you just have to figure out how to get there. Our best advice is to befriend a local or hire a guide.

You can access all the terrain below Rendezvous Bowl from the Sublette Quad. This lift also accesses the Cirque and, with a 15- to 20-minute climb, the Headwall. Or, try Dog Face and Bird in the Hand to the Dog Leg or veer off Pepi's Run into the Alta Chutes.

Jackson Hole opens its gates to unpatrolled backcountry for the season. The resort offers backcountry camps to teach proper skiing. It's worth it—participants get to ride early tram.

◆ **Advanced:** Advanced skiers can handle the tram runs, but before you jump aboard, test your skills on the dotted-blue-line runs in ungroomed Casper Bowl, Cheyenne Bowl or Amphitheater Bowl—all are shorter versions of the stuff you'll encounter off the tram. Think twice before venturing into the Hobacks: Once you're in, the only way out is ski to the base.

Rendezvous Trail and Grand let skiers play with jumping off the trail and skiing what they can see. On Apres Vous Mountain, St. Johns, Teewinot Face and Secret Slope are worth finding. Plunge into Saratoga Bowl, but veer skier's right as you head down or you'll have an awful traverse, perhaps even a hike, out. The terrain between Casper chair and Apres Vous is also fun: Try Sleeping Indian and Wide Open or hop into Moran Woods for a shot of trees.

■ **Intermediate:** Remember that 50 percent of that 2,500 acres is *not* black diamond. Even better, most of the tough stuff is completely separate from the easier runs—intermediates seldom have to worry about getting in over their heads. Stay on Apres Vous Mountain, with 2,170 vertical feet of terrain, and Casper Bowl, with its wide intermediate runs, sprinkled with a few advanced runs. Be forewarned that the Amphitheater, a major trail merge zone, would earn a black diamond on most other mountains. Ditto for Rendezvous Trail, off the Sublette Quad. Follow the solid blue lines for groomed terrain and the broken blue lines for ungroomed powder or bumps. If you're willing to ski ungroomed stuff, you'll run out of gas before you run out of terrain. Complimentary orientation tours for intermediate-level skiers depart the Mountain Host building daily at 9:30 a.m.

●● **Beginner:** Begin on the Eagle's Rest chair then move to the Teewinot Quad; both access Jackson Hole's easiest terrain. It's a big step from those gently undulating green-circle slopes to Jackson Hole's blues. Although the upper parts of Apres Vous and all of Casper Bowl are wide and groomed, they have a much steeper pitch than blues at other resorts, enough to intimidate many lower-level skiers. Our advice is to take a lesson or two to help with the tougher terrain. The resort has a program just for you (*see Lessons*).

● **Never-ever:** One surprise at Jackson Hole is its excellent learning terrain. The base of Apres Vous mountain has a fenced-in area, called Fort Wyoming, below the East's Rest Cut-off and the base area. It's served by a magic carpet. Faster skiers can't get in, so those just learning won't get nervous. Parents should take note that Jackson Hole's "Rough Riders" kids offering combines day care and children's instruction in one of the most innovative programs for young "never-evers" we have seen.

 ## Mountain layout—Snowboarding

If you've ever seen the surf movie, "The North Shore," where a kid who surfs in an Arizona wave pool moves to the North Shore of Waikiki to surf some of the hairiest waves in the world, then you're on your way to understanding how gnarly Jackson Hole really is. If you've only ridden in the East, or even some of the tamer mountains in Colorado, and you show up in Jackson, you're in for a BIG surprise.

Fully half of Jackson Hole's 2,500 acres is marked with one or two black diamonds, and with the mountain's no-rope-out-of-bounds clause, you can add the sickest off-resort backcountry riding available anywhere in the continental U.S. If you're not prepared, or experienced, there is an enormous probability of getting seriously hurt or killed, so be careful.

For a quick assessment of your skills, take the tram up the mountain for your first run. You'll quickly discover how good you really are. For the Hollywood huckers, there's Corbet's Couloir, a narrow passage that requires a 5- to 20-foot airborne entry into a usually tracked, steep mogul field. No way? Then consider the even more infamous S & S Chute or take the "easier" way down—Rendezvous Bowl, a huge face littered with gigantic moguls, bushes, rocks and, if you're lucky, powder. Follow that down to the Sublette chair and continue on to Dick's Ditch, or go to The Hobacks for some seriously ill powder on your way back to the base. If you've made it down on your first run without any fear, burning legs or slough slides, then move here now. You'll never be happy riding anywhere else—except maybe Alaska.

Most of the tough stuff is completely separate from the easier runs—intermediates seldom have to worry about getting in over their heads, which in this case is a very, very good thing. Apres Vous on it's own could hold itself as a very strong freeriding mountain, which is why you'll find the halfpipe over here, along with various hits and kickers built by the locals. We don't recommend building your own kickers, if you're busted, they'll pull your ticket. There are natural booters and kickers all over the place; try following some local riders around for the inside line. Don't miss Upper Dick's Ditch with a natural quarterpipe and halfpipe.

The base of Apres Vous has a fenced-in, beginner area, called Fort Wyoming, below the East's Rest Cutoff and the base area. It's served by a "Magic Carpet" moving sidewalk. Faster boarders can't get in, so those just learning won't get nervous.

Mountain rating

While there is an excellent learning area, it's a huge leap from the beginner trails off the Teewinot Lift to the intermediate trails on Apres-Vous. Beginners might want to head somewhere else after just learning to ski. Intermediates will find plenty of cruising terrain and lots to stretch their abilities. Advanced and expert skiers will quickly know that they have arrived in a heaven of sorts.

 ## Cross-country and snowshoeing

Jackson Hole has some of the most beautiful natural surroundings in the United States. Nordic skiers can strike out for marked trails in **Grand Teton or Yellowstone National Parks,** or try one of the five touring centers near Jackson and Grand Targhee. Trail passes generally are $10 or less for adults.

The **Saddlehorn Activities Center** (739-2629 or 800-443-6139) serves as the hub of the Nordic systems in Teton Village with 17 km. of groomed track. Because it is next to the downhill ski area, it has telemark lessons as an option. Rentals, full-day beginner group lessons, half-day lessons for other levels and private instruction are available, as are guided excursions into the backcountry of Grand Teton National Park. Trail fee is $10 for adults, and $5 for children and seniors. You can exchange your alpine lift ticket for a Nordic trail pass on the same day of purchase, so you can alpine ski in the morning and cross-country or snowshoe in the afternoon. Dog-sledding trips also are based here.

Other touring centers are **Spring Creek**, 20 km. with some fairly steep hills (733-8833 or 800-443-6139); **Teton Pines**, 14 km. of groomed skating and classic lanes on a golf course (733-1005 or 800-238-2223); and **Cowboy Village at Togwotee** (543-2847 or 800-543-2847), where trail fees are donated and you need your own equipment unless you're their guest.

 ## Lessons (2002/03 prices)

The ski/snowboard school is not only the place to get instruction, but it is also the place to engage a mountain guide. Jackson Hole's nooks and crannies can best be enjoyed with someone who knows them. To make reservations for any program including mountain guides call 739-2610 locally or (800) 450-0477.

Group lessons: Lessons cost $65 for a full day. Half day in the afternoon is $60 (beginner, with lift ticket) or $70 (intermediate, with lift ticket). Afternoon semi-private three-person groups are $85. A class with a max of four students is $85. Jackson Hole has a "Greens to Blues" class for those bored by the beginner trails but intimidated by the blues, for $70.

Never-ever package: Jackson Hole's Learn To Turn program is $65 and includes a guarantee that learners will be able to control speed and make turns after one day of lessons. Beginners can repeat these lessons for free until they "get it." For snowboarders, the resort offers Burton's innovative Learn-To-Ride program.

Private lessons: Normally given in a three-hour morning lesson. Three a.m. hours cost $290 and three p.m. hours are $255 for up to five skiers. Early "Tram Privates" start at 8:30 a.m. with four hours costing $345; a full day is $455 (the same as hiring a backcountry guide).

Special programs: There are many, such as instruction for the disabled (adaptive lessons questions are answered via a special adaptive hotline during the season), Backcountry Experience ($20 for four hours), Backcountry Camp ($500, three-day program), and Wild West Camps for ski and race, women ski, women snowboard, and steep & deep (separate ski and snowboard). These multi-day camps include coaching lifts, video, some meals and more.

Racing: There's a NASTAR course off the Casper Bowl Triple Chair. The resort offers race-training clinics for $220 for four-hour programs.

Child care (2002/03 prices)

Ages: 2 months to 6 years.

Costs: $90 for a full day and $65 a half day. Toddlers get lunch and a snack; parents must provide food for infants.

Reservations: Required, call 739-2691. Bring your child's immunization records. Kids Ranch children's programs are based at the Cody House, just above the gondola base.

Other options: For babysitting at your hotel or condo, call **Babysitting Service of Jackson Hole**, 733-0685 or (800) 253-9650; or **Childcare Services**, 733-5178. These services, members of the Jackson Hole Chamber of Commerce, have sitters trained in first aid and child CPR. **Baby's Away** (888-616-8495; 733-0387) rents and will deliver baby needs to your lodge, such as crib, stroller, car seat and toys.

Children's lessons: Rough Riders is for ages 3-6 and includes lift tickets. A full day is $90; half day is $65. Explorers (ages 7-14) is $99 for full day with lift ticket and lunch, $90 full day with lunch, $65 half-day lesson only. Team Extreme (ages 12-17) is a full-day program for advanced skiers and riders. It includes lift ticket and lunch for $99.

Lift tickets (2002/03 prices)

	Adult	Young Adult (15-21)	Child (Up to 14)
One day	$61	$48	$31
Three days	$174 ($57/day)	$131 ($44+/day)	$87 ($29+/day)
Five days	$280 ($56/day)	$210 ($42/day)	$140 ($28/day)

Who skis free: No one.

Who skis at a discount: Ages 65 and older ski at children's prices. Beginners pay a minimal lift ticket fee for the beginner lifts. Note: A photo ID is required to obtain young adult and senior rates.

Note: Jackson Hole's ticket includes all lifts.

Nearby resorts

The **Snow King Ski Area**—half the cost of Jackson Hole—is in downtown Jackson, about 12 miles from Jackson Hole Ski Resort. Sixty percent of its 400 acres is rated advanced, thanks to a north-facing slope that plunges 1,571 feet. It doesn't have a lot of green-rated terrain, primarily a catwalk that traverses the mountain from the summit to the base. Because it is so steep, always shaded and often icy, locals call it "Eastern skiing out West." This small town area is a great practice hill with a steep consistent pitch. Lift tickets for adults are $32; for kids ages 14 and younger and seniors 60 and older, $22. The hill is open for night skiing Tuesday through Saturday. You can buy a two-hour ticket for $15. Snow King's Web site is at www.snowking.com; e-mail is snowking@wyoming.com. SnowKing also has a multi-lane tubing park open weekdays from 4 to 8 p.m. and weekends noon to 8 p.m. The cost is $10 per hour for adults; $7 for kids.

Accommodations

Choose from three locations: Teton Village at the base of the slopes, with fewer restaurants and nightlife options; the town of Jackson, with lots of eating, shopping and partying, but 12 miles from skiing; or hotels, condos and a few fine resorts between the two. Shuttle buses connect the town and the ski area.

Call **Jackson Hole Central Reservations** (800-443-6931) for more information. This agency can book your entire trip, from airline tickets to activities. Other booking agencies are **Vacations Incorporated** (800-228-1025) or **Rocky Mountain Reservations** (800-322-5766). Too many hotels here have combined "Jackson Hole" with "Inn," "Lodge" or "Hotel." Another popular name is "Teton." When booking pay attention to the exact name and the location, or ground transportation could easily drop you and your luggage in the wrong place.

Teton Village

The following properties are all within steps of the slopes and each other, so the choice is on facilities or price rather than location. Most of these properties have ski packages.

Snake River Lodge & Spa (800-445-4655; $$$-$$$$) is just steps from the tram and gondola, the lodge includes a five-story spa with indoor-outdoor pool, whirlpools and water-falls; separate men's and women's spa floors, his with huge whirlpool tub with large-screen TV, hers with fireplaced lounge, both with therapy showers and hydro tubs. A full array of spa services is offered. Double rooms to three-bedroom suites are available.

The Bavarian-style **Alpenhof** (800-732-3244; 733-3242; $$-$$$$) is the closest lodg-ing to the lifts. It has an outstanding dining room. The casual Bistro, open for lunch and dinner, is also popular for apres-ski; snag an outdoor table in spring. Some of the 42 guest rooms have fireplaces. The hotel has a heated outdoor pool, Jacuzzi and sauna.

The Best Western Inn at Jackson Hole (800-842-7666; 733-2311; $$-$$$$) is conve-nient and slopeside, but showing its age. Rooms are spacious, and many have kitchenettes, fireplaces and/or lofts. Soundproofing between rooms is awful; you can eavesdrop on conver-sations in the rooms next door. It has two restaurants, a heated outdoor pool and hot tub. Exterior corridors mean that every time you leave your room, you step outside.

The Hostel X (733-3415; $) has some of the most inexpensive slopeside lodging in the United States. Rooms are spartan, but have private baths and maid service; amenities include a large lounge and game area and laundry facilities.

Village Center Inn (800-443-8613; 733-3155; $$), next to the tram, has 16 one- and two-bedroom units, some with lofts. **Crystal Springs Inn** (733-4423; $$) has 15 basic rooms.

Condominiums and **private homes** are available through Jackson Hole Resort Lodging (800-443-8613). Rates are about $125–$850 per night.

Jackson

Many of these accommodations also offer ski packages. All listed here are within a block of the public bus service to Teton Village unless noted.

One of the best, with a great location just off the main square, is the **Wort Hotel** (800-322-2727; 733-2190; $$$-$$$$), an 1880s-style, four-diamond AAA-rated hotel. Inside is the Silver Dollar Bar, with its curving bar inlaid with 2,032 uncirculated 1921 silver dollars.

Snow King Resort (800-522-5464; 733-5200; $$-$$$) is a large hotel with a pool, indoor ice rink, game and fitness rooms and more. It is several long blocks from downtown, but right next to the Snow King Ski Area, which has night skiing.

The Quality Inn 49er Inn and Suites (733-7550; $$-$$$) is a three-building complex conveniently located at the edge of town and a stone's throw from an express bus stop. Suites are spacious and feature a fireplace, large bathrooms, excellent fitness facilities and a hot tub. At the **Parkway Inn** (733-3143; $$-$$$) bed and breakfast, the decor is decidedly Victorian. Don't miss the granola and fresh-squeezed orange juice for breakfast, and check out the fit-ness center and pool, a great place to unwind after a long day of skiing.

Rusty Parrot Lodge (800-458-2004; 733-2000; www.rustyparrot.com; $$$$), the state's only year-round four-star, four-diamond hotel, has a country lodgepole pine décor. It also houses a day spa and a superb restaurant. It is a few blocks from town and near the bus stop.

Davy Jackson Inn (800-584-0532; 739-2294; www.davyjackson.com; $$–$$$), with its Victorian décor, has inviting rooms with down comforters (some have fireplaces too). The inn is three blocks to downtown and a block to the bus stop.

The Bunkhouse (733-3668; www.anvilmotel.com; $), a no-frills dorm in the basement of a motel comprises one 25-bed room, a separate room with couches for lounging and a kitchen area with microwave and refrigerators. There are separate men's and women's lavatories, and a laundromat. Cost is $22 per night, and reservations are not accepted.

Between downtown and the ski area

The **Red Lion Wyoming Inn of Jackson** (800-844-0035; 734-0035; $$–$$$$) and **The Best Western Lodge at Jackson Hole** (800-458-3866; 739-9703 $–$$$) are practically next door to each other on Broadway (Hwy. 89). Red Lion Wyoming Inn is decorated with antique reproduction furniture, but has no pool or hot tub (though some rooms have Jacuzzis). It serves a continental breakfast, but there is no restaurant. The Best Western Lodge at Jackson Hole (there also is a Jackson Hole Lodge, which is quite different) is a delight for children and has a swimming pool and hot tub, and the Gun Barrel Steak House is next door.

One of the best spots to see the rugged Grand Teton and its neighboring peaks is from the **Spring Creek Ranch** (800-443-6139; 733-8833; $$$–$$$$), atop the East Gros Ventre Butte, which blocks the view of Grand Teton from most of Jackson. The resort has luxurious hotel rooms, condos and houses for rent, a marvelous gourmet restaurant and unsurpassed views of the Jackson Valley, Grand Teton and the ski area. Shuttles to town and skiing are provided.

Next door is the ultra-exclusive **Amangani** (877-734-7666; 734-7333; $$$$). If you've got mega bucks, stay here; it has everything you could imagine wanting and then some, but if you have to ask, fuggedabowdit.

On Teton Village Road a few miles from the ski area and town is **Teton Pines Resort** (800-238-2223; 733-1005; $$$–$$$$). Better known for its summer activities, it is open in winter and has ski packages. The amenities list goes on and on: free pickup from the airport, free indoor tennis, use of a neighboring athletic club, daily continental breakfast, an excellent gourmet restaurant, 14 km. of cross-country trails, pool and hot tub.

The **Jackson Hole Racquet Club** (800-443-8613; $$–$$$$) is a relatively inexpensive condo cluster. It's just four miles to Teton Village, and there's a grocery store on the premises as well as a restaurant, bar and liquor store. The resort runs a free shuttle to the mountain.

Just below Teton Village is the **Wildflower Inn Bed & Breakfast** (733-4710; $$–$$$$), with in-room fireplaces, a shared whirlpool tub and fitness area, and fabulous breakfasts.

 # Dining

We start with dining at the ski area, and work our way toward town. If you're staying in Teton Village, be sure to spend at least one evening in town.

Teton Village

Gamefish (732-6040; $$$) at the Snake River Lodge and Spa the emphasis is on game and fish, presented with a Southwestern accent, such as Rocky Mountain Trout grilled with roast corn cakes and smoked tomato coulis. It's worth the splurge. Also at the elegant end of the spectrum is the **Alpenhof Hotel** (733-3462, $$), a quiet, genteel place. Start with lobster risotto and move onto a Caesar salad followed by pan-seared medallions of bobwhite quail.

The **Alpenhof Bistro** (733-3242; $$) serves entrees such as wild game loaf, salmon pasta and lamb cassoulet in a casual setting. The very funky **Mangy Moose** (733-4913; $-$$), is a three-fold find. Head downstairs to The Rocky Mountain Oyster for cheap eats for breakfast or lunch, to the restaurant for a steaks, chicken, game and fish choices (and an excellent salad bar) and to the Saloon for pizza and burgers and apres-ski. **Masa Sushi** (733-2311; $-$$), a tiny restaurant in the Best Western Inn, serves good sushi; reservations are essential.

For a truly unique dinner experience, make reservations well in advance for the **Solitude Cabin Dinner Sleighrides** (739-2603; $$$). The price is steep ($54.95 adults; $33.95 children younger than 10), but it includes a sleighride to an on-mountain cabin and a four-course meal. Live musical entertainment adds to the fun. Drinks aren't part of the fixed price, but you can bring your own (as long as you can handle the $5 cork fee).

You can grab a breakfast or lunch bagel in the **Bridger Center** locker area. For heartier quick morning eats, try the tramline burrito at **The Village Cafe**. Eat upstairs for fast service, head down for a more leisurely meal. You can get soups, salads, sandwiches, pizza by the slice and good veggie food (try the teriyaki tofu) here for lunch.

Jackson

For casual inexpensive dining, it's **Bubba's** (733-2288; $-$$), featuring heaping plates of "bubbacued" ribs, chicken, beef and pork. Try the Mexican for breakfast or sink your teeth into one of Bubba's oversized omelettes. No sense in giving you the phone number (it's at 515 W. Broadway), because Bubba's doesn't take reservations. Be prepared to wait, and while you do, send a member of your party down the street to the liquor store—Bubba's is BYOB.

Another casual place is **Mountain High Pizza Pie** (733-3646, $). **Joe's Pizza** (734-5637, $) is home of the "mean, green pesto pizza." **Nani's Genuine Pasta House** (733-3668; $$) and **Anthony's** (733-3717; $$) got raves from locals for its authentic Italian regional cooking. For Mexican, head to **The Merry Piglets** (733-2966; $-$$); for Thai, it's **Thai Me Up** (733-0005; $-$$).

Two new restaurants that have earned accolades from locals are **Koshu** (733-5283; $$) and **Rendezvous Bistro** (739-1100; $$). Koshu, part of the Jackson Hole Wine Company, serves a Latin- and Asian-inspired menu with such items as Spanish-style roasted sea bass, grilled black angus tenderloin with Thai salad and wok-fried green beans with hoisin and seasame. Rendezvous Bistro serves a menu ranging from fancy grilled cheese sandwiches and bistro meatloaf to grilled ahi tuna salad Nicoise and leg of lamb.

On the upper-scale end, choose from **Off Broadway Grille** (733-9777; $$-$$$) for entrées such as lamb tenderloin with a Mediterranean black olive tapenade, Thai-steamed seafood with Asian flavors or sauteed sea scallops and leeks in a creamy tomato-saffron sauce; and **The Blue Lion** (733-3912; $$-$$$), known for its roast rack of lamb. Both The New York Times and Food & Wine have recommended **terroir** (739-2500), where you can dine at the Chef's Counter overlooking the exhibition kitchen.

Cadillac Grille and **Billy's Burgers** (733-3279; $-$$$) share space; one serves game, steaks, wood-fired pizzas and the like; the other, well, burgers.

The hearty-breakfast king is **Bubba's**. For tamer breakfast fare try **The Bunnery** (733-5474) with excellent omelets, whole-grain waffles and bakery items, and **Jedediah's Original House of Sourdough** (733-5671) for superb sourjack pancakes.

Between town and the ski area

For excellent, elegant dining, the **Granary** (733-8833; $$$) at Spring Creek Resort is hard to beat. Another top choice is **The Grille at Teton Pines** (733-1005, $$-$$$) at the

Dining: $$$-Entrees $20+; $$-$10-20; $-less than $10.
Accommodations: (double room) $$$$-$200+; $$$-$141-$200; $$-$81-$140; $-$80 and less.

Teton Pines Resort, with a beautiful dining room and extensive wine list. **Stiegler's** (733-1071, $$) has specialties from owner Peter Stiegler's home in Austria.

The Mexican restaurant with the best reputation is **Vista Grande** (733-6964, $–$$). For casual dining, try the **Calico Italian Restaurant & Bar** (733-2460; $$), halfway between Jackson and Teton Village at a bus stop on Village Road.

If you're headed to Grand Targhee, **Nora's Fish Creek Inn** in Wilson (733-8288, $$ for dinner) is a local favorite for any meal, especially breakfast.

For more ideas, pick up a copy of the *Jackson Hole Dining Guide* or browse through the rack of business-card-sized menus at your hotel (an excellent idea other resorts might well use). **Mountain Express** (734-0123) will deliver to your hotel from a dozen eateries.

 ## Après ski/nightlife

In Teton Village the rowdiest spot by far for après-ski and nightlife is **The Mangy Moose**. **The Alpenhof Bistro** attracts a sedate group, as does the lobby bar in **Snake River Lodge**, where you can curl up in an oversized chair by the fire.

In town, **The Million Dollar Cowboy Bar** attracts tourists who love saddle bar stools and dancing to live Country & Western bands. It's cash-only, so leave the credit card at home. **The Silver Dollar Bar**, at the Wort Hotel, is similar, with 2,032 uncirculated 1921 silver dollars embedded in the bar. Plus it serves great buffalo burgers and Starbuck's coffee.

Sidewinders Tavern on Broadway is a sports bar with 28 televisions, pool tables, foosball, an arcade, separate cigar bar and more. It has live music several nights a week and attracts a youngish, blue-collar crowd. An even younger crowd that likes to party hard heads to the **Log Cabin Saloon** to shoot pool, play foosball and darts, and drink heavily. Another hot spot is the **Rancher** where drafts are $1 and mixed drinks $2 during Tuesday Night Town Meetings. **The Shady Lady Saloon** at the Snow King Resort has live entertainment several nights a week.

The trust fund crowd heads to the **Snake River Brewing Co.** for hand-crafted lagers and ale plus sandwiches, pastas and wood-fired pizza. **Koshu** is a laid-back wine bar.

Locals head to the **Stagecoach**, in Wilson, on Thursdays for disco night (honest!) and on Sundays, when the house band performs its mix of country-western, bluegrass and swing.

Other activities

Several unusual activities center around Jackson's abundant wildlife. The **National Museum of Wildlife Art** (733-5771) houses the nation's premier collection of fine wildlife paintings, sculptures and other art, some dating back 170 years. The excellent cafe overlooks the **National Elk Refuge** (733-0277), where 7,000 to 9,000 elk winter. Horse-drawn sleigh rides through the refuge are offered by the museum. Combination admission and sleigh-ride tickets are available.

An outstanding educational tour is offered through the **Great Plains Wildlife Institute** (733-2623). On the institute's wildlife spotting tours, you ride with a biologist to help note the location and numbers of various birds and animals. A four-hour tour costs about $70 for adults and $40 for adult-accompanied children aged 3–12, with snacks provided. Full day and multiday tours also are offered. We spotted bison, elk, eagles, moose, deer, bighorn sheep, trumpeter swans and pronghorn. Everyone gets to use binoculars and a powerful spotting scope for up-close viewing.

If you're a fan of classical music, the **Grand Teton Music Festival** (733-1128) stages a monthly concert series in Walk Festival Hall in Teton Village.

Horse-drawn **dinner sleigh rides** are offered by Spring Creek Resort (733-8833) and Solitude Cabin (733-6657). Bar-T-Five (733-5386) has a **winter dinner show** with a barbecue dinner and "yarn-spinnin' " leading the entertainment.

The Jackson Hole Nordic Center (739-2629 or 800-443-6139) has **dogsled tours** lasting anywhere from an hour to a day. The tours cover some 400 miles of scenic trails from the Shoshoni and Teton National Forests. Interested in more dog mushing? Then look into the Brooks Lake tour, a half-day trip to the historic Brooks Lake Lodge on the Continental Divide. Eight-time Iditarod veteran Frank Teaslee operates Jackson Hole Iditarod Sled Dog Tours (733-7388), with full and half-day options. We recommend the full-day trip ($224) into Granite Creek Canyon, which includes a soak in the hot springs and lunch. One child weighing less than 50 pounds is free with every two paying adults, and round-trip transportation from your lodging is available.

Other activities include **snowmobile excursions** to Granite Hot Springs, **helicopter touring and skiing** and, of course, nearby **Grand Teton** and **Yellowstone National Parks**. **High Mountain Heli-Skiing** (733-3274) has been operating for more than 25 years. A day trip delivers usually six runs of 12,000-15,000 vertical feet, with one guide per five clients. There's an indoor public **ice-skating** rink at Snow King Center (734-3000). Rendezvous Ski and Snowboard Tours gives daily **backcountry tours** in Grand Teton Park and Teton Pass, while Snow King Mountain Guides operates trips for Nordic and alpine skiers.

Shopping is plentiful. Wile away an afternoon browsing the boutiques, factory outlets and art galleries in Jackson. The covered wooden sidewalks encourage window shopping, even when it snows.

Getting there and getting around

By air: Five major carriers now serve Jackson Hole with jets: American, United, Northwest, Delta and Continental. There's non-stop daily service from Salt Lake City, Denver, Chicago, Minneapolis and Houston, plus weekend non-stop service from Atlanta and Newark. Check with the resort central reservations (phone number is in the stat box) for air bargains. This is a small airport, surrounded by towering mountains. It may be a good idea to build an extra day into your schedule heading in and out, especially if your travel requires several plane changes. And if weather grounds you, remember to ask about distressed traveler rates at local lodgings.

By car: Jackson is on Hwys. 89, 26 and 191 in western Wyoming. The town is 10 miles south of the airport, and Teton Village is 12 miles farther by Hwys. 89, 22 and 390.

Getting around: Rent a car. While buses run regularly, they can add up to 45 minutes to your commuting time during the busy après-ski period, and at night, buses from town to Teton Village run only once an hour. Unless you are used to driving steep Rocky Mountain passes, take the Targhee Express (733-3101) to Grand Targhee in snowy weather. It's $15 well spent.

Motorists, take note: Highway signs say little about the ski areas. From town, follow signs to Teton Village to get to Jackson Hole Mountain Resort, and to Wilson when driving to Grand Targhee.

Southern Teton Area Rapid Transit (START) buses run frequently between Jackson and Teton Village to 10 p.m. in ski season for a small fee. Study the bus schedule and get on an express bus if you want to minimize your commute. Another good deal: books of bus passes sold at most resorts. They can save you a few bucks off the published fare. Five companies provide taxi services and airport shuttles: Jackson Hole Transportation (733-3135), Gray Line (733-4325), Buckboard Cab (733-1112), All-Star Taxi (733-2888) and All Trans (733-1700).

North Lake Tahoe Area

Alpine Meadows

Squaw Valley USA

Northstar-at-Tahoe

Diamond Peak

Sugar Bowl

with

Reno, Nevada

ⓘ **Toll-free reservations:**
(888) 434-1262, North Lake Tahoe
(800) GO-TAHOE (468-2463), Incline Village/Crystal Bay
(800) FOR-RENO (367-7366), Reno
Internet: www.mytahoevacation.com (North Lake Tahoe)
www.renolaketahoe.com (Reno)
E-mail: info@mytahoevacation.com (North Lake Tahoe)
info@renolaketahoe.com (Reno)
Dining:★★★
Apres-ski/nightlife:★★(near the lake) ★★★★(Reno)
Other activities:★★★

Few regions on the North American continent have the ski-resort diversity of the Lake Tahoe region. When you consider the elements of a perfect ski vacation—variety of terrain, good snow, comfortable lodging, beautiful scenery, a wide choice of restaurants and nightlife, a myriad other activities, accessibility—Lake Tahoe would rank near the top in all but a couple of categories (and it would be above the median in those).

Lake Tahoe, one of the largest and most stunningly beautiful mountain lakes in the world, straddles the border of California and Nevada about 200 miles east of San Francisco. Tahoe has received accolades from travel writers for more than a century. Mark Twain was one of the first to note its beauty. In 1861, he wrote in *Roughing It*, Tahoe was "the fairest picture the whole earth affords." Because the lake is so deep and doesn't freeze, it retains its sapphire-blue color throughout the winter. Its name comes from a Washoe Indian word meaning "lake in the sky"—the lake is about 6,200 feet above sea level.

Tahoe is best divided into two regions for vacation purposes. Though you can run yourself ragged by trying to visit every major area in a week, it's better to concentrate on the North Shore or the South Shore. The two regions provide very different vacation experiences.

South Tahoe is densely developed, with high-rise casino-hotels hugging the California-Nevada state line, frequent big-name entertainment, and non-stop après-ski activity. It has three ski/snowboard resorts, one of which overlooks the twin towns of Stateline and South Lake Tahoe. Speaking in general terms, South Shore tends to attract first-time visitors who live outside California and Nevada, while the North Shore attracts fewer first-time visitors, but loads of Californians.

North Shore has history, is more spread out and a lot quieter, and has an amazing concentration of excellent skiing and snowboarding facilities. Resort skiing in California started in the North Lake Tahoe region in the late 1930s, when a group of investors, including Walt Disney, started Sugar Bowl. The 1960 Winter Olympics were staged at another North Tahoe resort, Squaw Valley. North Tahoe isn't as densely developed as the South Shore, but it covers a lot more miles of the lakeshore. Its Nevada side has casinos, but they are not as prominent as the ones at South Shore. The California side of North Tahoe is dominated by condos that are vacation homes for Northern Californians. There are restaurants and nightlife, but things get quiet once the sun goes down. The North Tahoe region has 11 Alpine ski facilities (the lake is visible from five of them) and six cross-country areas. The five largest Alpine resorts are Squaw Valley USA, Alpine Meadows, Northstar-at-Tahoe, Diamond Peak and Sugar Bowl. The nearby resorts of Mt. Rose, Boreal and Homewood also are worth a visit if you're in the region. The remaining three—Granlibakken, Tahoe Donner, Donner Ski Ranche and Soda Springs—are very tiny areas that destination visitors would be unlikely to visit.

North Lake Tahoe interchangeable lift tickets
(2002/03 prices)

The North Lake Tahoe Resort Association offers the Ski Tahoe North interchangeable ticket, valid anytime at Squaw Valley USA, Alpine Meadows, Northstar, Sugar Bowl, Mt. Rose, Homewood Mountain Resort and Diamond Peak, as well as five cross-country ski areas (Tahoe Donner, Lakeview, Northstar-at-Tahoe, Royal Gorge and Resort at Squaw Creek Cross-Country). Other options and deals are also available through this pass. Call (888) 434-1262 or stop by the North Lake Tahoe Resort Association Chamber of Commerce, 245 North Lake Blvd. in Tahoe City. Prices are: three-day package, $150; five-days, $250; seven days, $350.

Squaw Valley USA

Squaw Valley USA is the best-known resort in the region, since it hosted the 1960 Winter Olympics. It offers some of the finest skiing in the United States. There aren't many trail-cut runs here, just wide-open snowfields—4,000 acres of them. Anything within the boundaries can be skied by anyone daring enough to challenge the mountain. All levels can push their limits here—experts and beginners alike ride side by side on the cable car to the top.

In fact, Squaw boasts no named runs—the lifts have names and then skiers and riders can pick their own way down the mountain. Some might say "mountains," since Squaw skis more like a series of smaller resorts rather than one large entity.

Access starts at the base with the 28-person Funitel. Or board the 110-person cable car. Or start with the Squaw One high-speed quad and then connect to other lifts. Six separate peaks, each with every conceivable exposure, overlook Lake Tahoe.

The Funitel, which carries 15 people seated and 13 standing, replaced Squaw Valley's gondola and follows its course from the base to the Gold Coast facility. The Pulse, a custom gondola, connects the resort's two mid-mountain complexes at High Camp and Gold Coast. It has five cabins that operate with the push of a button. These lifts enable guests to take a mountain tour without putting on skis or a snowboard (of course, skiers and boarders will use them, too). They can ride the cable car to High Camp, the Pulse lift to Gold Coast, then download on the Funitel to the mountain's base.

Squaw has a good news/bad news situation. Phase I of Intrawest's new $250-million Village at Squaw Valley opened last season. Three buildings that house 139 condominiums, 19 shops and restaurants, and about 250 underground parking spaces are up and functioning, but the area is still a construction zone and will be during the 2002/03 season.

Mountain layout—Skiing

◆◆ **Expert** ◆ **Advanced:** Extreme skiers will be in heaven at Squaw. Thirty percent of the runs are either single- or double-black diamond. Two popular spots are the Palisades above Siberia Bowl and Eagle's Nest at the

Squaw Valley USA

Summit elevation:	**9,050 feet**
Vertical drop:	**2,850 feet**
Base elevation:	**6,200 feet**

Address: Box 2007, Olympic Valley CA 96146
✆ Area code: 530
Ski area phone: 583-6985
Snow report: 583-6955
ⓘ Toll-free reservations: (888) 766-9321 or 800-545-4350
Fax: 581-7106
E-mail: squaw@squaw.com
Internet: www.squaw.com

Number of lifts: 32–1 cable car, 1 Funitel, 1 Pulse, 2 high-speed six passengers, 4 high-speed quads, 1 quad, 8 triples, 10 doubles, 3 surface lifts, 1 magic carpet
Snowmaking: 10 percent
Total acreage: 4,000 lift-served acres
Uphill capacity: 49,000 per hour
Snowboarding: Yes
Bed Base: 3,500 within 3 miles
Nearest lodging: slopeside
Resort child care: Yes, 2 years and older
Adult ticket, per day: $48-$56 (01/02 prices)

Expert:★★★★★
Advanced:★★★★★ **Intermediate:**★★★
Beginner:★★★ **Never-ever:**★★★

top of KT-22. In fact, KT-22 has such a variety of terrain that some season-pass holders ski the peak exclusively. The Granite Chief, Headwall and Silverado lifts access some of the world's most challenging terrain. Locals will take you to terrain that resembles an elevator shaft.

■ **Intermediate:** Intermediate terrain has challenge and variety. Unfortunately, intermediates here don't get the big mountain feel that experts enjoy. Siberia Express accesses the largest intermediate bowl, advanced levels turn left getting off the lift, intermediates traverse to the right, which feeds into the Gold Coast terrain and other wide-open slopes. Newport, Gold Coast and Emigrant lifts offer acres of open-bowl intermediate terrain. Intermediates will like the Shirley Lake area served by a high-speed quad and a triple chair. For tougher runs, take the Headwall Express Lift, then opt for Chicken Bowl or drop over the back of the ridge to Sun Bowl, a beauty if conditions are right. Or, ride the KT-22 chair, head west on the Saddle Traverse, then drop into the Saddle, which is groomed.

The Mountain Run is a crowded end-of-the-day cruise: Top to bottom, it's a hefty 3-mile run. Another great cruise is Home Run. Or give the Olympic High ski run a try. It follows the route of the original 1960 Olympic men's downhill. It begins above the bottom shack of Headwall and heads to the base, bypassing the Mountain Run entirely.

●● **Beginner** ● **Never-ever:** Though Squaw Valley's well publicized steep terrain has given it a menacing reputation, it has a little-known surprise: This is a great spot for never-evers to learn. Squaw has a gentle bowl at the top of the cable car known as Bailey's Beach, served by two slow-moving lifts. Though Bailey's Beach is not physically separated from the other terrain, better skiers rarely use it. Beginners usually long to head toward any summit just like the big boys and girls, and here they can. They just ride the cable car up to High Camp (where they'll also find restaurants, shelter and an outdoor ice rink), and at the end of the day, ride the cable car back down.

Mountain layout—Snowboarding

Let's just say that Squaw is monstrous, and so are its parks and pipes. In various locations you'll find a superpipe, two halfpipes, a quarterpipe, plus terrain features like table tops, rails, rollers and volcanoes. One of the parks is lit until 9 p.m. and has a pumping sound system. The pipe sessions can definitely get heated—prepare to be humbled by locals. There's a reason many pros call Tahoe home.

But, as much fun as the manmade features are, Mother Nature's features still can't be beat here. As too many riders say with a big sigh, this place is so-o-o sick. The in-bounds riding gets insane and, unfortunately, gets tracked up quickly by hordes of riders who know all the mountain's secrets. When you have Sierra Cement at the lower elevations, book it to Granite Chief, where you'll find pow instead. And when it's freshies all over, you just can't go wrong, especially since they can be accompanied by bluebird days that make you swear you've died and gone to heaven. On those days, make sure to hike Granite Chief or high-tail it to the cornice on Siberia or seek out the Hanging Gardens. Gotta huck cliffs? Head to Palisades. One of those sick bump riders? Then Headwall's for you.

There's also great terrain for beginners and never-evers, and it comes with a jaw-dropping view of Lake Tahoe and the surrounding mountains. Squaw has a gentle bowl at the top of the cable car known as Bailey's Beach, and it's served by two lifts.

 Lessons (2001/02 prices)

Group lessons: Lower-intermediate to intermediate skier levels get instruction through a "Ski Your Pro" format, where instructors are assigned to training areas on the mountain, and skiers can join in on the hour for as long as they want for $38. Higher-level skiers get two-hour workshops on specific skills, such as moguls, powder or gate training, also for $38. A book of five two-hour lessons is $160.

Never-ever package: A Fun in the Sun Adventure Package that includes a beginner lift ticket, equipment rental and a two-hour lesson is $65 for skiing or snowboarding.

Private lessons: $79 an hour; $25 for each additional person. Multi-hour discounts available.

Special programs: Squaw Valley also has a full-service adaptive ski school.

Racing: A coin-op course is at the top of the Shirley Lake Express, $1 per run.

 Child care (2001/02 prices)

Ages: 2–3 years.

Costs: All-day care at the licensed Toddler Care center is $77 with lunch, activities and supervision, while half-day care is $56 (no lunch). A one-and-a-half-hour ski option for 3-year-olds is extra—call to get the price.

Reservations: Highly recommended; call (530) 581-7166. Parents must provide current immunization records. Children ages 4 and older enroll in ski school programs. The day care is located in the Children's Center, which is a one-stop area for kids' ski school and day care.

Other options: Baby's Away (530-581-3930) rents and will deliver baby items (cribs, strollers, toys, etc.) to your hotel or condo. For babysitting referrals, call (530) 587-5960.

Children's lessons: Ages 4–12 can take an all-day lesson, with lunch, lift ticket, activities and instruction for $77. The half-day price is $56 and includes a snack instead of lunch. Rentals are extra.

Lift tickets (2001/02 prices)

	Adult	Child (Up to 12)
One day	$56	$5
Three days	$147 ($49/day)	$15 ($5/day)
Five days	$240 ($48/day)	$25 ($5/day)

Who skis free: Ages 76 and older.

Who skis at a discount: Tickets for ages 65-75 and youth ages 13-15 are $28. Non-skiers can ride the cable car and gondolas for $16 for adults, $13 for seniors, and $5 for children younger than 13. Full-day lift tickets include night skiing until 9 p.m. (mid-December through mid-March). Night skiing only costs $20 for adults, $10 for seniors/youth and $5 for children.

Accommodations at the resort

Olympic Valley (the base-area town—Squaw Valley is the name of the resort) has several lodging choices. All have easy access to the slopes, but evening activities are limited. If you're staying here, it is best to rent a car if you'd like to explore dining and nightlife in Truckee and Tahoe City. For **central reservations** at Squaw Valley call (800) 403-0206. Generally, you can expect a range of $150 to $300 per night. Hotels are listed more or less in order from most expensive to least.

The **Village at Squaw Valley** (888-805-5022) has a brand new collection of condominiums across from the lifts, each with fireplace and balcony. The underground parking is breathtaking and very convenient. You can drive directly under your condo, park your car and never have to deal with it again.

The **PlumpJack Squaw Valley Inn** (800-323-7666 or 530-583-1576) opened a couple of years ago. This remodeled hotel, with 61 rooms, originally housed delegates to the 1960 Winter Olympics, and is right across from the cable car building. The rooms now have down comforters, hooded bathrobes and VCRs. A lap pool and two hot tubs further pamper the guest experience. The new lodging blends intimate country charm with the style and service of a grand Continental hotel. Its name honors Sir John Falstaff, Shakespeare's swaggering, high-living character. Its restaurant is excellent—details in the Dining section.

Resort at Squaw Creek (800-327-3353 or 530-583-6300) is a multistory luxury hotel that blends well with the valley. It connects with the ski area by its own lift, and is a self-contained resort, with five restaurants and three pools (one of which is open in winter), several hot tubs and spa, cross-country skiing and an ice-skating rink. The resort recently expanded and remodeled the Health and Fitness Center.

Squaw Valley Lodge (800-992-9920; in California, 800-922-9970) is only a few yards' walk from the lifts. The lodge boasts a fully equipped health club, free covered parking and kitchenettes in the units.

The **Olympic Village Inn** (800-845-5243 or 530-583-1501) has five hot tubs, and all units have kitchens. Rates: About $195 a night on weekends, $165 Sunday–Thursday.

Red Wolf Lodge (800-791-0081) at the base of Red Dog Chair next to the Children's Center has studio, 1- and 2-bedroom units with full kitchenettes.

Alpine Meadows

It's hard not to like Alpine Meadows. For every level, particularly intermediate and advanced, Alpine Meadows has something to offer. It has expert terrain, sweeping intermediate bowls, scenic trails, and a good beginner area. The view from the base lodge suggests that Alpine is a relatively small area. Not so. You'll see just how big it is when you take the Summit Six (a six-seater) and see it unfold beneath you. In the Lake Tahoe area, Alpine Meadows has traditionally been the ski area with the earliest and longest season (it's open well into May and some years, until July 4).

Recently, the oldest chairlift at Alpine Meadows, 34-year-old Weasel Chair, was replaced with a new triple chair named Hot Wheels. Hot Wheels not only takes visitors to the beginner terrain, but it also is a major access chair to the back bowls. Scott Chair, which accesses expert terrain, was upgraded from a double to a triple. The added weight of the triple chairs will allow the Scott Chair to run more often in bad weather, good news to experts who want to get to this area during a snowfall. It also speeds you toward the Lakeview Chair, which has great views of Lake Tahoe from the top.

 ## Mountain layout—Skiing

◆◆ **Expert:** This level has plenty of great bowl skiing and enough steeps to keep hearts in throats. Here's a route suggestion: Take the Summit Six and descend into the expert Wolverine Bowl, Beaver Bowl and Estelle Bowl (they're to the right as you ascend), then take the Summit Six again and cruise into the upper-blue territory of the Alpine Bowl. Finally, take the Alpine Bowl Chair and traverse to the Sherwood Bowls on the back side of the area or take the High Yellow Traverse to the Saddle Bowl. When you come up the Sherwood Chair, drop down Our Father—and you can say a few en route—then head to Scott Chair and try out Scott Chute for a direct plunge, or take it easy on tree-lined roundabouts. By then your knees will have earned a cruise. The Promised Land has great tree skiing for top skiers.

Alpine Meadows Facts

Summit elevation:	8,637 feet
Vertical drop:	1,802 feet
Base elevation:	6,835 feet

Expert:★★★★
Advanced:★★★★★
Intermediate:★★★★
Beginner:★★★
Never-ever:★★★
Address: Box 5279, Tahoe City CA 95730
☏ **Area code:** 530
Ski area phone: 583-4232
Snow report: 581-8374
ⓘ **Toll-free information:** (800) 441-4423
Fax: 583-0963

E-mail: info@skialpine.com
Internet: www.skialpine.com
Number of lifts: 12–1 high-speed six-person chair, 1 high-speed quad, 4 triples, 5 doubles, 1 surface lift
Snowmaking: 12 percent
Skiable acreage: 2,000 acres
Uphill capacity: 16,400 per hour
Snowboarding: Yes
Bed base: 10,000 (N. Lake Tahoe Area)
Nearest lodging: Tahoe City, 6 miles
Resort child care: None
Adult ticket, per day: $54 (01/02 prices)

◆ **Advanced:** Take your warm-up in Alpine Bowl, staying to skier's right on Rock Garden and Yellow Trail as you cruise down to the Hot Wheels chair. Then head for the Back Bowls. If there's a line at Hot Wheels, you also can reach the bowls via the Scott Chair through the blue-square Lakeview area to Ray's Rut. Depending on your mood, you can stay on the groomed Sherwood run to check out the scene, or traverse to the steeper Sherwood Face or South Face. You may want to stay here all day—one of our staffers did.

■ **Intermediate:** Plenty of terrain for this level off these lifts: Alpine Bowl, Roundhouse and Lakeview. The terrain off the Kangaroo lift is a short intermediate run, but much of it is devoted to race programs and the terrain park. All this activity creates a narrow descent, something many intermediates are uncomfortable with.

●● **Beginner:** Good terrain under the Meadows and Subway chairs.

● **Never-ever:** This level has a small but sheltered area close to the base lodge. The terrain is quite gentle and seldom used by better skiers.

 ## Mountain layout—Snowboarding

Riders will jump for joy when they see the new superpipe for 2002/03. It is together with the terrain park, Roo's Ride, off the Kangaroo lift. The pipe and terrain park also will be open for night riding 5–9 p.m. nightly, complete with an upgraded speaker system for tunes.

Even though Alpine Meadows is paying more attention to its manmade features, most riders agree that the natural terrain is the real reason to come here. If you like in-bounds hiking, this is the place for you. Unfortunately, you might be doing some hiking even if you're *not* looking for it: There are some flat spots and traverses that you might just find yourself cursing about. The biggest beware is traveling back from the Lakeview and especially the Sherwood lifts to the front side. It never hurts to ask one of the liftees, many of them snowboard and have helpful tips to make the trip less grueling.

The Bowls are great powder runs—with special kudos to Upper Beaver and Estelle Bowl—and there are plenty of steeps, gullies and nutty drops if you go looking for them. Mix it up with some of the tree runs such as Hot Wheels Gully, you'll be happy you did. If you're there after a fresh dump, look for the wind lips—you'll find yourself airborne for days—and see if you can find Munchkins and Outer Outer.

If you favor groomers, don't panic. Alpine does a real nice job and there's plenty to choose from all over the mountain. Beginners will find very gentle terrain and the learning area is sheltered from the rest of the trails.

 ## Lessons (2001/02 prices)

Group lessons: $34 for two hours, $20 for each additional two-hour session. Alpine also offers a coupon book of 10 two-hour lessons for $300 ($30 each). Anyone may use the coupons, so this is a good deal for families where everyone wants to take a refresher.

Never-ever package: A two-hour adult learn-to-ski or -snowboard program includes beginner lifts, equipment and instruction for $56. Two additional hours are $20. Same prices for lessons geared toward beginner-refresher and anyone still skiing and riding green runs.

Private lessons: For one person, $65 an hour, with discounts for multiple hours; all day is $340. For 2-4 people, one hour is $100, with discounts for multiple hours; all day is $420.

Special programs: Clinics for disabled skiers, women, or those who want to try shaped-ski techniques and various advanced skills such as powder, telemark, moguls and trees are also available. Most clinics cost $34. Five or more in a group can tailor their own program. Multi-day clinics on specific dates available also, call for details and prices. Telemark lessons are $34, including equipment rental, and are offered Saturdays and Sundays at noon and 1:45 p.m.

Racing: Daily race-training clinics are offered at $42, or you can buy a book of five sessions for $175. There is a race every Thursday, which costs $8 for two runs for all abilities with special prizes. Alpine Meadows also has coin-op racing.

Child care (2001/02 prices)

Alpine Meadows has no child care. Other options: **Baby's Away** (530-581-3930) rents and will deliver baby items (cribs, strollers, toys, etc.) to your hotel or condo. For **babysitting** referrals, call (530) 587-5960.

Children's lessons: Little Mountaineers for children ages 5–6 costs $79 for a full-day (including lunch, equipment, lift ticket and two 2-hour lessons); $52 a half-day. Half-day program is open to 4-year-olds, space permitting. Reservations are required, 581-8240. Private lessons for ages 4 and younger, $36 per half hour per person; lift ticket and equipment additional. Snowboard lessons for ages 4-6 are by private lesson only.

Junior Mountaineers is for children 7–12, skiing or snowboarding. A full-day program includes lunch, lift ticket and lessons, $79. Half-day cost is $52, includes a lift ticket. Never-ever packages cost the same. A 2 1/2-hour intermediate or advanced group lesson is available for $34 (not including lift ticket), at 10 a.m. or 1:30 p.m.

Lift tickets (2001/02 prices)

	Adult	Child (7-12)
One day	$54	$10
Two days	$102 ($51/day)	$20 ($10/day)
Three days	$153 ($51/day)	$30 ($10/day)

Who skis free: No one.

Who skis at a discount: Ages 65–69 pay $30; seniors 70 and older pay $8; teens 13–18 pay $42; 6 and younger pay $6. Parents can get an interchangeable ticket that can be traded between them for $54 a day.

Accommodations

Alpine Meadows doesn't have accommodations at the base, but has lodging-lift packages with hotels and condos in the region. Call **Alpine Meadows** at (800) 949-3296. A bed-and-breakfast package includes some two-dozen North Shore lodges, some starting at $59 per person, double occupancy, for lodging and a lift ticket.

Northstar-at-Tahoe

Northstar is a planned resort community, designed to make ski vacationing easy. Condos line the lower slopes, and the runs are laid out for excellent family skiing. The grooming is impeccable and the entire area management and operations are squeaky clean.

Northstar-at-Tahoe has undergone a dramatic transformation from a Casper Milktoast resort to a decent all-around ski and snowboard area. With the addition of the new Lookout Mountain runs, Northstar can take its place as a first-class resort.

You won't find bowls and cornices on Northstar's Mount Pluto, which makes the skiing here different than at Squaw or Alpine. Instead the skiing is all trail-cut with a bunch of awesome tree skiing. The tree skiing on Lookout Mountain rivals any found in the region. Combined with the widely spaced trees on the Backside, Northstar provides an excellent variety of tree skiing for everyone, from intermediates making their first forays into the woods to experts looking for the tightest glades they can ski.

Mountain layout—Skiing

◆◆ **Expert** ◆ **Advanced:** Lookout Mountain, with 200 acres of terrain and a high-speed quad is heralded as the expert section. There are five advanced/expert runs, named after the surrounding reservoirs Prosser, Stampede, Gooseneck, Boca and Martis. The trails can be classified as advanced, but trees are clearly expert. Stampede, Gooseneck and Boca are left to bump up while Prosser and Martis are groomed regularly. Here you'll find steep runs, trees, and great views overlooking Truckee's Martis Valley and the surrounding mountain peaks. After a storm, Northstar is one of the prime areas where you can enjoy powder through the trees long after Alpine and Squaw's powder has been skied off.

Northstar-at-Tahoe Facts

Summit elevation:	8,610 feet
Vertical drop:	2,280 feet
Base elevation:	6,330 feet

Expert:★★★
Advanced:★★★★
Intermediate:★★★★★
Beginner:★★★★★
Never-ever:★★★★
Address: Box 129, Truckee, CA 96160
☎ Area code: 530
Ski area phone: 562-1010
Snow report: 562-1330
ⓘ Toll-free reservations:
(800) GO-NORTH (466-6784)

Fax: 562-2215
E-mail: northstar@boothcreek.com
Internet: www.northstarattahoe.com
Number of lifts: 15–1 gondola,
5 high-speed quads, 2 triples, 2 doubles,
3 surface lifts, 2 magic carpets
Snowmaking: 50% of developed acres
Total acreage: 2,420 total acres,
500 developed acres
Uphill capacity: 21,800 per hour
Snowboarding: Yes
Bed Base: 5,500 at resort
Nearest lodging: Slopeside
Resort child care: Yes, 2 years and older
Adult ticket, per day: $56 (02/03)

On the Backside, you'll find long rides with moderately steep and sustained pitch off the back side via the Comstock Express. These runs make you feel as though you're in another mountain range, far away from crowds. Nine stretched-out swaths provide some of the West's longest continuous pitches, all served by the Backside Express high-speed quad. Though they're all labeled advanced runs, a strong intermediate will have no difficulty in good conditions. Sawtooth Ridge, off Challenger on the back side, has steep off-piste terrain. It's open at select times during the season and only advanced skiers are allowed.

Advanced skiers or those aspiring to the upper levels of intermediate will find some challenge in the drops off the East Ridge (labeled as black diamonds, but the mapmaker was being generous). Normally most of the runs in this section are groomed and the others have moderate bumps. Tonini's is the longest, but The Plunge is the steepest. The only bad part is that it's over too soon. Chute, Crosscut and Powder Bowl are also fun—short but sweet. If you're an air skier, you'll be disappointed. These blacks would be blues at Squaw.

■ **Intermediate:** This group will enjoy most of the mountain, particularly the smooth blues that descend from the two ridges into Main Street, an intermediate run that nearly every other run on the mountain feeds into. Avoid Main Street except when you need to get to a lift. Strong intermediates should try some of the black runs here. They will provide a good challenge to an intermediate looking to improve.

●● **Beginner** ● **Never-ever:** Northstar is the best never-ever and beginner resort in the region because its gentlest terrain is below the gondola, while all other runs are above it. Better skiers leave this area to the learners except at day's end, when some of them use it to practice tucks. Luckily for everyone, it's fairly flat, so no one can keep up excessive speed.

 ## Mountain layout—Snowboarding

If you like terrain parks and pipes, Northstar is right up your alley. You'll find seven terrain parks (not counting the kids' Paw Parks), a 17-foot superpipe and a halfpipe. Some of the parks have scaled-down features for beginners, Magic Moguls will remind you of a parking lot full of snow-covered VW bugs, and another is a snake-run with high walls. The Polaris Park pipe is lit for night riding on weekends and holidays. Northstar labels its parks on the trail map with happy faces, which makes them easy to find. As for Paw Parks, they're adventure zones for kids—pint-size terrain parks scattered across the mountain that include bumps, jumps, hideaways and snow play areas. Look for the paw prints on the trail map.

If you're craving serious steeps with sick air, you'll need to go somewhere else. Northstar is really geared more towards groomed cruising and woods riding with some good bumps through the center of Lookout Mountain.

After a storm, this is one of the prime areas where you can enjoy powder through the trees long after it's been tracked out at other Tahoe areas. On Lookout Mountain, riders claim Stampede, Gooseneck and Boca are divine. On the Backside, stick to the right side of the area where the trails drop right to the Backside Express Chair. If riders swing to the left down Challenger, they will face a long runout at the bottom of the area. Jibboom and Powder Bowl are some other favorites.

Stay on the front side if you like wide-open groomed runs for intermediates and beginners. The terrain here is mellow and will boost your ego. This is a good resort for learning to ride, too.

Lessons (2001/02 prices)

Group lessons: Free, 1.75-hour skill improvement clinics are held at 10 a.m. and noon for advanced-intermediate and higher levels, skiing and snowboarding, ages 13 and older. Sign up at the summit, first-come/first-served. Other group lessons are $30 for ages 13 and older.

Never-ever package: First-time students ages 13 and older get a 1.75-hour lesson (skiing or snowboarding) with beginner lift access and rental equipment for $65; those at the next level have the same program but with expanded lifts for $75. First Timer Ultimate Package is a 4-hour lesson, equipment, beginner lift access, lunch and goodie bag for $89.

Private lessons: For ages 13 and older, $75 per hour, with multi-hour discounts. Semi-private one-hour lesson, with 2-4 people, $125.

Special programs: Three-day clinics for women or men are offered a few times per year; call for specifics and pricing.

Child care (2001/02 prices)

Ages: 2–6 years (toilet-trained).
Costs: All day, $56; $68 to include 90-minute ski lesson (ages 3-6). Half day costs $33. The program combines skiing with other activities, including art, snow play, science, drama and language development.

Reservations: Recommended; call (530) 562-2278. Located in Clocktower Building in Northstar's Village. Hours: 8 a.m. to 4:30 p.m.

Other options: Baby's Away (530-581-3930) rents and will deliver baby items (cribs, strollers, toys, etc.) to your hotel or condo. For **babysitting referrals,** call (530) 587-5960.

Children's lessons: All-day program for children ages 5–12 is $82 with lifts, lessons, equipment and lunch. An afternoon-only program is $72. A novice's package for skiing or snowboarding, similar to the adults' program, costs $55. Children 13 and older enroll in adult programs. Meet at Starkids Center at mid-mountain.

Lift tickets (2002/03 prices)

	Adult	Child (5-12)
One day	$56	$17

Who skis free: Children under age 5 with a parent ski free.

Who skis at a discount: Ages 60–69 ski for $30 a day; 70 and older ski for $10. Unlimited gondola rides for non-skiers cost $10. Ages 13–22 ski for $44 a day.

Note: Northstar's parking lot sometimes fills on busy days, and cars are turned away at the entrance.

Accommodations at the resort

This area was created for condo living. The village has a convenient lodge, with rooms from $174 a night, two-night minimum. The condo rates range from $159 a night for a studio to $289 for a two-bedroom, two-bath unit. Northstar also has full-sized homes for rent, accommodating five to eight people for $379 to $669 a night. Packages can be arranged for whatever resort amenities you need—airfare, lifts, rentals and lessons are just some of the choices. **Reservations:** (800) 466-6784.

Diamond Peak Facts

Summit elevation:	8,540 feet	
Vertical drop:	1,840 feet	
Base elevation:	6,700 feet	

Expert:★ Advanced:★★★
Intermediate:★★★★
Beginner:★★★
Never-ever:★★★
Address: 1210 Ski Way
Incline Village, NV 89451
☎ Area code: 775
Ski area phone: 832-1177
Snow report: 831-3211

ⓘ Toll-free reservations: (800) 468-2463 or (800) GO-TAHOE
Fax: 832-1281 E-mail: info@diamondpeak.com
Internet: www.diamondpeak.com
Number of lifts: 6–3 quads, 3 doubles
Snowmaking: 75 percent
Skiable acreage: 655 acres
Uphill capacity: 9,800 per hour
Snowboarding: Yes
Bed Base: 6,000
Nearest lodging: About 1/4 mile away
Resort child care: Yes, 3 years and older
Adult ticket, per day: $41 (2002/03 price)

Diamond Peak

Bigger is not always better, nor desirable. For skiers and snowboarders who don't want the expansive terrain of most Lake Tahoe resorts, let us recommend Diamond Peak, a medium-sized but exquisite jewel that destination vacationers too often overlook.

Diamond Peak often is less crowded than the other large Tahoe areas and perfect for families. Visitors repeatedly remark that this is a very friendly area. Take a camera—the view is beautiful.

Mountain layout—Skiing

Diamond Peak was the first U.S. resort to install a "launch pad" loading system, a conveyor belt covered with a skiable felt surface. All of its quad chairs have this family-friendly loading system.

◆◆ **Expert** ◆ **Advanced:** Here's one of Diamond Peak's best-kept secrets: the tree skiing in Solitude Canyon and elsewhere throughout the ski area. Solitude is reached by a short hike over a knoll at the top of the Crystal Quad. The rest of the resort's terrain falls from a single ridge that starts at the summit and ends at the octagonal Snowflake Lodge overlooking Lake Tahoe. The canyons, glades and gullies off Crystal Ridge (a long blue run) are labeled advanced, but strong intermediates will have a blast on them; however, the tree skiing is definitely expert. At the other end of the resort, below the Snowflake Lodge, Oh God and G.S. provide some steep ungroomed pitches and good tree skiing.

■ **Intermediate:** This is a wonderful area for intermediates, especially families who don't want to worry about the kids taking a wrong turn and getting lost. The aforementioned Crystal Ridge is a 2.5-mile-long blue from the summit, with a stunning view of the lake. Golden Eagle Bowl provides intermediates a place to test their tree skiing. The lower-mountain runs off Red Fox also have a nice intermediate pitch.

●● **Beginner** ● **Never-ever:** This is a great learner's mountain more because of its friendly atmosphere and manageable size rather than its terrain (unfortunately, the amount of beginner terrain is a bit limited). Diamond Peak employs about 100 instructors—equal to much larger areas—another indication that it's a good place to learn.

Mountain layout—Snowboarding

The resort's terrain features attract boarders at every skill level, from first-timers to the most advanced. This is an excellent resort for riders who are ready to test themselves on the more adventurous terrain of canyons and gullies, since nothing here will give you the heebie-jeebies. Snowboarders also can find some alone time in the new "Glades," in the trees between The Great Flume and Thunder. Enjoy fantastic tree riding and untapped powder stashes. For boarders who like pulling some tricks, check out the new and improved terrain park and superpipe. The park is located on Spillway (at the bottom of The Great Flume) and includes tabletops, spines, hits and jumps, all over-looking beautiful Lake Tahoe.

Lessons (2002/03 prices)

Group lessons: Lessons are one hour and 45 minutes long. Cost is $24 (ski or snowboard); two sessions in the same day cost $37.

Never-ever package: Learn-to-Ski/Snowboard including beginner lifts, rentals and 105-minute lesson is $48.

Private lessons: $55-$65 an hour, depending on the time you take your lesson. Private adaptive lessons are available for disabled learners. Reservations required: (775) 832-1135.

Child care (2002/03 prices)

Ages: 3–6 years.

Costs: $42 for the morning or afternoon session; $65 for full day.

Reservations: Required for private lessons; call (775) 832-1130.

Note: Diamond Peak has the Bee Ferrato Child Ski Center, named for its director, a New Zealand native every kid will want to adopt as a grandmother. Check out the new Diamond Peak Kids Club, where by becoming a member, kids can participate in ski races and pizza parties throughout the season and their parents ski at a discount.

Other options: Baby's Away (530-581-3930) rents and will deliver baby items (cribs, strollers, toys, etc.) to your hotel or condo. For **babysitting referrals,** call (530) 587-5960.

Children's lessons: All-day groups for ages 7–12 cost $69 for skiers; $79 for snow-boarders. Ages 4–6 have full-day ski lessons with rentals and lunch for $79. Three-year-olds take private lessons. Reservations suggested for private children's lessons: (775) 832-1135.

Lift tickets (2002/03 prices)

	Adult	Child (6–12)
One day	$41	$15

Who skis free: Ages 5 and younger and 80+.

Who skis at a discount: Ages 13–17 pay $33; ages 60 and older pay $15. Parents can buy an interchangeable adult ticket for $41 that either of them can use—a good deal for those with toddlers. If you are planning on skiing more than just one day, consider the new Pass Stack program, where you can buy tickets in combination of three, five or seven, starting at just $99. Purchase tickets at any ticket window. Tickets are valid any day of the season. Check out www.diamondpeak.com for the latest deals. Last but not least, the ever-affordable Family Special Package starting at just $54 is one deal parents simply cannot pass up. The offer lets families customize a ticket package designed just for them. Packages available daily at any ticket window and valid for up to six persons with a maximum of two adults. Believe it or not, a family of four can hit the slopes for under $100.

Accommodations near the resort

Incline Village has several hotels and condo complexes. It also has private homes that can easily sleep 12–16 people. For **Incline Village** accommodations, call (800) 468-2463 (GO-TAHOE). The **Hyatt Regency Lake Tahoe Resort and Casino** (800-533-3288) is a four-star luxury hotel with rates from $135 to $705 a night. The good news is that the resort has just undergone a multimillion-dollar renovation and the new lobby and rooms are wonderful. The bad news is that the renovation will be continuing through the 2002/03 winter season, which means the pool will be shut down. However, the hotel has made arrangements to allow guests to use the excellent Incline Village recreation center. The **Inn at Incline Motor Lodge and Condominiums** (800-824-6391) has more modest facilities and rates starting around $70 a night. The **Tahoe Biltmore Casino** (800-BILTMOR) in Crystal Bay has midweek ski packages with Diamond Peak, including a lift ticket, lodging, a full breakfast and transportation to and from the slopes. Last season's price was $39 per night. The **Crystal Bay Motel** (702-831-0287) is an economy property from $35–$65 near casinos and **Haus Bavaria** (800-731-6222) is a European-style guest house with five rooms. The **Cal-Neva Lodge Hotel Spa Casino** (800-225-6382 or 800-CAL-NEVA) is split by the state line and once was owned by Frank Sinatra and visited by Marilyn Monroe. Rooms go for $85 to $289. Every room has a lake view, the best from the deluxe suites on the top three floors. There are also honeymoon bungalows with heart-shaped tubs, round beds and mirrored ceilings.

Sugar Bowl

Founded by Walt Disney, Sugar Bowl is one of the oldest resorts at Lake Tahoe and the oldest chair-lift-served resort in California. From the moment you step out of your car and board the Magic Carpet gondola to ride *down* across a pristine valley to the lifts, you feel you're stepping back in time. (If you are only coming to ski, it is recommended that you continue driving to the Mt. Judah parking area served with high-speed quads.)

Sugar Bowl Facts

Summit elevation: 8,383 feet
Vertical drop: 1,500 feet
Base elevation: 6,883 feet
Expert:★★
Advanced:★★★
Intermediate:★★★★★
Beginner:★★★★
Never-ever:★★★
Address: P.O. Box 5, Norden, CA 95724
☎ **Area code:** 530
ⓘ **Ski area phone/reservations:** 426-9000
Snow report: 426-1111

E-mail: info@sugarbowl.com
Internet: www.sugarbowl.com
Number of lifts: 14–1 gondola, 4 high-speed quads, 4 quads, 3 double chairs, 2 surface lifts
Snowmaking: 25 percent
Skiable acreage: 1,500 acres
Uphill capacity: 13,755 per hour
Snowboarding: Yes
Bed Base: 460
Nearest lodging: Slopeside
Resort child care: Yes, 3 years and older
Adult ticket, per day: $35-54 (02/03 price)

Sugar Bowl is another of Tahoe's overlooked ski areas, at least by destination skiers. That's a shame, because it has great variety. We recommend Sugar Bowl for a day's change of pace from the larger Tahoe resorts. However, remember that it's one of the first ski areas on the drive from San Francisco, Oakland and Sacramento and gets its big crowds on weekends so visit midweek if you can and take advantage of their $35 Tuesday through Thursday special ticket price.

Sugar Bowl has three peaks—Mt. Judah, with its own parking lot and base lodge; Mt. Lincoln; and Mt. Disney, reached initially by the Magic Carpet gondola. The three peaks are connected. This is one of the few ski areas where we agree with virtually all their trail ratings. Most of the lifts are high speed and a skier can pack in lots of vertical very quickly.

Mountain layout—Skiing

◆◆ Expert ◆ Advanced: Mt. Disney, one of three peaks at Sugar Bowl, has advanced runs off either side of a ridge. Mt. Lincoln also has advanced terrain dropping directly beneath the lift. There's an expert very steep cliff area, The '58 and The Palisades, to the right of the Silver Belt chair that's double diamond and comparable to the jumps at Squaw. There is some good tree skiing down the face off Crow's Nest peak or through Strawberry Fields.

■ Intermediate: From the top of the Disney Express head down the left side of the ridge along Crow's Traverse then drop down Pony Express, Montgomery and Upper Mac into Disney Meadows. Keep up your speed and stay high at the end of the run to avoid having to push to the lift.

From the top of the Mt. Lincoln Express, head to the right down Crowley's Run, Rahlves' Run and eventually head back to the base of the lift along Ridge Run or Silver Belt Finger.

The entire area served by Mt. Judah Express and Jerome Hill Express is an intermediate paradise, perfect for long cruising with occasional short steeps.

●● Beginner ● Never-ever: Beginners have beautiful long runs off the Christmas Tree and Mt. Judah chairs. An expanded novice area, Whitepine, at Mt. Judah is an excellent teaching area, segregated from the main ski trails.

Mountain layout—Snowboarding

Sugar Bowl has incredible natural hits and quarterpipes. Real experts should check out the 58's and Palisades off Mt. Lincoln, and the Sugar Bowl off the Disney Express. If that isn't enough there are two terrain parks on Mt. Judah and a halfpipe on Mt. Lincoln. The park for advanced riders has multiple tabletop and gap jumps, quarterpipes and spines. The second park is for less-advanced riders just learning to get their legs under them. Strawberry Fields and Crow's Nest Face are not to be missed on powder days. The groomers off the Jerome Hill Express are great for high-speed arcs. Remember to keep your speed up for the flat between the Mid Mountain Lodge and Village Lodge and at the bottom of the runs down from Crow's Nest.

Lessons (2002/03 prices)

Group lessons: $40 for two hours.
Never-ever package: The Fast Track package of lifts, two-hour lesson and rental (ski or snowboard) costs $65 for adults, $55 for young adults (13-22).
Private lessons: $70 an hour, with each additional person $20.

Child care (2002/03 prices)

Ages: 3–6 years.

Costs: All day is $70, and half day (without lunch) is $50. Sugar Bears Child Care is a licensed center with educational and recreational activities as well as skiing and quiet time. The program includes snacks, lunch and ski equipment.

Reservations: Suggested. Call the ski area.

Other options: **Baby's Away** (530-581-3930) rents and will deliver baby items (cribs, strollers, toys, etc.) to your hotel or condo. For **babysitting referrals,** call (530) 587-5960.

Children's lessons: All-day program for ages 6–12 is $70, which includes lifts, equipment, lessons and lunch. The Fast Track package for never-evers includes lift ticket, two-hour lesson and rental (ski or snowboard) and costs $60 for teens, $50 for children.

Lift tickets (2002/03 prices)

	Adult	Child (5–12)
One day	$54	$13
Two days	$100 ($50/day)	$22 ($11/day)

Who skis free: Children younger than 5 and ages 70 and older.

Who skis at a discount: Ages 60–69 pay $30; ages 13–22 pay $42. Adults who turn in their all-day lift ticket by 12:30 p.m. receive a credit coupon for $16 off another day's ticket. There's a special on tickets, Tuesday through Thursday, for $35 (excluding Christmas week Dec. 26 through Jan. 2, 2003).

Accommodations at the resort

Sugar Bowl has a lodge that is certainly unusual, and possibly unique at American ski resorts: a base lodge that also is a hotel. It is reached by the same four-passenger gondola that brings skiers to this part of the mountain. In addition to the usual services on the ground floor, Sugar Bowl's base lodge also has 27 rooms on the upper two levels. Though it was built in 1939, the rooms have been remodeled for a combination of historic charm and modern convenience. The dining room preserves the grace of a former era with its decor and jacket-required dress code. This is one of the more isolated and romantic settings in the ski world. Room rates, based on double occupancy, start at $95 per night. Bed-breakfast-lift packages, available Sunday through Thursday, non-holiday, are $255 double occupancy. Five-day ski weeks with two meals a day also are available; call for prices. Call (530) 426-9000 for reservations, well in advance.

Nearby resorts

Mt. Rose, Reno, NV; (775) 849-0704; (800) SKI-ROSE (754-7673)

Internet: www.skirose.com

6 lifts; 1,000 skiable acres; 1,440 vertical feet

Mt. Rose has the highest base elevation in the Tahoe area at 8,260 feet, which means it gets snow earlier than other areas (and gets snow when it's raining at lower elevations). It has two base areas, the result of Mt. Rose incorporating a neighboring ski area, Slide Mountain, several years ago. The Slide base area has primarily intermediate terrain with some advanced pitches, while the Rose side has very gentle beginner slopes, good intermediate trails and some long advanced runs.

Lift tickets (02/03): Adults, $45; Teens (13-17), $35; Children (12 and younger), $12.
Distance from Reno: About 22 miles on Hwy. 431.
Lodging information: (800) 367-7366 (FOR-RENO) or (800) 824-6348 (TAHOE-4-U).

Homewood Mountain Resort, Homewood, CA; (530) 525-2992
Internet: www.skihomewood.com
10 lifts; 1,260 skiable acres; 1,650 vertical feet
Homewood Mountain Resort, on the west shore of Lake Tahoe, is one of three Tahoe ski areas that can qualify for Best View Of The Lake honors. This area, though smallish by Tahoe standards, has more than 1,200 skiable acres accessible from either of two base areas called North Side and South Side. Child care starts at age 2 and is at the South Side Lodge.
Lift tickets (02/03): Adult, $42; Junior (11-18), $27; Senior (62+), $10. Kids 10 and younger ski free. Monday–Thursday (non-holiday) adults and juniors, $25; and seniors, $10.
Distance from Reno: About 50 miles from Reno via I-80 west and Hwy. 89 south.
Distance from Sacramento: About 120 miles via I-80 east and Hwy. 89 south.
Lodging information: (800) 824-6348 (TAHOE-4-U).

Boreal, Truckee, CA; (530) 426-3666
Internet: www.borealski.com
9 lifts; 380 skiable acres; 500 vertical feet
You can't miss Boreal when you're driving toward Tahoe from Sacramento. It is a wide ridge of fairly short ski trails right off I-80 on the Donner Pass. It's the closest resort to Sacramento and San Francisco. Boreal, purchased in 1995 by the company that owns Alpine Meadows, is very popular with riders, who like the short, straight runs off the summit and the eight Vans parks. Boreal also has runs down its back side.
Boreal has night skiing and a night halfpipe and terrain park. It is the home of the Western Ski Sport Museum, generally open during Boreal's ski hours.
Lift tickets (01/02 prices): Adults, $35; Adult night skiing, $22; Children (5–12), $10; Seniors (60–69), $20; Seniors night skiing, $16; Parents shared ticket, $35. Other ages, free.
Distance from Reno: About 45 miles west on I-80.
Distance from Sacramento: About 80 miles east on I-80.
Lodging information: (530) 426-1012.

 # Cross-country and snowshoeing

The Lake Tahoe region may have the greatest concentration of large cross-country ski areas in the U.S., with more than 800 km. of groomed trails. We have listed the bigger operations; local tourist offices can direct you to smaller and less expensive centers. Many of the ones we list here also have full-moon tours and snowshoe rentals and tours so call for information.

Six of these Nordic centers offer an **interchangeable trail pass**. They are Royal Gorge, Northstar-at-Tahoe, Spooner Lake, Squaw Creek Cross-Country, Tahoe Donner and Tahoe Cross-Country. The pass ranges from two days for $28 to six days for $66 and can be bought through the North Lake Tahoe Resort Association, (888) 434-1262 or (530) 583-3494. If you use the pass at Royal Gorge, there is a $4 surcharge.

Squaw Creek Cross-Country Ski Center (530-583-6300) is a small area at the Resort at Squaw Creek, which has rentals and lessons. Trails cover 18 km., are groomed daily, and range from beginner to expert. Trail fees are $12 for adults, $10 for children ages 12 and younger. Child care is available starting at age 4.

The largest private trail system in North America is in California at **Royal Gorge** (530-426-3871; 800-500-3871, nationwide; 800-666-3871, Northern California only; e-mail: info@royalgorge.com; Web site: www.royalgorge.com) just off I-80, west of Donner Summit at the Soda Springs exit. Royal Gorge has nearly 9,000 acres of terrain, and more than 300 km. of trails with a skating lane inside the tracks. They also make snow on some trails and use modern snowcats. Adult trail fees are $25, for teens (13–16), $12; with discounts for midweek, multiday tickets and skiers 65 and older. Ages 12 and younger ski free.

Royal Gorge has four surface lifts to help skiers up the tougher inclines. It is a full-service ski area, with rental equipment, ski school, ten warming huts, four cafes and a full-time ski patrol. Trailside lodging is at **Rainbow Lodge,** an historic 1920s B&B, or at **Wilderness Lodge,** a rustic retreat in the middle of the trail system. Book either through the ski area.

Northstar-at-Tahoe (530-562-2475) has 50 km. of groomed and marked trails. Trail fees: adults $20; children 5–12, $15; seniors 60-69, $10; seniors 70 and older, $5. Lessons (one-and-a-half hour) with equipment, $27. Rentals are available, as are snowshoe rentals. All are near the day lodge and downhill slopes. This is one of the gentler trail systems in the area—very good for families and those just learning.

Tahoe Donner Cross-Country Area (530-587-9484; e-mail: xcski@tahoedonner.com) is off I-80 at Donner State Park exit. This area has 100 km. of trails, all double-tracked with wide skating lanes, and a day lodge with cafe. Tahoe Donner has California's only lighted night cross-country skiing, Wednesdays and Saturdays. Day trail fees are $18 for adults, $14 for teens ages 13–17 and seniors ages 60–69. Those younger than 12 and older than 69 ski free. Cross-country gear, snowshoes and pulk sleds are available for rental.

Tahoe Cross-Country Ski Area (530-583-5475; formerly Lakeview Cross-Country), two miles east of Tahoe City, is a non-profit ski foundation. It has 65 km. of groomed skating lanes and tracks, a day lodge, cafe, lessons and rentals. Trail fees are $17 for adults, $12 for juniors 10–18 and seniors 60–69. Those older than 69 and younger than 10 ski free; call to inquire about bringing your dog. Snowshoes and pulk sleds also are available for rental.

Spooner Lake Cross-Country (775-887-8844, recording; 755-749-5349, live voice) on Hwy. 28, about a half-mile north of Hwy. 50, has more than 80 km. of trails, nearly all of which are machine groomed, with one 19-km. backcountry trail. Adult trail fees are $16.50; less for ages 7–15. Children younger than age 7 ski free. Lessons and cross-country gear, snowshoe and pulk sled rentals are available; you also can rent a backcountry cabin.

Accommodations

The North Shore is relatively quiet. The accommodations below generally run less than $150; however, the more luxurious lodging will top out closer to $200. The North Shore has bed-and-breakfast inns, cabins on the lake, plush or spartan condominiums, and medium-sized casino hotels—a place for everyone. The best source for lodging-and-lift packages that include interchangeable lift tickets for several North Tahoe resorts is **North Lake Tahoe Resort Association Lodging Information & Reservations,** (888) 434-1262 or (530) 583-3494; its Web site is www.mytahoevacation.com. The agency also can suggest private homes and condos.

The most upscale bed-and-breakfast is the **Rockwood Lodge** (530-525-5273), originally built in the mid-1930s. There are five rooms, two with private bath. It has antique furnishings, plush carpet, brass-and-porcelain bath fixtures, and down comforters on the beds. The lodge is next to the Ski Homewood Ski Area, on the west shore of Tahoe about seven miles south of Tahoe City. **Note:** This is a No-Smoking inn and does not accept children.

Dining: $$$$ Entrees $30+; $$$-$20-30; $$-$10-20; $-less than $10.
Accommodations: (double room) $$$$-$200+; $$$-$141-$200; $$-$81-$140; $-$80 and less.

The **Mayfield House** (530-583-1001), another B&B, was once a private residence in Tahoe City. The atmosphere is elegant and romantic, and full breakfasts come with the rate. Some rooms have a private bath.

Other B&Bs that are recommended are **The Cottage Inn** (530-581-4073; 800-581-4073) in Tahoe City; **The Shore House** (530-546-7270; 800-207-5160) in Tahoe Vista; or **Tahoma Meadows Bed & Breakfast** (530-525-1553) in Homewood.

Just south of Tahoe City is the **Sunnyside Lodge** (530-583-7200, or in California only, 800-822-2754), directly on the lake. There are 23 rooms, all with a lake view and a few rooms have fireplaces. No. 39 makes a great honeymoon suite—it has a four- to six-week waiting list. This is an excellent property with a lively après-ski bar and a good restaurant, the Chris Craft.

Perhaps the most luxury for the money on the North Shore can be found in the **Tahoe Vista Inn & Marina** (530-546-1515) in Tahoe Vista. The six units here are spectacular and sited directly on the lake. Rates range from about $160 a night for the smallest unit to $240 for a one-bedroom suite with a panoramic lake view.

The **Cal-Neva Lodge Hotel Spa Casino** (800-225-6382 or 800-CAL-NEVA) is split by the state line and once was owned by Frank Sinatra and visited by Marilyn Monroe. Every room has a lake view, the best from the deluxe suites on the top three floors. There are also honeymoon bungalows with heart-shaped tubs, round beds and mirrored ceilings.

The **Granlibakken Resort & Conference Center** (800-543-3221) in Tahoe City is a great place to stay. Lodging is in 160 privately owned suites and townhouses and some feature a kitchen and fireplace. Sizes start at one bedroom and top out at a six-bedroom, six-bath townhouse. Two saunas and an outdoor spa are on site. The lovely complex sits on a hill among towering pines and red firs, next to the site of a former ski jump used for the 1932 Olympic tryouts. Two cross-country ski trails and a beginner's Alpine hill also are on site. Ski packages are available with Squaw Valley and Alpine Meadows.

For families or anyone looking for a great deal, **North Lake Lodge** (530-546-2731), in Kings Beach only a few feet from the shore, is one of the oldest hotels but still in great shape. Continental breakfast is included and the shuttlebuses stop just across the street.

River Ranch (530-583-4264) on Hwy. 89 near Alpine Meadows is another moderately priced lodge. This historic ski lodge sits on the banks of the Truckee River and rooms are furnished with early American antiques. Continental breakfast is included, and the shuttles for Squaw Valley and Alpine Meadows are nearby. A rushing river lulls you to sleep.

Away from the lake in Truckee, but convenient to Northstar and Sugar Bowl, is the **Truckee Hotel** (530-587-4444), which has been welcoming guests since 1873. Mostly it housed timber and railroad workers, but one of the residents was a madam who reportedly ran a little business on the side. It has been renovated, but you'll still feel like you're sleeping in the Old West. Some rooms have baths—the old-fashioned, claw-footed kind. Some rooms have private baths, some don't. Some rooms are large enough to sleep six. Moody's Bistro serves lunch and dinner.

The **Richardson House** (888-229-0365; 530-587-5388) is a B&B in Truckee that was built in the 1880s as a private residence. It has been fully restored. Six of the eight rooms have private baths. A full breakfast buffet is included, as well as 24-hour access to the "refreshment center." Beds and comforters are feather-filled.

Another recommended lodge is the **Best Western Truckee-Tahoe Inn** (530-587-4525) with 100 rooms and complimentary breakfast.

Accommodations—Nevada Northeast

Reno offers big-time casino atmosphere closer to the North Shore and at lower prices than you'll find surrounding the lake. Reno also has a planetarium and two major museums, and is 30–45 minutes by car from the North Shore resorts. This is a good place to stay if you want to save some serious money and have a big enough group to split a rental car cost. Some hotels have ski shuttles, but most visitors here probably will want a car. **Reno Central Reservations** is at (800) 367-7366 (FOR-RENO).

Dining (530 area code unless noted)

Dining is in the midst of a renaissance in North Lake Tahoe. The old Mom'n'Pop places are giving way to some upscale gourmet eateries. All restaurants are within a half-hour drive of each other. They are listed geographically—Very North Tahoe, Tahoe City, Truckee, Incline Village and Squaw Valley.

Very North Lake Tahoe (Carnelian Bay, Tahoe Vista, King's Beach, Crystal Bay)

Le Petit Pier (546-4464; $$$$) in Tahoe Vista presents upscale French cuisine. Locals refer to this restaurant as "where to go on a very special date." Reservations needed.

Spindleshanks (546-2191; $$$), in Tahoe Vista, has been awarded "Best Wine List" for the past two years. The food is also excellent at somewhat reasonable prices. The place gets packed. It was the hottest restaurant on the lake last ski season. Call for reservations or go early. On Wednesdays, when the appetizers are half price all evening at the bar, get a spot there and order a couple or so to make a nice light dinner.

The Soule Domain (546-7529 or 775-833-0399; $$$) in Crystal Bay receives consistent raves from people at both ends of the lake. The menu hasn't changed for years but it seems to work. Just across the highway is the new **Lake Tahoe Brewing Company** (775-831-5822) with pub fare and fresh-brewed beer. The casinos on the Nevada border serve inexpensive breakfasts, lunches and dinners. Try **Lakeview Dining Room** at the Cal-Neva Resort (775-832-4000), the **Steak and Lobster House** at the Crystal Bay Club (775-831-0512), or the **Cafe Biltmore** at the Tahoe Biltmore (775-831-0660).

In Kings Beach, **Jason's Beachside Grill** (456-3315; $$) has moderate fair with lots of burgers around $8 and entrees $10-20. In Tahoe Vista, **Boulevard Cafe** (546-7213; $$) gets regular mention from locals for good Italian-influenced meals.

For sushi head to **Hiro Sushi** (546-4476) in Kings Beach, where you should order the all-you-can-eat menu (you only have an hour to stuff it in). The caterpillar rolls, made with eel, look just like caterpillars right down to the antenna. The best Mexican in the area is **La Mexicana** (546-0310) in Kings Beach.

Lanza's (546-2434; $-$$), an institution in Kings Beach, also has excellent Italian fare at family prices. **Gar Woods Grill** (546-3366; $$) in Carnelian Bay serves a California grill menu. For pizza head to **C.B's Pizza** (546-4738; $) in Kings Beach or **Jiffy's Pizza** in Tahoe Vista (546-3244). **Steamer's Beachside Bar and Oven** (546-2218) was voted best pizza on the North Shore by Tahoe.com.

For breakfast try the **Old Post Office** (546-3205; $) at Carnelian Bay and order the deluxe French toast or create your own omelet. Or try the **Log Cabin** (546-7109; $$) in Kings Beach where you can get lobster and shrimp scrambles, trout benedict and fancy pancakes. The $1.99 breakfast served 24/7 at the **Tahoe Biltmore** (800-BILTMORE) is a real bargain.

Dining: $$$$ Entrees $30+; $$$–$20-30; $$–$10-20; $–less than $10.
Accommodations: (double room) $$$$–$200+; $$$–$141-$200; $$–$81-$140; $–$80 and less.

Tahoe City and nearby

Wolfdales (583-5700; $$$$) in Tahoe City is superb. Reservations are suggested. **Christy Hill** in Tahoe City (583-8551; $$$$) is a real find. Christy Hill offers superb lake views in an intimate, casually elegant atmosphere. The menu, which changes several times each week, is loaded with the freshest fish and specialty produce. The restaurant is open for dinner only from Tuesday through Sunday. Call for reservations.

Truffula (581-3362; $$$$) in Tahoe City is a gourmet find. The tiny place serves "wild food from land and sea" in a modern atmosphere.

Black Bear Tavern (583-8626; $$–$$$) is in an historic A-frame log building with knotty-pine walls and a large stone fireplace. South of Tahoe City on Hwy. 89, it features top-rate dining at moderate prices—steak, chicken, and fresh salmon and swordfish when available. Portions are large, but save room for apple crisp, an old German recipe smothered in vanilla ice cream.

Swiss Lakewood Restaurant (525-5211; $$$) in Homewood is Lake Tahoe's oldest and one of its finest dining experiences with impeccable service. Cuisine is French-Swiss and classic continental. Closed Mondays, except holidays.

Yama Sushi and Robata Grill (583-9262) in the Lighthouse Shopping Center is a classic sushi restaurant but it also includes grilled meats, fish and vegetables.

Sunnyside (583-7201; $$$) has good meals and a great setting. The crab legs are wonderful and on Wednesdays fish tacos rule.

Za's (583-1812; $$) in Tahoe City serves moderately priced Italian. **Jake's on the Lake** (583-0188; $$) in Tahoe City has an American menu. For Mexican with a big dose of margaritas and a shoulder-to-shoulder crowd on weekends, a good choice is the **Hacienda del Lago** (583-0358; $) in Tahoe City in the Boatworks Mall. **Coyotes Mexican Grill** (583-6653; $$-$$$) is another Mexican place that is now recommended by return visitors and locals alike. **Blue Agave** (583-8113; $$) has been described as an upscale Taco Bell.

River Ranch (583-4264; $$–$$$) at the access road to Alpine Meadows has been there for years and still gets great reviews. In the spring sitting by the river is a joy. Another Tahoe original is the **Old European Restaurant and Bar/Pfeifer House** (583-3102), just north of Tahoe City on the road to Alpine and Squaw, with its traditional German meals.

For lots of good food at very reasonable prices try **Bacchi's** (583-3324; $) for Italian; **Fast Eddie's Texas Bar-B-Que** (583-0950; $–$$) where the food is voluminous; or **Bridgetender** (583-3342; $) for great half-pound burgers and an extensive beer selection.

Fiamma (581-1416; $$), in the middle of town, has a wood-fired pizza oven. Also try **Lakehouse Pizza** (583-2222; $$) for a great lake view or **Squaw Valley Pizza** (583-4787; $) at the entrance to Alpine Meadows resort.

For breakfast head to **The Fire Sign** (583-0871; $), about 2 miles south of Tahoe City, where many believe the best breakfasts and lunches in the region are served, or go to **Rosie's Cafe** (583-8504; $), where breakfast is a locals' affair. Near Alpine Meadows, try **The Alpine Riverside Cafe** (583-6896; $–$$) for breakfast and lunch.

Truckee

Moody's Bistro and Lounge (587-7619; $$$$), in the Truckee Hotel, is the new kid on the block run by a locally well-known chef. **Pianeta** (587-4694; $$$) serves an excellent Italian menu. **Dragonfly** (587-0557; $$$), upstairs on Truckee Row, has an interesting Asian menu with dishes from Japan, Thailand, China and Vietnam. **OB's** (587-4164; $$), decorated with old farm antiques, serves creative cuisine (example: potato-asparagus soup with nutmeg) at cheap prices. **El Toro Bravo** (587-3557; $$) has excellent Mexican portions that locals claim is the best Mexican on the North Shore. **La Bamba** (587-3516) has, perhaps, the least expensive Mexican. **Java Sushi** (582-1144) serves what its name implies. Try the Friday Night Special served every night. They also serve tempura, teriyake and broiled salmon. **Coffee And** (587-3123; $) serves meatloaf, chops and steak for down-home lunches. For pizza, try **Pizza Junction** (587-7411) where they make Truckee River Beer, head to **Pacific Crest** (587-2626) for a wood-fired pizza or stop by **Villaga Pizzeria** (587-7171).

On the other side of the tracks try **Andy's Truckee Diner** (582-6925; $) and **Taco Station** (587-8226; $).

Truckee may be the breakfast capital of the country. The **Squeeze In** (587-9814; $$) in Truckee is where the list of omelets requires a speed-reading course. The Squeeze In has all the atmosphere you could want in a breakfast joint, built in a former alley and only 10 feet wide. On weekends, expect to wait a while—this place is popular. Down the street, and very "atmospheric" as well, you'll find **Wagon Train** (587-7574; $) and **Coffee And** (587-3123; $), which both serve up a good basic breakfast. For pancakes and French toast head to the Coffee And.

Incline Village

On the northeastern side of the lake, in Incline Village, go to **The Lone Eagle Grill** at the Hyatt Regency (775-832-3250; $$$$) for some of the best food on the Nevada lakeshore. The soaring stone and timber and the massive fireplace blend with magnificent views across the lake at sunset, and the cuisine and wine list provide accomplished accompaniment.

Le Bistro (775-831-0800; $$$$) across the street from the Hyatt is considered the best restaurant on the lake by some locals. As the name implies, the focus is on French fare.

Also in Incline Village, try **The Big Water Grille** (775-833-0606; $$$), at the bottom of the hill at Diamond Peak. A Native American name for Lake Tahoe, the Big Water features an eclectic menu and spectacular lake views—the perfect setting for romantic dinners, après-ski relaxation and group gatherings. The menu features American Contemporary cuisine with Mediterranean and Pacific-Rim influences.

Cafe 333 (775-832-7333; $$$) in Incline Village, written up in *Bon Appetit* several times, is favored by Incline locals. It has French country decor and a moderately priced menu.

The Wild Alaskan Fish Company (775-832-6777; $$) is one of the top spots for excellent seafood on the lake. It's just plain good.

Ciao Mein Trattoria (775-832-3275; $$) in the Hyatt has a menu that is half Italian and half Chinese. **Azzara's** (775-831-0346; $–$$) in Incline Village serves good, reasonable Italian food. **Austin's** (775-832-7778; $) gets raves for meatloaf and homemade soups. **Stanley's** (702-831-9944; $) is an Incline institution for Sunday breakfast and Friday night local entertainment in the bar. **Jack Rabbit Moon** (775-832-3007; $$) gets the nod for dinner from knowledgeable locals. **Hacienda de La Sierra** (775-831-8300) is a top Mexican spot.

Squaw Valley

PlumpJack Squaw Valley (583-1576; $$$$) is an extraordinary dining experience in a style that is as unique as the cuisine is delicious. The wine list is carefully selected and prices are very reasonable, given the high quality. Reservations suggested.

Balboa Café (583-5850; $$$$) in the Village at Squaw Valley is owned by the same team who owns PlumpJack Squaw Valley (if you're familiar with San Francisco, you'll also be familiar with the fine reputation of their two restaurants there).

Dining: $$$$ Entrees $30+; $$$–$20-30; $$–$10-20; $–less than $10.
Accommodations: (double room) $$$$–$200+; $$$–$141-$200; $$–$81-$140; $–$80 and less.

Glissandi at the Resort at Squaw Creek (581-6621; $$$$) brings New York and San Francisco style and service, all overlooking Squaw Valley. Reservations suggested. Also in the hotel, Ristorante Montagna's (581-6619) serves a California/Italian fusion cuisine. Try Graham's at the Christy Inn (581-0454; $$$) for gourmet southern European meals.

Après-Ski/nightlife

At Squaw, local hangouts include the bar at PlumpJack, Bullwackers at the Resort at Squaw Creek, Bar One, Plaza Bar at the Olympic House and the Red Dog Saloon at the Opera House. River Ranch on the Alpine Meadows access road was voted to have the top après-ski in North Lake Tahoe. Go before sunset to enjoy the winter wonderland scene across the Truckee River.

In Tahoe City, places to head include Pete'n'Peter's, Rosie's Café, Pierce Street Annex (behind Safeway near the Boatworks Mall, voted best pick-up place), or Jake's on the Lake. Hacienda del Lago in the Boatworks has nachos 'til 6 p.m. Sunnyside, just a couple of miles south of Tahoe City on the lake, has a lively bar. For the best live music, try Sierra Vista, adjacent to the Boatworks Mall. An offbeat après-ski spot is Naughty Dawg on the main road in Tahoe City, where you can get munchies and specialty drinks served in dog dishes. Watch out for the "shotskis"—'nuff said.

In Truckee, there's music at Bar of America, Tahoe Taps and the Pastime Club on Commercial Row. The Cottonwood Restaurant overlooking Truckee on Hwy. 267 has jazz.

The casinos on North Lake Tahoe have entertainment every night. Sure bets are the Cal-Neva Lodge (775-832-4000), The Crystal Bay Club (775-831-0512), Hyatt Lake Tahoe and the Tahoe Biltmore (800-245-8667). Call to see what shows are currently performing. The Tahoe Biltmore also has an excellent pool hall.

Spindleshanks bar is a great après-ski spot where drinks and appetizers are half price every day during happy hour. On Wednesdays the appetizers are half price all evening.

Incline locals hang at Bigwater Grill, Frederick's at the 7/11 Plaza, Hacienda de la Sierra, Rookie's Sports Grill, Crosby's and Legends. Cutthroats in the Hyatt Regency also gets rocking après-ski.

With all these bars check the local papers for their half-price appetizer days.

Other activities

Squaw Valley's High Camp at the top of the cable car has ice skating, snowtubing, dining and more. Polaris Park, located mid-mountain at Northstar, has lighted snow play areas for tubing, snow biking and other activities. It is open weekends and holidays, 3 to 9 p.m. Sleigh rides are available at Northstar-at-Tahoe, (530) 562-2480, and in the Squaw Valley meadow, (530) 583-6300. The region also has snowmobiling, scenic flights, hot-air balloon rides, horseback riding, sleigh rides, bowling, movies and health clubs.

Snowfest is North Tahoe's winter carnival, usually in late February/early March. Call (800) 824-6348 or (530) 583-3494 for a complete list of things to do.

At Diamond Peak, check out the Incline Village Recreation Center, which has aerobics, basketball court, weight room, European sauna and an indoor pool among its amenities. Visitors can use the facilities for $10 per day or $25 per week. Discounts are available for children, teens, seniors and families. Another spot for family fun is Bowl Incline with more than bowling. You'll find pool tables, other pinball gizmos, video poker built into the bar and a golf simulator where you can play seven world-class courses. Greens fees are $24 per hour and it takes about an hour to play 18 holes. The **Incline Village Cinema** is an excellent movie theater.

There are also plenty of **casinos** on the north shore. The Tahoe Biltmore is a favorite of locals for slots and poker. The Hyatt Regency Lake Tahoe is also an excellent casino and has prehaps the best shows. The best **shopping** is in the Boatworks Mall.

 ## Getting there and getting around

By air: Reno-Tahoe International Airport has more than 100 nonstop flights a day from various parts of the country. The airport is 45 miles from Squaw Valley USA.

By train: Amtrak serves Truckee and Reno on the California Zephyr line, running from Oakland to Chicago. Call (800) 872-7245.

By bus: Shuttles run from almost every major hotel to each major ski resort. Check for schedules when you arrive.

Sierra Nevada Gray Lines (800-822-6009 or 775-329-1147) operates a daily ski shuttle between Reno and Alpine Meadows as well as Northstar-at-Tahoe (except Saturdays). Squaw Valley USA (800-446-2928) operates a Reno/South Lake Tahoe Shuttle from mid-December through the end of March. Tahoe Casino Express (800-446-6128) runs between Reno airport and South Shore for about $17 each way.

By car: Driving time from Reno is about an hour to any major North Shore resort. San Francisco is about four hours away via I-80 to the North Shore. During storms, the California Highway Patrol doesn't let drivers come up the mountains without chains or a 4-wheel-drive vehicle, so be prepared.

Squaw Valley is on Hwy. 89 South (runs between I-80 and Hwy. 28, which hugs the North Shore). It's the third Truckee exit on Hwy. 80 coming from Reno and the second coming from San Francisco. The only resort with signs on the Interstate is Squaw Valley.

Alpine Meadows is just south of Squaw Valley on Hwy. 89.

Northstar-at-Tahoe is on Hwy. 267 (runs between I-80 and Hwy. 28, which hugs the North Shore). Coming from Reno, follow signs to Lake Tahoe/Hwy. 267. If you miss the Hwy. 267 turnoff, take the Hwy. 89 exit and then turn left on West River Road. This takes you into Truckee. Turn right at Hwy. 267.

Diamond Peak is on Hwy. 28 in Nevada on the lake's northeast side at Incline Village. From Reno take Hwy. 395 south then turn off at the Hwy. 431. There are signs to Lake Tahoe/ Incline Village and Mt. Rose.

Tip: If you are driving a rental car from Reno on I-80, headed west toward Northstar, Squaw or Alpine, you may pass through a California agricultural checkpoint. If you do, get off the freeway at the next stop and turn around. That checkpoint means you just missed the turnoff for Hwy. 89 South, just like one of our staffers did. The signs are dimly lit at night and tough to see a couple of hours before sunset.

Getting around: As much as we hate to recommend adding more auto pollution to this pristine location, rent a car. Public transportation is getting better, but not yet to the point where we can honestly recommend using it exclusively. If you stay near one of the ski resorts, your dining and evening options would be limited. Squaw Valley, Alpine Meadows, Sugar Bowl, Diamond Peak, Northstar and Homewood all have shuttles from North Tahoe towns.

South Lake Tahoe Area

Kirkwood

Heavenly

Sierra-at-Tahoe

ⓘ Toll-free reservations:
(800) AT-TAHOE (288-2463)
Internet: www.virtualtahoe.com
Dining:★★★
Apres-ski/nightlife:★★★★★
Other activities:★★★

Few regions in the world have what South Lake Tahoe does: almost 10,000 acres of lift-served terrain that annually receives an average of 40 feet of snow, a stunning alpine lake—72 miles of shoreline—that never freezes, and sunny skis over 300 days a year. Add to this entertainment like Natalie Merchant, Blues Traveler, Smash Mouth, and Willie Nelson (all bands that played here in 2002), 24-hour access to slot machines and casino table games, and lots of great food. And did we mention that South Lake Tahoe is just over an hour from a major international airport? Paradise, eh?

Better still, you can pick your style of vacation. Part of the town lies in Nevada, so if you like to stay up late dancing and gambling, you can book a room at one of four giant, high-rise casino hotels. A few steps across the Nevada/California state line, which runs right through town, life is quieter. Two Marriott properties opened in fall 2002 near the state line. Here, you can enjoy the hustle and bustle of the south shore's casino nightlife—just two blocks away—shop in one of the retail stores in the new complex, or sit back and quietly soak in the area's innate beauty. Or stay in one of the many, many smaller inns and motels lining South Lake Tahoe Boulevard (a.k.a. Highway 50).

When you're ready for the slopes, you can pick from three resorts: Heavenly and Kirkwood, two of the largest Tahoe resorts, and Sierra-at-Tahoe, just 12 miles down the road. Heavenly is the most popular Tahoe resort with out-of-towners, probably because you can see its runs rising above town. Kirkwood has a well-deserved reputation for awesome terrain and massive amounts of snow, and the near completion of the mountain village at its base is metamorphosing it into a year-round resort. You also shouldn't miss Sierra-at-Tahoe, known for its tree skiing and a locals' favorite.

Of note to families: Heavenly and Sierra-at-Tahoe are the only two resorts in the entire Tahoe area that offer state-licensed child care for children under age 2. For this reason, their day care centers fill up fast, so book early. Other options are noted in the child care sections for each resort.

A word on phone numbers: Though the South Shore appears to be one big town, it's two towns in two states. If you're staying on the Nevada side, you'll need to dial the area code before all California phone numbers, and vice versa. Kirkwood is in another area code, 209.

Heavenly Resort

Heavenly is big. It ranks Number One at Lake Tahoe for highest summit elevation (10,040 feet), greatest vertical rise (3,500 feet, though not all of it is "working vertical") and longest run (5.5 miles). Heavenly has some good expert terrain—Mott Canyon on the Nevada side, and its famous face run, Gunbarrel, on the California side. Other than that, however, the resort is most appropriate for intermediates and advanced skiers.

www.resortspace.com

Heavenly is also the only two-state mountain resort—you can start out from either California or Nevada. The new gondola provides direct access from the center of the South Lake Tahoe/Stateline district to the resort, and the 12-minute ride gives skiers and riders a killer view of the lake. But more parking is available at the California base just up Ski Run Blvd. On busy weekends, skiers and snowboarders who are looking to avoid crowds can start from the Nevada side; take the Kingsbury Grade to either the Stagecoach or Boulder bases.

But mostly, Heavenly is the view. The most spectacular view of Lake Tahoe—perhaps the most awesome view from a ski area summit anywhere—is at the top of the Sky Express. From here on a sunny day just after a storm, the lake looks like a brilliant blue sapphire, nesting in soft folds of white velvet. Pack a camera or stop at one of the photographers lining Ridge Run.

Mountain layout—Skiing

◆◆ **Expert:** The California base strikes awe in all but the best skiers because the world seems to drop straight down into Lake Tahoe. Gunbarrel and East Bowl are 1,700-vertical-foot-high straight ladders of bumps, often with dangerous-looking rocky protrusions in early winter or late spring. But true experts should head to the Nevada side. From the gondola, take the Tamarack Express chair, then cruise down to the Dipper Express. From here, traverse to Milky Way Bowl, which has arguably the best snow at the resort. Then enter Mott Canyon via designated gates 5 or 6. Hully Gully and Pinenuts are double-diamond runs and will allow you to do some reconnaissance on the canyon's north-facing chutes. But if you're already uncomfortable, don't try Bill's, Snakepit, or The Y—listed in order of difficulty and accessed via gate 1. They are three of the steepest lift-served runs in the west. Killebrew Canyon is even more treacherous. Only venture here if you have a change of underwear.

◆ **Advanced:** If the bumps on the California face look too menacing, head to the Sky Express chair, right off the gondola down Von Schmidt's Trail. From the top of the Sky Express, the best of the California side opens up. After you have admired the view of Lake Tahoe, drop down Ellie's if you are looking for bumps. When Ellie's is groomed, it's a screaming cruiser. Then strike out for Nevada, where 50 percent of the terrain is. You get to the Nevada side from the top of Sky Express; go left along the Skyline Trail. As you near Milky Way Bowl, look to your right for tracks leading into the trees and follow them. After a short traverse you will end up near the top of the bowl. Those coming off the Dipper chair on the Nevada side can use the same traverse. The daring may want to test their mettle in Mott Canyon. But if the view of the canyon makes you tremble, return instead to the Dipper Express for a run in the Dipper Bowl. Avoid the Galaxy chair; it's a slow lift that serves relatively flat terrain.

■ **Intermediate:** If you want long smooth cruising, head to the right from the Sky Express when you get off the chair and steam down Liz's, Canyon, Betty's or Ridge Run.

The Nevada side has even better cruisers. From the top of the Dipper Express are the Big Dipper and Orion's. The Galaxy Chair is a good spot for low intermediates to gain confidence. With its meandering intermediate runs, it also is a great hideaway for families with small children. For a cruise that takes forever, take Olympic Downhill to Stagecoach Base.

●● **Beginner** ● **Never-ever:** Though Heavenly is exactly that for intermediates and up, never-evers should pick another resort for their skiing baptism. Except for a tiny learning section at the California base, Heavenly's green terrain is smack in the middle of the boarding area for four lifts. People dart in every direction, making a most intimidating scene. However, everyone—non-skiers included—can ride the tram or gondola to admire the view of the lake. If you must take your first lesson here, go to the Boulder base area on the Nevada side, where there is a gentle slope and more room to spread out.

Note: The gondola stops downloading people at 4 p.m., so be sure you wind your way back to the top of the gondola before then (via 49er, Sam's Dream, Cascade, or the California Trail). Signage is good at Heavenly, so you shouldn't have trouble finding it.

Mountain layout—Snowboarding

Riders don't come here for terrain parks and halfpipes, they come for the steeps, powder-filled canyons and powder stashes in the woods. The biggest bummer is the terrain layout isn't exactly snowboarder-friendly—the traverses are flat, flat, flat, and you have to do a lot of strapping and unstrapping to move around the mountain. But, all that work is worth it, especially after a powder dump.

General consensus among riders is the California side is too bumped up (stay away from Gunbarrel and East Bowl if you hate bumps like most riders do), so the Nevada side is the place to play. Mott Canyon and Killebrew Canyon have the steepest terrain at Heavenly. But beware: by steep, we mean *way* steep. For strictly trees, head to Dipper Knob Trees and the area known as the "western perimeter" (off Olympic Chair, ride the ridge to the trees, where you'll find natural hits, waves and lots of powder). On the California side, the best woods are Skiways and Maggie's Canyon (both reached by the Sky Express lift).

Other playgrounds include the numerous hits in Sand Dunes, the waterfall in North Bowl trees and the natural pipe left of Sky chair. Stick to Stagecoach and Olympic lifts if you want to carve your brains out. And if you must head to the terrain park, ride the trees on the northeast side of it instead. By the way, there's a new halfpipe on California Trail. Never-evers should pick another resort for their snowboarding baptism.

Heavenly Resort Facts

California Side—
Summit elevation: 10,040 feet
Vertical drop: 3,500 feet
Base elevation: 6,540 feet
Nevada Side—
Summit elevation: 10,040 feet
Vertical drop: 2,840 feet
Base elevation: 7,200 feet
Expert:★★★★
Advanced:★★★★
Intermediate:★★★★
Beginner:★★   Never-ever:★
Address: Box 2180, Stateline, NV 89449
✆ Area code: 775
Ski area phone: 586-7000
Snow report: 586-7000, press 1

ⓘ Toll-free reservations:
(800) 243-2836 (2-HEAVEN)
E-mail: info@skiheavenly.com
Internet: www.skiheavenly.com
Number of lifts: 29–1 aerial tram, 1 gondola,
1 six-passenger high-speed chair, 5 high-speed quads,
8 triples, 5 doubles, 8 surface lifts
Snowmaking: 69 percent of trails
Total acreage: 4,800 patrolled acres
(1,084 skiable trail acres)
Uphill capacity: 41,000 per hour
Snowboarding: Yes
Bed Base: 22,000 in S. Lake Tahoe
Nearest lodging: At base of gondola
Resort child care: Yes, 6 weeks and older
Adult ticket, per day: $52-57 (01/02)

Lessons (2001/02 prices)

Group lessons: For levels higher than advanced beginner, ski and snowboard clinics (called Mountain Adventure Clinics) cost $49. If you also need rentals and/or a lift ticket, ask about packages. You also can buy a three- to five-day clinic booklet at a discount. The booklet does not have to be used on consecutive days. Heavenly also packages lessons with lift tickets or rental equipment.

Never-ever package: A two-hour Perfect Turn clinic, rentals and access to the beginner lifts is $79, ski or snowboard. Ask about multiday savings.

Private lessons: $85 per hour. Discounts offered for multiple hours and for early-morning or late-afternoon lessons. Reservations suggested. Call (775) 586-7000, Ext. 6218.

Special programs: Heavenly has special theme clinics, such as Mott and Killebrew guided tours for experts, carving clinics, and clinics for women. Perhaps the most popular is Carver's Paradise, which gets you on the mountain a half-hour before the lifts open, clearly the best way to catch fresh powder and corduroy. Call for prices, dates and reservations on all these programs.

Racing: A coin-op course is on the Yahoo run on the California side, for $2 per run.

Child care (2001/02 prices)

Ages: 6 weeks to 6 years.

Costs: Full-day program costs $75; half-day, morning or afternoon, costs $55. Both include lunch. Ski instruction/day care combo programs also are available for ages 3 and older.

Reservations: Strongly recommended. Call the resort at (775) 586-7000. The child-care center is at the California base.

Other options: Bright Beginnings (775-588-5437) is a state-licensed day-care center in Stateline (just north of the casinos) for ages 6 weeks to 12 years. The center is open Mon.-Sat., 8:30a.m.-4:30 p.m., and the staff is very friendly. Reservations are required; full day including lunch costs $70. Or call the Heavenly child care center for a list of **babysitters,** but expect to pay $15/hour for a sitter. **Baby's Away** (800-446-9030) rents and will deliver baby items (cribs, strollers, toys, etc.) to your hotel or condo anywhere in the Lake Tahoe area.

Children's lessons: Full day for ages 4–13 is $116, including instruction, equipment, lunch, snacks and lift access. Ages 7-13 can take snowboard lessons for the same price. The afternoon session costs $76, and does not include lunch. A Tag-A-Long private lesson allowing the parent to participate with their child is 75 minutes long and costs $85.

Lift tickets (2001/02 prices)

	Adult	Child (6-12)
One day	$57	$29
Three of four days	$162 ($54/day)	$81 ($27/day)
Five days	$260 ($52/day)	$125 ($25/day)

Who skis free: Children ages 5 and younger ski free with a paying adult.

Who skis at a discount: Young adult (ages 13–18) ski for $47 a day; $132 for three days; $210 for five days. Ages 65 and older ski for child prices. A tram ride for nonskiers is $18 for adults and $12 for children. A gondola ride costs $20 for adults, $12 for children (kids under 5 are free) and $18 for seniors.

Kirkwood

The lovely drive through Hope Valley to Kirkwood from South Lake Tahoe takes only about 45 minutes, but it is light-years away in altitude and ambiance. Kirkwood has no bright lights, no ringing jackpots, no wide blue lake, no high-rise buildings and no urban noise. Instead, you have the feeling that you are entering a special secret place, known to a select few. Yet you're at one of Tahoe's "big six" resorts.

As you drive up the access road from Highway 88, it's easy to see why this giant bowl was chosen for a ski resort. Skiers and snowboarders have left their tracks on every slope leading down to Kirkwood Village. No town existed before the resort came to fruition in 1972, and whatever you see was built (and is still being built) for a purpose: to improve the skiing and riding experience. Not that there was much to improve. Kirkwood sits in a natural basin with a base elevation of 7,800 feet—the highest in the Tahoe area. In a mountain range known for heavy powder (a.k.a. Sierra cement), Kirkwood's snow is often lighter and fluffier and more abundant than the other Tahoe resorts. Consequently, the resort frequently stays open into May with good late-season conditions.

Terrain-wise, Kirkwood is the most balanced resort in the Tahoe region. It has one of the best learning areas in the country; several gentle runs off to one side, away from the main traffic, are served by their own lift. Kirkwood will thrill any expert, even super-expert, with its steeps and dozens of chutes. And it offers great terrain for all ability levels between those extremes. The only complaint we've ever heard about Kirkwood is its slow lifts. Of its 10 chairlifts, only one is an express quad. But we hear upgrades are planned in the future.

Mountain layout—Skiing

Kirkwood has both named and numbered its lifts. Locals and staff tend to use the numbers, so we list those in parentheses in the terrain description.

◆◆ **Expert:** Kirkwood locals know to follow the sun. Take The Reut (Chair 11) and traverse under Norm's Nose. Make a few turns down this wall and head to Caples Crest (Chair 2). Then drop into the backside (watch for Bud's Alley to the right or you'll end up below the Sunrise lift). As you ride up the painfully slow

Kirkwood Facts

Summit elevation:	9,800 feet
Vertical drop:	2,000 feet
Base elevation:	7,800 feet

Expert:★★★★★
Advanced:★★★★★
Intermediate:★★★★★
Beginner:★★★★
Never-ever:★★★★★
Address: Box 1, Kirkwood, CA 95646
Area code: 209
✆ **Ski area phone:** 258-6000
Snow report: 877-KIRKWOOD (877-547-5966)

ⓘ **Toll-free reservations:** (800) 967-7500
Fax: 258-8899
E-mail: kwd-info@skikirkwood.com
Internet: www.skikirkwood.com
Number of lifts: 12–2 quad, 7 triples, 1 double, 2 surface lifts
Snowmaking: 5 percent
Skiable acreage: 2,300 acres
Uphill capacity: 17,905 per hour
Snowboarding: Yes
Bed Base: 2,000 in resort, 22,000 in S. Lake Tahoe
Nearest lodging: Slopeside, ski-in/ski-out
Resort child care: Yes, 2 years and older
Adult ticket, per day: $49-$54 (02/03)

Sunrise chair, you can scout for untracked powder (or read the historical trivia posted on the lift towers). Since it takes three chairs to get here (four if you miss Bud's Alley), and the Sunrise chair closes when it's too windy, powder often remains for days after a storm. But beware, it can be heavy too. To return to the front side, drop down to Thunder Saddle and pick one of four north-facing chutes to return to the main base area.

Then, pick from the Wagonwheel/The Wall (Chair 10) or Cornice (Chair 6) lifts. Both serve steep, wide-open bowls and white-knuckle chutes. For a real thrill, traverse from Chair 10 to the top of Notch Chute in The Sisters. If you can handle the "step" that's been carved into the chute, you're there. Cornice serves single-diamond runs that feel like double-diamonds (e.g., Lost Cabin). From the top of Cornice, you can also traverse right to Palisades Bowl for some good powder shots. One final note: Pay attention to signs warning of cliffs. What looks like a simple trail on the map may in reality be a tight plunge through a cliff band.

◆ **Advanced:** Both Sentinel Bowl and Zachary are groomed every day, a draw for anyone looking for super-smooth steeps. If you want bumps, try Olympic, Look-Out Janek, or Monte Wolfe, on either side of the Cornice Chair. The Reut (Chair 11) has some great cruisers—black on the map, but a solid intermediate could handle them. Don't miss runs on the back side, served by the Sunrise chair. Return to the front side via the Iron Horse chair.

■ **Intermediate:** Intermediates can stay on the lower sections of the face, using Hole'n'Wall (Chair 7) and Solitude (Chair 5), or work their way over Caples Crest (Chair 2) to the Sunrise section, where there's plenty of groomed intermediate terrain. The entire lower mountain, with just a couple of exceptions, is perfectly suited for intermediates. When you're ready to test your black-diamond skills, try the runs off Chair 11.

●● **Beginner:** Beginners will find gentle trails served by Snowkirk Chair (Chair 1) to the east, and Bunny Chair (Chair 9) and Hole 'n' Wall (Chair 7) at the far west.

● **Never-ever:** Never-evers should head straight for the Timber Creek Lodge, a right-hand turn before you reach the main parking lot (there's a sign). Here novices will find a rental shop and ticket window, plus Chairs 9 and 7 (Bunny and Hole'n'Wall) that serve novice and low-intermediate terrain. Experienced skiers should park in the main lot and get their tickets in the main lodge farther down the road, but if there's a novice in your group, you can get to the main area using Chair 7. Kirkwood has—by far—the best setup for novices in the South Tahoe region.

 # Mountain layout—Snowboarding

Kirkwood has the best pow in Tahoe—sick, dry and fluffy—and tons of gullies that are Mother Nature's very own halfpipes and quarterpipes. Kirkwood also gets high marks for its freestyle terrain park, reached by Caples Crest (Chair 2), and the halfpipe, reached by Solitude (Chair 5).

Besides the obvious double-black shots off Wagonwheel/The Wall (Chair 10) and the back side just waiting to be explored, experts will find some of the best riding off the Cornice chair (Chair 6), which also serves Palisades Bowl, to the far right on the trail map. Getting here requires a bit of a traverse and some hoofing, but you'll find great powder shots. Some favorite spots on the back side served by Sunrise (Chair 4): Drop the cornice at the spot called The Wave or float the chutes to the right of Thunder Saddle. Beware of the long flat back to the lifts after dropping off the saddle.

Chomping at the bit to carve some nice arcs? You'll find nice long, grooved runs here too. Stay on the lower sections of the face, using Hole'n'Wall (Chair 7) and Solitude (Chair 5), or work your way over Caples Crest (Chair 2) to the Sunrise section, where there's plenty of groomed intermediate terrain. Never-evers should head straight for the Timber Creek Lodge. Kirkwood has—by far—the best setup for novices in the South Tahoe region.

Lessons (2002/03 prices)

Group lessons: Kirkwood's Ski and Board School offers clinics for all levels. These are 110 minutes long, cost $40, and are designed to smooth out rough edges, rather than teach the basics from scratch.

Never-ever package: A First Time ski package including a two-hour lesson, beginner lift ticket and rental equipment costs $75. The first-time skier program uses the Elan PSX 133 cm. short carving skis that accelerate learning by adding stability and providing an early introduction to the sensation of "shaping" turns. Learn-To-Snowboard packages with a 2.5-hour lesson, beginner lift ticket and rental equipment are $75.

Private lessons: $85 for an hour, $25 each additional person.

Special programs: There are programs for women, all-mountain day camps, and Kirkwood Explorers that tackles non-groomed terrain. Call for dates and prices.

Child care (2001/02 prices)

Ages: 2–6 years, toilet-trained.
Costs: All day is $75 including lunch, a half day $55.
Reservations: Recommended; call (209) 258-7274. Licensed child care for infants can be arranged with an outside agency at (209) 258-8783.

Other options: If you are staying in South Lake Tahoe, **Bright Beginnings** (775-588-5437) is a state-licensed day-care center in Stateline (just north of the casinos) for ages 6 weeks to 12 years. The center is open Mon.-Sat., 8:30a.m.-4:30 p.m., and the staff is very friendly. Reservations are required; full day including lunch costs $70. Or ask the Kirkwood child-care center for a list of **babysitters;** expect to pay $15/hour for a sitter. **Baby's Away** (800-446-9030) rents and will deliver baby items (cribs, strollers, toys, etc.) to your hotel or condo anywhere in the Lake Tahoe area.

Children's lessons: Ski lessons for ages 4–12 and snowboard lessons for ages 7–12 include rental equipment, lunch, lessons and lifts for $80 for a full day and $65 for a half day. The package for those who have equipment is $70 for a full day, $55 for a half day. Ages 13 and older are considered young adults and enroll in the adult lessons. Kirkwood's children's center is located in the Timber Creek novice area.

Lift tickets (2002/03 prices)

	Adult	Child (6-12) and Seniors (70+)
One day	$54	$12
Three days	$156 ($52/day)	$36 ($12/day)
Five days	$245 ($49/day)	$60 ($12/day)

Who skis free: No one.
Who skis at a discount: Ages 5 and younger, $6; ages 60–69, $29; young adults 13–24, $43.

Accommodations at Kirkwood Resort

If you want big-mountain skiing and a get-away-from-it-all location, stay slopeside at Kirkwood. The village has many new condos, shops, and services such as an ice rink and recreation center/swim complex. Phase One of the village is now complete and includes **Snowcrest Lodge, The Mountain Club** and the **Lodge at Kirkwood.** Just completed in 2002 is the **Meadow Stone Lodge,** just steps from the lifts. Perhaps the best part about the new village is that it's, well—new. All the rooms feature modern interiors, have a prime location on the slopes and make efficient use of space. Of the other condo-complexes on the Meadow Side, the top choice is **Sun Meadows,** which is across from the Solitude and Cornice chairs and about as centrally located as you can get in Kirkwood. The second choice is **The Meadows,** between Timber Creek and the Cornice Chair. Rates range from $159-249 for a studio to $550-600 for a three-bedroom condo. Packages—particularly midweek stays—bring down the cost. Reservations: (209) 258-7000 or (800) 967-7500.

For a classic Sierra experience, book a cabin at **Sorensen's Resort** (800-423-9949; 530-694-2203; www.sorensensresort.com; $$-$$$$). Nestled beneath a cliff in the Hope Valley 14 miles from Kirkwood, Sorensen's is a secluded, quiet camp bustling with winter activity, including cross-country skiing.

Sierra-at-Tahoe

Sierra-at-Tahoe often is overlooked by destination skiers to the South Shore. What a shame. Sierra-at-Tahoe has more than 2,000 vertical feet and 2,000 acres, and the tree skiing is some of the best in the country. Roughly 1,500 of the 2,000 acres are in the trees, old growth fir trees that, as one local put it, seem "strategically placed." Just 12 miles south (about 30 minutes), this fun, big resort has an intimate feel. The resort has opted to invest its money into on-mountain upgrades; consequently you won't find any lodging or even a mountain village at its base. You *will* find a compact base area that's easy to get around, fabulous terrain, an efficient lift network, and great customer service, thank you very much.

Mountain layout—Skiing

◆◆ **Expert:** Forget trails. Head for the trees, particularly on a powder day. In West Bowl, the trees between Horsetail and Clipper hold almost unlimited stashes. When you hit the lift line, don't bail. Head back into the trees on the other side for a secret area of more untracked, creamy powder. The terrain around the Grandview Express gets tracked quickly, but you can still find fun in the trees between Preacher's Passion and the Tahoe King lift. It's steep and littered with giant boulders that, when covered with 10 feet of snow, resemble giant gnomes. Consider it nature's terrain park. Higher up, dive into the trees before Upper Dynamite. An opening referred to as Daylight Chute isn't on the map. Five backcountry access gates were recently opened. Access is free with the purchase of a lift ticket, but know about avalanche safety and come equipped. Guided tours are available daily.

◆ **Advanced:** Sierra-at-Tahoe has a good collection of bumped-up black-diamond trails off the Grand View Express. Eastabout, Castle, Preacher's Passion and Dynamite all cascade roughly 1,300 vertical feet. Also try Clipper and Horsetail in the West Bowl.

■ **Intermediate:** This is a wonderful area for intermediates. West Bowl will fast become the favorite area of the mountain for this level. Lower Main is a steep, groomed run that rises above the day lodge. It's gotta be the toughest blue run here. If you see this trail and gulp, don't worry. Fun awaits in West Bowl. The Backside is another good spot for intermediates looking to test their powder skills.

●● **Beginner:** Sugar 'n' Spice is a 2.5-mile, easy cruise from the summit. Ride the Grand View Express chair and take a moment to look at the view of the lake (much better on the roof deck of the Grand View Grill). As you descend Sugar 'n' Spice, stay a good distance from the snowbank on the left edge of the run, especially when it gets to be head-high. Hot shots like to shoot out of the trees between this run and Upper Snowshoe. Fortunately, Sugar 'n' Spice is plenty wide. Stay to the middle or the right and give the idiots some room.

Upper Snowshoe is another good beginner run, but be sure to turn right at Marten to meet up with Sugar 'n' Spice, or you'll be on Lower Snowshoe, a blue run. Another chair that serves good beginner terrain is Rock Garden.

● **Never-ever:** This is a great learner's mountain. Sierra-at-Tahoe has a super learning slope called Broadway, right at the day lodge and served by its own quad chair.

 Mountain layout—Snowboarding

Sierra-at-Tahoe has three terrain parks, all marked with icons on the trail map. The advanced terrain park is on The Alley and has three rail slides, two hits, two tabletops (with multiple hits) and a 17-foot superpipe. Aspen/Aspen West also has a superpipe. Intermediates should head to the park on Upper Main, where you'll find four big tabletops. Beginners can try the berms and rollers in the park on Wagon Trail. Like riding in the trees? About 1,500 of the 2,000 acres here are woods, and powder stashes often stay hidden in the old-growth forest for days after a storm. Ride the Grand View Express or West Bowl Express and just jump into the trees—anywhere. Five backcountry access gates were recently opened. Access is free with the purchase of a lift ticket, but know about avalanche safety and come equipped. Guided tours are available daily.

Sierra-at-Tahoe Facts

Summit elevation:	8,852 feet
Vertical drop:	2,212 feet
Base elevation:	6,640 feet
Expert:★★	
Advanced:★★★★	
Intermediate:★★★★	
Beginner:★★★★	
Never-ever:★★★★	

Address: 1111 Sierra-at-Tahoe Rd. Twin Bridges, CA 95735

✆ Area code: 530
Ski area phone: 659-7453
Snow report: 659-7475

ⓘ **Toll-free reservations:** 800-AT-TAHOE (288-2463)
Fax: 659-7749
E-mail: sierra@boothcreek.com
Internet: www.sierratahoe.com
Number of lifts: 9–3 high-speed quads, 1 triple, 5 doubles
Snowmaking: 10 percent
Skiable acreage: 2,000 acres
Uphill capacity: 14,921 per hour
Snowboarding: Yes
Bed Base: 22,000 in S. Lake Tahoe
Nearest lodging: About 12 miles away
Resort child care: Yes, 18 months and older
Adult ticket, per day: $50 (2001/02 prices)

Lessons (2001/02 prices)

Group lessons: FREE lessons for strong intermediate through expert skiers or snowboarders are offered twice a day on a first-come basis for ages 13 and older; sign-up and meet at the top of the West Bowl Express. Break-through packages for advancing beginners through lower intermediates, 1.5-hour lessons cost $32 for lessons only; $88 with lifts and equipment.

Never-ever package: A First Time package including beginner lifts, rentals and two-hour lesson is $65 for skiers or snowboarders. A two-day package is $105.

Private lessons: $70 an hour, with discounts for additional hours or early-bird lessons.

Child care (2001/02 prices)

Ages: 18 months–5 years.
Costs: $85 for full day (full day includes lunch); call for half-day rates.
Reservations: Recommended; call (530) 659-7453.

Children's lessons: All-day ski or snowboard instruction (including lunch, rentals, lift ticket) is $85 for ages 4–12; $75 for afternoon half day (with no lunch).

Lift tickets (2001/02 prices)

	Adult	Child (6-12)
One day	$50	$10
Two of three days	$86 ($43/day)	$22 ($11/day)
Three of five days	$125 ($41+/day)	$33 ($11/day)

Who skis free: Younger than 6.

Who skis at a discount: Ages 70 and older pay $12; ages 60-69, $29; young adults ages 13-22, $40; multiday discounts available.

Cross-country and snowshoeing

The Lake Tahoe region may have the greatest concentration of large cross-country ski areas in the U.S., with more than 800 km. of groomed trails. Most of that is on the north end of the lake, but South Shore has a good network of trails, too. Most also allow snowshoes.

Sierra-at-Tahoe (530-659-7453) has more than 3 miles of groomed snowshoeing trails with daily rentals available.

Spooner Lake Cross-Country (775-887-8844, recording; 755-749-5349, live voice) on Hwy. 28, about a half-mile north of Hwy. 50, has more than 80 km. of trails, nearly all of which are machine groomed, with one 19-km. backcountry trail. Adult trail fees are $16.50; less for ages 7-15. Children younger than age 7 ski free. Lessons and cross-country gear, snowshoe and pulk sled rentals are available; you also can rent a backcountry cabin.

Kirkwood Cross-Country (209-258-7248) has 80 km. of machine-groomed tracks, skating lanes and three interconnected trail systems with three warming huts, including the 1864 Kirkwood Inn, a trappers' log cabin full of nostalgia. Rental gear includes cross-country, telemark, snowshoes and pulk sleds. Lessons are also available. Adult trail fees are $20, ages 13-18 and 65+ are $15, children 7-12 are $6, children 5 and younger are free.

Heavenly's Adventure Park (775-586-7000) at the top of the gondola includes a cross-country skiing and snowshoeing center. You'll find 5 km. of groomed trails that meander through the forest and provide awesome views from nearly 3,000 feet above Lake Tahoe. Prices for both activities are $20 for a day or $10 for two hours and include rental equipment.

Hope Valley Cross-Country Ski Center (530-694-2337) is near the junction of Highways 89 and 88. It has about 100 km. of marked trails, a quarter of which are groomed. Trail fees are by donation. Lessons and rentals are available. The trails at **Sorensen's Resort** (800-423-9949; 530-694-2203) hook into this system.

Camp Richardson Resort (530-542-6584) in South Lake Tahoe has a cross-country ski center with lessons, rentals and trails along the Lake Tahoe shoreline. It's been voted "Best XC ski trails" by Tahoe locals.

Accommodations

South Shore accommodations divide into four categories: the multistory casinos hugging the Nevada border for great views and nonstop nightlife; the top of Kingsbury Grade, near the base of Heavenly's Nevada side, for upscale condominiums and top-quality hotels; along the California lake shore for moderately priced motels; and at Kirkwood to escape the hustle and bustle. **Central Reservations for South Lake Tahoe** is at (800) 288-2463 (AT-TAHOE). Sunday through Thursday nights, you can get extremely good deals. Packages can run as low as $69 per person, per night, double occupancy. If you're here Friday and Saturday, however, prices double or sometimes triple. South Shore has a wide variety of lodging, so tell the agent how much you want to spend.

Many destination visitors like to be smack in the middle of the action. If you're in that group, try **Harveys Resort & Casino** (800-648-3361 from outside Nevada or 775-588-2411 from Nevada; $$–$$$) and **Harrah's Casino Hotel** (800-648-3353 or 775-588-3515; $$–$$$$), which have everyone's highest ratings, from AAA to Mobil. Other casino-hotels within walking distance of the state line are **Caesars Tahoe** (800-648-3353 or 775-586-2000; $$–$$$$) and the **Horizon Casino Resort** (800-648-3322; $$–$$$$). Ask for a lakeview room with a balcony at the Horizon.

On the California side, several beautiful hotels have been built in the past few years. The newest among them is the **Marriott Grand Residence Club** (866-204-7263; $$-$$$$) in the new Park Avenue development at the base of Heavenly's gondola. It features in-suite kitchens, laundry service, a ski-check room, as well as a number of retail shops. It's also the closest hotel to Heavenly's gondola, which gives skiers and sightseers a jaw-dropping view of the lake in its 12-minute journey from downtown to the slopes.

Also near the gondola is one of our favorite places, the **Embassy Suites Lake Tahoe Resort** (800-362-2779; 530-544-5400; www.embassytahoe.com; $$–$$$). Just 50 feet from the nearest casino, this property was chosen No. 1 in the 108-hotel Embassy Suites chain in a survey of 40,000 guests. It has an indoor atrium, pool and spa, an exercise center and on-site restaurant. Cooked-to-order breakfast and a free happy hour are included in the rates.

The California side of South Lake Tahoe has many hotels and motels lining Hwy. 50. Among the best are two Best Western properties—**The Timber Cove Lodge** (800-528-1234 or 530-541-6722; $–$$$), located on the beach; and **Station House Inn** (800-822-5953 or 530-542-1101; $$–$$$), within walking distance of the casino area, on the California side of the border. Two miles from the casinos, **Inn By The Lake** (800-877-1466; 530-542-0330; $–$$$) sits almost at the shore (although on the wrong side of Hwy. 50). It has 100 guest rooms (including nine suites with kitchens, but many of the regular guest rooms are large and have refrigerators), a free continental breakfast with enough selections to keep you full until lunch, heated pool, and bi-level hot tub. It's also one of the stops on the free shuttle to the slopes.

Embassy Vacation Resorts (800-362-2779; 530-541-6122; $$$-$$$$) is a 300-suite resort with timeshare condos and all the amenities. At the intersection of Hwy. 50 and Ski Run Boulevard, it is close to the lake, the ferry dock and Heavenly's slopes.

For the rustic-minded, try the **Historic Camp Richardson Resort** (800-544-1801; $$–$$$). The cabins have large fireplaces, spacious living rooms and full kitchens. Perfect for couples traveling together or families who enjoy various outdoor sports. Onsite sledding, snowshoeing, cross-country trails and wilderness sleigh rides complete this seasonal resort. The historic hotel and beachside inn provide more "civilized" accommodations.

Adjacent to the Lakeside Beach is the funky **Royal Valhalla Motor Lodge** (800-999-4104; 530-544-2233; $-$$$), just two blocks from the casinos in a quiet neighborhood. Some rooms have kitchens and most have wonderful lake views. .

Lakeland Village (800-822-5969; 530-544-1685; $$–$$$$) has a hotel and condominiums on the lake with shuttlebus service to Heavenly and Kirkwood. The units range from studios to a lakefront four-bedroom, three-bath unit. For those who want a room 150 yards from Heavenly's California base, the **Tahoe Seasons Resort**, with 160 suites, has received good reviews from everyone locally (530-541-6700; $$–$$$$). Another possibility is the **Holiday Inn Express** (800-544-5288; 530-544-5900; $$–$$$$).

One for couples only: The **Fantasy Inn** (800-367-7736, 530-541-4200; $$$–$$$$) has about 60 rooms designed for romance. Tahoe had another Fantasy Inn a while back that was quite tacky, but this one is very tastefully done. Each room has one bed in a choice of several shapes (round, heart-shaped, water or regular mattress, king-size), a private spa for two, an in-room music system with 30 channels, adjustable peach-colored lighting and showers with double shower heads. Sixteen of the rooms have themes, such as Rain Forest (plants and rattan decor), Caesar's Indulgence (a sexy black decor), and Romeo and Juliet (the honeymoon suite we didn't see because it was continually booked during our visit). A wedding chapel is on the premises. Theme suites are in the $245–$295 range. Ask about special ski and/or wedding package rates.

Dining

For the best restaurants in the higher priced category:

Evan's American Gourmet Café (542-1990; $$$) on State Route 89 has become one of the best-liked restaurants on the South Shore. The chef prepares California Cuisine with an unusual flair. Expect to pay for his efforts, but they are reported to be well worth it. **Primavera Restaurant** (775-586-2000; $$–$$$) in Caesars Tahoe serves Italian poolside in an atmosphere reminiscent of quaint European cafés with excellent service, quality and wine list. For a superb meal, great wine list and attentive service—with a beautiful view—head to **Friday's Station** (775-588-6611; $$$) at the top of Harrah's casino-hotel. Other recommendations are **Fresh Ketch** (541-5683; $$$) for fish; **Dory's Oar** (541-6603; $$$) for steaks and seafood; or **ECHO Restaurant & Lounge** (543-2140, $$–$$$) in the Embassy Suites hotel for its delicious American fusion cuisine.

For good reasonable restaurants, try: **The Cantina Bar and Grill** (544-1233; $) for Mexican, **Scusa** (542-0100; $$) for Italian (a local favorite), **Sato Japanese Restaurant** (544-0774 or 775-588-1914 in the Horizon Casino; $–$$) for surprisingly good sushi specials, the **Shoreline Café** (541-7858; $$) for good pasta specials and an extensive kids' menu, or **The Tudor Pub** (541-6603; $-$$), upstairs from Dory's Oar, for fish & chips and European beers on tap. Of the casinos' affordable buffets (and there are many), we enjoyed **Harveys** (775-588-2411; $) reasonably priced seafood buffet with large portions.

Dining: $$$-Entrees $20+; $$-$10-20; $-less than $10.
Accommodations: (double room) $$$$-$200+; $$$-$141-$200; $$-$81-$140; $-$80 and less.

Others to try are **Beacon** (541-0630; $$-$$$), at Camp Richardson, with blackened prime rib a specialty; and **Nephele's** (544-8130; $$), which serves California cuisine in a cozy setting. Next door to Nephele's is an outstanding restaurant called **Café Fiore** (541-2908; $$). It doesn't seat many, so reservations are a must. The food and the wine list are superb.

Sprouts (541-6969; $) is another local favorite. The extensive menu includes rice bowls, hummus melts and lasagna. Don't miss the smoothies, especially if you're ailing after a long night. A shot of wheatgrass might cure all. A small eclectic café with an island atmosphere (check out the salt and pepper shakers on each table), **Freshies** (542-3630; $) is another good bet for fresh, healthy food. In keeping with the name, the café offers half off soups on powder days.

For great breakfasts head to the **Red Hut Waffle Shop** (541-9024; $), where you can pack into a small room and listen to the talk of the town. Another branch is on Kingsbury Grade (775-588-7488, $), handy for skiers heading to the Nevada side of Heavenly. At **Heidi's** (544-8113, $), get anything from dozens of types of Belgian waffles to chocolate pancakes. If you're in over the weekend you must go to **Llewellyn's** (775-588-2411; $$) at Harvey's Resort Hotel for Sunday brunch; food is flavorful, and the view breathtaking. If you're a jetlagged easterner and wake up at 4 a.m., head to one of the casino's 24-hour restaurants. The Horizon's **Four Seasons** serves a basic breakfast, and you can pick up a latté at **Starbucks** in the hotel lobby.

And just in case you crave a malt "so thick it holds the straw up," go to the **Zephyr Cove Resort**. Try the banana-chocolate shake. **Alpen Sierra Coffee Roasting Company** (544-7740), at Highway 50 and Pioneer, was voted "Best Coffee House in South Lake Tahoe" and offers locally roasted mountain coffee.

At Heavenly, table linen lunch service is offered at **Monument Peak Restaurant** ($–$$) at the top of the tram. **East Peak Lodge** ($) and the **Sky Deck** ($) both have outdoor lunch service and sun-drenched tables, but we recommend bringing your own food.

The best on-mountain lunch we had was at Sierra-at-Tahoe. We had a delicious Thai chicken wrap (kind of like a burrito), washed down with a Sierra Nevada Pale Ale at **The Sierra Pub** in the day lodge. The pub serves several microbrews and wine by the glass, as well as nonalcoholic beverages. The resort also has a grill-style restaurant at the summit, and fresh-ground coffee and fresh-baked goods in the day lodge.

If you're staying at Kirkwood, you'll probably discover the places to eat on your own— not a big selection, but all are pretty good. **Off the Wall Bar & Grille** in the Lodge at Kirkwood has California-style gourmet cuisine in a comfortable cozy atmosphere. **Bub's Sports Bar & Grill** ($-$$) across the street from the Cornice Express is where the locals eat, and you'll soon discover why. The burgers and sandwiches go a step beyond the usual bland slopeside cuisine. Also try **Kirkwood Inn,** built in 1864 by Zachary Kirkwood and in operation ever since, featuring hearty meals such as steaks and seafood. Look for the bullet holes left in the walls from Prohibition days. A mile east of Kirkwood on Hwy 88 is the **Caples Lake Resort** for fine dining overlooking scenic Caples Lake. At the **General Store** you can find inexpensive sandwiches and fresh cookies—great for a slope-side picnic.

 Après-ski/nightlife

Head to **Chevy's** immediately after skiing or stop in the **California Bar** at Heavenly's Base Lodge. If you want quieter après-ski with a flickering fireplace, stop in at **Christiana Inn** across from the Heavenly ski area. Kirkwood's **Bub's Sports**

Bar & Grill has an extensive appetizer and happy hour menu. You'll also find dart boards, a pool table, big-screen TVs and a stage for live music.

Later in the evening, **Nero's 2000** in Caesar's Tahoe Casino Hotel has dancing seven nights a week, and live music on the weekends. They have reggae on Mondays and Alternative Night on Wednesdays. **The Pub at Tahoe** (formerly McP's—new name, same place!), a great Irish pub near the state line, has terrific live music (listenable rather than danceable), pool tables on the first floor, and is packed every night. Other spots recommended by locals are **Mulligan's** and **Hoss Hogs**. The **Goalpost Restaurant & Bar** in Stateline is the hot spot for the late-late crowd.

And of course, the **casinos** have musical reviews that are extravaganzas of sight and sound. Some shows run through the season; others are top-name singers and comedians who do one or two shows. Check a local newspaper for up-to-date listings.

Other activities

South Tahoe has tons to do, but space doesn't permit us to list all the options. Ask your hotel concierge for suggestions.

Ice skating is at the South Tahoe Ice Center, also called STIC (530-542-4700). Figure and hockey skates are available for rent, and the Tahoe Lakers pro hockey team plays on Friday and Saturday nights. Call Lake Tahoe Balloons (530- 544-1221) for **balloon rides** and Lake Tahoe Adventures (530-577-2940) for **snowmobiling**. The Husky Express (775-782-3047) takes people **dog sledding** in the Hope Valley for $85/person. Camp Richardson (530-541-3113) has **sleigh rides** through meadows; reservations required.

Heavenly's Adventure Park (775-586-7000) at the top of the gondola includes lift-accessed snow tubing. New at Kirkwood for 2002/03 is **ice skating** at the rink in the pedestrian village. Kirkwood also offers **dogsledding, sleigh rides, sauna and massage,** the **Swim Complex** with an Olympic-size pool and workout facilities, and a family **tubing hill.**

A few **factory outlets**—Bass, Geoffrey Beane, Van Heusen, Big Dog, Adidas/Salomon—have opened at "The Y" (the intersection of Hwy. 50 and 89 south of town). For a **massage**, make an appointment with the Bodymind Studio (530-541-5041) in the Timber Cove Lodge.

Weddings aren't your everyday optional ski activity, but if you're thinking of getting married with little fuss, this is one of the best spots to do it. More than 20 wedding chapels dot the area, but probably the nicest ones are in the big hotels. Most have wedding concierges to plan every detail. You also can be married outdoors, either by the lake or on the slopes. California marriage licenses cost about $50; Nevada licenses are a bit less, plus no blood test is required. For more information, contact the Lake Tahoe Visitors Authority at (800) AT-TAHOE (288-2463).

Getting there and getting around

By air: Reno-Tahoe International Airport has more than 100 nonstop flights a day from various parts of the country. The airport is 55 miles from South Lake Tahoe. The Lake Tahoe Airport, near South Lake Tahoe, has limited service from California. Buses and hotel shuttles take skiers to the resorts from both airports. Tahoe Casino Express (800-446-6128; www.tahoecasinoexpress.com) runs 18 times daily between the Reno airport and South Shore for $17 one-way or $30 round-trip.

By boat: The Hornblower Tahoe Queen, an authentic Mississippi sternwheeler, double-decked and heated, takes South Shore skiers and snowboarders across Lake Tahoe to Squaw

Dining: $$$-Entrees $20+; $$-$10-20; $-less than $10.
Accommodations: (double room) $$$$-$200+; $$$-$141-$200; $$-$81-$140; $-$80 and less.

Valley (buses take skiers from the dock to the ski areas). Call (530) 541-3364. Round-trip fare is about $25. Another paddlewheeler, the M.S. Dixie II, based at Zephyr Cove in Nevada, does daily cruises of Emerald Bay for adults and children, and Saturday night dinner cruises for adults during the winter. For fares and schedules, call (775) 588-6644.

By bus: Shuttles run from almost every major hotel to the resorts. Check for schedules when you arrive. Most of the shuttles are free.

By car: Driving time from Reno is about an hour and ten minutes. San Francisco is about four hours away (that's the way Californians describe driving distances) on Hwy. 50. Sierra-at-Tahoe is 12 miles south of the lake on Hwy. 50. Kirkwood is on Hwy. 88 (follow signs from South Lake Tahoe). During storms, the California Highway Patrol doesn't let drivers come up the mountains without chains or a 4-wheel-drive vehicle, so bring chains or be sure the car rental agency provides them. Or take the shuttle on snowy days.

Getting around: Bring a car if you intend to move frequently between the south and the north shores; otherwise, a car is optional. We'd say have one if you like to roam far afield at night. If not, you can walk to restaurants and nightspots near your hotel and use the ski shuttles during the day.

Mammoth Mountain
June Mountain
California

Summit elevation:	**11,053 feet**
Vertical drop:	**3,100 feet**
Base elevation:	**7,953 feet**

Address: Mammoth Mountain, Box 24; Mammoth Lakes Visitors Bureau, Box 48; both Mammoth Lakes, CA 93546

✆ **Area code:** 760

Ski area phone: 934-2571 & 800-MAMMOTH (626-6684)

ⓘ **Toll-free snow report/information:** (888) SNOW-RPT (766-9778)

Toll-free reservations: (888) GO-MAMMOTH (466-2666) and (888) MAMMOTH (626-6684)

Fax: 934-7066

E-mail: info@mammoth-mtn.com

Internet: www.visitmammoth.com (town); www.mammothmountain.com (ski area)

Dining:★★★
Apres-ski/nightlife:★★★
Other activities:★★★

Expert:★★★★★
Advanced:★★★★★
Intermediate:★★★★★
Beginner:★★★
Never-ever:★★★

Number and types of lifts: 30—2 gondolas, 1 six-pax chair. 8 high-speed quads, 1 quad, 8 triples, 6 doubles, 4 surface lifts

Skiable acreage: 3,500+ acres

Snowmaking: 25 percent

Uphill capacity: 56,600 per hour

Snowboarding: Yes, unlimited

Bed base: 30,000

Nearest lodging: slopeside

Resort child care: Yes, newborns and older

Adult ticket, per day: $46–$60 (02/03 prices)

June Mountain Facts

Summit elevation: 10,135 feet

Vertical drop: 2,590 feet

Base elevation: 7,545 feet

Number and types of lifts: 7—2 high-speed quads, 5 doubles

Skiable acreage: 500+ acres

Uphill capacity: 10,000 per hour

Bed base: 2,000 local

No mountain is better named than Mammoth. When you stand at the base lodge and scan the mountain, you can't even see a quarter of the ski terrain. The encircling ridge, all above treeline, promises dramatic skiing, but what you can't see is even better. Lower peaks such as Lincoln Mountain, Gold Hill and Hemlock Ridge, all with groomed swaths and moguled canyons, stretch six-and-a-half miles in width. Mammoth is one of the nation's largest winter resorts in size, and at times it's the nation's busiest, with more than 14,000 skiers and riders swooping over its slopes on an average weekend.

Its season runs from early November through June—legitimately. Mammoth often relies on its 430 acres of snowmaking to be open by Thanksgiving, but snow often falls by early November. Skiing and riding here on the Fourth of July is a well-loved tradition among the diehards who haven't had enough.

Mammoth attracts people who want one thing: to ski or snowboard. There isn't much at the top of the mountain road to distract you. There is a labyrinthine base lodge with ski school, lift ticket windows, rental shops and hundreds of lockers for locals and visitors. Across the parking lot is the Yodler chalet, brought piece by piece from the Alps and rebuilt to house a restaurant and bar. Slopeside is the Mammoth Mountain Inn.

At the bottom of the mountain road lies the small but spread-out town of Mammoth Lakes. Juniper Springs Lodge and Sunstone, Mammoth's new premiere lodging facility, boasts ski-in/ski-out access. Mammoth is now owned in part by Intrawest, a ski and golf resort company based in Vancouver. Intrawest plans to build a large, slopeside pedestrian village with 1,000 residential units and 140,000 square feet of retail stores over the next 10 years. The first phase of the Village at Mammoth is scheduled to open in early 2003.

Until that village is completed, being a pedestrian at Mammoth will continue to be tough. As the town grew to support the ski area's success, newcomers haphazardly transplanted Southern California sprawl and mini-malls to the mountains. Most visitors come by car from Southern California, but the few who don't will feel the need for wheels—not much is within easy walking distance. However, there is a free town shuttlebus that runs day and night.

If size intimidates you, Mammoth's little sister June Mountain, a half-hour drive from Mammoth Lakes, will appeal to you. Its Old World village atmosphere in a sheltered canyon is on a more human scale. That is not to say it's a puny resort: it has eight chair lifts and a 2,590-foot vertical rise (as opposed to 3,100 feet at Mammoth).

Mountain layout—Skiing

This mountain is very, very large. Almost everything goes by number. The mountain is crisscrossed with a network of chair lifts numbered in the order they were built. It makes perfect sense to visitors who grew up with the mountain, but it's confusing to the first-time visitor who hears regulars planning their day football-quarterback style, "Take one to three, then back side to 23, down the ridge to 14, then to 13 and lateral to 19." Now that the resort has installed several high-speed lifts and given them names, regulars still refer to the lifts by their former number, which makes it even more confusing for the first-time visitor. For the record, Chairs 1, 2, 3, 4, 6, 11, 16 and 18 all have names now, and exist only in the memories and automatic brain-recall of Mammoth regulars.

If you come on a weekend, avoid the Main Lodge at the top of the mountain road (unless you're staying at the slopeside Mammoth Mountain Inn). Tickets are sold (in order as you come up the road) at Little Eagle Lodge next to Juniper Springs Lodge, Canyon Lodge, The Roller Coaster lift, Stump Alley Express and the Main Lodge. Little Eagle Lodge and the Canyon Lodge are actually off the main road to the ski area, so ask someone to direct you. To avoid weekend crowds, take Chairs 9, 25, 22, 21, 12, 13 and 14, listed from left to right on the trail map.

Never-evers should go to Canyon Lodge or Main Lodge. Those with a little experience also can start at Little Eagle Lodge on the Eagle Express.

◆◆ **Expert:** Expert yaa-hoo skiers will strike out for the ridge, reachable by the gondola or a series of chairs. From the ridge, any chute or path will open into a wide bowl. Mammoth's signature run, a snarling lip of snow called Cornice Bowl, looms large in every expert's memory bank. Other runs dropping from the ridge are considered steeper and more treacherous. Reached from the gondola, Hangman's Hollow—Mammoth's toughest—is an hour-glass-shaped chute hanging from the summit and bordered by wicked rocks. At its narrow part there's space for only one turn—a perfect one. Other expert shots are off Chair 22, and on powder days you can often find untracked or less-tracked snow on the far east Dragon's Back off Chair 9, or the far west Hemlock Ridge above Chair 14.

◆ **Advanced:** One of the most popular advanced areas is the group of bowls available from Face Lift Express (formerly Chair 3). They're great warm-up runs for experts, but plan to get here early on weekends. This high-speed lift has helped lessen the formerly outrageous lines (that's our term; one of our favorite Mammoth employees describes it as "healthy"), but it is still busiest on weekend mornings around 9:30 a.m. Midweek, no problem.

A slightly less busy alternative is triple-Chair 5, the next chair to the left on the trail map, or Chair 14, to the far right on the map. Chairs 22 and 25, which provide access to Lincoln Mountain and its intermediate runs and advanced chutes, rarely have lines.

When you feel like attacking the ridge, head to Dave's Run. Off the gondola, traverse the ridge to trail-map left, then drop down when the pitch isn't sheer vertical. Dave's is still pretty steep, but of the single-black options off the ridge, it's usually the least crowded. If you have any doubts, ride the gondola back down to Mid-Chalet, or take the upper-intermediate ridge trail to the Chair 14 area.

■ **Intermediate:** The middle part of the mountain is still above treeline, so those at this level have plenty of room to traverse on the single-black runs. Hidden canyons like Lower Dry Creek (off the Face Lift Express) are full of swoops and surprises, and require tighter turns. For long cruising, head to Eagle Express. Other intermediate playgrounds are served by the tree-lined runs from The Roller Coaster and Canyon express quads and Chairs 8, 20 and 21. At the other edge of the area is Chair 12 and the drop over to Chairs 13 and 14.

●● **Beginner:** If you aren't a first-timer, but still practicing turns, the runs near Canyon Lodge are best. Trails such as Hansel and Gretel weave gently through evergreens, providing sheltered slopes for learning, away from the speed demons. When you're ready for the next step, Christmas Tree, a long run under Eagle Express, is pretty gentle. This part of the mountain gets soupy in the afternoon on warm days, however. If you're intimidated by crowds, and you're trying to step up to the intermediate level, avoid Stump Alley and Broadway, both usually packed with speeders.

● **Never-ever:** The never-ever slopes are off the Discovery Chair at the Main Lodge and Chair 7 from the Canyon Lodge, separated from the hot shots.

June Mountain: June Mountain has none of the high broad bowls that make Mammoth Mountain famous. The steepest terrain at June, The Face, is as steep as anything at Mammoth. Because it is on the lower mountain, it unfortunately doesn't keep the snow as long as the upper runs. Since June is more sheltered than Mammoth and none of its slopes is above the tree line, June tends to hold powder longer than Mammoth's more exposed bowls and the snow doesn't crust up so quickly. There's a great view of June Lake from the upper runs.

Though June has a few expert drops, this level will be bored quickly. Intermediates will have a ball, however. Schatzi is a fantastic and long cruiser, and Matterhorn often is totally deserted. Beginners should stick to the mid-mountain, though Silverado is a gentle, long and uncrowded trail from the Rainbow Summit.

 Mountain layout—Snowboarding

So you're a leap-of-faith kind of rider? The plunge off the summit ridge offers a slew of descents with one thing in common: All are so sickeningly steep you can easily reach out and touch the snow while turning. Want to test Newton's theory of gravity? Drop into the steeps of Climax, pop the cornice into Dave's Run, dance between the rocks in The Wipeout Chutes or huck into Hangman's Hollow. If you really want to shake up your innards, dart through the rocks at the top of Phillipe's and straight-shoot it all the way to the bottom.

Mammoth is definitely one of the carving capitals of the West, so check out the arcs and deep trenches below while riding up the chair, and then slice some yourself. St. Anton, Stump Alley and Gremlin's Gulch are just three of the carving runs to hit. Just make sure to get up early if you expect freshies or perfect corduroy. For long mellow cruisers with a view, explore the backside off the Face Lift Express, wander through Dry Creek's canyon and natural gullies, or ride Ricochet's open glades.

Main Park is arguably one of the best freestyle areas in North America. There's big air to be had off a slew of spines, gaps and tabletops. New this year, you'll find a super-duper-pipe—with walls that are a soaring 22 feet high—making it the largest kind of pipe in North America (superpipes generally have 15-foot walls). Mammoth has two other parks: South Park, on Roller Coaster West, is geared for intermediates, and Canyon Lodge Park has a beginner pipe and smaller-scaled terrain features. No wonder riders are raving about this place! June Mountain also has a superpipe and a snowboard park with jumps, rails and table-tops.

Mountain rating

No matter what level you're at, you won't be shortchanged. First-time visitors should pack a trail map. (Seriously. One of our staff writers has skied here for two decades, but she still carries a trail map—and occasionally uses it.) If you're with a group, decide where to meet if you get separated. We usually pick a centrally located chair, rather than Mid-Chalet or the Main Lodge, which are usually loaded with bodies looking for other bodies. We just stay on the runs under that chair and watch from the lift until we all hook up.

June doesn't have Mammoth's range of terrain, but most skiers and boarders will enjoy it. The pace at June is slower and the crowds considerably fewer. It is a very good choice for mid-winter Saturdays and holiday periods, as well as for families with young children who ski faster than their parents (it's difficult to get lost at June, but very easy at Mammoth).

 ## Cross-country and snowshoeing

Twenty-five miles of groomed trails, actually summer roads, wind around four of the dozen or more high Alpine lakes for which the town of Mammoth Lakes is named. **Tamarack Lodge** (934-2442; 800-237-6879), a 75-year-old summer hunting and fishing lodge now owned by Mammoth Mountain, maintains these trails and charges $18 for access ($13 for ages 10–17 and seniors; free if younger than 9). The Lakes Basin includes many trail heads into the backcountry, where no fee is charged. Rentals and lessons are available. On weekends it's advisable to reserve.

 ## Lessons (2002/03 prices)

Programs are the same at Mammoth or June unless otherwise noted. At Mammoth, lessons are available at both the Main Lodge and the Canyon Lodge. For reservations or questions call 934-0685 for the Main Lodge, 934-0787 for The Canyon Lodge. For June Mountain Ski School call 648-7733.

Group lessons: A three-hour lesson is $55 per person.

Never-ever package: Rentals, lift ticket and three hours of lessons are $81 for skiers and snowboarders.

Private lessons: $120 for one hour for one to five people. Discounts are offered early in the morning, and a two-hour private at 2 p.m. costs $130.

Special programs: There are many, including three-day camps for various groups and skills that cost $260. Call the ski school for dates.

Racing: Mammoth has a well-established racing heritage. It has hosted World Cup races, and several U.S. Ski Team coaches and executives call this resort home. Self-timed courses at Mammoth or June cost $1 per run. Racing clinics are available.

Child care [2002/03 prices]

Ages: Newborn to 12 years.

Costs: $65 for a full day, $45 for a half day. Fees include snacks and lunch, except for infants. Day care can be combined with ski and snowboard school for ages 4–12. They get supervised activities from 8 a.m. to 4:30 p.m., including a lesson and rentals, for $105 if the child is aged 4–6 or is an older beginner; ages 7–12 who have skied or snowboarded before pay $131.

Reservations: Strongly advised, six to eight weeks ahead. Day care is located at both The Small World Day Care Center at Mammoth Mountain Inn (934-0646), just across the street from the Main Lodge, and the child care center at June Mountain (648-7609).

Mammoth has helmet rentals for the kids ($5), and pager rentals for the adults ($2).

Children's lessons: The Woollywood Ski School teaches kids 4–14. Full-day packages (lessons, lunch, lift ticket) for skiing or snowboarding (minimum age for the latter is 7) are $90. Lessons alone cost $35 for two hours, $55 for three hours.

Lift tickets [2002/03 prices]

	Adult (19+)	Teen (13-18)	Child (7-12)
One day (weekends, holidays)	$60	$45	$30
One day (non-holiday weekdays)	$57	$43	$29
Three days (non-holiday)	$159 ($53/day)	$120 ($40/day)	$80 ($26+/day)
Five days (non-holiday)	$233 ($46+/day)	$175 ($35/day)	$118 ($23+/day)

Who skis free: Children ages 6 and younger and seniors 80 and older ski free, as do never-evers taking a ski school lesson.

Who skis at a discount: Ages 65 and older ski for child prices. A beginner lift ticket costs $25 and is valid on Chair 7 and the Discovery Chair.

Lift tickets may be used at either Mammoth or June; however, a June-only ticket (not valid at Mammoth) costs $45 for adults, $40 for ages 19-23, $35 for teens 13–18, $25 for kids.

Ticket offices at Mammoth are at the Main Lodge, the Canyon Lodge and Little Eagle Lodge. Additional satellite offices at two lifts—The Roller Coaster and Stump Alley Express—are open weekends and holidays.

Note: The multiday rates listed here are non-holiday. During holidays, regular per-day rates apply, though you still can buy a multiday ticket.

Accommodations

Mammoth Mountain Inn (934-2581; 800-MAMMOTH; $$–$$$$) is the most convenient. The inn is owned by the ski resort, and includes a restaurant, two small sundries stores, and the resort's child-care facility. Lodging is deluxe to moderate and includes hotel rooms and condos. The better rooms are in the main building.

The new slopeside **Juniper Springs Lodge** and **Sunstone** (760-924-1102; 800-MAM-MOTH; $$$-$$$$) feature deluxe condominium-style rooms with full kitchen, gas fireplaces and balconies, plus there are two heated outdoor pools, two Jacuzzis, a fitness center and underground parking. There's a coffee shop in the lobby, and next door in Little Eagle Lodge you'll find Talon's Restaurant, open daily during the winter for breakfast, lunch and dinner.

Lincoln House and **White Mountain Lodge** (800-MAMMOTH; $$$-$$$$) will be the first buildings to open in the new Village at Mammoth. The one-, two- and three-bedroom units are scheduled to open March 2003.

We list just a few of the places to stay in town. As a starting point, call **Mammoth Lakes Visitors Bureau** (888-466-2666) for a reservation referral. Generally, condos start at about $100 per night, while hotel accommodations—we use the term loosely, as Mammoth currently has more motels than true hotels—can be found for less than $80 per night. Sunday through Thursday stays are quite a bit cheaper than Friday and Saturday.

Mammoth Lakes has been called Condo City of the Sierras. Just beyond the central part of town, **Snowcreek** (934-3333; 800-544-6007; $$-$$$$) is huge and wooded with an athletic club that includes racquetball and basketball. It's actually a neighborhood. Units are spacious one-, two- and three-bedroom loft style.

Closer to the slopes, next to The Canyon Lodge, are many large condominium complexes with a range of units. Try **Mountainback** (934-5000; 800-468-6225) or **1849 Condominiums** (934-7525; 800-421-1849; $$$–$$$$).

In the middle of town, only a walk to restaurants and a shuttle to the lifts, you'll find **Sierra Nevada Rodeway Inn** (934-2515; 800-824-5132; $–$$$) has hotel rooms and chalet units. Check out **Alpenhof Lodge** (934-6330; $–$$$) and the **Snow Goose Inn** (934-2660; 800-874-7368; $–$$$), one of a few bed-and-breakfast inns in town, decorated with antiques, with breakfast served communally in a friendly atmosphere.

Mammoth has several inexpensive motels that offer rooms at $50 to $100 per night, including **Mammoth Thriftlodge** (934-2416; 800-525-9055), **Econo Lodge/Wildwood Inn** (934-6855; 800-845-8764) and **Swiss Chalet** (934-2403; 800-937-9477; $–$$). **Ullr Lodge** (934-2454; $) has rooms with private baths, rooms that share baths and dorm bunks.

June Mountain: The newest lodging in June Lake (the town where June Mountain is located) is among the nicest we've seen in this region. **Double Eagle Resort & Spa** (648-7004; $$$) has several two-bedroom cabins (all No Smoking), plus an on-site restaurant called Eagle's Landing that serves delicious meals and has a magnificent view of the surrounding peaks.

June has two large condominium complexes, with prices starting at less than $100 midweek and $135–$150 weekends. **Interlaken** has studios to three-bedroom units. **Edgewater** has only one size unit, suitable for six to nine people. All other lodgings at June are small and quaint, even funky. **The Haven** has studios for about $70. Call **June Lake Properties Reservation** at (800) 648-5863 (648-JUNE) or **Century 21 Rainbow Ridge** at (800) 462-5589 for condominium reservations.

Also try **Fern Creek Lodge** (800-621-9146; $–$$$), **Whispering Pines** (800-648-7762; $–$$), or **Boulder Lodge** (970-648-7533; $–$$).

Dining

Mammoth Lakes has nearly 60 dining options, from gourmet French cuisine to delicatessen sandwiches and quick take-out. The best gourmet food in town, according to locals, is at **Skadi** (934-3902; $$), with a romantic atmosphere. Another excellent choice for fine dining is **Cervino's** (934-4734; $$), with two recent *Wine Spectator* magazine Awards of Excellence on the wall and a menu that leans toward Northern Italian cuisine.

For the most romantic (and expensive) dining, head out to **Lakefront Restaurant at Tamarack Lodge** (934-3534; $$$) where the menu is basic but the presentation excellent. The atmosphere is Old World in a small dining room decorated with photos of movie stars who used to hang out here. Another top choice, with one of the best wine lists in town, is **The Restaurant at Convict Lake** (934-3803; $$$), four miles south of Mammoth Lakes on Hwy. 395. Look for the Convict Lake turnoff just south of the airport. The Restaurant at Convict Lake is under the same ownership as Cervino's, and it, too, has received two *Wine Spectator* Awards of Excellence.

Nevados (934-4466; $$) has been one of Mammoth's top restaurants for more than 20 years. For steaks, prime rib and seafood, head to **Whiskey Creek** (934-2555; $$), **The Mogul Restaurant** (934-3039; $$) or the **Chart House** (934-4526; $$). Although Mogul has built its long-time reputation as the best traditional family Mammoth steak house, we give best marks to the grilled seafood appetizers and entrees. Your friendly server doubles as your chef. The Mogul also has a children's menu. **Ocean Harvest** (934-8539; $$) is the prime seafood restaurant, offering fresh fish caught from the owner's boat.

Families (or anyone with limited funds) will want to stop in at **Berger's** (934-6622; $-$$) for big, big portions. The tuna salad is massive and you can have not only burgers, but also chicken, salad or Canadian stew. Another family spot is **Angel's** (934-7427; $$) with great ribs, beans and barbecue.

Locals consider **Nik-N-Willie's Pizza** (934-2012; $) the best in town. Pizzas also are featured at **Giovanni's** (934-7563; $) or **Perry's Italian Cafe** (934-6521; $). The best Mexican food is at **Roberto's** (934-3667; $) with homemade tortillas and authentic big servings. Other Mexican-food choices are **La Sierra's** (934-8083; $-$$) or **Gomez's** (924-2693; $).

Grumpy's (934-8587; $) holds the distinction of the town's best fried chicken, also the best cole slaw, all presented in a big-screen TV, No Smoking, sports-bar atmosphere.

Shogun (934-3970; $) has Japanese cuisine and a sushi bar. Try **Matsu** (934-8277; $) for inexpensive Chinese-American. **Austria Hof** (934-2764; $$) and **Alpenrose** (934-3077; $$) serve German and Austrian specialties.

The best breakfast in town is served at **Good Life Cafe** (934-1734; $), which has a very diverse early-morning menu, and also offers lunch-type meals. Locals also recommend **The Stove** (934-2821; $), with biscuits 3 or 4 inches high. Another restaurant with hearty breakfasts is **The Breakfast Club** (934-6944; $) at the intersection of Old Mammoth Road and Highway 203. Coffee lovers, your choices are **Looney Bean** (934-1345; $) on Main Street next to the Chevron station or **World Cup Coffee** (924-3629; $) on Old Mammoth Road across from the movie theater. Both have in-house bakers for rolls and muffins. For very good baked goodies and good gourmet coffee, try **Paul Schat's Bakery and Cafe** (934-6055; $) on Main Street, which serves breakfast on weekends; fresh-baked goodies daily.

For lunch or evening dining at the mountain, the best bet is the **Mountainside Grill** (934-0601) in the Mammoth Mountain Inn. Or head over to the more crowded **Yodler** (934-0636). Other on-mountain lunch best bets are the **Mill Cafe** at the base of Stump Alley Express and the **Canyon Lodge**. The Main Lodge has rather so-so cafeteria food.

In June Lake, the best dining is at the **Eagle's Landing Restaurant** (648-7897; $$) at the Double Eagle Resort and Spa. Other choices are **Fern Creek Grill** (648-7897) for break-

Dining: $$$-Entrees $20+; $$-$10-20; $-less than $10.
Accommodations: (double room) $$$$-$200+; $$$-$141-$200; $$-$81-$140; $-$80 and less.

fast, burgers, steaks and chicken; or The **Sierra Inn Restaurant** (648-7774) which has a slightly more upscale menu. The best dining is still in Mammoth Lakes.

 Après-ski/nightlife

Lively après-ski gets under way across the parking lot from the Main Lodge at the **Yodler** or in the **Thunder Mountain Bar** in the Main Lodge, decorated with photos of early Mammoth days. At the Canyon Lodge base area, try **Grizzly's**. **Slocum's** in town is the après-ski hangout for ski patrol and instructors. At **Austria Hof**, there's usually live entertainment after the lifts close. Entertainment is also at Mammoth Mountain Inn's **Dry Creek Bar**.

La **Sierra's** is the latest hot spot. Mammoth's longtime meet market (you may meet someone whose parents used to party hardy here in their younger days) is **Whiskey Creek,** which serves six microbrews. There's plenty of nighttime hoopla at **Grumpy's**. Featured are five giant-screen TVs, pool, foosball, inexpensive chili and burgers. Visiting Brits like this place, and also hang out at the **Clock Tower Cellar** at the Alpenhof Lodge.

 Other activities

Snowmobiles can be rented from DJs Snowmobile Adventures (935-4480; www.snowmobilemammoth.com) or Mammoth Snowmobile Adventures (934-9645) or Center Street Polaris (934-6888). The area has about 300 miles of snowmobile trails, some signed and groomed, others not. **Bobsledding or tubing** down a designated track is available through Sledz (934-7533). **Dogsled rides** are offered by Dog Sled Adventures (934-6270).

Hot-air balloon trips with High Sierra Ballooning Company (934-7188) take off from Mammoth Meadow. **Snowcreek Athletic Club** (934-8511) has a variety of indoor and outdoor facilities. **The Monkey Bar** (934-2776) offers an indoor climbing wall and **Golf 'n' Games** (924-1082) has indoor miniature golf and an arcade for kids of all ages.

Mammoth's **shopping** is oriented as much for the local population as for tourists. You won't find many trendy boutiques here, though there is a factory outlet center on Main Street, and many small shopping malls scattered throughout town. Mammoth Lakes also has two **movie theaters** (one with two screens), Minaret Cinemas and Plaza Theater (both at 934-3131). The Mammoth Times, the local newspaper, is a good source for special events listings.

 Getting there and getting around

By air: The nearest major airport is Reno, 165 miles away. Rent a car for the drive south, because ground transportation is spotty, and you probably will want a car in Mammoth. Mammoth's air service information changes frequently, so for the latest news, call the Mammoth Lakes Airport (760-934-3825), Mammoth Lakes Visitors Bureau, (888) 466-2666 or consult the MLVB Web site (www.visitmammoth.com).

By car: Mammoth is 325 miles north of Los Angeles on Hwy. 395, and 165 miles south of Reno on the same road. June Mountain is 20 miles north of Mammoth Lakes off Hwy. 395.

Getting around: The resort operates a free shuttle that runs throughout the town and to Mammoth's Main Lodge (four miles out) and to the Canyon Lodge and Juniper Springs. A nightly shuttle makes loops around town until midnight during the week, 1 a.m. on Friday and Saturday nights, or call Mammoth Shuttle (934-3030) or Sierra Express (924-TAXI; 924-8294). Most visitors have a car.

California
regional resorts

Bear Valley, Bear Valley, CA; (209) 753-2301
Internet: www.bearvalley.com
11 lifts; 1,280 skiable acres; 1,900 vertical feet

Bear Valley is one of those word-of-mouth ski areas beloved by those who know it's at the winter terminus of Highway 4. This area has many things to like: 360 inches of snow annually; a town just big enough to provide lodging, food and alternate activities (cross-country skiing, ice skating and most snow sports); and an enticing advanced and expert area called Grizzly Bowl that makes up about 30 percent of the terrain. The Grizz is below the base area, and that's its drawback. With no snowmaking coverage and an elevation of 6,600–7,750 feet, Grizzly Bowl isn't always open. However, the upper mountain is covered by snowmaking and has a few black-diamond runs amid its great beginner and intermediate terrain. A good area for families, Bear Valley has child care starting at age 2 on weekends and holidays. It also sells an "Interchangeable Parent Ticket" for $40 that may be used by two parents who are taking turns caring for an infant.

Lift tickets (01/02 prices): Adults, $43; Young adult (13-23), $36; Children (7-12), $15; Seniors (65-74), $10; Super seniors (75+) and children younger than 7, free.

Distance from San Francisco: About 190 miles east on I-580 and I-205, north on I-99, then east on Hwy. 4. Bear Valley is on the west slope of the Sierra Nevada and not accessible from Tahoe or Mammoth.

Lodging information: On the Web site, or press 5 after calling the recorded information line to get phone numbers for various hotels and condos. Two recommendations: The Bear Valley Lodge (209-753-2327) is three miles from the slopes (as close as you can get) and smack in the center of the little town. About 25 miles down Hwy. 4 is The Dorrington Hotel & Restaurant (209-795-5800), a charming shared-bath B&B in a historic house. The restaurant is worth a stop.

Badger Pass, Yosemite National Park, CA; (209) 372-1000
Internet: www.yosemitepark.com/html/badgerpass.html
5 lifts; 10 trails; 800 vertical feet

This is a tiny, 67-year-old ski area best suited for beginners, patient intermediates and families with young children. Though Badger Pass is charming (and the employees are wonderful), what makes it a great winter weekend destination is not the downhill skiing. It's special because it's inside Yosemite National Park. The park's legendary crowds disappear in the winter, so you'll share the majesty of the Yosemite Valley with a comfortable number of humans. Activities include ranger-naturalist snowshoe walks, ice skating, sightseeing tours and lots more.

Yosemite has a renowned cross-country ski center headquartered at Badger Pass with lessons, 40 km. of machine-groomed track and another 150 km. of marked trails, including a 17-km. skating lane on the rim of the Yosemite Valley to Glacier Point.

336 • California Regional Resorts

Lift tickets (01/02): Adults, $3; Children (12 and younger), $16; Seniors 65+ pay adult price on weekends and holidays but ski free midweek/non-holidays.
Distance from San Francisco: About 230 miles east on I-580, I-205 and Hwy. 120.
Distance from Los Angeles: About 290 miles north on I-5 and I-99, then east on Hwy. 41.
Note: Hwy. 120 between Yosemite and Lee Vining is closed in winter, making Badger Pass inaccessible from Mammoth.
Lodging information: (209) 252-4848.

Snow Summit, Big Bear Lake, CA; (909) 866-5766
Internet: www.snowsummit.com
12 lifts; 230 skiable acres; 1,200 vertical feet
Big Bear Mountain, Big Bear Lake, CA; (909) 585-2519
Internet: www.bearmtn.com
12 lifts; 198 skiable acres + 550 off-piste acres; 1,665 vertical feet

Southern Californians just don't know how good they have it. On a sunny winter day, it is entirely possible to spend the morning skiing at Big Bear (as the locals call it) and the afternoon playing a round of golf in Palm Springs or surfing in the Pacific Ocean. These neighboring ski areas, in the mountain town of Big Bear Lake, are less than a two-hour drive from the fabled desert resort in one direction and the beach in the other.

The Big Bear areas, though at an altitude of between 7,000 and 8,800 feet, rely heavily on snowmaking to cover the runs. Both are snowmaking experts and have a reliable water supply from Big Bear Lake. Even if the season has been dry, you'll find surprisingly good snow on the runs. And if the winter has been a wet one, the conditions can be quite good.

The terrain is largely intermediate-level, with a couple of runs at each that qualify as advanced, not expert. Snowboarding is hugely popular here, with boarders constituting nearly half of the business. The town has many lodging and restaurant options and a charming, walkable downtown.

Neither area has child care; lessons start at age 4. Snow Summit signed a purchase agreement to acquire Big Bear Mountain in late summer 2002; if the purchase goes through, the two mountains will offer an interchangeable ticket for the 2002/03 season.
Lift tickets (01/02 prices): Snow Summit: Adults, $41 ($50 holidays); Teens (13-19), $34 (pay adult prices on holidays); Children (7-12), $13 ($21 holidays). Kids younger than 7 always ski free with paying adult. Night skiing tickets available. Big Bear: Adults, $39 ($49 holidays); Teens (13-19), $34 (pay adult prices on holidays); Children (6-12) and super seniors (70+), $12 ($20 holidays). Kids younger than 6 always ski free with paying adult.
Distance from Los Angeles: About 110 miles east on I-10, I-215, Hwy. 30, Hwy. 330 and Hwy. 18.
Distance from Ontario (nearest commercial airport): About 60 miles by I-10, I-215, Hwy. 30, Hwy. 330 and Hwy. 18.
Lodging information: Big Bear Lake Resort Association's Lodging Referral Service, (909) 866-5671 or 800-4-BIGBEAR (244-2327); check out their Web site at www.bigbearinfo.com.

Alyeska

Alaska

Summit elevation (lift-served): 2,750 feet
Vertical drop: 2,500 feet
Base elevation: 250 feet

Address: P.O. Box 249
Girdwood, AK 99587
☎ Area code: 907
Ski area phone: 754-1111 or (800) 775-6656
Snow report: 754-7669 (SKI-SNOW)
ⓘ Toll-free reservations: (800) 880-3880
Fax: 754-2200
E-mail: info@alyeskaresort.com
Internet: www.alyeskaresort.com

Expert:★★★
Advanced:★★
Intermediate:★★★★
Beginner:★★★★
Never-ever:★★

Number and types of lifts: 9–1 60-passenger tram, 1 high-speed quad, 2 quads, 3 doubles, 2 surface lifts
Skiable acreage: 1,000 acres
Snowmaking: 42 percent
Uphill capacity: 10,355 per hour
Snowboarding: Yes
Bed Base: 533
Nearest lodging: slopeside, hotel
Resort child care: Babysitting services
Adult ticket, per day: $36-$46 (02/03)

Dining:★★★★
Apres-ski/nightlife:★★
Other activities:★★★

It's easy to miss the turn off Seward Highway to Alyeska. Chances are you'll be mesmerized by the jaw-dropping views over fjord-like Turnagain Arm, a tidal basin where the mountains literally plunge to the sea.

Just 40 miles southeast of Anchorage, Alyeska offers convenient, big-mountain skiing without the threat of altitude sickness. A 60-passenger tram and the high-speed quad that services the summit mean lift lines are short on weekends, nonexistent midweek. And they have plenty of snow: It averages more than 700 inches of snow each season, and had a high of 1,116 inches a couple years back.

The riches extend to the resort itself, where the Alyeska Prince Hotel provides luxurious accommodations at the tram base. The tram zips up 2,028 feet of Alyeska's 2,500 foot rise in just three-and-a-half minutes.

Contrary to popular opinion, the weather in this part of Alaska is quite tolerable in winter, with temperatures an average of 10 to 30 degrees Fahrenheit. And here's a real bonus for late-night revelers: Lifts don't even open until 10:30 a.m., meaning you can sleep in, have breakfast *and* get first tracks. Normal closing time is 5:30 p.m., but on Friday and Saturday nights from mid-December until mid-March, the lifts remain open to 9:30 p.m.

Nearby Anchorage is a bustling city with plenty to keep residents entertained through the long winter nights. Alaskans are particularly good at winter celebrations. We recommend visiting in late February during Fur Rendezvous, Anchorage's winter festival (see Other Activities), or early March, to coincide with the Anchorage start of The Iditarod dogsled race. By that time of year, the temperatures start to rise (average high is 30 degrees Fahrenheit; -1 degrees Centigrade) and daylight hours increase (almost 13 hours).

Alaska is one of the most spectacularly beautiful spots on Earth, winter or summer. The incentives for a winter visit are it's low season, so the price is right; crowds are light; and you can ski. Just keep in mind that Anchorage and Alyeska are one time zone beyond the West Coast of the United States. So if it's 9 a.m. in Los Angeles and noon in New York City, it's 8 a.m. at Alyeska.

Mountain layout—Skiing

◆◆ **Expert** ◆ **Advanced:** The high-speed quad Spirit of Alyeska carries skiers 1,411 vertical feet to the top of the lift-serviced terrain, which is at the base of the Alyeska Glacier. Up here it's wide-open, above-treeline skiing. The entire 2,500 feet of vertical is skiable in one continuous run, with intermediate to super-expert pitch depending on your choice of route.

You also can hike to the 3,939-foot summit of Mt. Alyeska, where expert-level Glacier Bowl and the Headwall await.

From the quad, experts can go right and drop down Gail's Gully or Prospector and take a gully left or right of Eagle Rock, then back to the quad. Experts willing to work can take the High Traverse from the quad, arcing through The Shadows between Mt. Alyeska and Max's Mountain, and dropping down through open steeps; or continue over the ridge to find steeps and a short section of gladed skiing on Max's Mountain (when opened by the ski patrol).

The lower half of the North Face makes it possible to ski double-black terrain from the upper to the lower tram terminal. You can scout out this gnarly area riding up the tram. The upper part,Tram Pocket, is above treeline; the lower part is heavily forested with two trails—Jim's Branch and Last Chance. Descend Tram Pocket, then cut over to the rest of Alyeska's runs to avoid the gladed area below. The North Face is open when conditions permit.

■ **Intermediate:** Alyeska also has an unusual combination of open bowl skiing and trails through the trees directly under Chairs 1 and 4. Intermediates can take the new quad chair, drop into the bowl and ski whatever they can see. It doesn't take much judgment to figure out whether you are getting in over your head, and this bowl gives you plenty of room to traverse out of trouble. The bowl funnels into Waterfall and ends on Cabbage Patch.

For intermediates taking the Spirit quad chair to the top of the resort, swing left when you get off the chair and follow the Mighty Mite. This takes you past the Glacier Express restaurant in the Glacier Tram Terminal, and back to the quad by three intermediate routes, or tip down South Face (very steep and ungroomed).

●● **Beginner:** Beginners should stick to the area served by Chairs 3 and 7. The area is pretty big, but unfortunately used by everyone on their way home.

● **Never-ever:** Don't make the long trip to Alyeska solely to learn to ski. Not a huge amount of easy terrain, plus the flat light problem, could put a serious crimp in those plans. If "the Alaska experience" (scenery, dogsledding in Iditarod country, being able to brag you "survived" Alaska in winter) is your main goal, then definitely make the trip. You can find some great things to do off the slopes while everyone else skis.

Mountain layout—Snowboarding

Alyeska's machine-built terrain park below Eagle Rock has several table-tops, rails and quarterpipes. It's the best bet on icy days. Throughout the season, the resort builds one or two halfpipes near the top of Chair 4 that are well maintained with a halfpipe groomer. Better yet, because of Mt. Alyeska's natural topography—with its steep vertical and rocky slopes—the entire mountain becomes a natural terrain park under a blanket of snow.

Cat trails cut across several sections of the upper part of the mountain, creating a series of awesome cat-track jumps. You can catch great air coming off the cat track just above Gun Mount 2. Jumps in "The Fridays" on North Face are a snowboarder's dream, as are hits on Half Moon and Horseshoe off the Silvertip Run. Many aren't on the trail map, so ask the locals and they'll gladly share some secret spots. Heading down the mountain is Lolo's Leap, with 10- to 30-foot drops into the trees.

Two spots to keep speed up or you'll be walking: Going into Ego Flats in the bowl area and on the Prince Run heading back to the tram base and the Alyeska Prince Hotel.

In spring, wait until after noontime for the snow to soften for the best riding. The best-kept local's secret at Alyeska is anytime it's raining on the bottom, you can count on it dumping lots of fresh pow up top!

Mountain rating

Intermediates will have a field day, especially with the wide-open bowls and spectacular views from the top of the Spirit quad. Experts have some good drops but the real challenge of Alyeska is the tremendous variety of terrain and snow conditions from top to bottom. Snow may be groomed, cut up or untouched. Sometimes it's powder at the top, moistening to mashed potatoes at the bottom.

Cross-country and snowshoeing

The 10-km. **Winner Creek trail** leaves from Alyeska's base and wanders through woods, across meadows and up and down gentle hills. The trail is not groomed, and locals recommend it for snowshoeing. Groomed and tracked trails are in the nearby **Moose Meadow** area—locals will point you there. It's groomed and tracked. Rental equipment is available at the Alyeska Prince Hotel's rental shop. In spring, you need to wait late enough into the morning for the ice cover to melt. Lessons are $40 an hour, $20 for extra students. Since they're not regularly scheduled, make advance reservations with the ski school by calling 754-2280.

If you are a serious cross-country enthusiast, Anchorage is the place to go. About 115 km. of groomed cross-country trails are in **Kincaid, Russian Jack** and **Far North Bicentennial parks**. Kincaid Park is the best developed, with more than 1,500 acres covered by trails for all abilities. The Nordic Skiing Association of Anchorage (561-0949; grooming report, 248-6667) maintains the trails, all supported by donations and volunteer labor (Hint: If you use the trails, please make a donation.). NSAA puts out a great map of the trails, printed on a water-resistant paper.

Lessons (2002/03 prices)

Group lessons: Alyeska packages its ski and snowboard lessons, a real benefit for those traveling from the Lower 48. For example, adult intermediate and advanced skiers can get a lesson, lift ticket and rentals for $60, or the lesson alone for $33. (The snowboard price is $63 for the package, $33 just for the lesson.)

Never-ever package: Never-evers pay $50 for a ski ticket-lesson-rental package, snowboard novices pay $55; for the lesson alone for both groups, it's $30. If you're not ready to ride Chairs 3 or 7 at the end of the lesson, the afternoon lesson is free.

Private lessons: Skiing, telemarking or snowboarding cost $50 an hour, $30 for extra students. Telemarking lessons are not regularly scheduled, so make advance reservations with the ski school, 754-2280. If you're enrolled in a private lesson, ask about discounted lift and rental prices.

Special programs: The Challenge Alaska Adaptive Ski School, a chapter of Disabled Sports USA, provides skiing for the disabled: all disabilities, all ages, by reservation only. A skier with a disability, and buddy, may buy discount lift tickets and rent adaptive ski equipment. Open daily, usually December 15 to April 15. The Alyeska Price Hotel and Tramway are fully wheelchair-accessible, and Challenge Alaska has material on other wheelchair-accessible accommodations and amenities. Challenge Alaska, Box 110065, Anchorage, AK 99511-0065; 563-2658; fax 561-6142.

Racing: A $1-per-run race course is open on selected dates.

Child care (2002/03 prices)

Ages: 6 months to 10 years.

Costs: For Little Bear's Playhouse: $35 full day, or $5 an hour, for all ages. For Alyeska Prince Hotel babysitting: $5 one-time fee, plus $8 an hour for one child; $10 an hour for two children; $12 an hour for three children.

Reservations: For Little Bear's, it's a good idea; call 783-2116 or ask when you reserve lodging. Little Bear's Playhouse, Inc. is a licensed child-care facility in Girdwood, the town where Alyeska is located. Girdwood's public transportation is virtually nonexistent. You may need to transport your child to and from the center; ask about that when you call. Little Bear's is open 7 a.m. to 6 p.m. weekdays, 10 a.m. to 6 p.m. on Saturdays, from Dec. 22, 2001 through April 20, 2002 (closed on Sundays). Babysitting service may be available by appointment, three days in advance, through the Alyeska Prince Hotel's guest service desk; call 800-880-3880 or 754-1111.

Children's lessons: Cubs and Super-Cubs caters to ages 3–4 learning to ski; Mini-Riders is for ages 5–7 learning to snowboard. Prices are $30 for skiing and $35 for snowboarding, includes lift ticket, one-hour lesson and rental; available only on weekends and Anchorage School District holidays. First Tracks is offered for ages 5–13 for skiing and 8-13 for snowboarding, offered daily and during Anchorage School District holidays. A two-hour lesson, all-day lift ticket and rental package ranges from $40–$45, depending on ability level; add $5 for snowboarding. If you don't need rentals, ask about discounted pricing. The children's programs are popular—try to make reservations (754-2280).

Lift tickets (2002/03 prices)

	Adult	Child (8-13) & Senior (60-69)
One day	$46	$21
Three days*	$102 ($34/day)	$52 ($17+/day)

Who skis free: Children 7 and under when skiing with a ticketed adult.

Who skis at a discount: Ages 70 and older ski for $8. Students (14–17) with ID pay $28 for day tickets. Beginner lift tickets (Chairs 3 and 7) cost $19. Adult guests of the Alyeska Prince Hotel pay $36 per day for all lifts and all hours. A family of four skis for $108 per day.

Note: Keep in mind that Alaskan winter days are shorter than they are farther south. The lifts don't start running until mid-morning at 10:30 a.m., but the "ski day" ends at 5:30 p.m. (Daylight lingers for about 90 minutes after the sun sets in early February, and you can see very well.) Night skiing on 27 trails covering 2,000 vertical feet runs Fridays and Saturdays

4:30–9:30 p.m. mid-December through mid-March: Adults $19, children and seniors $13. Late-night skiing (8-9:30 p.m.) is $10 and tickets can be extended to 9:30 p.m. for just $10. *The best deal on multiday tickets comes with lodging-lift packages.

Accommodations

The **Alyeska Prince Hotel** (800-880-3880, 754-1111; $$$–$$$$) is a self-contained resort. Packages are the way to go, and package rates begin at $199 per room per night, single or double occupancy. This package includes lodging, breakfast for two and two adult all-day lift tickets. That's an excellent deal for a hotel that has a $1,200-per-night Royal Suite. There is no charge for up to two children under age 18 staying in the same room in existing bedding with a maximum of two adults. The hotel architecture is spectacular in the mold of the grand Canadian lodges. Though the hotel has 307 spacious rooms, several restaurants, shops and other guest facilities, it has a very intimate feel. The Alyeska Tramway is right outside the door, or you can ride Chair 7 to the lower-elevation terrain at the ski area's base.

Other than the hotel, lodging is in condos or bed-and-breakfast inns. The **Winner Creek Bed & Breakfast** (783-5501; $–$$) is a new log lodge owned by 30-year Alaska residents Victor and Kim Duncan. It's within walking distance of Alyeska. **Alyeska Accommodations** (783-2000) is a place to start, or you can get a list of B&Bs on the Girdwood community Web site, www.girdwoodalaska.com. B&B rates range from $45-$125 per night, based on double occupancy; condos range from $125-$250.

The larger bed base is in **Anchorage**, a 35- to 55-minute drive depending on weather. We expected lodging prices to be rock bottom in winter, but Anchorage does a steady convention business then. Prices aren't as high as they are in summer, but most are in the $100 to $200 per night range. For more lodging options check the excellent free Visitors Guide, available by writing to the **Anchorage Convention & Visitors Bureau**, 524 W. Fourth Ave., Anchorage, AK 99501-2212. Phone: 276-4118, fax 278-5559, Web site: www.anchorage.net.

Dining

In the Alyeska Prince Hotel the **Pond Cafe** ($-$$) serves breakfast, lunch and dinner with a California-Alaskan menu—try the caribou stew with a big sourdough cheese roll and lots of vegetables. We heartily recommend the **Katsura Teppanyaki** ($$$), open for dinner five nights a week. It seats about 20 diners around a U-shaped table facing the chefs who prepare the meals in front of you. The four-diamond **Seven Glaciers Restaurant and Lounge** ($$$) on the second level of the Glacier Terminal at 2,300 feet has a view that is beyond belief and the gourmet meals are excellent. Call 754-2237 for reservations at all three. **The Bake Shop** (783-2831; $) in the ski area base lodge has superb soups, sandwiches and sticky buns. Lots of locals, ski instructors and patrollers eat here.

Alyeska vicinity: Perhaps the best restaurant in the area is the **Double Musky Inn** (783-2822; $$$), a mile from the lifts on Crow Creek Road. It's mind-boggling to find Cajun food in Alaska (go for the French Pepper Steak). Service is great and the decor is a delight—Mardi Gras beads everywhere and posters on the ceiling. Dress is casual—some Alaskans wear muddy boots to dinner. Busy nights may require a two-hour wait, but it's worth it. (They served 340 dinners on Valentine's Day, 1997—many to lovers who made the drive from Anchorage.) No reservations, opens at 5 p.m.; closed Mondays.

Chair Five (783-2500; $-$$), in Girdwood next to the Post Office, is casual and big on burgers and pizza, but also offers prime rib, halibut and a tasty, very spicy chicken jalapeño.

Dining: $$$-Entrees $20+; $$-$10-20; $-less than $10.
Accommodations: (double room) $$$$-$200+; $$$-$141-$200; $$-$81-$140; $-$80 and less.

The Mediterranean pastas and sandwiches are good, too. **Turnagain House** (653-7500; $$-$$$), a white-tablecloth restaurant looking out on Turnagain Arm halfway to Anchorage, has a reputation for fine seafood and other dishes with excellent service.

Anchorage: A special-occasion restaurant for locals is **Simon & Seafort's Saloon & Grill** (274-3502; $$-$$$). It specializes in seafood and steak. Take a walk through the bar and try to find the on-purpose errors in the paintings. Ask for a table next to the large picture window, and get there before dark so you can admire the view across Knik Arm. Other choices for fine dining are the **Marx Brothers Cafe** (278-2133, reservations required; $$-$$$) for inventive continental cuisine and impeccable service in a cozy frame-house setting which reminds us of a small New England inn; or the **Corsair** (278-4502; $$-$$$), with continental cuisine offered by owner Hans Kruger. The style is elegant and the wine list is excellent. Expect to spend the whole evening.

For great views, especially at cocktail time, try the top-floor **Crow's Nest** (276-6000; $$$) at the Hotel Captain Cook, or **Top of the World** (265-7111; $$$) in the Hilton. **Josephine's** (276-8700; $$$) in the Sheraton also has a view, and is a good choice for Sunday brunch.

Many Japanese have settled in Anchorage, and restaurants such as **Akaihana** (276-2215; $$) and **Tempura Kitchen** (277-2741; $$) are among the Asian eateries. They offer tempura, sukiyaki and other cooked dishes as well as sushi and sashimi. Anchorage also has Thai, Chinese and Korean restaurants.

For moderately priced, delicious food—and great beer—head to **The Glacier Brew House Restaurant** (274-2739; $$) on Fifth Avenue.

Families should head to **Sourdough Mining Co.** (563-2272; $) for great ribs and corn fritters; **Hogg Brothers Cafe** (276-9649; $) for wow omelets; the **Royal Fork Buffet** (276-0089; $) or **Lucky Wishbone** (272-3454; $) for the best fried chicken. **Gwennie's Old Alaska Restaurant's** (243-2090; $) costumed staff serves big breakfasts and sandwiches midst historic photos.

Après-ski/nightlife

The **Aurora Bar and Lounge** in the Alyeska Prince Hotel might have TV going in the bar and sometimes some singing. The lounge is quieter, with a stone fireplace and comfortable sofas and chairs. For après-ski, head to the **Sitzmark Bar** at the base of Chair 3 for burgers and live bands on Friday and Saturday nights during ski season. The **Double Musky** and **Chair 5** also have taverns.

Anchorage has a highly developed nightlife and cultural scene, a legacy of pipeline days, long winter nights, and generous doses of oil patch money. The city reportedly had an orchestra before it had paved streets.

We love wacky watering holes that have unique character. Anchorage has two great ones, but one is closed most of the winter, unfortunately. For loud rock and dancing try **Chilkoot Charlie's**, 2435 Spenard Rd., "where we cheat the other guy and pass the savings on to you." (They sell T-shirts with that slogan—it's a great souvenir.) Chilkoot's is huge—six bars with about 30 beers on tap, two stages (the night we were there during Fur Rondy, one stage had a rockin' band and the other had the Fur Bikini contest), pool tables and games, and sports on TV (though it's impossible to hear the audio). Generally, the ratio of men to women is about seven to one, and any attire goes—one February night, we saw people dressed in gym shorts; others in business suits and cocktail dresses. **Mr. Whitekeys' Fly By Night Club** is famed for its Spam appetizers, the Spamtones and satirical Whale Fat Follies show. The club does a "Christmas in Spenard" show, but after that, it's closed for the winter but opens in the spring.

Humpy's on Sixth Avenue has 36 beers on tap and occasional live entertainment. For quieter dancing and a slightly older clientele try **Legends** at the Sheraton or **Whale's Tail** at the Hotel Captain Cook, or the lounge at the **Golden Lion Best Western**. For country music, head to **Last Frontier Bar** or **Buckaroo Club**.

For theater, opera, drama and movies, buy the local newspaper (*Anchorage Daily News*). There's a Friday morning entertainment tabloid that's very helpful. You be surprised at the visiting artists and productions at the **Alaska Center for the Performing Arts** downtown. For recorded information, call 263-2901.

 ## Other activities

The variety of winter activities is staggering. We have room to list just a sampling. We encourage you to get the excellent free Visitors Guide from the **Anchorage Convention & Visitors Bureau**, 524 W. Fourth Ave., Anchorage, AK 99501-2212. Telephone: 276-4118; fax: 278-5559; Web site: www.anchorage.net.

Think of Alaska in winter and you think of **dogsleds.** Call Chugach Dog Sled Tours in Girdwood near the ski area (783-2266 for reservations, last-minute calls don't work; or make reservations through the guest services desk at the Alyeska Prince Hotel). If you're staying in Anchorage, drive about 20 minutes to the hamlet of Chugiak to Mush a Dog Team-Gold Rush Days (688-1391). As you travel the trail, you'll see a recreation of an Alaskan gold miner's camp. You'll be amazed at how cramped and cold those unheated tents must have been.

Dogsled races are a focal point of **Fur Rendezvous,** held annually in mid-February. The World Championship Sled Dog Race is the sprint (some sprint—25 miles a day for three days) counterpart to the more famous endurance race, **The Iditarod,** which follows Fur Rondy on the first Saturday in March. Fur Rondy also has fireworks, a snow sculpture contest, a small carnival, a snowshoe softball tournament (hilarious for spectators) and the World Championship Dog Weight Pull, a contest detailed in Jack London's book, *Call of the Wild.* Alaskan Natives come from all parts of the state for Fur Rondy, and many wear traditional fur parkas, stunning works of art with intricate patterns. By the way, if seeing people wearing fur offends you, don't come at this time. You'll only work yourself into a lather over something that has kept native Alaskans warm for centuries. If you're a dog lover, don't miss the start of The Iditarod, when about 1,500 sled dogs are parked on main street in downtown Anchorage. Early in the morning, you can visit with the dogs and the mushers.

Several companies offer **flightseeing tours** via helicopter or fixed-wing planes. It is the best way to see Alaska's spectacular mountains and glaciers and well worth the cost. We flew with Era Helicopters (800-478-1947, 248-4422; www.eraaviation.com) into the rugged Chugach Mountains that border Anchorage. On an overcast day, you'll gain an appreciation for the arduous conditions that 19th-century mushers endured to bring supplies over mountain passes from Seward to Anchorage. On a clear day, you'll see Mt. McKinley off in the distance, its broad hulk standing apart from surrounding mountains. Alpine Air (783-2360) operates airplane tours out of Girdwood. Prices begin at $69 for a one-hour tour and they will pick-up at the Alyeska Prince Hotel.

Alyeska offers **snowcat skiing and heliskiing** with more than 750 square miles of backcountry slopes. Chugach Powder Guides (783-4354) operates out of the Alyeska Prince Hotel. A full-day heli-skiing package is $650, with a guarantee of 16,000–20,000 vertical. A full-day snowcat package is $150 standby, $195 by advance reservation. **Tandem paragliding** with a certified pilot 2,300 feet above the ski area is another thrill for visitors. Available daily in summer and by appointment in winter. Call Alyeska for more details, 754-2275.

Backcountry skiers can explore the region with Alaska Off Piste (441-2249), an adventure skiing and alpine guiding company based in Girdwood. Per person rates are about $175 for one, $125 for two and $100 for three or more for a day trip.

The **Anchorage Museum of History and Art** (343-4326) is a must-see, with displays that show 10,000 years of Alaskan civilization, from ancient days through the Gold Rush and the great earthquake of 1964. The **Alaska Native Heritage Center** (330-8000 or 800-315-6608) provides an introduction to Alaska's native population. Although it's not fully open in winter, special events and art shows are reason enough to visit. If you're in law enforcement, don't miss the **Alaska State Trooper Museum** (800-770-5050) that tells the history of the state's law enforcement through exhibits, memorabilia and photographs.

In Seward, two hours' drive south of Alyeska Resort, you can visit the **Alaska Sea Life Center** (224-6300), funded by Exxon Valdez oil spill restoration funds and dedicated to understanding and maintaining the integrity of Alaska's marine ecosystem. It's a combination aquarium and museum, with interactive exhibits, displays and touch tanks for children. Renown Charters and Tours (800-655-3806 or 224-3806) offers an exciting **wildlife cruise** that circumnavigates Resurrection Bay and touches briefly into the Gulf of Alaska; transportation is available from the Alyeska Prince Hotel. The **Big Game Alaska Wildlife Center** (783-2025), just 10 miles south of Girdwood, is dedicated to the rehabilitation of orphaned and injured animals. Here you can get close enough to pet moose, Sitka deer, caribou and reindeer. Also on premises are birds of prey, buffalo and muskox. It's open daily, 10 a.m.–4 p.m. Admission is $5.

If you need another reason to visit Alaska in the winter, the **Northern Lights** might be it. If you've ever seen photos of the aurora borealis, with its green, blue and red streaks of light across an ink-black sky, you have an inkling of how magnificent this phenomenon is. For forecasts on when to plan your trip to maximize the chances of seeing the Northern Lights, go to this Internet site: www.geo.mtu.edu/weather/aurora. The Alyeska Prince Hotel has a unique Northern Lights wake-up service and a 7-minute electronic display of the aurora on the ceiling of the hotel's three-story lobby.

Getting there and getting around

By air: Anchorage is served by many major airlines. East Coast skiers who want to make the trek to Alyeska would be well advised to find a travel agent who specializes in Alaska in order to find the best airfares and packages.

By car: Alyeska Resort is 45 miles south of downtown Anchorage. Get on Gambell Street south, which becomes the Seward Highway, Route 1, along Turnagain Arm, which has one of the highest tides in the world. The drive is quite scenic; try to alternate drivers so everyone can admire the view. Bring your camera and lots of film for the Dall sheep, moose, bald eagles, beluga whales and bore tides often seen along the way. Turn left at the Girdwood/Alyeska highway turn-off, the resort is 3 miles up the road.

Getting around: If you stay in downtown Anchorage or at the Alyeska Prince Hotel, you can get by without a car. Alaska Sightseeing or The Magic Bus (268-6311) can take you from the city to the resort with advance reservations. Ask at the hotel desk. Otherwise, you'll need a car. The Alyeska area (the town of Girdwood) doesn't have a local transportation system. However, the hotel runs a continuous free shuttle during mountain operations and in evenings by request. If you want to try some of the restaurants we listed, such as the Double Musky, make arrangements with the bell desk.

"Interior" British Columbia

Big White Ski Resort
Sun Peaks Resort
Silver Star Mountain Resort

From British Columbia's west coast, the mountain ranges roll east in ascending waves until they reach the Rocky Mountain peaks on the Continental Divide. The Divide forms the southern border between British Columbia and Alberta. British Columbia is the heli-skiing and Nordic touring center of the known ski universe, and that's in addition to the 35 or so alpine ski areas. There are a slew of heli-skiing outfitters and nearly 30 Nordic destinations. British Columbia covers 366,000 square miles, and more than 90 percent of that is provincial forests and parks. As Vancouver writer Steve Threndyle said, "B.C. is one of the few places in the world where people can still seek out an endless amount of recreational challenge in a vast, uncompromising wilderness setting."

The British Columbia highlands and plateaus take moisture from the Pacific storms that drop dryer snow in the Monashees, Selkirks, Kootenays and Purcells on their way to the Rockies. The skiing experience in western Canada has its own fingerprint, its own special flavor with an inviting appeal to skiers from eastern North American, Europe and Australia. It can be a bit like traveling to a foreign country. Distinctions range from snow to snacks, lodging to location. When you're in the West, informality is the rule, friendly folks the reason. After you've visited three of the up-and-coming resorts in this region—Big White Ski Resort, Sun Peaks Resort and Silver Star Mountain Resort—we think you'll agree that this is some of the most memorable skiing there is.

Big White Ski Resort

Big White, now the fifth-largest ski area in Canada, overlooks the Okanagan Valley and its 100-mile-long Okanagan Lake and the spectacular Monashee Mountain Range. Though it's been around for nearly 40 years, it's been only in the last decade that it's grown into full resort status. The Okanagan Valley is the hot winter destination in the West, and many advise getting here soon while it's still relatively affordable.

Big White boasts, "We use only dry, natural Okanagan Powder." The village sits at 5,700 feet (B.C.'s highest base area) and lifts carry skiers up to 7,600 feet. That's about the same elevation as Whistler Blackcomb, but the air and snow are considerably dryer this far inland. One of Big White's signature features is its tree skiing.

The resort has already pumped in $100 million and with more skiable terrain than Sun Valley, it's a good investment. For Australians, Big White is the second-biggest destination ski resort in B.C., behind Whistler Blackcomb. The resort now has an eight-passenger gondola, an adventure park with a tubing park and lodge, and new slopeside accommodations.

New for 2002/03, 100 new slopeside lodging units are scheduled for completion. If you haven't heard the news already, Big White just purchased nearby Silver Star Mountain Resort. With one lift ticket, skiers and snowboarders now have access to almost 6,000 acres of

Big White Ski Resort Facts

Summit elevation: 7,606 feet

Vertical drop:	2,550 feet
Base elevation:	5,706 feet (Village base);
	4,950 feet (Westridge base)

Address: Box 2039, Station R, Kelowna, B.C., Canada V1X 4K5

Area code: 250   Ski area phone: 765-3101

Snow report: 765-7669 Fax: 765-1822

Toll-free reservations: (800) 663-2772

E-mail: bigwhite@bigwhite.com or cenres@bigwhite.com for reservations

Internet: www.bigwhite.com

Expert:★★★   Advanced:★★★★

Intermediate:★★★★

Beginner:★★★★ Never-ever:★★★

Number of lifts: 11–1 8-passenger high-speed gondola, 4 high-speed quads, 1 quad, 1 triple, 1 double, 1 T-bar, 2 surface lifts

Snowmaking: No

Skiable acreage: 2,565 acres

Uphill capacity: 23,400 per hour

Snowboarding: Yes

Bed base: 11,000

Nearest lodging: Slopeside lodging, ski-in/ski-out

Resort child care: 18 months to 6 years

Adult ticket, per day: $51-$55 (02/03, Cdn$, without tax)

Dining: ★★★ (resort), ★★★ (region)

Apres-ski/nightlife:★★★ (resort), ★★★ (region)

Other activities: ★★★

---

skiable terrain. Up to 16 airport and inter-resort ground shuttles each day, plus an inter-resort helicopter service, will ensure seamless transfers between Big White and Silver Star. The new inter-mountain helicopter shuttle service is the first of it's kind in Canada: A helicopter is based at each resort, on stand-by each day for scenic joy-flights, inter-mountain shuttles, airport shuttles and winery tours.

Mountain layout–Skiing

◆◆ **Expert:** Experts normally like the Gem Lake Express runs. Goat's Kick, left of the Ridge Rocket Express, is an especially fun challenge. Going to the right from the Alpine T-bar gets you into Parachute Bowl.

◆ **Advanced:** Natural hits and drops fall off the side of Perfection, Falcon Glades and around Westridge. For bumps, try Dragon's Tongue.

■ **Intermediate:** Good warm-up runs are the Sun Run from the top of the Alpine T-bar, Exhibition, Highway 33, Serwas and Sundance. There's also fine terrain off the Rocket and Powder chairs. Roller Coaster, Blue Sapphire and Kalinas Rainbow come recommended. International is an intermediate bump run. The blue ratings in the Black Forest are low-end.

●● **Beginner:** Millie's Mile, named after the owner's granddaughter, runs alongside the Black Forest Express. All lifts serve at least one green run.

● **Never-ever:** A complete learn-to-ski facility, in a private teaching area, is at the base of the gondola. Hummingbird, served by the Plaza Chair, is designated for first-timers only. Woodcutter is also excellent, but mind the traffic.

Mountain layout–Snowboarding

The mountain has a world-class competition halfpipe and a quarterpipe for beginners that is lit for night moves. Easy Street has a permanent boardercross course. Big White also has a boardercross training facility.

Freeriders have a good time most anywhere on the mountain. Particularly popular is the Sun-Rype Bowl and the adjacent Black Bear run, both reached by the Gem Lake Express. The bowl is a big gentle swoop of a run that can get you into some trees known as the Black Bear Glades. Also reached from Gem Lake Express is the single-black Blackjack, a good long fall-line run. The only double-blacks are reached by the Alpine T-bar. There are some gentle ways down if you change your mind, but at least have a look on the way up into Parachute Bowl.

Mountain rating

The mountain is big, with plenty of terrain to explore. Trails are mixed by ability level on almost every lift, so riders of all ability levels can take the same lift up together and meet again at the bottom. A few lifts serve primarily one ability level—the Power Chair serves mostly black runs, while Ridge Rocket Express has mostly blue runs under its airway. Big White has a separate learning area at its base. You'll find the toughest stuff off the Alpine T-bar at the summit. Grooming reports are posted at the top of each chair.

Cross-country and snowshoeing

Big White has 25 km. of trails, mostly groomed except for the backcountry double-black diamonds. The beginners' trail is a 4.3-km. loop from the Plaza Chair. Cross-country skiing is included with lift tickets. If skiers head down-mountain from the mid-mountain day lodge, the Plaza Quad Chairlift back up is free.

Lessons (2002/03 Cdn$, without GST)

Group lessons: A 2-hour lesson costs $39; multiday rates available.
Never-ever package: A two-hour learn-to-ski lesson costs $49; learn-to-snowboard costs $59. Includes Plaza lift ticket and rentals.
Private lessons: All day, $350; half-day afternoon, $160; half-day morning, $205; two hours, $149; one hour, $79. Early-bird private lessons available 8:45-9:45 a.m., $64.

Child care (2002/03 Cdn$, without GST)

Ages: 18 months to 6 years.
Costs: Hourly rate is $12; $55 for a full day (lunch included).
Reservations: Recommended. Call 765-3101.
Children's lessons: Ages 4-12, full day is $63, half day is $42 (rentals are extra). Program for kids ages 4-6 includes indoor play time. For kids ages 4-12, a two-hour learn-to-ski lesson costs $45 (includes Plaza lift ticket and gear rental); learn-to-snowboard for kids 7-12 costs $53. A note about the kids' instruction center: It's recognized as a top program for kids. Security is tight. Parents are given pagers.

Lift tickets (2002/03 Cdn$, without GST)

	Adult	Youth (13-18)	Child (6-12)
One day	$55	$47	$29
Three days	$159 ($53/day)	$135 ($45/day)	$81 ($27/day)
Five days	$255 ($51/day)	$215 ($43/day)	$125 ($25/day)

Who skis free: Children 5 and younger.
Who skis at a discount: Seniors 65+ pay $38 for a one-day ticket, $108 for three days, and $170 for five days.

Note: Six-out-of-seven-days flex passes are available as of opening day: $318 for adults, $270 for youth, $162 for children, and $216 for seniors ages 65+. Big White has night skiing, 5 p.m.–8 p.m., Tuesday to Saturday, from mid-December to end of March.

 ## Accommodations

Lodging in the mountain village ranges from hostels, hotels and condos to private chalets, all ski-in/ski-out. **Big White Central Reservations** (800-663-2772 in North America) is a one-stop shop for your accommodation and package vacation needs. You can also visit the Web site for accommodation details.

Chateau Big White ($$–$$$$) is close to all amenities in the Village Plaza. Room types include deluxe rooms with two queen beds, loft suites with double and queen beds, and one- and two-bedroom suites. All rooms have gas fireplaces and kitchenettes with microwaves and fridges. The hotel has a lounge, four-star restaurant, underground parking and hot tub.

The **Inn at Big White** ($$–$$$$) is the most-requested property. This hotel has 100 rooms and suites, an outdoor pool and hot tub, fitness room, restaurant and lounge. **White Crystal Inn** ($$–$$$$), a luxury inn in the heart of the Village, is recently renovated and includes cable TV and phones in the rooms, fine dining and a great slopeside lounge.

Premium condominiums, all new or recently built, range in size from one to four bedrooms, feature full bathrooms and kitchens, and are centrally located with ski-in/ski-out convenience. Some units have gas fireplaces, balconies and private hot tubs. Choose from **Stonebridge Lodge** ($$–$$$$), **Trappers' Crossing** ($$$–$$$$), **Timber Ridge** ($$$–$$$$), **Treetops** ($$$–$$$$), **Black Bear** ($$$–$$$$), **Grizzly Lodge** ($$–$$$$), **Snowy Creek Lodge** ($$$–$$$$) and the **Blacksmith Lodge** ($$$–$$$$).

Chateau On The Ridge ($$$–$$$$) has condos with kitchens, gas fireplaces and outdoor common hot tubs. **Das Hofbrauhaus** ($–$$$) is slopeside and has an indoor pool, hot tub and racquetball courts, plus a restaurant and lounge. **Eagles Resort** ($$$–$$$$) has 20 three-bedroom condos with gas fireplace and kitchens, plus a large hot tub on the property. **Graystokes Inn** ($$) has one- and two-bedroom condos, plus a common outdoor hot tub. **The Moguls** boasts fabulous views of the Monashee Mountains, an indoor hot tub and sauna.

The Legacy ($$–$$$$) consists of luxury one-, two- and three-bedroom condos with full kitchens and gas fireplaces, covered balconies and covered parking stalls. The **Monashee Inn** ($$–$$$) has an unsurpassed view of the Monashee Mountains. **Plaza On The Ridge** ($$–$$$$) is right on the ski run and features six outdoor hot tubs. Each unit has a fireplace and spacious kitchen. The **Ponderosa Inn** ($–$$$) is on the Easy Street ski run. It's family oriented with a hot tub and sauna.

Ptarmigan Inn ($$–$$$) is next to the village and has hot tubs, a plunge pool and sauna. One- and two-bedroom units are available. **Snow Pines Estates** ($$–$$$$) has nice big chalets, either single-family or duplex, all with ski-in/ski-out access.

In the heart of the Village, the **Whitefoot Lodge** ($–$$) features a hot tub, sauna, cold plunge, elevator, and laundry. Some rooms have kitchenettes. It has an indoor hot tub, sauna, restaurant, lounge and grocery/liquor/video store.

The **RV park** ($) provides easy access to the Black Forest Express lift. It has 32 full-service hookups with water, sewer, 30-amp electrical and cable TV. A chalet, hot tub and washroom with showers are on-site. Rates are $30 per night (Cdn$).

The cheapest digs are at **Big White Hostels** (765-2100; $), a.k.a. **Bumps** and **Bumps Too**, where you get a dorm bunk from $15 per night (Cdn$), plus there's a common room with cooking facilities and Internet access is available.

Dining

Unlike most other ski resorts, you don't have to drive or even walk more than a block or so to find a great meal. All restaurants are located in or near the village center and represent a swell variety of offerings.

Beano's (765-3101 ext. 291; $), located smack in the middle of the main ticket/rental building, serves the best coffee, the best soup and the best sandwiches in the village. It's also an Internet cafe. Beano's owners are usually on site waiting on friendly Big White CEOs, managers and ski school directors enjoying their morning javas. Big White's owners and family live just across the street and like to check out what's happening with their guests and staff each morning. Drop by and say hello, lodge a complaint or give a suggestion. They'll be glad you did.

Snowshoe Sam's (765-1416; $$-$$$) is a legend at Big White. This multistoried establishment, up a flight of steps in the village, concentrates mainly on steaks and chops, although their seafood and pasta are quite good. You'll need dinner reservations, especially on the weekend. It's packed! Their claim to fame is their Gunbarrel Coffee. It's as much of a show as it is an after-dinner drink. Your waiter pulls up alongside your table with a 22-shotgun and pours flaming Grand Marnier down the barrel into a glass with brandy, cacao and whipped cream! The restaurant, which originated in Apex, sells the most Grand Marnier in Canada.

The **Swiss Bear Dining Room** (491-7750; $$-$$$) in the Chateau Big White serves authentic Swiss cuisine, specializing in delicious fondues. Reservations recommended.

The **Powder Keg** (491-2009; $-$$), in the Inn at Big White, is a great family restaurant specializing in authentic Greek cuisine. The grill serves breakfast, lunch and dinner with an interesting menu (some good veggie choices). The bar offers typical pub food like wings, dips and sandwiches and a great view. Dinner reservations are recommended.

De Montreuil's (491-9690; $$), in the White Crystal Inn, is a beehive at lunch serving a variety of tasty homemade soups and sandwiches. Dinners feature a European flair and an interesting wine list, mostly Canadian, Australian and Californian.

Coltino's Ristorante (765-5611; $$), at Raakel's Hofbruahaus, serves Italian fare as well as Alberta beef. **Raakel's** next door has après-ski where they serve some mean salads, burgers and pizzas. They also offer the usual pub fare of wings, fries, even poutine—that typical French Canadian dish of French fries topped with cheese curd and steaming hot gravy.

Après-ski/nightlife

Big White has seven lounges and bars. Live bands perform regularly. **Snowshoe Sam's** is commonly thought of as the best ski bar in Canada, and we agree. It has DJ entertainment, live bands and games of chance. **The Powder Keg**, in the Inn at Big White, is a great après-ski spot. **Raakel's Ridge Pub**, in Das Hofbrauhaus, has dancing. In Whitefoot Lodge, there is a **market** (765-7666) with everything from liquor to video rentals.

Other activities

Head to the Adventure Centre (765-8888) to find **Big White Dogsledding Adventures** for "mush your own dog team" tours, the **Mega Snow Coaster tube ride** with 10 lanes and lifts, **snowmobile tours, sleigh rides, ice skating** and **snowshoeing**. Also **Scenic helicopter tours** are available from the resort, or take a local **winery tour** (the region produces very good wines).

Dining: $$$–Entrees $20+; $$–$10-20; $–less than $10.
Accommodations: (double room) $$$$–$200+; $$$–$141-$200; $$–$81-$140; $–$80 and less.

Weekly activities include a **torchlight parade and fireworks, Carnival Night** and **Bingo Night.**

An interesting little tidbit is that the **Whitefoot Medical Clinic** (765-0544) operates in the village from 3–6 p.m. for medical services. Appointments are preferred, but not required.

Getting there and getting around

By air: Kelowna International Airport is an hour's drive from Big White and less than an hour's flight from Vancouver, Calgary or Seattle. It's served daily by Air BC (Air Canada) and Horizon Air (5 daily flights) and WestJet (3 daily flights). U.S. Customs is right in Kelowna. There are even direct flights from Toronto and Hamilton, Ontario. Big White's airport shuttles serve the ski area; $36.95 adult and $25.50 junior (6–12) for one-way tickets, and $59.95 adult and $42.50 junior round-trip.

By car: Big White, in the heart of the Okanagan Valley, is 33 miles from Kelowna. It's 134 miles from Kamloops; 407 miles from Calgary; 278 miles from Vancouver; and 346 miles from Seattle.

Getting around: Big White has a Budget rental agency on the mountain. One-way rentals to and from the airport can be booked through Central Reservations. No car is needed at Big White unless you plan to visit Kelowna (33 miles).

Sun Peaks Resort

Summit elevation: 6,824 feet	**Number of lifts:** 10–4 high-speed quads, 1 quad, 1 triple, 4 surface lifts
Vertical Drop: 2,891 feet	
Base elevation: 3,933 feet	**Skiable acreage:** 3,408 acres

Address: #50-3150 Creekside Way, Sun Peaks, B.C., Canada V0E 1Z1
Area code: 250
Ski area phone: 578-7842   **Fax:** 578-7843
Snow report: 578-7232
Toll-free reservations: 800-807-3257
E-mail: info@sunpeaksresort.com
Internet: www.sunpeaksresort.com
Expert: ★★★
Advanced: ★★★★
Intermediate: ★★★★
Beginner: ★★★   **Never-ever:** ★★★

Snowmaking: 80 acres
Uphill capacity: 9,000 per hour
Snowboarding: Yes
Bed base: 3,800
Nearest lodging: Slopeside, ski-in/ski-out
Resort child care: 18 months-5 years
Adult ticket, per day: $52 (02/03; CdnS, without tax)

Dining: ★★★★ (resort), ★★★ (region)
Apres-ski/nightlife: ★★ (resort), ★★ (region)
Other activities: ★★★★

Sun Peaks Resort

As for Sun Peaks, its strides toward the future of skiing began with Nippon Cable's purchase of the former Tod Mountain in 1992. So far, more than $225 million has gone into the re-do, with $70 million more on the way. Al Raine and his Olympic ski-race-champion wife, Nancy Greene Raine, who helped build Whistler to the international destination it is today, call Sun Peaks home, and Nancy is the director of skiing. As a matter of fact, Sun Peaks is often called the next Whistler. That's stretching things a bit—a whole lot, in fact. But don't let that stop you. It's a very nice chunk of mountain village and resort, with nothing to apologize for. It has huge bowls, wide runs, steep chutes and an abundance of glades.

Sun Peaks has big news for the 2002/03 winter season: They are opening a new peak, Mt. Morrisey, and adding almost 1,000 acres to the resort's skiable acreage. Sun Peaks Resort is now ranked the largest ski area in the interior and the second largest in British Columbia, behind Whistler.

The resort has one of five North American detachable quads with a bubble, the 1.5-mile Sunburst Express. Off to its right are six single-diamond steeps, all in a row, plus one blue steep. Beginners have their own separate area near the Village Day Lodge in front of Nancy Greene's hotel. It's very much out of the way. Snowboarders have a couple of halfpipes and an obstacle course off to the side of the intermediate runs served by the Sundance Express. Just a warning: If you use lifts as meeting places, be aware that Sun*dance* and Sun*burst* chairs unload at different points.

"Friendly, chatty Kamloopsians will have you loading up the U-haul and moving west within one Sun Peaks chairlift conversation. They wrote the book on civic pride." This is how *Ski Canada Magazine* describes local Sun Peaks skiers and snowboarders in a recent "Best of Canadian Skiing" issue. Those locals began the ski area in 1961, with volunteers carving many of the runs that are skied today.

Mountain layout—Skiing

◆◆ **Expert:** The really advanced runs—the bowls, chutes and head walls—are up off the higher chairs and T-bar. Hat Trick, to the right of the Crystal triple chair, dumps you unceremoniously into the woods.

◆ **Advanced:** The six chutes to the right of the Sun*burst* Express are big favorites, but you'll have a fine ol' time in the Burfield Quad region. Off Juniper Ridge, to the left, are several challenging runs.

■ **Intermediate:** The Sun*dance* Express, to the right, gets you to the top of Sundance Ridge, where three blue runs (Grannie Greene's, Sun Catcher and Sunrise) begin. If you take the Sun*burst* Express, there are several good blue runs on the left. Higher up, even to the top of the West Bowl T-bar, there are lots of blue runs.

●● **Beginner:** Except for the West Bowl T-bar and Crystal Chair, there are green runs descending from every lift. One of the most fun is the 5-miler that starts at the top of the Burfield Quad. If you want to do it again, be sure to take the Burfield Outrun under the Sunburst Express and back to the bottom of the Burfield.

● **Never-ever:** The area right in front of Nancy Greene's hotel is all for you. The three runs—Sunbeam, Gentle Giant and Cowabunga—cannot terrorize you, guaranteed.

Mountain layout–Snowboarding

Sun Peaks has two halfpipes and one terrain park. The terrain park is 2,500 feet long and is served by a high-speed quad. At 20 acres, it's one of North America's largest snowboard parks. Sun Peaks is a popular stop on the FIS Grundig Snowboard World Cup. The six single-blacks to the right of the Sunburst Express chair are a fair challenge and can keep a freerider busy all morning. Up higher, the Crystal Bowl, between the Crystal and Burfield chairs, is wide and single-black steep. If it's too much, and you want to avoid the Head Walls, blue-diamond Crystal Run is good for bailing.

Mountain rating

It's trite to say it, but this mountain has something for every skier and rider. It's a big mountain, but not hard to know after your first morning. Everyone who has skied before will benefit from a few warm-up runs off the Sun*dance* Express. That will be the comfort zone for most of us. The rest of you will want to hustle over to Tod Mountain across the way. Just stay out of the closed woods area at the bottom of the Crystal Chair.

Cross-country and snowshoeing

Sun Peaks has 40 km. of cross-country trails, half wilderness trails and half track-set trails and skating lanes. Rentals and lessons are available. Snowshoeing, alone or with a guide, follows dedicated trails with bird feeding stations, wildlife viewing and a snow cave. Rentals include snowshoes, gaiters and an interpretive map. Tours include snowshoes, gaiters and headlamps for evening tours.

Just 25 minutes from Kamloops is **Stake Lake Trails** (fax, 579-5653; snow phone, 372-5514), with 45 km. of well-groomed classic and skating tracks. It's run lovingly by the Kamloops Overlander Ski Club.

Lessons (2002/03 Cdn$, without GST)

Group lessons: A two-hour group lesson for novice through intermediate, $32. Top of the World Clinics for advanced skiers is 2 hours, $39.

Never-ever package: A three-hour lesson plus lunch, rentals and lift ticket, $60.

Private lessons: For a one-hour lesson, $65; a two-hour lesson, $125; a half-day lesson, $175 (up to 3 people); an all-day lesson, $285 (up to 3 people). Early risers can take a one-hour lesson for $49.

Special programs: Take a one-hour private lesson with Olympian Nancy Greene, $125 for up to two people, each additional person is $27; reservations required.

Child care (2002/03 Cdn$, without GST)

Ages: 18 months to 5 years.

Costs: Full day is $49 with lunch; half day is $26 with snacks only; $9 an hour with two-hour minimum.

Reservations: Call 578-5433.

Children's lessons: Sun Kids is for ages 6-13. Full day with lunch, $59; half day, $35. Lift ticket and rentals are extra. Sun Tots, for ages 3-5, is half-day program that costs $35, includes lunch, lessons and snowplay; or choose a 90-minute lesson in the afternoon, $25.

Lift tickets (2002/03 Cdn$, without GST)

	Adult	Youth (13-18)	Child (6-12)
One day	$54	$47	$29
Three days			
Five days			

Who skis free: Children 5 and younger.

Who skis at a discount: Seniors 65 and older, $38.

Accommodations

Kids 12 and younger stay and ski free at Sun Peaks (one per adult). All hotels are ski-in/ski-out; many other properties are as well. **Central Reservations,** (800) 807-3257, can arrange lodging, activities, rentals, lift tickets and more. **Nancy Greene's Cahilty Lodge** (578-7454; $$-$$$$) is practically on the slopes. Nancy's gold and silver Olympic medals are displayed in the lobby. It's a condominium lodge with hotel rooms, studio units and large family units. The lodge has a fitness center, hot tubs and restaurant.

The deluxe, full-service **Sundance Lodge** (578-0200; $$-$$$$) sits right at the base of a chair lift. Some of the units have kitchens, and all have coffee makers and microwaves. You'll find a fitness center, restaurant and shops.

The new 226-room **Delta Sun Peak Resort** ($$-$$$$) includes laundry facilities, an indoor/outdoor pool, three hot tubs, fitness center, spa, steam room and sauna, babysitting, game rooms, restaurants and a nightclub.

The **Woodlands Fireside Lodge** and **Woodlands Hearthstone Lodge** (578-8588; $$-$$$) are both full-service hotels with deluxe studios and suites. All suites have kitchens or kitchenettes and fireplaces. Plus there's a restaurant, fitness center and whirlpools. **The Heffley Inn** (578-7878; $$) is a 26-room, European-style hotel with a whirlpool, sauna and steam room. There's also a restaurant.

The **Sun Peaks International Hostel** (578-0057, www.sunpeakshostel.com; $) is a large rustic lodge and offers slopeside accommodation from $20 per person (Cdn$). Amenities include a fully equipped kitchen, commissary, large lounge area, Internet access, private and semi-private rooms, and ski/snowboard storage lockers.

Dining

Bento's Daylodge, east of the Village Daylodge, is an OK quick cafeteria stop in your busy ski day. The **Sunburst Daylodge**, mid-mountain, is a cafeteria with great views. In the Sundance Lodge, you'll find the **Bolacco Café** and **Bottom's Bar & Grill**. Bottom's is charmingly noisy. High-country-style AAA Canadian beef is the specialty at the **Heffley Steakhouse**. You quickly learn to trust the local McDonnell brothers' eclectic fusion menu at **Macker's Bistro & Bar,** located in Nancy Greene's Cahilty Lodge. Imaginative continental cuisine is served in the **Val Senales Dining Room.**

Après-ski/nightlife

Things are kind of quiet here at the end of the day, and that quiet is best experienced at the **Stube** in Sun Peaks Lodge. For a livelier time, head to **Bottom's Bar & Grill** or **Masa's Bar & Grill** in the Village Daylodge. Or try the new nightclub **Club Mac Daddies.**

Other activities

At Sun Peaks' **Annual Icewine Festival**, held in late January, participants stroll between village hotels and restaurants where 15 Okanagan Valley wineries are featured. Festival events included a wine tasting, a winemasters' dinner, a seminar and an awards presentation. Festival activities are scheduled for the late afternoon and evening to allow for skiing, dogsledding, snowshoeing and other winter fun.

Dining: $$$-Entrees $20+; $$-$10-20; $-less than $10. (Cdn$)
Accommodations: (double room) $$$$-$200+; $$$-$141-$200; $$-$81-$140; $-$80 and less. (Cdn$)

Two outdoor **skating rinks** are located at the Sports Centre, which offers drop-in hockey, skate rentals, stick rentals, and more. When you're done skating, relax in the **outdoor pool** or **hot tub**.

One-hour **dogsled rides** leave from the horse barn at the east end of the village. You can even mush your own team if you're age 14 or older. Tours are offered Tuesday to Sunday at 10 a.m., noon and 3 p.m. Visit the **Resort Activity & Information Centre** in the Village Day Lodge for tickets, or phone 578-5542. **Sleigh rides** leave from the Village Day Lodge; choose between valley tours or evening dessert rides.

Sun Peaks Snowmobile Tours supplies helmets with visors and all exterior clothing (except gloves). Drivers must have a driver's license; passengers need only be legal age, or have parental consent. Choose from a regular snow machine or high-performance.

Getting there and getting around

By air: Kamloops Airport is served by two airlines, Air Canada via Central Mountain Air (888-247-2262 in Canada; 800-776-3000 in the U.S.) and Canadian Regional (800-665-1177 in Canada; 800-426-7000 in the U.S.). Both have connections into Kamloops Airport several times daily from Vancouver, Calgary and Edmonton. For shuttle service from the Kamloops Airport to Sun Peaks, call 319-3539. Cost is $27 one way. Children 12 and younger ride free.

By car: Sun Peaks is a 45-minute drive from Kamloops. From Vancouver it's 4 hours, from Seattle it's 5 hours, and from Banff it's 6 hours.

Getting around: There are regular shuttles (Wednesdays & Saturdays; 800-807-3257) to and from Whistler, the BC Ski Country resorts, plus the airports in Kamloops, Kelowna and Vancouver. At Sun Peaks there is no need for a car.

Silver Star Mountain Resort

Summit elevation:	**6,280 feet**
Vertical Drop:	**2,500 feet**
Base elevation:	**5,280 feet**

Address: Box 3002,
Silver Star Mountain, B.C., Canada V1B 3M1
Area code: 250
Ski area phone: 542-0224
Snow report: 542-1745
Toll-free reservations: (800) 663-4431
Fax: 542-1236
E-mail: star@skisilverstar.com
Internet: www.skisilverstar.com
Expert:★★★★ **Advanced:**★★★
Intermediate:★★★★
Beginner:★★★
Never-ever:★★★★

Number of lifts: 10–1 six-person high-speed chair, 1 high-speed quads, 1 quad, 2 doubles, 3 T-bars, 2 magic carpets
Snowmaking: No
Skiable acreage: 2,725 acres (+340 acres off-piste)
Uphill capacity: 14,700 per hour
Snowboarding: Yes
Bed base: 3,200 on mountain; nearby RV camping
Nearest lodging: Slopeside, all ski-in/ski-out
Resort child care: 18 months to 6 years
Adult ticket, per day: $51-$55 (02/03 CdnS, withouth tax)

Dining:★★★
Apres-ski/nightlife:★★
Other activities:★★★

Silver Star Mountain Resort

First-time visitors to Silver Star love the frontier ambience of the 1890s Victoria Gaslight village. With a street full of unique wooden buildings in surprising colors, and no cars, Silver Star has a compact touch of elegance, even with eight hotels, restaurants, plenty of shopping and an aquatic center.

Silver Star is highly rated for family skiing. It's the fourth-largest downhill ski resort in British Columbia, behind Whistler Blackcomb, Sun Peaks and Panorama. The resort gets 23 feet of snow, and the average snowpack is 9 feet deep. Silver Star is usually the first British Columbia ski resort to open. The south-facing Vance Creek area consists of gentle slopes and nicely groomed cruisers, while the Putnam Creek face is renowned for its deep powder and challenging terrain. The town of Vernon is at the mountain's base, 14 miles away.

Last season, a new high-speed six-passenger chair, the Comet Express, replaced the Vance Creek quad. Also the Putnam Creek Express quad was replaced with a faster high-speed quad and renamed the Powder Gulch Express. If you haven't heard the news already, Big White just purchased Silver Star. With one lift ticket, skiers and snowboarders now have access to almost 6,000 acres of skiable terrain. Up to 16 airport and inter-resort ground shuttles each day, plus an inter-resort helicopter service, will ensure seamless transfers between Big White and Silver Star. The new inter-mountain helicopter shuttle service is the first of it's kind in Canada: A helicopter is based at each resort, on stand-by each day for scenic joy-flights, inter-mountain shuttles, airport shuttles and winery tours.**Getting around:** There are regular shuttles (Wednesdays & Saturdays; 800-807-3257) to and from Whistler, the BC Ski Country resorts, plus the airports in Kamloops, Kelowna and Vancouver. At Sun Peaks there is no need for a car.

Mountain layout–Skiing

From the top of the Summit Chair and the Vance Creek Express, you can see Sun Peaks and Big White. That's on a clear day, of course. From here, it's a 5-mile run to the bottom of Aunt Gladys at the Putnam Creek station.

◆◆ **Expert:** Don't delay—head straight to the Putnam Creek side and scout the Back Bowl. Look for Free Fall, Where's Bob, Black Pine and Kirkenheimer. Then work your way over to the other side of the Powder Gulch Express to 3 Wisemen, Headwall and Chute 5.

◆ **Advanced:** There are plenty of single-blacks on both sides of the mountain. Be sure to test yourself on Caliper Ridge, a trail that runs under the Powder Gulch Express.

■ **Intermediate:** Gypsy Queen, reached via Bergerstrasse from Paradise Camp, is the most popular blue run on the mountain. Another really great one, on the opposite side of the Powder Gulch Express, is Sunny Ridge. It takes off to the left just before Paradise Camp.

●● **Beginner:** If you want to get high on the mountain, you can't go wrong taking the Powder Gulch Express. From the top, Bergerstrasse/Aunt Gladys make a sweet 5-mile green run. You can also take the Main St. Skiway straight to the village.

● **Never-ever:** The area served by the Town T-bar is fenced to keep out the speedy interlopers, so it's a good place to make those initial turns.

Mountain layout–Snowboarding

Silver Star's halfpipe and terrain park are both located on Big Dipper, reached by riding down next to the Yellow Chair. The terrain park has a variety of manmade features for all skill levels. A second halfpipe is lit for night riding. It's served by the Summit Chair and is between Show Off and Milky Way. New for 2002/03 another terrain park was built. The boardercross track is between Milky Way and Exhibition, near the Vance Creek Express.

On the Putnam side, watch out for the Bergerstrasse flats above Paradise Camp. Once beyond it though, there are plenty of single- and double-black runs that will keep your inner freerider happy. The runs all are served by the Powder Gulch Express. Just take Aunt Gladys to the left and pick your chute.

Mountain rating

Silver Star's two mountain faces ensure that skiers or boarders of all abilities will find what they need. The Vance Creek side offers long, rolling cruisers. The Putnam Creek side is a little wilder with groomed and ungroomed double-blacks, glades and bumps.

Cross-country and snowshoeing

Part of the **National High Altitude Training Center**, Silver Star's cross-country trails attract skiers from around the world. Many of them are Olympic athletes in training. There are two fully certified biathalon ranges here too (one with 22 lanes). Lessons are available daily. The trails at the resort are skating groomed, and 4 miles are lit for night skiing. Guided snowshoe tours also are available. The network of trails includes the adjoining **Sovereign Lakes Cross-Country** system, for more than 105 km. of groomed and track-set skiing heaven, with several warming huts along the way. Silver Star's adult (ages 19-69) one-day trail tickets cost $16; all other ages pay $8. If you want a dual pass to ski both networks, it's $20 for adults (19-69), $10 for all other ages.

Lessons (2001/02 Cdn$, without GST)

Group lessons: A two-hour lesson, beginning at 10 a.m., $39.
Never-ever package: Discover Skiing includes lift, 90-minute lesson and rental, $35; Discover Snowboarding, $55.
Private lessons: 90-minute lesson, $89; two-hour lesson, $119; full day, $289.
Special programs: Ski Weeks include five two-hour group lessons, social events, a fun race and video analysis for $159 (all age categories).

Child care (2001/02 Cdn$, without GST)

Ages: 18 months to 6 years.
Costs: $39 half day, $59 full day, $9 lunch option.
Reservations: Mandatory; call 558-6028.
Children's lessons: Children ages 3-10, full day (includes a four-hour group lesson), $59. Half-day (includes a two-hour group lesson), $39. A full-day package for Adventure Week includes five four-hour lessons and lunches, $249; a half-day package includes five two-hour lessons, $159. Youth ages 11-18 have lessons tailored after adult programs: two-hour group lesson, $39; Discover Skiing includes lift, 90-minute lesson and rental, $35; Discover Snowboarding, $55; Ski Weeks include five two-hour group lessons, social events, a fun race and video analysis for $159.

Lift tickets (2002/03 prices Cdn$, without GST)

	Adult	Youth (13-18)	Child (6-12)
One day	$55	$47	$29
Three days	$159 ($53/day)	$135 ($45/day)	$81 ($27/day)
Five days	$255 ($51/day)	$215 ($43/day)	$125 ($25/day)

Who skis free: Children 5 and under.
Who skis at a discount: Seniors 65+ pay $38 for one day, $108 for three days, $170 for five days.

Accommodations

All Silver Star hotels are centered around the main village. All accommodations can be booked through **Silver Star Central Reservations,** (800) 663-4431.

Creekside condominiums (877-630-7827; 558-7825; $$$-$$$$) have one- and two-bedroom units, a fireside lounge and an outdoor hut tub patio. The **Grandview** (877-630-7827; 558-7825; $$$) condominium complex has 33 two-bedroom units, each with a view of the Monashee Mountains. **Mountain Vacation Homes** (800-489-0599; 542-2459; $$$$) rents private homes located in residential areas on-mountain with easy access to lifts and village. There also is a 47-site **RV park** in the ski area.

The **Silver Lode Inn** (800-554-4881; 549-5105; $$-$$$) is a Swiss-style hotel with 32 rooms, some with kitchenettes, fireplaces and Jacuzzis. The **Lord Aberdeen Apartment Hotel** (800-553-5885; 542-1992; $$$-$$$$) has private-entrance, one- and two-bedroom apartments, each with a full kitchen. The hotel has a sauna and shops downstairs.

The **Silver Star Club Resort** (800-610-0805; $$-$$$$) has outdoor rooftop hot tubs on its three buildings. The Vance Creek Building has hotel rooms only, but most units in the Chilcoot and Silver Creek buildings have full kitchens.

The **Pinnacles Suite Hotel** (800-551-7477; $$$$) sits on the edge of the ski runs and has units with up to four bedrooms. **Putnam Station Inn Hotel & Restaurant** (800-489-0599; 542-2459; $$-$$$) features a unique railroad atmosphere, plus an outdoor hot tub under the water tower, Craigellachie Dining Room and the Cellar Lounge wine bar.

Samesun Ski Hostel (877-56CARVE; $-$$) offers ski-in/ski-out accommodations with hot tubs, free breakfast and linen service. Private or family rooms available; there's also the option of dormitory rooms.

Dining

Bugaboos Bakery Café, (545-3208; $-$$) noted for its award-winning strudels and coffee, is a European-style café. **Paradise Camp** ($), at the Powder Gulch Express mid-station, is good for an informal lunch or snacks. Some ski writers think it's the best place on the continent to enjoy a beer in the spring. In the Townhall day lodge, the **Town Hall Eatery** ($-$$) is the locals' hangout.

In the Silver Star Club Resort you'll find the full-menu/lounge **Clementine's Dining Room** (549-5191; $-$$), **The Italian Garden** (549-5191; $-$$) and the **Vance Creek Saloon** ($-$$), serving light meals and snacks until midnight. Don't miss the **Aberdeen Deli Company** (260-4904; $). Soups are a specialty and there's a wide variety of homemade fare.

More upscale is the **Craigellachie Dining Room** (542-2459; $$) in the Putnam Station Inn. It has a full Okanagan wine list and a full menu selection. Uh-oh…*Ski Canada* magazine

Dining: $$$-Entrees $20+; $$-$10-20; $-less than $10.
Accommodations: (double room) $$$$-$200+; $$$-$141-$200; $$-$81-$140; $-$80 and less.

voted the Craigellachie the "Best Kids' Restaurant." Also in the Putnam, **The Okanagan Wine Cellar** ($$) is an intimate wine bar with light meals. The **Silver Lode Inn Dining Room** (549-5105; $$-$$$) features Swiss and international cuisine and a buffet dinner on Thursday evenings.

Après-ski/nightlife

Be sure to check out the *Entertainment Weekly* when you check in. It lists the special après-ski activities that vary from week to week. Meanwhile, head over to the **Vance Creek Saloon** where there's entertainment to be had Wednesday to Saturday. **Charlie's Bar** is quieter and more cozy. It's off the Silver Lode Inn Dining Room.

Other activities

Silver Star's **Adventure Park** has a lift-served Tubetown, skating pond, Mini-Z snowmobile park for kids, horse-drawn sleigh rides, snowmobile tours and snowshoe excursions. The **National Altitude Training Center** has a climbing wall (lessons available); there's also either a feature activity or a movie in the auditorium almost every night. The **village** has a liquor store, ski & snowboard shop, clothing & gifts shop and a grocery store. Guided **snowmobile tours** are available. You can also take a ride through the village in a **horse-drawn carriage**.

Getting there and getting around

By air: Kelowna International Airport is about an hour's drive from Silver Star and a short flight from Vancouver, Calgary or Seattle. It's served daily by Air Canada and Westjet. Horizon has five non-stop flights daily from Seattle—a 50-minute flight. Airport shuttles serve the resort from the Kelowna airport (prices in Cdn$, including GST): Adult/youth round trip, $60; child round trip; $43; children 5 and younger ride free. Reservations required, call Central Reservations at 800-663-4431.

By car: Silver Star is 40 miles northeast of the Kelowna airport. The resort is 6 hours from Vancouver and 7 hours from Seattle.

Getting around: Silver Star's village is complete, so there is no need to have a car. A taxi loops continuously throughout the resort until 10 p.m. daily.

Red Mountain

British Columbia, Canada

Summit elevation: **6,800 feet**
Vertical drop: **2,900 feet**
Base elevation: **3,900 feet**

Address: P.O. Box 670
Rossland, B.C., Canada V0G 1Y0
✆ **Area code:** 250
Ski area phone: 362-7384
Snow report: 362-5500; (509) 459-6000 (U.S.)
ⓘ **Toll-free information:** (800) 663-0105
Toll-free reservations: (877) 969-SNOW (7669)
Fax: 362-5833
E-mail: info@ski-red.com
Internet: www.ski-red.com
Expert: ★★★★★
Advanced: ★★★★★
Intermediate: ★★★
Beginner: ★★ **Never-ever:** ★

Number and types of lifts: 5–3 triple chairs, 1 double chair, 1 T-bar
Skiable acreage: 1,200-plus
Snowmaking: None
Uphill capacity: 6,150 skiers per hour
Snowboarding: Yes
Bed base: 300 rooms within 6 miles
Nearest lodging: slopeside, mountain inn
Resort child care: Yes, 18 months and older
Adult ticket, per day: $45 (02/02 Cdn$ without GST)

Dining: ★★★★
Apres-ski/nightlife: ★
Other activities: ★★

The charming town of Rossland and its surrounding mountains were settled by goldminers in 1897. Today it still has a gold-mine feel thanks to an unpretentious, friendly ski resort called Red Mountain. This resort epitomizes how skiing used to be—inexpensive, with friendly locals, low-frills, surprisingly excellent restaurants and a pure adrenaline rush from top to bottom.

Nancy Greene trained on Red, and won Olympic gold in 1968. Kerrin Lee-Gartner, also from Rossland, did the same in 1992. In fact, Red Mountain has contributed more skiers to Olympic and World Cup competition than any other mountain in North America. Red Mountain's casualness is appealing. Even today, maps don't show boundaries. This is the kind of place you come to if you want to ski or board all day long, have something to eat, wash it down with a cold beer, flop into bed at night, then do it all again the next day.

A free Snow Host service is available to newcomers, and it's smart to take the tour. The Snow Hosts will take you around the mountain, but are forbidden to take skiers down the extreme steeps and tight trees. Hire a guide for access to the best spots. A Michigan skier leaving after his first visit to Red summed it up, "What you see is not what you ski. Get a local or a guide to show you the way into the best runs."

New for 2002/03, the resort is cutting glades on the northeast side of Red Mountain, and we all know north-facing aspects always mean great snow. The glades are between Sally's Alley and War Eagle. Anyone who's skied this area before knows there are some skiable sections, but often you end up in really tight trees. The goal is to open up this entire side of the mountain so the glades are nicely spaced from top to bottom. The glades are accessed from the top of Red Mountain and exit onto Dale's trail—a cat track that takes you back to the Red Chair. While the pitch is the same as Sally's Alley (a blue run), the glades will be designated black diamond, and possibly some double-black diamond, because of the trees. Also new winter activities include heli-skiing and cat-skiing, backcountry tours and moonlight snowshoeing tours (see *Other Activities* and *Cross-country and Snowshoeing*).

Mountain layout–Skiing

Red Mountain consists of two distinct mountains: Red Mountain and Granite Mountain, both of which offer 360 degrees of skiing terrain. The Paradise Area is part of Granite.

◆◆ **Expert** ◆ **Advanced:** Red has a few short and steep runs at the tippy top. Don't forget to check out the new gladed area between Sally's Alley and War Eagle. The real experts will want to head to Granite for fabulous tree skiing, chutes, glades, steeps and cliff bands. The Orchards, Chutes of Pale Face, Cambodia, Needles, Short Squaw, Beer Belly and the Slides are just some of the runs where experts will shine and many advanced skiers may be humbled. Bump enthusiasts can test their skills on Gambler Towers and Centre Star, while powder hounds will find secret stashes in Papoose Bowl, Sara's Chute and Beer Belly.

Tree skiing is a big draw here. No point in choosing a favorite run through the woods, because you may never find it again—skiers who have worked here for years still find new routes. Some locals come up in the summer and cut their own trails to open up secret stashes they discovered earlier. Skiers are advised to double up in the woods.

■ **Intermediate:** On Granite, head to the Paradise Triple chair. Groomed runs such as Southern Belle, Southern Comfort, Gambler and Ruby Tuesday—among others—let you cruise and take a dip into the trees where you feel comfortable.

This is a wonderful resort for skiers learning to ski in the woods. The trees are evergreens, and mostly large ones, with plenty of space in between them—the intimidation factor is as close as it comes to zero.

● **Beginner:** The beginner area is nicely separated from the rest of the mountain. Stick to the T-bar or the Silverload triple chair for a good spot to learn the basics. Terrain for those shifting from beginner to intermediate is limited.

●● **Never-ever:** Plenty of skiers learn here. Stay with the T-bar and Silverload triple.

Mountain layout–Snowboarding

The woods here are what appeal to freeriders. Caution: Many trails through the woods are unmarked, ungroomed and unpatrolled. Don't ride alone. Red is one mountain where hiring a local guide can make a big difference in your vertical day. For starters, try Meadows, Mini Bowls, and Inagadadavida. Check the day's grooming report before tackling Main Run and Schuss. Maggie's Farm is considered advanced-intermediate because of the tricky tree riding.

This is a wonderful resort for snowboarders learning to ride in the woods. The trees are evergreens, and mostly large ones, with plenty of space in between them—the intimidation factor is as close as it comes to zero.

Beginners should stay on the open slopes or practice off the T-bar. Of course, riding a T-bar on a snowboard is one of the toughest things you can do, so once you're up top the rest is easy. Strong-legged beginners like Long Squaw, a 5-mile cruiser that wraps around Granite Mountain.

Mountain rating

Red Mountain is exceptional for advanced-intermediates to experts. Skiers and snowboarders will find plenty of trees and very steep terrain. Solid intermediates will be pushed to their limits. Lower-intermediates and beginners may be discouraged by the lack of gentle slopes, but adventurous souls will thrive here.

Cross-country and snowshoeing

Blackjack Cross Country Ski Club across the road (362-9465), has 40 km. of trails. About 25 km. are groomed, both double-tracked and for skating. Trails wind past hemlock stands and frozen beaver ponds. Day passes cost $7 or five days for $30 (Cdn$).

New this year, take a **moonlight snowshoe tour** on the mountain (362-3325; moonwalks@telus.net). Choose from six different walks ranging from three to five hours and starting at $39; includes snowshoes, poles, headlights, shuttle to the mountain, and a warm-up with refreshments.

Free cross-country skiing on tracks set after every snowfall is available 28 km. north of Rossland (on Hwy. 3B) in the **Nancy Greene Provincial Park.** The 45 km. of trails are maintained by the Castlegar Nordic Ski Club. There are also tracks set after snowfalls on the **Centennial Trail,** which run from the upper part of Rossland to Red Mountain, for free cross-country skiing.

Lessons [2002/03 prices Cdn$, including GST]

For lessons or guides call (800) 663-0105 ext. 235, or email at snowschool@ski-red.com.

Group lessons: $30 for two hours on skis or snowboard; $100 for a four-pack of lessons.

Never-ever package: $45 for the first and second day skiing or snowboarding (lifts, lesson and rentals; T-bar and Silverlode only).

Private lessons: One hour, $50; three hours, $125. Guiding costs $125 for three hours (1-2 persons), $20 for each additional person. Guiding is for expert skiers and snowboarders only.

Child care [2002/03 prices Cdn$, including GST]

Ages: 18 months to 6 years.

Costs: Full day (4+ hours), $35; half day (less than 4 hours), $20. Most bring lunch, but lunch is available for an extra cost.

Reservations: Recommended. Call (800) 663-0105 ext. 237. The child-care center also can provide a list of babysitters.

Children's lessons: For ages 3–6, a two-hour afternoon lesson with hot cocoa break is $30; an all-day program with lessons and day care is $45 per day (lunch $3 extra). Kids 7–15 get full-day group ski lessons for $60. Reservations are required.

Lift tickets (2002/03 prices Cdn$, not including GST)

	Adult	Child (7-12)
One day	$45	$24
Three days	$122 ($40.67/day)	$65 ($21.67/day)
Five days	$203 ($40.60/day)	$108 ($21.60/day)

Who skis free: Children ages 6 and younger and seniors ages 75 and older.

Who skis at a discount: Skiers age 65–74 pay $29. Teens 13–18 pay $37 a day, $100 for three days and $167 for five days. A beginner-lifts ticket is $10 (for T-bar and Silverload lifts).

Accommodations

Red Mountain Central Reservations can book all travel, lodging and ski packages. Its toll-free number is (877) 969-7669, or call 362-5666 if you are calling from another continent and can't access the toll-free number. We list a few choices, but there are others. Prices at Red Mountain are very reasonable, generally less than $100 per night (Cdn$).

Carolyn's Corner and **The Lofts** (866-475-4733; $$$) are luxury two- and three-bedroom condominiums at the base of the mountain. They all include hot tub, full kitchen, heated bathroom floors, pre-ordered groceries, gas fireplaces, garage and full laundry. The condos are ski-in with a short walk to the lifts (just on the other side of the parking lot). The Lofts sleep up to six; Carolyn's Corner condos sleep up to eight.

The **Ram's Head Inn** (362-9577; $$) is only a short walk from the base area. This comfortable country inn is No Smoking with 14 units, hot tub, sauna, bountiful breakfast, recreation and a ski wax room in a cozy setting. The tiny, six-room, **Red Shutter Inn** (362-5131; $–$$) is right in the ski area parking lot with hot tub and sauna. The inn doesn't have a shuttle to the airport per se, but they will pick guests upon request.

The 67-room **Uplander Hotel** (362-7375; $–$$) in town has sizeable rooms and great dining. The **Thriftlodge** (362-7364; $–$$$) is a bit out of the center of town, but has some No-Smoking rooms, large outdoor hot tub and a good restaurant with Swiss specialties. The **Rossland Motel** (362-7218; $) has rooms with kitchens; perfect for families.

Rossland also has a series of B&Bs. Try **Angela's Place** (362-7790; $–$$), **Mountain Comfort** (362-9004; $–$$) or **Sleeping Bear** (362-7646).

The **Mountain Shadow Youth Hostel** (362-7160 or 888-393-7160; $) has rooms for $17 a night (Cdn$). Most bunks are shared with five others but there are a couple of private rooms. Kitchen facilities are open to all.

Dining

This town is a major surprise when it comes to dining. At least three of the restaurants—Olive Oyl's, Mountain Gypsy and Louis Blue Room—serve diverse, upscale and contemporary cuisine that seems out of sync with the rustic mountain, mining town. Call for reservations.

Perhaps the finest cooking is found at **Olive Oyl's** (362-5322; $$–$$$). Next try **Mountain Gypsy** (362-3342; $$–$$$). Then head to the **Louis Blue Room** in the Uplander Hotel (362-7375; $$–$$$). These eateries offer excellent wines and dinner entreés such as salmon, prawns, sirloin steaks and tender lamb chops. Leave room for desserts at each establishment.

We're told that in true Rossland tradition, the new **Idgies Restaurant** (362-0078; $$) serves wonderful wine and creative food with a "world flavor." The **Flying Steamshovel**

(362-7323) is a lively pub and Mexican restaurant with great views. **Sunshine Café** (362-7630) has basic burgers and pasta in major portions.

For a full breakfast head to **Amelia's** in the Uplander Hotel, the **Sunshine Café,** or **Sourdough Alley** in the base lodge. **Clansey's** is the locals' hangout and offers full breakfast and lunch menu. **Alpine Grind Coffee Shop** dishes out hot and cold breakfasts. Try the awesome Belgian waffles served on weekends.

Après-ski/nightlife

For immediate après-ski, head to the **Rafter's Lounge** upstairs in the base lodge. By 5 p.m., the action has headed to Rossland. The Uplander Hotel's **Powder Keg Pub** has terrific jazz every Wednesday and live music on most weekends. The **Flying Steamshovel** is another gathering spot, but the action is mostly where you and your friends get together.

Other activities

The Rossland Arena has **hockey games, curling matches** and public **ice skating.** High Mountain Adventures (362-5342) has **snowmobile tours** and rentals.

New for 2002/03, Red Mountain and Snowwater Creek Lodge, in the Bonnington Mountain Range, have teamed up to offer single- and multi-day **heli- and cat-skiing** packages. Guests will be transfered to Snowwater via helicopter direct from Red Mountain. Book through Red's Guest Services, (800) 663-0105 ext. 233.

At Rossland Mountain Adventures (877-550-6677; www.rosslandmtadventures.com) guides provide **backcountry tours and clinics.** They have a variety of tours to choose from: single day, yurt and lodge touring, women only, and custom packages, to name a few. They also teach courses in orienteering, avalanche awareness and wilderness first aid. The guides are an impressive bunch, you'll even recognize some of their names. Ladies have the opportunity to take a women's only extreme skiing clinic with Alison Gannett and Kirsty Exner.

Rossland has a small collection of **shops.** Browse through Mainstage Gallery for local art, GoldRush Books and Espresso for you know what, the Cellar for Canadian-made gifts, and both the Legacy Gift Room and Feather Your Nest for unique home décor stuff.

The biggest party of the year is the **Winter Carnival** for three days near the end of January with a snow sculpture contest, dances and other festivities. Call 362-5399.

Getting there and getting around

By air: The airport in Castlegar, 20 miles north, is served by Air Canada Jazz from Vancouver and Calgary. Hotel pickup and rental cars are available, or call Castlegar Taxi, 365-7222. The nearest airport with U.S.-carrier service is Spokane, 125 miles south.

By car: Red Mountain is 3 miles from the City of Rossland; only 10 miles from the Canada-U.S. border on Hwy. 3B. From Spokane, take Hwys. 395 and 25 north to Rossland.

Getting around: We recommend a car for off-slope exploring. The town bus and hotel shuttles only go to the mountain in the morning around 8:30–9:30 a.m. and have pickups in the afternoon when the lifts close around 3:30 p.m.

Dining: $$$-Entrees $20+; $$-$10-20; $-less than $10. (Cdn$)
Accommodations: (double room) $$$$-$200+; $$$-$141-$200; $$-$81-$140; $-$80 and less. (Cdn$)

Whistler Blackcomb
British Columbia, Canada

Whistler Resort Facts

Address: 4545 Blackcomb Way, Whistler, BC, Canada V0N 1B4 (resort)
4010 Whistler Way, Whistler, BC, Canada V0N 1B4 (Tourism Whistler)
✆ **Area code:** 604 **Ski area phone:** 932-3434 **Snow report:** 932-4211 **Fax:** 938-5758
ⓘ **Toll-free reservations:** (800) 944-7853 (800-WHISTLER)
Internet: www.whistler-blackcomb.com (resort) or www.tourismwhistler.com (Tourism Whistler)
Bed Base: 5,000+ **Nearest lodging:** Slopeside, hotel and condos
Resort child care: Yes, 3 months and older **Snowboarding:** Yes
Adult ticket, per day: $61-$62 (01/02 Cdn$ prices; including G.S.T. tax)

Dining:★★★★★ Apres-ski/nightlife:★★★★★ Other activities:★★★★★

Whistler Mountain Facts

Base elevation: 2,140 feet (Creekside)
Vertical drop: 5,020 feet
Summit elevation: 7,160 feet
Number of lifts: 16—1 10-person gondola,
1 6-person gondola, 6 high-speed quads,
2 triples, 1 double, 5 surface lifts
Snowmaking: 4 percent
Skiable acreage: 3,657 acres
Uphill capacity: 29,895 per hour
Expert:★★★★★
Advanced:★★★★★
Intermediate:★★★★★
Beginner:★★★
Never-ever:★★★

Blackcomb Mountain Facts

Base elevation: 2,214 feet (Village)
Vertical drop: 5,280 feet
Summit elevation: 7,494 feet
Number of lifts: 17—1 eight-person gondola,
6 high-speed quads, 3 triples, 7 surface lifts
Snowmaking: 11 percent
Acreage: 3,414 skiable trail acres
Uphill capacity: 29,112 per hour

Expert:★★★★★
Advanced:★★★★★
Intermediate:★★★★★
Beginner:★★★★
Never-ever:★★

Whistler has consistently been rated as the most popular ski resort in North America, according to most ski and travel magazine surveys. There are several reasons for this: two mountains with the largest vertical drop on the continent (over 5,000 feet for each); tremendous bowl skiing; and runs that wind down the mountain seemingly forever—the longest run on each mountain is 7 miles. To top it off, the town has a people-friendly four-village base area with lodging, restaurants and nightclubs—all within walking distance (the main areas of Whistler Village are designed for pedestrian-only traffic). Both mountains now belong to Intrawest and are known as Whistler Blackcomb, making them the one great resort that most tourists always knew they were.

Generally, Whistler (the name most folks use for this two-mountain resort) gets rave reviews, but two drawbacks that come up most often by word of mouth sound worse than they really are. One is Whistler's weather. Located close to the Pacific Ocean at a low base altitude at just over 2,000 feet, Whistler can get heavy rain or dense fog at times. But, the weather at the bottom isn't always what's at the top—it may be raining in Whistler Village, but snowing (or even sunny) on the summit. Crystal-clear, sunny days are a frequent surprise, especially later in the season, and on those days skiing conditions are just awesome. Skiers will some-times cite horrendous lift lines (primarily at base areas early in the morning) as the other problem, but in reality the few lines that develop look longer than the actual wait, thanks to high-speed lifts at the three base areas.

This is one of the most international ski resorts, attracting skiers from Australia, Asia, Europe and Latin America as well as North America. Whistler Village is European-style, built to house, feed and amuse tourists. It's huge. Whistler has almost 100 restaurants and bars; more than 200 shops; plus more than 100 condos, B&Bs, lodges and hotels offer upwards of 5,000 units, with more being built.

There are four villages in the valley: Whistler Village, where all the new development started, is the closest neighborhood to the main lifts for both mountains. Stroll the cobble-stone streets, window-shop or have a latte in one of the many outdoor patios along the way. Two first-class hotels—the Pan Pacific and the Westin—were recently built here. Market-place (formerly known as Whistler North) is where the locals go for the essentials. Along with a host of goods and services, you'll also find the post office, a grocery store and a liquor store. Upper Village, the Blackcomb base, is the site of the elegant Fairmont Chateau Whistler and several excellent cafes and restaurants. And Whistler Creek, the original Whistler base on the south end of the valley, is undergoing a major rejuvenation. It's home to the legendary, origi-nal—and recently renovated—Dusty's Bar & BBQ, as well as the new Legends and First Tracks Lodge, Whistler's premiere suite property. Town Plaza connects Whistler Village and Marketplace, and is lined with hotels, restaurants and shops. You can also walk over the covered bridge to the Upper Village for some great shopping and fabulous food. Each of these villages is about a five-minute walk from the others, while Whistler Creek is a five-minute, $8 taxi ride south.

Whistler Mountain has a new high-speed quad, the Fitzsimmons Express, starting at the Whistler Village base area. The Village quad (with a bubble), which alleviates congestion, ends at mid-station near the Children's Learning Center and connects to the second, the Garbonzo Express, which recently replaced the triple Black Chair. Four gladed runs off the Tokum and Bear Paw areas were cut in the north-facing Garbonzo Basin. This provides a third point of access to the alpine via Franz's chair and also opens more mid-mountain terrain that can be skied when the high alpine is shut down due to bad weather. You also can take the Whistler Gondola out of the village—it ends at the Roundhouse Lodge and accesses greens, blues, blacks and double-blacks. New for 2002/03: Grooming for intermediates extends into alpine areas that, in the past, have only been accessible to advanced and expert skiers.

 ## Mountain layout—Skiing

Tips: There are more tree runs, more cut trails on Blackcomb. Whistler has more alpine bowls. On days with poor visibility, you can often navi-gate better on Blackcomb. On sunny days, Whistler has more spectacular views, especially in the bowls. On snowy days, if you're skiing Whistler, just ride Big Red and Garbonzo.

But ski both mountains. Part of the appeal is to stand on one mountain and look across the steep Fitzsimmons Valley at the runs of the other—to chart out where to go or gloat over where you've been. Both mountains offer complimentary tours for intermediates and experts, which may be the best way for those new to this resort to learn their way around. Tours meet outside the Roundhouse Lodge on Whistler (at the top of the Village Gondola) and at the Rendezvous on Blackcomb (at the top of the Solar Coaster) at 11:30 a.m. Meeting places are at the Guest Services Centers on top of both mountains, but be sure to check current meeting spots with Guest Services at the base ticketing areas.

◆◆ **Expert** ◆ **Advanced:** At Whistler, start at the Whistler Village Gondola and take a speedy ride up 3,800 vertical feet to the Roundhouse Lodge. Ascending over so much terrain, you'll think you're at the summit, but one glance out the gondola building reveals a series of five giant bowls above the treeline. These spread out from left to right and are all served by the Harmony Express and Peak Chair. On busier days, take the Fitzsimmons quad out of the Village, then the Garbonzo Express to get up on the mountain. Ski the top, especially late morning. Stay in the alpine and plan to eat a late or early lunch to avoid the crowds.

Experts will pause just long enough to enjoy the view and then take the Peak Chair to the 7,160-foot summit and turn left along the ridge to drop into Glacier Bowl. Or they'll do the wide mogul apron, Shale Slope, in upper Whistler Bowl, rest awhile at the ridge and then have another go below Whistler Glacier.

Though most of the expert playground is above treeline, the lower mountain has a few advanced challenges, most notably the Dave Murray Downhill. Hook up with a local and explore the mid-mountain glades here—especially on snowy days. The glades are significant in this region of the mountain—try the trees off Seppo's or the glades of Club 21 and Side Order—all accessed by the underused Garbonzo Chair.

But wait, there's another whole mountain. Blackcomb's gondola, Excalibur, is just to the left of Whistler Mountain's base, right next to the Whistler Gondola in the village. A high-speed quad, Excelerator, at the top of the gondola, connects skiers to another high-speed quad, Glacier Express, going to the glacier at the summit.

Another fast way up Blackcomb Mountain is on the speedy Wizard Express, a sleek quad with an aerodynamic Plexiglas windscreen that also keeps out the rain, which can be a soaking menace at the 2,200-foot base area. At the top of the lift, 2,230 feet higher, you're still not halfway up the mountain. Hop on Solar Coaster, next to the Wizard Express unloading area, for another 2,000 feet. Here at Rendezvous Restaurant are routes for all abilities.

To get into the wide-open territory from Rendezvous, take Expressway, a lazy beginner's traverse, to 7th Heaven Express. That lift takes you to Mile High summit. From there, the routes off the back side into Horstman and Blackcomb Glaciers give the feeling of being hundreds of miles into the wilderness. Jersey Cream and the Glacier Express sort of go side-by-side, although Glacier Express accesses much more terrain.

While going down the spine off the back of Horstman, keep to the left and peer over the cornice into the double-black-diamond chutes. Just seeing the abyss—or seeing someone hurl himself into it—gives quite a rush.

The best known of these severe, narrow chutes is Couloir Extreme. The entry requires a leap of faith and skill. Nearby is Cougar Chute, also a double black. One of the most difficult chutes on the mountain is Pakalolo, which is very narrow and steep with rock walls on either side. "You don't want to miss a turn," a local says. Another, called Blowhole, drops from the trail leading to the Blackcomb Glacier from the Horstman Glacier. The runs from Spanky's ladder offer some of the best expert skiing in North America.

■ **Intermediate:** With the installation of the Peak Chair at Whistler, crews also developed some easier beginner and intermediate runs down from the top of the Peak. Frontier Pass, a blue run, and Matthew's Traverse, a green, give easier access to Whistler Bowl, West Bowl, Bagel Bowl and over to the Harmony Chair. The Saddle, a stunning groomed blue run down from the Peak, gives you a sense of what this alpine is all about (this season there will be more similar alpine groomed pitches such as on Shale Slope and Bagel Bowl). It puts you back at the bottom of the Peak Chair but with lots of other options like heading down to the Fitzsimmons Chair or farther down. There are two other intermediate ways down. One, Highway 86, is to the right of West Bowl, keeping to the ridge around Bagel Bowl instead of dropping in. The other is Burnt Stew, arguably the most scenic on the mountain. It goes high and wide off to the left of Harmony Bowl, sometimes flattening into a bit of a trudge. Reached by a long cat track that loops behind the bowls, its views are dominated by the imposing Black Tusk peak. Of the bowls at the top, Symphony is the by far the mildest.

If you want to know what skiing a distance of 5 miles feels like, take the Alpine T-bar near Roundhouse Lodge and turn right to find the bronze plaque identifying Franz's Run, one of the longest ski trails in North America. Any intermediate will enjoy this one. Local tip: If you're up early, check the grooming map and if either Franz's or Dave Murray Downhill is groomed, do a 5,000-vertical-foot cruiser from "peak to creek." This will make your day.

At Blackcomb, intermediates will love the trails off the Jersey Cream Express. They are wide and as smooth as the name implies. The runs under the Solar Coaster Chair also are good blues. Off the top of the Crystal Chair, you can find some remote, hidden blues like Trapline, Ridge Runner, Rock'n Roll and Backstage Pass. When the crowds hit, venture over to this country where you'll never have a line-up and enjoy beautiful cruisers and undulating terrain—perfect for intermediates. Ski Crystal and Excellerator together for the best blues.

Intermediates can easily handle runs in the 7th Heaven area and on the two glaciers. In fact, the long run down the Blackcomb Glacier on a bluebird day is a fine memory.

●● **Beginner:** At Whistler, Matthew's Traverse from Peak Chair to Burnt Stew is designed just so beginners can experience the alpine (return from the top of Harmony via Pika's Traverse). You also will find green-circle routes down from the Roundhouse, which is, after all, more than 3,800 feet above the village. Check the daily grooming report before you launch and take a trail map. Once you're on an intermediate trail, there's usually no escape. On a beginner's first day, it's better to go to Whistler's mid-mountain first. Take the Whistler Village Gondola to the Roundhouse Lodge and then ski down Ego Bowl under the Emerald Express lift to Upper Olympic to the Goldola's mid-station stop. And on sunny days for beginners, Burnt Stew Trail on Whistler will make your day. Local tip: For the ski down to the village, Crabapple, when groomed, is a great option since few people ski it. At the end of the day, the best advice is to download on the gondola. A beginner's legs are usually tired anyway and the descent may be busy, so enjoy the ride and save your legs for the next morning.

A surprise for Blackcomb beginners is Green Line. This takes off from the upper terminal of 7th Heaven Express and goes top to bottom on trails that are groomed daily. It's a thrilling way for beginners to do big-mountain skiing, but getting down, down, down may take all day. Another easy descent from the Hut is Crystal Traverse. It winds below the glaciers, becomes the Crystal Road and passes the Glacier Creek Lodge before joining Green Line two-thirds of the way down.

● **Never-ever:** At Blackcomb, the learning areas are at the base and are ccompletely sectioned off. Blackcomb's Magic Castle and Adventure Centre and Whistler's Family Zone on the Emerald Express offer great terrain for those just starting out. At Whistler, the never-ever area and Children's Learning Center is at the gondola's midstation, about 1,000 feet higher than the base. The Whistler beginner's area is more secluded and all classes fit into one gondola. Definitely an easier and more secure experience for the never-ever. All learning areas are covered by snowmaking and are fairly isolated from high skier traffic.

Mountain layout—Snowboarding

Most riders, especially freeriders, prefer the Blackcomb side because of the preponderance of fall-line runs. The Whistler side was originally designed with the mountain's contours in mind, but a lot of fall-line runs have been added in recent years to even the score.

Blackcomb Mountain features the World Cup Half Pipe (actually a superpipe) and Snowcross Track just below the immense terrain park on Catskinner. The Blackcomb terrain park is in two sections: the Nintendo Terrain Park Zone for intermediates and Highest Level for experts. Highest Level is sort of a gated community, with a guard at the gate. You'll find only black and double-black features here. To get in you are required to have a $15 photo season pass around your neck (available from Guest Relations after reading park rules specific to Highest Level and signing a waiver) and a helmet.

Some flats to avoid, unless you just have to go across to the 7th Heaven Express, are 7th Avenue and Expressway to the right of the Catskinner Chair. Blackcomb cruisers like the runs around the Jersey Cream Express chair and the Jersey Cream Wall have some nice little jumps when the snow is fresh.

Whistler Mountain grooms its competition-grade halfpipe nightly. It's accessible from the top of the Emerald Express chair, and just below it is the 'Family Zone' area leading back to the Emerald Express. Ridge riding and plenty of bowls can be reached from the top of the Harmony Express chair.

Mountain rating

When you ask locals which mountain they prefer, you get mixed responses. Even super experts have reasons for enjoying both, and intermediates will have a field day on either set of slopes. Beginners can have a good time on either, especially because they can get down from the summits (and it's always fun to get to the top). This is one of the best resorts for non-skiers, because of the many enjoyable activities off the mountain, and because non-skiers can ride the gondolas to admire the views.

Cross-country and snowshoeing

Nordic skiing is available on the municipal **Lost Lake Trails,** 32 km. of double-tracked trails with a skating lane. Trails are well marked, and start right from the main parking lots in the village. Trail passes are Cdn$10, $4 after 6 p.m. and free for kids after dark. At night, a 4-km. stretch of trail is lit until 10 p.m. The log hut at Lost Lake is a great rest stop. Call Cross Country Connections at 905-0071 for conditions or information. Most avid cross-country skiers travel north to the Cariboo region and the **100 Mile House,** with more than 150 km. of groomed tracks. Call 898-2420 or HELLOBC (435-5622) for more information on those facilities.

Snowshoe treks are offered by Outdoor Adventures at Whistler (932-0647) at the midstation of the Whistler Village Gondola and possibly from the Blackcomb side this season as well. Snowshoeing is also offered in other areas of the Whistler Valley including the ancient cedar forest.

Lessons [2001/02 prices; Cdn$ without GST]

Prices are for regular season, and are higher for peak periods and lower for value periods. It's best to call ahead for information and to reserve a space in a class, (800) 766-0449, or locally, 932-3434.

Group lessons: There are full-day and afternoon adult workshops in parallel skiing, bumps, powder and steeps. A full-day lesson costs $115; afternoon lesson, $95. Snowboarders can choose from freeriding, carving, boardercross or freestyle workshops. Full-day lesson costs $93; afternoon lesson, $83.

Never-ever package: The ski program is a full-day class using special Rossignol short skis; cost includes lesson, rentals and lift ticket. One day costs $115, three days cost $315. Snowboarding lessons for adult beginners (average age is getting closer to 40) use specially designed Burton boards and cost $103 for one day and $285 for three days; includes lessons, lift ticket and rentals. **Private lessons:** Skiers pay $365 for a half day; $545 for a full day. Snowboarders pay $209 for two hours; $305 for three hours; $489 for a full day.

Special programs: Multi-day camps focus on women, skiers and riders wanting to reach a higher level. Racing and other topics are available. Call for details and prices.

Racing: Whistler has a NASTAR course under the Green Express chair. Blackcomb has two NASTAR courses, one on Springboard under the Solar Coaster Express, and the other on Cougar Milk in the Jersey Cream area.

Child care [2001/02 prices, Cdn$ without GST]

Ages: 3 months to 3 years.
Cost: Full day is $89, includes lunch and snacks.
Reservations: Required; call (800) 766-0449 or 932-3434. This is designed specifically for each age group. Whistler/Blackcomb's child-care centers are near the Whistler Village Gondola base building, near the Creekside Gondola and at the base of the Wizard Express (Upper Village Blackcomb base). **Other options:** The Fairmont Chateau Whistler and other major properties highly recommend the **Nanny Network** (938-2823) for babysitting. **Babysitting Whistler** (902-2229; www.babysittingwhistler.com) is a new company that provides 24/7 sitting services and other activities for kids. The **Whistler Activity Center** (932-2394) can also refer you to other babysitting services. **Babies on the Go** (894-0092) rents and will deliver baby needs to your lodge, such as crib, stroller, car seat and toys. **Fun for Kids** (932-2115) does rent strollers, but it's basically a clothing store.

Children's lessons: Full-day lessons for ages 3–12 years (in various programs separated by age and ability). Ages 3-4 years pay $89; ages 5-12 pay $86. Lunch is included, but lift tickets and rental equipment (children's rental package includes a helmet) are extra. A popular program for ages 3–12 is a five-day camp that starts each Monday; call for prices. Teen programs (ages 13–17) are offered daily, $86 for a full day including lunch. Five-day teen camps cost $409 (lessons only).

Lift tickets [2001/02; Cdn$ without GST]

	Adult	Child (7–12)
One day	$65	$31
Three days	$195 ($65/day)	$93 ($31/day)
Five days	$315 ($63/day)	$153 ($30+/day)

Who skis free: Children ages 6 and younger.

Who skis at a discount: Teens (13–18) and seniors 65 and older ski for $53 for one day, $158 for three days, $259 for five days. Super seniors (75+) can purchase a $99 season pass with unlimited use—great even for visitors planning to make one multiday trip for the season.

Note: Tickets are good at either mountain, and prices are a little higher during the week between Christmas and New Year's Day.

Accommodations

Lodging varies from dorm bunks to European-style B&Bs to luxury hotels. Most guests stay in the village condominiums. Lodging has become quite expensive at Whistler, though you may be able to find some bargains off-season or with lift-and-lodging packages. The best starting point is **Whistler Central Reservations**, (800) WHISTLER (944-7853) or **Resort Reservations** at (888) 284-9999. Taxes of 17 percent will be added to lodging bills—10 percent hotel and the 7 percent Canadian Goods and Services Tax (GST). During holiday periods (generally late December), seven-night minimum stays are given priority, as a general guideline. The www.whistler-blackcomb.com vacation planner allows guests to book all aspects of a vacation to Whistler, including air, lodging, car rentals, equipment rentals, lift tickets and ski & snowboard school. For those of you traveling with Fido, check out Puppyzone.com, a listing of hotels that take dogs (this is a dog-friendly resort so you'll find quite a few).

First Tracks Lodge at Whistler Creek ($$$-$$$$), Whistler's most exclusive suite experience, is opening for the 2002/03 season at Creekside. **Legends** ($$-$$$$) also is opening. Both feature upscale ski-in/ski-out lodging with access to Creekside Gondola.

The all-suite **Westin Resort & Spa** (888-634-5577; 905-5000; $$$-$$$$), now about three years old, is mountainside in Whistler Village with a world-class spa and health club.

The **Fairmont Chateau Whistler** (800-606-8244; 938-8000; $$$-$$$$) has 558 rooms in 12 stories with an expansive sun deck stretching below the high turrets.

Another full-service property is **Delta Whistler Resort** (800-515-4050 from the U.S. and Canada; 932-1982; $$$-$$$$), with 292 rooms, 30 percent of which are kitchen-equipped suites. Their sister property in Whistler, the **Delta Whistler Village Suites** (800-268-113, 905-3987; $$$-$$$$) also offers kitchen facilities.

The **Summit Lodge** (888-913-8811; 932-2778; $$$-$$$$), nestled in the heart of Whistler's Marketplace, is a quiet, luxurious boutique retreat with 81 fireplace suites. This is not your cookie-cutter lodging. The facility also offers *en suite* massage, an outdoor heated pool, hot tub, sauna, workout room and shuttle service to the ski lifts.

The **Pan Pacific Lodge** (888-905-9995; 905-2999; www.panpac.com/hotels; $$$-$$$$) is a high-end hotel. It has 121 suites with gas fireplaces, kitchens, floor-to-ceiling windows and soaker tubs.

The secluded **Residence Inn by Marriott Whistler/Blackcomb** (800-777-0185; 905-3400; $$$-$$$$), with 186 units, is up at the end of Painted Cliff Road on the Blackcomb side beside the Wizard Express lift and alongside the Lower Cruiser run.

Pinnacle International Resort (888-999-8986; 938-3218; $$$-$$$$), on Main Street in Village Centre, bills itself as Whistler's first "boutique/romance hotel." It has suites with queen beds and double Jacuzzis close to the fireplace.

The **Glacier Lodge** (866-932-2343; 932-2343; $$$-$$$$) $$$-$$$$), at the Blackcomb base right next to Chef Bernard's deli, features suites with kitchens, gas fireplaces, balconies, living rooms, data port telephones, duvets and all the usual high-end amenities.

The **Crystal Lodge** (800-667-3363; 932-2221; $$$–$$$$) has 137 rooms. Cozy common areas around the fireplaces give a European atmosphere. Families who don't mind a longer walk to the village center may find the **Tantalus Lodge** (800-268-1133 from the U.S. and Canada; 932-4146; $$$–$$$$) a comfortable alternative to staying in the heart of the village. The **Hearthstone Lodge** (800-663-7711; 932-6699; $$–$$$$), the **Listel Whistler Hotel** (800-663-5472; 932-1133; $$$–$$$$), and the **Blackcomb Lodge** (800-667-2855; 932-4155) all offer good accommodations within walking distance of the main village.The **Holiday Inn SunSpree Resort** (800-229-3188; 938-0878; $$$–$$$$) is in Whistler Village Centre. Its suite design is very imaginative, and maids are not allowed to use sprays in certain "allergy-free" rooms. The **Coast Whistler** (800-663-5644; 932-2522) is well placed, just off the hubbub of the central core, but with nice views of the Whistler Golf Course. The **Edgewater Lodge** (888-870-9065; 932-0688; $$$–$$$$) is on a peninsula of Green Lake, bordering a golf course. Great for those who want luxury and no village bustle.

The least expensive accommodations are a few minutes' drive outside the village at **Shoestring Lodge** (932-3338; $$) offering dorm beds for $30 per night and twin or queen rooms at $109. All have kitchens. **Whistler Resort and Club** (932-2343; $$–$$$) has rooms from $85 a night, depending on the season. Two dormitory lodges and a youth hostel have beds at about $28 a night—**Fireside Lodge** (932-4545), **UBC Lodge** (604-932-6604; $) and **Whistler Hostel** (932-5492). Whistler also has upscale B&Bs. These are located in residential areas outside the village and usually have no more than eight rooms. Most have private baths. Rates start at about $125 Cdn$ and include breakfast. Ask for those with BC Accommodations approval. **Durlacher Hof** (932-1924; $$$–$$$$) is the genuine B&B article for skiers wanting an Austrian lodging experience. At the door, you swap your boots for boiled-wool slippers. Each of the eight rooms has its own bath and extra-long beds. They can accommodate 16 to 20 guests total. Breakfasts are always spectacular, as only the Austrians can do, and on occasion, visiting celebrity chefs prepare dinner on the weekends.

Dining

For years locals have recommended the **Rimrock Cafe and Oyster Bar** (932-5565) in Highland Lodge as the best restaurant in town. It is located at Whistler Creek, about a half-mile south of the village. Well-prepared seafood is complemented by an extensive wine list. **Les Deux Gros** (932-4611; reservations) is another local favorite for the best in French fare. It's about a mile south in Twin Lakes Village and is not usually listed in restaurant guides.**Bearfoot Bistro** (932-3433; $$$–$$$$) next to the Listel Whistler Hotel has come a long way since it opened in 1996. Once a simple French bistro, the main restaurant is now a high-end French restaurant offering a fixed-price accomplished gourmet chef's menu that begins with 1,600 wines and a French tradition called "sabering." Guests can "saber" a bottle of champagne in a celebratory ceremony by running a sword along the seam of a champagne bottle and blow the cork against a distant wall to cheers of other diners. There is no menu per se but trust the chef with a multi-course dinner of oysters with Nashi pear, bronzed sea scallops, black cod, Ontario squab, loin of wild Arctic caribou, sorbet and soups, petit fours, all courses accompanied by friendly wines from the huge cellar. Where else could you get Dom Perignon by the glass? There's a less formal (and less expensive) wine bar with the same kitchen and a simpler bistro menu here too.

Aubergine Grill (935-4344; $$–$$$) at The Westin has magnificent views and specialty seafood menus. Next door enjoy simpler fare from the **Firerock Lounge** (935-4345). If you're

---

Dining: $$$-Entrees $20+; $$-$10-20; $-less than $10. (Cdn$)
Accommodations: (double room) $$$$-$200+; $$$-$141-$200; $$-$81-$140; $-$80 and less. (Cdn$)

into beef, don't miss the classic **Hy's Steakhouse** (905-5555; $$-$$$; reservations recommended) on the corner of Village Gate Blvd. and Northlands Blvd. Their slogan is "tender steaks and stiff drinks" and they're not kidding. **Val d'Isère** (932-4666; $$-$$$), now in the Town Plaza, features fine French cuisine and has a strong local reputation.

Umberto Menghi, an Italian chef whose TV cooking show is popular in Canada, presides over two restaurants in Whistler—**Trattoria Di Umberto** (932-5858), more casual, and **Il Caminetto Di Umberto** (932-4442; $$-$$$), more formal, where Italian Tuscan cuisine is featured. Locals call Umberto "our Emeril." Reservations recommended at both.

Umberto's head chef for 16 years, Mario Enero, now owns **La Rua** (932-5011; reservations recommended), one of the top-rated spots in all of Whistler. **Araxi** (932-4540; $$-$$$; reservations recommended), on the village square, specializes in West Coast fare and serves creative fish, meat, vegetarian and pastas. A great place to people-watch.

Quattro's (905-4844; $$-$$$), in the Pinnacle Hotel, is one of the most popular (and well-deservedly so) Italian/Mediterranean restaurants in the development north of the main village. It has an innovative kitchen and a 600-plus wine list.

The Old Spaghetti Factory (938-1081; $-$$) in the Crystal Lodge has moderate prices as does **Evergreens** (932-7346; $-$$) in the Delta Whistler Resort. Evergreens has a fine daily buffet breakfast for $18.95; Sunday, $26. Right next door along the same promenade, the **Cinnamon Bear Sports Bar** (932-1982; $) serves typical bar fare, burgers, pizzas and salads from 11 a.m. to 11 p.m. **The Keg** (932-5151; $-$$) at Whistler Village Inns and Suites has good steaks, seafood and basic American-type food.

Auntie Em's Kitchen (932-1163; $), in the Village North Market Place, is a way-above-average deli with a deep menu featuring monster vegetarian sandwiches, matzo-ball soup, breakfast all day, and good breads and sweets. **Ingrid's Village Café** (932-7000; $) on Skier's Approach near Village Square, is a local legend in Whistler. In business since 1986, meet the whole family as you enjoy a huge breakfast for cheap in their cozy deli. It's probably the best breakfast in Whistler Village.

Caramba (938-1879; $-$$), in Town Plaza, serves great putanesca pasta, wood-fired pizzas, and a Caramba salad (chicken, butter lettuce, peanut sauce), all at reasonable prices.

Shakespeares (935-1743; $-$$), above the Royal Bank in the village, serves good value for the Whistler dollar. Known as the home of savory meat and veggie pies, soups and sweets, this Brit establishment offers comfort food for a reasonable price.

On the Blackcomb side, top dining spots are the **Wildflower** (938-2031; $$-$$$) in the Fairmont Chateau Whistler for fresh seafood and Pacific Northwest cuisine, and **Portobello** (938-2040; $$), which also has an extensive deli counter where you can order out. **Monk's Grill** (932-9677; $$-$$$) features USDA steaks.

A locals' favorite Thai restaurant, **Thai One On** (932-4822; $$) features nicely priced dishes for eat-in or take-out. **Zeuski's Taverna** (932-6009; $$), in the Whistler Town Plaza, has moderately priced Greek food.

Visiting Japanese tourists means excellent Japanese restaurants. **Sushi Village** (932-3330; $$-$$$) is legion. For steaks cooked Japanese steakhouse-style, it's **Teppan Village** (932-2223) or the very popular **Sushi Ya** (905-0155; $$-$$$) in the Marketplace area. They do take out as well. A new sushi restaurant is scheduled to open in First Tracks Lodge at Creekside this winter, as well.

Moderate-priced dining is also available. **The Crab Shack** (932-4451; $$) across from the conference center has affordable steaks, chicken and pasta. **Milestones** (938-4648; $-$$) has a huge family- and casual-style menu, plus the Palomino Bar.

A number of restaurants with international themes have gained popularity in Whistler. In the Pan Pacific Lodge, **Dubh Linn Gate Old Irish Pub** (905-4047; $$), an authentic Irish pub, has a country feel and the best draft beer selection in Whistler. Choose from 50 whiskies and 16 beers on tap while you dig the live music. **Crepe Montagne** (905-4444; $$) at Market Pavillion serves up French everything: music, language and savory crepes. Get a taste of Austria at **Bavaria** (932-7518; $–$$$) where schnitzels and fondues rule. **The Amsterdam Cafe** and **La Bocca** (932-2112) are primo people-watching spots, both facing Whistler Village Square, the heartbeat of Whistler.

For a simple, cozy meal, sneak into **"Gone Bakery & Soup Co."** It has a reader board of daily deli specials. There's good food on the mountains, too. For fine dining, stop for lunch at **Christine's** (938-7437) in the back of Rendezvous Lodge on Blackcomb. (In the "Standing Room Only" room in the Rendezvous Lodge, there's a Telus cell phone that allows you to phone free to any number in Whistler and Vancouver.) Reservations are a good idea here.

For those who prefer brunch to breakfast, **The Crystal Hut** on Blackcomb has the best choice on the mountain.

The Roundhouse Lodge at the almost-top of Whistler boasts four restaurants including **Pika's** (905-2373), still perfect for families craving burgers and fries or gourmet baked potatoes and home-made soup. Try **Steeps Grill** (905-2379) for a simple menu of barbecue, soups, stews, salads and the only place in the lodge where you can buy spirits. **Mountain Market** offers open cafeteria-style dining with your pick of pastas, paninis, fish & fries, salads and deli sandwiches by the inch! **Paloma's** features Italian fare.

Eager skiers and riders can board the Whistler Village Gondola at 7:15 a.m. for a first tracks buffet breakfast at the **Roundhouse Lodge** and first rights to the runs ($14.95 Cdn$, lift ticket extra; through mid-April). Locals hail this as the best breakfast in town.

On the Blackcomb side at the Glacier Creek Lodge, you can choose from market-style dining at the International Plaza or grab a taste of West Coast specialties at the BC Eatery, at the entrance level. Condo renters: The Grocery Store in the village will deliver groceries to your condo for your arrival. Call 932-3628 with a grocery list. Other options for groceries: Food Plus (932-6193), open 24 hours, is located in Creekside; IGA Plus (938-2850) in the Marketplace; and Nester's Market & Pharmacy (932-3545) 1 km. north of the village—"Where the locals shop." Nester's will also deliver for a $75 order or more.

Après-ski/nightlife

Après-ski spills out onto the snow from **Garibaldi Lift Co. Bar and Grill** at Whistler Village Gondola base and **Merlin's** at Blackcomb. Both are beer-and-nachos spots with lively music. **Citta** in the center of Whistler Village is also a good après-ski site. Don't miss their newly renovated atrium. **Dubh Linn Gate Old Irish Pub,** an Irish pub in the Pan Pacific Lodge, is catching on for immediate fun when the lifts close. Enjoy a rousing atmosphere with Celtic music, 50 whiskies and 16 beers on tap.

Things don't slow down when the lifts close. Whistler has happening nightlife—from hot and heavy to sweet and subdued. Among the 100+ bars and restaurants, some of the most popular include **Maxx Fish,** a dance club with a wild interior paint job, next to the new **Amsterdam Cafe** in Village Square. It's Whistler's funkiest local hangout for night time mingling. Drop into a deep couch or pull up a bar stool beside a famous local athlete. **Tommy Africa's** is in the main Whistler Village, under the Pharmasave and behind the zebra poles. It's a treasure hunt to find, but it's the "best place to dance in Whistler" as voted by the locals—and our staff!

Dining: $$$-Entrees $20+; $$-$10-20; $-less than $10. (Cdn$)
Accommodations: (double room) $$$$-$200+; $$$-$141-$200; $$-$81-$140; $-$80 and less. (Cdn$)

If keeping in step with the go-go girls is too tough, belly up to one of the five bars for fuel. **The Savage Beagle,** near the Village Center, has been recently renovated. This dancing heaven favors funk and acid jazz in a double-decker, double-loud lounge in the middle of Whistler. More people watch than dance, but the dancers have all the fun. Open until 2 a.m.

Moe Joe's, across from **Buffalo Bill's** (also a big bar scene for the 30+ crowd, but get there early), is near the conference center just off the main Village Square. While you're in the conference center neighborhood, look for "The Shack," **Crab Shack**, that is. It serves up live music, great pub food and a fresh oyster bar. Search out the legendary **Garfinkel's** featuring music for the younger crowd in the Delta Whistler Village Suites.

Dusty's Bar & BBQ at Creekside is still the local's choice. Newly renovated, Dusty's is home to award-winning barbecue, a relaxed atmosphere and stellar live music. Now here's some local lore: The DJ station in the bar houses one of the original gondolas named for Seppo, who set up the first Whistler gondola way back in 1966. On site at one of the less expensive lodges in Whistler, **The Shoestring Lodge**, is the oldest pub in Whistler. A kilometer north of the village is **The Boot Pub** where many locals hang our. It has great live entertainment.

For a more civilized après-ski or evening drink, snuggle in at the Fairmont Chateau Whistler's expanded **Mallard Bar** just off the hotel lobby with a view of Blackcomb Mountain. Or check out the **Cinnamon Bear Bar** in the Delta Whistler Resort. **The Firerock Lounge** at the Westin Resort & Spa is in the heart of Whistler Village. **Black's Pub** on the square in the Westbrook Hotel is just 20 yards from the gondola bases. You'll get 180-degree views and have your pick of 99 beers and 45 scotches.

Check the Pique newsmagazine for the weekly entertainment listings.

Other activities

The resort puts on a **Fire & Ice Show** each Sunday during the winter months at 6:30 p.m. to welcome guests.

Heli-skiing is offered by Whistler Heli-Skiing (932-4105), which also features **scenic flights.** Hundreds of miles of logging roads are accessible for **snowmobiling**. Cougar Mountain Wilderness Adventures (932-4086) and Blackcomb Snowmobiles Ltd. (932-8484) have tours several times a day, and evening rides. Canadian Snowmobile Adventures (938-1616) offers luxury evening dinner tours up Blackcomb Mountain.

Daily and multi-day **backcountry ski & snowboard tours** are available through Spearhead Mountain Guides (905-9033), Whistler Alpine Guides (938-3228) and Callaghan Country Wilderness Adventures (938-0616).

Whether you're new to the sport or an experienced climber, **ice climbing** with Whistler Alpine Guides (938-3228) will provide an experience you can take back to the water cooler.

Whistler is in a Coastal Temperate Rainforest. Cable between trees across Fitzsimmons Creek with **Zip Trek** (866-935-0001) on a 2 1/2-hour tour, offered year-round. Zipsters are attached by body harness and carabiner to a steel pulley system.

Covered **tennis** courts are at the Delta Mountain Inn. **Ice skating, swimming** and drop-in **hockey** take place at Meadow Park Sports Centre (935-PLAY) a few miles north of the village. **Sleigh rides** are offered by Blackcomb Sleighrides (932-7631) and Whistler Outdoor Experience Co. (932-3389). Visit the **Great Wall Climbing and Guiding Centre** (905-7625) where you can literally climb the wall (in the Westbrook Hotel, lower level). The **Whistler Activity and Information Centre** (932-2394) provides information and reservations. **Intrawest Activity Centre** (935-4528) can book activities as well.

Shopping is plentiful and we could write an entire chapter! But just enjoy the thrill of discovery. Here are a couple of secret cheap and invaluable finds for those of you renting equipment or suffering boot pain: Wild Willies Ski Club (938-8036) has three stores in Whistler where you can find the best price points for renting equipment and also some good buys. McCoo's (932-2842), in the main village, has a tiny work bench in the back and a treasure of a bootfitter named George, who works miracles on those pain-causing ski boots. Surefoot (938-1663) in the main village also will do a great job of re-fitting your ski boots.

Explore Canadian-made gifts at Skitch Knicknacks and Paddywacks. At the Roots store (the designer of the U.S.A. Olympic team's uniforms) in Whistler Village you just might find some memorabilia from Salt Lake City. And if you're looking for that perfect outfit, don't miss Open Country in The Fairmont Chateau. They have what everyone in Canada is wearing…washable leather! Jeans, slacks, jackets. Yes, just throw those garments in the washing machine and the dryer. Too good to be true.

Expressions provides a great rainy day activity: You Paint It Ceramics. You pick a pattern, or do a freehand paint job, and pick up your creation after the glaze is fired. It's in the Stone Lodge. If you're into authentic Northwest Coast art, the Black Tusk Gallery at the Summit Lodge in Whistler North is a must. Experience the works of leading native artists in the forms of potlatch masks, totem poles, bowls, jewelry and sculptures.

Getting there and getting around

By air: Most major airlines fly to Vancouver. Allow plenty of time in the Vancouver Airport, both arriving and leaving for customs.

Whistler Air (888-806-2299) offers a twice-daily service between downtown Vancouver and Whistler, plus a charter service that's available from two airports—Victoria and Seattle. The float planes leave from Coal Harbor in downtown Vancouver for a 30-minute ride over some fabulous countryside at 9:30 a.m. and 5 p.m. daily; $125 per person one way. The return flights leave Whistler at 8:30 a.m. and 4 p.m. daily for Vancouver. Don't forget your passport.

Perimeter's Whistler Express (877-317-7788; Whistler 905-0041; Vancouver 266-5386; www.perimeterbus.com) connects from the Vancouver Airport to Whistler 12 times a day, with the last bus leaving at 12:30 a.m. Fare is about $55 one way. Reservations are required by noon, one day prior. **Note on ground transportation:** The Perimeter bus picks up only at certain hotels. If you are staying somewhere that isn't on their list, you must get yourself and your bags to a pickup point on time. So keep that in mind as you make lodging reservations. **Whistler Star Express** (685-5600; 905-7688) also shuttles between the airport, Vancouver and Whistler for $55 one way (children 5-11, $34 one way), reservations required.

By train: The most scenic way to travel is to board BC Rail's passenger trains (800-663-8238; 984-5426). Trains leave North Vancouver at 7 a.m. daily, arriving at 9:45 a.m. They depart Whistler at 6:40 p.m. and arrive at North Vancouver at 9:15 p.m. Advance reservations are required, one day prior. Roundtrip fare is about $69 for adults, $44 for children ages 2–12. Taxis go from the airport to the train station and a bus picks up train passengers at several downtown locations. Call (800) 663-8238.

By bus: Greyhound Canada operates from the Vancouver bus depot at Main and Terminal, and charges about $21 one way; $42 round trip (call 800-661-8747, 932-5031). You can also check www.greyhound.ca.

Getting around: For local cabs, call Whistler Taxi (932-3333). There's a free Village Shuttle and a local transit bus as well (932-4020).

Oregon regional resorts

Timberline Lodge, Timberline, OR; (503) 622-7979

Internet: www.timberlinelodge.com

6 lifts—4 high-speed quads, 1 triples, 1 double; 1,430 lift-served acres; 3,590 feet vertical

Timberline is known for its summer skiing and beautiful, historic lodge. Timberline was the continent's first ski area to offer lift-served summer skiing, and now more than 50,000 skiers come each summer. The Palmer Snowfield, at 8,500 feet above sea level, has a steady pitch at the advanced-intermediate level. It's challenging enough that you'll find World Cup ski racers from several countries practicing technique. A high-speed quad, Palmer Express, allows Timberline to keep the terrain open nearly the entire year, and gives the area the greatest vertical drop in the Northwest—3,590 feet. The deep snows of winter sometimes require cat drivers to dig out the lift, the upper terminal of which is inside the mountain. Spring skiing is incredible off this lift. Palmer runs through Labor Day every year, conditions permitting (and they usually do).

Half of Timberline skiing is still below tree line and the main lodge, but few experiences in the skiing world match a ride up the Magic Mile Super Express and the Palmer Express to the top of the Palmer Snowfield. The original Magic Mile lift was the second ski lift in the country, after Sun Valley's. Silcox Hut, which served as the original top terminus and warming hut, has been restored and is open to overnight groups. Below the Timberline Lodge are many blues and greens, with a few short blacks. The trail system between the trees makes each run feel like a wilderness excursion.

Timberline has two terrain parks to challenge everyone from the amateur to the professional level. The terrain parks and halfpipe are accessed by the Stormin' Norman high-speed quad chairlift

Lift tickets (02/03): Adult day tickets, $39.

Distance from Portland: 68 miles.

Lodging information: (800) 547-1406

Mt. Hood Meadows, OR; (503) 287-5438 in Portland or (503) 337-2222 at mountain

Internet: www.skihood.com

12 lifts—4 high-speed quads, 6 doubles, 3 surface; 2,150 lift-served acres; 2,777 feet vertical

Mt. Hood Meadows has by far the most varied terrain of the Mt. Hood ski areas and is as big as many Western destination resorts. Heather Canyon has always been the favorite for experts, when it is open. Now three of its entry runs—Twilight, Pluto and Moon Bowl—are winchcat-groomed, which means advanced and upper-intermediate skiers can go where they before had feared to tread. Snowcat skiing adds another 1,020 feet of vertical drop.

A favorite intermediate area is under the Hood River Express chair, called "Hurry" (for its initials—HRE). The entire HRE pod is designated slow speed for families and novice skiers and snowboarders. Beginners have the runs under the Daisy, Buttercup and Red chairs. Mitchell Creek Boulevard, reached from the Red chair, is particularly great for kids. Night skiers are served by four chairlifts near the lodge, one of them a high-speed quad.

Meadows has a lot of what you'd have to call "free range" terrain. Most anywhere is good for riding and most of the mountain rides big. The east-facing runs between the Cascade

Express and the boundary—more of a face actually—are all smoothies, good for working on the turns and swooping back and forth. Between the Cascade Express and the Mt. Hood Express are six little bowls and patches of trees—all single-black runs. For the real deal, head to the experts-only Heather Canyon, the bulk of it reachable from the Morning Star Express. Absolute Magnitude is the best to jump into from the Shooting Star Ridge. For the upper canyon, you have to take Cascade Express and turn right. Things are steeper up here, starting with A-Zone and 7151. To start way high with the runs into Super Bowl, you must take the Super Bowl Snow Cat up 1,700 feet of vertical from the top of Cascade Express. The ride costs $10 per trip. Meadows also has a groomed halfpipe, a natural halfpipe and three terrain parks. There's nice terrain for beginners too.

Lift tickets (01/02): Adult day tickets, $44; children, $25 per shift.
(Shifts are 9 a.m.–4 p.m., 11 a.m.–7 p.m., and 1–10 p.m.)
Distance from Hood River: 35 miles.
Lodging information: (800) 754-4663

Mt. Hood SkiBowl, OR; (503) 272-3206

Internet: www.skibowl.com
9 lifts—4 high-speed quads, 4 doubles, 5 surface; 960 lift-served acres; 1,500 feet vertical

Mt. Hood SkiBowl is gaining a reputation for challenging ski runs with the addition of its Outback area and 1,500 feet of vertical reached from Upper Bowl. The mountain is now rated at 60 percent expert, but the 65 runs have enough variety for all skills. Beginners have some nice terrain, although the unloading ramps on the Multorpor side can be steep and intimidating for those at this level.

Mt. Hood SkiBowl claims to be America's largest night-skiing area by virtue of the number of lights. It illuminates 34 runs, including some truly steep black-diamond runs. It also emphasizes ski racing, with programs for a variety of age groups.

The Multorpor side and the Outback are favorites. The Terrain Park, on Lower Surprise, features a halfpipe, hips, lips, rollers and spines. The Stump Garden is a boarder-cross course, accessible from the Cascade chair. Both areas are open to skiers and boarders.

Lift tickets (01/02): Adult day tickets, $23-$32.
Distance from Portland: 68 miles.
Lodging information: no central reservations

Mt. Bachelor, Bend, OR; (541) 382-2442

Internet: www.mtbachelor.com
12 lifts—7 high-speed quads, 3 triples, 2 surface; 3,686 lift-served acres; 3,365 feet vertical

Mt. Bachelor is not your typical mountain. At other resorts, the highest point often is difficult to distinguish from neighboring summits, which may be just a few feet higher or lower. But Mt. Bachelor, a stately volcanic cone that is part of the Cascades mountain range, rises from Oregon's high desert and is visible for miles in every direction.

On the eastern side of the Cascades, where snow falls lighter and drier than at other northwestern resorts, Mt. Bachelor has become a popular destination for western skiers and snowboarders. Despite no on-mountain lodging and little nightlife, Mt. Bachelor attracts visitors with its dependable snowpack, clear dry air, average daytime winter temperatures of 26 degrees, and fine skiing and snowboarding from early November to July.

Visitors should keep in mind that all that snow results from a lot of storms, and winds often close the Summit Express chair, a high-speed quad to the 9,065-foot treeless summit. An average stormy day brings winds of 60 to 70 miles per hour, which can kick up ground blizzards where the snow swirls into a whiteout six feet high. (Visibility is usually better lower on the mountain, where the ski trails are protected by trees.) But when the weather is clear and you're standing on top, you can see California's Mt. Shasta 180 miles to the south. That view, most commonly seen in spring, is fantastic.

Between the Outback and Red chairs is an unusual geologic feature, a lone cinder cone. It's not lift-served, so powder lasts there until it's wind-packed. By getting up a head of steam from Leeway, skiers can swoop up nearly two-thirds of the way and climb the rest.

Mt. Bachelor's Northwest Express Quad serves 400 acres of tree skiing and open-bowl terrain in an area called the Northwest Territory. When the Summit Express is open, experts should head for it. The steepest descent is through The Pinnacles, a jagged rock formation reached by a 150-foot hike from the top of the lift, then across the broad ungroomed expanse of Cirque Bowl. Next might be Cow's Face, far to the left of Summit Chair, steep but smooth. Because it's unknown to many skiers, it doesn't get carved into moguls, but wind packs it hard. You usually can find moguls on Grotto, Canyon and Coffee Run, all off the Pine Marten chair.

This mountain is best suited to intermediates. The Outback Express, with a 1,780-foot vertical rise, serves excellent intermediate runs. From this chair, Boomerang is the only run rated black, and it parallels the lift. One blue run, Down Under, often is left ungroomed for mogul enthusiasts. Other popular chairs for intermediates are the Pine Marten Express and the Skyliner Express. Old Skyliner, off the Pine Marten chair, has marvelous dips and rolls— far more fun than the usual freeway design of many intermediate trails.

For beginners green-circle trails descend from every lift except the Summit and Outback chairs. More difficult trails are on either side, funneling the faster skiers away from those still learning to control their turns.

Mt. Bachelor has an excellent and extensive program for snowboarders at all levels, including the High Cascade Snowboard Camp, an adult seven-day camp offered before Christmas and twice in April.

The resort has a superpipe built to Olympic specifications, 400 feet long with 17-foot walls. You'll find it next to the Pine Marten lift. A superpipe cutter will keep it in tip-top shape. The terrain park this season covers an entire trail near the Skyliner Express and is about 6,300 feet long spread across 20 acres. It includes jumps, quarterpipes, spines, hips, table tops and rails. Those just getting started will find appropriately sized features near the bottom of the Sunshine Accelerator.

Most freeriding takes place in the Outback, which is loaded with trees and fall-line runs. For your final run in the Outback, try to take the Outback Express back up to Pine Marten Lodge. If you take the Northwest Express Quad up, you have to traverse the Northwest Crossover, and it's a bit flat. The New Summit Express gets you to the Peak of Mt. Bachelor, well above treeline. There are some good steeps in The Cirque. Everything else up there to the left of the Express is gentle terrain.

Lift tickets (02/03): Adult day tickets, $44.
Distance from Portland: 162 miles.
Distance from Bend: 17 miles.
Lodging information: (800) 800-8334

Crystal Mountain
Washington

Summit elevation: 7,012 feet
Vertical drop: 3,100 feet
Base elevation: 4,400 feet

Address: 33914 Crystal Mountain Blvd., Crystal Mountain WA 98022
✆ Area code: 360
Ski area phone: 663-2265
ⓘ Reservations: 663-2558, 663-2262 or (888) 754-6400
Snow report: (888) SKI-6199 (754-6199)
Road conditions: (800) 695-7623
Fax: 663-3001
E-mail: comments@skicrystal.com
Internet: www.skicrystal.com
Expert: ★ ★ ★ ★
Advanced: ★ ★ ★ ★
Intermediate: ★ ★ ★ ★ ★
Beginner: ★ ★ ★
Never-ever: ★ ★ ★ ★ ★

Number and types of lifts: 10–2 six-passenger high-speed chairs, 2 high-speed quads, 2 triples, 3 doubles, 1 surface lift
Skiable Acreage: 2,300 (including 1,000 backcountry)
Snowmaking: 1.3 percent
Uphill capacity: 19,110 per hour
Snowboarding: Yes
Bed Base: About 350 (176 rooms)
Nearest lodging: Slopeside, cabins
Resort child care: None
Adult ticket, per day: $44 (02/03)

Dining: ★ ★ ★ ★
Apres-ski/nightlife: ★ ★
Other activities: ★

When the weather is right and the snow is deep, hardcore skiers from all over the West Coast beam themselves to Crystal for unparalleled skiing. The terrain is steep and thrilling, and there's enough of it to keep the adrenaline rushing all day. There's enough snow too, often 12 feet deep at the top. The average annual snowfall is 380 inches.

Crystal Mountain is Washington's only destination Alpine ski resort, just a 90-minute drive from Seattle.

No new lifts or construction took place during the summer of 2002, but very big plans are afoot pending approval by the U.S. Forest Service. Future plans call for an all-season 80-passenger tram, mid-mountain restaurant, and the conversion of many of the fixed-grip chairs to high-speeds.

With two high-speed, six-person lifts and two high-speed quads, skiers and snowboarders can now exhaust themselves on Crystal's nearly 2,600-foot vertical—the most in the state.

Mountain layout—Skiing

Experts may only see one-third of the trails designated for them, but they'll find their real thrills in the backcountry here. And there's something to be said for a mountain dwarfed by nearby 14,410-foot Mt. Rainier.

◆◆ **Expert** ◆ **Advanced:** Black-diamond runs are a whopping 43 percent of the terrain. That high percentage is because of the 1,000 skiable acres in the inbounds backcountry areas, most of which is not lift-served. It's the kind of terrain that is out of bounds at most ski areas—woods, chutes and steep bowls. With the new winch-cat groomers, expect to see corduroy on runs like Iceberg Gulch, Green Valley and Deer Fly.

■ **Intermediate:** Blue runs make up another 37 percent of Crystal's 2,300 acres. However, runs are fairly short, such as Lucky Shot, Little Shot and Gandy's Run, all from Summit House. For a longer run, ski Green Valley from the right of Summit House to the base of the Green Valley chair and continue to the base area on Kelly's Gap Road.

●● **Beginner** ● **Never-ever:** Beginners can have fun on Broadway and Skid Road, both served by the new base-area lift, The Chinook Express. Never-evers have their own Meadow and Fairway runs served by Discovery chair. Child novices now have a "moving carpet" lift called the Kid Conveyor instead of a handle tow.

Mountain layout—Snowboarding

Crystal has woods, ridges and carving slopes that keep freeriders coming back. A lot of intermediate and advanced riders enjoy the up-mountain area off Green Valley Chair, reached by taking Chinook and Rainier Express chairs.

Both the Rainier Express to Summit House and the Green Valley Chair to Grubstake Point will get you to the Northway Ridge and Northway Notch. From those you turn right to the double-black-diamond bowls of North Country, which is only open if the Ski Patrol says it is. This is legal backcountry boarding at its best, with the added bonus of a shuttle ride from the bottom of Lower Northway back to the main lift area. It operates daily.

For the acrobatically inclined, the terrain park and halfpipe are next to the Quicksilver Chair. The Quicksilver beginner run is also right next to the chair.

Mountain rating

Crystal is best for expert and advanced skiers and riders because of the backcountry terrain, and for beginners who have good terrain, including a 3.5-mile run, Queens. Intermediate terrain is good, but we wish the trails were longer.

Lessons (2002/03 prices)

Group lessons: $35 for a two-hour session, $45 for four hours; add $40 for ticket and gear rental.

Never-ever package: Two-hour lesson, lift ticket and rental gear, $39, skiing or snowboarding. The four-hour version is $10 more.

Private lessons: For up to two people, one hour, $65; two hours, $120; three hours; $175; full day, $300. A one-hour lesson before 10 a.m. or after 2 p.m. costs $55. Add $10 per hour for each extra person.

Racing: Crystal has a coin-operated course for $1 per run.

Child care (2002/03 prices)

The resort does not offer non-skiing child care.

Children's lessons: Ages 4–11 for skiers and ages 7–11 for snowboarders. Includes lift, lesson and supervision. Lunch is included in the full-day session. Full day $65; half day $45. Rental equipment costs $10.

Lift tickets (2002/03 prices)

	Adult	Youth (11-17)
One day	$44	$34

Who skis free: Ages 10 and younger (limit of two kids per paying adult; after that, $22 per child).

Who skis at a discount: Seniors 70 and over, $13. Beginner-only lift tickets (Discovery Chair) are $20. Crystal Mountain does not sell multiday tickets, but a book of five adult all-day vouchers saves about $4 per day. The vouchers may be used by anyone and are sold at the mountain during the afternoons or at Costco.

Accommodations

Lodging is walking distance from the slopes. Three hotels and 96 condominiums vary widely in styles and prices, from about $50 for a double with a shower down the hall in the **Alpine Inn** ($–$$$) to around $363 for a **Crystal Chalet** ($$–$$$$) condo on the weekends. Parking Lot B has 21 **RV hookups** (first-come, first-served) $20 per night each; more on holidays.

For hotels, call (888) SKI-6400 or 663-2262. For condos, call **Alta Crystal Resort** at (800) 277-6475 or 663-2500; or **Crystal Mountain Lodging Suites** at (888) 668-4368 or 663-2558.

Dining/après-ski/nightlife

Restaurants cater to both the white-linen and take-out crowds, with rustic dining, a cafeteria and après-ski lounges in between. **Sourdough Sal's** has live entertainment most Friday and Saturday evenings, full cocktail service and a great view of the slopes. The **Snorting Elk Cellar** in the Alpine Inn is like a Bavarian Rathskeller. It's always the place to gather after a great day on the slopes. The Elk has a terrific selection of microbrews, full cocktail service and expanded food service to the bar from its own deli.

Summit House, a rustic dining lodge at the top of the Rainier Express lift (6,872 feet), serves gourmet pizzas and pastas along with soups and salads, but the main attraction is the view of Mount Rainier, so close it looks as if you can touch it. **Alpine Inn Restaurant,** open for breakfast and dinner daily, has fine foods and wines. It's across the wooden footbridge tucked into the woods.

You can find all your essential grocery, bakery, beer and wine needs at **The Market at Crystal Mountain.** Bonus: The Market serves espresso and gourmet hot dogs.

Other activities

You'll find a hot tub, sauna, showers and game room at **East Peak Massage and Fitness** (663-2505), located next to Silverskis condominiums above Parking Lot C.

Getting there and getting around

By air: Seattle-Tacoma airport is served by most major airlines.

By car: Crystal is 76 miles southeast of Seattle and a 64-mile drive from Sea-Tac Airport. Drive south on I-5 from Seattle, take Exit 142 east to Auburn, Hwy. 164 to Enumclaw, and Hwy. 410 east to Crystal Mountain Boulevard.

By bus: Service from Puget Sound is available on the Crystal Mountain Ski & Snowboard Express from December to March. Call (800) 665-2122, 8 a.m. to 5 p.m.

Dining: $$$–Entrees $20+; $$–$10-20; $–less than $10.
Accommodations: (double room) $$$$–$200+; $$$–$141-$200; $$–$81-$140; $–$80 and less.

Washington State Regional Resorts

Mt. Baker, Bellingham, WA; (360) 734-6771; (360) 671-0211 (snow reports)

Internet: www.mtbakerskiarea.com

10 lifts; 1,000 acres; 1,500 vertical feet

Mountain resorts need snow, and this resort in the northwest corner of Washington State gets more of it than any other. This is not hype. During the 98/99 season, Mt. Baker set a new world record, certified by the National Oceanic and Atmospheric Administration, for a winter season's snowfall of 1,140 inches. So if you're looking in your atlas to find this wonder of white, we should tell you that the ski area is not actually located on the 10,778-foot volcano of the same name. It's on an arm of 9,127-foot Mt. Shuksan, one of the most photographed mountains in the world. It's also one of the most listened to, since its careening chunks of steep glacial avalanche can be seen and heard for miles around (they're well out of the ski area, so no worries, mate). But imagine the thrill of witnessing a slide from a distant chair lift.

In an era when smaller ski hills and non-destination resort ski areas are disappearing, Mt. Baker's success is an exception. Location, location and location, between Seattle and Vancouver, B.C., has a lot to do with it, but the main ingredients are the average annual 645-inch snowfall and its "non-corporate" style of management. It's just funky.

Mt. Baker added an award-winning day lodge, two quad lifts and expanded intermediate terrain a few years ago. Now, even on record days lift lines never top five minutes. Last season, the resort upgraded Chair 2 to a quad, with easy loading and unloading ramps. Chairs 4 and 5, adjacent doubles from the base of Honkers over Gabl's to the natural halfpipe on the Shuksan side, are being replaced by a quad for the 2002/03 season. At press time, names being considered for the new chair were Chair 4.5 and Chair 9.

Newcomers sometimes have a tough time figuring how to get back to the Heather Meadows Base Area, because everywhere they go takes them farther away. With 1,000 acres to play with, that doesn't sound likely, but the ski area is laid out over two mountains, the Pan Dome side and the more popular Shuksan (pronounced SHUCK-sun) side. Shuksan has the heaviest-duty terrain for snowboarders under the new quad chair and the gentlest groomed slopes for beginners and intermediates.

World-champion snowboarders practice regularly at Mt. Baker and live nearby. Aside from the abundant snow, a main attraction for snowboarders is the natural halfpipe. Starting from the top of the newest Shuksan quad, it follows a creek bed for a few hundred yards and is normally buried under 20 feet of snow. The halfpipe is the site of the annual Mt. Baker Legendary Banked Slalom snowboard competition. The January event, launched in 1984, has earned a national reputation, attracting riders from all over the U.S., Canada and Europe. Baker also has a groomed permanent halfpipe, 600 feet long, 80 feet wide and 10-12 feet high, just to rider's right of Chair 7 on the White Salmon Side.

The Pan Dome side, served by Chairs 1, 2, 3 and 6, is for the mogul bashers and chute shooters. Hot skiers can play here endlessly challenging the steep and deep. Every time experts take one run, they are sure to find another just as hairy. Shuksan has more wide-open, powder bowl type of terrain.

The out-of-bounds areas are extremely attractive at Mt. Baker and many pass the signs and do the hikes. But avalanches are a problem out of bounds, and sometimes people die. In recent years, quite a few people have lost their lives when they left the ski area's boundaries and got caught in snow slides. If you ride a chairlift to go out of bounds, you must have an avalanche transceiver and know how to use it. You also must have a partner, a shovel, and knowledge of your route, the terrain, avalanche conditions and predictions.

Nearly 70 percent of Mt. Baker's terrain is labeled blue or green. Chairs 7 and 8 expand the Shuksan possibilities, but beginners may want to avoid Chair 8 for the time being—its terrain is mostly intermediate. The ride, however, rivals Blackcomb's Jersey Cream Express Chair for the majestic view of the mountain ridges past the area boundary at Rumble Gully.

On the Pan Dome side, beginners can easily get back to the lodge on the Austin and Blueberry runs. The signage is good, but don't follow tracks or other skiers if you don't know where they're going. You may end up on steep Pan Face or unmapped places called Rattrap and Gunbarrel. The ski patrol performs rescues on icy crags that are best avoided.

The learning areas are near the Heather Meadows base lodge and the White Salmon Day Lodge, served by chairs 2 and 8. The slopes are long and gentle, not sectioned off, but not used by more accomplished sliders. Snowboard novices—some of whom feel immortal rather than timid—use this slope. Timid novices probably are better off learning elsewhere.

Mt. Baker has long been popular with snowboarders, even in the early days of the sport. In the old snowboarding days, snowboarders were carving turns here even where the ski patrol would rather not go. They opened new terrain within the boundaries and so helped skiers improve their skills. There were only a few boarders then; now they're up to 70 percent of the mountain's business, at least.

"Of my 100 deepest powder days in the last 20 years, 80 of them have been at Mt. Baker Ski Area," a local powderhound and heli-skier recently said. The challenge is to pick your days carefully and finish your skiing by 10:30 in the morning, when the runs are packed out. And take note: About 70 percent of bodies at Baker are on boards.

Lift tickets (02/03 prices): Weekend/Holiday: adults (16-59), $36; youth (7-15)/senior (60-69), $28; kids 6 and younger ski free & seniors 70+ pay $10. Weekday: adults (13-61), $24; youth (7-12)/ senior (62-69), $20; kids 6 and younger ski free & seniors 70+ pay $10.

Distance: The Mt. Baker Ski Area is at the end of the Mt. Baker Hwy., 56 miles east of Bellingham, I-5, Exit 255. The drive from Bellingham takes about 90 minutes; from Seattle, allow three hours; and from Vancouver, B.C., two hours.

Lodging information: Mt. Baker Lodging (800-709-7669 or 360-599-2453; $$–$$$$), in Glacier, rents vacation houses, from cedar cabins to large-group chalets, all with kitchens and fireplaces. The **Mt. Baker Chalet** (800-258-2405 or 360-599-2405; $–$$$$), at Mile Post 33 on the Mt. Baker Hwy. at the west end of Glacier, has 20 cabins and condos. The **Snowline Inn** (800-228-0119 or 360-599-2788; $–$$) rents studio units for up to four people and condo loft units for two to 10 people. **Mt. Baker Bed and Breakfast** (360-599-2299; $-$$) at 9447 Mt. Baker Highway near Glacier features three non-smoking rooms with views of the mountain, a hot tub, terry cloth robes and a five-course breakfast.

The Summit, Snoqualmie Pass, WA; (425) 434-7669; (206) 236-1600 (info line)

Internet: www.summit-at-snoqualmie.com
22 lifts; 1,916 acres; 2,200 vertical feet

The Summit comprises four separate ski areas, all within a mile of each other on Snoqualmie Pass. Three are connected by trails, and the fourth, Alpental, is a mile away on another face. The four areas—Alpental, Summit West, Summit Central and Summit East—share an interchangeable lift ticket and offer a free shuttle so skiers can get from one to the others. Our stats reflect the combined lifts and acreage, while the vertical listed is for Alpental. The vertical drop at the other three areas varies from 900 to 1,080 feet.

Alpental has the most rugged reputation, Summit West features gentle green and blue runs, Summit Central has mostly gentle terrain with a few serious black-diamond drops off the ridge, and Summit East has some great tree runs and a snowboard halfpipe among its attractions. At least one of the areas (sometimes two) is closed every weekday, but the entire complex is open weekends and holidays. (Call or visit the Web site for the specific schedule.) A Nordic ski area offers 55 km. of trails. Child care starts at 6 months and is offered at Summit West and Summit Central; make reservations. Night skiing operates until 10:30 p.m. (9 p.m. Sundays) on any mountain open that day. Night child care is available by reservation.

Lift tickets (01/02 prices): Weekend/Holiday: adults (13-61), $38; youth (7-12)/senior (62-69), $25; children 6 and younger & super seniors 70+, $8. Weekday: adults (13-61), $31; youth (7-12)/ senior (62-69), $21; children 6 and younger & super seniors 70+, $8.

Distance from Seattle: About 50 miles east on I-90.

Lodging information: Best Western Summit Inn, (800) 557-7829. Visit the resort's Web site for a listing of private homes available for rent.

Stevens Pass, Skykomish, WA; (206) 812-4510

Internet: www.stevenspass.com
10 lifts; 1,125 acres; 1,800 vertical feet

The geographical elevation combined with dry wind from the east make the snow conditions nearly perfect throughout the operating season. The annual average snowfall is 450 inches and snowpack is 105 inches.

The upper-front of Big Chief Mountain is steep and dense with Alpine conifers and a few skinny runs, providing the most challenging terrain at Stevens. The lower-front of Big Chief has one open intermediate run. The backside of Big Chief, called Mill Valley, faces south and has lots of very open runs and is popular among Stevens die-hards. On the front of Cowboy Mountain lies the most intermediate runs and lighted night-skiing terrain. From the top of Cowboy, amazing scenery and backcountry access is possible, as well as more challenging experts terrain. In the heart of the base area is the beginner terrain and tube city.

The night terrain offers something for everyone—two lighted high-speed quads combined with four additional lifts offer access to 12 major runs through 400 acres. Night operations run seven nights a week from 4–10 p.m. Tube City is also lighted until 9 p.m.

The Kid Zone Childcare accommodates kids ages 3–12 years old (must be toilet trained). The Stevens Pass Nordic Center, 5 miles east of the resort on Hwy. 2, has 30 km. of groomed cross-country and snowshoe trails.

Lift tickets (02/03 prices): Weekend/Holiday: adults (13-61), $44; children (7-12), $28; senior (62-69), $31; seniors 70 and over, $7; ages 6 and under, $5.

Distance from Seattle: About 78 miles northeast on Hwy. 2.

Lodging information: SkyRiver Inn is in Skykomish, (800) 367-8194 or (360) 677-2261. Leavenworth, a tourist town with an Alpine Bavarian theme, is 35 miles east of Stevens Pass. For lodging information in Leavenworth, call Bavarian Bedfinders at (800) 323-2920, or the Leavenworth Chamber Of Commerce at (509) 548-5807. The resort's Web site also has a complete lodging section.

Sugarloaf/USA
Maine

Summit elevation: 4,237 feet
Vertical drop: 2,837 feet
Base elevation: 1,400 feet

Address: RR 1 Box 500, Carrabassett Valley, ME 04947
☏ **Area code:** 207
Ski area phone: 237-2000
Snow report: 237-6808
ⓘ **Toll-free reservations:** (800) 843-5623 (THE-LOAF) or (800) 843-2732 (THE-AREA).
Fax: 237-2718
E-mail: info@sugarloaf.com
World Wide Web: www.sugarloaf.com/
Expert:★★★★★
Advanced:★★★★★ Intermediate:★★★★
Beginner:★★
Never-ever:★★

Number and types of lifts: 14–2 high-speed quads, 2 quads,1 triple, 8 doubles, 1 surface lift
Skiable acreage: 1,400 acres
Snowmaking: 92 percent
Uphill capacity: 21,805 per hour
Snowboarding: Yes
Bed base: 5,400
Nearest lodging: Slopeside, condos and hotel
Resort child care: Yes, 10 weeks - 5 years
Adult ticket, per day: $53 (02/03)

Dining:★★★★
Apres-ski/nightlife:★★
Other activities:★★

If you approach Sugarloaf by daylight, the first view is a jaw-dropper. As you round Omigosh! corner on Route 27, the mountain looms with runs snaking down from the crown in every direction. Sugarloaf is a major mountain, with more than 2,800 feet of continuous skiable vertical and the only above-treeline lift-serviced skiing in the East and the legendary Snow-fields. The variety of skiing goes beyond its already impressive size: Each of the mountain's many runs has its own unique twists and turns, and the skiing is "boundary to boundary" which includes off trail between the trees. As one guide put it, "Sugarloaf not only has good uphill capacity, it has exceptional downhill capacity, too." Sugarloaf is a skiers' and riders' mountain, with plenty of challenge for those who seek it.

Because it faces north toward the nearby Canadian border, Sugarloaf does not have an overabundance of sunshine. This, combined with its high latitude and elevation, means big natural snowfalls that come early and stay late. It's not unusual for the season to begin in early November and last into May. When the sun peeks over the north side in March and April, Sugarloaf is a favorite spring skiing and partying spot.

Terrain is just one of the reasons many loyal skiers don't hesitate to drive an extra hour or so to get here. Sugarloaf skiers are a different breed, with more in common with those who ski Vermont's Jay Peak than with sibling Sunday River, two hours south. Another plus: Most of the employees are Maine natives who love the mountain and want others to love it, too.

Sugarloaf may be in the boondocks, but its compact base village provides a choice of independent restaurants and bars, a handful of shops, an arcade, health club, two hotels and plenty of condos, all of which are either on the shuttle route or lift serviced. Indeed, this is one mountain where it's easy for family members to separate for the day and regroup for lunch or after skiing or riding. The Anti-Gravity Center, at the base of the access road, provides a place to work off any energy not burned on the slopes. This center boasts one of the highest indoor climbing walls in New England as well as an indoor skating part, basketball court, weight room, trampolines and more.

Mountain layout–Skiing

◆◆ **Expert:** This is a good all-around mountain for any level of skier, but what sets it apart is that it has enough steep and challenging runs to keep experts happily banging the boards all day. In addition to more than 500 acres of classic wooded New England ski trails, Sugarloaf also has 80 to 100 acres of treeless snowfields at the summit, where experts can experience western-style, open-bowl skiing. Powder collects on the Backside, but the front face has some of the steepest terrain in New England; White Nitro literally falls away beneath you. The downside is that only one lift, a fixed-grip quad, services the summit. Although it is much more reliable than the gondola it replaced, it still shuts down on occasion due to high winds.

Experts can easily figure out where to ski. Double-diamond on the trail map is the honest truth. Steep black runs beckon from the summit, and most also can be accessed from the East Spillway double chair. In general, the runs get more difficult the farther east you venture. Given the boundary-to-boundary policy, Sugarloaf has quite a few glades, too. For a challenge, try Rookie River, Cant Hook or Max Headroom.

◆ **Advanced:** The blacks down to the King Pine quad are all sweet and steep, if a little short. Bump monkeys should head for Choker, a natural snow trail on this side of the mountain, or to Skidder on the west side; groomers are under orders not to touch these trails. Ripsaw, Bubblecuffer and Upper Winter's Way, all natural snow trails, are also off limits to groomers. Narrow Gauge is perhaps the 'Loaf's most famous trail. It's the only trail in the East is FIS approved for all Alpine disciplines.

■ **Intermediate:** Advanced intermediates will find that they can handle most of the single-diamond blacks on this mountain. With a few exceptions, the western half of the mountain is an intermediate playground. Tote Road and Timberwind are both long (Tote Road is 3.5 miles), wide cruisers that wind from the summit to the base—skiers can be on these trails for a half hour, notes one regular. Hayburner and King's Landing both swoop down a continuous fall line, making them ideal for cruising.

●● **Beginner:** At the base of the mountain, beginners will find the very broad and very gentle Boardwalk run. Those looking for a little more challenge graduate to the paths from the top of the Double Runner chairs and from there to the Wiffletree quad. Terrain off the Bucksaw chair offers even more challenge: a steeper pitch or narrower trails. To escape crowds, head to West Mountain, suitable for advanced beginners and lower intermediates.

● **Never-ever:** First-timers start on the long, gentle Birches slope, served by two chair lifts, Snubber and Sawduster. This is a great learning slope with only one caveat: It also is the access slope for a lot of slopeside lodging, so first-timers should quit a little early.

Mountain layout–Snowboarding

SuperQuad area: Double Bitter or Wedge are winding and narrow, with natural bank turns and drop-offs. Skidder has a natural quarterpipe, rider's right. King's Landing and Hayburner have natural knolls. Sugarloaf's Superpipe, built for competition, is one of the biggest, longest and most consistent in the East. It's followed by the Stomping Grounds, a double-black diamond terrain park. At the right-hand cutoff to Candyside is a super kicker onto a steep, smooth landing.

West Mountain is ideal for novices and lower intermediates, with long, gentle cruising trails that incorporate some steeps at the beginning. West Mountain trail also has some nice banks on the rider's left, but beware of the clearance underneath the double chair and be sure to cut right toward Windrow near the end of the steeps to avoid the flats. Scoot, located below Bullwinkle's, has a BorderX course, with bank turns, lips and a practice park with 15-foot hip jumps, then successive tabletops.

King Pine area: Misery Whip is at most 9 feet wide and usually ungroomed and full of huge whale-size bumbs of stored-up snow. Take Boomauger to gain speed and lay down huge carves. Rip Saw and the Rip Saw Glades have nice drop-offs on rider's left at the beginning. Exit the King Pine Bowl from the top, heading left toward Spillway. From the bottom, the only way out is Crosshaul, which is long, flat and torturous.

Locals can be found almost anywhere in glades that they have spent the summers working on with their own chainsaws. Unbeknownst to the rest of the world, these glades include some of the biggest cliff drops on the East Coast, but don't waste your time looking for them on a map. If you're lucky, you may follow a pack of riders into the woods at exactly the right moment, but be ready to keep up.

Mountain rating

A giant in terms of vertical (a continuous 2,820 feet), Sugarloaf/USA is a favorite for eastern experts and advanced skiers thanks to its great tree, mogul and open-bowl skiing. Traditional New England skiers will find those classic narrow winding trails they love, while intermediates and beginners will find plenty of wide open cruising. Though just one (albeit impressive) peak, Sugarloaf/USA offers as much variety as its once rival and now fellow American Skiing Co. resort, Sunday River.

Cross-country

The **Sugarloaf/USA Outdoor Center** (237-6830) is the largest and most complete in Maine, with 105 km. of trails groomed with double tracks and lanes for skating. Most of the trails are well suited for beginners and intermediates. The center is off Rte. 27, south of the resort access road. Three trails reach it from the resort's lodging facilities and the village area. The center also has a lighted Olympic-sized outdoor skating rink and a 6,000-square-foot lodge with a giant fireplace, a south-facing deck, and food and drink at the Klister Kitchen, a locals' favorite.

Group and private lessons are available, as are equipment rentals. The all-day trail fee is $16 for adults, $10 for ages 13–18 and $10 for ages 6–12 and 65 and older. Multiday ticket holders may exchange a day of downhill for a day of cross-country including trail fee, lesson and equipment. Exchange tickets at the guest services desk in the base lodge.

Lessons (2002/03 prices)

Group lessons: The ski school uses the Perfect Turn® program. It combines state-of-the-art ski technique and educational theory. Perfect Turn has 10 levels of clinics. For lower intermediates and above, the clinics normally last 90 minutes with a maximum of 11 clients. Enrollees watch a short video that demonstrates various ability levels. This eliminates the "ski-off," which can take up 40 minutes of a two-hour lesson. Clinics meet three times each morning and cost $25. The ski school uses the Perfect Turn® program.

Never-ever package: Perfect Turn levels for never-evers to beginners are 90 minutes to two hours. The $65 Level-1 package includes the clinic, shaped skis, boots and poles, and a lift ticket for learning lifts. The resort guarantees Level 1 skiers that they will be able to ride a lift, turn and stop by the end of the clinic, or they can repeat it free or get their money back. Levels 2–3 cost $70 per clinic, or three for $150. New skiers start on shorter shaped skis on learning terrain, then graduate to longer skis on more challenging terrain.

Learn-to-Ride programs start at $65 and include coaching, equipment and a lift ticket. **Private lessons:** $65 per hour.

Special programs: The Women's Turn program offers three- and five-day programs with at least five instruction hours on the snow and after-ski activities. The cost is $380 for three days and $670 for five, which includes clinics, lift tickets, lunch and activities. Special 90-minute Women's Turn clinics are $25.

Child care (2002/03 prices)

Sugarloaf's spacious child center is staffed by caring and nurturing workers. Some vacationers come here specifically because it is so good. **Ages:** 10 weeks to 5 years.

Costs: Full-day, $48; half day, $30. Full day with skiing, $63, half day with skiing, $47. **Reservations:** Required; call (207) 237-6959.

Note: There are children's activities every night except Sunday in the Mountain Magic Room in the base lodge. Ages 5–12 have one type of activity, while teens do something else. Examples include games and movies for the young set, and skating, dances, Wallyball games (a volleyball-type game played on a racquetball court) and PG-13 movies for the teens.

Children's lessons: Perfect Kids programs are available for those ages 3-17 and range in price from $49 for half day to $62 for full day with lunch. Register at the Perfect Turn desk or in the Magic Mountain room in the base lodge. Moose Alley is a special kids-and-instructors-only section of the mountain where kids can do some controlled tree skiing. Activities are available for teens, ages 15-18, through the Mountain Experience program.

Lift tickets (2002/03 prices)

	Adult	Junior (6-12)	Young Adult (13-18)
One day	$53	$36	$48
Three days	$147 ($49/day)	$96($33/day)	$132 ($44/day)
Five days	$235 ($47/day)	$150 ($30/day)	$210 ($42/day)

Who skis free: Children ages 5 and younger; however, they must have a lift ticket, which can be obtained at a ticket window.

Who skis at a discount: Ages 65 and older ski or ride for the junior price. College students can ski or ride for $26, with ID card, during special college breaks, call for details.

Accommodations

Sugarloaf is a planned condominium community. The central village blends in well with the overall environment. Make reservations using the toll-free numbers listed in the stat box at the beginning of this chapter.

The **Grand Summit Resort Hotel** ($$$$) is the centerpiece of the Alpine village. The slopeside **Sugarloaf Inn** ($$$$) has a New England inn ambiance, but is in need of a face lift.

The Sugarloaf Inn offers packages that include ski lessons and use of the Sugarloaf Sports & Fitness Club, with pool, spas, massage therapy, tanning beds, exercise equipment and indoor racquetball and squash courts.

More than 900 condo units are spread throughout the resort, all designed so skiers and snowboarders can slide back to their lodging. (Not all have lift access, but a shuttle runs from the lodging to the lifts.) Families like the **Gondola Village** units because they are close to the state-licensed child-care facility. The **Bigelow, Snowflower** and **Commons** units are more luxurious, **Sugartree** units offer easy access to the health club and **Snowbrook** has its own indoor pool.

The resort has an RV parking area serviced by lifts.

Kingfield, 15 miles south of the mountain, offers more affordable lodging. **Three Stanley Avenue** (265-5541; $) is a Victorian-style B&B where rooms have private or shared bath.

In Stratton, seven miles north, the **Spillover Motel** (246-6571; $) has clean rooms at reasonable rates. For budget accommodations, call The **Widow's Walk** (800-943-6995 or 246-6901; $), a no-frills bed and breakfast, also in Stratton.

Dining

Sugarloaf is compact, but it has 18 eateries that range from pizza and burgers to fine dining. The best part is many offer ski-in/ski-out lunches, a big plus for those who dislike crowded base lodges. For dinner, reservations are normally essential.

In the base village, you can't miss with **Gepetto's** (237-2192; $-$$). This family-friendly restaurant has been one of the region's most popular for more than 20 years, and it offers an express lunch soup-and-salad bar. For pizza or burgers in a homey, noisy atmosphere, try **The Bag and Kettle** (237-2451; $-$$), locals call it The Bag. You can rate the local talent on Blues Monday while eating a Bag-burger and get the lore of Sugarloaf from the locals. **D'Ellie's** (237-2490; $), a small, mostly take-out restaurant, has excellent homemade soups, sandwiches and salads. There's an express line for soups and drinks, but get sandwiches early and stash them away to avoid a long wait during peak lunch hours or order in the morning for later pickup. It also serves a hearty breakfast. If your idea of breakfast is a cuppa Joe and a bagel or muffin, head to **Java Joes**. For fine dining and atmosphere, make reservations at The **Seasons** (237-6834; $$-$$$) at the Sugarloaf Inn.

For an English pub experience, take the shuttle to **Theo's Microbrewery & Pub** (237-2211; $-$$), where the Sugarloaf Brewing Company peddles its wares. On Wednesdays, Saturdays and other nights during vacation weeks, take a snowcat to **Bullwinkle's** (237-6939; $$$$), Sugarloaf's on-mountain restaurant, for a five-course, fixed-price candlelight dinner.

Hug's (237-2392; $-$$), about two miles from the mountain's access road, is a popular choice for traditional Italian food served family style at reasonable prices. Even more kid-friendly is **Tufulio's** (235-2010; $-$$), located in Carrabassett Valley.

In Kingfield: **One Stanley Avenue** (265-5541; $$-$$$) is the best and most expensive restaurant in the region. Chef Dan Davis serves a creative menu of regional cuisine prepared in classic ways. If you're passing through town early in the morning, fill up at **The Kingfield Woodsman** (265-2561; $), where they start serving breakfast at 5 a.m.

In Eustis, 11 minutes north of Sugarloaf, the **Porter House** (246-7932; $$) draws diners from Canada, Sugarloaf and Rangeley and with good reasons: Excellent food, an award-winning wine list, a homey atmosphere and choices for every appetite.

Dining: $$$-Entrees $20+; $$-$10-20; $-less than $10.
Accommodations: (double room) $$$$-$200+; $$$-$141-$200; $$-$81-$140; $-$80 and less.

Après-ski/nightlife

On sunny days, après-skiers crowd the decks of The **Beach** or The **Bag.** The hot spot for live music and dancing at night is the **Widowmaker Lounge.** For a more subdued atmosphere, try the **Sugarloaf Inn,** home of the **Shipyard Brewhouse** or The **Double Diamond Steakhouse and Pub** in the Grand Summit Resort Hotel.

    Judson's Motel, on Rte. 27, is a favorite with UMaine and Colby College students. Pre-teens have **Pinocchio's,** with video games, pinball and board games.

 ## Other activities

Sugarloaf has a **Turbo Tubing** park with its own lift and four 1,000-foot chutes. The park is open Wednesday–Saturday for two sessions daily, 3–5:15 p.m. and 6–8:15 p.m. The fee is $10 per session. The new **Anti-Gravity Center,** at the base of the access road has an indoor climbing wall, skating park and track as well as trampolines, a weight room and multi-use basketball court. The resort also has a health club with an **indoor pool** and **outdoor hot tubs.**

    Dogsledding, horse-drawn sleigh rides, snowmobiling, snowshoeing, ice fishing and **skating** are among the activities that Sugarloaf Guest Services can arrange (237-2000).

    Special events: Sugarloaf rolls back prices during **White White World Week,** held in late January. The annual **Reggae Weekend,** usually in mid-April, is a two-day bash with indoor and outdoor reggae bands. Book well in advance, as it usually sells out.

    Shopping: The village has several shops. Pat Buck's Emporium features handcrafted items by Maine artisans as well as Geiger clothing and other items. Goldsmith Gallery sells gold and silver jewelry, photo frames, and similar items.

 ## Getting there and getting around

By air: The closest commercial airport is the Portland International Jetport. The Augusta airport is serviced by U.S. Air/Business Express. Bangor International Airport also is serviced by major airlines. Guests who fly into Bangor or Portland and who reserve lodging & lift stays through Sugarloaf/USA reservations can reserve transportation at the time of booking.

    By car: Take I-95 north to Augusta, Rte. 27 through Farmington and Kingfield. Or take the Maine Turnpike to the Auburn exit, Rte. 4 to Farmington and Rte. 27 through Kingfield. The drive is about two-and-a-half hours from Portland.

    Getting around: A car is optional—nearly everything in the resort is within walking distance. A free on-mountain shuttle runs on weekends and during holiday periods and is on call during the week. To do anything away from the resort complex, you will need a car.

Nearby resort

Maine Saddleback, Rangeley, ME; (207) 864-5671

Internet: www.saddlebackskiarea.com
3 lifts, 2 tows; 41 trails; 110 acres; 1,830 vertical feet
What a sleeper! Underdeveloped, uncrowded, untamed are the words most often used to describe this area located in prime snowmobiling territory, just 45 minutes from Sugarloaf. This is a mountain where you can find powder stashes long after they've been exhausted at Sugarloaf or Sunday River. It's an old-fashioned, family area, where it seems everyone knows just about everyone else. The sun-soaked base lodge is always filled with brown-bags at lunch, and this isn't discouraged. Purchase a chocolate-chip cookie in the cafeteria, and the workers may even offer to warm it up for you so the chips are all melty.

Even in a bad snow year, Saddleback is blessed with an abundance of snow, an average of 200 inches each year. The lift, snowmaking and grooming crews are primarily locals who take pride in their jobs and know that if they don't provide a good day's skiing, they'll be taken to task by their friends and neighbors. Smiles are genuine; greetings warm.

The downside: The lifts are antiquated, and the only way to the summit is a T-bar.

In general, trails get progressively more difficult as you progress from east to west, with the most expert terrain on the top third of the mountain. It's worth it to brave the feisty Wells-Fargo T-bar, itself sometimes a black-diamond run, for the views from the summit. From here you can look over the wind-stunted trees across the Rangeley Lakes to the Presidential Range and Mt. Washington. When Muleskinner is open, it's a true double-diamond thriller: steep, narrow and twisting and punctuated with moguls, trees, rocks and other obstacles. It gives a taste of Saddleback's potential terrain, as most of the developable terrain is west of this trail. Experts can have fun in the Nightmare Glades and on Bronco Buster.

The lower two chairs and Pony Express T-bar reach three quarters of the terrain, primarily beginner and intermediate slopes and trails, all cut long before the days of snowmaking. Most are narrow, winding through birches and hardwoods, offering peaks of Saddleback Lake and the surrounding wilderness.

The lower third of the mountain is ideal for beginners. Saddleback's wide-open, gentle learning slope with its own chairlift, Gold Rush, attracts those wishing to learn the sport far from prying eyes. This is also a good place to learn to ride a T-bar, a skill that still comes in handy at some resorts.

Saddleback finally settled its long-running dispute with the Appalachian Mountain Trail, which means it's now free to develop. The ski area has the potential to be one of the biggest in the East, but it is for sale. Stay tuned to see what develops here.

The resort has on-mountain condominium lodging, but you'll have to make your own entertainment here when the lifts shut down. Rangeley, seven miles from the base, is a good-sized town with at least a dozen restaurants and a good range of lodging.

Lift tickets: Adults, $49; Children (7-13), $32; students and seniors, $43. Midweek tickets are $32 for everyone. Half-day tickets are available.

Distance from Boston: About 5+ hours. Take 95 North to the Maine Turnpike, get off at Exit 12 and follow Route 4 north through Farmington to Rangeley.

Lodging information: For the limited number of condos on the mountain (400 trailside), call the ski area number, (207) 864-5671. To reach the Rangeley Chamber of Commerce, call (800) 685-2537.

Sunday River
Maine

Summit elevation: 3,140 feet
Vertical drop: 2,340 feet
Base elevation: 800 feet

Address: P.O. Box 450
Bethel, ME 04217
☎ **Area code:** 207
Ski area phone: 824-3000
Fax: 824-5110
Snow report: (207) 824-5200;
ⓘ **Toll-free reservations:** (800) 543-2754
E-mail: info@sundayriver.com
Internet: www.sundayriver.com
Expert:★★
Advanced:★★★
Intermediate:★★★★
Beginner:★★★★★

Number of lifts: 18–4 high-speed quads,
5 quads, 4 triples, 2 doubles, 3 surface lifts
Snowmaking: 92 percent
Skiable acreage: 663 acres
Uphill capacity: 32,000 per hour
Snowboarding: Yes
Bed base: 6,000 on mountain; 2,000 nearby
Nearest lodging: Slopeside
Resort child care: Yes, 6 weeks to 6 years
Adult ticket, per day: $47-$53 (02/03 prices)

Dining:★★
Apres-ski/nightlife:★★
Other activities:★★

Sunday River, just outside of Bethel and tucked against the Sunday River, is maturing and that's a good thing. Baby Boomers who came for the guaranteed snow and the extensive terrain and who bought the mountain's many condos are still coming, but now they're bringing their grown children and even grandchildren. Sunday River is ready for them with a wide variety of steeps, intermediate cruisers, learning slopes, glades and terrain for every level.

In Maine (just six miles from the picturesque New England village of Bethel), the resort and its trails spread out with a spectacular view of New Hampshire's White Mountains. Sunday River, for all its vertical, is very horizontal—It is more than three-and-a-half miles across its eight separate peaks. Veterans of the mountain can readily recite the trails that move skiers from one peak to the next, but those new to Sunday River might want to study the trail map extensively before venturing out. This is especially true if the desire is to ski or board from one end (White Cap) to the other (Jordan Bowl).

This sprawling resort lacks a true center. There are three separate base lodges: South Ridge, Barker Mountain and White Cap. South Ridge is the hub. It houses the ski school, Maine Handicapped Skiing program and a grocery store. The North Peak Lodge is reasonably accessible from all but White Cap peak, which makes it a great mid-morning or luncheon meeting place

Skiing/riding is definitely the emphasis at Sunday River. Plan to get good and tired doing it because Sunday River, with its spread-out base and separate ski-in, ski-out condo complexes, tends to be rather quiet at night, especially midweek.

Known for its impressive snowmaking and lift system, Sunday River can suffer from its own popularity. While lift lines are seldom long, its trails do get full. To avoid crowds, the recommendation is to start your day at Jordan Bowl and make your way back across the general flow of traffic (an ideal scenario for those staying at the Jordan Grand Hotel).

Mountain layout–Skiing

♦♦ Expert ♦ Advanced: Oz is a playground for high-level sliders. Served by a fixed-grip quad, it features a 500-yard-wide steep swath with tree islands and glades. You won't find the trails zigzagging across the fall-line; Oz is a collection of straight, fall-line, tree-studded drops.

Aurora Peak, served by a fixed quad chair and a triple chair, is still the spot to find tough skiing. Northern Lights, rated blue on the map, provides an easier way down the mountain, though it's no stroll through the park. Celestial, reached from Lights Out, is one of the nicest gladed trails. It starts out steep and wide, but mellows and narrows as you descend.

From the top of Barker Mountain a steep trio—Right Stuff, Top Gun and Agony—provide advanced skiers long, sustained pitches. Agony and Top Gun are premier bump runs. Right Stuff is a cruiser early in the day after it's been groomed, but normally develops moguls by afternoon. Tree-skiing fans will find the Last Tango glade between Right Stuff and Risky Business. This black-diamond, natural slalom area is the gentlest and most spacious of the resort's nine mapped glades. Though it's not particularly steep, it's tight. A work road about two-thirds of the way down allows skiers to bail out onto Right Stuff. Those who continue through the trees will find the terrain getting steeper and narrower. If you're less than an expert, you won't have much fun on Last Tango's lower third.

From the top of Locke Mountain, T2 plunges down the tracks of an old T-bar providing a spectacular view of Bethel, the valley and Mt. Washington.

The White Heat run is a wide swath straight down the mountain from the peak of White Cap. Double-diamond Shockwave, considered by many locals as tougher than White Heat, offers 975 vertical feet of big bumps and steep pitches. Two gladed areas, Hardball (skier right) and Chutzpah (skier left), start out deceptively mellow and open-spaced, but watch out. Technically, they are the most demanding on the mountain.

■ Intermediate: Advanced intermediates are at home at Sunday River. The top of North Peak has the largest concentration of blue runs, though there's an intermediate way down from the top of every peak, and for the most part, these are wide, undulating trails, such as Obsession off White Cap. Jordan Bowl provides some of the best blue-square cruising in New England down Excalibur and Rogue Angel, with the wide-open Blind Ambition glade accessed by the mellow cruiser Lollapalooza. An advanced-intermediate trail is Monday Mourning, which starts out steep and wide but mellows near the end, where the race arena is located. Lower intermediates can head to the White Cap quad (far left on the map) and enjoy the relatively mellow Moonstruck, Starburst and Starlight runs. Off Barker Mountain, Lazy River is narrow by Sunday River standards and a fun cruise, but it can be strewn with people during busy times as it's the main route to adjoining Spruce Peak.

●● Beginner: Once a skier is past the basic snowplow and into stem christies, much of Sunday River beckons. The North Peak triple chair opens long practice runs like Dream Maker. Lollapalooza, the green-circle trail in Jordan Bowl, is "like Dream Maker on steroids," as one frequent visitor said. It's long and wide with great views, but not a trail that beginners should start out on; the upper part can get bumped up on busy days, and probably should have a blue rating. Farther down it's quite mellow.

● Never-ever: First-timers start on Sundance and then have the entire South Ridge area to practice linking their turns. Twelve beginner runs in the South Ridge area are serviced by a high-speed quad, a triple, a double and a surface lift. This area can be crazy, though, as it is the resort's hub.

Mountain layout–Snowboarding

Sunday River is good for riders of all ability levels, and its parks reflect that. Beginners have Whoville, at South Ridge. The double-barrel mini halfpipes (two back-to-back mini halfpipes with a spine in between where they meet) here are a good place to practice balancing in the pipe and making turns at the top of the 3.5-foot walls. Intermediates have a park on American Express, with challenging rails and hits. The Park, on White Cap, has multi-leveled jumps, side hits and rails. Experts have Rocking Chair, on Barker Peak. It's location on a chairlift means riders better be able to put on a show or risk the jeers from those above.

Serious pipe riders find the Superpipe on the lower right of Monday Mourning. This pipe gets bigger every year. There's no lift serving just this pipe, so you'll either have to hike it or do laps on Chair #1 down Ecstasy and Monday Mourning. You also can get to it from Cascades: Watch for a cut-over on riders' left. Note: Sunday River is the site of the 2003 USASA National Championships. A second halfpipe will be built for the event, March 23-30.

Some favorite riders' trails are on Jordan Bowl, which is a pain in the glutes, calves and feet to get back from. You either have to hike to the #13 lift, which brings you to a somewhat maneuverable pitch, or chance the possibility of having to unstrap and skate your way over the dreaded Kansas trail, a long and almost uphill traverse (We're definitely a long way from home, Toto). Other flat spots to avoid at all costs are Three Mile Trail, Southway and Easy Street. For bumps, try Agony; for trees, head into Wizard's Gulch; for cruising, you can't beat Cascades or Obsession.

Mountain rating

Sunday River offers a vast amount of terrain for all skiing levels. Beginners can start on the lower mountain area, then work their way up to the intermediate trails in the North Peak area. Intermediate and advanced skiers have lots of options on every one of eight peaks. Experts will find super steeps, glades and monster bumps on Oz, Jordan Bowl, Aurora Peak, Barker Mountain and White Cap. The resort's snowmaking system is one of the best and biggest anywhere, and its lift system moves skiers and riders quickly and efficiently. It's important to keep a trail map handy to navigate from one side of the resort to the other. It can feel as if you're spending more time getting from one place to another rather than skiing.

 # Cross-country and snowshoeing

Sunday River does not have a dedicated cross-country center, but this part of Maine is known for some of the best Nordic skiing and snowshoeing options in New England within an hour's drive (see also the Mt. Washington Valley chapter and The Balsams listing under regional New Hampshire resorts). Golf course skiing, with some wooded trails, is available at the **Bethel Inn Cross-Country Ski Center** (824-2175). The center has 40 km. of marked and groomed trials, 30 of which are groomed for both diagonal and skate skiing. It has rentals, lessons and evening sleigh rides. The Bethel Inn also has instruction in telemark. If you're a novice Nordic skier, this is a great place to learn, because many of the trails are quite gentle. Midweek, the trail fee is also good for entrance to the outdoor heated pool, sauna and fitness center, until 4 p.m.

Closest to the slopes, the **Sunday River Ski Touring Center** (824-2410) is run by the Sunday River Inn, located on the Sunday River access road. It has 40 km. of groomed and tracked trails, as well as 2 km. lit for night skiing. It's family oriented, with warming shelters, an overnight yurt, a groomed dog trail, a downhill practice area and instruction. Ice skating, snowshoeing, sleigh rides and an outdoor hot tub and sauna round out the amenities.

Owned by a former cross-country ski racer, **Carter's Cross-Country Ski Center** (539-4848) has two locations. One, on Intervale Road, is just five miles from Sunday River, and has great views of the downhill area. It has 60 km. of trails for all levels (half groomed) and has a back-country experience with rustic get-away cabins. Carter's Cross-Country Center in Oxford, off Rte. 26, provides another alternative for skinny skis, with 25 km. of tracks.

Telemark Inn (836-2703) has wilderness cross-country skiing with unlimited backcountry skiing into the White Mountain National Forest. The inn also has 20 km. of groomed trails.

Guided fireworks showshoe treks depart from the Snow Cap Lodge at **Sunday River** on Thursdays and Sundays.

Lessons (2002/03 prices)

Group lessons: The Sunday River Ski and Snowboard School created the innovative teaching program called Perfect Turn®. It combines state-of-the-art ski technique with state-of-the-art educational theory. The Sprint Perfect Turn Discovery Center offers one-stop shopping: lift tickets, lessons and rental equipment are all in one spot.

Perfect Turn has eight levels. For lower intermediates and higher, the clinics normally last 90 minutes with a maximum of six skiers. Skiers watch a short video that demonstrates various levels of skiing ability. The video eliminates the "ski-off," which usually takes up about 40 minutes of a two-hour lesson. Clinics run about every half hour and cost $30.

Never-ever package: The package includes the clinic, shaped skis, boots and poles, a lift ticket for the South Ridge and North Peak. It costs $65 for Level 1. Sunday River guarantees Level 1 skiers that they will be able to ride a lift, turn and stop by the end of the clinic, or they can repeat it free or get their money back. The second and third lessons cost $85 apiece.

Private lessons: $70 per hour, additional person is $40; all day costs $380, additional person is $165.

Racing: A course is on Race Arena, adjacent to the Monday Mourning trail. It is available for private groups by appointment and open to the public on a limited basis.

Child care (2002/03 prices)

Ages: 6 weeks to 6 years.
Costs: All-day programs are $50, including lunch, and half-day programs are $30 for older toddlers. Discounts apply for siblings. Bring diapers, formula and food for infants.

Reservations: Advised midweek, required weekends. Call 824-5959. The main child care facility is at South Ridge. Child care, day and evening, also is available at the Grand Summit Resort Hotel and the Jordan Grand Resort Hotel.

Children's lessons: Sunday River's children's programs are among the best-organized and smoothest-running at any resort. The flow from equipment rental to classes is outstanding and all facilities are separate, which makes dealing with youngsters much easier.

Age 3 starts with Tiny Turns, an hour of private instruction with a half- or full-day session in day care. The private clinic is $30 if the child is registered in day care; otherwise, the clinic cost is the regular private rate.

Mogul Munchkins is for ages 4–6; Mogul Meisters is for those 7–12 years of age.

Perfect Kids clinics cost $60 for a full day, $69 with rental equipment, $92 with rental and lift ticket. Half-day clinics are $30, $42 with rental equipment.

Lift tickets (2002/03)

	Adult	Young adult (13-18)	Child (6-12)
One day*	$53	$48	$35
Three days	$147 ($49/day)	$132 ($44/day)	$96($32/day)
Five days	$228 ($46/day)	$206 ($41/day)	$148 ($30/day)

*Midweek tickets are $1 to $2 less; holiday tickets are $1 to $2 more.

Who skis free: Children ages 5 and younger with parent.
Who skis at a discount: Ages 65 and older ski for child rates.
Multi-resort discounts: Sunday River is one of the American Skiing Company (ASC) resorts. ASC has set up a discount lift ticket Web site at www.sundayriver.com/metickets.html.

Accommodations

The Summit hotels and condominiums are the most convenient to the slopes. But Bethel also has a group of excellent B&Bs and old country inns. Call **central reservations** (800-543-2754).

The **Jordan Grand Resort Hotel and Conference Center** ($$–$$$$) is slopeside to Jordan Bowl, but miles by car or shuttle to the rest of the resort. Enjoy whirlpool spa, indoor/outdoor pool, full-service health club, restaurants, child care. Be forewarned: The walls are not well soundproofed.

The **Grand Summit Resort Hotel and Conference Center** ($$–$$$$) is trailside with a 25-meter heated outdoor pool, athletic club and one of the resort's better restaurants. The **Snow Cap Inn** is a short walk from the slopes and the **Snow Cap Ski Dorm** next door offers affordable digs. All but the dorm offer packages with lift tickets.

Sunday River has nine condominium complexes throughout the resort; all are convenient to the slopes and have trolley service. **Locke Mountain Townhouses** are the most upscale, but hard to get, with the ideally located **Merrill Brook** condominiums not far behind.

In Bethel, the **Bethel Inn and Country Club** (824-2175; $–$$$) has old-style atmosphere. Renovated rooms are first rate; others barely make the grade. The rates include breakfast and dinner. The inn also has a cross-country center and health club (see *Cross-country)* and a shuttle to the ski area.

L'Auberge (824—2774 or 800-760—2774; $$), located in a renovated barn just off the Bethel Common, has a French country-style flavor, boasts an excellent restaurant and welcomes kids. The **Four Seasons** is in an old elegant building with excellent French cuisine (824-2755 or 800-227-7458; $$–$$$). The **Sudbury Inn** (824-2174; $$–$$$), which has vastly improved under new ownership, has one of the best restaurants in town as well as Sud's Pub, a popular watering hole. The **Holidae House** (824-3400; $–$$) is filled with Victorian-era antiques and elaborate decorating touches. The newly renovated **Gideon Hastings House** (824-3496; $$) has two suites with whirlpool tubs and a casual restaurant downstairs.

The **Victoria Inn** (824-8060 or 888-774-1235; $$-$$$$) is an ornate country inn/B&B in a magnificent Queen Anne-style house. The bedroom-with-loft suites in the attached carriage house are ideal for families. The restaurant is also open for dinner.

The **Briar Lea** (877-311-1299 or 824-4714; $$) has six rooms with private baths, two of which can be connected as suites for families. The inn also has a good restaurant, with a children's menu, and inn guests can order whatever they want from the menu for breakfast.

Less than a mile from the area, the **Sunday River Inn** (824-2410; $–$$$) is a traditional lodge with large living room with fireplace. Family-style breakfast and dinner are included. There is cross-country skiing (see *Cross-country*), ice skating, snowshoeing, ski-jouring (harnessed dogs pull a person on skinny skis), plus a wood-fired hot tub and sauna. Choose from dorm rooms, rooms with shared or private baths. Shuttles take guests to ski.

Information about **other lodging** is available through Sunday River's central reservation line (800-543-2754) or the Bethel Area Chamber of Commerce (824-3585).

Dining

Although Sunday River is striving to improve its dining, the food is still usually described as expensive and awful. One budding dining adventure is an evening **dinner snowcat ride** to the North Peak Lodge for dinner, followed by fireworks. It is offered most weekends and holidays.

Legends (824-3500, ext. 5858; $$$), in the Summit Hotel, is the closest you'll come to fine dining. **Walsh and Hill Trading Company** (824-5067; $$–$$$), in the Fall Line Condominiums, serves steaks and seafood. **Rossetto's Italian Restaurant** (824-6224; $$–$$$), in the White Cap Lodge, is open for dinner daily as well as for lunch on weekends and holidays.

Foggy Goggle ($–$$), in the South Ridge base, is packed for lunch, with good reason. The **Peak Lodge and Skiing Center** ($–$$) at the summit of North Peak, is a popular lunch spot with a giant deck. **BUMPS!** ($-$$) in the White Cap Lodge serves a pub menu which should be avoided unless you're starving.

The **Matterhorn** (824-6836) and the **Great Grizzly American Steakhouse** share a large barn on Sunday River's access road. The former serves brick-oven-baked pizza and fresh pasta and the latter serves steak (of course) and nightly specials. Get there before 6 p.m. and your dessert is free. At the base of the access road is the **Moose's Tale** (824-3541; $–$$), located in the **Sunday River Brewing Company**. According to locals, it now serves food worthy of its excellent on-premise-brewed ales.

In Bethel, the **Sudbury Inn** (824-6558; $$–$$$) and the **Bethel Inn** (824-2175; $$–$$$) serve excellent food in refined dining rooms. For authentic French cuisine, head to **L'Auberge** (824—2774 or 800-760—2774; $$–$$$). The **Victoria Inn** (824-8060; $$–$$$) offers fine dining in an elegant setting. (It's suffered recently from rapidly changing management; ask locals before making reservations.)

The menu at the **Gideon Hastings House** (824-3496; $$) ranges from gourmet pizzas to filet mignon. **Sud's Pub** ($–$$) is popular for après-ski and pub food. The **Briar Lea** (877-311-1299 or 824-4714; $–$$) is a good choice for a nice meal in an unfussy setting. It also has a children's menu. Back in business again, but under new ownership, is **Mother's** (824-2589; $–$$), which serves a wide-ranging menu of soups, salads, sandwiches and other specialties.

Après-ski/nightlife

If you strike it rich, you may find midweek action at Sunday River and in Bethel, but the real fun heats up on weekends.

Immediate après-ski is at the base of the slopes. **Foggy Goggle,** in the South Ridge base area, is the liveliest of the mountain spots. Try the **Barker Brew Haus** in the Barker Mountain base area or **BUMPS!** at the White Cap Base Lodge. Off mountain, head to the **Sunday**

Dining: $$$–Entrees $20+; $$–$10-20; $–less than $10.
Accommodations: (double room) $$$$–$200+; $$$–$141-$200; $$–$81-$140; $–$80 and less.

River Brewery or Sud's Pub, in town. On the access road, the Matterhorn is an all-ages bar with 48-ounce Glacier Big Bowl drinks and extensive beer choices, including Guinness.

At night, BUMPS! has bands on weekends and comedy on Tuesdays. The crowd leans toward young. The Sunday River Brewery has live music and excellent homemade brew. Downtown, the Backstage usually has karaoke during the week, with Country & Western and rock'n'roll bands on weekends. It also has the only pool tables in town. Sud's Pub has bands ranging from blues to bluegrass. For local flavor, come on a Thursday for Hoot Nite, an open-mike forum that has been running for 16 years. A more sedate crowd fills Legends at the Summit Hotel for its acoustic music. It has family entertainment every Saturday.

Other activities

Swimming pools and saunas are in virtually every resort condominium complex. Guests staying at the few condos that don't have them get privileges at nearby complexes. The ski dorm has video games and pool tables.

You can take BMW test drives from the Grand Summit and Jordan Grand hotels and even sign out a vehicle to go into Bethel for dinner.

The White Cap Base Lodge houses the Nite White Cap Fun Center for families. Activities here include an arcade, a lighted tubing park and skating rink. Guided snowshoe tours are also available. Tube, skate and snowshoe rentals are available. Fireworks take place here every Thursday and Saturday evening.

Bethel Station, about four miles from Sunday River, has a four-screen movie theater.

Arrange snowmobile rentals and tours through Sun Valley Sports (824-7533) or Bethel Outdoor Adventures (824-4224), which also offers snowshoeing tours. Indoor laser tag, miniature golf and rock climbing are available at B.I.G. Adventure Center (824-0929). For one-day or multiday, fully-outfitted dog-sledding trips, call Mahoosuc Guide Service (824-2073), located in Grafton Notch.

Bethel has unusual shops. Bonnema Potters sells pottery depicting the Maine landscape. Mt. Mann is a native gemstone shop. Samuel Timberlake makes fine reproduction Shaker-style furniture.

Getting there and getting around

By air: Portland International Jetport is 75 miles from Sunday River. Private pilots can land in Bethel. Bethel Express Corporation will pick up from either airport by reservation (824-4646).

By car: Sunday River is in western Maine an hour and a half from Portland and three-and-a-half hours (with no traffic) from Boston. From I-95, take Exit 11 in Maine to Rte. 26 north, continue to Bethel, then take Rte. 2 six miles north to Sunday River.

RV parking, no hookups, is allowed in designated parking areas at the resort. An RV park is also at White Birch Camping, in Shelburne on Rte. 2.

Getting around: The Mountain Explorer public transit system provides free transportation between the resort and the village of Bethel. It operates weekends from Thanksgiving to Christmas, then daily through March, from 7 a.m.-midnight. Pick up a schedule at the resort or local lodgings.

During the regular season, on-mountain, trolley-car transportation between the base areas is quite good. The shuttle loop expands to include the condos at night. In shoulder season, the mountain shuttles are by request only.

Mt. Washington Valley

New Hampshire

Attitash, Cranmore and Wildcat and five touring centers
Also: Black, King Pine and Shawnee Peak

Mt. Washington Valley Facts

Address: Chamber of Commerce
P.O. Box 2300, N. Conway, NH 03860
ⓘ **Toll-free information:**
(800) 367-3364
Dining: ★★★★★
Apres-ski/nightlife: ★★★★
Other activities: ★★★★★

✆ **Area code:** 603
Phone: 356-5701
Fax: 356-7069
E-mail: info@mtwashingtonvalley.org
World Wide Web:
www.mtwashingtonvalley.org
Bed base: 7,500+

If anyone wants skiing and a whole lot more, Mt. Washington Valley is the place. Here, the craggy White Mountains form a valley dominated by the imposing Mt. Washington, the East's highest peak at 6,288 feet and world renowned for its wicked weather. Seven downhill ski areas are within easy driving distance, offering a variety of terrain and skiing experiences. Add the Jackson Ski Touring Foundation (one of the world's best cross-country trail systems), the Great Glen Trails Outdoor Center, Bear Notch Ski Touring, Mt. Washington Valley Ski Touring and Snowshoe Center and a myriad indoor and outdoor activities, and you've got a vacation that shouldn't be missed.

This was a destination resort long before anyone came here to ski. A quarter century before the Civil War, fashionable Northeasterners started coming here for the summer to beat the heat, to meet Hawthorne and Emerson, watch Bierstadt paint his mountain landscapes and find suitable husbands for their daughters. Today, the few remaining grand old hotels have been brought up to date to add their charm to the mix of condos, motels, country inns and B&Bs. The Valley, as locals call it, is still busier in the summer months than in the winter.

Legends of the early days of skiing, the late '30s, surround you. Ride up the Wildcat summit quad and look back at the fantastic bulk of Mt. Washington with its huge, scooped-out ravines. This is hallowed ground, where Toni Matt on his wooden boards schussed over the Tuckerman headwall in one long arc to win the 1939 Inferno race, summit to base in six and a half minutes; a record that still stands.

Most of all, what made this area one of the pioneers of downhill skiing in America is the Eastern Slope Ski School, founded by Carroll Reed. This is where the Arlberg method of ski instruction was introduced to North America by Benno Rybizka and his Austrian teacher, the great Hannes Schneider, who was released by the Nazis in return for banking concessions.

Restaurants, many of them tucked into the tiny country inns or restored barns in the Valley, are world class and have acknowledged gourmet reputations. Besides the skiing, picturesque inns and tempting restaurants, there are scores of tax-free factory outlet stores in Conway and North Conway, making the region a top shopping destination.

No single ski resort in the Valley is a worthy winter destination by itself, but as a group of resorts, combined with the Valley towns and the surrounding cross-country trails, Mt. Washington Valley becomes a formidable vacation force. Other winter resorts across the United States and Canada would struggle to offer as complete and varied an experience. This is a wonderful place to come and ski, snowboard or cross-country. We've always complained that one thing that would make it a bit more enticing would be some cooperation between the ski areas, hoteliers and merchants to make this valley a true regional resort, and we're thrilled to hear that work has begun on an interchangeable ticket.

Attitash Bear Peak

 ## Mountain layout–Skiing

Just west of Glen on Rte. 302 in Bartlett, Attitash Bear Peak is an all-around, two-mountain resort with a few expert touches. The Attitash side still features a warren of narrow New England trails filled with history, and the newer Bear Peak trails provides cruising terrain plus some glades.

Ptarmigan, on Attitash, is supposed to be one of the steepest trails in New England, but it is manageable for good intermediates because of the elbow room on the run. The rest of the mountain is enough to keep 80 percent of skiers perfectly satisfied, with Northwest Passage to Cathedral and Saco to Ammonoosuc providing inspired cruising, while Idiot's Option and Grandstand are favorites for those seeking a knee workout. The problem with the Attitash side of the mountain is the lack of a high-speed, base-to-summit lift.

Not so on the Bear Peak side, where there's a high-speed quad backed by several other chairlifts. Bear Peak features Illusion, Avenger, Kachina and Myth Maker: a foursome of cruising delight (the diamonds shouldn't scare any strong intermediate away, unless the trails haven't been groomed). Seeking more challenge? Jump into the peak's ever-expanding glades.

The Attitash base is the primary one. Here you'll find the massive Adventure Center that houses all of the Learn to Ski and Ride programs and children's programs. Lessons, rentals and child-care are all under one roof, and just outside, beginners have a new "Snowbelt" lift. First-timers graduate from that to the adjacent, protected learning slope served by a triple chair. From there, they move on to beginner trails around the neighboring Double-Double lifts. Attitash has created a family fun zone in this area.

If you're parked at Bear Peak or staying in the Grand Summit at its base, the quickest way back to Attitash is to take the base-to-base shuttle.

 ## Mountain layout–Snowboarding

Attitash has a terrain park on Thad's Choice and this season will build a Superpipe on Lower Ptarmigan. The easiest access to the terrain park is via the double 4 and 5 lifts or from the summit; avoid trying to get there from the quad, it's way too much work. The park has a good variety of well-built jumps that are both good on approach and landing. Attitash employs a full-time park and halfpipe groomer as well as park rangers who patrol these areas.

Bear Peak is best for free riding, carving and glades. Illusion has great rollers and whoop-de-doos, while Avenger is great for speed runs. If you're looking for challenge, head into the glades. The transitions between Attitash and Bear Peak are the only flat areas. When riding from Attitash to Bear Peak, avoid Bearback and ride the quad instead. When riding from Bear Peak to Attitash, avoid Bear Right to Stonybrook. Instead, when you see the bridge, take Bear Notch Pass to Stonybrook Bypass. Here, it's worth it to unstrap and walk the 50 feet to the top of the bypass. From there on, it's all downhill.

Lessons (2002/03 prices)

Group lessons: $30 per 90-minute session for levels 2-8.
Never-ever packages: The Guaranteed Learn to Ski and Learn to Ride package includes rentals, lifts and lessons for $155.
Private lessons: $65 per hour for one student. Early bird/last run (before 9 a.m. or after 2 p.m.) is $50.

Child care (2002/03 prices)

Ages: 6 months to 6 years.
Cost: $45 per day, including lunch; $8 per hour. Tiny Turns, an intro to skiing program designed for kids ages 3-5, costs $60 an hour, $40 for children enrolled in child care.
Reservations: Recommended, call 374-2368.
Children's lessons: $75 full day, $55 half day; includes lessons, lift ticket and rentals.

Lift tickets (2002/03 prices)

	Adult	Young adult (13-18)	Child (6-12)
One day	$49*	$44	$32
Three days	$129	$99	$69
Five days	$209	$139	$109

*Note: Adult one-day tickets cost $53 during these holiday periods: Dec. 26-Jan. 1, Jan. 18-20 and Feb. 15-21.

Who skis at a discount: Students with college ID ski for same price as Young Adults. Seniors ages 65-69 ski for $32 any day; 70 and older pay $15 any day. Multi-day E tickets and midweek tickets purchased online at www.attitash.com at least 14 days in advance offer an additional 10 percent off the already discounted multi-day price.

Cranmore Mountain Resort

Mountain layout–Skiing

Cranmore is one of the oldest ski resorts in the nation. Its good balanced terrain, modest size (yet with an extensive trail system) and convenient location practically in the center of North Conway also makes it an ideal mountain for young and growing families, and its sunbathed, lower elevation means its the warmest of all the valley areas. Cranmore skis larger than it is, and has both nice open slopes (don't miss the back or East side of the mountain) as well as classic, skinny New England trails.

As part of the family of Booth Creek Resorts (Loon Mountain, an hour away, and Waterville Valley, an hour-and-a-half, are sister resorts), Cranmore now calls itself a "snowplay" resort rather than just a ski resort. In addition to the standard skiing and snowboarding, Cranmore offers tubing and snowtoys such as snowbikes, snowscoots and ski foxes that give its clientele an alternate way to get down the mountain. Cranmore has lift-serviced tubing on eight groomed lanes Fridays, Saturdays and during holiday weeks.

Attitash Bear Peak Facts

Summit elevation:	**2,300 feet**
Vertical drop:	**1,750 feet**
Base elevation:	**550 feet**

Expert:★★
Advanced:★★★
Intermediate:★★★★
Beginner:★★★★
Never-ever:★★★★★
Address: P.O. Box 308, Barlett, NH 03812
Ski area phone: 374-2368
Snow report: 374-0946
ⓘ **Toll-free reservations:** (800) 223-7669
E-mail: info@attitash.com
Internet: www.attitash.com
Number and types of lifts: 12–2 high-speed quads,1 quad, 3 triples, 3 doubles, 3 surface lifts
Skiable acreage: 280 acres
Snowmaking: 98 percent
Uphill capacity: 14,385 per hour
Snowboarding: Yes
Bed base: 1,600 **Nearest lodging:** slopeside
Resort child care: Yes, 6 months and older
Adult ticket, per day: $49–$53 (02-03)

Wildcat Facts

Summit elevation:	**4,062 feet**
Vertical drop:	**2,112 feet**
Base elevation:	**1,950 feet**

Expert:★★★ Advanced:★★★
Intermediate:★★★★
Beginner:★★★
Never-ever:★★★
Address: Rt. 16, Pinkham Notch, Jackson, NH 03846
Ski area phone: 466-3326
Snow report: 1-888-SKI WILD
ⓘ **Toll-free reservations:** 1-800-255-6439
E-mail: through Web site
Internet:www.skiwildcat.com
Number and types of lifts: 4–1 high-speed quad, 3 triples
Skiable acreage: 225 acres
Snowmaking: 90 percent
Uphill capacity: 7,200 per hour
Snowboarding: Yes
Bed Base: None at the area
Nearest lodging: AMC, about a quarter-mile
Resort child care: Yes, 6 months and older
Adult ticket, per day: $42-$52 (02/03)

Mountain layout–Snowboarding

The Mt. Dew Code Red right Nites Fun Zone, located on the South Slope, has been designed with the entry level or intermediate skier or rider in mind. It's filled with gentle rolls, banked corners and manageable terrain features. There's also a halfpipe directly in front of the base lodge.

Lessons

Group lessons: Quick Tip lesson is $25. A package including lift ticket plus rental equipment or Quick Tip lesson is $52, with both, it's $62.
Never-ever packages: Adult two-hour Getting Started lesson, $35; with lift ticket and rental equipment, it's $62.
Private lessons: $55 per hour for one student.

Child care (2001/02 prices)

Ages: 6 months to 5 years.
Cost: $50 for a full day or $8 per hour. The second child in the same family pays half price.
Reservations: Recommended, call 800-SUN-N-SKI (800-786-6754), ext. 8541 or 8542.

Telephone area code: 603 (unless in Maine where 207 is noted)

Cranmore Facts

Summit elevation: 1,700 feet
Vertical drop: 1,200 feet
Base elevation: 500 feet
Expert:★ **Advanced:**★★
Intermediate:★★★★
Beginner:★★★★
Never-ever:★★★
Address: Skimobile Road,
N. Conway, NH 03860
✆ **Ski area phone:** 356-5544
Snow report: 356-7070

Toll-free reservations: 800-SUN N SKI (786-6754)
Internet: www.cranmore.com
Number and types of lifts: 7–1 high-speed quad, 1 triple, 3 doubles, 2 surface lifts
Skiable acreage: 185 acres
Snowmaking: 100 percent
Uphill capacity: 7,500 skiers per hour
Snowboarding: Yes
Bed base: 250
Nearest lodging: slopeside
Resort child care: Yes, 6 months and older
Adult ticket, per day: $32 (01/02)

Children's lessons: $55 half day, $60 full day. A child's all-day lift ticket with rental equipment and full-day lesson is $78, with half-day lesson it's $68.

Lift tickets (2002/03 prices)

Adults tickets cost $32 and ticket for children ages 6–12 cost $18, any day. Children ages 5 and younger ski free.

Wildcat Mountain

Wildcat Mountain has no condominiums or trophy ski houses lining its trails, no fancy base village with shops and restaurants, therefore giving a taste of what skiing used to be like. What you'll find is back-to-basics skiing with old-style trails that ebb and flow with the mountain's contours. It's a true skiers' mountain. When you sink your teeth into Wildcat, it often bites back.

Wildcat sits across a narrow ribbon of highway from Mt. Washington, home to some of the highest recorded winds in the world. While Mt. Washington's summit, at 6,288 feet, is higher than Wildcat's, at 4,062, the stunted evergreens coated with rime ice on both give testament to the harshness of the environment. Wildcat can be brutally cold, but the location and elevation does have a silver lining: The scenery is magnificent and snow is plentiful — an average year yields at least 15 feet — and it comes early and stays late, often well into May.

Wildcat has made major progress in the past few years. Investments in snowmaking and grooming equipment have helped tame the conditions. Trees have been thinned to create glades. Trails have been widened, making them easier for lower-level skiers to navigate. Even the once wild and woolly Wildcat Trail is less menacing. It's been widened, but it's seldom groomed, so it still growls. The base lodge has been rebuilt. Best of all, a high-speed quad now zips skiers and riders from base to summit in a little over six minutes.

Mountain layout–Skiing

Wildcat deserves its reputation as an experts' mountain, but it's much more than that. The Snowcat area, with its own triple chair and trails, is an ideal place for first-timers and shaky beginners, and the 2.75-mile cruise down

Polecat from the summit gives advanced beginners an authentic alpine experience.

Intermediates have plenty to play on here, too. The Tomcat triple reaches about two-thirds of the way up the mountain and are a good retreat when the wind blows hard and cold, perhaps shutting the summit quad. The Bobcat triple reaches a little below midmountain and provides access to the narrow trails at Wildcat's core, two glades and the Bobcat slope and the Cheetah slope, which is often used for races.

From the summit, experienced back-country enthusiasts can take the plunge to the village of Jackson. The Wildcat Valley Trail, cut in 1972, descends 3,245 vertical feet over 17.8 km. Be sure to check conditions first with the Jackson Ski Touring Foundation (383-9355), and never ski this trail alone: it is not patrolled and has natural hazards (the first corner alone is enough to make you religious).

Confirming that religious experience is Lynx: It might just convince you that Wildcat is God's chosen mountain. For decades, Lynx has been the 'Cat's most popular trail. It's easy to see why. Lynx plays with you, dropping quickly at the summit, then rolling around a few bends before dropping and rolling again. A different view, changed terrain or a trail split hover around every bend. When taken from summit to base, there are few trails in New England that can compare for range of terrain and the sheer joy of skiing.

Mountain layout–Snowboarding

Wildcat has doubled the size of its terrain park, located on the Bobcat trail. You'll find eight or nine snow features here as well as a halfpipe. The best trail is the Lynx due to its contours and fall-line riding. Keep your speed up at the bottom of Wild Kitten to get back to the lift without hoofing it.

Lessons (2002/03 prices)

Group lessons: $30 per session.
Never-ever packages: $59, including rentals, lifts and lessons. The First Tracks Pass Program, for ages six and older, comprises four consecutive lessons, with lessons and rentals, for $199. Complete all four, and you get a free season pass as well as a discount book.
Private lessons: $54 per hour for one student.

Child care (2002/03 prices)

Ages: 2 months to 6 years.
Cost: $54 for a full day (with lunch), $27 for a half day (without lunch).
Reservations: Recommended, required for children younger than 18 months; call (800) 255-6439.
Children's lessons: $84 full day, includes lunch, $74 half day; includes lessons, lift ticket and rentals.

Lift tickets (2002/03 prices)

	Adult	Teen (13-17)	Junior (6-12)
One day (weekend/midweek)	$52/$42	$42/$36	$25
Two-day (weekend)	$72	$72	$50
Two-day (midweek)	$52	$52	$50

Who skis free: Children age 5 and younger with a ticket-holding parent. Anyone on his or her birthday, with valid ID.

Who skis at a discount: Seniors (65 and older) and college students ski for Teen prices. Everyone on Sunday afternoons: noon to close is $15. Two ski for $52 on nonholiday Wednesdays. Pass-holders from other alpine resorts get 50 percent off Sunday-Friday.

Mt. Washington

A trip to Tuckerman Ravine on the east side of Mt. Washington is a rite of spring for New England's skier and riders. Called the birthplace of extreme skiing, skiers have hiked into this snow-filled glacial cirque since 1914, and in the 1930s, races were even held here. The first giant slalom in the U.S. was held in Tuckerman's, as well as a truly sick event called the American Inferno, which started at the very summit of Mt. Washington and ended 4,200 feet lower at Pinkham Notch. The only trick is that you get to Tuckerman's the old-fashioned way: You climb it. From the Pinkham Notch Visitor's Center, a wide trail climbs 2 miles to a hut called HoJo's. Although visitors are no longer allowed to sleep (or even warm up) in the hut, it has camping and outhouse facilities. From here, the floor of the Ravine is reached via a steep hike.

Although skiing Tuck's is only for experts as it ranges anywhere from 40-55 degrees in pitch, less experienced folks still make the trek either to watch or ski the shallower terrain close to the ravine floor. Most people head straight for Lunch Rocks, an outcropping on the right as you hike in. From here, you can kick steps into the snow and hike up any of the gullies or the famous headwall. The aerobically ambitious can hike all the way to Mt. Washington's summit and ski the more gentle snow fields above the Ravine. But remember, the only way back down is via the Ravine's precipitously steep terrain. At day's end, you either ski down the Sherburne Trail or, if snow is thin, hike down the way you came. For weather and trail information, call 466-2721.

Cross-country and snowshoeing

Jackson Ski Touring Foundation (383-9355 or 800-927-6697; Box 216, Jackson, N.H. 03846), on Rte. 16A, is a mecca for Nordic skiers with more than 150 km. of trails (87 km. are groomed), suitable for all ability levels. Country inns are spaced throughout the region. The base lodge is around the corner in Jackson Village, directly across from the Red Fox Pub.

Mt. Washington Valley Ski Touring and Snowshoe Center (356-3042; Box 130, Intervale, N.H. 03845) has more than 65 km. of inn-to-inn trails, plus ski school and rentals. It also offers guided start-gazing tours and animal-tracking clinics.

The Appalachian Mountain Club (466-2721) maintains a network of touring trails radiating from the AMC Camp at Pinkham Notch. About 7 km. are rated Easiest or More Difficult (requiring skills up to a strong snowplow and step-turn), but about 40 km. are rated Most Difficult, with long challenging hills and narrow trails.

Great Glen Trails (466-2333) has 40 km. of cross-country skiing and snowshoeing trails at the base of Mt. Washington, which translates into jaw-dropping scenery all around you. Telemarkers, cross-country skiers and snowshoers can take a snowcat partly up the Mt. Washington Auto Road, then ski down; sightseers also are welcome. The resort recently added a snowtubing park.

Bear Notch Ski Touring Center (374-2277) is one of the valley's best kept secrets. With a truly beautiful setting just north of Bartlett Village (Rte. 302), the 60 km. of Bear Notch trails offer uncrowded wooded scenery.

The **Nestlenook Recreation Center** (383-9443), also in Jackson, has 35 km. of touring tracks that wind through its 65-acre farm. **Purity Spring Resort** (800-373-3754 or 367-8896), near Madison, has 15 km. of groomed and tracked trails. Rentals and lessons are available.

Accommodations

Accommodations in the Mt. Washington Valley are among the most extensive in skidom if you like romantic, tiny country inns and bed-and-breakfast establishments. You won't find high-rises, but great old historic inns accommodate those who prefer the atmosphere of a large resort hotel. The Valley also has plenty of moderately priced motels suitable for families

For condominiums, chalets and motel suites, call **Top Notch Vacation Rentals** (383-4133, 800-762-6636; $-$$$$), which works with properties all up and down the valley. **Luxury Mountain Getaways** (603-383-9101, 800-472-5207; $$ - $$$$) has everything from 1-bedroom condos to luxury villas. **Attitash Mountain Village** (603-374-6500; 800-862-2600;$-$$$$), across the road from the area, has inexpensive motel packages to upscale 3-bedroom condos.

For lodging information (but no reservations), call the **Mt. Washington Valley Chamber of Commerce** at (800) 367-3364 or visit its Web site. Lodgings are listed by region:

Bartlett (Attitash/Bear Peak Resort)

Right at the base of Bear Peak, the ski-in/ski-out **Grand Summit Resort Hotel** (364-1900 or 800-223-7669;$$-$$$$) provides all amenities for skiers from saunas and hot tubs to fitness rooms and restaurants. **The Bartlett Inn** (374-2353, 800-292-2353;$-$$) is informal and comfortable with family cabin units and cross-country trails out the back door.

Gorham (Wildcat)

If you are skiing at Wildcat, this town, just to the north of the valley, is where to stay. The **Royalty Inn** (466-3312 or 800-437-3529; $-$$) has 90 rooms of varying sizes that are all very spacious and well kept. Kitchenettes are available, but have a stovetop without an oven. The family-owned **Town & Country Motor Inn** (466-3315 or 800-325-4386; $) is a bit older and simpler, with 70s decor and smaller rooms. Families will want to stay in the same building that houses the pool, video games, sauna and Jacuzzi. Children age 15 and younger stay free. The inn also has dorm-style accommodations starting at $15 per person.

Pinkham Notch (Wildcat)

To be really close to Mt. Washington, and to get a head start if you're climbing, skiing, or using its cross-country trails, there's the **Joe Dodge Lodge** (466-2727; $) at Pinkham Notch, run by the Appalachian Mountain Club, with room for 104. The two-, four- and five-bunk rooms are simple, and rates include either one or two meals. Three public rooms have fireplaces; one has a well-used piano, another is stocked with games and activities for children and the third has a library.

Jackson Village

This town is the home to a collection of old-time mansions, hotels, farms and houses that have grown into upscale B&Bs. Most ooze country touches, are filled with antiques and charm and offer dining on premises.

The Inn at Thorn Hill (800-289-8990 or 383-4242; $$$–$$$$), with views of Mt. Washington, is elegant without being stuffy. Rates include breakfast and a three-course dinner.

Eagle Mountain Resort (383-9111; for reservations, 800-966-5779; $–$$$) is one of those lovingly restored classic 19th-century resort hotels. Children age 15 and younger stay free if sleeping in existing beds.

The Wentworth Resort Hotel (383-9700 or 800-637-0013; $$$–$$$$) is one of the best values in the area and also has some of the nicest rooms as well as a top-notch dining room. Renovated rooms are spacious, have big hot tubs and some have gas fireplaces. Rates include two meals. The Jackson Ski Touring base is right next door.

The Christmas Farm Inn (383-4313 or 800-443-5837; $$–$$$) is a cluster of buildings around a larger house, each as quaint as the next. All rates include breakfast and dinner. A 15-percent service charge and taxes will be added to your bill.

The Inn at Jackson (383-4321 or 800-289-8600; $–$$), is right through the covered bridge. The country breakfast will get you up in the morning and keep you going all day.

Whitneys' Inn (383-8916 or 800-677-5737; $$–$$$), is a restored, 1840s farmhouse at the base of Black Mountain, allowing Alpine and cross-country skiing from the door.

The Crowes' Nest (603-383-8913; 800-511-8383, $–$$) is a more recent addition to the Jackson B&B scene, a stone's throw from the Jackson Ski Touring Foundation's trails.

Intervale

The 1785 Inn (800-421-1785 or 356-9025; $–$$$) is a country inn with what has been called the best view of the valley. It also boasts an excellent dining room that is open to the public for dinner, and one of the most extensive wine lists in New England.

The Langley House (356-9060; $–$$) has five recently redecorated rooms as well as a restaurant and bar. It's on Rte. 16A in Intervale. You can cross-country ski or snowshoe right out the back door of The Forest Inn (356-9772; 800-448-3534; $$), a cozy B&B also located on 16A, and The New England Inn (603-356-5541; 800-826-3466; $$–$$$$), also in the same vicinity, has everything from inn rooms to romantic cabins and a deluxe lodge, plus a lively pub and a dining room.

North Conway

With a few exceptions, North Conway's lodging is more motels and hotels with national chains being recently added to the lodging mix.

Stonehurst Manor (356-3113 or 800-525-9100; $–$$) was created from a turn-of-the-century mansion that belonged to the Bigelow family of carpet fame. It is still manorial. The setting, rooms and restaurant are absolutely elegant. Breakfast and dinner meal plans are optional. The Buttonwood Inn, North Conway (356-2625 or 800-258-2625; $$–$$$), is tucked in the woods with cross-country skiing from the back door; ask about the family suites. Rates include a full breakfast and afternoon snacks. The Eastman Inn (356-6707 or 800-626-5855; $–$$) is a B&B with 14 rooms in one of the oldest houses in town, newly restored with antique charm. Breakfast with waffle irons almost at your table is superb.

North Conway Grand Hotel (800-648-4397; in New Hampshire 356-9300; $$–$$$$) at Settlers' Green in North Conway, handy to all the best outlet stores, children younger than 17 stay free. White Mountain Hotel and Resort (356-7100 or 800-533-6301; $–$$), is at the foot of Whitehorse Ledge, the enormous, sculptured, granite cliff you see from all North Conway. The views back across the Valley toward Cranmore are unmatched. Don't miss the lavish Friday seafood buffet. The Eastern Slope Inn Resort (356-6321 or 800-862-1600; $$), in the heart of North Conway, is a classic New England inn. The Green Granite Inn (356-6901 or 800-468-3666; $–$$) is on Rte. 16 on the mile-and-a-half shopping strip. It has

Dining: $$$–Entrees $20+; $$–$10-20; $–less than $10.
Accommodations: (double room) $$$$–$200+; $$$–$141-$200; $$–$81-$140; $–$80 and less.

an indoor pool and a hot tub, and evening movies and children's programs are offered during weekends and vacation periods. **Mt. Washington Valley Motor Lodge** (356-5486 or 800-634-2382; $$) is a pleasant surprise for families with clean basic rooms and a swimming pool. **The Holiday Inn Express Hotel & Suites** (356-2551, 800-465-4329; $$-$$$) is on the strip but in a quiet spot behind one of the town's oldest cemeteries. Kids younger than 18 stay free. **Red Jacket Mountain View** (356-5411 or 800-752-2538; $$-$$$$), is a rambling building and some loft rooms and townhouses, both good for families. It has panoramic views and an indoor pool and hot tub. **The Briarcliff** (356-5584, 800-338-4291; $-$$), updated from a classic 1950s motel is affordable and convenient.

For rock-bottom prices, head to **Hostelling International-White Mountains** in Conway (447-1001;$) or the **Ski Dorm** (800-356-3596 or 356-2044;$) at the Cranmore Mountain Lodge with bunk and breakfast.

Dining

Mt. Washington Valley has a number of excellent restaurants. Those noted in the next three paragraphs serve meals worth a special trip. The **Rare Bear**, **Bistro** and **Black Bear Pub** are at The Bernerhof (383-4414; $$-$$$), in Bartlett on Rte. 302. **Stonehurst** (356-3113; $$) and **The 1785 Inn**, in North Conway (356-9025; $$-$$$), have excellent cuisine. In Jackson, **The Christmas Farm Inn** (383-4313; $$-$$$), **The Inn at Thorn Hill** (383-4242; $$$), **Wentworth Resort Hotel** (383-9700; $$-$$$), and **Wildcat Inn and Tavern** (383-4245; $$) are all fairly expensive and serve gourmet meals.

If you're willing to travel to the outskirts of the valley, you can get fine gourmet dining with great winter views at the **Notchland Inn** (374-6131; $$-$$$), in Hart's Location; the **Snowvillage Inn** (447-2818; $$$), in Snowville; and the **Oxford House Inn** (207-935-3442; $$-$$$), over the border in Fryeburg, Maine.

For more down-to-earth meals, try the **Red Parka Pub** (383-4344; $$) for great barbecued spare ribs and prime rib. It doesn't take reservations; expect up to an hour wait on Saturday nights. **Moat Mountain Smoke House & Brewing Co.** (356-6381, $$), at the northern edge of North Conway, lists wood-grilled or smoked entrées, such as salmon, brisket, port and ribs, as well as lighter fare such as pizza and quesadillas. **Monte Bello** (356-6668; $$-$$$) serves the best Italian meals in town. **Bellini's** (356-7000; $-$$) serves massive portions of southern Italian cooking while **Marcello's** (356-2313; $$) is more northern Italian.

Coyote Rose (356-7673; $$), in the center of North Conway, serves creative Southwestern fare and magnificent margaritas. The **Red Jacket Mountain View** (356-5411; $-$$), which looks like any other giant hotel from the outside, serves very good food. **Horsefeathers** (356-6862; $-$$), in North Conway, is perhaps the most popular spot in town. For a good time and plenty to eat, it's hard to beat, but it you're looking for gourmet, pass this one up, the menu promises more than it can deliver. **Delaney's Hole-in-the-Wall** (356-7776; $-$$), a big locals' haunt, inexplicably has a southwestern flair. Head to the **Shannon Door Pub** (383-4211; $) for Irish entertainment and good thin-crust pizzas. Pizza, from thin-crust to deep-dish, is found at **Elvio's** (356-3208; $).

For casual meals, **Brandli's Pizza Pasta Grill** (356-7878; $-$$), in Settlers Green, meets the test of good and cheap and lots to eat. For Mexican, locals head to **Margarita Grille** (383-6556; $-$$), formerly Margaritaville, just beyond the Red Parka, on Rte. 302, in Bartlett, or to **Cafe Noche** (447-5050; $), in a brightly colored building on Main Street, Conway.

The **Muddy Moose** (356-7696; $$) has affordable prices as well as some exotic choices, such as Wild Boar Marsala or Venison Pasta. On particularly crowded weekends in the Valley, head to **the Red Fox Pub & Restaurant** (383-6659; $$), in Jackson. With seating for 200, chances are you won't have to wait. Look for a great choice of microbrews. The Sunday Jazz Brunch here is a locals' favorite and a bargain at $5.95 per person.

For breakfast, head to **Gunther's** (356-5860; $), for giant waffles and pancakes (356-5200; $) or **Peaches** (356-5860; $), both on the main drag in North Conway. An all-day breakfast spot, **Guldie's** ($), is on the Rte. 16 strip. In Jackson, we recommend **Yesterday's** (383-4457; $) or the **Wentworth Resort Hotel** (383-9700), which serves an exceptionally good breakfast for $8.

If you're staying in Gorham, try **Welsh's** (466-2206; $), a family restaurant that serves hearty breakfasts and lunches. The oversized muffins and charbroiled burgers are delicious. **Libby's Bistro** (466-5330; $$), on Exchange Street, serves an ever-changing menu of creative entrees such as duck au poivre with a balsamic rhubarb sauce and strawberry rhubarb chutney. At the **Appalachian Mountain Club** (466-2727; $$), meals are served family-style: a great way to meet some new friends.

Après-Ski/nightlife

One of the best ski bars in the country is the **Red Parka Pub**, which offers lively après-ski and then nightlife activity into the wee hours. Something is happening every night, and its informal style runs to beer served in Mason jars to vintage skis and creative license plates covering the walls. On nights when there is no live music, live comedy or a movie is often featured.

The place to be in Jackson is the **Wildcat Tavern**, where folk rock is served on weekends. On Friday and Saturday nights, **Horsefeathers**, in North Conway, hops, and the **Up Country Saloon** has live dance music. Locals hang out in **Hooligans**, **Horsefeathers** and **Delaney's Hole-in-the-Wall**, all in North Conway.

Other activities

The **Cranmore Sports Center** (356-6301), at Cranmore base, is a huge all-season facility, with indoor tennis courts, pool, aerobics classes, steamroom and sauna. It is also home to a huge (30 by 40 feet) indoor climbing wall. Classes are available through **International Mountain Climbing School** (356-6316). The owner, Rick Wilcox, has climbed Mt. Everest. **Eastern Mountain Sports** (356-5433) is in the Eastern Slope Inn. Both offer a range of winter climbing and hiking programs, including ice-climbing instruction, ascents of Mt. Washington and traverses of the Presidential Range.

The **Appalachian Mountain Club** (466-2721) has an active schedule of courses and workshops on ski touring, snowshoeing, avalanches and more.

Take a **sleigh ride** in the Valley, try Nestlenook's horse-drawn sleigh (383-0845) or The Stables at the Farm off West Side Road (356-4855).

Cranmore, Black Mountain, King Pine and Shawnee Peak have very active **tubing** hills. In Conway, visit the Ham Arena (447-5886) for indoor **ice skating**. It has open skating, rentals and concessions. Two-hour skating lessons start at $4 for children and $5 for adults. Call ahead for public skating hours. You can also ice skate in Jackson, North Conway and at King Pine's covered ice arena (free with a lift ticket).

At the **Weather Discover center** (356-2137), you can experience what it felt like to be atop Mt. Washington when those famously high winds blew.

For bargain hunters, Mt. Washington Valley may have the best **shopping** of any ski resort in the nation, with more than 100 factory outlets and no sales tax. The area also has

Dining: $$$-Entrees $20+; $$-$10-20; $-less than $10.
Accommodations: (double room) $$$$-$200+; $$$-$141-$200; $$-$81-$140; $-$80 and less.

many unusual boutiques with creative gift items. Stop by the Chamber of Commerce in North Conway and pick up a Visitor Guide or map and guide to shopping.

Getting there and getting around

By air: The closest airport is Portland, Maine, with major airline service from all over the country. It is about a 90-minute drive from North Conway. Manchester Airport, in New Hampshire, is served by Southwest, US Air, MetroJet, United, Continental Express, ComAir and Business Express/Delta Connection, and is about a two-hour drive.

By car: The Mt. Washington Valley is 140 miles north of Boston. Take I-95 to Rte. 16, then north on 16/302. An alternate route is I-93 north to Rte. 104 to Rte. 25 to Rte. 16 and on to North Conway. From Portland, follow Rte. 302.

North Conway has been notorious for its weekend traffic jams going through town. The new North-South connector road is scheduled to be complete to North Conway Village by August 2002, offering a good alternate route for those coming from the north or the south. Even so, be patient if you're behind the wheel at 4 p.m., when the lifts close. Or, if you are driving from the Jackson/Wildcat/Attitash Bear Peak end of town to the south, take West Side Road to avoid most of the shopping traffic and the North Conway crowds.

Getting around: Bring a car or call F.A.S. T. Taxi (356-0000).

Other Mount Washington Valley Resorts

Black Mountain, Jackson, NH

800-698-4490 or 383-4490; Internet: www.blackmt.com

4 lifts—1 triple, 1 double, 2 surface lifts; 140 trail acres; 1,100 vertical feet

Black Mountain, a compact ski area at the top of Jackson Village on Rte. 16B, may be the best place in the valley for beginner lessons and family skiing. Wide open Whitneys' Hill was the site of the first ski lessons in the Valley, in 1936, and it's still an ideal place to take your first turns or have your children take theirs. The best beginner trails down the mountain are Sugarbush and Black Beauty, while Upper Galloping Goose and Mr. Rew offer some short expert fun. Upper intermediate or expert skiers can play in the glades. Located on the Jackson Ski Touring trail system, Black has more than its share of telemark skiers, both beginner and experts; its top-to-bottom Skinny Ski Inferno is a classic event. Finally, Black Mountain's southern exposure provides a warmer place to ski when it's just too cold at other valley areas.

Lift tickets: (01/02 prices) $32 adults weekends, $20 weekdays, $20 Juniors (18 and younger and 65+) weekends, $15 weekdays. Children 5 and younger ski free. The Passport, a day ticket valid for two adults and two juniors on a holiday, costs $89.

Lessons: Group lessons: $25 per 90-minute session. Never-ever packages: $45 midweek, $55 weekend and holiday, for ages 13 and older, for skiing; $50, $60 for snowboarding. Price includes rentals, lifts and lessons. Private lessons: $40 per hour for one student.

Lodging information: 800-698-4490.

Purity Spring Resort/King Pine Ski Area, East Madison, NH

(800) 373-3754 or 603-367-8896; Internet: www.kingpine.com

6 lifts — 2 triples, 1 double, 2 surface; 350 vertical feet; 35 skiable acres

This small area, part of family-run Purity Spring Resort, has a modest vertical drop, but for those just starting out and parents who want to keep an eye on young children, it is an ideal resort. On-mountain lodging, a health club with indoor pool and packages that include lodging, skiing, meals and full use of the resort's facilities make this a good value for young families. King Pine does have one short, steep trail, reportedly one of the steepest in the state, but top-level skiers are better off somewhere else. Night skiing is available Tuesdays, Fridays, Saturdays and holidays, and the resort also has 15 km. of groomed and tracked cross-country trails. Other activities include snow tubing, snowshoeing and ice skating.

Lift tickets (01/02 pricing): $29 for adults weekends, $22 weekdays. Kids (6–12) ski for $20 weekends, $14 midweek. Night skiing: $16 adults, $12 children. Kids 5 and younger ski free.
Lessons: Group lesson: $20. Private lesson: $40. Never-ever package: A ski lesson is $40 for adults, $33 for ages 6-12, $24 for age 5 and younger. Snowboard lessons are $44 for adults, $40 (ages 8-12). Package includes beginner lift ticket, rentals and lesson.
Distance from Boston: About 2.5 hours via I-95, Rte. 16, Rte. 25 and Rte. 153.
Lodging information: (800) 373-3754.

Shawnee Peak, Bridgton, ME

(207) 647-8444; Internet: www.shawneepeak.com

5 lifts; 35 trails; 225 acres; 1,300 vertical feet

About a 30-minute drive from North Conway, this family resort in Bridgton, Maine, offers fantastic views across Maine flatlands and lakes to the White Mountains. It has excellent snowmaking and a twice-a-day grooming program that allows for "first tracks" twice daily, if you're lucky. The mountain is primarily a day trip for Portland-area residents, but its terrain offers a bit of something for everyone, and it's very popular with families. The toughest runs at the top and left side of the mountain as you look at the trail map, and wide-open beginner slopes to the right (or west). Excellent, tight gladed areas are nestled between the two sides of the mountain. Most of the trails to the left are New England-narrow. Upper/ Lower Appalachian is a great steep cruiser with fantastic views that uses almost all the mountain's vertical. Shawnee features the most extensive night-skiing facilities in New England with a lighted vertical drop of 1,300 feet covered by 17 trails. New this season is a 68,000-square-foot learning area.

Lift tickets (01/02 prices): $41 weekends/holidays and $30 midweek for adults; $26 on weekends/holidays and $21 weekdays for ages 6–12 and 65 and older. Children age 5 and younger ski free when accompanied by a paying adult. Night skiing (daily, except Sunday, 4–10 p.m.) is $21 for adults and $19 for juniors/seniors. Other tickets available include Twilight (12:30-10 p.m.) and day/night (9:30 a.m.-10 p.m.) The $45 Saturday Night Special lets you ski all night Saturday and all day Sunday. The beginner lift is free anytime.
Distance from Boston: About 3 hours. Take 95 North to 295 to the Forest Ave./Route 302 West exit and follow Rte. 302 through Bridgton. The access road is approximately 6 miles beyond downtown.
Lodging information: For the limited number of condos on the mountain, call the ski area, (207) 647-8444. For lodging in North Conway, call the Mt. Washington Valley Chamber of Commerce, (800) 367-3364.

Bretton Woods

New Hampshire

Summit elevation:	3,100 feet
Vertical drop:	1,500 feet
Base elevation:	1,600 feet

Address: Route 302, Bretton Woods, NH 03575
☎ **Area code:** 603
Ski area phone: 278-3320
Snow report: 278-3333
ⓘ **Toll-free reservations:** (800) 258-0330
E-mail: skibw@brettonwoods.com
Internet: www.brettonwoods.com
Expert: ★
Advanced: ★
Intermediate: ★ ★ ★
Beginner: ★ ★ ★ ★
Never-ever: ★ ★ ★ ★ ★

Number and types of lifts: 8–3 high-speed quads, 1 quad, 1 triple, 1 double, 2 surface lifts
Acreage: 375 trail acres
Snowmaking: 95 percent
Uphill capacity: 8,000 per hour
Snowboarding: Yes
Bed base: 3,400+
Nearest lodging: slopeside
Resort child care: Yes, 2 months and older
Adult ticket, per day: $49-$57 (02/03 prices)
Dining: ★ ★ ★ ★
Apres-ski/nightlife: ★ ★
Other activities: ★ ★ ★

Bretton Woods is a well-known name in the history of the United States. The grand Mount Washington Hotel, a National Historic Landmark, first opened to summer guests in 1902. It was the setting for the 1944 International Monetary Conference, where the gold standard was set, and the American dollar was established as the backbone of the international exchange system. In 1999, the resort completely winterized the hotel to welcome cold-weather guests and initiated one of the largest expansions of any ski area in New Hampshire. Those who haven't visited Bretton Woods recently are in for a surprise. It now has the most skiable acres of any area in New Hampshire, although it retains the laid-back, family-friendly atmosphere.

The resort's expansion to West Mountain added some short-but-sweet steeps and fun glades, and last year it added 30 acres of steep, wooded terrain in Rosebrook Canyon, including 10 tree chutes. For this season, Bretton Woods has upgraded the West Mountain quad to a high-speed lift and replaced the Crawford double chair with a quad. The latter, which services beginner terrain, will be free for all ages. It also is constructing a new halfpipe and terrain park and has added a Pipe Dragon to its grooming fleet. A much-needed expansion of the base lodge will add some space this season, with construction ongoing through the winter.

Given its remote location and its high-speed quads, liftlines are rare. The location and elevation have another benefit: When it's raining or sleeting elsewhere, it's often snowing at Bretton Woods. Perhaps the area's biggest attribute, though, is the view. From the slopes, the Presidential Range of the White Mountains dominates the skyline, with the majestic Mount Washington Hotel lying below its namesake peak.

Mountain layout–Skiing

This is a mountain that was designed for beginners and intermediates but now has a growing assortment of glades and short steeps to provide a thrills. So many glades have been added that you could practically spend an entire day sliding a different glade on each run. The traditional Bretton Woods trails, such as Sawyer's Swoop, Big Ben and Range View, have been joined with an excellent series of expert glades in the newly developed West Mountain and Rosebrook Canyon. The trail names sound more sinister than they really are; however they do offer a quantum leap in difficulty over previous Bretton Woods trails. You don't have to be an advanced skier to sample the glades. Some are pretty open, so you can pop in and out of them off intermediate trails to experiment. With the new terrain, virtually everyone can enjoy skiing this area without feeling like they've done it all. Only extreme-skiing junkies will be out of place and probably won't be found here unless they are skiing the trees out of bounds.

Mountain layout–Snowboarding

Cruising riders will love this resort. It's also a great place to learn the sport. Bretton Woods is rebuilding its halfpipe and terrain park as last year, these were yawners. Fun terrain can be found in the trees, where there are plenty natural hits for jumping and spinning. When riding back from West to the main base area along Crawford Ridge, it's important to get your speed up and maintain it. Another place to maintain enough speed to get across the flats is near the bottom of Two Miles Home.

Mountain rating

This is a perfect place for beginners and a wonderful place for intermediates to cruise and feel great about their sport. Advanced skiers and riders will find some challenge in the glades. This is an ideal area for families or those traveling in groups of mixed abilities or varying age groups.

Cross-country and snowshoeing

The 100 km. of cross-country and snowshoeing trails, located on the grounds of the Mount Washington Hotel, offer 1,700 acres of spectacular scenery. The trail system is dotted with a series of restaurants and lounges. Intrepid cross-country skiers can glide from the top of the Bretton Woods ski area back to the hotel. This area averages 200 inches of snow every year.

Trail fees are $15 for adults (ages 13–64) and $9 for juniors (ages 6–12) and seniors (ages 65 and older). Children (5 and younger) ski free. Snowshoers can use the skate lanes of the cross-country trails with a trail pass. Complimentary guided hour-and-a-half ski tours through the Ammonoosuc Valley available. They leave from the Nordic Center daily.

There is a cross-country ski school and a telemark ski school as well. Atlas snowshoes are available for sale or rent. The variety and extent of trails rivals that of the nearby Jackson Ski Touring and Vermont's Stowe system.

Lessons (2002/03 prices)

Group lessons: $29 for 90 minutes.
Never-ever package: This includes equipment, all-day lessons and a limited lift ticket for $55 per day.
Private lessons are $65 per hour.
Special programs: Intermediate programs include equipment, lessons and lifts for $79.

Child care (2002/03 prices)

Ages: 2 months to 5 years.

Costs: The Babes in the Woods program with stories, crafts and games is $59 for a full day (8 a.m.–4:30 p.m.) with lunch and $45 for a half day, a.m. or p.m. Hourly prices are $12 with a two-hour minimum.

Snow Play and Ski Readiness all-day care with a gentle introduction to skiing, for children ages 5 and younger, is $87 for a full day (8 a.m.–4:30 p.m.) with lunch or $69 for the morning only.

Reservations: Required; call 278-3325.

Children's lessons: The Hobbit Ski and Snowboard School (ages 4–12) has ski and snowboard lessons including lunch and rentals for $87 full day, $69 half day. Snowboard programs are for ages 8–12. Reservations are required for snowboard programs: call 800-278-3345.

Lift tickets (2002/03 prices)

	Adult	Teen (13-18)	Junior (6-12)
One day (weekend)	$57	$46	$34
Three days (weekend)	$146	$118	$87
Five days (weekend)	$214	$173	$128

Who skis free: Younger than 6 ski free. Use of the Crawford Beginner quad chair is free.

Who skis at a discount: Seniors 65 and older ski for $15 midweek, non-holiday. On non-holiday Wednesdays, two ski or ride for $49. The $199 Bold and the Beautiful Midweek Season Pass is an interchangeable pass good at Bretton Woods or Cannon Mountain (on sale at the Bretton Woods ticket offices throughout the season). Midweek non-holiday tickets are $49 for adults, $39 for teens and $29 for juniors for one day; $94, $79 and $69 respectively for three days; $149, $124 and $105 respectively for five days.

Note: Night skiing is offered Friday and Saturday and nightly during holiday weeks. A twilight ticket, valid 2-9 p.m., is $35; a night ticket, valid 4-9 p.m. is $19.

Accommodations at the resort

Be sure to ask about packages, as Bretton Woods offers plenty, including themed weekends such as ballroom dancing and more. The **Mount Washington Hotel** ($$$-$$$$) is one of the most breathtaking hotels in the country. The grand dining room and period decor add to the magic. Staying here is a step back in time with excellent service and a touch of elegance.

The restored 1896 **Bretton Arms Country Inn** ($–$$), a National Historic Landmark, has spacious rooms, old fashioned charm and an excellent dining room.

The **Lodge at Bretton Woods** ($–$$) is a good choice for those on a budget. Rooms are nice, but not fancy; there's an indoor pool; and guests have full use of all Bretton Woods facilities, including the shuttle bus and the sports center.

Bretton Woods also has a grouping of townhouses. All Bretton Woods properties can be reached through (800) 258-0330 or 278-1000. In winter, the ski area provides complimentary shuttle buses to and from the slopes.

Other area accommodations

Built of granite, the **Notchland Inn** (374-6131 or 800-866-6131; $$–$$$$), in Bartlett, has 13 rooms, all with fireplaces. It has a hot tub, skating, and cross-country skiing from the door.

The Inn at Forest Hills (823-9550, fax 823-5555; $–$$) is a beautifully restored, English Tudor-style B&B built into a house which was once part of the grand Forest Hills Hotel. It's just about a mile from the village of Franconia, on Rte. 142, heading toward Bethlehem.

The Mulburn Inn (869-3389; $) is another B&B in a great Tudor-style setting with oak staircase and stained glass windows. It's located in Bethlehem, once considered one of the fresh-air centers of New England, only about 10 minutes from Bretton Woods.

Six miles north of the region at the crest of Sugar Hill, you'll find the **Sunset Hill House** (800-786-4455 or 823-5522; $–$$), a restored turn-of-the century inn built in 1882 in the era of Grand Hotels and Resorts. You can still stay in luxury and elegance, with wonderful views of the Presidentials. This mountain resort also has 30 km. of cross-country tracks (free for guests, $6 trail fee for others). Call for ski-and-stay programs.

Dining

The opulent **Main Dining Room at the Mount Washington Hotel** (278-1000; $$-$$$) provides a unique and grand setting for any meal complete with serenading orchestra, daily menus and an extensive wine list. Proper attire is required (gentlemen, that means jackets). For gourmet cuisine in a more intimate, century-old atmosphere, try the **Bretton Arms Restaurant** (278-1000; $$-$$$). Many locals say it's the best restaurant at the resort.

Other spots recommended by locals for fine dining are **Sunset Hill House** (823-5522; $$–$$$) and **Notchland Inn** (374-6131 or 800-866-6131; $$–$$$) in Hart's Location.

On the mountain, the **Top o' the Quad Restaurant** ($$) serves casual lunches daily, with views of Mt. Washington's summit. Back down the mountain, only a quarter-mile from the slopes, try **Darby's Diner** ($-$$) for traditional diner fare. **Fabyans Station** ($-$$) is a good eatery in an old railroad station. In Franconia head to **Hillwinds** ($$).

Après-ski/nightlife

Bretton Woods is not known for wild nightlife, still there's enough to keep most guests happy. You can dance to a dinner orchestra or head down into the stone depths of the Mount Washington hotel to the Cave Lounge.

Other activities

The Mount Washington Hotel has plenty of non-skiing activities including **horse-drawn sleigh rides**, a **skating rink**, and an **indoor pool** and **outdoor heated pool**. The resort also has a tubing area and a separate sports center with indoor pool, racquetball courts, exercise and weight rooms, Jacuzzi and sauna. Nearby Cannon is home to the **New England Ski Museum,** a collection of ski memorabilia well worth a brief visit. **Cannon's tram** is open for non-skiing sightseers for $9 a ride.

The Rocks Estate in Bethlehem has **sleigh rides** and offers some **forestry-related activities**, being owned by the Society For The Protection of New Hampshire Forests. Call (800) 639-5373. The Sunset Hill House, about six miles north of Cannon and the Old Man of the Mountain, has **sleigh rides** and **ice skating**. Call (800) 786-4455 or 823-5522.

Nearby Twin Mountain is one of New England's top **snowmobiling** areas.

Dining: $$$–Entrees $20+; $$–$10-20; $–less than $10.
Accommodations: (double room) $$$$–$200+; $$$–$141-$200; $$–$81-$140; $–$80 and less.

The factory outlet bonanza of North Conway with phenomenal tax-free **shopping** is 30 miles southeast of Bretton Woods.

Getting there and getting around

By air: Boston's Logan Airport is 150 miles away from the area. Manchester Airport, 100 miles south, is serviced by Southwest, MetroJet, Comair, Continental Express, Delta's Business Express, USAir, and United. The airport phone number is 624-6556; its Internet address is www.flymanchester.com.

By car: From I-93 heading north, Bretton Woods is on Rte. 302: take Exit 35 to Rte. 3, which meets Rte. 302 at Twin Mountain.

Getting around: A car is a necessity to reach the resort conveniently, but a shuttle bus operates throughout the resort.

Cannon Mountain

New Hampshire

Summit elevation: 4,146 feet
Vertical drop: 2,146 feet
Base elevation: 2,000 feet

Address: Franconia Notch State Park
Franconia, NH 03580
✆ **Area code:** 603
Ski area phone: 823-8800
Snow report: 823-7771
Fax: 823-8088
ⓘ **Toll-free reservations:**
(800) 227-4191
E-mail: info@cannonmt.com
Internet: www.cannonmt.com
Expert:★★
Advanced:★★
Intermediate:★★★★
Beginner:★★★
Never-ever:★★★

Number and types of lifts: 8–1 70-person aerial tram, 2 high-speed quads, 3 triples, 2 surface lifts
Acreage: 163 skiable acres
Snowmaking: 95 percent
Uphill capacity: 11,000 per hour
Snowboarding: Yes
Bed base: 13,000 nearby
Nearest lodging: about 1/2 mile
Resort child care: Yes, 6 weeks and older
Adult ticket, per day: $34-$45 (02/03)

Dining:★★
Apres-ski/nightlife:★
Other activities:★★

State-owned Cannon Mountain, located in breathtaking Franconia Notch, is the farthest north of the three resorts that line Interstate I-93. It's also the most historic. The first racing trail in North America, now called the Taft Slalom, was cut into Cannon in 1933 and brought several major races to Cannon, including the National Alpine Championships. The aerial tramway was also the first in North America and opened for business in 1938. In 1980, the tram was updated to the current 70-person model, but the old tram houses still remain at the base and summit, and the resort still enjoys the charm of the early skiing days. Not as popular as Loon or Waterville, Cannon has a devoted following that appreciates its historic significance. An added plus is the New England Ski Museum, located adjacent to the tram base.

Besides the Tramway Base Station (off Exit 2) Cannon's main base lodge, the Peabody Base Area, is off Exit 3. Long known by experts as one of the most challenging mountains in the East, Cannon enlarged its beginner and intermediate terrain. The Brookside novice slope, served by its own triple chair, was added below the Peabody Base Lodge, as well as a new building to house children's programs. Parkway and Lower Cannon, both beginner runs, were widened, and Lower Cannon was divided by netting, with one side designated for lower-level skiers (unfortunately, it is difficult to tell which side is which). The state also blasted 35,000 cubic yards of granite to widen Middle Ravine and Middle Cannon, both mid-mountain inter-mediate trails. Big Link, which brings skiers and riders back to the Cannonball Express Quad (serving the summit), was also widened.

But experts, do not despair. With a 2,146-foot vertical served by the 70-passenger tram, the challenge is still there. The summit is also accessible via a high-speed quad that takes intermediates and experts from the Peabody Base Area over halfway up the mountain to access the expanded terrain or the summit trails via the Cannonball Express Quad. A triple chair lifts experts from the Peabody Base Area to the famous Front Five trails. Beginners can also use this triple to access the gentler terrain nearer the base.

Though that three-letter word "ice" sometimes has been associated with the mountain, Cannon takes mountain preparation very seriously and added four groomers to its squadron last year. Of Cannon's 163 acres, 95 percent are covered by snowmaking, and its higher base altitude often finds it enjoying snow while other nearby mountains have rain. The trails are narrower in legend than they are in reality, and the mountain can actually be skied by most intermediates. This is still a place for advanced skiers to play and intermediates to push themselves.

When the weather is good, skiers and riders also flock to Cannon for the sheer scenic beauty. From the summit, you can see all the way to New Hampshire's Presidential Range. You also see no signs of civilization except for the highway and base lodges. Lodging is available 15 minutes south in Lincoln or Woodstock or about 5 minutes north in Franconia.

Mountain layout–Skiing

◆◆ **Expert** ◆ **Advanced:** Experts can either take the tram or the Peabody Express Quad. From the quad, skiers and riders can reach the summit via the Cannonball Express Quad. The Profile Trail, right under the summit express quad, is a wide, straight trail that takes you down almost to mid-mountain. Or you can experience New England skiing the way it used to be, by winding down Skylight or Upper Ravine. From the tram's summit station, Upper Cannon, Tramway and Vista Way are all intermediate trails that are challenging but certainly negotiable. The steepest is Upper Cannon, which offers New England-style steeps and whoop-dee-do turns—almost too many to count—through the high-elevation scrubby pines.

The Front Five, as known to locals, are the intimidating-looking trails seen from the highway. These are accessed via Paulie's Extension or Lower Cannon. Three of them, Avalanche, Paulie's Folly and Zoomer, are marked black and rightfully so, especially Zoomer's bumps, and all five look as if they plunge straight into Echo Lake. The other two, Rocket and Gary's, have less pitch and no bumps. None is as frighteningly steep as it appears, and it's easy to return to the tram from any of them.

■ **Intermediate:** Although touted as an expert's mountain, intermediates will find plenty of terrain to suit their skills. From the summit, you can take either Vista Way, Tramway (the widest of the three) or Upper Cannon. These feed into a collection of intermediate runs, including Middle Cannon and Middle Ravine. Or from the top of the Cannonball Express Quad, treat yourself to Upper Ravine, which swoops its way through the subalpine forest. Intermediates wishing to return to the tram without scaring themselves on the Front Five can follow the Tram Cutback from Gary's, the easiest of the Front Five.

●● **Beginner:** The bottom half of Cannon has five long runs that will suit beginners: Toss-Up, Lower Cannon (now divided into two halves to, in theory, keep faster skiers segregated from beginners), Parkway, Gremlin and Turnpike. The Eagle Triple Chair from the Peabody Base Area is the best way to access this terrain. More daring beginners can take the Peabody Express Quad. A slew of intermediate runs feed into the beginner trails.

● **Never-ever:** The Brookside learning area adjacent to the Peabody Base Area opened last year and is ideal for never-evers. The area is segregated from the rest of the mountain (so experts won't zoom through). It is serviced by its own triple chair lift as well as a surface lift.

Never-evers can rent equipment and sign up for lessons at the Brookside Learning Center to the right of the Peabody Base Lodge parking area.

Snowboarding

Cannon has terrain park and a halfpipe.

Mountain rating

This is the toughest mountain in the region. It is a good place to come to test your skiing and riding. The steeps can take your breath away and with ice they are a true challenge. Beginners and uncertain intermediates will probably have more fun at nearby Bretton Woods.

Cross-country

The Franconia Village X-C Ski Center (800-473-5299) has 105 km. of trails, 65km of which are groomed and tracked. Ski, stay and sleigh packages are available through the Franconia Inn at the same telephone number.

Lessons (2002/03 prices)

Group lessons: $25 per session; $100 for book of five lessons.

Never-ever package: Introduction to Skiing or Snowboarding is $49 and includes a lesson, ski or snowboard rental and Brookside lift ticket. A follow-up Refresher course is also $49.

Private lessons: $45 for one hour, $70 for two hours, plus $25 for each additional hour and $10 for each additional person per hour. An Early Bird discount of $35 per hour applies to lessons at 8:45 a.m. A half-day lesson is $95; a full-day lesson is $160. Best deal: 3-person private lesson for $75, plus $25 for each additional person. A half-day private lesson is $95 and a half-day semi-private lesson for two is $125.

Other: All-day ski guides are available for $275 for up to six people.

Racing: Recreational racing is offered weekends and holidays at 1 p.m. at $1 per run. Training sessions are at 10 a.m. and cost $20.

Child care (2002/03 prices)

Ages: 6 weeks and older.

Costs: For children 6 weeks to 1 year: $9 per hour; $25 per half day; $50 per full day. For children older than 1 year: $8 per hour; $23 for a half day, $48 for a half day with private lesson; $45 for full day with lunch, $65 for full day with lunch and private lesson.

Reservations: Advised; call 823-8800.

Children's lessons: Cannon Tykes, for ages 3-4: $30 private lesson with rentals. Cannon Kids (for skiers ages 4-8) and Mountain Explorers (for skiers and riders ages 8-12) have morning and afternoon sessions with all-day ticket is $60; morning or afternoon session with all-day tickets is $50; afternoon session with afternoon ticket is $40. Five-day program with two sessions daily and lift ticket is $250. Five-day program one session daily and lift ticket is $225. Rental equipment for all programs is $10.

Lift tickets (2002/03 prices)

	Adult	Teen (13-19)	Child (6-12)
One day, weekend/midweek	$45/$34	$37/$23	$29/23

Multiday tickets: Skiers who arrive at the ticket window with the previous day's lift ticket still attached to their clothing get a $5 discount.

Who skis free: Ages 5 and younger when with a ticketed adult.

Who skis at a discount: Ages 65 and older ski at child rates. On Tuesdays and Thursdays, two people can ski for $40 (excluding Dec. 26 and 31). On Feb. 18 and 20, two ski or ride for $45.

Accommodations

Cannon has no slopeside lodging, but nearby Lincoln and Woodstock (about 15 minutes south) and Franconia (about 5 minutes north) have accommodations to suit just about any needs. Please consult the chapter on Loon for recommended accommodations in the Lincoln/Woodstock area, or call Lincoln/Woodstock Central Reservations at (800) 227-4191.

Long known as a ski town, Franconia has several quaint New England Inns, the nicest being the **Sunset Hill House** (800-786-4455 or 823-5522; $–$$) and the **Franconia Inn** (800-473-5299 or 823-5542; $$-$$$). Located just outside Franconia on historic Sugar Hill (the site of the first ski school in North America), the Sunset Hill House is a restored farmhouse built in 1789 that has wonderful views of the Presidentials and the Green Mountains. The Franconia Inn is a lovely turn-of-the-century inn with hand-hewn beams in the cozy lobby and a sunny dining room. Some of the rooms have been renovated recently; others still have quaint old bathrooms with claw-foot tubs. Both the Sunset Hill House and Franconia Inn offer cross-country skiing (free for guests, $8 trail fee for others). Of note, the Franconia Inn is located on Rte. 116 2.5 miles south of Franconia. Unless your car has good suspension, we recommend you take I-93 to Franconia, then follow signs for Rte. 116. There is a short-cut from Cannon off Rte. 18, but the road gives new meaning to the term "frost heave."

The Inn at Forest Hills (800-280-9550 or 823-9550; $–$$) has been beautifully restored by Joanne and Gordon Haym. The English Tudor-style B&B is built into a house which was once part of the grand Forest Hills Hotel. We hear the full New England breakfast with a gourmet twist is not to be missed. The inn is located just about a mile from the village of Franconia, on Rte. 142, heading toward Bethlehem.

Among the least expensive places to stay are the **Hillwinds Lodge** (800-906-5292 or 823-5551; $-$$), which is owned by the same people who own the Franconia Inn; **Parker's Motel** (800-766-6835 or 745-8341; $), which is about five miles from Cannon Mountain, the **Riverbank Motel** (800-633-5624 or 745-3374; $) or the **Cannon Mountain View Inn** (800-823-9577 or 823-9577; $), right off Exit 37 in Franconia. We also hear that the **Kinsman Lodge** (823-5685, fax 823-9512; $) is a casual and affordable B&B located on Easton Road in Franconia.

About 30 minutes north is the newly renovated and reopened Mountain View Grand (603/837-2100 or 866-484-3843; $$-$$$$). This sprawling historic hotel now houses a European-style spa on the fourth floor and has a fitness center, indoor pool and steamroom on the lowest level. The potential is great, but the service to date has been poor to uneven.

Dining

For elegant dining experiences, locals recommend the **Sunset Hill House** (823-5522; $$), which also has great views of the Franconia Range, and the **Franconia Inn** (823-5542; $$-$$$), which has a bright, sunny dining room. Both establishments require reservations, even if you are staying there.

For more traditional fare, head to the **Village House** ($-$$) in downtown Franconia or **Hillwinds** ($$), which specializes in grilled steaks and seafood.

For breakfast, head up Sugar Hill outside Franconia to **Polly's Pancake Parlor** (823-5575; $). Or drive a few miles up I-93 to Littleton and the **Littleton Diner** (444-3994; $), a traditional old diner car where you can get a great breakfast.

If you are staying in the Lincoln/Woodstock area, please see our chapter on Loon for dining recommendations in the area.

Après-ski/nightlife

With no restaurants nearby, Cannon is not exactly bustling with après-ski activities. But down the road in Franconia, try Village House, a comfortable lounge with a lot of classic ski history and an evening entertainer who plays après-ski at the mountain's lounge. Or try Hillwinds, a large bar and lounge with live entertainment and a huge crowd on weekends.

Other activities

The **New England Ski Museum** sits adjacent to Cannon's Tramway Base Station and has a collection of ski memorabilia well worth a visit. The museum is open noon-5 p.m. Friday-Monday, and admission is free. **Cannon's tram** is open for non-skiing sightseers for $9 a ride.

The **Rocks Estate** in Bethlehem, on a hilltop about 10 miles from Cannon, has **sleigh rides** and offers some forestry-related activities, since it's owned by the Society For The Protection of New Hampshire Forests. Call (800) 639-5373.

The Sunset House in Sugar Hill outside Franconia on Rte. 117 has **sleigh rides** and **ice skating**. Call (800) 786-4455 or 823-5522.

Getting there and getting around

By air: Boston's Logan Airport is about 145 miles away from Cannon and the Franconia area. Manchester Airport, 85 miles south, is serviced by Southwest, MetroJet, Comair, Continental Express, Delta's Business Express, USAir, and United. The airport phone number is 624-6556; its Internet address is www.flymanchester.com.

By car: From I-93 heading north, Cannon is visible from I-93 just north of Franconia Notch State Park. Take Exit 2 for the Tramway Base Station, Exit 3 for the Peabody Base Area.

Getting around: As there is no on-mountain lodging, a car is a necessity.

Dining: $$$-Entrees $20+; $$-$10-20; $-less than $10.
Accommodations: (double room) $$$$-$200+; $$$-$141-$200; $$-$81-$140; $-$80 and less.

Loon Mountain

New Hampshire

Summit elevation: 3,050 feet
Vertical drop: 2,100 feet
Base elevation: 950 feet

Address: RR1, Box 41
Lincoln, NH 03251
✆ **Area code:** 603
Ski area phone: 745-8111
Snow report: 745-8100
Fax: 745-8214
ⓘ **Toll-free reservations:**
(800) 229-7829
E-mail: info@loonmtn.com
Internet: www.loonmtn.com
Expert:★ **Advanced:**★★
Intermediate:★★★★
Beginner:★★★★
Never-ever:★★★

Number and types of lifts: 9–1 gondola,
1 high-speed quad, 2 triples, 3 doubles,
2 surface lifts
Acreage: 275 skiable acres
Snowmaking: 98 percent
Uphill capacity: 10,550 per hour
Snowboarding: Yes
Bed base: 13,000
Nearest lodging: slopeside
Resort child care: Yes, 6 weeks - 8 years
Adult ticket, per day: $40-$51 (02/03)
Dining:★★★
Apres-ski/nightlife:★★★
Other activities:★★★

Easy accessibility, good terrain and a beautiful natural setting combined with the nearby re-sort town of Lincoln, with its shops, restaurants, inns and motels, have contributed to Loon Mountain's popularity. Like many of the other ski resorts in the White Mountains, Loon has decent vertical. Many of the runs maintain their pitch from top to bottom (unlike some resorts where most of the runs wash out to beginner terrain near the base). Although the mountain's black-diamond terrain will keep experts entertained, overall Loon is an intermediate's moun-tain. The blue runs are true intermediate runs, and beginners who have ventured into interme-diate terrain may find that Loon's blue squares test their limits. Loon has two base areas, separated by parking lots but connected by a steam train that shuttles skiers and riders back and forth, a real hit with children.

The resort enjoys some of the friendliest staff around, which keeps skiers and riders coming back. It also offers plenty of family-friendly activities, including snow-tubing (both day and night), snow toys, a climbing wall, an ice skating rink and horseback riding year-round.

When it comes to lodging, the resort is a behemoth. It's one of the few resorts where the bed base is larger than the lift capacity. This has created crowded conditions at times. Fortu-nately, Loon has made a number of improvements during the past few years. Among these were trail improvements to relieve congestion in high-traffic stretches, new lifts to get people up the mountain faster, more snowmaking coverage and a dedicated learning area. Loon also has extended tubing to daytime hours on the Little Sister trail near the gondola.

Another plus: Loon Mountain limits lift ticket sales to keep the mountain experience positive. Continued improvements have meant the sold-out signs quit coming out every week-end; now it's about four days per season, with perhaps 10 near-sellout days. To ensure that you'll get a lift ticket on those busy days (normally holiday weekends), you can reserve tickets with a major credit card ahead of time; call (800) 229-LOON (5666) or log onto www.loonmtn.com. The Unconditional Satisfaction Guarantee also ensures you'll like the conditions or you'll ski or ride free on your next visit.

Loon is owned by Booth Creek Ski Holdings, which owns nearby Waterville Valley, Mt. Cranmore in the Mt. Washington Valley as well as resorts in the West. The three New Hampshire areas have interchangeable lift tickets and season passes.

Mountain layout–Skiing

◆◆ **Expert** ◆ **Advanced:** North Peak runs are challenging and well removed from lower-intermediate traffic. The steeps are there, but half the bumps are groomed out. To reach North Peak, take the gondola, then ski down Big Dipper, Triple Trouble or Angel Street to the North Peak Triple Chair. In fresh snow, experts will like the three tree-skiing areas: One is accessed off Upper Flying Fox, another off Angel Street and the third off Haulback between Lower Flume and Lower Walking Boss.

■ **Intermediate:** Loon is loaded with intermediate terrain. The intermediate runs are good and solid, with no expert surprises around the next clump of trees. The upper trails are a bit twisted, narrow and seemingly undirected, but they open onto a series of wide intermediate pistes. Flying Fox is a delightful cruise with old-fashioned twists and turns through the trees and granite boulders. Depending on snow conditions, skiers can link up with the West Side trails via Upper Speakeasy, or they can drop down to the parking lot on any of the wide cruising runs (Rumrunner is a good choice, if there isn't a race on it), and ride the steam train the 100 yards to the adjacent base area and the gondola.

If you want to sample trees, try Misgiving Link and Scaler off Grand Junction.

●● **Beginner:** The center of the mountain, serviced by the Seven Brothers triple chair, has good intermediate trails that advanced beginners can handle. The east side of the chair has beginner runs such as Grand Junction, The Link, Brookway, and Lower Bear Claw.

● **Never-ever:** Never-evers have an improved learning area to the right of the Governor Adams Base Lodge.

Mountain layout–Snowboarding

Riders can get easy access to the Loon Mountain Park by taking the Kanc Quad or the Seven Brothers lift. The gondola is also an option if you don't mind the long run from the summit to the top of the park, located between Lower Picked Rock and Picaroon. Jumps range in difficulty from one that gives newbies just a few inches of air under their boards to a hit-it-for-all-you're-worth-and-hope-you-make-it-to-the-landing kicker. That monster has a perfect transition and a nice smooth landing. The Superpipe could use more frequent grooming. The park ends with two rails. A big plus here is that you can hit most of the park's features in each run.

Picaroon, which runs under the gondola, is narrow and had plentiful rollers. For glades, try Bucksaw, off North Peak.

Mountain rating

This is a great mountain for intermediates and with the new learning area it has fine terrain for never-evers and early beginners. Experts and Advanced skiers seeking challenges will have more fun up the Interstate at Cannon or testing themselves in the extensive trees at Bretton Woods.

Cross-country and snowshoeing

The **Loon Mountain Cross-Country Center** (745-8111, ext. 5568) has 35 km. of groomed and tracked trails that wind along the scenic Pemigewasset River. Children ages 5 and younger and seniors 70 and older ski free.

Lessons (2002/03 prices)

Group lessons: $33 for 2 hours.

Never-ever package: For skiers or riders, this includes equipment, all-day lessons and a limited lift ticket for $69 per day. Enroll at either rental shop.

Private lessons: $69 an hour; $40 for additional hours, $40 for each additional person.

Racing: A race course is served by the Seven Brothers lift.

The Burton Method Center pairs snowboard instruction with equipment progression.

Child care (2002/03 prices)

Ages: 6 weeks to 8 years.

Costs: Half day, $39; full day, $59.

Reservations: Required; call 745-8111. Hours: 8 a.m. to 4:30 p.m. Loon has a spacious Children's Center near the Governor Adams Lodge.

Children's lessons: Full day for age 3 including lunch and lifts is $89; half day $69. Full day for children ages 4–6 costs $89; $69 half day. An Adventure Ski Camp for ages 7–12 groups children by ability level. Price is $89 a day, including lunch; $69 for a half day. All children's lessons are run out of the Children's Center, which also houses a rental shop for skiers and boarders to age 6. Reservations are required for all programs, call 745-6281, ext. 5160 or 5162. Camps are not available during holidays or peak periods.

Lift tickets (2001/2002 prices)

Weekday Prices	Adult	Young Adult	Child (6-12)
One day	$43	$36	$29
Three days	$114 ($38+/day)	$95	$81
Five days (midweek)	$164 ($32+/day)	$135	$114

Who skis free: Children ages 5 and younger.

Who skis at a discount: Ages 70 and older pay $10 midweek (non-holiday), but pay the regular adult price on Saturday, Sunday and holidays.

Weekend prices (02/03) are $54 for adults, $48 for young adults, $36 for children. Holiday rates are about $2 extra.

Note: Ticket sales are cut off after approximately 6,000 have been sold. To reserve tickets, parking or ski rentals in advance by major credit card, call (800)-229-LOON (5666) or visit www.loonmtn.com.

Accommodations

The **Mountain Club on Loon** (800-229-7829 or 745-2244) is a ski-in/ski-out property with everything under one roof, from parking to swimming pool, fitness club to restaurants. One problem: Many of its rooms have a double Murphy bed with two small day beds along the windows. This arrangement is fine for couples, or for a family with young children, but it is awkward for two adults who don't want to sleep in the same bed. Instead, request two rooms that, when adjoined, make a suite. Loon also has condominiums. Make reservations through the Mountain Club.

Reservations and information for many of the properties in Lincoln and Woodstock can be obtained through the **Lincoln/Woodstock Central Reservations** at (800) 227-4191.

The **Comfort Inn** (800-228-5150 or 745-6700; $$) is right off I-93 at Hobo Railroad. It has both regular hotel rooms and one-bedroom suites with kitchenettes. Two prominent properties right on the Kancamagus Highway (Main Street) in Lincoln are **The Mill House Inn** (800-654-6183 or 745-6261; $-$$$) at The Mill and the **Nordic Inn** (800-536-1038; $-$$), which offers condominiums (studios-3 bedrooms). The **Rivergreen Resort Hotel** (800-654-6183 or 745-2450; $$-$$$), owned by the same group that owns The Mill House Inn, is also a condominium hotel. The last in a trio of "Mill" properties is **The Lodge at Lincoln Station** (800-654-6188 or 745-3441; $$-$$$), a hotel situated on the Pemigewasset River. Accommodations are studios to one-bedroom suites. These properties are about one mile west of Loon.

Another couple of miles away from Loon is **The Woodstock Inn B&B** (800-321-3985, 745-3951; $-$$), a typical New England lodge. The main building is more than 100 years old with no two rooms alike. You'll find the rooms tucked under the rafters, some with private bath, some with shared, a few with hot tubs, all with casual charm. The restaurant in the front of the inn is one of North Woodstock's most elegant; the one in the station at the rear is one of the town's liveliest.

Wilderness Inn B&B (745-3890; $-$$) is run by the Yarnells, a couple who make families with youngsters welcome in their house. Parents note: This place has laundry facilities! The B&B is only steps from the center of North Woodstock, which is filled with shops and restaurants.

Three motelish properties along Rte. 3 in Lincoln, one exit up I-93 from Loon, join for advertising and have similar accommodations with mostly identical prices, but each has slightly different amenities. **Indian Head Motel Resort** (800-343-8000, 745-8000; $$) is one of the centers of après-ski action with live bands and a great ice-skating pond and cross-country trails. **The Beacon** (800-258-8934, 745-8118; $-$$$ has indoor tennis and large indoor pools, but attracts the bus-tour crowd. **Woodward's Motor Inn** (800-635-8968, 745-8141; $-$$) is the most family oriented. It has the area's only racquetball court and the best steaks in the region. Another reasonably priced motel along this stretch of Rte. 3 is the **Drummer Boy Motor Inn** (800-762-7275 or 745-3661; $-$$$). All are located off I-93's Exit 33.

Dining

The most elegant dining experience in the Lincoln/Woodstock area can be found at the **Woodstock Inn's Clement Room** (745-3951; $$-$$$), which gets high ratings from locals for its informal dining with style. The Woodstock Inn also serves great daily breakfasts as well as a fabulous weekend brunch.

At Loon Mountain, try **Seasons on Loon** (745-8111; $$) or **The Black Diamond Bar** ($-$$), both at the Mountain Club. Locals claim the **Open Hearth Steak House** (745-8141; $$) at Woodward's Motor Inn has the best steaks. **Gordi's Fish and Steak House** (745-6635; $-$$) is family-oriented and features Maine lobster and steaks. The **Olde Timbermill** (745-3603; $$) in The Mill is set in a modernesque, barn-like building that is also one of the nightlife centers in Lincoln.

Truant's Tavern (745-2239; $-$$) serves clever dinner entrées in a mock schoolhouse atmosphere; drinking in class was never so much fun. The bar hops on weekends. **Woodstock Station** (745-3951; $-$$), in an old train station on Main Street, offers a creative menu of

Dining: $$$-Entrees $20+; $$-$10-20; $-less than $10.
Accommodations: (double room) $$$$-$200+; $$$-$141-$200; $$-$81-$140; $-$80 and less.

reasonable meals, from meatloaf to Mexican, makes its own beer and is a local favorite. **G.H. Pizza** (745-6885; $) serves traditional and gourmet pizza, as well as hot and cold subs. Locals agree that the best pizza in town is found at **Elvio's Pizzeria** (745-8817; $). We're also told **Chieng Gardens** (745-8612; $-$$) in Lincoln Square offers decent Chinese food.

For breakfast try **Sunny Day Diner** (745-4833; $) or **Peg's Place** (745-2740; $), both in North Woodstock. For good coffee, head to either **Java Joe's** ($) in The Depot or the **Pycolog Bakery Café** (745-4395; $). Both coffee places have excellent pastries, too.

 ## Après-ski/nightlife

After skiing at Loon, head to the **Black Diamond Bar in the Mountain Club** for good weekend entertainment and a quiet après-ski spot. The **Paul Bunyan Lounge** at the Octagon base has a young, rowdy crowd and really rocks. Or head to **Babe's** at the Governor Adams Lodge.

North Woodstock-area locals set up party camp at **Truant's Tavern** and the **Woodstock Station**. **Gordi's Fish and Steak**, in Lincoln, has great munchies. **Indian Head Resort**, in Lincoln, offers good après-ski. From Wednesday through Sunday, live bands rock the joint. The **Tavern Sports Bar** is a low-key darts, video game and pool hall. Downstairs, the **Olde Timbermill** has the area's best singles action, with bands on weekends.

 ## Other activities

Shopping: The town of Lincoln has several specialty shops worth a look, including some factory outlets, along the Kancamagus Highway in town. The factory outlet bonanza of tax-free North Conway is 35 miles east of town, but the drive takes about an hour in winter.

Loon Mountain has **skating, day and night tubing** and après-ski **entertainment** for families.

Profile Mountaineering, in Lincoln, offers introductory **ice climbing** and **winter mountaineering**. Alpine Village has a **rock-climbing wall**, as does the Pemi Valley Rock Gym (745-9800) in Woodstock. Alpine Adventures (745-9911) in Lincoln offers guided **snowmobile tours**. Creations in The Depot has **make-your-own pottery**. Lincoln also has four **movie theaters**.

Getting there and getting around

By air: Boston's Logan Airport is 140 miles away from Loon. Manchester Airport, 80 miles south, is serviced by Southwest, MetroJet, Comair, Continental Express, Delta's Business Express, USAir, and United. The airport phone number is 624-6556; its Internet address is www.flymanchester.com.

By car: From I-93 heading north, Loon Mountain is about 2 miles up the Kancamagus Highway (Route 112) from Exit 32 in Lincoln.

Getting around: A car is a necessity unless you stay in the Lincoln-Woodstock area. Lincoln-Woodstock has a shuttle service and taxi, available anytime.

Waterville Valley

New Hampshire

Summit elevation: 4,004 feet
Vertical drop: 2,020 feet
Base elevation: 1,984 feet

Address: One Ski Area Rd., Waterville Valley, NH 03215
☎ **Area code:** 603
Ski area phone: 236-8311
Snow report: 236-4144
Fax: 236-4344
ⓘ **Toll-free reservations:** (800) GO-VALLEY (468-2553)
E-mail: info@waterville.com
Internet: www.waterville.com
Expert: ★
Advanced: ★★
Intermediate: ★★★
Beginner: ★★★
Never-ever: ★★★

Number and types of lifts: 11–2 high-speed quads, 2 triples, 3 doubles, 4 surface lifts
Skiable acreage: 225 acres
Snowmaking: 100 percent
Uphill capacity: 15,187 per hour
Snowboarding: Yes
Bed base: 2,500
Nearest lodging: quarter mile
Resort child care: Yes, 6 months - 4 years
Adult ticket, per day: $47 (01/02 price)
Dining: ★★★★
Apres-ski/nightlife: ★★
Other activities: ★★

Waterville Valley is the first "big" resort you come to as you drive north on I-93 from southern New Hampshire or Massachusetts, making it one of the most popular ski resorts in New Hampshire. Besides its location, the resort gained its reputation from staging more than 10 World Cup ski races over the past quarter century. (Waterville founder Tom Corcoran finished fourth in the 1960 Olympic giant slalom.) Though many of the trails are well suited for racing, in truth, the resort is better known as an intermediate's mountain. In recent years, its reputation has changed to that of a family resort. Still, it enjoys significant vertical for an eastern resort, and it uses it well. Almost all the trails follow the fall line, and they maintain their pitch almost from top to bottom.

Waterville Valley is sufficiently self-contained so that most visitors, once they enter, do not venture any farther than the slopes, just a short shuttlebus ride away from the lodging in and around Town Square, where you'll find shops, restaurants and bars. Most of the off-slope activities are in Town Square, including cross-country skiing, sleigh rides and a huge sports complex with indoor and outdoor swimming pools, tennis, squash and racquetball courts and indoor track. There is an indoor skating rink and a handful of shops here, too.

On the mountain, Waterville has one fairly large base area, making it ideal for families who don't want to get separated amidst multiple base lodges. Two high-speed quads start right outside the base lodge, one being Quadzilla. Despite its scary name, the lift is decorated like a happy dog wearing a whirly-bird beanie. You can tell how windy it is by how fast the propeller turns! The other quad, White Peak Express, takes skiers and riders *almost* to the summit. The High Country Double services the three uppermost intermediate slopes when wind (and snow) conditions are right.

Waterville Valley belongs to the Booth Creek resort family, which means it offers a wide variety of snow toys and tubing, as do its sister New Hampshire resorts, Cranmore and Loon Mountain. Lift tickets are interchangeable at these three resorts.

Mountain layout—Skiing

◆◆ **Expert** ◆ **Advanced:** One of the toughest runs, True Grit, develops big moguls and drops down the Sunnyside face. With several tough rollers and steep pitches, the World Cup Slalom Hill is a good place for experts to test their carving skills. There's also a tree-skiing area off Lower Bobby's Run; it starts about halfway down the trail on the left. An interesting note—Bobby's Run (both Upper and Lower) was named after the late Senator Robert Kennedy, who frequented the resort after it opened in 1966.

■ **Intermediate:** Waterville's trails are not New England's typical steep and narrow pistes. Most are wide swaths through the trees, and there's elbow room and a chance to check out the slope before committing to the fall line again.

Two former tough mogul runs, Ciao and Gema, now are groomed daily. Such trails as White Caps, Sel's Choice, Old Tecumseh and Tippecanoe are intermediate and advanced playthings. Upper Bobby's Run is a great intermediate trail, but if you don't want to find yourself on a black diamond or double-diamond mogul trail (Lower Bobby's), make sure you take a strong left to Terry's Trail or Old Tecumseh.

Something more resorts should do: Waterville has a designated "easier mogul field." For those wanting to move to the next level, this is great practice.

●● **Beginner:** Beginner terrain at Waterville is limited, and beginners who have skied blue runs at other resorts might find Waterville's intermediate terrain challenging. But the Valley Run is a beginner/lower intermediate heaven with enough width to allow skiing for a couple of days down different sections. This run is now served by Quadzilla, a high-speed quad that takes skiers to the top of the run in 4.5 minutes.

● **Never-ever:** Never-evers have a small area with a separate lift.

Mountain layout—Snowboarding

Waterville Valley has enough diversity and runs to keep any rider happy for a least a day. It hosts competition ranging from amateur events to the World Quarterpipe Championships. The Exhibition Terrain Park & Halfpipe, located right above the base area, has a Superpipe, a couple of jumps, hip, two rails and a quarterpipe. Unfortunately, the elements aren't set up so that you can hit all of them in one run. While Exhibition has its own surface lift, if you access the top of the park from Psyched, you'll gain two extra hits. A second terrain park, The Boneyard, was the first terrain park in the East.

Kids have their own terrain park, Little Slammer, where they can train for the big stuff.

Oblivion, a winding trail with banked sides, is the trail of choice for many riders. Carvers head to World Cup. Also popular are Sel's Choice and the glades off True Grit.

Mountain rating

Unless you have young children, you might find Waterville a bit limiting for a week's vacation, but it can be a lot of fun for an extended weekend. There is a little bit of something for everyone, but the emphasis is on "little bit" if you are an accomplished skier. Though the area made its name in the race arena, there is little more than those few good racing trails. That said, the black diamonds are really black diamonds, and the blue squares are true intermediate runs, making them challenging for beginners. This makes Waterville Valley feel like a bigger mountain than it really is.

Cross-country and snowshoeing

Waterville has 105 km. of trails, 70 of which are groomed and tracked for skating and classic skiing through the White Mountain National Forest. This cross-country center and the trail system is considered one of the best in New England by Nordic aficionados.

Rentals and lessons are available, as are guided cross-country and snowshoe tours for all levels and ages. Call 236-4666 for more information. Cross-country trail fees are included as part of the Winter Unlimited lodging package. Otherwise, daily tickets cost $14 for a full day, $10 for a half day. Rentals cost $18 for classic equipment, $22 for skate ski equipment.

Lessons (2001/02 prices)

Group lessons: $28 for 2 hours. This year Waterville will also offer free from-the-summit clinics for upper-intermediate and advanced skiers. The one-hour clinics will meet twice daily in the afternoon.

Never-ever package: Skiing or snowboarding, $62 for lower mountain lift ticket (includes J-bar, Lower Meadows and Valley Run J-lift), two lessons and equipment. A special Passport provides two follow-up days for *$XX*.

Private lessons: $65 an hour plus $35 for each added hour and $35 for each added skier.

Racing: A recreational course on Utter Abandon has races Wednesdays, Fridays, Saturdays and Sundays.

Child care (2001/02 prices)

Ages: 6 months to 4 years.

Costs: All day is $42, with multiday discounts. Half day is $32, hourly is $10 (2-hour minimum). Lunch is $5, or children may bring their own.

Note: Women's Wednesdays include free child care (max. two kids per ticket), 50-percent off half-day or full-day kids camps, 50-percent off group lessons, free use of the athletic club and more with the purchase of non-holiday Wednesday ticket.

Reservations: Required if you want to ensure a space. Call 236-8311, Ext. 3196. Waterville has two nurseries at the base area.

Children's lessons: Kids Camps lessons costs $63 a day for ages 3–5. Rental equipment is $15 extra; lunch is also extra. Programs for ages 6–8 and 9–12 cost $51 a day, not including lift ticket. Rentals cost an additional $16, and lunch is extra. Call for half-day prices.

Lift tickets (2001/02 prices)

Weekend Prices	Adult	Teen (13-18)	Child (6-12)
One day	$47	$41	$15
Three days	$115 ($38+/day)	$102 ($34/day)	$45 ($15/day)
Five days	$168 ($33+/day)	$142 ($28+/day)	$75 ($15/day)

Holiday prices are higher. Lift tickets may be used at Loon and Mt. Cranmore.

Child ticket includes use of snowtoys and tubing in Exhibition Park from 9 a.m. to noon.

Who skis free: Kids 5 and younger ski free anytime. Waterville often runs a Kids Ski Free promotion (for ages up to 12) when parents buy multiday lodging packages; ask about it.

Who skis at a discount: Ages 65 and older ski at children's rates Monday-Friday and non-holidays. Midweek one-day prices are $40 for adults, $33 for teens, and $15 for children.

Midweek three-day prices are $105 for adults, $86 for teens and $45 for children. Midweek five-day rates are $149 for adults, $120 for teens and $75 for children.

 ## Accommodations

Waterville Valley has 2,500 beds in its Village, located about 1.5 miles from the slopes. To make reservations at any of the Waterville Valley accommodations listed below, call (800) GO-VALLEY (468-2553) or 236-8311. The "Winter Unlimited" package is all inclusive, offering all of Waterville's winter activities plus lodging for one price. With one call, you can book lift-and-lodging packages, kids' snowsports lessons and child care.

The **Golden Eagle Lodge** with condominium suites features a distinctive design reminiscent of the turn-of-the-century grand hotels at the White Mountain resorts.

Additionally, Waterville has three hotel properties and four groups of condominiums, all located in the valley. The **Valley Inn and Tavern** operates as a country inn with rates that can include meals, and the **Black Bear Lodge** is more hotel-like. All are in the same price range with two-day lodging and lift weekend packages starting at around $80 for rooms in January (per person, double occupancy) and averaging around $150 during the regular season (February and March, excluding President's Day week). The **Best Western/Silver Fox** offers continental breakfast and is the most economical place to stay. **Condominiums** are also available.

 ## Dining

The most elegant dining experience in Waterville Valley can be found at the **William Tell** (726-3618; $$-$$$) on Rte. 49 just down the valley from the resort. The William Tell has a strong Swiss-German accent with excellent wines.

On Saturday nights, take a 30-minute snowcat ride up the slopes to the **Schwendi Hutte** (236-8311, ext. 3000). The food is some of the best in the valley, as is the ambiance. Reservations are required, and the snowcat ride and meal cost $65/person.

The **Wild Coyote Grill** (236-4919; $-$$) in the White Mountain Athletic Club is the best restaurant in Waterville Valley Village. The menu offers nouveau cuisine with a Southwestern flair, and the calimari is a specialty. Or head to **Latitudes** (236-4646; $) for moderately priced family fare. For pizza, call **Olde Waterville Valley Pizza Co.** (236-3663; $). **Valley Inn** (236-8336; $$) and **Diamond Edge North** (236-2006; $$) are also located in Town Square, but we have yet to eat at either.

Lunch can be purchased at any of the four on-mountain restaurants. The **Schwendi Hutte,** at the top of the White Peak Express Quad, is the best of the lot: Don't miss the lobster bisque. On sunny spring days, head for BBQ on the deck of **Sunnyside Up** on Valley Run. The base area has a cafeteria, pizza corner and **T-Bars**. The food at T-Bars is nothing to write home about, but the ski memorabilia lining the walls is interesting.

For breakfast, pick up coffee and pastries at the **Waterville Coffee Emporium** (236-4021; $) or the **Jugtown Sandwich Shop** (236-3669; $). The Coffee Emporium also cooks up omelets, eggs, French toast and waffles. Both are located in Town Square.

 ## Après-ski/nightlife

Waterville now has a collection of bars in Town Square, each with slightly different après-ski. They are all within a few steps of each other. **Legends 1291 Latitudes** and **Diamond's Edge** serve a good time, and later in the evening they stand in the same order, ranging from loud disco and rock to quieter music. **T-Bars**, at the mountain, has the normal collection of skiers for après-ski until 5:30 p.m.

Just down the road from Waterville, on the way back to the interstate, try the **William Tell**, for a cozy quiet après-ski, or the **Mad River Tavern**, for a more raucous setting. Both have popular dinner menus.

Other activities

Waterville Valley has **sleigh rides** and an **indoor fitness center** with pool, track, weight rooms and more, as well as a covered ice arena for **skating.**

The resort also offers a full recreation program that includes activities for toddlers, youngsters and teens such as ice cream socials, basketball and dances.

Waterville Valley's Town Square has several specialty **shops** selling books, souvenirs, gifts, clothing and jewelry.

Getting there and getting around

By air: Boston's Logan Airport is 130 miles south of Waterville Valley. Manchester Airport, 70 miles south, is serviced by Southwest, MetroJet, Comair, Continental Express, Delta's Business Express, USAir, and United. The airport phone number is 624-6556; its Internet address is www.flymanchester.com.

By car: From I-93 heading north, Waterville Valley is 11 miles up Rte. 49 at Exit 28.

Getting around: Waterville Valley is self-contained and offers a shuttle from the Village to the slopes. It's wise to take the shuttle, since parking at the ski area can be a nightmare, although valet parking is available for $15. If you plan to venture away from the Village or want to try to Loon, Cannon and Bretton Woods farther north, a car is a necessity.

Dining: $$$-Entrees $20+; $$-$10-20; $-less than $10.
Accommodations: (double room) $$$$-$200+; $$$-$141-$200; $$-$81-$140; $-$80 and less.

New Hampshire Regional Resorts

The Balsams Wilderness, Dixville Notch, NH; (603) 255-3400; (800)
255-0800, NH; (800) 255-0600 U.S. and Canada
Internet: www.thebalsams.com
4 lifts: 2 triples, 1 double, 1 surface; 13 trails; 87 acres; 1,000 vertical feet

When you need to be pampered, owe your loved one a romantic weekend or want a family vacation without hassle, The Balsams Wilderness delivers. This remote resort, situated on a private, 15,000-acre estate located in far northern New Hampshire, easily earns its four-star rating. This is not, however, a ski resort. Rather, it's a resort where skiing is just one of many amenities. The mountain is small, but crowds are rare here.

The Balsams Wilderness is one of New Hampshire's surviving Grand Resort Hotels. It resembles a Disney Castle, with turrets and towers, porches and balconies, and huge public rooms rambling from one to another. It's also the site of the first-in-the-nation primary, and the Ballot Room is a history lesson in itself. Guestrooms are mostly understated with an old fashioned charm complemented with some amenities. Only a few rooms have televisions, but there is a big screen in the TV room.

Almost everything is included in one daily, per person rate: meals, skiing, entertainment and more. Guests are pampered with attentive service. Award-winning chefs prepare a full breakfast buffet (or you can order from the menu) and five-course dinner daily. You can put your car keys away once you check in, and you don't even need to carry your wallet. Children's programs, which even include mealtimes as well as skiing, keep the youngsters occupied so the parents can relax or take part in other planned activities. And when the kids are in bed, the hotel offers movies in a full-size theater, dancing and entertainment nightly in two lounges and often the ballroom, too.

Oh, yeah, we shouldn't forget the skiing. The alpine trails are varied, the people are very friendly (they are really up in the woods!) and the area gets lots — and we mean lots — of snow. This year the Balsams is replacing two ancient lifts, a double and a T-bar, with triple chairs. One will access the summit. Expert skiers will not be tested at the Balsams, but will enjoy the narrow twisting Notch and the glades off of it. The terrain is primarily intermediate, but these long winding trails just invite leisurely cruising. The other triple will serve the sunbathed beginner's slope, which is completely separate from the main mountain and has been recontoured for a continuous and perfect learning grade.

The Balsams also has 90 km. of cross-country trails with one circuit that has a vertical drop of 1,000 feet on trails 20 and 19 (the less daring can ski on the golf course). Trails are 12-feet wide and have two diagonal lanes and one skate lane. The resort also has a topographical trail map, so you should be able to avoid that big drop if you so desire. An ice-skating rink, 30 km. of designated snowshoeing trails, horse-drawn sleigh rides and a natural history program with guided tours round out the outdoor experience. If you still have energy to burn, there's a small fitness center, and the hotel usually offers a morning exercise program.

Lift tickets: $35 for adults weekends, $30 midweek; $25 for children weekends, $20 midweek. (Skiing is complimentary for hotel guests.)
Distance from Boston: About 220 miles north via I-93 (to Exit 35) then Rte. 3 to Colebrook and Rte. 26 to Dixville Notch.
Lodging information: (800) 255-0800, NH; (800) 255-0600, U.S. and Canada.

Mt. Sunapee, Mt. Sunapee, NH; (603) 763-2356

Internet: www.mtsunapee.com

10 lifts; 61 trails; 1,510 vertical feet, 220 skiable acres

New management, the same group that runs Okemo Mountain, has energized family-friendly Mt. Sunapee with a great, cheerful atmosphere and more than $14 million in improvements since 1999. The most noticeable signs of rebirth are the 25,000-square-foot base lodge with expanded food service and seating, a ski shop, Learning Center desk and Guest Services area; the high-speed quad that powers skiers to the summit in less than six minutes; and the snow quality, backed by impressive snowmaking and grooming.

Mt. Sunapee is a family mountain attracting a loyal following of skiers who like its New England feel and its close proximity (less than two hours) to Boston. The mountain skis a lot bigger than it is, with two different base areas and a separate beginner area. Cross-country skiing is available nearby. Mt. Sunapee is also the base for the New England Handicapped Sports Association (NEHSA), which provides programs for skiers with physical and mental challenges.

Lift tickets: Adults, $51 weekend, $48 weekday; Young Adult (13–18) and Senior (65-69), $44 weekend, $38 weekday; Junior (7-12) and Senior (70+) $34 weekend, $30 weekday. Children ages 6 and younger ski free with a ticked adult. Mt. Sunapee has a conditions guarantee. If you are not satisfied with the conditions within the first hour of your ski day, you may return your ticket for a voucher to come visit on another day of the current season.

Distance from Boston: About 90 miles via I-93, I-89 and Rte. 103.

Lodging information: A selection of B&Bs, inns, hotels/motels and condos is available through the Mt. Sunapee referral service: www.mountsunapee/lodging.com

Ragged Mountain, Danbury, NH; (603) 768-3475 or (603) 768-3600

Internet: www.ragged-mt.com

9 lifts: 1 six-pack, 2 triples, 2 doubles, 4 surface; 50 trails; 1,250 vertical feet; 225 skiable acres

Ragged is a sleeper. This small, but mighty mountain is packed with excellent terrain on three peaks for beginning through advanced skiers. It oozes New England charm. Its white clapboard base facilities resemble a farmhouse complex, complete with barn, and are spacious and comfortable. Good grooming and 95-percent snowmaking coverage provide a memorable experience, and trails run the gamut, from tight and twisting to wide cruisers to glades. There's also a terrain park and a halfpipe.

Ragged's owners are committed to building a solid resort, and in 2001 it installed a high-speed six-passenger chairlift that whisks skiers to the summit in four-and-a-half minutes. Ragged has a total of seven peaks peaks to develop, and so far its tackled just three of them. This season expect improved snowmaking and base lodge upgrades.

Lift tickets: (02/03) Weekends and holidays, Adults, $45, $32 midweek; Teens (13-18) $37, $29 midweek; Youth (6-12), $30, $25 midweek. Skiers ages 5 and younger and 72 and older ski free; Seniors (65-71) receive a 50-percent discount.

Distance from Boston: About 100 miles via I-93 to Rte. 4 West to 104 East.

Lodging information: (800) 887-5464; Ragged Mountain condos: (800) 400-3911.

434 • Regional Resorts – New Hampshire

Gunstock, Gilford, NH; (800) GUNSTOCK or (603) 293-4341
Internet: www.gunstock.com
6 lifts; 47 trails; 220 acres; 1,400 vertical feet

Gunstock is a family-friendly resort with a historic stone-and-timber lodge and winter sports that stretch into the night hours for all ages. This is a mountain for those who love to cruise. Trails are maintained by Gunstock's Groom On Demand program; when the mountain needs attention, the cats go out. Advanced skiers can ski through glades on Middle Trigger and find bumps on Red Hat or Flintlock Extension. Intermediate glades can be found on Middle Recoil. Beginners have their own separate area at the Ski Learning Center, with handletow and new conveyor lift, and the Gunshy chairlift. Snowboarders will find a 600-foot halfpipe and a terrain park. Night skiing is open on 15 trails served by five lifts. Snow tubing is available day and night. Snowshoers and cross-country skiers can enjoy 52 km. of trails for hiking, skating and gliding. The surrounding N.H. Lakes Region has thousands of rooms and plenty of restaurants as well as other activities such as ice fishing and snowmobiling.
Lift tickets: Adults, $46 weekend, $36 weekday, $20-$22 night; teens and seniors (65-69), $36 weekend, $15 midweek, $15-$26 night; Child (6–12) $26 weekend, $16 weekday, $14-$15 night. Skiers and riders ages 5 and younger and 70 and older ski free. The $129 Sunday Family 4-Pack includes two adult and two teen/child tickets; some holiday restrictions apply.
Distance from Boston: About 90 miles via I-93 and Rtes. 3 and 11A.
Lodging information: (603) 293-4341 or (800) GUNSTOCK (486-7862).

Lake Placid/Whiteface

New York

Summit elevation:	4,386 feet
Vertical drop:	3,166 feet
Base elevation:	1,220 feet

Address: Olympic Regional Development Authority (ORDA), Olympic Center, Lake Placid, NY 12946

✆ Area code: 518

Ski area phone: 946-2223

ORDA phone: 523-1655

Snow report: 946-7171

ⓘ Toll-free information: 800-462-6236

Fax: 523-9275

E-mail: info@orda.org

Toll-free reservations:
(800) 447-5224 (800-44-PLACID)

Internet: www.orda.org (ORDA) or www.whiteface.com www.lakeplacid.com (Lake Placid Visitors Bureau)

Expert:★★★★
Advanced:★★★★
Intermediate:★★★
Beginner:★★★   **Never-ever:**★★

Number and types of lifts: 10–1 eight-passenger, heated gondola, 1 high-speed quad, 1 quad, 1 triple, 5 doubles, 1 surface

Acreage: about 210 acres

Snowmaking: 99 percent

Uphill capacity: 13,270 skiers per hour

Snowboarding: Yes

Bed base: 5,000

Nearest lodging: 1/2 mile in Wilmington, about 9 miles in Lake Placid

Resort child care: Yes, 12 months and older

Adult ticket, per day: $48–$56 (02/03 price)

Dining:★★★
Apres-ski/nightlife:★★★
Other activities:★★★★★

Strictly in terms of skiable terrain, Whiteface would fall somewhere in the middle of the pack of Northeast resorts, but it more than compensates through its dramatic vertical drop: the biggest in the East at more than 3,400 feet. The surprisingly normal and quiet village has been host to two Winter Olympics, 1932 and 1980, and the 2000 Winter Goodwill Games. The memories these stir, combined with the plethora of winter sports activities available, set Lake Placid apart as a winter sports mecca.

From the moment you drive past the dramatic Olympic jumps, just south of the village, you know this isn't an ordinary winter vacation spot. The Olympic Regional Development Authority (ORDA) operates the multi-facility recreational area, and more world-class winter sports athletes still train and compete here than anywhere else in the free world. The extent of the facilities also attracts competitions in all of the Olympic winter sports, so athletes of all ages and abilities fill the town throughout the season, constantly renewing the village's Olympic atmosphere.

Like many Eastern mountains, Whiteface stands unshielded, lording over a vast valley of forests and frozen lakes. Its position makes for some of the most spectacular views in the world, but winter winds do whip across that valley and up the walls of Whiteface with regularity. For many veteran eastern skiers, the complaint about Whiteface has been that it's too often windblown, cold and icy. This is not just myth. The cylindrical building at the summit is a weather research center. Of course, you can't fault any area for bad weather, and on an ideal day, Whiteface comes close to being as good as it gets in the East, and spring here can be especially good.

Whiteface itself is not in Lake Placid at all, but nine miles to the northeast, officially in the town of Wilmington. Most visitors stay in Lake Placid because that is where the major action is. Apart from shops and restaurants galore, there is the Verizon Sports Complex, six miles to the southeast. Two other big draws: 31 miles of groomed cross-country trails and the bobsled run that offers a half-mile "adrenaline injection" for $40 a pop. For the uninitiated, bouncing off the walls here is not unlike being the pinball in a game played by unseen Nordic giants. Of course, no one in their right mind would want to experience firsthand the thrill of being launched off the 120-meter ski ramp at nearby Intervale, but you can get a breathtaking perspective on that madness by taking the elevator 26 stories to the observation deck at the top. The $8 ticket, thankfully, is round-trip.

Back on Main Street, the town itself is dominated by the arena where America watched its Cinderella hockey team enter the history books with the "Do you believe in miracles?" victory over the heavily favored Russian team in 1980. Wonderfully situated on Mirror Lake, Main Street makes up in charm and bustle what it lacks in quaint. For a relaxing afternoon, take a dogsled ride across the lake or a three-mile walk around. Daytime or evening, many people find both relaxation and exercise on the Olympic oval (where Eric Heiden won five gold medals), lulled into an easy rhythm by the sharp scrape of their skates over the quarter-mile loop. Another favorite is the nighttime toboggan slide down a floodlit ramp out onto the darkness of frozen Mirror Lake. A word of caution: Wear old clothes!

Mountain layout–Skiing

◆◆ **Expert** ◆ **Advanced**: Whiteface is proud of its challenging terrain and is looking for adrenaline seekers to give trails such as Cloudspin and Skyward, where the Olympic downhill races started, a try. For certifiable experts who don't mind a hike to truly challenging terrain, the Slides is the real deal on days when conditions permit. The black-diamond trails off Little Whiteface—Approach, Upper Northway, and Essex—are often left to bump up, providing accessible challenging terrain for advanced skiers. Whiteface has serious tree skiing, too—13 acres of black and double-black glades can be found off Little Whiteface Mountain.

■ **Intermediate:** Take the Cloudsplitter gondola from the base or the Little Whiteface double from the midstation to the top of Little Whiteface. An observation platform just off to the left at the top of this double chair gives you an unparalleled view of the lakes and valley. Then try the snaking Excelsior run, which twists back down to the midstation. You can cut the rounded corners of this baby like a bobsled, choosing your own pace. After that warm-up, tackle Paron's Run or The Follies from the tip-top of Whiteface (Summit Quad). Before this run was added several years ago, intermediates had no way to enjoy either the awe-inspiring view or best-in-the-East vertical available from the top of the mountain.

Whiteface has added a new high-speed quad this season that will service the novice and intermediate terrain on the mountain's lower half.

●● **Beginner** ● **Never-ever**: These levels have a secluded area, the Mixing Bowl. Novices and families will enjoy New Boreen trail, located below the midstation lodge and accessed by a high-speed quad. The run's average width is 100 feet over approximately a 2,200 foot length.

Mountain layout–Snowboarding

The Brookside terrain park offers a quarter mile of hits, table tops, rails, picnic tables and other varieties of airtime. Both the halfpipe and terrain park have proven to be quite attractive not only to snowboarders, but to the burgeoning freeskiing crowd as well. The halfpipe has hosted events such as the Winter Goodwill Games and the Paul Mitchell Board Frenzy Tour. When cruising down Excelsior run, keep up your momentum after the eighth and ninth corners so you can ride out the short flat.

Mountain rating

Whiteface is one of those rare mountains that has more to offer experts and beginners, with less in the middle range for true intermediates. Experts will find much of the upper half of the mountain challenging. Beginners will find almost everything accessed by the new quad much to their liking. Intermediates probably will feel bored by most of the lower half of the mountain and stretched by much of the upper but can push themselves into the advanced stage on Little Whiteface. Be ready for a variety of conditions. The mountain is high enough that winter conditions on the top can give way to mushy corn snow by the time you reach the bottom.

Cross-country and snowshoeing

Lake Placid stands as a major cross-country destination with 455 km. of trails. Foremost is the **Verizon Sports Complex** (523-2811), site of the Nordic and biathlon races during the 1980 Olympics. It has cross-country skiing you are unlikely to find elsewhere: 50 km. of marked trails that average 15 ft. wide, regularly groomed and patrolled; bridges built especially for cross-country skiers so you don't have to worry about traffic; snowmaking (5 km.); and emergency phones. The complex has 10 marked loops offering one expert, six intermediate and three novice tours with additional expert skiing on the Porter Mountain racing loops.

The **Lake Placid Resort** (523-2556) has 25 km. of trails and connects with the more secluded Jackrabbit Trail (ski conditions: 523-1365). The trail, 50 km. long, runs from Keene through Lake Placid and Saranac Lake.

Snowshoeing trails crisscross the entire **High Peaks Wilderness** area—get maps and advice at the local Eastern Mountain Sports Store on Lake Placid's Main Street or head to the Dewey Mt. Ski Center that offers snowshoe trails in addition to cross-country skiing. For a more controlled snowshoe experience complete with bonfires to roast marshmallows and educational stops on the trail, stop at the **High Falls Gorge** center. Here you can follow a marked trek around the Ausable River gorge and be welcomed back with complimentary hot chocolate or coffee. Just south of Whiteface, High Falls Gorge is something different for families. Reservations recommended on weekends (946-2278).

Lessons (2002/03 prices)

Group lessons: $30 for two hours, $50 for two four-hour lessons and $70 for three two-hour lessons.

Never-ever package: A two-hour group lesson with pass and equipment rental is $75 for skiers or riders for one day, $135 for two days and $315 for five days. It puts new skiers on the short skis called Snowblades and guarantees that in five days they'll be able to ski from the top of Little Whiteface.

The Parallel to Perfection program includes rentals, lifts and lessons. Cost is $99 for one day, $188 for two days; $425 for five days.

Private lessons: $70 an hour; $110 for two hours; $60 for an additional person.

Child care (2002/03 prices)

Ages: 1–6 years.

Costs: $30 per half day or $50 per day per child, with lunch included in full-day price.

Reservations: Recommended; call 946-2223.

Note: The expanded Bunny Hutch at Easy Acres is complete with a children's drop-off, adjacent parking for parents, a large nursery, children's rentals and an outdoor terrain garden. New this winter is a Magic Carpet lift.

Children's programs: Four-hour lessons for ages 7–12 are $89 with lunch and indoor supervision included. The Easy Acres and Family Learning Center has its own parking area, base lodge, lifts and trails and is completely separate from the main ski trails of Whiteface, although the lift and trail network allows parents to ski or ride to and from it.

Play 'n' Ski is for children ages 4–6. The drop-off area has adjacent parking. Half-day programs are $50. A full-day program costs $80 (including lunch). Reservations recommended. For more about the children's program, call 946-2223.

Lift tickets (2002/03 prices)

	Adult	Child (7-12)	Teen (13-19)/Senior (64-69)
One day	$56*	$29	$46
Three days	$150 ($50/day)	$81 ($27/day)	$127 ($42+/day)
Five days	$240 ($48/day)	$131 ($26+/day)	$207 ($41+/day)

Who skis free: Children aged 6 and younger when accompanied by an adult, and ages 70 and older.

Who skis at a discount: Active military pay $30 any day. Super Sunday Specials (Jan. 5, 26; March 2) pricing is $30 per adult and $15 for juniors. Ask about lodging packages. Holiday pricing is higher.   *Ski America & Canada estimate

Accommodation

Some of the larger hotels centered around the town of Lake Placid tend to be of the modern franchise variety. An important exception is the **Mirror Lake Inn** (523-2544; $$$$), a traditional lodge right on the lake shore that's probably the finest overnight in the area. The New England-style exterior continues inside with antiques, chandeliers and mahogany walls. The inn also has an indoor pool, whirlpool, sauna, health spa and game room. The two restaurants include one of the best in town, with candlelight dining overlooking the lake.

If snowshoeing or cross-country is your main interest or if you just want to experience the traditional Adirondack Lodge atmosphere, try the **Lake Placid Lodge** (523-2700; $$$$); it has cross-country skiing from the door. Expanded from an 1882 lodge, it is filled with the Adirondack twig-and-birch furniture and massive stone fireplaces and has lodge rooms, suites and separate cabins. A little more affordable are the **Mt. Van Hoevenberg Cabins** (523-9572; $$), with an outdoor sauna and a games room, and **Trail's End Inn** (576-9860; $-$$$), in Keene Valley, which has a hot tub.

The **Lake Placid Resort Holiday Inn** (523-2556 or 800-874-1980; $–$$$), in the town center, is Lake Placid's largest hotel. All 209 rooms have refrigerators and microwaves, and some have a Jacuzzi tub and fireplace. It has a large indoor pool and complete health club, cross-country trails and two restaurants, including one of the area's finest. The **Best Western Golden Arrow** (523-3353 or 800-582-5540; $$–$$$) is on the lake with spectacular views and has an indoor pool, Jacuzzi, sauna, weight room, and racquetball courts. Also boasting similar amenities is the **Lake Placid Hilton Resort** (523-4411 or 800-755-5598; $$–$$$), with two indoor pools and private balconies for each room with a view of the lake. The hotel's bed-and-breakfast package is quite popular. There are also a **Ramada Inn** (523-2587 or 800-741-7841; $–$$$) and a **Howard Johnson Resort Inn** (523-9555 or 800-858-4656; $$–$$$) in town.

Skiers on a budget should try the **Edge of the Lake Motor Inn** (523-9430; $$), **Art Devlin's Motor Inn** (523-3700; $$-$$$), **Town House Lodge by the Lake** (523-2532; $-$$$), **Alpine Air Motel** (523-9261; $–$$$), the **Econo Lodge** (523-2817; $–$$$), and the **Wildwood** on the Lake (523-2624; $-$$$).

If you want to stay right by Whiteface, book a room at the **Ledgerock** (946-2379 or 800-336-4754; $-$$$), a family-owned and operated 19-unit motel, right opposite the entrance to the mountain in Wilmington. The view from the spacious rooms looks just like the trail map.

Dining

For an upscale culinary treat in a quintessential Adirondack setting, head to the **Lake Placid Lodge** (523-2700; $$$$). If your wallet can't quite handle it, try just stopping in for an après-ski drink in the fireplaced bar overlooking the lake.

The **Great Adirondack Steak and Seafood Company** (523-0233; $$), right in the middle of Main Street, serves beer brewed on premises and honest hearty food.

Every Wednesday, January through March, the **Alpine Cellar** restaurant has a Bratwurst Night with traditional German fare and oom-pah-pah accordian music. Wash it all down with your choice of 80 different beers.

The **Charcoal Pit** (523-3050; $$-$$$) has been charbroiling steaks and chops for 25 years. **Veranda** (523-3339; $$), next to the Holiday Inn, has a great view to go with fine food.

Nicola's Over Main (523-4430; $$) has wood-fired pizza and a Mediterranean slant. **The Great American Bagel Factory** (523-1874; $-$$) is American-meal-on-the-fly with bagels, specialty coffee and sandwiches. On the way into the village, try the **Downhill Grill** for lunch (523-9510; $-$$). Its menu reflects the decor: old ski memorabilia and Mexican. No ski town is complete without an inexpensive Italian restaurant featuring pizza—**Mr. Mike's Pizza** (523-9770; $) takes care of that craving. Original soups and arguably the best burger in town can be found at **Cameron's Restaurant.**

In Wilmington, is the upscale and excellent **Hungry Trout** (946-2217; $$) specializing in, you guessed it, fish. In the same neighborhood is the **Wilderness Inn** (946-2391; $$-$$$), where steak lovers will want to try the sandwich on the bar menu.

Après-ski/nightlife

Lake Placid is large enough to generate its own heat as a nightlife center, drawing not only out-of-town vacationers but also the locals. Because Whiteface lies separated from the town, however, most of the après-ski action is in the base lodge. **Steinhoff's** and **R.F. McDougall's**, at the Hungry Trout just down the road from Whiteface, are also good for an après-ski drink.

Dining: $$$-Entrees $20+; $$-$10-20; $-less than $10.

Accommodations: (double room) $$$$-$200+; $$$-$141-$200; $$-$81-$140; $-$80 and less.

Late night, the young with dancing feet head to **Mud Puddles**, on the side street next to the speed skating oval. High-tech disco gear is on full display around the dance floor. Most of the other nightlife action centers around the main hotels. **Roomers**, next to the Best Western, the **Dancing Bears Lounge** at the Hilton and the **Zig Zag's** are popular spots along Main Street. The **Lake Placid Pub and Brewery**, with its downstairs companion **P.J. O'Neils**, is on Mirror Lake Drive, up from the speed-skating oval.

Anyone looking for a quieter, more middle-aged nightspot should head for **The Cottage,** across the street from the Mirror Lake Inn. The fire's always going, and the sunset view of the lake and mountains is postcard perfect. It also serves good burgers.

 ## Other activities

Lake Placid is nothing *but* other activities. The half-mile **bobsled rides** at Verizon Sports Complex (six miles from the village) are $40 per person and a must for any Lake Placid visitor. Just relax and enjoy; they provide a professional driver and a brakeman. Rides on the new combination bobsled/luge track are by reservation only (523-4436).

Tours of the **Olympic Jumping Complex,** with chair lift and elevator ride, cost $8 for adults, $4 for children and seniors. Hours are 9 a.m. to 4 p.m. **Tubing**, near the jumps, is offered when conditions and schedules permit. The **Olympic Speed Skating Oval** is open for public skating 7–9 p.m. daily and 1–3 p.m. on Saturdays and Sundays (523-1655). The cost is $5 for adults and $3 for juniors. Operating hours for the **toboggan run** on Mirror Lake are Wednesday, 7–9 p.m., Friday, 7–10 p.m., Saturday noon–4 p.m. and 7–10 p.m., and Sunday noon–4 p.m. The charge is $3 for adults, $2 for children, and $3 for the toboggan rental. The new **Lake Placid Winter Passport** includes a day of cross-country or snowshoeing and admission to the jumping complex, museums and public skating. The passport also qualifies you for a $10 discount on the half-mile bobsled ride and a 10-percent discount at the ORDA store.

Get into the real spirit of things by visiting the **Lake Placid Winter Olympic Museum,** with displays from the 1932 and 1980 Winter Olympics. It's open daily. Admission is $3 for adults and $2 for juniors. Call 523-1655 ext. 263 for more information.

 ## Getting there and getting around

By air: Continental commuter service serves Adirondack Airport, 16 miles away on Rte. 86 in Saranac Lake. Air-ground packages are being developed. Private planes can use Lake Placid Airport.

By train: Trains stop at Westport on the New York City–Montréal line. There has been a shuttle bus from the train station to the resort in the past, but in our experience this is not a convenient way to reach Lake Placid. If you plan to travel this way, ask the Lake Placid Visitors Bureau (phone number in the stat box). Amtrak has ski packages; call (800-872-7245; spells USA-RAIL) for more info.

By car: From the south, take Exit 24 (Albany) off the New York State Thruway (I-87). Take Northway (still I-87) to Exit 30, follow Route 9 north two miles to Route 73 and continue 28 miles to Lake Placid. From the west, take I-90 (NY State Thruway) to Exit 36 (Syracuse) for I-81. Follow I-81 north to Watertown, go east on Route 3 to Saranac Lake, then take Route 86 east to Lake Placid.

Getting around: It's about a 10-mile drive to both Whiteface and Mt. Hoevenberg from the center of Lake Placid. A free shuttlebus connects the town with the outlying facilities, from Christmas to Easter.

Québec City, Canada

Mont-Sainte-Anne, Stoneham, Le Massif

Québec City Facts

Address: Greater Quebec Area Tourism and Convention Bureau, 835, avenue Wilfrid-Laurier, Quebec (Quebec) G1R 2L3

ⓘ **Toll-free reservations:** (800) 665-1528

Dining:★★★★

Apres-ski/nightlife:★★★★★

Other activities:★★★★★

✆ **Area code:** 418

Phone: 649-2608

Fax: 522-0830

E-mail: bit@riq.qc.ca

World Wide Web: www.Quebecregion.com

Bed base: 11,200

Québec is a city that not only embraces winter; it celebrates it. Founded in 1608 by the French navigator, geographer and explorer Samuel de Champlain, Québec is the only walled city in North America north of Mexico. Perched atop a 350-foot-high cliff overlooking the St. Lawrence River, it immerses North American visitors in French history and culture, providing a taste of Europe without jetlag. As one of our contributors noted, it's like France without the attitude.

Drive down Grande Allée, enter Old Québec through Porte (gate) Saint-Louis and descend into the 18th century. The narrow streets are lined with stately old homes, many of them now gourmet restaurants and boutique hotels. You half-expect to see horse-drawn carriages clacketty-clacking along *les rues*. Don't worry if your French is rusty (or non-existent); almost everyone on the front lines of tourism speaks at least some English. And here's a real plus: Winter is low season in Québec City. With the exception of Winter Carnival weekends, lodging rates are at their lowest.

Although you may have the city to yourself in the low season, you'll feel a certain *joie de vivre*. Everywhere you turn there's an activity: tobogganing, sleigh rides, ice skating, ice climbing, snow rafting, dogsledding, cross-country skiing, you name it. Québec is alive with culture, too. The calendar is punctuated with festivals, and the city dotted with 27 museums. With more than 4,900 restaurants representing 85 different ethnic styles, the city is also renowned for its cuisine. Old Québec is home to over 100 restaurants, most of them excellent.

Beginning the last weekend in January, Winter Carnival is a 17-day party presided over by the jolly snowman ambassador Bonhomme. The world's biggest winter festival, *les Québecois* party in style. Nearly everyone wears the red, white and black sash that is the signature of Quebec, and the city is full of dancers, singers, bands, ice sculptures and parades. Perhaps the craziest, but most hotly contested, event is the canoe race across the ice-choked St. Lawrence.

Don't miss Québec's little Champs Élysées, Grande Allée, near the Parliament. Private homes once owned by judges and members of Parliament have been converted to discos, restaurants and other outlets for traditional nightlife. Cartier Avenue is great for shopping, and Petit Champlain, one of North America's oldest shopping streets, is lined with boutiques and galleries and feels like pure Europe. It can be reached by the funicular, a cable car straight down from outside Le Chateau Frontenac, for $1.50 each way.

Mt. Sainte Anne Facts

Summit elevation:	**2,625 feet**
Vertical drop:	**2,050 feet**
Base elevation:	**575 feet**

Expert:★★★★
Advanced: ★★★★
Intermediate: ★★★★★
Beginner: ★★★ Never-ever: ★★★★
Address: 2000, Beau Pre, C.P. 400,
Beaupre (Quebec) Canada G0A 1E0
✆ Area code: 418
Ski area phone: 827-4561
Snow report: (888) 827-4579 or 827-4579
Fax: 827-3121
ⓘ Toll-free reservations: (800) 463-1568 or (827-5281

E-mail: info@mont-sainte-anne.com
Internet: www.mont-sainte-anne.com
Number and types of lifts: 13–1 high-speed 8-passenger gondola, 1 high-speed quad with bubble cover, 1 high-speed quad, 1 quad, 1 triple, 2 doubles, 6 surface
Skiable acreage: 428 acres
Snowmaking: 80 percent
Uphill capacity: 18,560
Snowboarding: Yes
Bed base: 2,000
Nearest lodging: slopeside
Resort child care: Yes, 6 months-10 years
Adult ticket, per day: $39-$47 (02/03 prices without GST)

Mont-Sainte-Anne, the largest ski resort in eastern Québec, and Stoneham are about 30 minutes away, while Le Massif is a little less than an hour-long drive. Each resort has its own nearby lodging, though without the big-city activities. A three-area ticket, nicknamed Carte Blanche, offers skiers and snowboarders a multi-day, multi-destination ticket between Mont-Sainte-Anne, Stoneham and Le Massif for only US$30 per day, per adult (assuming the exchange rate holds). With Carte Blanche, visitors staying in downtown Québec City hotels can also use the Winter Express shuttle to get to the mountains for just a few dollars more.

Mont-Sainte-Anne

Drive east along the St. Lawrence, and you'll soon reach Mont-Sainte-Anne, Québec City's largest ski area. With 2,050 feet of vertical, it's impressive, big-mountain skiing with a lift system to match. Trails drop from summit to base at almost a constant pitch, with only a short run-out to the lift. The trail ratings aren't inflated here, and experts won't get bored; seven of the mountain's trails are true double diamonds, some with challenging bumps and/or glades, and 10 are F.I.S.-approved race trails. But this isn't to say beginners and intermediates will be intimated. There are plenty of wide cruising runs and gentle beginner trails spread across the mountain's three faces. All that and an excellent terrain park and monstrous halfpipe make it a good choice for all ability levels. In general, the slopes increase in difficulty as you move from east to west.

The South Side faces the St. Lawrence River, where all base facilities are located. It also bakes under the sun, so the snow is often heavier (or harder) here. The North Side, or the backside, has a high-speed quad and a small lodge. The West Side is dedicated to backcountry skiing and riding on natural snow.

Mont-Sainte-Anne's riverside location delivers plenty of snow, an average of 160 inches a year. When the wind whips up the river, though, it's a bone-chilling and damp cold, so go prepared.

This resort lets you get a good taste of winter Québecois-style. Don't miss the sugarhouse on the La Pichard trail, where you can taste such treats as maple sugar on snow. You can try paragliding, ice skating, snowshoeing or dogsledding, all served with a French accent. Mont-Sainte-Anne's cross-country center is the largest in Canada and second largest in North America.

Mountain layout—Skiing

♦♦ **Expert**: West of the gondola on the South Face is an expert's playground, with serious single- and double-black trails and glades. This is steep terrain with a continuous fall line. La Super S is long and smooth and steep; its evil twin, La S, is the same, but with bumps. For even more challenge, head into the woods on La Brunelle. Two lifts, La Trip, a triple, and La Sainte-Paix, a double, service this area. If you're hot in the bumps, strut your stuff on La Gondoleuse, under the L'Etoile-Filante gondola. For a backcountry experience, head to the West Side.

♦ **Advanced**: On the South Side, take La Crete to La Beauregard for a long, steep, fast cruise. These are two of the 10 FIS-certified race trails on the mountain. La Pionniere, just east of the gondola, has the feel of an old-style New England trail as it twists its way down the upper third of the mountain.

On the North Side, L'Archipel and La Surprenante are good choices. If you want to escape the crowds, take L'Amarok on the West Side, which is served only by a T-bar.

■ **Intermediate**: While experts and advanced skiers head west off the gondola, intermediates should head east (on the South Side), or over the top to the North Side. Warm up on Le Gros Vallon or La Beaupre on the South Side. Be sure to take at least one run on La Pichard to stop by the sugar shack for a maple-syrup treat. On cold days, ride either the gondola, L'Etoile-Filante, or L'Express du Sud, a high-speed quad with a bubble cover to shield the wind. Don't miss the North Side's great cruising trails and the intermediate-level glades, La Vital-Roy or La Sidney-Dawes. The snow is often softer here.

●● **Beginner**: The eastern edge of the mountain on both the South and the North sides is where you'll find the easiest trails. Take the gondola up, then work your way down La Familale on the South Side, L'Escapade and La Ferreolaise on the North Side, then return to the South Side on Le Chemin Du Roy, which wraps slowly and gently from the North Side summit to the South Side base. The Enchanted Forest, off Le Ferrelolaise, has enjoyable trails through the trees for beginners.

● **Never-evers**: Choose from three free surface lifts in the ski school area at the mountain's base. After mastering these, take the gondola to the summit and meander down the mountain's longest trail, Le Chemin du Roy.

Mountain layout–Snowboarding

Mt. Ste. Anne's 282,500-square-foot, mountain-top terrain park, La Grande Allée, is perfectly situated under La Tortue lift, a quad chair lift on the South Side. This is a fun park, with numerous jumps of varying types and difficulty, a few rails and a fun box. It's a good idea to take a run through to check the jumps before hitting them full speed, as many are not what they first appear. The park has a fairly mellow pitch, so you'll want to maintain speed; expect to miss some hits if you fall, as you'll need time to build speed again. The park is also home to Dragon's Cradle, a beginners' halfpipe. For serious air, head to the Dragon's Den halfpipe, which is designed according to World Cup standards and has been the site of World Cup events. Both halfpipes and the terrain park are lit for night riding.

Cross-country and snowshoeing

Superlatives are all one hears for the **Mont-Sainte-Anne Cross-Country Centre**, 7 km. from the downhill area. With 224 km. of trails through the Laurentian forest, this center is the largest in Canada, second only to California's Royal Gorge in North America, and not to be missed just for the *joie de ski* Canadians exude on cross-country trails.

The Mont-Sainte-Anne Cross-Country Centre has plenty of trails for all abilities. A choice of varying length trail loops make it easy to adjust your outing to your ability and stamina. Skating skiers will find a whopping 125 km. of trails groomed for them.

The area's base lodge has an extensive ski school, a small cafeteria, a waxing room and a cross-country boutique with rentals, which include a baby glider to pull along your youngster if you choose not to leave him or her at the Alpine area day care.

A day trip for the not-faint-of-heart is the trek along the powerline (Sentier du Versant Nord) to the base of the north side of Mont-Sainte-Anne Alpine area. Though it's about a 7 km. trek, all uphill, the reward is the superb scenery along the way and a nice lunch at the Chalet du Versant Nord. And then there's skiing downhill all the way back to the base lodge.

Mont-Sainte-Anne also has 20 km. of snowshoeing trails. Try the guided tours with a Swiss fondue dinner at La Crete summit lodge, on Tuesday nights.

Lodging opportunities at the cross-country area include the unique B&B, L'Auberge du Fondeur (827-5281; 800-463-1568) right on the trails, or the Ruisseau Rouge and Le Chaudron shelters along the trails. These rustic shelters each can accommodate up to eight skiers and are equipped with a woodstove so skiers can cook their own meals. Reservations are required (827-4561, ext. 408), but there is no charge for their use with purchase of a two-day or more ski pass.

Lessons (2002/03 prices in Cdn$ without GST)

Group lessons: Offered for age 15 and older. Two-hour session is $49 in the morning and $41 in the afternoon. For four days or more, there's a 10-percent discount off regular group rates.

Never-ever package: Discover Skiing is a three-step beginner program, with each lesson lasting 1.5 hours. Initiation is $51 and includes equipment and access to beginner slopes at the mountain's base. Discovery is $51 and includes equipment and a lift pass. Autonomy is $65 and includes equipment, lift pass and a bonus card. Discover Snowboarding is a two-step program, with each lesson lasting 1.5 hours. Rookie is $51 and includes equipment for one-half day and access to beginner slopes at the mountain's base. Liberty is $51 and includes equipment for a half day and a full-day lift pass. Beginners age 15 and older can also take the Three-Day Introduction to Snowboarding Camp for $230. It includes nine hours of instruction, equipment, lift passes for days two and three and a bonus card.

Private lessons: One person for one hour is $65; a second person or additional half hour is $42. First Tracks private clinics are offered on the Gros Vallon trail for intermediate and advanced levels. The cost is $61, for one or two, which includes access to the lift 15 minutes before it officially opens. Last Track private clinics are available after 3 p.m. for $61 for one or two. Neither the First or Last Tracks clinics are available during peak periods. Semi-private lessons are given in the afternoon for up to three people; $99 for two hours, $150 for three. A Pro for the Day is available for $222 for one student, $278 for two and $309 for three or more.

Special programs: Adult Head Tyrolia Snowsports Academy for intermediate level and better skiers. A morning session is $43, afternoon is $36, five-day membership is $199; includes access to all Snowsports Academy sessions and demo equipment. Check schedule to see which sessions are offered on each day. These include technical freeskiing, short turns, terrain adaptation, supervised GS gate training, gates with coaching, and carving.

Note: Prices have been rounded to the nearest whole dollar.

Child care [2002/03 prices in Cdn$ without GST]

Mont-Sainte-Anne's award-winning Children's Centre houses a nursery, day care, ski and snowboard lessons, Kinderski program, equipment rental, a trail reserved exclusively for children, indoor and outdoor playgrounds, a video and music hall and lunch.

Ages: 6 months to 10 years.

Cost: $45 per day for the first child in a family (the cost decreases by $5 for each additional child from the same family). Hourly rate is $10. Or $100 for four days.

Child care at Mont-Sainte-Anne is wisely split into two sections: the day care center for those ages 2-10 and the nursery for babies ages 6-24 months. Day care in the nursery without skiing is available for children 7 months-6 years. Open 9 a.m. (8:30 on weekends) to 4:15 p.m., the Children's Centre is in the same building as the Ski & Snowboard School (note: it is a bit of a climb for a little one). There is at least one caretaker for every three babies, who have their own nap, play and feeding area. The nursery can accommodate up to 12 children daily.

Older children can choose to just play indoors, or they can opt for an outside activity, which can include skating, sliding, skiing or a sleigh ride. Parents may also decide to enroll their child in the Youth Camp program to get them started in skiing.

Children's lessons: Children who are ready to try skiing on a limited basis can be enrolled in 5-STAR Camp, which includes day care, a 45-minute lesson, equipment, lunch and a Snowsports School T-shirt. Three year-olds can also be introduced to skiing without day care through a special 45-minute clinic. The cost for 5-STAR Camp is $67; the 3-year-olds 45-minute private lesson costs $36. (Prices rounded to nearest dollar.)

Youth Camp combines four hours of ski lessons for youngsters ages 4-6 years with lunch, arts and crafts, movies and daycare before and after the lessons, running from 9 a.m. to 4 p.m. Cost is approximately $70 per day, $60 per day for four days or more.

Adventure Camp is for ages 7-14 years and runs from 10 a.m. to 3 p.m. Children learn to ski or snowboard, exploring a variety of terrain, including an introduction to the Snowpark. Cost is $64 per day, $55 per day for four days or more.

The children in Youth and Adventure Camps have meeting areas separated by ages. All instructors speak both French and English.

Lift tickets [2002/03 prices in Cdn$ without GST]

Weekend prices:	Adult	Young Adult (14-22)	Child (7-13)
One day	$47	$37	$25
Three days	$129	$105	$69
Five days	$195	$162	$103

Who skis free: Children age 6 and younger. Beginners ski on three lifts at no charge.

Who skis at a discount: Seniors age 65 and older ski for Young Adult rates. Disabled skiers and riders also ski at a discount.

Note: Night skiing, half-day and other tickets are available. Ticket prices have been rounded to nearest dollar.

Accommodations at the resort

The suites at the full-service, ski-in/ski-out **Chateau Mont-Sainte-Anne** (800-463-4467 or 827-5211; $$-$$$$), next to the gondola base, is unfortunately starting to show its "crow's-feet" and could use some refurbishing. Rooms are spacious and all have balconies and kitchenettes; loft suites also have fireplaces. You'll find a health club, indoor pool, hot tub and sauna, restaurant and lounge here too.

The family-friendly **Hotel Val-des-Neiges** (888-554-6005 or 418-827-5711: $$-$$$) is five minutes from the base lodge (shuttles available to both Mt. Ste. Anne and Le Massif) and has an indoor pool, whirlpool and sauna, lounge with deli menu, dining room and full-service spa. The hotel has just finished a major renovation and has whirlpool baths in 48 of its 220 rooms. Fireplace suites and condos are also available. Ski packages with breakfast and dinner begin at $90 per person, per day.

For condominium lodging, try **Chalets Mont-Ste-Anne** (800-463-4395 or 827-5776; $-$$), next to the Chateau; the ski-in/ski-out **Village Touristique Mont-Ste-Anne** (800-463-7775 or 827-2002; $$-$$$); the Swiss-style **Chalets Montmorency** (800-463-2612 or 826-2600; $-$$$), 800 yards from the lifts and with a free shuttle; or the stone Québecois-style **Chalets Village** (800-461-2030 or 650-2030; $-$$$), each chalet with fireplace, double whirlpool or sauna and multiple bedrooms and bathrooms.

Dining

Le Colette (826-1963; $$-$$$) is an intimate restaurant specializing in French cuisine and game and **Café Suisse** (826-2184; $-$$) serves fondue, in St-Ferreol-les-Neiges. Snowshoe from the top of the gondola to **La Crete Lodge** (827-4561, ext. 0; $$$) for Swiss fondue on Tuesday nights. You ride the gondola to the summit, then snowshoe to the lodge for a fondue dinner. It's a great family activity.

In Beaupre: **L'Aventure** (827-5748; $-$$) is a lively bar and restaurant with an excellent view of the mountain. It serves an eclectic selection including Mexican and Italian favorites. The menu at **Le St-Bernard** (827-6668; $-$$) lists steaks, pizzas and pastas. **Auberge La Camarine** (800-567-3939 or 827-1958) serves progressive French cuisine.

Après-ski/nightlife

At Mont-Sainte-Anne, the place to head immediately after skiing is the **Chouette Bar**, in the main lodge at the base of the mountain. It has pool tables, music and dancing to a disc jockey. The **T-Bar** in Chateau Mont-Sainte-Anne is a good spot to stop later on for a relaxing drink in a more genteel atmosphere. On Wednesday through Saturday nights, entertainment is provided by a singer or musician.

Other activities

Mount-Sainte-Anne has a **skating** rink at the base. Skating, **dogsledding, paragliding** and **sleigh rides** can be arranged at the area. **Snowmobiling** and **karting** on ice are available nearby. For information on all, call 827-4561.

The Charlevoix region has deep roots in its Catholic religious heritage. In every parish you can visit the church of each village, but don't miss a trip to the spectacular **Basilica Sainte-Anne-de-Beaupré** (827-3781) on your route between Québec City and Mt. Ste. Anne.

Stoneham Facts

Summit elevation:	**2,075 feet**
Vertical drop:	**1,380 feet**
Base elevation:	**695 feet**

Fax: 848-1133
Internet: www.ski-stoneham.com

Expert ★
Advanced ★
Intermediate ★★★★
Beginner ★★★★
Never-ever ★★★★
Address: 1420, chemin du Hibou,
Stoneham, PQ, Canada G0A 4P0
✆ Area code: 418
Ski area phone: 848-2411
Snow report: 848-2415
ⓘ **Toll-free reservations:** (800) 463-6888

Number and types of lifts: 9-1 high-speed quad,
3 quads, 1 double, 4 surface lifts
Skiable acreage: 328 (daytime), 183 (nighttime)
Snowmaking: 86 percent
Uphill capacity: 14,200 per hour
Snowboarding: Yes, unlimited
Bed base: 500 at base;
10,000 in Quebec City, 20 minutes away
Nearest lodging: Slopeside
Resort child care: Yes, age 2 1/2 and up
Adult ticket, per day: S37 (02/03 CdnS w/o GST)

It's one of 20 pilgrimage shrines in Québec. The original burned to the ground in 1927. This replacement is magnificent, immense and there's a fair touch of whimsy in the floor tiles depicting the seven deadly sins.

Getting there

Take Rte. 138 from Québec City to St.-Anne-de-Beaupre, then Rte. 360 to the resort.

Stoneham

As you near Stoneham, don't be fooled. The resort is much larger than the few trails you see directly ahead. Thirty trails stretch across three mountains. The emphasis here is not on how big the vertical drops are (they range from 1,140 to 1,380 feet), but on how much terrain the connected mountains deliver. Known as more of a family resort, Stoneham has terrain for everyone, from double-diamond glades to leisurely cruisers. Advanced skiers on multi-day vacations will soon want to escape to Mont-Sainte-Anne or Le Massif. Kids will find a lot of activities to keep them occupied.

Situated in a sun-filled, wind-protected horseshoe valley, Québec locals head to Stoneham when the temperatures drop or the wind is howling. The emphasis here is on having fun, whether on the slopes or in the restaurants and bars. Don't let the very English sounding name of the mountain mislead you; Stoneham is *trés* French with many of its patrons speaking only French (most mountain personnel are bilingual, however). But that's good news, because as one regular Stoneham skier told our Ski America writer, "The French know about food, and they know about fun."

Part of the fun (or not) is figuring out the trail map. Stoneham shows four mountains on the map. Although locals refer to them by number, the map fails to list these numbers. One is the farthest to the left, followed by two, then four. Number six, with a potential vertical drop of 1,514, is detailed on the map, but the trails aren't cut nor is the lift in. All of this leaves one wondering: So what happened to three and five? This seemingly haphazard numbering also

Dining: SSS-Entrees $20+; SS-S10-20; S-less than S10. (CdnS)
Accommodations: (double room) SSSS-S200+; SSS-S141-S200; SS-S81-S140; S-S80 and less. (CdnS)

plagues the trails, which are numbered from 1 to 61. If you actually take the time to count, there are only 30 trails listed on the map.

Sixty percent of the mountain is lit every evening of ski season and that includes two colorfully lighted halfpipes and a snow-tubing area. With its party reputation, a visit for the nighttime skiing (because you'd *have* to stop for some refreshments afterwards) is a must for anyone on a ski vacation to the Québec City region. In fact, the resort is more crowded at night; 85 percent of the people on the hill are snowboarders!

Mountain layout—Skiing

◆◆ **Expert:** Experts will want to head straight for mountain four. Little grooming is done here, and the trails are steep, skinny and bumped. Trails 47, 48 and 49 are legitimate double blacks. They are left *au natural*, so you want to be on the look out for stumps, rocks and other such obstructions in lean snow years.

◆ **Advanced:** Stoneham is primarily a family mountain and even double-black-diamond trails 45 and 46, though steep, are easily maneuverable for upper-intermediate skiers. If you like glades, head for trail 19 (the black diamond 19, not the green circle 19).

■ **Intermediate:** The entire mountain is an intermediate's playground. Even the bump runs, glades and, as mentioned earlier, the groomed double-black-diamond trails should be tried and conquered. Undulating terrain and wide-open trails call for lots of top-to-bottom GS runs. For challenging fun, ski trails number 41 and 42, both are long with steep pitches that mellow then drop again for little adrenaline rushes.

●● **Beginner** ● **Never-ever:** Although considered a family mountain, Stoneham is surprisingly lean on true beginner terrain. Peaks one and two have a couple of top-to-bottom green-circle trails (trails 19 to 6 and 6 top to bottom), but even these have places that may challenge real beginners. But the wide-open area served by a quad and two Poma lifts right in front of the main base lodge gives a non-threatening place for beginners and never-evers.

Mountain layout—Snowboarding

Our Ski America riders loved Stoneham, which boasts an excellent halfpipe as well as plenty of terrain features. If you're experimenting with air, head to trail 9, where there's a full line of jumps. For more advanced hits and rainbow and kinked sliders, cut over to trail 18 and head down 7B to 7. More terrain features can be found on 4B.

For continuous fun, just do laps on the A quad, which accesses a beginner double barrel slider, some of the biggest hits on the mountain and the appropriately named Superpipe.

This park opens with three nice tabletop hits and a straight rail; all ideal for warming up for what's below. The next section of the park has a straight rail that leads into a kinked rail followed by a rainbow slider and finishes with a tabletop. The biggest thrills are at the park's base, where the hits are bigger—tables and rails, including an S rail—and where the mountain's well-maintained Superpipe is located. If you choose to ride the pipe, you miss a couple of the bigger tables. One plus, Stoneham grooms twice daily.

Sous Bois is a natural terrain park. This wide, long glade is full of little hits, chutes through the trees, rolling turns and a few gentle moguls.

Lessons [2001/02 prices in Cdn$ without GST]

Private lessons: $30 per hour for one plus $15 for each additional person; $51 plus $22 for a two-hour lesson; $79 plus $34 for a three-hour series; $129 plus $41 for a five-hour series and includes the lift ticket for the length of the lesson. Special equipment rental rates are available. A private one-hour lesson with equipment rental and lift ticket is $55 for skiers, $61 for snowboarders.

Group lessons: Adventure Package is an intensive four-hour lesson (from 10 a.m. to 3 p.m.) plus lunch with your instructor. These are prices for youths ages 7–17; adults are about 5 percent more. One day costs $49 without lift ticket and $57 with lifts; two-day are $91 without lifts and $106 with lifts; and five-day programs are $213 without lifts and $252 with lifts.

Note: All lessons are by reservation only, call 848-2415, ext. 537

Child care [2002/03 prices in Cdn$ without GST]

Ages: 1 month-12 years.
Costs: First child for one day is $25 with lunch, with the second child from the same family costing $20. The half-day prices are $15 and $12 respectively, and the hourly rate is $7 for infants 12 months and under, $5 for those over 1 year.
Reservations: recommended.

Day care has bilingual caregivers, but most of the children on any given day speak only French. Open from 8:30 a.m.–5 p.m., the center is located just a few steps from the main base lodge, but the walk to the actual skiing can be a bit of a trek for little ones. It has a large game room and separate sleeping and eating rooms, as well as a nifty adjacent outdoor playground. For those with young children, the day care center will arrange baby-sitting if you call ahead.

Children's lessons: Stoneham offers the Kid Island, a program to introduce young children to skiing. The program is offered three ways: half-day (8:30 a.m.–noon or 1 p.m.–5 p.m.), with a two-hour ski or snowbird lesson, equipment rental, a snack and daycare for $32; two-thirds day (8:30 a.m.-2 p.m., or 11 a.m.-5 p.m.), which is the same as half-day with lunch for $37; or full-day (8:30 a.m.-5 p.m.), with a pair of two-hour lessons, rentals, snacks, lunch and daycare for $48. Multi-day rates are available. For children just starting out, the ratio is two children per instructor, with never more than four children per instructor as the child progress. (Note: we've rounded prices up to the nearest dollar).

Lift tickets [2002/03 prices in Cdn$ without GST]

Weekend prices	Adult	Student (14-22/65+)	Youth (7-13)
One day	$37	$29	$17
Evening	$22	$19	$13
Three days	$108	$77	$45

Note: Because of night-skiing, Stoneham offers a variety of tickets including the longer day ticket (9 a.m.-6 p.m.), a day-to-evening ticket (12:30 p.m. - closing), a half-day (12:30-4:30) and an evening ticket (3 p.m.-closing). Consecutive multiday tickets include night skiing and may be bought to seven days.
Who skis free: Children ages 6 and younger.

Accommodations at the resort

The practical **Hotel Stoneham** is an anchor in the ski area's mini-village and offers 60 spacious rooms where children younger than age 18 stay for free when sharing a room with their parents. The ski area also rents out about 100 condos through Condominiums Stoneham. These vary in size from studios to four bedrooms and are located at the base of the slopes. Attractive ski-and-stay packages are available. (Example: two adults, two children for two nights in a hotel for $173.) Reservations at both hotel and condos may be made by calling 848-2411 or 800-463-6888.

If not staying slopeside, the best option is to stay in Québec City, although the nearby town of Ste-Foy (25-30 minutes away) offers a **Holiday Inn** (653-4901; 800-463-5241), a **Comfort Inn** (872-5038; 800-267-3837), the **Hotel Plaza** (658-2727; 800-567-5276), **Hotel Québec** (658-5120; 800-567-5276) and **Hotel Universel** (653-5250; 800-463-4495).

Dining

Try the cafeteria in the base lodge or Charlie's Grocery in the village, which offers freshly baked bread and cookies in addition to cold cuts, cheeses and some take-out. Lunch and light snacks are also available in **Le Bar Le 4 Foyers** (the bar of the four fireplaces) in the base lodge, a place for meeting people, dancing, and playing pool.

For more substantial dining, try **Le Pub St-Edmond**, more geared to night-time snacks after skiing than full meals; the Italian cuisine at **Le Capriccio** with 16 different choices of thin crust pizza including the Veniccia with smoked snails and oysters; and **Feu Follet**, with such exotic dinner offerings as bruchetta of alligator and ostrich ravioli, is also recommended for Sunday brunch. All of these options are within easy walking distance of each other in Stoneham's base village. See *Québec City dining* for some of the best dining choices.

Après-ski/nightlife

Because the base area is so small, it may be hard to believe that the Québecois leave Québec City and head here to have fun, but that's what they do. **Le Bar Le 4 Foyers**, a funky Irish pub, brings in a wide range of musical performers, including the requisite rock bands and a disco night on Thursdays. It serves basic pub fare and screens nonstop snowboard flicks on the TV. There's also a pool table in the back room. **Le Pub St-Edmond**, on the other end of the village (a five-minute walk), offers a little more mellow fare, with folk and oldies plus a wide selection of beers. Skiers will find that even with a language barrier—many of Stoneham's regular skiers speak no English—après-ski conviviality prevails, and trying to make your French understood after a few drinks is actually fun.

Other activities

Stoneham has three slopes that are specially equipped for **tubing**, with a lift and a cabin shelter and snack area designed for the enjoyment of this activity. **Ice skating** as well as an indoor **climbing wall** are available. For **snowmobiling**, go to Lac Beauport to Nord Tour (841-2810) for rentals.

Shopping: The mini-village has two small stores: Boutique Sports Alpins offers gifts and interesting ski items, and La Shop is for snowboarders.

Getting there and getting around

Stoneham is 20 minutes from Québec City via Hwy. 73 North, taking the Stoneham exit.

Le Massif facts

Summit elevation: 2,645 feet	**Toll-free reservations:** (877)-LeMassif (536-2774)
Vertical drop: 2,526 feet	**E-mail:** info@lemassif.com
Base elevation: 118 feet	**Internet:** www.lemassif.com
Expert: ★★★ **Advanced:** ★★★★	**Number and types of lifts:** 5–2 high-speed
Intermediate: ★★★	quad2, 1 double chair, 2 surface
Beginner: ★★	**Skiable acreage:** 220 acres
Never-ever: ★	**Snowmaking:** 75 percent
Address: 1350 Rue Principale, C.P. 47, Petite-Riviere-	**Uphill capacity:** 7,220 per hour
Saint-Francois, Quebec , Canada G0A 2L0	**Snowboarding:** Yes, unlimited
Area code: 418	**Bed base:** 873
Ski area phone: 632-5876; (877) 536-2774	**Nearest lodging:** one-half mile
Snow report: 632-5876; (877) 536-2774	**Resort child care:** Yes, 3 years and older
Fax: 632-5205	**Adult ticket, per day:** $42 (01/02)

Le Massif

Perched on the edge of the St. Lawrence River, Le Massif is a must-visit ski resort. From the moment you step out of your car at the new summit area — the most direct access to the resort from points west — you are struck with the awesome views and the resort's natural beauty. It's calm, quiet, peaceful. And the trails appear to just plunge 2,500 feet directly down into the ice-choked St. Lawrence, referred to as the sea, given its 10+-mile width here. As you ski or ride down La Petite Riviere, a classic first-run trail, a fishing trawler or cargo ship might pass silently right beneath you. Little wonder that Le Massif and its surroundings are located within a UNESCO World Biosphere Reserve. Le Massif's owners have honored this beauty by developing the area in harmony with nature. The three lifts are, for the most part, hidden in the trees, and the trails follow the natural fall lines of the three connected mountains.

Le Massif has the highest vertical drop east of the Canadian Rockies and, because of its riverfront location, it receives abundant snowfall. Legend has it that when the area's mascot owl, Le Grand Duc, circles, the area will receive at least 30 centimeters of snow within 48 hours. It is one of eastern Canada's great secrets, but not for long. In late 2001, Le Massif unveiled a spectacular summit lodge built to take advantage of the endless views up and down the St. Lawrence. In addition, the resort added a second high-speed chairlift, with midway loading. This lift serves new trails on Cap Maillard, including the La Charlevoix downhill racing trail. Le Massif is now site of Canada's national training center for downhill and Super G. The resort also added nine more trails and additional snowmaking and extended and improved the double chair.

When you visit, don't pack a lunch. The cafeteria food here is among the best and the most reasonably priced we've seen: On our last visit, we had escargot over angel hair pasta and Charlevoix sausage with fresh local cheeses.

Mountain layout—Skiing

◆◆ **Expert:** La "42," an ungroomed, natural-snow trail, snakes its way down the eastern edge of the mountain. It's punctuated with bumps, stumps, narrow chutes and steep drops, and clinched with the area's trademark jaw-dropping views of the St. Lawrence. Le Sous-Bois ("glades" in French) is relatively tame by comparison. La Tremblay, a single black, can be challenging since it's rarely groomed. For a short, steep thrill, take the plunge on La Pointue.

Le Massif's expansion added a new peak with a summit that was built up using rocks dug out of a nearby lake. We understand why this peak was chosen for a new Canadian Alpine Team training trail. The trails here boast a sustained pitch that quickly accelerates you to rocket speed as you hurtle toward the river, so don't let their single-diamond designation deter you from testing them. Le Charlevoix is the training trail and the peak's only double-diamond run.

♦ **Advanced** ■ **Intermediate**: With nary a bump in sight, this mountain is nirvana for cruisers. The black diamond and blue square designations seem almost arbitrary. Three-fourths of the runs are meticulously groomed, and only occasional steep pitches give pause to an intermediate skier. The runs are long (2.36 miles, the longest), so rest stops allow for spectacular views of the ice-capped St. Lawrence. Concentrate your efforts on the middle quad chair, Le Grande-Pointe Express, for the best vertical and choice. La Petite Riviere, a blue, is a sweet way to launch your day with spectacular drop-dead views of the river.

●● **Beginner:** New beginner trails have been added off the double chair according to the trail map. However, the leap from never-ever to intermediate is a big jump, and Le Massif really doesn't have good beginner terrain for those who need to practice wedge turns. Trails that start out fine for beginners all finish along narrow trails where upper level skiers race back to the lift. It is unsettling.

● **Never-ever:** Previously, we recommended that never-evers avoid this mountain and that only adventurous beginners consider it. But Le Massif has added a new never-ever area with its own surface lift near the summit day lodge.

 ## Mountain layout–Snowboarding

Le Massif is ideal for carving deep arcing turns. For bumps and trees, ride the double lift, chair B, and yo-yo on Le Sous Bois and La Tremblay. Le Massif has two terrain parks, one on La Grande Pointe and the other at the bottom of L'Ancienne. However, La "42" and Le Sous-Bois are natural terrain parks. There is no halfpipe. Early in the season, the traverse over to the new high-speed quad, lift C, is a miserable hike.

 ## Cross-country and snowshoeing

Le Massif is developing a new cross-country network at the top of the ridge, about a mile behind the new ski lodge with a base on the access road from Québec City.

For those staying in the Malbaie area, the 160 km. of cross-country and snowshoeing possibilities are extensive and well developed in the **Parc Regional du Mont Grand-Fonds**. Trails for every level of cross-country skier loop around lakes and past four chalets where skiers can rest and imbibe.

Lessons (2002/03 prices in Cdn$ with GST)

Group lessons: Includes two-hour lesson, lift ticket and equipment rental for the day; $35 for skiing, $55 for snowboarding.

Private lessons: Many options are available. A two-hour lesson with lift ticket and equipment rental for the day is $55 for skiing, $64 for snowboarding. A one-hour private lesson is $39, plus $15 for each additional person. Two consecutive hours is $69, a three-hour booklet is $109. A five-hour booklet is $165.

Special programs: A 2.5-hour adaptive lesson for handicapped skiers including lift ticket and equipment for the full day is $36. A companion skis for free.

Child care (2002/03 Cdn$, with GST)

Ages: Ages 6 months-10 years.

Cost: The full-day program with lunch runs from 8:30 a.m.-4:30 p.m. and costs $20; half-day (8:30 a.m.-12:30 p.m., or 12:30 p.m.-4:30 p.m.) is $14. Hourly day care is available for $7; a separate lunch can be bought for $5.

Reservations: Required; call 632-5876 or 1-877-LeMassif (536-2774). Le Massif has a new day care center in its new mountaintop lodge. It comprises one large room and can handle 21 children. Comfortable furniture is set about, and a crib area is condoned off by curtains. Equipment rental is located across the hall.

Children's lessons: A semi-private lesson can be added to the day-care program; the one-hour, morning or afternoon session costs $15.

The resort has a new beginners' area that's convenient to the children's room, and the introductory Iniski ($35) or snowboarding Inisurf ($44) program includes a two-hour lesson, lift ticket and equipment rentals for the day; lessons are at 10 a.m. and 1 p.m. Special four-day programs for ages 7-16 years are offered from 10 a.m.-3 p.m. during holiday periods for $99.

Lift tickets (2001/02 prices Cdn$ without tax)

Weekend	Adult	Young Adult (17-23)	Child (7-16)
One day	$37	$30	$31
Three day	$100	$82	$57
Five day	$151	$123	$86

Who skis free: Children ages 6 and younger.

Who skis at a discount: Ages 55 and older ski at young adult rates.

Note: Rates are rounded to the nearest dollar.

Accommodations and dining near the resort

Le Massif offers skiing packages at bed and breakfasts, inns and motels as well as chalets and villas in nearby towns; most also include dinner for guests and are also open to the public for dinner, which is why we've combined dining and lodging in one section.

Baie-Saint-Paul, with a population of about 6,000, is the largest town and offers the best variety of dining and lodging as well as nightlife. For regional information, call (800) 667-2276. Good choices here are: **Maison Otis** (435-2464 or 800-267-2254; $$$-$$$$) pampers guests with one of the region's best dining rooms, a full-service spa, a cozy lounge, a lively pub and even a discoteque. It also has an indoor pool, saunas and whirlpool tub. Rooms vary greatly, from cozy to sprawling; some with fireplaces and hot tubs. Rates include a choice-of-menu breakfast and a four-course dinner. **Auberge La Grande Maison** (800-361-5575 or 435-5575; $$-$$$), built in 1913, was previously a hospital and is now a charming bed and breakfast run by a local family. **Auberge La Pignoronde** (888-554-6004 or 435-5505; $$-$$$) sits on a hillside overlooking the town and bay and is some of the closest lodging to Le Massif. This charming inn, with a good restaurant and an indoor pool, is a good choice for families. A variety of meal plans are available. **Le Saint-Pub Microbrasserie Charlevoix** (240-2332; $-$$) brews its own beers and serves a menu that includes pasta and seafood.

La Malbaie, 45 minutes east of Le Massif, has an excellent selection of chic lodging as well as a small ski area, Grand Fonds (see nearby skiing, below). The grandest lodging is at **Le Manoir Richelieu** (665-3703 or 800-866-5577; $$$$), a four-star, five-diamond Fairmont resort with all the amenities you would expect, as well as a casino and full spa. Other on-site activities include cross-country, snowmobile and snowshoe trails, a skating rink, sleigh rides and dogsledding. The resort sits on the bank of the St. Lawrence River, providing magnificent views from many rooms. Le Manoir offers ski packages with Air Canada that include tickets at Le Massif and/or Mont Grand Fonds.

Auberge des 3 Canards (665-3761; 800-461-3761; $$$–$$$$) just down the hill from the Manoir Richelieu, rivals its larger and more famous neighbor. All rooms have spectacular views to the river and its acclaimed dining, prepared by long-time Chef Eric Betrand from Strasbourg, France, has won numerous awards. Deluxe rooms come with Jacuzzis for two and a fireplace. The manager, Guy Lépine, is one of the finest hoteliers we have encountered.

L'Auberge des Peupliers (888-282-3743 or 665-4423; $$$-$$$$) sits high atop a hill overlooking the St. Lawrence River and is one of the oldest guesthouses in the Charlevoix region. Rooms are a pleasant mix of antique and rustic, but include all the modern amenities you're accustomed to having. Sauna and indoor Jacuzzi, plus spa services available upon request. Breakfast and a five-course gourmet regional dinner prepared by a renowned chef are included.

One of the best reasons to visit Canada in the winter is to get low-season rates at high-end resorts. One such place is the Relais & Chateaux property **La Pinsonnière** (800-387-4431 or 665-4431; $$-$$$$), a charming country inn hugging the shore in La Malbaie. Impeccable service, fine cuisine and a flair for romance define its character. Here you can dreamily relax with a special Valentine package offered throughout February: two nights, a continental breakfast in bed, a five-course dinner, champagne, oil massages, and a gift. Dinner might be extra tender lamb raised locally as a specialty of the house, accompanied by libations from the 12,000-bottle wine cellar of mostly French wines. A most impressive collection of masterpieces from regional artists hangs on the walls of the dining room and throughout the inn.

Other activities

The Charlevoix region is a paradise for outdoor activities. **Snowmobiling** is extremely popular here, as is **dogsledding**. Your hotel should be able to make arrangements. The Fairmont Manoir Richelieu has a **casino** and **spa.** Spa services are also available at the Centre Santé Beauté Francine Thibeault, in Baie-Saint-Paul (435-6028).

Take a **scenic drive** along the St. Lawrence River from Pointe-au-Pic to Baie-Saint-Paul, through St. Irénée, known for the famous music academy Le Domaine Forget, and its river beaches. A spectacular descent brings you to the tiny 200-person town of Saint-Joseph-de-la-Rive, where a free ferry plies the route to Isle-aux-Coudres. Try the pastries at Boulangerie Laurentide, visit the Maritime Museum and see handcrafted papermaking at Papeterie Saint-Gilles. In Baie Saint-Paul, stop at the La Laiterie Charlevoix, where you can see cheesemaking in process and purchase fresh cheese. A must-top for chocoholics is the Chocolaterie Cynthia, on rue St. Jean-Baptiste (240-2304). For a break, enjoy lunch at surprising Joe's Deli Bar Smoked Meat, where the sandwiches are massive and tasty (and Joe is friendly and speaks English).

The Charlevoix region's magnificent scenery and intriguing lights attracts many important painters. Dozens of **art galleries** dot the entire route from Malbaie. Baie-Saint-Paul has 20 galleries, although not all are open in winter. Many artists are represented at Galerie d'Art Iris, 30 rue St. Jean-Baptiste. La Maison de René Richard is worth a visit to see the development of one of Canada's most renowned artists. Le Centre d'Art has changing exhibits. Guy Pacquet often opens his home studio to visitors; the views are breathtaking, the artwork spectacular.

Nearby skiing

Parc regional du Mont Grand-Fonds, La Malbaie, Charlevoix (Quebec); (418) 665-0095

Internet: www.quebecweb.com/montgrandfonds
1 quad, 2 T-bars; 14 trails; 1,095 vertical feet

Mont Grand Fonds, located just 15 minutes from Le Manoir Richelieu, skis bigger than it actually is. Crowds are rare, which is a good thing since there's only one quad and one T-bar. The atmosphere is laid back, the views over the St. Lawrence are terrific, and the trails were cut for maximum sun exposure. Trails to the right of the lifts, as you look up at the mountain, are primarily intermediate, with a few gentle beginner trails, while those to the left provide more challenge. Glades start out open and inviting, but get tighter and steeper as you descend. This is an excellent family mountain, and its proximity to the fabulous Manoir is ideal. With the exception of glades cut down the center of the mountain this is a piece of cake. **Note:** Lifts open at 10 a.m. on weekdays, 9 a.m. on weekends. There is no day care available at the area. Grand Fonds also has 160 km. of groomed cross-country trails with four heated warming huts and a special bird-watching area.

Lift tickets (01/02): Adults, $30; Student (16–22), $22; Child (6-15) $20. Half-day rates available.

Distance from Québec: 90 miles via Rte. 138.

Lodging information: See Manoir Richelieu, above.

Getting there

Le Massif is 45 miles east of Québec City on Rte. 138.

Québec City Accommodations

Le Chateau Frontenac (800-441-1414 or 692-3861; $$-$$$$), perched on the edge of the Cap Diamant promontory in Old Québec's upper town, is the grande dame of Québec City. It is historic, formal, elegant and full-service. Rooms vary greatly, from small to spacious, some offering magnificent views of the St. Lawrence. Most packages here include the hotel's bountiful buffet breakfast, enough to fuel you through most of the day. Ask about the skiing package, which includes breakfast, lodging and lift tickets for two. The hotel has a health club with indoor pool and a full-service spa. Also full service are the **Québec Hilton** (800-445-8667 or 647-2411; $$-$$$$), and **Hotel Loews Le Concorde** (800-235-6397 or 647-2222; $$-$$$$), both in old Québec, but outside the city walls.

Some of the top hotels in town are termed boutique hotels. The following five, all in the Vieux-Port area, are among the city's best places to stay.

Hotel Dominion 1912 (692-2224; $$-$$$), perhaps the best of the lot, is ultra modern yet hidden in an old factory. Glass showers and sinks highlight the bathrooms, and the beds

Dining: $$$-Entrees $20+; $$-$10-20; $-less than $10. (Cdn$)
Accommodations: (double room) $$$$-$200+; $$$-$141-$200; $$-$81-$140; $-$80 and less. (Cdn$)

are covered with mounds of down. The spacious rooms have Bose Wave Radios and 27-inch TVs. Breakfast is a non-stop Continental affair.

The intimate **Auberge Saint-Pierre** (888-268-1017 or 694-7981; $$-$$$) is built in a 1821 buiding that once housed an insurance company. It has original brick and mortar walls, steam-heat radiators and bathrooms that were once safes. A full, hot breakfast from the menu is included in the rates.

The **Auberge Saint-Antoine** (888-692-2211 or 692-2211; $$-$$$), in a restored 19th-century maritime warehouse, is an elegant retreat offering warmth and intimacy. Some rooms have river views. Rates include an extravagent continental breakfast and 24-hour snacks. For a real kick, reserve the James Bond suite.

Hotel Le Clos Saint-Louis (694-1311; $$-$$$) is a romantic 25-room hotel filled with period antiques. Rooms are spacious, each with private bath, and the hotel, built as a stately home in 1844, opens directly onto one of the old city's main streets (two blocks from Le Chateau Frontenac). Continental breakfast included.

Hotel Le Priori (692-3992; $$-$$$) has small rooms but much larger suites.

Small hotels within the city walls are the **Hotel Clarendon** (888-554-6001 or 692-2480), the **Hotellerie Fleur-de-Lys** (800-567-2106 or 694-0106; $$$-$$$), and the **Manoir de l'Esplanade** (694-0834).

Hotel La Maison Acadienne (800-463-0280 or 694-0280; $-$$) serves a Continental breakfast and also has packages with Mont-Sainte-Anne.

The recently renovated **Hotel Manoir Victoria** (800-463-6283 or 692-1030; $-$$$), in the old city, is a good choice for families. Also popular with families is **L'Hotel du Vieux-Québec** (800-361-7787 or 692-1850; $$-$$$).

Auberge Louis Hébert (525-7812; $$), on the Grande Allée, the heart of Québec City's nightlife, also has a good restaurant. Prices for the 8 rooms and 4 salons start at $95 for two, including breakfast. As is true of much of old Québec, the comforts are modern within 17th-century walls.

Small inns and bed and breakfasts are clustered around the Frontenac and offer simple rooms, usually with breakfast, at affordable rates. Try the **Hotel Manoir de la Terrasse** (694-1592 $), the **Manoir Ste-Genevieve** (694-1666 $-$$) or the **Chateau Bellevue** (800-463-2716 or 692-2573 $-$$)

Three hostels provide bottom-dollar lodging: **Centre International de Séjour de Québec** (694-0755, $), which has a cafeteria and 243 beds in 8- to 12-bed dormitories; **Auberge de la Paix** (694-0735; $), which has 14 rooms with two to eight beds, a kitchen and where rates include breakfast; or **Association du YWCA de Québec** (683-2155; $), with shared bathrooms, swimming pool and self-service kitchen.

For something completely different, consider one night at the new **Ice Hotel** (www.icehotel-canada.com; $$$). Constructed and furnished completely of snow and ice, this hotel, a sister to the original ice-hotel in Sweden, opens in January and closes approximately three months later, when it melts. Guests are provided with sleeping bags guaranteed to keep them warm to 30-degrees below zero. Other amenities include a cinema, two art galleries, an ice bar and heated bathrooms. Rates include breakfast — in a warm restaurant.

Québec City dining

You have to work to get a bad meal in this city. Almost all restaurants post their menu outside the door, and most include a *Table d'hote*, or set menu, usually with appetizer, entrée and dessert, for a fixed price.

For traditional Québecois cooking like *grandmere* used to make—pea soup, onion soup, meat pies, fish and game dishes and for dessert, maple syrup pie—dine at **Aux Anciens Canadiens** (692-1627; $$$). Five cozy dining rooms on two floors have been built in one of the oldest houses in the city, Maison Jacquet. The building was constructed between 1675-76 with thick stone walls, wainscoting and recessed cupboards. The lunch menu (normally less than $15) is served from noon until 6 p.m. making for an affordable and hearty early supper for skiers returning from the slopes.

Next door, **Restaurant Continental** (694-9995; $$$-$$$$) prepares Québec's only true upscale French cuisine with flambé tableside service. The other top spot in the upper old town is **Le Saint-Amour** (694-0667; $$$$).

One of our favorite restaurants in Vieux-Québec is **Auberge du Trésor** (694-1876; $$-$$$) which serves mussels (*moules*) that were the best we've eaten this side of the Atlantic Ocean. For more than 45 years, **Au Cafe Suisse** (694-1320; $$) has been serving Swiss fare, such as fondue, raclette and grillades. **Au Parmesan** (692-0341; $$), with an accordianist and lots of singing locals, serves Italian meals. **Restaurant Gambrinus** (692-5144; $$-$$$), overlooking the Place d'Armes, is an excellent Italian restaurant with a French flair and good seafood. A strolling musician performs at night.

There's no graffiti at **Graffiti**, (1191 Cartier Ave; 529-4949; $$-$$$), but an eclectic array of art adorns the brick and warm wood walls. French and Italian cuisine make up the two menus—à la carte and table d'hote. Don't miss the apple tart with maple sauce, a to-die-for house specialty. Brunch in the atrium room is a popular Sunday event. We're told this is one of the city's best, and after dining here, we won't argue the point.

Two restaurants, in the Vieux-Port neighborhood, also vie for best in Québec: **Initiale** (694-1818; $$$$) and **Laurie Raphaél** (692-4555; $$$$).

Also in the same Vieux-Port area you'll find the more casual art deco **L'Echaudé** (692-1299; $$-$$$) serving nouvelle French cuisine, and **Cafe du Monde** (692-4495; $$), with its bistro atmosphere and affordable wines, which fills with locals each evening. **Piazzetta** (692-2962; $-$$) only steps away is an inexpensive choice for creative focaccio and pizzas (we loved the apple and pork pizza).

Rue Petit-Champlain has several good eateries. **Marie-Clarisse** (692-0857; $$$), at the base of the funicular and the bottom of the Breakneck Stairs, is well respected for fish and seafood. **Cochon Dingue** ($$) offers a wide-ranging, bistro-style menu in a busy atmosphere and serves excellent breakfasts. Kids under 10 pay $5 for a complete meal. Try the Mussels Extravaganza for $20.95. Pastas begin at $18.95. There are now three Cochon Dingue restaurants: 46, boul. Champlain (692-2013); 46, René-Lévesque O. (523-2013); and 1326, av. Maguire (684-2013). **Le Petit Cochon Dingue** (OK, Cochon Dingue means Crazy Pig; 694-0303) is a traditional pastry shop with a bakery, café and sandwich shop. The donuts are, well, old-fashioned, and you can't beat the raisin buns anywhere. **Le Lapin Sauté** (692-5325; $$) is popular for breakfast but avoid it for dinner.

In the old train station, Gare du Palais, **l'Aviatic Club** (522-3555; $$$) looks like an officers' mess and serves specialty foods from five continents. The Tex-Mex is quite good and theThai food and sushi are good sellers. Stay awhile and join the nightlife.

Dining: $$$-Entrees $20+; $$-$10-20; $-less than $10. (CdnS)
Accommodations: (double room) $$$$-$200+; $$$-$141-$200; $$-$81-$140; $-$80 and less. (CdnS)

Le Café du Monde (692-4455; $$), in the lower town, is a chatty bistro with a fine menu. We suggest the mussels followed by either chocolate mousse cake or apple rum cake.

Along the Grande Allée, start the night with dinner at **Louis-Hébert** (525-7812; $$-$$$) and you'll be well situated to enjoy this street's hearty nightlife afterward. This is where the cognoscenti dine...the Members of Parliament, the crème de la crème. The service is exquisite, as is the food. Allow a long evening for your dining experience and don't be afraid of asking for special plates. There is also a swell boutique hotel above the cookery. Take in a view of the whole city from **Astral** (647-2222; $$$), the revolving restaurant atop Loews Le Concorde hotel. It takes about one hour for it to make a complete circle. A buffet is served every Saturday night, and the Sunday brunch is in a class of its own. Reservations are a must. If you're holding out for a carbo feed, head to the **Place du Spaghetti** (694-9144).

La Maison de Serge Bruyere (694-0618; $-$$$) houses three restaurants under one roof. The most famous, **La Grande Table**, has four-diamond fine dining. The others are the **Bistro Livernois** and the **Cafe Bruyere**.

For simple, Mediterranean-style fare, head to **Freres de la Cote** (692-5445; $-$$), a lively restaurant with an open kitchen and wood-burning ovens. **Portofino Bistro Italiano** (692-8888; $-$$), in the center of Old Québec, is a good choice for pizza. The Pizza Grizzly (with smoked salmon) is particularly tasty.

If you're a bit adventurous, visit a **sugar shack**: Follow signs for a *cabane a sucre*. Most open only when the sap is running. The fare usually includes crepes, eggs, meat pies, meats, toast, baked beans, all topped with maple syrup and flavored with music and dancing.

 # Québec City Après-ski/nightlife

Québec City has so much to offer you could spend most of your ski vacation in the city without even venturing to the slops. We've selected just a sampling of what you can do.

On the Terrasse Dufferin there is a not-to-be-missed, exciting **toboggan** ride that is open most days from 11 a.m to 11 p.m. Cost is only $1.50 per rider. You can **ice skate** for $5 per hour with skates at a rink nearby.

The **funicular** (692-1132) is the shortest link between Dufferin Terrace at the Château Frontenac and Quartier Petit-Champlain in the lower city. This landmark and unique transportation vehicle provides commanding views of the St. Lawrence River. It is wheelchair accessible. Take a **ferry ride** across the river for a spectacular perspective of the walled city. It leaves every half hour during the day and every hour at night (644-3704).

The frozen falls at **Montmorency Falls Park** (663-3330) are one-and-a-half times higher than Niagara Falls. Cable cars, bridges lookouts and trails make it possible to get close to the falls. For **ice climbing**, L'Ascension (647-4422) rents equipment and provides guides.

At Village Vacances Valcartier (844-2200), 20 minutes north of the city, **go snow rafting, sliding** and **tubing** on 38 slides; **skate** through a forest; **race go-karts** on an ice-covered track; **snowmobile, ride horseback, dogsled** or take a **sleigh ride**.

In the city, you can **cross-country ski** on the Plains of Abraham (649-6476 for information, 648-4212 for trail conditions) or **snowshoeing** or take a **sleigh ride** (687-0707). Duchesnay Station Ecotouristque, surrounding the Ice Hotel, 20 minutes north of Québec, has 150 km. of cross-country trails that wind almost exclusively through evergreens. Side-by-side tracks make cross-country for couples enjoyable. In the spring a stop at the sugar house is a good time.

The Greater Québec area is home to 1,512 km. of **snowmobile trails**. For rentals and guided tours, try Laurentides Sports Service Inc., in Charlesbourg, 849-2824; Location S.M. Sport, in Loretteville, 842-2703; or Dion Moto, 337-2776.

The history and culture of the region is captured in many museums and interpretation centers throughout Old Québec City. Begin with a three-site ticket ($8.50) for the **Musée de la Civilisation** (85 rue Dalhousie, 643-2158), **Musée de l'Amérique Française** (2 côte de la Fabrique, 692-2843) and **Centre d'Interprétation de Place-Royale** (27 rue Notre-Dame, 646-3167). You'll be swallowed up in human adventure, the origins of the French-speaking world and 400 years of Place-Royale — the first permanent French settlement in North America established in 1608. (Winter hours,10-5 Tues.-Sun., admission is free every Tuesday). Also worth visiting: **Musée du Québec** (643-2150), the national art gallery partly housed in a former prison annexed to the 1933 museum by a glassed-in space (open until 9 pm on Wed.); **Musée du Fort** (692-2175) with a sound and light show on the famous battles of the city; and **Musée d'art Inuit Brousseau** (694-1828), the first museum dedicated exclusively to Inuit art and culture. The **Citadelle** (694-2815) is the largest military fortification in North America still occupied by regular troops and the official residence of Governor General of Canada. It was built in 1820-1832 to protect the city from invaders.

The narrow streets of Le Quartier Petit Champlain, in Vieux Québec, are lined with ancient stone buildings housing boutiques with traditional and contemporary Canadian artwork, crafts, clothing and more. Artists sell their work on pedestrian alleyway, Rue du Trésor, off Place d'Armes. The Galeries de la Capitale not only has 250 shops, but an amusement center. Boutique Metiers d'Art at 29, Notre-Dame, has a vast collection of local and regional art. Potenciel L'Art de la Table, 27 Petit Champlain, is a cook's heaven of upscale tools, cookbooks and trinkets for the kitchen. Zazu Boutique, 31, Petite Champlain, just down the narrow street, features one-of-a-kind Montreal and Quebec designer woman's clothing, such as hand-stitched parkas and coats with fur hoods and fashionable outer clothing for the below zero temperatures in Quebec.

Getting there and getting around

By air: Jean-Lesage International Airport in Québec city is served by Air Canada, Continental, Air Atlantic, American Airlines, Air Transat and Air Canada. HiverExpress operates a winter shuttle from the airport to the city for $24.50 each way; or take a cab, call 525-5191; or rent a car.

By car: Stoneham is 20 minutes from Québec City via Hwy 73 North, taking the Stoneham exit. To get to Mont-Sainte-Anne, take Rte. 138 from Québec City to St.-Anne-de-Beaupre, then Rte. 360 to the resort. It's about a half hour away. Le Massif is 45 miles east of Québec City. Take Route 138 to Petite-Riviere-Sainte-Francois, then follow signs to Le Massif.

Getting around: For those without a car, the HiverExpress runs shuttles from downtown hotels to Mt. Ste. Anne from mid-November to April. It costs $22 round trip or $17 one way; call 525-5191. Shuttles leave Québec city at 8:30 a.m. and return around 4:30 p.m. For the return trip, shuttles leave the ski area at 9:30 a.m. and return at 3:30 p.m. Thursday to Sunday there is an additional departure from Québec at 10:30 a.m. Reservations are compulsory (before 7 a.m. on the day of the trip) and may be made through your hotel. Shuttles to Stoneham also are offered; and another shuttle connects at Mt. Ste. Anne to Le Massif. The Orleans Express operates between Mont-Sainte-Anne and Québec City on Fridays, Saturdays and Sundays; phone 525-3000.

Eastern Townships, Canada

Mont Orford, Mont Sutton
with Owl's Head and Bromont

Eastern Townships Facts

Eastern Townships Tourism Association
Address: 20, rue Don-Bosco Sud,
Sherbrooke (Quebec) J1L 1W4
Email: tce@tourisme-cantons.qc.ca
Internet: www.tourisme-cantons.qc.ca
Phones: (819) 820-2020, (800) 355-5755
Fax: (819) 566-4445

Quebec Tourism:
Address: P.O. Box 979,
Montreal, (Quebec) H3C 2W3
Email: info@tourisme.gouv.qc.ca
Internet: www.tourisme.gouv.qc.ca.
Phones: Canada and US, 1-877-BONJOUR
(1-877-266-5687); France, 0-800-90-77-77;
Belgium, 0-800-78-532
Fax: (514) 864-3838

The Eastern Townships' marketing efforts would have you believe that the four ski areas in the region—Sutton My Mountain Resort! (that's its official name, we'll call it Sutton from here on), Orford, Bromont and Owl's Head—are right next door to each other, but in reality they are from 20 to 45 minutes away from each other on dry roads. Don't let that deter you, this is a beautiful region for a vacation, and we don't think you'll be disappointed. As with any resort in Quèbec, the French-Canadian culture is everywhere: That means fabulous food, first-rate service, French spoken all around you and an overall feeling of vacationing in France.

The Eastern Townships comprise dozens of quaint little towns ripe with history, so try to find time to explore the region in your car. The original residents were Abenaki Indians, and the names they gave to places and bodies of water remain, including Memphremagog, the lake that serves as a centerpiece to the region's winter resorts. Eventually Canada became a British colony and, not surprisingly, loyalists from the American Revolution fled to Quèbec, soon to be followed by other Americans looking for cheap land. In the 1850s the French-speaking residents arrived, and by the early 1900s most of the population was francophone.

That said, each resort has a different feel and flavor. Mont Orford, Sutton and Bromont are dominated by the French experience (in fact, Bromont is rather intimidating because the resort's signs don't have an accompanying English translation, while Sutton and Orford are much more accommodating). On the other hand, at Owl's Head everyone speaks English and switches to French if necessary.

Adventurous intermediates and better who enjoy the challenging terrain at Mont Orford and Mont Sutton should consider spending a day at nearby Jay Peak Resort, Vt.

If you're planning to visit all the areas, consider the interchangeable Ski East Pass. It's a multiday ticket of four consecutive days or more that offers full interchangability with Sutton, Mont Orford and Owl's Head (Bromont does not participate). It can be purchased at any of the participating resorts. Four days cost $134 for adults, $88 for children ages 6 to 13.

Please make note of the different area codes.

Mont Orford Facts

Summit elevation: 2,800 feet
Vertical drop: 1,772 feet
Base elevation: 1,082 feet
Address: 4380 Chemin du Parc, Orford, PQ;
Mail: C.P. 10, Magog, PQ Canada J1X 3W7
Area code: 819
Ski area phone: 843-6548
Toll-free reservations: (800) 567-2772
Snow report: 843-8882 or (800) 567-2772
Fax: 847-2487
E-mail: info@mt-orford.com
Internet: www.mt-orford.com
Number and types of lifts: 8—2 quads, 1 triple, 3 doubles, 1 T-bar, 1 surface lift

Skiable acreage: 244 acres
Snowmaking: 85 percent
Uphill capacity: 11,400 per hour
Snowboarding: Yes
Bed Base: 170 slopeside; 5,000 in Orford-Magog area
Nearest lodging: Condos, walking distance
Resort child care: Yes; 2 years and older
Adult ticket, per day: $39 (02/03 Cdn$ with GST)

Expert: ★★★★
Advanced: ★★★★
Intermediate: ★★★★
Beginner: ★★★ **Never-ever:** ★★★

Mont Orford

Mont Orford is operated under a long-term lease on government land within Parc du Mont-Orford. The resort is spread across three separate mountain peaks and has fabulous terrain for all abilities. Adventurous skiers will be challenged here, and you'll be completely surprised by that because at first glance, the mountain looks rather tame. The trails are long, giving skiers and riders maximum use of the vertical drop, and they follow the contours of the mountain. The glades are really tight woods, where trees may be thinned a bit, but the mountain is left alone. Certainly the best time to hit this mountain, if you're planning to check out the woods, is when there's fresh powder, so keep in mind that Orford gets fresh snow on days when nearby resorts may get rain.

Mountain layout—Skiing

◆◆ Expert ◆ Advanced: Triple-diamond labels are a bit hyped, but experts won't be disappointed either. Take La Quatuor lift to the top of Mont Giroux, and warm up on Slalom: When we skied it, there was new powder and the workout left us huffing and puffing with screaming quads. Riding up Le Quad du Village, you'll realize what you're up for as you look at the bodies littered across Sherbrooke below (probably thought they'd take a break from the glade skiing—hey, it's a trail, how hard can it be?). Once you unload from Le Quad du Village, you'll find a steep headwall to skier's right. If you're looking for woods (as if you'd be over here for any other reason), stay along the top of the headwall and keep your eyes peeled for the entrance; you'll probably notice people peering down the ravine that gets you into the woods. A new experience for us: Once you're in the woods, you'll see signs for various woods shots off the woods shots. It doesn't matter which way you go, it's all good. Ledges and boulders simply add to the thrill of the woods skiing here. By the way, if it's in-bounds, you can ski it. There are about 12 unnamed glades as well; be nice to the locals, and maybe they'll give you a private tour.

For those who prefer trails to woods, don't worry, be happy. Trois-Ruisseaux and Maxi on Mont Orford are especially delightful, and both are groomed in the middle of the day, which is a treat since these are popular trails. Trois-Ruisseaux is a winding trail, narrow in spots with nice steep pitches. Maxi, on the other hand, is steep and goes straight down the mountain. Watch out, you'll pick up lots of speed before you know it. Two new advanced trails have been recently added: L'ecureuil, parallel to Maxi, leads into the gently gladed intermediate Arcade; and Porc-épic winds steeply along skier's right.

■ **Intermediate**: The intermediate trails on Mont A.-Desrochers are winding and rolling, sometimes narrow, but with a steady pitch and no unexpected steeps. A wonderful experience! Because the chair is a bit out of the way, you'll find these trails relatively uncrowded. Grande Coulée on Mont Orford is a nice cruiser, but it has a steep section that might intimidate some intermediates (if it's windy, some parts get windswept and icy too). Wondering if you might like woods skiing? Arcade is a gentle glade to skier's right after unloading La Mi-Orford chair. If you're having fun, try Escapade, a short glade.

●● **Beginner** ● **Never-evers**: Talk about being friendly to novices: Beginner trails are groomed during the day, if it's a snowy day. The scenic 4 Km. is a narrow cat track from the top of Mont Orford that eventually widens and has fabulous views of nearby Lake Memphremagog and Owl's Head in the distance. A real surprise is that the north side of Mont Giroux, which is covered in black on the east side, has trails that are loads of fun for beginners. Take the Le Quatuor lift and head straight, or skier's right. They're separate from expert trails, so you don't need to worry about hotshots. The learning area is at the base of Mont Giroux and has its own lift.

Mountain layout–Snowboarding

The snowboard park is halfway down on the intermediate-rated Magog trail, which can be accessed directly from the top of Le Quatour lift or by following Jean-Davignon. The park is isolated from other runs, has a variety of hits, carries on for a decent distance and finishes with a long halfpipe. That said, Orford's contour varies from narrow to wide to narrow, and much is covered with ledges, rocks and double-fall lines that make it a natural terrain park. Almost all of the glades on Mont Giroux dump onto Passe-Montagne, a long, flat beginner trail that might require some hoofing to get back to the lift. Don't let that stop you if you like glades, some riders say it's a nice relief after the tough workout they just had in the woods! Want to reach warp speed? Head to Maxi and Trois-Ruisseaux.

Lessons (2002/03 prices in Cdn$, with GST)

Group lessons: Priced according to your requirements.
Never-ever package: Never-evers can take a 90-minute class that includes a full-day lift ticket and rentals, $55. *Reserve 24 hours in advance.*
Private lessons: One-hour lesson is $39, two hours is $71. Additional skier is $19.

Child care (2002/03 prices in Cdn$ with GST)

Ages: 2 years and older.
Costs: $21 for a full day, lunch is an additional $4. The hourly rate is $5.
Reservations: Required.
Children's lessons: Age 3 and older. Kids 3 to 6 years old get a 60-minute ski lesson, rentals and day care for $55 for the full day or $59 with lunch. *Reservations 24 hours in advance are required for all lessons.*

Lift tickets (2002/03 prices in Cdn$ with GST)

	Adult	Junior (6-13)
One day	$39	$22
Three days	$109	$65
Five days	$160	$110

Who skis at a discount: Children 5 and younger pay $5; students age 14 to 21 with I.D. pay $31; seniors age 65 to 69 pay junior rates; seniors age 70 and older pay $5.

Accommodations at or near the resort

The full-service **Auberge Estrimont** (800-567-7320, 819-843-1616; $$$), just minutes away from the mountain, has made about $1 million in renovations, with more to come. If you don't mind some minor annoyances that haven't yet been repaired, you'll enjoy staying here. Our suite had a sunken living room, fireplace, balcony and small refrigerator. Massage and spa services also are available. The over-priced and uninspired **Manoir des Sables** (800-567-3514, 819-847-4747; $$$) has 117 deluxe rooms and suites and is set on its own private lake and golf course. Some rooms have a fireplace, Jacuzzi and mini-bar. Service was spotty and lukewarm at best, and the atmosphere was similar to a Holiday Inn. Those who prefer condominium lodging should look to **O'Berge du Village** (888-326-1252, 819-868-1252; $$-$$$), which has fully-equipped units overlooking Lake Memphremagog, is within walking distance of downtown and has ready access to the town's ice skating path.

Dining at or near the resort

On-mountain, you'll find a pub and a cafeteria with seating in several areas on different levels, so finding your friends is a like playing hide-and-seek).

La Loyaliste at Auberge Estrimont (819-843-1616; $$-$$$) serves excellent regional cuisine in a cozy dining room with a fireplace. If you're a chocoholic, you'll want to order Le Diable, a rich chocolate mousse filled with chocolate sauce-absolutely to die for. **Les Jardins at Manoir des Sables** (819-847-4747; $$-$$$) also focuses on regional cuisine with a French influence. It sets a sumptuous buffet breakfast as well (try the paté). In town, **Restaurant Do** (819-843-9570; $$) is a small Vietnamese restaurant serving excellent food with either a fixed price menu or à la carte in a comfortable and friendly atmosphere. Some Continental dishes, such as rack of lamb, are also available.

For a much more casual meal, head **to Rôtisserie St-Hubert** (819-847-3366; $-$$). The kids will be happy in the playroom while you drink St.-Hubert private-label beer (on lees, so it's light and somewhat like champagne), munch on the teaser appetizers that allow you to sample two or three of your choice (you *must* try the fried corn tortillas stuffed with spiced jalapeño cream cheese) and indulge in the scrumptious rotisserie chicken.

Après-ski/nightlife at or near the resort

The on-mountain **Slalom Pub** has been renovated and has happy hour from 4-6 p.m., dinner, live entertainment and games. The other choice is to head to nearby Magog, where a variety of pubs and restaurants line the main street. Among the noteworthy are **The Liquor Store,** the jazz bar **Le Chat du Mouliniere** and **Café St. Michele**, where live folk music is featured. Or, simply walk along until you find a place that meets your fancy.

Sutton Facts

Summit elevation:	**3,175 feet**
Vertical drop:	**1,500 feet**
Base elevation:	**1,675 feet**

Address: 671, chemin Maple, Sutton, PQ Canada JOE 2K0
Area code: 450
Ski area phone: 538-2545
Toll-free reservations: (800) 663-0214
Snow report: (514) 866-7639
Fax: 538-0080
E-mail: Through the Web sites
Internet: www.montsutton.com (resort); www.sutton-info.qc.ca (town & township)

Number and types of lifts: 9–1 high-speed quad, 2 quads, 6 doubles
Skiable acreage: 174 acres
Snowmaking: 60 percent
Uphill capacity: 11,800 per hour
Snowboarding: Yes
Bed Base: About 650 in Sutton (275 rooms)
Nearest lodging: Slopeside
Resort child care: Yes; 2 years to 5 years
Adult ticket, per day: $42 (02/03 Cdn$ with GST)

Expert: ★★★★
Advanced: ★★★★
Intermediate: ★★★★
Beginner: ★★★★ **Never-ever:** ★★★

Sutton My Mountain Resort!

A trip to Sutton is a step back in time. The resort made its debut in 1960 and still has some of its original chair lifts, which you board after working your way through a lift line of wooden fences and passing ticket-checker booths that look like little red-trimmed log cabins. All around you, skiers and riders decked out in the latest gear and apparel chatter away in French. Which reminds us to tell you that Sutton and the nearby town may just be one of the friendliest places we've ever visited. Everyone seems to know everyone, and if they don't know you, they act like they do. By the way, just say *bonjour* or *merci* and everyone happily switches to English (yes, your accent *will* give you away!).

At first glance, Sutton appears to be a small area, but it skis like a large resort. Trails and glades take you all over the mountain before reaching the bottom. Ability levels are generally separated from each other: Beginner terrain is on the far right; intermediate terrain is in the middle; expert terrain is to the far left. Two lifts in the middle of the mountain also serve beginner terrain.

Glades, or *sous-bois,* clearly set this mountain apart from others. They are thinned enough to groom—not often, because they're most fun in the powder. The glades were cut in 1960, long before other resorts even thought of such a thing. Trails follow the true fall line. You're constantly winding your way down the mountain. Trails are also usually left *au naturel*—only 13 are groomed nightly, and fewer than that on a powder day. Are you getting the message yet? This charming retro resort gets a lot of powder, and that's what the skiers here like, so the owners don't mess with it. Speaking of the owners, the same family that opened the resort still runs it, with great affection and respect for the mountain and its guests.

Mountain layout–Skiing

We'd be doing you a real disservice if we told you to use a trail map while skiing this mountain. Our usual MO of telling you which trails to ski and which ones to skip is meaningless. The locals are proud to say you can ski this mountain for years and never come down the same way. And we believe it! For truly, the way to ski this mountain is to merely follow where your skis take you, and they take you to a different place every time. No one here skis just one run to the bottom, they slip into glades and cut under lifts and dart down the bottom sections of trails and catch air over boulders, usually skiing at least four trails and *sous-bois* before reaching the bottom. It's an exhilarating experience, whether you're a beginner or an expert. And the separation of ability levels ensures you won't end up somewhere you shouldn't be.

◆◆ **Expert** ◆ **Advanced:** The primary bunching of double-diamond terrain is off of Lift IV-West, where Bo-Real runs directly under the lift, unleashing some serious dips and drops. We particularly like #29, Sous-bois Poma, and #28, Challenge, both of which are narrow trails that bring back the glory of old-time eastern skiing. Look also for a cluster of shorter double-diamonds at skier's far right atop Chairlift VII (numbers 51-55). To reduce the challenge a notch, try single-diamonds Escapade (#42) and Miracle (#44), accessed from Chairlift V.

■ **Intermediate:** The best part of the intermediate- and beginner-rated runs is that, along with their easier pitch and groomed surfaces, they each yield Sutton's signature sensibility: experiencing a real adventure by skiing through the wooded, natural environment. The majority of intermediate trails are grouped off of Lift II, the area's only high-speed quad. We particularly enjoyed #16, Alouette, and #18, Sous-bois II, because they evoked the true Sutton spirit.

●● **Beginner** ● **Never-evers:** While this spaghetti-mess of a trail mix may sound intimidating to novices, the area actually serves beginners well. Three sections are devoted to green-rated runs. One is reached from the III chairlift, which is located not far from the main base lodge and travels slightly less than halfway up the mountain. From here, there's easy access to runs numbered on the trail map from #22-26. Even shorter, absolute novice runs are found off Lift II-West, just in front of the main base lodge, where Numbers 9, 13 and 15 are located.

Mountain layout–Snowboarding

Mont Sutton has a Skill Zone, or terrain park, but most riders are here for the natural terrain. You won't be disappointed either: You'll find natural river beds, boulders, drop-offs, trees and dips. And no flats. This mountain really wants you to ride it!

Lessons (2002/03 prices Cdn$ with GST)

One of the country's best technical ski instructors, Guy Duquette, is director of the Ski and Snowboard School. He has been a member of the Canadian Exhibition Team at Interski, which consists of CSIA's top 10 technical ski instructors, since 1987.

Group lessons: A four-hour lesson costs $45.

Never-ever package: The learn-to-ski package costs $39.95 and includes a 90-minute lesson, rentals and lifts; learn-to-snowboard costs $49.95. Reservations required. The program allows for three lessons at this price.

Private lessons: One-hour lessons cost $39, each additional person is $14. Also six hours of lessons for the price of five, $195.

Special programs: Ski or snowboard week is 16 hours of lessons, video instruction, racing and awards. Minimum of four per group. $299 for adults, ages 65 and older pay $249.

Dining: $$$-Entrees $20+; $$-$10-20; $-less than $10. (Cdn$)

Accommodations: (double room) $$$$-$200+; $$$-$141-$200; $$-$81-$140; $-$80 and less. (Cdn$)

Child care (2002/03 prices Cdn$ with GST)

Ages: 2 to 5 years.
Costs: Full day, $16; hourly rate, $3. Parents are responsible for picking up their children for lunch.
Reservations: Not required.
Children's lessons: Kids 3-5 years old are introduced with a day care program that includes two hours of lessons. Full day, $59 (parents responsible for lunch); half day, $35. Equipment is extra. Kids 6 years and older sign up for adult classes and will be grouped by age (see *Lessons* above). The ski or snowboard week for ages 6-17 includes 16 hours of lessons, video instruction, friendly race and awards. With a minimum of four per group, the cost is $229.

Lift tickets (2002/03 prices Cdn$ with GST)

	Adult	Junior (6-17)
One day	$42	$30
Three days	$108	$77
Five days	$166	$110

Who skis free: Kids ages 5 and younger.
Who skis at a discount: Ages 65 and older ski for junior rates.

Accommodations at or near the resort

You can book your Sutton-area lodging through Sutton Accommodation (800-663-0214, ext. 4), a separate entity from Sutton. The only slopeside accommodations are found at **Auberge La Paimpolaise** (800-263-3213, 450-538-3213; $), a charming 28-room inn, reminiscent of a Swiss chalet. After a tough day on the slopes, head to the large outdoor Jacuzzi and ask one of the friendly staff to bring you a tasty local beer.

Just down the road, **Auberge des Appalaches** (877-533-5799, 450-538-5799; $) is a cozy inn owned by long-time locals Micheline Côté and Daniel Martin, who do everything possible to make you feel at home. There are 13 tastefully decorated rooms with private baths and stunning views. The couple guide evening snowshoe tours for guests on the trails of Parc Environment Naturel de Sutton, which are accessed from their property. They also have snow tubing and snow volleyball.

The picturesque **Auberge West Brome** (888-902-7663, 450-266-7552; $$-$$$$) is about 10 minutes away in West Brome. This upscale country inn has hotel rooms as well as one- and two-bedroom condo suites with a nice-sized kitchen, fireplace and balcony that are great for families. Some suites also have whirlpool baths. Breakfast is delivered to your room or condo. If you're traveling with kids, the **Hotel Horizon** (877-538-3212, 450-538-3212; $$) is not only family-friendly and located just a kilometer from the ski hill, but has the all-important indoor pool.

Dining at or near the resort

Mont Sutton has four **cafeterias**, two at the summit of lifts and two at the base. Our favorite is **Altitude 840 m.**, where you can have pulled pork and fries in front of a roaring fireplace while you look out at the valley below.

Auberge La Paimpolaise (450-538-3213; $$) is a casual restaurant that serves yummy regional and European cuisine. It can get very busy, since it's at the base of Mont Sutton, but there's a lively après-ski bar for a drink while you're waiting. **Auberge des Appalaches** (450-538-5799; $$) is another casual restaurant that serves fine European cuisine. No wonder, the chef is from Paris. Ask for a table next to a window so you can watch the sunset. **Auberge West Brome** (450-266-7552; $$-$$$), a rustic turn-of-the-century farmhouse in nearby West Brome, provides an intimate but casual setting for friends and family. A wonderful plus, you can choose from five kinds of sauces for your meat or seafood: five pepper, peanut, Thai, satai or Indian. In the town of Sutton, chefs Karen Anderson and Pierre Tétreault, trained in France and Rome, bring superb French cuisine to **Auberge Le St-Amour** (888-538-6188; 450-538-6188; $$$-$$$$). The comfortably elegant dining room is decorated with hand-painted reproduction frescos from Impressionist masters.

Après-ski/nightlife at or near the resort

The slopeside **Auberge La Paimpolaise** is the obvious place to head. The après-ski crowd here is loud and lively. Make sure to ask about the local beers. **Auberge des Appalaches**, just down the road, also has several tasty local beers on hand, plus loads of toys and board games for people of all ages, perfect for families or groups looking for friendly competition and laughter.

Cross-country and snowshoeing

Parc du Mont-Orford (819-843-9855) has 87 km. of trails for both classic and skating. Upon entering the Mont Orford entrance to the park, turn right to Le Cerisier Visitor's Center. Trails range from flat and gentle alongside a lake to steep and challenging as they climb up Mont Chauve. Snowshoers and winter hikers are welcome. Cross-country gear and snowshoe rentals are available.

Park Environment Naturel de Sutton (450-538-4085) has 20 km. of snowshoeing trails and 40 km. of cross-country skiing trails. Winter hikers also are welcome. The trail network was founded by Daniel Martin, who owns the Auberge des Appalaches just down the road from Sutton. Stop by the auberge to purchase trail maps and access the trail network.

Getting there and getting around

By air: Fly into Montreal's Dorval International Airport or Burlington (VT) International Airport. If you arrive from outside Canada, you'll need a passport or birth certificate for customs. You'll need to rent a car either way.

By car: If you're coming from the United States, you'll need a birth certificate to cross the border. The resorts are fairly spread out, and the travel directions vary considerably according to where you're going. The best bet is to ask your lodging for directions and/or print off a map from the resort's or lodging's Web site. Access from the major northeastern U.S. metro areas is relatively easy, via interstates 89, 91 and 93. Here's a general rule of thumb for travel time: The resorts are about an hour from Montreal, one to two hours from Burlington, seven from Boston and nine hours from New York.

Getting around: You'll need a car. Everything is spread out, and you'll want to explore the surrounding area and visit the various resorts.

Dining: $$$-Entrees $20+; $$-$10-20; $-less than $10. (CdnS)
Accommodations: (double room) $$$$-$200+; $$$-$141-$200; $$-$81-$140; $-$80 and less. (CdnS)

Owl's Head; (450) 292-3342

Internet: www.owlshead.com

8 lifts—2 high-speed quads, 6 doubles; Skiable acreage, 86; 1,772 feet vertical

Owl's Head is named after the Abenaki Indian's greatest chief, Owl, whose spirit will live forever through the naming of the mountain in his honor. The resort is something of a charming throwback. The ski area has the feeling of an old-time ski club, with it's simple, wooden base lodge and lack of intrusive slopeside development. Inside the base lodge, regulars take their places on long wooden benches lining the walls to change their boots and exchange pleasantries.

The minute you get off the lift, any lift, you'll be awestruck by the fabulous views from the top of this hump of a mountain that rises above a rather flat section of the region. Lake Memphremagog is below the base, and you often feel as if you'll ski right off the edge of the mountain into the lake. No kidding: The magnificent views are comparable to skiing in the Tahoe region of California. This is a lovely mountain; perfect for families and groups that want gentle skiing and nicely groomed trails. However, it *is* small, and most will not want to ski here for an entire week unless they have young children.

◆◆ **Expert ◆ Advanced:** Owl's Head has some genuine steeps, but they're short and won't entertain experts for very long. Advanced skiers will find a few ways to test themselves. For true steeps, however short, the narrow Grand Allée reaches 47 degrees and The Wall of Death, on Colorado, reaches 43 degrees. Newport Express, a short, narrow double-diamond, is known to locals as Higgins' Hazzard, after an instructor from nearby Jay Peak, Vt., who broke body parts several different times here (don't worry, he seems to be the only one who can't get this run down right). Single-diamonds Lake View and Le Loup reveal terrific lake views, and Bois du Loup presents a small tree-skiing adventure. Kamikazee, under the main high-speed quad, is popular for black-diamond cruising.

■ **Intermediate:** Lily's Leap is a must-ski: As it winds down the mountain from the top it offers amazing views of the lake far below. Centennial, which meanders across the mountain and provides access to virtually every other run on the mountain, is loads of fun. We thoroughly enjoyed Upward Trail, a wide, well-groomed cruiser that had a nifty little bump field at the bottom. When you're ready to challenge yourself, try the single-diamond trails.

●● **Beginner ● Never-evers:** This mountain is well-suited for beginners and never-evers. While some beginner runs feed higher-level skiers to the base, there are no hotshots here. You won't find beginner trails from the top, so head to wide-open Chouette and Panorama, each with its own lift, for magnificent lake views. Proficient beginners will want to go to the top and take Lily's Leap. Never-evers are well served by Cindy's Slip, Winker and Petite Allee, which are also served by their own lift, one that's easily accessible from the base lodge. This double is being replaced by a quad chair for the 2002-03 season, which should help ease congestion at the base area.

Lift tickets: Adults, Cdn$34, Juniors (6–13), Cdn$22 (with GST)

Lodging information: Owl's Head Auberge (800-363-3342, 450-292-3342; $-$$; ✕ ℗⊛) has 20 rooms on the top floor of the base lodge. The meal plan includes breakfast in the cafeteria and dinner in the dining room. **Owl's Head Apartment Hotel** (800-363-3342, 450-292-3318; $-$$) has 36 units, ranging from 1 to 3 bedrooms. Condos have a fully equipped kitchen and fireplace, most have a balcony. Guests have access to a solarium lounge and mini-spa with whirlpool and sauna, as well as a laundry room.

See Eastern Townships Accommodation section as well.

Bromont; (450) 534-2200

Internet: www.skibromont.com

4 lifts—1 high-speed quad, 2 doubles, 1 surface lift; 174 skiable acres; 1,329 feet vertical

Bromont, the Eastern Township ski area closest to Montreal, can be a very busy place, particularly at night. Québécois are well-known for their love of night-skiing, and Bromont fills that fancy very well. About 75 percent of the terrain, including the Free Zone terrain park, is lighted for night skiing, which goes till 10 p.m. Sunday through Thursday and 10:30 p.m. Friday and Saturday. Proximity to Montreal ensures steady business and a lively night life.

Although the trail map is dominated by diamonds, the trails are really intermediate. Experts and advanced skiers will find that the cruisers are a great way to give tired legs a break after skiing hard all week at Mont Orford or Mont Sutton. Grooming is meticulous, and on weekends, trails are groomed three times a day. A new high-speed quad lift has been installed for the 2002/03 season. It runs alongside the existing quad on the Versant du Village, significantly enhancing uphill travel. The mountain has a lower elevation than other resorts in the area, so it often rains here when it snows elsewhere. Bromont gives you 30 minutes to test conditions—if you're not pleased, exchange your ticket for a coupon to return at no extra charge. Most skiers will want to spend only a day here because of limited terrain.

◆◆ **Expert** ◆ **Advanced:** The trail map shows a multitude of single-diamond runs, a few double-diamonds and three triple-diamonds. These designations can be deemed somewhat over-stated, but there are some nice short adventurous shots. In the Versant du Lac section, trails are still being developed, but there currently exists a mix of relatively narrow advanced and intermediate runs that have been developed to give an old-fashioned feel to the skiing.

■ **Intermediate:** Because of the extensive grooming, solid intermediates will be able to ski most, if not all, of the mountain. Knowlton will let you run your skis at maximum speed. Montreal and Cowansville have some surprising changes in pitch that will keep you on your toes. You'll find short sections of some trails are left to bump up, but there's bail-out room if you get intimidated.

●● **Beginner** ● **Never-evers:** The learning area is on its own peak, Mont Soleil, and is served by a chair lift and a Magic Carpet. The trails here are gentle and will boost any novice's ego. This area gets afternoon sun, a real plus since that's when snow normally firms up on the main mountain. If you're feeling adventurous, try St.-Bruno and St.-Hubert, which are wide-open, winding trails with pockets of scattered trees.

The terrain park, Free Zone, has rails, table tops, a quarterpipe and jumps, plus it's lighted for night riding. There's always a lot of activity here, so if you're yearning to learn new tricks or make friends with other riders, this is where you should head. The meticulous grooming on the mountain means lots of fun for riders, whether you're looking to make perfect carving arcs or catch air off plateaus and dips. Beware of the long flat at the bottom of Cowansville and Montreal heading back to the lift. If you're a beginner with some snow time under your boots, you'll enjoy the beginner terrain, which has a steady and sometimes rolling pitch without flats to stop you dead in your tracks.

Lift tickets: Adults, Cdn$36; Juniors (6–13) Cdn$21 (with GST).

Lodging information: Le Château Bromont (800-304-3433, 819-534-3433; $$$-$$$$) gives you luxury without airs, creating a delightfully elegant atmosphere and experience just minutes from the slopes. Some rooms have fireplaces and whirlpools. Don't miss out on the variety of treatments available at the Spa.

See Eastern Townships Accommodation section for more options.

Tremblant

Québec, Canada

Summit elevation:	3,001 feet
Vertical drop:	2,131 feet
Base elevation:	870 feet

Address: 3005, Chemin Principal
Mont-Tremblant, Quebec, Canada J0T 1Z0
☎ **Area code:** 819
Ski area phone: 681-2000
Snow report: (514) 333-8936 (Montreal)
ⓘ **Toll-free information and reservations:**
(800) 461-8711 or 681-2000
Fax: 681-5996
E-mail: info-sac@intrawest.com
Internet: www.tremblant.ca (ski area) or
www.tremblant.com (region)
Expert:★★★ **Advanced:**★★★★
Intermediate:★★★★
Beginner:★★★★
Never-ever:★★★

Number and types of lifts: 14—1 high-speed,
eight-person gondola; 5 high-speed quads; 1 quad;
3 triples; 3 magic carpets; 1 cabriolet
Acreage: 604
Snowmaking: 80 percent
Uphill capacity: 27,230 skiers per hour
Snowboarding: Yes
Bed base: 3,500-plus at resort base
Nearest lodging: slopeside, hotel & condos
Resort child care: Yes, 12 months and older
Adult ticket, per day: $59 (01/02 price)

Dining:★★★★
Apres-ski/nightlife:★★★
Other activities: ★★★

Heading north out of Montreal, it's hard to believe that you're anywhere near mountains worth skiing. Montreal is flat, flat, flat. But about 30 minutes into your drive, you catch glimpses of oddly shaped hills bursting out of the flatness, almost like giants trying to punch their way through the ground to catch a breath of fresh air. Suddenly, you are surrounded by these funky hills, and it occurs to you: There are ski trails etched out of the trees, and beautiful homes dot the hillsides (see end of chapter for a description of these five ski areas). This is just the beginning of what turns into a breathtaking drive through and around hills, mountains, valleys and lakes.

Tremblant is the highest peak in the Tremblant Provincial Park. Tremblant, a French word that has its roots in Algonquin legend, means Trembling Mountain: The mountain shook, as though by an angry god, from the Laurentian Shield's release from the weight of the arctic glacier. The tiny town of Tremblant is a few miles from the resort, but slopeside you'll find a charming European-style village that gives you everything you need while vacationing here (but don't miss a visit to the nearby town). When the brightly colored tin roofs of the mountain village glisten in the sunlight, they look like a bag of Skittles spilled across the snow. If you've ever been to Quebec City, you'll be convinced it's been moved to the mountains. During a marketing presentation, resort officials talked about how the village designers wanted to blend manmade structures with nature, to provide intimate surprises with every turn. My first thought was "what a bunch of marketing gibberish," but as I later wandered through the 18th-century-style village, I saw they had accomplished *exactly* what they had set out to do. The landscape changed with virtually every step, and I saw glimpses of the mountain, or the lake at the foot of the mountain, or welcoming courtyards overlooked by colorful balconies, or rows of roofs tumbling down the mountainside like dominos towards the lake.

This is one of the historic peaks in North American skiing. It began in the 1930s—in 1932, if you count Tremblant's founding from its inaugural Kandahar downhill ski race; or in 1938, the hectic year that Philadelphia millionaire Joe Ryan hiked to the top of Mont Tremblant, purchased it and opened North America's second true winter resort (Sun Valley was the first, two years earlier).

The complete resort experience includes the old village of Tremblant and the picturesque town of St. Jovite, dripping with Quebecois culture and the French language. Though the employees speak English, the native language here is French, and you will earn big smiles from locals if you give it a try. You get all the fun and excitement of trying out a foreign language with none of the frustration of not being understood. The entire experience is steeped in romance, so you'll win extra brownie points if you bring your lover here. Plus, there's little or no jet lag for North Americans. Keep in mind though, that the summit consistently registers the coldest temperatures south of Hudson's Bay.

 ## Mountain layout–Skiing

Tremblant is a hulk of a mountain with skiing on four faces. The trail map proclaims North and South sides, but these would be more accurately portrayed with designations Northeast and Southwest. It is easy for skiers to follow the sun: Simply ski on the North Side in the mornings to catch the sun and then move to the South Side for the afternoons.

The resort recently added a true south face, Versant Soleil, with 15 intermediate and advanced trails and glades. Most trails are groomed daily, but since 60 percent of the area consists of glades, don't expect buffed snow in the woods.

Most skiers and boarders start from the South Side, where the base village is. However, on crowded days many savvy locals make the 15-minute drive to the parking lot on the North Side, where they can avoid the crowds and get first crack at skiing in the sun.

◆◆ **Expert:** The most challenging sections of the mountain are in the sectors called The Edge and Versant Soleil. The Edge is reached by the Letendre trail, which starts halfway down the North Side and brings skiers to the base of the Edge quad chair. This chair serves only expert and advanced terrain. Only one trail, Action, is cut; the other descents are through the trees. The gladed skiing in Reaction and Sensation is cut wide enough for strong intermediates, but the glades dropping to the right down Emotion will push experts to their limits. Also on the North Side are Tremblant's major bump runs and super steeps. If you want to drop down steep bumps, try Dynamite, the steepest in eastern Canada, and Expo, beneath the lift and wide enough for big wipeouts. The drop down Devil's River and into the woods at Boiling Kettle is a rush.

Versant Soleil, accessed by the Le Soleil lift, is 80-percent expert with the bonus of sunshine. Black and double-black runs take you through fall-line glades. We didn't find any truly tough glade skiing here, but it was all rollicking fun.

◆ **Advanced:** For the most part, the single blacks are excellent choices for advanced skiers and riders, especially those who are just moving up a category from intermediate. Just beware of the many skiers and riders who shouldn't be on these trails; for some reason, lots of beginners seem to think they can handle them. It should be noted that we found quite a range among Tremblant's single-black diamond trails: some a challenge worthy of the rating, such as Banzai and Le Tunnel; others that could have been rated blue-square cruisers, such as Geant; and Dernier Cri, which we thought barely deserved a blue rating.

Kandahar is a ripping groomed cruiser. There are steep drops off the catwalk down Vertige (a double diamond) and Dunzee (both get bumped up in spring). They are easily avoided, if you prefer. Ryan is one of the original trails, narrow and twisting with short, very manageable stretches of steeps that earn its lower section a double diamond. Ryan is very much like an old-fashioned New England ski trail, but it's nothing compared to Dynamite; consider it a narrow advanced cruiser. But if you think Ryan is challenging at the top, you can bail out on blue-square Charron before you get to the narrow part.

■ **Intermediate:** On the South Side, Grand Prix, Beauvallon and Alpine are great wide-open cruising runs. The Cure Deslauriers trail, toward the lower part of the mountain, has been contoured to form snow waves; it's kind of a skier's terrain park. Kandahar, though rated black, is groomed. It has one fairly steep section, but is a good choice for upper-intermediates. At the end of the day, Johannsen—a short blue stretch at the base that funnels everyone off the mountain—gets bumped and/or mushy, depending on temperatures.

The North Side appears tough on the trail map, but is more intermediate than advanced. Stick to the far right or far left and you can't go wrong. Geant, Coyote and Duncan Haut are all fine for confident intermediates, and in some respects, are better than Beauchemin and Lowell Thomas, which are rated blue and get a lot more traffic.

Intermediates can ski the Le Soleil lift on a blue from the top down Franc Sud and Tobaggan, which runs into Tapecul to the bottom of Le Soleil lift. You can continue down La Carriole and along the run-out, Sentier des Pruches, right to the upper village.

●● **Beginner:** Le P'tit Bonheur takes beginners from the top of the North Side to the easiest mid-mountain trails. Still, most will stick to the South Side. From the top of the Flying Mile lift, beginners head left to La Passe and Nansen bas or they can head right down Standard and Biere-en-bas (named after a shortcut secretly cut by a racer when the staff would race down at the end of the day for beers; winner got to drink for free). Finally, take the big step to the top of the mountain and head down La Crête and all of Nansen. All in all, this is a fantastic area to start, but stick to Nansen or Roy Scott at the end of the day to avoid the crowds.

● **Never-ever:** Novices start on the free Magic Carpet lifts near the bell (the ski school meeting place). After never-evers master the terrain served by the Magic Carpets, they advance to the Flying Mile lift and Nansen.

 ## Mountain layout–Snowboarding

Gravity Park is on the North Side. The area is groomed by a state-of-the-art Scorpion snowpark grooming machine and has a super halfpipe, quarterpipe, rollers, tabletops, spines, bankturns and two rails sections. The park is reached by, and runs alongside of, the Lowell Thomas lift, putting you in full view of folks on the lift. The end of the run flattens out, so most boarders walk back up.

Boarders also ride The Edge and Versant Soleil for the glades. If you like screaming cruisers, Tremblant doles out some of the best. Start with any of the trails off Le Soleil—especially Laurentienne with its rolling dips for air and Tobaggan—and work your way around the mountain. Try to avoid Geant on the North Side, it has a very lo-o-o-ong run-out.

Mountain rating

Because of the near-continuous fall line with little run-out at the base, Tremblant skis even bigger than it is. The mountain is good for experts, great for advanced and intermediate skiers (though we're still a bit puzzled over some of the trail ratings), very good for beginners and acceptable for never-evers.

Weather can be brutal. We've heard many stories of days when the mercury drops well below zero (and that's Fahrenheit we're talking about), so bring warm clothes. We've also visited in late January, when the snow phone reported severe winds and only one lift open. Call ahead and be prepared to spa or shop; customer service will give you a break on your lift ticket. If you prefer milder weather, springtime skiing at Tremblant is a true delight.

 # Cross-country and snowshoeing

Canadians have serious winters so they definitely take all of their winter sports seriously. Case in point: the abundant and varied cross-country choices available to visitors to the Tremblant region.

More than 260 km. of cross-country trails are scattered in the region, most of which are found in **Parc du Mont-Tremblant** (688-2281). A ski pass is $15 at Parc du Mont Tremblant. Trails wind through maple and birch forests and provide views of wildlife and lakes.

There are two networks of marked, patrolled and groomed trails. The La Diable network has nine trails totaling 49 km. with six heated huts along the way. The La Pimbina network has seven trails, 30 km. all together, with two heated huts. Trail fees are $10 for adults and $6 for children younger than 12, those ages 65 and older and anyone in a group of 20 or more. Snowshoeing trail passes are $4. Skis and snowshoes are available for rent, and you can also arrange a trip on marked but ungroomed trails to backcountry bunkhouses.

To get away from all civilization, except for a few strategically located heated huts, head to the Parc du Mont-Tremblant and plan to make a day of it (or two days if winter camping and "an intense encounter with our Quebec winter," as they put it, appeals to you). This vast reserve offers two reception centers, complete with ski and snowshoe rentals and 150 km. of trails, 49 km of which are marked. Pack a lunch and ski out to one of the heated huts; trail loops of varying degrees of difficulty and length may be chosen. If you're lucky, trail guides will stop by a hut to tell you more about the history and the wildlife of the region.

The **Domaine St-Bernard** is owned by the Mont-Tremblant Municipality. It offers a network of more than 100 km. of trails, with 50 km. double-tracked and 12 km. skate groomed. The undulating trails are known for their magnificent vistas, but, alas for the novice skier, the majority of these vantage points are located on diamond and double-diamond trails.

Choose in-village, inn-to-inn trails in the Mont Tremblant/St. Jovite region, a wilderness trek in the nearby Parc du Mont-Tremblant or experience the longest linear park in North America, the 200-kilometer "Le P'tit Train du Nord," that runs from Saint-Jerome through Mont Tremblant to Mont-Laurier. St. Jerome to Ste. Agathe is for cross-country skiing, and Ste. Agathe to Mt. Laurier is for snowmobiling.

Popular choices for the average cross-country skier, who will still get his or her share of magnificent views and occasional sightings of wildlife, include the winding Domaine St. Bernard, the Jack Rabbit and skiing on the Gray Rocks golf course. A portion of Le P'tit Train du Nord linear park is also incorporated into these trails.

Lessons [2001/02 prices in Cdn$, taxes not included]

Group lessons: $46 for a 90-minute session, two sessions offered each morning; $41 for afternoon. Group lessons are one instructor with four students, making it easy for instructors to give tips while riding Tremblant's gondola.

Never-ever package (lifts, lesson and rentals): Discover Skiing and Snowboarding, also called Magic Trax 1, costs $59 for a morning lesson, $49 in the afternoon. Magic Trax 2 takes beginners to the mountaintop. It's $69 in the morning, $59 in the afternoon.

Private lessons: $89 for a morning hour, $72 in the afternoon.

Special programs: Ski Week is 14 hours of skiing or snowboarding with the same instructor for $217. The program also includes a welcome reception, race, dinner and souvenir video tape. Book at least seven days in advance for a discount.

All private or group instruction can be taken on normal skis, shaped skis, snowboard or Snowblades.

Racing: The Chrono-Course is open every day on Promenade.

Child care [2001/02 prices in Cdn$, without taxes]

Ages: 12 months to 6 years.

Costs: $32 for a half-day, $38 for a half-day with lunch. $49 for a full day with lunch. Multi-day packages, with lunch, are $45 per day.

Reservations: Call (888) 736-2526. Or, check with the concierge at your hotel or condo for babysitting services that come to your room.

The Kidz Club is at the base of the gondola lift, adjacent to the magic carpet beginner's lift and hill.

Children's lessons: Ages 3-12 pay $83 for a full day, including lunch. Tremblant offers Kids Ski Weekends (7 hours over two days) for $166 for 3- and 4-year-olds, $153 for 5- to 12-year-olds, lunch included, and Ski Weeks (four days with lunch included) for $287 for ages 3-4, $265 for ages 4-12. Note: you can save up to 13 percent on these programs if you reserve at least seven days in advance. All children's instructors carry radio phones so that they can be located quickly in case of an emergency, and pagers are offered to parents. Prices for all children's programs are lower if pre-booked, call (888) 736-2526.

Lift tickets [2001/02 prices in Cdn$, with taxes]

	Adult	Child (6-12)
One day	$59	$30
Three days	$161 ($53+/day)	$87 ($29/day)
Five days	$265 ($53/day)	$144 ($28+/day)

Who skis free: Children 5 and younger. The Magic Carpet beginner's lift also is free.

Who skis at a discount: Skiers 65 and older pay $40. Students aged 13–17 ski for $40.

Note: These are prices rounded to the nearest Canadian dollar. These prices include the 7 percent federal GST and the 7.5 percent provincial tax in this section.

Accommodations

Tremblant Reservation Call Center (800-461-8711) can reserve anything at the resort. **Mont Tremblant Reservations** (888-857-7967) can book all lodging and has good travel, lodging and ski packages. Call (800) 567-6760, or dial 425-8681. We list lodging choices in the base-area village, but there are less expensive alternatives nearby.

Staying in the base village is the way to go. At the upper end of the village, the luxurious **Fairmont Tremblant** (800-441-1414 or 681-7000; $$$-$$$$) is a magnificent stone and timber structure with ski-in/walk-out access, shops and restaurants, as well as a health club with indoor and outdoor heated pools, whirlpools, sauna, steam baths and an exercise room.

Le Westin Resort (866-681-8898 or 681-2000; $$$$) is another high-end property with ski-in/ski-out access, this time a condo-hotel featuring 126 rooms, an outdoor saltwater pool, 24-hour room service and a world-class spa. Lots of mahogany and rich colors.

The all-suite **Le Sommet des Neiges** (800-461-8711 or 681-2000; $$$) is just 100 feet from the Express Gondola. Suites have one to three bedrooms and include fireplace, fully equipped kitchens, washer and dryer. Exercise room, outdoor whirlpool and indoor parking.

The **Marriott Residence Inn, Manoir Labelle** (866-836-3030 or 681-4000; $$$-$$$$) is at the lower end of the village. Includes continental breakfast.

La Tour Des Voyageurs (800-461-8711; $$$-$$$$) is a condominium hotel adjacent to the Cabriolet lift with ski-in/ski out access, a swimming pool, whirlpool and exercise room.

Le Country Inn & Suites by Carlson (800-461-8711 or 681-2000; $$$-$$$$), formerly the Kandahar Resort Hotel, has comfortably appointed, spacious suites and hotel rooms, most with fireplaces and fully equipped kitchens. Sauna, outdoor whirlpool, exercise room and indoor parking. Includes continental breakfast.

The slopeside **Lodge de la Montagne** (800-461-8711 or 681-2000; $$$-$$$$) houses country-style condominium units, many with gas fireplaces and fully equipped kitchens. Sauna, outdoor whirlpool, exercise room and indoor parking.

Lining the cobblestoned street that leads from the Chateau to La Tour Des Voyageurs are three- to four-story buildings that house restaurants and shops on the ground floor and condominiums above. The **Saint Bernard, Johannsen and Deslauriers condos** (800-461-8711; $$-$$$) are very roomy and beautifully furnished.

Other condo complexes are within two miles and have shuttle service to the slopes. **Pinoteau Village** (800-667-2200; $$$-$$$$) and **Condotels du Village** (800-567-6724; $-$$) have kitchens, balconies and fireplaces. Pinoteau Village has cross-country trails outside its doors, while the Condotels have a clubhouse with a sauna, hot tub and exercise room.

Mont Tremblant Reservations also can book the **Club Tremblant** (800-567-8341; $$$-$$$$), where rates include breakfast and dinner and lifts; **Gray Rocks** (800-567-6767; $$-$$$$), which has its own small ski area and specializes in the all-inclusive, heavy-on-socializing Ski Week; the luxurious **Intrawest Resort Club** (800-799-3258; $$-$$$$) or several condos, cozy inns, motels and historic lodges in the villages of Mont Tremblant and St. Jovite.

Hotel packages at the resort include a passport in the value season. This includes four hours of snow toy trials, one overnight ski tuneup, 90 minutes of ski tips with an instructor and free Kidz Club for children ages 6 and younger. Advanced reservations are required.

For budget travelers, The 84-bed **Mont-Tremblant Youth Hostel** (425-6008; $) offers four- to 10-bed dorm rooms as well as private rooms; all with shared baths. The lodge is in the village of Mont-Tremblant, just 3 kilometers from the mountain, and a shuttle (fee) stops at the front door. A fully-equipped kitchen is available, but the hostel offers an inexpensive Continental breakfast. Guests can relax in a common room with TV, a reading room with library and Internet access or the English pub with pool table. The pub serves alcohol and is open to guests only.

Dining: $$$-Entrees $20+; $$-$10-20; $-less than $10.
Accommodations: (double room) $$$$-$200+; $$$-$141-$200; $$-$81-$140; $-$80 and less.

Dining

Most of the restaurants have moderately priced food, and you can have lunch-type foods for supper, if you like. At the foot of the Gondola Express in the pedestrian village, there are a number of **outdoor BBQ venues**, in the springtime. At outside grills you can get a hot dog with chips, hamburgers or grilled chicken for less than $5. Most restaurants on the Place St. Bernard have an outdoor grill blazing on a sunny day.

Near the Place St. Bernard: At the **Al Van Houtte at Mt. Tremblant** you can get soups, bagels, salads, beers, coffee and muffins. **Les Delices du St. Bernard** (681-4555; $-$$) is a deli offering cheeses, pates and cold cuts, sandwiches, fresh breads and other dishes.

For the town's best coffee and a good selection of pastries, visit **Au Grain de Cafe** (681-4567; $), just off the plaza.

The atmosphere at **Mexicali Rosa's** (681-2439; $$-$$$) is cozy-ethnic, but the food is fair, especially for those who live in the Southwest. Try the deep-fried ice cream, if you dare, or concentrate on the sangria and margaritas.

Le Shack Resto-bar (681-4700; $-$$) has a breakfast buffet and is the spot for people-watching during lunch or an apres-ski beer or two. In Vieux-Tremblant: **Cafe Bistro Ryan** (681-4994; $-$$) is for late-night munchies, open from 7 a.m. to 4 a.m.!

The three owners of **Creperie Catherine** (681-4888; $) used to cook aboard ships. Now, they offer Bretonne-style crepes with any kind of filling you could possibly dream up in a delightful indoor/outdoor building. It's a great stop for breakfast and desserts.

Microbrasserie La Diable (681-4546; $-$$), or "Microbrewery of the She-devil," serves light meals of European sausages alongside their six unique craft beers, brewed right on the premises. Be sure to note alcohol percentages listed on the menu as well and order accordingly. Don't mistake a 4 percent Diable for an 8.5 percent Extreme Onction!

La Savoie (681-4573; $$-$$$) serves traditional French Alps fare in a cozy French Alpine setting. Everything on their menu is "all-you-can-eat" and prices are per person. Strictly for an elegant yet relaxed lunch and dinner. The communal dining experience is great. If you sit next to the cheese warmer you'll become an expert in preparing raclette. Or be the one to cook meals on the hot rock.

La Grappe a Vin ($-$$) is an intimate wine bar where you can order 40 wines by the glass and another 130 by the bottle; choose from 20 ports, 50 scotches and 30 imported beers. In addition an oyster bar, wild game pates, local cheeses, fresh soups and salads are available. It's fun apres-ski and perfect for a light dinner.

If you're after a true feast, the high end **Soto Restaurant Sushi Bar** (681-4141;$$$) in Le Westin Resort specializes in Japanese cuisine with emphasis on sushi, sashimi and maki.

Windigo at the Fairmont Tremblant (681-7685; $$$) lays out a sumptuous and tasty theme buffet, or try the a la carte menu or table d'hote.

The Pizzateria (681-4522; $$) has such enticing flavors floating from their doors, you'd be hard-pressed not to stop in. Order to take out or be seen on their strategically placed outdoor deck, perfect people-watching territory. The house specialty at **La Chouquetterie** (681-4508; $), which translates as sugar tree, is the cream puff, Tropez style. **Queues de Castor** (681-4678; $), also known as Beavertails, is a tiny take-out spot. The traditional Canadian pastry, called a Beavertail because that's what it looks like, is a sinfully yummy. **The Coco Pazzo Deli** (681-4774; $) sells cheeses, salamis, prosciutto and dry pastas. It's around the corner from their restaurant, also called Coco Pazzo ($$) where the menu includes roasted rack of lamb, spice rubbed and grilled veal chop and herb-encrusted sea bass as well as pastas.

Les Artistes (681-4606; $-$$) serves traditional French bistro food. Sample offerings at the wine bar or sit outside on their corner terrace overlooking Lake Miroir. Smoked meats are a specialty in the Laurentians, and **Moe's** (425-9821; $-$$), in nearby St. Jovite, has the best in the region.

On the hill: For lunch, the non-smoking **Grand Manitou,** on top at 3,000 feet (the highest peak in the Laurentians), should satisfy most appetites. It features a meal of the day, for $7 or $10, sandwiches to order, pizza, fries and hot dogs.

Après-ski/nightlife

We list these in order from the quieter, mellow spots to the noisy party places. Since many of the hot spots also are restaurants, see the *Dining section.*

On sunny days, the best apres-ski is in the **Place St. Bernard,** where a stage often is set up with a live band cranking out the tunes. People sit in chairs with a brew and enjoy the sun, listen to the music and watch everyone looking for their friends.

La Grappe a Vin is the place to go for fine wine or liquors and light fare. The mountaintop bar in the **Grand Manitou** is open for apres-ski. **Microbrasserie La Diable** has canned music, good sausages for late-night snacks and six beers brewed on the premises. Blues bands play every Friday and Saturday.

Le Shack is a bit louder and often has a live band on the weekends. The whimsical décor of trees and flying geese overhead makes you feel like you're outdoors. The dancing never stops here, so be prepared for a lot of apres-ski exercise. Shooters are served in the traditional Quebec glass ski boot.

Cafe de l'Epoque in Vieux Tremblant sports strobe lights, loud live music (also CDs) and lots of bodies pressed together on the crowded rustic wood dance floor. OK at night, but a bit of a pit when exposed to daylight. **P'tit Caribou** is also in Vieux Tremblant and consistently gets high ratings from Ski Canada. Great, loud music and bar-top dancing by go-go girl wannabes. The people and the noise create the wild party ambience. You'll feel like you're 20 again, be ready to stay up far too late into the night.

Other activities

You can take a **sleigh ride,** go **ice skating** on Lac Miroir, go for a **dogsled ride** (you can mush the dogs yourself) or zip around on a **snowmobile.**

For a true Nordic experience, visit nearby **Le Scandinave** (425-5524) and wallow in the Scandinavian baths. The theory is simple: warm up your body, then close your skin's pores by chilling the body rapidly, then relax in a heated environment. Start in a Finnish sauna or steam bath, then plunge into cold water by running under a waterfall, diving into a pool or dipping into the river that runs through this forest retreat. To warm back up, sit in the outdoor Jacuzzi or return to the sauna or steam bath. Repeat all this as necessary! Two or three hours of this surprisingly affordable indulgence leaves you thoroughly refreshed .

The **Spa-sur-le-Lac at Club Tremblant** (425-8341) offers a more traditional experience with 11 body care and aesthetic rooms and a beauty salon. The Fairmont Tremblant also has a complete **spa** (681-7680) with facials, manicures, massages and the like.

The Source (681-5668), billed as "A Lake in the Laurentians," lets guests escape winter. This family-oriented spa includes an exercise room and a lake created to evoke the Laurentian outdoors complete with beach, waterfall and Tarzan-style rope swing.

The village has about 60 **shops.** Some of the fanciest are in the Chateau Mont Tremblant, with a nice cafe in the middle of the lobby. Chocoholics will want to make fast tracks to the

Dining: $$$-Entrees $20+; $$-$10-20; $-less than $10.
Accommodations: (double room) $$$$-$200+; $$$-$141-$200; $$-$81-$140; $-$80 and less.

Rocky Muontain Chocolate Factory, where you'll find smooth chocolate, deliciously creamy fudge, and crunchy toffee. The village also has a two-screen **movie theater.**

To book any activity, call the MTA central reservation numbers: 800-567-6760 or 425-8681. For more information, you can reach the tourist bureau at Tremblant at 425-2434.

Getting there and getting around

By air: Montréal has the nearest major airport, 75 miles away. Air Canada has many direct or non-stop flights from the United States. Northwest Airlines, KLM and most major airlines serve this major international airport.

By car: From Montréal, take autoroute 15 north to Sainte-Agathe, where the 15 merges with 117. Continue on autoroute 117 north past St. Jovite. About two kilometers (a little more than a mile) past the town, at the light, turn right on Montée Ryan (there's an Ultramar gas station on the left). Follow signs to Tremblant.

Getting around: Most visitors arrive by car, so rent one if you fly into Montréal. And then to get some use from the car, we suggest side trips to Mont Tremblant Village and St. Jovite, or even some of the smaller ski areas in the surrounding area.

Packing tip: Bring shoes with good traction. The cobblestone street is fairly steep. Though it has shallow steps built along each side, most people walk in the street (no vehicles are allowed). It can be slippery late at night and early in the morning.

Nearby skiing: Gray Rocks

Internet: www.grayrocks.com
5 lifts — 1 quad, 3 doubles, 1 surface; 22 trails; 620 feet

Gray Rocks is a mouse compared to Tremblant: It has 620 feet of vertical and four chair lifts. When you stand at Tremblant's summit, you can see Gray Rocks' 22 compact runs a few miles in the distance. It may look small, but Gray Rocks is a mouse that roars. Good trail planning and maintenance makes Gray Rocks ski like a much bigger mountain. Trails wrap around the mountain, rather than plunge straight down, and they incorporate the natural features of the terrain.

This is one of the best learning mountains in North America, and Gray Rocks has capitalized on that strength by carving out a big slice of the student skier market. The success of its Learn-to-Ski Week is overwhelming, with thousands of North Americans taking lessons every season. Lessons are not only for timid never-evers. Skiers of every level are faced with a challenging week of perfecting technique. Ski Weeks have been offered since 1951 and include everything: lodging, meals, instruction, video analysis, lift tickets, access to Le Spa fitness center and indoor pool, gratuities, a souvenir pin and photo, and full social calendar and activities.

Part of the success is creating group camaraderie, on and off the slopes. Since people learn best when they are relaxed and having fun, Gray Rocks considers its off-slope program as important as the lessons on the hill. Nightly entertainment, oui. But après-ski also has such creative alternatives as a cooking course, French lessons, wine-and-cheese get-togethers, classical guitar concerts, sleigh rides, a spa and fitness center-the list goes on. Gray Rocks has a day care and "Ski'N'Play" program for children, and it even has a pet kennel.

Gray Rocks also offers an all-inclusive "ski getaway" (room, meals, entertainment, gratuities, skiing, fitness center), with the option to add lessons and clinics.

The best deal here is a package, in which lift tickets valid at Gray Rocks and its sister resort, Mont Blanc, are included (call 800-567-6767 for reservations). Ski Week prices begin at $1,116 (Cdn$; 01/02 prices) per person, double occupancy.

Jay Peak
Vermont

Summit elevation: 3,968 feet
Vertical drop: 2,153 feet
Base elevation: 1,815 feet

Address: 4850 VT. Rte. 242, Jay, VT 05859
✆ Area code: 802
Ski area phone: 988-2611
Snow report: 988-9601
ⓘ Toll-free reservations: (800) 451-4449 (outside Vermont) or 988-2611
Fax: 988-4049
E-mail: info@jaypeakresort.com
World Wide Web: www.jaypeakresort.com

Expert:★★★★★
Advanced:★★★★★
Intermediate:★★★
Beginner:★
Never-ever:★

Number and types of lifts: 8–1 60-passenger aerial tramway, 1 high-speed quad, 2 quads, 1 triple, 1 double, 1 T bar, 1 Magic Carpet
Skiable acreage: 385 (plus 200 acres off-piste)
Snowmaking: 80 percent
Uphill capacity: 10,615 per hour
Snowboarding: Yes
Bed base: 1,000+ slopeside; 1,500 in area
Nearest lodging: slopeside
Resort child care: Yes, 2 to 5 years
Adult ticket, per day: $53 (02/03 price)

Dining:★★
Apres-ski/nightlife:★
Other activities:★

If you're looking for some of the East's best woods and most powder, come to Jay Peak Resort. Long before it was popular for Eastern resorts to cut glades, Jay's locals were sneaking into the woods to cut their own lines. After the resort president's son was caught skiing out of bounds, the resort cut some glades and opened them to the public, making tree skiing legit.

Since 1990, the resort has cut 21 glades and two extreme chutes, plus there's an additional 200 acres of backcountry terrain. Become familiar with Jay's woods-skiing policy—be an expert skier/rider in a group of three or more, and if you go out of bounds you are responsible for your own actions and cost of rescue. This is serious skiing and riding, with all the dangers inherent in backcountry terrain, so always carry a backpack containing emergency equipment in case you get injured or lost and have to stay on the mountain overnight.

As for snow, they call it the "Jay Peak cloud," which hovers over the mountain and dumps a foot or more of snow on days when skies are clear just five miles away. The 2000/01 season was a record year for Jay, blanketing the mountain with 571 inches (within two weeks, one storm brought 46 inches and another dumped 54 inches), more than any other resort in the country. Even in a "poor" snow year, like the 2001/02 season, Jay received 414 inches.

You've heard the old New Englander saying: "You can't get they-ah from hee-ah." While it's a bit of a trek and a lot of back roads to get to Jay, it's well worth the effort. Most of the time, you have the mountain practically to yourself. Even on powder days, you can catch freshies all day long. During holiday weekends, you'll wonder why you ever went anywhere else. Of course, this is when the locals complain about the oh-so-long 15-minute wait to ride up the lift.

People who come to Jay are here for the mountain's challenging and exciting terrain, so this isn't a good vacation for a group that includes non-skiers and non-riders. There's not a whole lot to do in the area. This is rural Vermont at its best, quiet and relaxing, with a focus on outdoor activities and recreation. Come if you want to ski or ride your legs off, settle into a Jacuzzi afterwards, then go to sleep early to get up early in the morning to do it all over again.

A high-speed detachable quad services terrain on the right side of the mountain previously accessed only from the Tram. Locals refer to the Green Mountain Flyer as the Green Mountain Freezer: You'll understand once you crest the ridge and get a full blast of the wind off the lake. The biggest drawback to Jay's layout is that there are only three ways to work your way across the mountain — Northway, Goat Run and Vermonter — they can get crowded and the snow gets skied off.

This season, Jay has replaced the Metro T-bar with a quad chair, giving beginners access to more terrain. Also new is a never-ever magic carpet lift. We hope they'll give the base lodges and hotel a facelift soon.

If you're here for a week, you might want to consider taking a day or two to ski Quebec's Eastern Township resorts (see Eastern Townships chapter).

Mountain layout–Skiing

◆◆ **Expert** ◆ **Advanced:** Experts who have never been here may very well quake in their boots when they see what Jay considers single-diamond terrain. The Face, The Saddle and Tuckermans Chutes are rock-and-tree-stub strewn, forcing you to pick your way over some gnarly stuff to get to the goods. All this in full view of the folks riding up the Tram. But the real challenge is in the woods. Warm up in Hell's Woods, Buckaroo Bonzai, Everglade and Beaver Pond Glade, then head to Timbuktu and Valhalla. Locals groaned loudly when Jay officially opened Beyond Beaver Pond Glade last season because it's just about the only piece of "unofficial woods" left on the mountain, but it remains pretty much untouched since you have to hike a bit to get there (or know the shortcut to it, and we're not telling). Keep an eye out for locals, who are more than willing to share their secret stashes if they see that you know what you're doing in the trees. There's plenty of in-bounds woods skiing to keep you grinning for a week, so don't go out of bounds unless you're with someone who knows the area.

Kitzbuehl is a tight bumped run that'll leave you huffing and puffing. River Quai and Green Beret (when it's open) are both truly hairy trails. Powerline is rated intermediate, but we think its monster moguls and double fall line make it tougher than that.

Advanced skiers ready to push themselves will want to take a glade technique lesson and head into the woods. You can always try out the "kiddie" glades mentioned below and see if you're ready first. Tree skiing opens up a whole new world of skiing and riding, it's just you and Mother Nature at her best. One of our expert staffers made her first foray into the woods several seasons ago and now we're lucky when she skis on a trail with us.

■ **Intermediate:** Jay is a great place for intermediates who are comfortable with their ability and want to put themselves to a challenge. Most intermediate trails here would be rated for advanced skiers elsewhere. One writer's niece and nephew, who are used to skiing at Mount Snow, found the narrower trails and wide-open "kiddie" glades (Kokomo, Moon Walk and Bushwacker) to be great fun.

We recommend warming up on Ullr's Dream (slip into Kokomo if you want to avoid the long flat at the end), JFK or Northway to Angel's Wiggle. To take in the amazing 360-degree views from the top to Mt. Mansfield, Québec's Eastern Townships, Lake Champlain, Mt. Washington and Montréal, ride up the tram and head down Vermonter. Goat Run is another fun trail, but gets iced up and moguled on heavy-traffic days.

Most advanced-intermediates will enjoy the groomed black-diamond trails off the Jet Triple Chair, once they make it past the somewhat-steep top sections. A favorite is Derick Hot Shot, a narrow winding trail that gets moderate bumps on high-traffic days. If you get to the top of the Jet and decide the terrain looks too steep, take Montrealer and choose from some wonderful intermediate terrain like Northway, Paradise Meadows, lower Kitzbuehl and Angel's Wiggle. (We wish this area of the mountain were served by its own chair.)

●● **Beginner:** Beginners have very limited terrain. The beginner area is served by a quad chair. However, higher-level skiers and riders have to use those trails to reach the Tram and Green Mountain Flyer. All this can be very intimidating. Once you ride up one of the main chair lifts, you're faced with intermediate terrain that can be very overwhelming if you're not a daring person.

● **Never-ever:** There is a new dedicated learning center with a magic carpet at the base of Tramside.

Mountain layout—Snowboarding

Jay has a terrain park on Lower Can Am, but most riders come for the glades, chutes and off-piste terrain. Make sure to read the skiing description; it applies to riders too. Experienced woods riders will quiver with excitement upon discovering the natural halfpipe in Canyonland: We dare you to find it. Ullr's Dream is a great warm-up run, but duck into Kokomo to avoid the lo-o-ong flat at the bottom. Riders coming out of Beaver Pond Glade and Beyond Beaver Pond Glade hook back up to Ullr's, so you'll also want to heed that warning (plus Beyond has its own unavoidable flat that will have you hoofing back to the trails). If you're looking to make sweeping arcs, head to wide-open Jet and Haynes. If they're too steep for your taste, take Montrealer to Angel's Wiggle, then take the Wiggle all the way down or choose from Lower Milk Run and Hell's Crossing to Paradise Meadows. The beginner area is now served by quad chair and there is a dedicated learning center with a magic carpet.

Mountain rating

Jay Peak is the perfect mountain for skiers and riders who are adventurous intermediates and better. Most trails are cut classic New England style, meaning narrow and winding. The glades and chutes are so enticing, experts will ski and ride till they drop from exhaustion. Beginners and never-evers may want to go someplace else to prepare for this mountain.

Cross-country and snowshoeing

Jay Peak has 20 km. of cross-country skiing that network into 200 km. of touring trails in the area. Jay recently purchased new trail-grooming and track-setting equipment. Instruction and rentals are available. A trail pass is $5.

Two-hour, naturalist-led tours on snowshoes are scheduled throughout the week in the afternoons and evenings. Cost is $12 per person and includes guide, snowshoes, headlamps, boots and poles. Check with the Ski School Desk to register. Extended or group tours also can be arranged. For those who want to head out on their own, snowshoe rentals are available anytime through the snowboard shop.

Hazen's Notch Cross-Country Ski & Snowshoe Center (326-4799), about 10 miles away in Hazen's Notch, is owned and operated by the nonprofit Hazen's Notch Association. The 64 km. of groomed and backcountry trails include 16 km. of snowshoe-only trails. For 2002/03 the intermediate Westside Trail will be reopened. The views alone are worth the trip, plus the high elevation ensures bountiful snow. You'll find ski and snowshoe rentals, plus instruction by appointment. Ask about naturalist-guided snowshoe tours and full-moon snowshoe tours. Adult passes cost $10, children $5 (2002/03 prices).

Lessons (2002/03 prices)

Group lessons: Two-hour ski or snowboard lesson, $25 US/$32 CDN. Multiday packages available.

Never-ever package: Two-hour ski or snowboard lesson with rental and use of beginner lifts, $40 US/$50 CDN. Multiday packages available. GETSkiing program uses short skis or Snowblades to help you learn to ski or improve technique, $25 US/$32 CDN.

Private lessons: One-hour ski or snowboard session, $48 US/$60 CDN. Private telemark lessons also available.

Special programs: Glade Skiing Techniques are two-hour sessions on days when glade skiing is best and for advanced skiers only, $25 US/$32 CDN. Backcountry Adventure gives guided tours of popular off-piste areas. You must be a very experienced skier or rider; the ski school has the option to disqualify participants, $45 US/$59 CDN. Advanced skiers can go for the First Tracks program with a ticket purchased the day before, getting you up the first tram at 8:15 a.m. weekdays (7:45 a.m. weekends) for a guided tour down the untouched mountain. Cost is $5 US/$7 CDN.

Racing: Racing Camps for recreational skiers feature gate running and on-hill training. JAYSTAR races at 1 p.m. on Thursday, Friday and Saturday, $5 for two runs. Special JAYSTAR Clinic available just prior to race time.

Child care (2002/03 prices)

Ages: 2 to 5 years old.
Cost: $40 all day (does not include cost of lunch); $20 half day.
Reservations: Recommended.

Note: Guests staying at Hotel Jay and Jay Peak Condominiums receive free day care for children ages 2 to 5 years old. Evening supervised dinner is also available. Preregistration is advised. Infant care is available on a fee basis with advanced reservations.

Children's lessons: Kinderschool Ski Program for ages 3–5, includes lift ticket, $30 US/$39 CDN. Preregistration is required. Mountain Explorers, a full-day program for ages 5–10 costs $47 US/$60 CDN plus lift tickets. Miniriders is the same program, only for snowboarding. Mountain Adventurers, a full-day program for ages 10–16, $47 US/$60 CDN plus lifts.

Other programs include snowskating, snowshoeing, cross-country skiing, torchlight parades, and First Tracks. Multichild discounts and multiday packages available.

Lift tickets (2002/03 prices)

	Adult	Junior (7–14)	Toddler (6 and younger)
One day	$53	$39	$6

Who skis at a discount: Seniors 65 and older ski for $12 US/$15 CDN. College students with an ID ski for $30 US/$40 CDN. Vermont residents pay $36 for one-day adult, $30 for a junior and $6 for a toddler.

Note: When staying for more than one day, the wise move is to buy a lodging package that includes tickets: Children younger than 14 stay and ski free, teenagers 15–18 stay and ski for US$50 per day when sharing their parent's room or condo.

Accommodations

Jay Peak Resort assists guests in arranging lodging, air travel, train travel, shuttle van service to the airport and train station and rental cars. Jay Peak is overall a bargain. The best deal is to stay in the slopeside hotel or condos. During non-holiday weeks, children 14 and younger stay and ski free, and teens 15–18 stay and ski for $50 US per day, when sharing the same room or condo with their parents (meals are extra). Five-day stays and longer include a half-day complimentary ticket that can be used on the day of arrival beginning at 12:30 p.m.

If you have kids ages 7 and younger, stay at **Hotel Jay** (800-451-4449 or 988-9601; $– $$). It provides complimentary child care from 9 a.m. to 9 p.m., including a supervised dinner. A sauna, Jacuzzi, family room with fireplace and game room are available. Five-day packages for a family with two adults cost $571 US per adult (includes meals for adults).

Slopeside condos range from luxury to economy. Five-day packages, including lodging and lift tickets, range from $583 to $820 US per adult. Meal plans are available. Nicest are the recently built **Village Townhouses** ($$). Deluxe accommodations can be found at **Mountainside, Trailside** and **Slopeside** condos ($$–$$$). **Mountainside Studios** and **Stoney Path** are perfect for small families or couples ($$–$$$).

There are also a variety of chalets, cabins, motels, hotels, inns and B&Bs in the area. Jay Peak Resort can assist you, or call the Jay Peak Area Association at 800-882-7460.

The Black Lantern Inn (326-4507 or 800-255-8661; $-$$), about 20 minutes down the road in Montgomery, is a beautifully restored stagecoach stop originally built in 1803 and now listed on the National Historic Register. The inn has 10 rooms and six deluxe suites with fireplaces and Jacuzzi bathtubs; all decorated with Vermont antiques.

Phineas Swann Bed & Breakfast (326-4306; $$), a bit closer in Montgomery Center, is an 1890s gingerbread Victorian inn that includes suites in its carriage house with a Jacuzzi, fireplace, queen-size bed and TV/VCR. Gourmet breakfast and afternoon tea is served.

The Inn at Trout River (326-4391 or 800-338-7049; $-$$), also in Montgomery Center, is a rambling Victorian with queen-size beds, down quilts, feather pillows, flannel sheets and private baths. The main dining room and sitting room have fireplaces, a Montgomery Soapstone Stove warms up the split-level living room and library.

Dining

Each lodge has a cafeteria that serves breakfast and lunch, and the food is quite good. For heartier and tastier on-mountain meals, **Hotel Jay** is the place for breakfast and **The International Restaurant** dishes out a satisfying lunch. Hotel Jay has a fixed-price, gourmet dinner for about $22 that's very good. Children's menus also are available.

Don't miss dinner at **Zack's on the Rocks** (326-4500; $$), in nearby Hazen's Notch. The dining experience is as much of an adventure as a day on the mountain: You'll feel like you've wandered through the woods and discovered someone's secret garden, complete with vines and flowers draping from the ceiling and employees who remind you of free-spirited wood sprites. You'll first be seated at the piano bar, where you'll find yourself chatting freely with the other patrons as you agonize over the menu. When your appetizers are ready, you're led to your table by Zack, ringing a brass bell and usually attired in a purple flowing gown that reminds you of Merlin. And, oh, what a wizard he is in the kitchen!

Dining: $$$-Entrees $20+; $$-$10-20; $-less than $10.
Accommodations: (double room) $$$$-$200+; $$$-$141-$200; $$-$81-$140; $-$80 and less.

Several local inns are renowned for their gourmet meals and appropriately, reservations are suggested. Try **The Black Lantern Inn** (326-4507; $$), where the menu changes nightly and is served by candlelight. The food, cozy atmosphere and prices here rival any you'll find across the border in Quebec. **Lemoine's** at The Inn at Trout River (326-4391; $$) is another palate-pleasing experience.

For something less pricey, consider the pub menu at **Hobo's Café** at The Inn at Trout River (326-4391; $-$$). Another good bet is **The Belfry** (326-4400; $-$$), just down the mountain road toward Montgomery Center, where you'll find their extensive menu written on a blackboard at the entrance.

Ask at the hotel front desk to find out about favorite restaurants in nearby Québec. You'll find French cuisine at affordable prices because of the exchange rate.

Après-ski/nightlife

The **Golden Eagle Sports Bar** and the **International Bar,** both in the Tram base lodge, and the **Sport Lounge at Hotel Jay** are the on-mountain places to head when you quit the slopes. We recommend taste-testing the Vermont microbrews. Live entertainment, Karaoke nights and theme parties are frequently scheduled. **The Belfry**, just down the mountain road toward Montgomery Center, has a good selection of beers and local microbrews on tap and in the bottle.

Family activities include ice skating, snowcat rides, naturalist-led snowshoeing treks, welcome parties, sing-a-longs and bonfire parties. Teens will find special activities just for them such as movie nights, bowling, snow volleyball and dances.

Other activities

Guided **snowmobile** tours into the surrounding mountains and valleys of the Northeast Kingdom are available for varying lengths of time. Reservations are required, call the Jay Peak reservations line.

Shopping: There are a few shops in Jay worth visiting, such as The Snow Job (where you'll get the best tunes around) and the Jay Country Store, but if you're planning to take a shopping excursion, we suggest heading to Burlington, Montréal or Magog. In the spring, visit one of the nearby maple sugar shacks.

Getting there and getting around

By air: Burlington International Airport is served by Continental, Delta, Jetblue, United and USAir. Resort shuttle service and special Thrifty Car Rental rates are available. It takes 1.5 hours to drive from the airport to the mountain.

By car: Jay Peak Resort is on Rte. 242 in northern-central Vermont, just below the Canadian border, about equidistant between I-91 and I-89. Sample driving times: Boston, 3.5 hours; Albany, 4.5 hours; New York City, 6.5 hours; Toronto, 7 hours; Montréal, 1.5 hours.

By bus: Vermont Transit serves nearby Newport from all major New England points. Ground transportation available.

By train: AMTRAK Vermonter to St. Albans, 45 minutes away. Ground transfers available to Jay Peak.

Getting around: Bring a car if you want to venture off mountain.

Killington/Pico

Vermont

Summit elevation: **4,215 feet**
Vertical drop: **3,050 feet**
Base elevation: **1,165 feet**

Address: Killington Road
Killington, VT 05751
✆ **Area code:** 802
Ski area phone: 422-3333
Snow report: 422-3261
ⓘ **Toll-free reservations:** (800) 621-6867
(621-MTNS)
E-mail: info@killington.com
Internet: www.killington.com
Expert:★★
Advanced:★★★
Intermediate:★★★★
Beginner:★★★★
Never-ever:★★★

Number and types of lifts: 32–2 gondolas,
6 high-speed quads, 6 quads,
6 triples, 4 doubles, 8 surface lifts
Acreage: 1,182 skiable acres
Snowmaking: 70 percent
Uphill capacity: 52,973 per hour
Snowboarding: Yes
Bed base: 5,500 (base), 18,000 (region)
Nearest lodging: Walking distance
Resort child care: Yes, 6 weeks to 6 years
Adult ticket, per day: $52-$64 (02/03)
Dining:★★
Apres-ski/nightlife:★★★★
Other activities:★★

Tucked beneath Vermont's second-highest peak, the Killington Basin is a natural place for a ski resort. The K-1 gondola carries skiers and riders to the highest lift-served skiing in the state (yes, even higher than on Stowe's Mt. Mansfield). If it's snowing anywhere in the state, it's probably snowing here. The basin receives, on average, 250 inches of snow each year. If the snow doesn't fall from the sky, Killington/Pico makes it fall from its guns. With one of the world's largest snowmaking systems, the resort literally blankets its seven mountains in white.

Thanks to its prodigious snowmaking capacity, Killington/Pico is usually open longer than any resort in the East, sometimes as long as eight months. Even during drought years, when other resorts are hamstrung by dry rivers and snowmaking ponds, Killington can cover most of its terrain, thanks to a pipeline that brings water up to the slopes from a local reservoir. From the cool days of autumn, when skiers and snowboarders make a few turns down a white strip high on the mountain, framed by fall foliage, to the carefree days of late spring, long after mud season, Killington attracts those who can't wait for winter and are sad when it's over.

Spring is probably the best time to ski or ride at Killington/Pico. Crowds gather on the deck of the Bear Mountain Lodge, hooting and hollering as up-and-coming bump skiers rip it up—or flail—on the legendary Outer Limits trail, the longest, steepest mogul slope in the East. The smell of burgers on the grill wafts into the air, beer is plentiful (for age 21 or older), and everyone is having a good time. It's like a giant frat party on the slopes.

Killington, though, is not all things to all people. Weekend warriors flock to the slopes, and the chaos is sometimes dangerous. Snowshed (the beginner area) is dubbed "Bloodshed" by the locals. Furthermore, navigating the morass of terrain has made more than one skier or rider wish they had their own GPS system. Experts often find themselves zooming down beginner runs because they have missed their black-diamond choice. Worse still, beginners find themselves stranded on black-diamond runs in an attempt to reach their cars at day's end. To add to the confusion, Killington boasts five base areas. (Note: the Sunrise Base Area on Rte. 100 is now closed, and lift service is no longer available.) Killington does provide shuttle service at day's end for those who have taken a wrong turn and ended up at a base different from where they parked in the morning.

Only about 1,500 feet of Killington's 3,050-foot vertical drop is working vertical, and only three trails, mostly beginner, meander the last 1,500 feet down to the true base on Rte. 4. People looking to avoid the crowds at the other Killington base areas often park here, take the gondola to the mountain(s) proper, then tolerate the long, slow run back down at day's end.

To avoid confusion or ending up on those flat run-outs when you'd rather be bashing serious bumps, we recommend signing up for one of the free Meet the Mountain tours, which leave from the Snowshed Base Lodge every Monday, Tuesday, Friday and Saturday at 9:45 a.m., and every Monday afternoon at 12:45 p.m. The tour guides, Killington's volunteer ambassadors, will show newcomers how best to take advantage of Killington's trails without getting lost or stuck in the thickest crowds.

Or you can ski Pico, a physically separate mountain from Killington's other five. The resort added Pico to the "family" in 1996, but the planned interconnect never materialized. Even though it's 10 minutes away by car, Pico is still worth visiting. Considered by many locals as a feather in the Mother Ship's cap, Pico has 2,000 feet of vertical, 48 trails and some very interesting (and often uncrowded) terrain.

Note: Though we would prefer to give you separate stats for Killington and Pico, the resort's policy is to provide combined stats, as if it were already one resort, so that's what we list. We refer to Killington/Pico when we're talking about the whole enchilada (this introduction, primarily), and Killington or Pico when talking about each one individually. Lift tickets are valid at both areas, but if you plan to ski just Pico, you can purchase a Pico-only pass that's about $15 cheaper than the full pass. Another option is to order a free Pico card on-line (www.killington.com), and use it to take $10 off the lift ticket price. Public transportation between the two is via The Bus, which charges $1 and stops at several locations along the Access Road. Catch it at the Snowshed Base Lodge.

 ## Mountain layout–Skiing

Killington's terrain is almost too sprawling to describe. The resort has five separate base areas (six, including Pico.) Three are clustered within striking distance at the top of Killington Road—Snowshed and Rams Head are across the street from one another, and Killington base is just a bit up the road. Bear Mountain, home of the famed Outer Limits bump run, is on Bear Mountain Road off Rte. 4 (note: occasionally, snowtires or chains are required on the Bear Mountain Access Road). Also off Rte. 4 is the Skyeship Base Station, a good choice for those who don't want to hassle with traffic on the Access Road, but the run down at day's end is less than scintillating.

◆◆ **Expert** ◆ **Advanced:** Between Snowdon Mountain and Killington Peak is some of the toughest terrain. The Canyon quad chair services this area for access to double-diamond Cascade, Downdraft, Double Dipper and Big Dipper Glade.

Skye Peak is one of the most popular sections of the mountain. Ovation, Superstar, Skyelark and Bittersweet are all fairly easy expert trails that are covered with plenty of manmade snow. Superstar is usually the last trail to close in the spring and is the scene of the downhill ski leg of the Killington's Memorial Day Weekend Triathlon.

From the top of Skye Peak, advanced skiers can drop down Skyeburst and Wildfire by following the Skye Peak quad. This connection is not recommended for lower intermediates because it leads to the Bear Mountain quad, which services good advanced and expert terrain. From the top of the Bear Mountain quad, skiers can descend the double-diamond pitch of Devil's Fiddle or loop in the opposite direction down Wildfire, an easier single-diamond run with some bumps. For mogul hounds, the real thrill is to drop directly under the chairlift and challenge Outer Limits. If you ski it on one of the rare days it's groomed, and if you fall, you may slide all the way to the bottom, much to the amusement of the crowds watching from the base and the chair lift.

After a good snowfall, head to Pico and get fresh tracks down the gnarly Giant Killer or Upper Pike. Upper KA and Sunset 71, narrow trails reminiscent of the early days of New England skiing, wind down from the top of Pico and offer interesting knolls, twists and turns.

■ **Intermediate:** Don't be alarmed by the black diamonds on the Killington trail map. Many of their single-black diamond runs would be blue cruisers at other resorts, and indeed, we've been told that many of them have been relabeled as such.

The Rams Head high-speed quad chair covers mainly beginner and intermediate trails. Capers, a gentle trail, is a good warm-up cruiser. The Snowdon area is another cruiser's delight. It's served by two chairs from the base area and a mid-mountain Poma lift on Bunny Buster. Highline and Conclusion are good advanced cruising runs with excellent pitch. Bunny Buster and Chute are similar but with a more mellow slope.

Needle's Eye drops beneath the second section of the Skyeship gondola and is a nice wide cruiser as is the aptly named Cruise Control. A trip back up the Needle's Eye Express quad will put skiers back on Bittersweet for a cruise to the Killington Base Lodge or Snowshed.

Pico is home to 49-ner, a cruiser that offers superb views from the top of Pico. Beginners will find the top part of this blue square challenging, though.

●● **Beginner:** Green trails lead from all six interconnected peaks, which allows beginners the panoramic vistas and thrill of skiing from the summit, not possible at areas where the upper-mountain trails are reserved for seasoned skiers. Beginners beware: It's easy to get lost at Killington on these meandering trails. If it's the end of the day, consult your map frequently to make sure you'll end up at the same base area as your car, or be prepared to hop on the shuttle.

● **Never-ever:** Killington, in theory, has a perfect learning area: Snowshed. Served by three chairlifts, this gentle slope is a segregated beginning area. But the top of the trail is accessible from the upper part of the mountain, which can make Snowshed exceedingly crowded and not just with other beginners. Experts often fly down the slope. Consider learning at another resort or head to Pico, where beginners learn at the more isolated Bonanza area.

Mountain layout–Snowboarding

This is quite a confusing mountain for first-time Killington riders. Half of our snowboard writer's day was spent stopped and studying the trail map, trying to figure out where she was and how she got there, when she wanted to be two peaks over. If you're going to make the most of your time here, either take a free "Meet the Mountains" tour or befriend a local. Be aware that some roped-off trails are not visibly marked until it's too late — around a bend or over a knoll — which means you'll have to hike a few feet back to the open trail.

Do find your way to Killington's tight terrain features. Both the Superpipe and the terrain park were ranked best in the Northeast in a recent national skier/boarder opinion survey. One trip through The Beach terrain park, at Snowshed base area, is all it takes to realize that

Killington's Park and Pipe crew aren't just doing it for the fame; they're serious riders and hardcore jibbers who want to make it fun for everyone. Transitions between jumps are smooth, and the crew works harder on the landings than average. Good chance you'll see crew members hand-grooming park features or testing the product. The park includes a straight rail, rainbow slider, funbox and various jumps, many of which have two, differently sized approaches; one for the intermediate jumpers and one for advanced. One drawback about the park is that it's in a beginner's learning area. Our rider encountered sliders who had yet to master turns slideslipping in the park; a major hazard for all. Beginning riders will find a mini terrain park on Snowshed that has much smaller features.

The massive 450- by 55- by 15-foot Superpipe is at rider's left off the K-1 gondola. Pico has a terrain park on Panhandler.

Mountain rating

Overall, intermediates won't tire of Killington. Advanced skiers will have a lot of fun in select areas such as Skye Peak, Bear Mountain and Killington Peak. Though experts will find no extreme skiing, they can find glades (called fusion zones) that will test them, such as Low Rider on Snowdon and Julio on Killington Peak. Weekend crowds could prove daunting to beginners and never-evers, but if you learn to ski during midweek, you will find Snowshed acceptable.

Cross country and snowshoeing

Near the base of the Killington Access Road, **Mountain Meadows Cross Country Ski Resort** (775-7077) has 56 km. of trails meandering across Kent Lake and through surrounding forests. The Center also has a 1.2-km. loop with an extensive snowmaking system. When snow is lean, Mountain Meadows is one of the few cross country ski resorts that opens. **Mountain Top Cross-Country Ski Resort** (483-2311), in Chittenden, has 110 km. of trails, 40 km. of dual-set tracks and 0.5 km. of trails with snowmaking. Both areas have rentals, lessons, ski shops and warming huts. Mountain Meadows offers dogsled tours, and Mountain Top offers sledding and horse-drawn sleigh rides.

Trailhead Ski Touring Center in Stockbridge (746-8038) has 60 km. of trails, with 35 km. groomed and 35 km. tracked. In Woodstock, the **Ski Touring Center** (457-2114) has 75 km. of trails, lessons and rentals.

Lessons (2002/03 prices)

Group lessons: The Killington Skier Development Program uses the innovative teaching program called Perfect Turn®. Perfect Turn has 10 levels. For lower intermediates and higher, the two hour clinics, for levels 2 through 8, are offered at 10 a.m. and 1 p.m. and cost $34 for one day. There are also five-day programs.

Never-ever package: The resort has a well-designed Perfect Turn Learn-to-Ski Center at Snowshed. Five-day ($239) first-time packages for skiers and riders include lift, clinic and equipment.

Private lessons: A one-hour clinic is $89 for one person, $138 for two. A two-hour lesson is $149 for one, $218 for two. Three- and six-hour clinics also are available.

Special programs: Too many to list here. Among the topics are moguls, women's instruction, racing, adaptive instruction for the disabled and even instruction for instructors.

Racing: None for public participation. Call the Alpine Training Center (422-6797) near the Killington Base Lodge for information on clinics and programs.

Child care (2002/03 prices)

Ages: 6 weeks to 6 years.
Costs: $69 per day (with lunch) and $48 per half day (no lunch). Multiday discounts available.

Reservations: Required; call (800) 621-6867.

Note: All-day programs run from 7:45 a.m. to 4:30 p.m. on weekends, and 8 a.m. to 4:30 p.m. midweek. Parents must supply food and beverage for children 23 months and younger. The Friendly Penguin Children's Center is located in the Rams Head Family Center.

Children's lessons: Programs for ages 2–3 include lessons, lunch and equipment for $99 for a full day, $66 for a half day. Programs for older children, with lessons and lunch but no equipment, run $89 for a full day and $64 for a half day for ages 4–6, and $101 for a full day and $74 for a half day for ages 7–12. Multi-day rates are available. Teens 13–17 can take part in The SnowZone, which offers skiing, snowboarding and skiboarding, and other popular trends in snow sports in either half-day ($34) or full-day ($68) sessions. Prices do not include lift tickets in the SnowZone program. One-, three- and seven-day programs are also available.

Lift tickets (2002/03 prices)

	Adult	Teen (13-18)	Child (6-12)
One day	$64	$58	$40
Three days	$168 ($56/day)	$150 ($50/day)	$102 ($34/day)
Five days	$260 ($52/day)	$230 (46/day)	$155 ($31/day)

Who skis free: Children 12 and younger ski free when accompanied by an adult who buys a Monday-Friday five-day pass or longer.

Who skis at a discount: Ages 65 and older, same price as teens. Pico Card holders ski for $10 off the Pico-only lift ticket price of $48 Sunday and $45 Monday through Friday, nonholiday. To order a free Pico Card, log onto www.killington.com.

Accommodations

Killington has very little slopeside lodging and no real ski-in/ski-out options; on-mountain condos are ski-in, but not ski-out. To make reservations for the **Killington Grand Resort Hotel, Killington Resort Villages** and most properties, call the **Killington Lodging Bureau** (800-621-6867).

Killington Resort Villages has good values and the best location, with nearby athletic club facilities, some nightlife and an excellent shuttlebus system. Of the condo complexes here, **Highridge** units are by far the most desirable. **Sunrise**, at the base of Bear Mountain, is another good choice. Other condos include **The Woods at Killington**, which boasts Jacuzzis and saunas and a complete spa, and **Mountain Inn** and the **Cascades Lodge**, which are very convenient but basic. The Cascades has a nice indoor pool, and the Mountain Inn has some of the best nightlife, when the bar is hopping.

The **Killington Grand Resort Hotel** ($$–$$$$), near the base of Snowshed, is the newest lodge in the area. It has 200 units from hotel rooms to penthouses, and the accommodations are more on par with what you'd find at a Comfort Inn. Also on site are a full-service restaurant, outdoor heated swimming pool, health club and "slopeside" location. (In truth, you have to walk across a snowmaking pond on a long pedestrian bridge to reach the slopes.) When you reserve a room, make sure you ask for a "hotel room" or "suite." Most of the "studio" rooms only have sofa or Murphy beds.

Dining: $$$-Entrees $20+; $$-$10-20; $-less than $10.
Accommodations: (double room) $$$$-$200+; $$$-$141-$200; $$-$81-$140; $-$80 and less.

The top hotel on the mountain road at Killington is **The Inn of the Six Mountains** (800-228-4676 or 422-4302; $$–$$$), with a 65-foot indoor lap pool, exercise room and frequent shuttles to the slopes. Rates include breakfast. **The Red Clover Inn** (775-2290 or 800-752-0571; $$$–$$$$) is five miles from the Killington Access Road and is hard to find, but we think it's the best in the area. Situated on 13 acres, this farmhouse estate has private baths, country decor and handmade quilts in each room. Room rates include breakfast and dinner, and the food is superb. Another favorite is **The Inn at Long Trail** (775-7181 or 800-325-2540; $-$$). One of Vermont's first ski lodges, the inn still maintains its cozy, rustic feel. The 19 rooms are small, but the inn has a devoted following. Rates include breakfast and dinner.

Of the other properties on Killington Access Road, **The Red Rob** (422-3303; $$), **Killington Village Inn** (422-3301; $$–$$$) and **Chalet Killington** (422-3451; $$) rate in that order. The food is reportedly best at The Red Rob. Rates include breakfast at The Red Rob and Chalet, and breakfast and dinner at the Killington Village Inn. The **Birch Ridge Inn** (422-4293; $$$-$$$$), also on the Access Road, was created from a former executive retreat. The A-frame design gives it an alpine flair, and the cuisine earns highs marks from gourmands. Near the base of the Killington Road is the **North Star Lodge** (422-4040; $-$$), which has a pool and shuttle service and is surrounded by good restaurants.

The Grey Bonnet (775-2537; $-$$) on Rte. 100 north received numerous recommendations. There is a nice indoor pool, sauna and pub. Rates include breakfast and dinner. You will need a car to get to the ski area.

The Cortina Inn (773-3333 or 800-451-6108; $$$–$$$$), on Rte. 4, a mile past Pico, is very good. It has a health club, pool, spa, two restaurants, children's activities on holiday weekends, and many large suites. **The Vermont Inn** (775-0708 or 800-541-7795 ; $$–$$$$), with 18 rooms, fireside dining, and everything homemade, is a charming New England country inn. Breakfast and dinner are included in the rates, and the food is excellent. The inn is located just over one mile west of Pico on Rte. 4.

A favorite luxury spot of ours is the **Woodstock Inn and Resort** (800-448-7900; $$$–$$$$), about 17 miles east of Killington. Rooms are cozy and beautifully decorated, with hand-stitched quilts on each bed. The dining room wine list has 184 selections, both foreign and domestic. Midweek, the inn has a very attractive package with downhill skiing at nearby Suicide Six or cross-country skiing at the Woodstock Ski Touring Center.

Dining

The Killington area has more than 100 restaurants and bars. The best in the area—ranked among the top in the nation by *Food and Wine* and *Condé Nast Traveler*—is **Hemingway's** (422-3886), one of only two four-star restaurants in Vermont. The prix fixe four-course menu ranges from $50–$65.

Our other favorites are **The Summit** (422-3535), an award-winning restaurant with a menu that changes nightly and a great wine list; the top-rated **The Vermont Inn** (800-541-7795 or 775-0708), with fine formal dining; and the award-winning **Red Clover Inn** (775-2290), where the rack of lamb is exceptional. The **Birch Ridge Inn** (422-4293; $$$) has a small, but highly acclaimed restaurant. **Jason's** (422-3303) in The Red Rob has excellent Northern Italian food, and **Zola's Grille at the Cortina Inn** (773-3333) serves a blend of Northern Italian, French bistro, and Mediterranean cuisine in a casual atmosphere. Reservations are required at all restaurants but Zola's.

McGrath's Irish Pub (775-7181) at The Inn at Long Trail serves a wonderful Guinness stew and shepherd's pie in its funky pub and restaurant built into a cliff. Service can be slow, but the food is hearty and tasty. We have not eaten at **Ovations** (422-5001), at the Killington Grand Resort Hotel, but it advertises a family-oriented menu. At **Charity's** (422-3800), the bar is cozy and welcoming, the portions healthy and the menu of steaks, BBQ and Italian dishes such as Tortellini Siciliano and Shrimp Diavlo can appease virtually any hungry skier's appetite. Avoid the prime rib though; it's tough.

Lots of locals recommend **Choices** (422-4030) on the Killington Access Road.

For restaurants a bit kinder to the budget: **The Wobbly Barn Steakhouse** (422-3392) is known for steaks and a great salad bar (no reservations). **Mrs. Brady's** (422-2020) serves the "basics" (salads, burgers, roast turkey and monster sandwiches). **Pizza Jerks** (422-4111) and the **Outback Pizza** (422-9885), both on the Access Road, serve decent 'za. A new place, **Ralphies** (422-2345), does take-out only gourmet pizza.

For breakfast, locals head to **Peppers** at the nightspot Outback. Portions are massive, and it caters to the hung-over. Another choice is the **Waffle House**. If you're looking for a good cup of coffee or a quick breakfast, head to the **Sun-up Bakery**, but be forewarned: If there's 10-inches of fresh snow, the staff often shuts the doors and skis for a few runs. On a sunny day, head to **Raul's Burrito Stand** at the base of the Needle's Eye chair.

Après-ski/nightlife

Killington's après-ski scene, strung out along the Access Road, is often voted number one in the nation, with the atmosphere generally raucous and young, and the festivities often driven by excellent bands, some nationally known. Après-ski at the mountain includes the **Mahogany Ridge** at the Killington Base Lodge, the **Long Trail Brew Pub** at Snowshed and the **Bear Mountain Lounge** at, you guessed it, the Bear Mountain Base Lodge.

Immediate après-ski action on the Access Road can be found in **Charity's**. **Outback Pizza** is highly recommended for its happy hour(s) as well. It's a favorite locals' hangout on weekdays, with $5 all-you-can-eat pizza on Monday nights; entertainment and dancing extend into the evening on weekends. A new local hotspot is the **Lookout Bar and Grill**, where Skiddy, one of Killington's best local bump skiers, rules the bar. For rowdy après-ski and then dancing to loud music, head to the **Wobbly Barn Steakhouse**. Big name bands often lead the line-up on busy winter weekends at **The Pickle Barrel**, which has a lively happy hour with dancing later in the evening. It's a favorite among the young college crowd.

Those older than 30 may want to opt out of the mosh pits at Wobbly Barn and the Pickle Barrel, and head down the road to **The Grist Mill**. This restaurant/bar has earned a reputation in recent years as the place for slightly "more mature" skiers, but don't let that fool you: Maturity at Killington is strictly relative. The place rocks on weekends, when live music and dancing is featured, and its circular bar and layout is perfect for checking out the action and general people-watching. Plus, for our money the Grist Mill makes the area's most toe-curling Goombays, a local concoction of fruit juices and various flavors of rum. Two Goombays and you'll understand why this rates as the unofficial drink of the official après-ski/nightlife capital of the East.

Casey's Caboose is a favorite locals' haunt with killer spicy buffalo wings. An older, quieter set meets at the **Summit** for happy hour. When the bar at the **Mountain Inn** has live entertainment, it's great fun.

From Pico, head a few yards up Rte. 4 to The Inn at Long Trail, nestled right into the apex of Killington Pass. McGrath's Irish Pub here serves Guinness ale on tap. Live entertainment, performing on a stage built right into the cliff, keeps the bar full on weekends at St. Paddy's Day.

 ## Other activities

Snowshed also has an **indoor rock climbing wall** (773-3343) that's open daily. The **Killington Peak Restaurant** at the top of the K-1 Gondola serves dinner Wednesdays only. The fixed-price dinner, ($30-or-so for adults and $15-or so for children) includes a ride to the top in a gondola. Reservations are required, 422-6780. Farther down the Access Road, an **outdoor skating rink** can be found below the Summit Lodge on Grist Mill Pond. For **snowmobiling information** call the Cortina Inn, 773-3333, or Killington Snowmobile Tours, 422-2121.

The **Spa at The Woods** is a full service European spa at The Woods Resort & Spa. Treatments include hot stone therapy, citrus body polish, seaweed body mask, herbal wraps and paraffin treatments.

Shopping is plentiful, bus as spread out as the resort. The Killington Shops at the Shack, several outlet-style stores now owned by the ski resort, are at the intersection of Rte. 4 and the Killington Access Road. In Killington, stop at the Greenbrier Gift Shop for handcrafted items and gourmet ware. Nearby Bridgewater has an old mill that now houses about 10 shops including a bookstore, Miranda Pottery and Charles Shackleton Furniture. Woodstock, about 17 miles east of Killington on Rte. 4, is one of Vermont's most beautiful villages and is packed with **art galleries** and shops. Even farther east on Rte. 4 in Quechee is the Simon Pearce **glass-blowing** workshop and store.

Getting there and getting around

By air: Major airports are located in Burlington, VT, Albany, NY, and Manchester, NH. Burlington is about a 90-minute drive from Killington, while Albany and Manchester are each about 2 hours. Green Mountain Limousine Service (773-1313) runs transfers from the Burlington airport for $330 for two, round-trip, plus 15-percent driver gratuity. Thrifty Rental Cars has an office at the Inn of the Six Mountains. Major car rental companies are also available at the Burlington, Albany and Manchester airports. Other airports with commercial service are Rutland (USAir Express), 30 minutes away, and West Lebanon, NH (Delta), a 45-minute drive.

By car: Killington is at the intersection of Rtes. 4 and 100 in central Vermont near the city of Rutland, about three hours northwest of Boston. Pico is located about three miles west of the Access Road on Rte. 4.

By train: Daily service is available on Amtrak's Ethan Allen Express from New York City to Rutland, with bus service or car rental to Killington. Train-lodging-lift packages are available. Call (800) USA-RAIL (872-7245) for train info, or Killington Travel Service (800-621-6867) for package info.

Getting around: Bring or rent a car or use the Killington Shuttle bus service. Though you may not use your car to move between your lodging and the slopes, Killington is very spread out, and you may want to visit the attractions nearby.

Mad River Valley
Sugarbush & Mad River Glen

Waitsfield/Warren Region
Vermont

Dining: ★★★★
Apres-ski/nightlife:★★
Other activities:★★
ⓘ Toll free reservations: (800) 828-4748
Internet: www.madrivervalley.com

Sugarbush

Summit elevation: 4,135 feet
Vertical drop: 2,650 feet
Base elevation: 1,485 feet
Expert: ★★★★★
Advanced: ★★★★
Intermediate:★★★★
Beginner: ★★★★
Never-ever:★★★★
Address: 2405 Sugarbush Access Road
Warren, VT 05674-9572
✆ Area code: 802
Ski area phone: 583-6300
Snow report: 583-SNOW
ⓘ Toll-free reservations: (800) 53-SUGAR
Fax: 583-6303
Internet: www.sugarbush.com
Number and types of lifts: 18–4 high-speed quads, 3 quad chairs, 3 triples, 4 double chairs, 4 surface lifts
Skiable Acreage: 432
Snowmaking: 61 percent
Uphill capacity: 24,363 per hour
Snowboarding: Yes
Bed Base: 6,600 (2,200 on mountain)
Nearest lodging: Slopeside
Resort child care: Yes, 6 weeks and older
Adult ticket, per day: $48-$57 (02/03)

Mad River Glen

Summit elevation: 3,637 feet
Vertical drop: 2,000 feet
Base elevation: 1,637 feet
Expert: ★★★★★
Advanced: ★★★★
Intermediate:★★★
Beginner: ★★★
Never-ever: ★
Address: PO Box 1089
Waitsfield, VT 05673
✆ Area code: 802
Ski area phone: 496-3551
Snow report: 496-3551
ⓘ Toll-free information: (800) 850-6742
(area Chamber)
Fax: 496-3562
E-mail: ski@madriverglen.com
Internet: www.madriverglen.com
Number and types of lifts: 5–3 double chairs, 1 single chair, 1 surface lift
Skiable Acreage: about 115
Snowmaking: 15 percent
Uphill capacity: 3,000 per hour
Snowboarding: No
Bed Base: 6,600
Nearest lodging: About a quarter-mile
Resort child care: Yes, 6 weeks and older
Adult ticket, per day: $42 (02/03)

Once the playground for the well-to-do, the out-of-the-way Mad River Valley gradually fell out of favor with the "in" ski crowd and became the place that time forgot. This has been a good thing. The valley remains free of large chain hotels and other ski resort sprawl, and the ambiance is classic New England: clapboard houses, quaint inns, restored barns and picture-postcard downtowns in the two villages that make up the valley, Waitsfield and Warren.

American Skiing Company acquired Sugarbush in the mid-1990s, adding high-speed lifts, more snowmaking and new trails, but it (thankfully) left the soul of Sugarbush untouched. ASC sold to a trio of locals in 2002, in a move welcomed by the valley. Sugarbush's trails, at least many of the ones in the Lincoln Peak area, are steep and narrow. It's no wonder that the resort is home to extreme skier John Egan of Warren-Miller-movie fame. This is old-time New England skiing at its finest.

Serious skiers will find more of the same seven miles up the road at Mad River Glen. The Alta of the East, Mad River Glen is the way skiing used to be. Home to one of the few single chairs left in the country, Mad River has almost no snowmaking and no condos. Narrow trails cut down the thickly wooded mountain are merely suggestions of where to ski. Diehards ski all over Mad River Glen, through trees, over frozen waterfalls and down cliffs. Its terrain attracts such a devoted following that Mad River is America's only skier-owned, nonprofit cooperative. For co-op share information, call the resort.

But beginners, don't despair. Both Sugarbush and Mad River have plenty of trails marked with green circles and blue squares. And everyone will enjoy the relatively uncrowded slopes, because the valley is still off the beaten path.

Sugarbush

Mountain layout–Skiing

Sugarbush is divided into two separate areas, Lincoln Peak and Mount Ellen, connected by a 10-minute ride on rollercoaster-like, high-speed quad chair lift. Each of these mountains is then subdivided further into ski areas with their own distinct flavors. Lincoln Peak alone has four separate mountains, ranging from the extreme runs of Castlerock Peak to the relatively gentle slopes of North Lynx Peak. Mt. Ellen, one of few mountains in Vermont over 4,000 feet, has three double-diamond runs plummeting off its summit complemented by good cruising terrain below.

◆◆ **Expert** ◆ **Advanced:** At Lincoln Peak, the runs served by Castlerock lift are very black and no place for the timid. The entire Castlerock area offers narrow New England-style steeps, and if you are lucky the Castlerock run will occasionally be groomed, making for a heavenly smooth steep. The Castlerock double chair is popular with those in this ability level, so be aware that sometimes there is a wait, usually not more than eight to 10 minutes. The benefit is that these narrow trails do not fill up with yahoo skiers. You have to want to be there to end up at Castlerock.

From the summit of Lincoln Peak and the top of the Heaven's Gate triple, experts can drop down Ripcord or Paradise, two double-black-diamond runs that frequently bump up. The more wide-open Organgrinder (the old gondola lift line), which we dubbed "Organ Donor," is a wide, steep run that dares you to ski fast. Stein's Run, accessible by either the Super Bravo Express or the Valley House Double chair lifts, is another long, steep, bumped-up run. Egan's Woods, to skier's left of Stein's Run, is no doubt where extreme skier John Egan plays.

Mt. Ellen is primarily an intermediate playground, though the double blacks at the top—F.I.S., Black Diamond, Exterminator and Bravo (the latter a single diamond)—are among the toughest in New England.

■ **Intermediate:** Intermediates should start at the Super Bravo chair on Lincoln Peak, then traverse to the Heaven's Gate triple. Once at the summit, take Upper Jester, a run full of fun switchbacks that take you back to the top of the Super Bravo lift. From here, choose from Downspout, Domino, Snowball, Murphy's Glades or Lower Jester. On a busy day, these runs are crowded with skiers. Intermediates also tend to flock to the North Lynx triple on the upper part of North Lynx Peak. Here, the views are good, and the runs sometimes bump up.

The slopes tend to be less crowded on the lower part of North Lynx Peak and parts of Gadd Peak. Eden, a tree-skiing area on Gadd Peak, is the place to learn to navigate glades. Spring Fling is wide-open and attracts few skiers and is great for long, fast turns.

Mt. Ellen also has wide-open cruising runs. On the map, the intermediate runs from the top of the Summit quad chair seem relatively short, but the map is misleading. The Rim Run, connecting to Upper Lookin' Good, Lower Rim Run, Cruiser and Straight Shot, is one of the classic cruising runs in the United States. The other intermediate section is Inverness, served by a quad chair.

●● **Beginner:** North Lynx Peak on the far right side of the Lincoln Peak is a good place for beginners. Start on Pushover and Easy Rider and then graduate to Slowpoke and Sleeper. At Mt. Ellen, Walt's Trail is a long green run from the top of the Inverness chair.

● **Never-ever:** Lincoln Peak has Easy Rider, a gentle slope served by a double chair. Mt. Ellen has Easy Street and Sugar Run, off to one side and also served by a double chair.

Mountain layout–Snowboarding

Terrain park fans should park at the Mt. Ellen base, because that's where the park is located. Getting to the park from Lincoln Peak requires a long, cold lift ride or taking the base-to-base trolley. The upper section of the park is located on Whichway and the lower section is on Crackerjack. Maintain your speed when crossing the flats between Whichway and Crackerjack, but watch for the Slide Brook quad, which unloads just before the flattest section. The best jumps and rails last season were on Crackerjack. Last season Sugarbush did not have a halfpipe, even though its literature indicated that one was located on the lower part of Straight Shot. We suggest halfpipe riders call before coming to confirm one exists.

Free riders will find great trails off the Super Bravo quad and Heaven's Gate triple. Our rider last season wished there were more snow because the trees looked good. The only trail that will leave you hiking here is Lower FIS; even if you hold speed you'll be booting out and kicking. It's worth it on a powder day, because this is a quiet trail that holds freshies late, but you will have to hike out. There are a few traverses where you'll need to keep up speed: Bailout from Castlerock Run to Heaven's Gate is not all that bad, a little speed will get the job done. The Northway, from Exterminator to the Inverness lift at Mt. Ellen, is long and somewhat flat as well, but speed should carry you, provided the surface is groomed, otherwise, you'll hike. Reverse Traverse, from the top of Stein's Run over to Murphy's Glades, is tough because you really can't get a lot of speed to go the distance. Instead, head down Snowball to Spring Fling.

Lessons (2002/03 prices)

Group lessons: $35 for all levels except never-evers. A Value Pak of 5 two-hour clinics costs $155.

Never-evers: Learn-to-Ski or Ride clinics include lesson, lifts and rentals and costs $70 for the first day, $75 for the second, and $85 for the third. Or you can buy all three days for $205.

Private lessons: $80 an hour; $130 for two hours; $180 for five hours; $295 for full day.

Special programs: Sugarbush offers a morning powder clinic and afternoon clinics for bumps or steeps. Multi-day clinics for snowboarders, women and expert skiers or riders, called Snow Sports University, are also available. Call 888-651-4827 for reservations.

Child care (2002/03 prices)

Ages: 6 weeks to 6 years.

Location: Sugarbush Village (a group of condos to the far right past the main parking lot at Lincoln Peak).

Cost: Day Care Cubs (6 weeks–6 years) get a non-ski program for $68 full day, $48 half day. Multiday pricing is available. Reservations required; call 802-583-6717.

Note: You can park at Sugarbush Village, but make sure you have a lift ticket already and be prepared to push and skate your way uphill to the lift.

Children's lessons: Children are divided into age groups for instruction. Microbears for 3-year-olds combines day care with some skiing: $80 full day, $60 half day. Minibears for 4-6-year-olds combines ski lessons with play activities: $85 full day, $65 half day. Sugarbears, ages 7–12, get ski or snowboard lessons: $85 full day, $65 for half day. Full-day children's programs include lunch and lift tickets, plus equipment for the age 6-and-younger crowd. Reservations required; call 888-651-4827. Lessons for every group but Microbears start at the Gate House Lodge at Lincoln Peak. Microbears are located at child care.

Lift tickets (2001/02 prices)

	Adult	Young Adult (13-18)
One day, weekend/midweek	$57/$48	$49/$42
Three days	$138 ($46/day)	$120 ($40)
Five days	$222 ($44/day)	$193 ($39)

Note: Three- and five-day rates are rounded to the closest dollar.

Who skis free: Children ages 5 and younger.

Who skis at a discount: Sugarbush lowers ticket prices for adults in its Value Season, (opening through mid-December and in April). Children, ages 7–12, pay $35 for a midweek day, $37 for a weekend day, $90 for three days and $142 for five days. Ages 65 and older ski for the child's price.

Note: The Valley of the Giants, a joint ticket for Mad River Glen and Sugarbush, is available when skiers purchase accommodation for three nights or more in the valley. The joint lift ticket allows skiers to choose where they want to ski in the valley each day. Make sure to ask about this special lift ticket when you make reservations.

Mad River Glen

Mad River Glen is a throwback to earlier ski days, and as one of our contributors put it, "It's the type of skiing that made my mother give up the sport." The ski area prides itself on being tough, and the bumper sticker, "Mad River Glen: Ski It If You Can," is all too true. Trail ratings are not inflated, and even the beginner trails here might be graded intermediate elsewhere. But MRG fans love this area and have shown their devotion by buying shares of this now skier-owned resort. And yes, we mean *ski* resort; snowboards are not allowed. MRG is traditional (it's one of two areas in the nation with a chair lift for solo riders), natural (little snowmaking, combined with plenty of tight tree skiing), hard-corps (the ski shop at the base sells T-shirts with the slogan, "Friends don't let friends get first tracks") and homey (skiers with serious tracks to carve have got to love a cafeteria with peanut-butter-and-jelly sandwiches to go). It's a mountain for serious skiers, not posers. Leave your Bogner suit on the hanger and don some wool pants. You'll fit right in.

Mountain layout–Skiing

◆◆ **Expert** ◆ **Advanced:** Experts will be happy just about anywhere at Mad River Glen, especially after a snowstorm when the bumps become gigantic. One nice feature that's a throwback to tradition is the area's refusal to make much snow. All of the expert terrain is covered with natural snow (when it falls), so it bumps up nicely and doesn't get as icy as the East's other resorts.

While the line for the single chair is usually about 10 minutes long, it can approach 45 minutes on peak holidays and good powder days, and the real experts happily wait. From the top of this historic lift, experts can immediately drop down the Chute under the lift or traverse to Catamount Bowl, one of the most wide-open runs on the mountain. For more of a challenge, find a guide or hook up with a local and venture into the area called Paradise, entered by dropping down an 8-foot waterfall. Ask around for Octopus's Garden and the 19th and 20th Holes. If you look like you know how to ski, a local may direct you to these. At the single chair's midstation, tree skiing beckons through the Glades to the right as you ski off the chair. Experts with tired legs can traverse on Broadway and drop down wide-open Grand Canyon.

■ **Intermediate:** Mad River Glen is not known for its cruiser runs, and if intermediates find themselves at the top of the single chair, they have only one route down, upper Antelope, which splits into Catamount after a few turns. Both runs are quite narrow, and intermediates should beware: About halfway down, Antelope veers off into the woods and gets steeper, and, hard to believe, even narrower. Unless you're up for a challenge, follow Broadway under the lift, and head to the other side of the mountain.

Intermediates will find a better selection of terrain off the Sunnyside Chair. Quacky to Porcupine is a nice run. Bunny will also take you from Quacky to the base. To the right of the chair is a series of expert trails, Panther, Partridge, Slalom Hill and Gazelle, most of which empty into Birdland. Confident intermediates will find these runs challenging, if not downright scary, and a missed turn may mean you have to side-slip into a trail.

If you feel like you're ready to tackle MRG's classic terrain (i.e., the woods), give yourself a sampler. From the top of the Sunnyside chair, take Fox to the big intersection and traverse straight into the woods. The trees soon open up into the Glades. If this trail seems fun, congratulations! You're ready for the tough stuff. If you're intimidated, bail out on Bunny.

●● **Beginner:** Birdland is ostensibly the beginner area, but to get there, you have to have good route-finding skills. Otherwise, you'll find yourself at the top of an overly-moguled expert pitch vowing to give up the sport. Take the Sunnyside chair to the top, then follow Fox to Snail, catwalks that will take you to the land of green circles. Granted, Duck, Lark, Robin, Wren and Loon are for beginners, but intermediates will find the pitch is comfortable. Learn to ski here, and little will daunt you elsewhere.

● **Never-ever:** Mad River Glen is not the best place for a first-timer.

Lessons (2002/03 prices)

Mad River Glen has a ski school that, like the area, marches to its own drummer. The Beginner "You Can" Learn to Ski Package, including a beginner ticket, two-hour lesson and rentals, is $55 for either alpine or telemark. A follow-up two-hour lesson on the same day costs $35. Private lessons cost $55 for one hour, $90 for two hours.

Child care (2002/03 prices)

Ages: 6 weeks to 6 years.

The Cricket Club Nursery (496-2123) offers infant care for children 6 weeks to 18 months for $55 for a full day, $40 for a half day, $100 for two days. Childcare for children ages 1 to 6 years costs $50 for a full day and $35 for a half day, $90 for two days. The Ski and Play introduction to skiing program is $65 for a full day with lunch and two lessons, $120 for two days. A half day with one ski lesson is $45. This program takes place in the special Callie's Corner kids' area and includes use of a handle tow. Children ready for more advanced skiing should register in the Chipmunk program (*see below*). The Nursery does not take reservations, but if you check your child into the nursery on Friday and pay for two days, you're guaranteed a spot on Saturday. Or if you call at 8:15 a.m. and say you're on your way, they will hold a spot for your child. Call 496-3551, ext. 20.

Lessons: Ducks is for first-time children ages 6-12; Chipmunks is for ages 4-7; Panthers is for ages 7-12. Programs run from 10 a.m. to 3 p.m. A full day is $60 with lunch, half-day is $30, without lunch. Kids who know how to ski can sign up for the Freestyle Team and learn to attack Mad River's moguls. Private lessons for kids cost $35 per hour.

Lift tickets (2002/03 prices)

	Adult	Junior (6-15)/Senior (65-69)
One day	$42	$30
Three days	$117 ($39/day)	$81 ($27/day)
Five days	$195 ($39/day)	$135 ($27/day)

Who skis free: Ages 70 and older. Children 5 and younger are issued a free ticket when skiing with a paying adult.

Who skis at a discount: If you buy a two-day ticket, you get $2 off the price each day. For a three-day or longer ticket, you get $3 off the daily price.

Note: Ski the Valley is a joint ticket for Mad River Glen and Sugarbush available when skiers purchase accommodation for three nights or more in the valley. Make sure to ask about this special lift ticket when you make reservations.

Cross-country and snowshoeing

The **Blueberry Lake Cross Country Ski Center** (496-6687) has 23 km. of trails, beginner to expert, groomed for skate skiing and classic. Dogs are permitted. **Ole's Cross Country Center** (496-3430; near the airport) has 50 km.

of groomed trails on rolling terrain. Ole's also has snowshoeing and a Rossignol demo center. The **Inn at the Round Barn Farm** (496-2276) cross-country area, with 15 km. of groomed trails, is linked with Ole's.

Snowshoe treks (583-0381) are available from the summit of **Sugarbush**'s Mt. Ellen to Lincoln Peak. Free, guided treks begin at the base of Lincoln Peak. **Mad River Glen** has just under five miles of snowshoe trails on the mountain. These trails connect with Vermont's famed Long Trail. It also offers snowshoe naturalist programs. Or arrange **treks** through Vermont Pack & Paddle (496-7225) and Clearwater Sports (496-2708). Snowshoers who want to strike out on their own can take advantage of a variety of **backcountry trails** in the region. A trail map is available from the Sugarbush Chamber of Commerce.

Accommodations

This area has some of Vermont's finest country inns and B&Bs, all of which can be booked through Sugarbush Chamber of Commerce (800-828-4748; spells 82-VISIT; or www.madrivervalley.com), Sugarbush Central Reservations (800-537-8427; spells 53-SUGAR) or call the inns directly.

Topping the list, **The Inn at the Round Barn Farm** (496-2276; $$–$$$$), a mile from Rte. 100, across the covered bridge, on East Warren Road is one of the best B&Bs we've seen anywhere in ski country. The farmhouse has been made into an elegant, spacious, 11-room bed-and-breakfast. It is peaceful and quiet, strictly No Smoking, with children discouraged. The stunning Richardson Room with Vermont-made canopied king bed, skylights, gas fireplace, oversized Jacuzzi and steam shower is top-of-the-line. There are 30 km. of cross-country tracks outside the door.

The Pitcher Inn (496-6350 or 888-867-4824; $$$$) is luxury in the tiny village of Warren, with eight rooms in the main inn and two suites in an adjacent barn. This is a member of the Relais & Chateaux properties.

Tucker Hill Inn (496-3983 or 800-543-7841; $-$$), two miles from lifts, has 22 rooms and a steakhouse restaurant. **The Waitsfield Inn** (496-3979 or 800-758-3801; $-$$), in the center of Waitsfield Village, started life in the 1820s as a parsonage, was a sleeping-bag dorm for young skiers in the '60s and '70s and is now a quaintly elegant 14-bedroom B&B. It now has a restaurant, too.

The Sugartree Inn (583-3211; $$) has award-winning breakfasts and a collection of rooms, ranging from large with canopied beds and/or fireplace to small; all are most pleasant. The inn is only a quarter mile from Sugarbush's slopes. **The Featherbed Inn** (496-7151; $$), on Rte. 100 only a stone's throw from the resort access road, is a restored 1806 house with 10 spacious guest rooms, all with private baths and luxurious featherbeds, plenty of space to spread out and to-die-for breakfasts.

West Hill House B&B (496-7162; $$-$$$) has seven bedrooms all with private baths. **Beaver Pond Farm Inn** (583-2861; $-$$) is right on the cross-country trails of the Sugarbush golf course. **1824 House Inn** (496-7555; $) has eight rooms just north of town with featherbeds and an outdoor hot tub.

The nicest full-service hotel property is the **Sugarbush Inn** (583-6114 or 800-53SUGAR; $$) on the access road. The inn and its 46 rooms are well-kept but nondescript.

Closer to Sugarbush resort you'll find **Sugar Lodge** at Sugarbush (800-982-3465; $-$$), only a half mile from Lincoln Peak. The **Weathertop Lodge** (800-800-3625, 496-4909; $-$$), on Rte. 17 between town and Mad River Glen, is an affordable B&B.

Dining: $$$-Entrees $20+; $$-$10-20; $-less than $10.
Accommodations: (double room) $$$$-$200+; $$$-$141-$200; $$-$81-$140; $-$80 and less.

The **Inn At The Mad River Barn** (496-3310; $-$$) has rustic but spacious rooms and some of the best lodging food in the valley (both in quantity and quality). To stay here is to step into a wonderful 1940s ski lodge.

Families will want to check into **John Egan's Big World** on Rte. 100 (496-5557; $-$$) or the **Hyde Away Inn and Restaurant** (496-2322; $-$$) on Rte. 17. Both are great spots for children and close to the slopes. The Hyde Away has become the favorite locals' hangout for shooting pool.

Of the condominiums in the **Village at Sugarbush**, the most luxurious are the **Southface Condominiums** with hot tubs in each unit and a shuttlebus ride from the slopes. The Snow Creek condos are ski-in/ski-out, but you have the noise of snow guns at your back window during snowmaking operations. The **Paradise** condos are newer but a good walk from the slopes; however, they have a reliable, free shuttle service. The **Summit** units are roomy, and **Castle Rock** condos are close to the slopes. **Unihab** looks like boxes stacked on one another, and the small **Middle Earth** condos are 10 minutes from the lifts. Rates range from $145 for a one-bedroom in value season to $635 for a four-bedroom during holidays. Guests may use the indoor pool, tennis, racquetball, squash courts, aerobics, Jacuzzi, steam room and Nautilus equipment at the Sugarbush Sports Center for an additional fee.

Almost as close to the lifts as Sugarbush Village units is **The Bridges Resort and Racquet Club** (583-2922 or 800-453-2922; $$-$$$$), with tennis courts and an indoor pool. These units are quieter than the mountain units and have wonderful amenities as well as a regular shuttle.

Skiers heading for Mad River Glen should check into the unfortunately named **Battleground** condos on Rte. 17 (496-2288 or 800-248-2102).

 ## Dining

The Mad River Valley has more than 40 eating establishments, many of them offering excellent food. Most of them require reservations, so call before venturing out.

The top of the line is **Chez Henri** (583-2600; $$-$$$) in Sugarbush Village at the base area of Lincoln Peak. The oldest restaurant in the valley, it captures a true French bistro feeling, with low ceilings and a flickering fire. The owner, Henri Borel, personally greets guests and makes them feel at home. He also supervises the excellent wine selection. Chez Henri features lunch, fondue in the late afternoon, then dinner until 10 p.m.

The **Spotted Cow** (496-5151; $$-$$$), run by Jay and Renata Young, has gained a reputation for some of the best food in the valley. Pricey to be sure. Don't miss the Bermuda fish chowder; it's worth the trip to Waitsfield.

The **Pitcher Inn Restaurant** (496-6350; $$$) has courted the gourmet crowd, but to mixed reviews. Meals here are served in an attractive traditional dining room overlooking the Mad River in Warren Village. The wine cellar boasts 3,500 bottles.

John Egan's Big World Pub & Grill (496-3033; $$) serves excellent food and is a great place to bring the family.

The **Common Man** (583-2800; $$) has attracted a faithful clientele and has a reputation for good food, but for the money, it's not quite as "common" as the name implies. The atmosphere is what might be called a New England Baroque barn with crystal chandeliers.

The **Warren House** (583-2421; $$), down a driveway to the left as you approach the Sugarbush parking lot, has developed lots of fans and offers an eclectic menu rivaling any in the area, along with a good wine list.

Michael's Restaurant (496-3832; $$), at Powderhound Lodge on Rte. 100, serves dishes such as Grown-Up Grilled Cheese, Lobster Shepherds Pie and Green Mountain Jambalaya.

The **Steak Place at Tucker Hill** (496-3025; $$) serves beef in front of a flickering fireplace under a beamed ceiling. It also has light apres-ski and late-night fare.

Millbrook Country Inn (496-2405; $$), on Rte. 17, has a small dining room with a fireplace, original art and antiques. The meals are prepared from local organic produce.

Miguel's Stowe Away (583-3858; $-$$) serves plentiful Mexican food at affordable prices, guaranteeing that this place is normally packed.

Mad River Barn Restaurant ($) has a popular Saturday buffet and serves dinners Sunday through Friday from 6:30 to 8 p.m.

A Sugarbush tradition worth the effort is the **American Flatbread Kitchen** (496-8856; $), open only on weekends, at the Lareau Farm Country Inn. Be ready for a long wait (anywhere from 30 to 90 minutes).

For families out to stretch the budget and still get good wholesome food, try the **Hyde Away** (496-2322; $-$$), on Rte. 17. **BonGiorno**'s (496-6265; $), also on Rte. 17, is the place to head for pizza and affordable pasta, with delivery as well. For simple quick food, try **The Den** (496-8880; $-$$) on Waitsfield's main street. **Jay's** (496-8282; $) doesn't claim to be anything fancy but is a good spot for family fare.

For breakfast, try the **Hyde Away** or **Pepper's Restaurant** (583-2202; $) at Pepper's Lodge. The **Mad River Barn** lays out excellent homemade muffins and jams and serves only real maple syrup.

New this year is **Pete's Eats**, located in the same building as the Mad Mountain Tavern. You can get breakfast while having your skis tuned at the shop next door. Try two eggs, coffee, toast and hash browns with a quick edge and wax for $10.99.

The **Valley Pizzeria** (496-9200; $) makes real brick-oven, hand-thrown pizza. It's as close to Jersey pizza as you'll ever find in Vermont, one local tells us. Seating is limited; get it to go.

Condo dwellers can pick up basic staples, baked goods, beer and wine at the **Paradise Deli & Market** (583-2757) on the access road. The deli also has dinners-to-go. There are two supermarkets in town. **Shaw's** is to Sugarbush as **Mehuron's Market** is to Mad River Glen. Shaw's has the better produce. Mehuron's is the local's choice, the bonuses here are the butcher and fish departments.

 Après-ski/nightlife

Après-ski starts at the base lodges, which do booming business at the bar as the lifts close. **Chez Henri's Back Room** is the on-mountain après-ski hangout and can rock all evening. **The Hyde Away** is where you will find the locals; the **Blue Tooth** on the access road is most popular with tourists. On weekends try the **Sugarbush Inn** for a slightly more upscale, older crowd.

The base area bar at Mad River Glen, **General Stark's Pub**, follows the retro atmosphere of the area with plenty of fun in an old-time bar. After leaving Mad River Glen, the next place to stop is the **Mad River Barn**. The bar there looks like an old Vermont bar should look: moose head hanging over the fireplace, hunting scenes on every wall, big couches and stuffed chairs, wood paneling and bumper pool or shuffleboard.

Gallagher's recently had a much-needed facelift. In the evenings, it has dancing with a mix of music from rock to country-rock and an interesting crowd. **Mad Mountain Tavern**,

Dining: $$$-Entrees $20+; $$-$10-20; $-less than $10.
Accommodations: (double room) $$$$-$200+; $$$-$141-$200; $$-$81-$140; $-$80 and less.

across from Gallagher's, is popular with the dancin' crowd because of live music on weekends.

Other activities

The Sugarbush Sports Center and the Bridges Resort and Racquet Club have various **sports and exercise facilities**.

Winter Wonderland (800-53-SUGAR), owned by the resort, located at the Sugarbush Golf Course on Golf Course Road, offers evening sleigh rides for $10 a person or a **sleigh ride/dinner combination** for $40 a person. During the day they have **snowmobile rides**.

Sleigh rides and skijoring (496-7141) can be arranged at the Vermont Icelandic Horse Farm in Waitsfield. (Skijoring here involves being pulled behind a horse or snowmobile while on skis.) Other farms offering sleigh rides are the Mountain Valley Farm (496-9255).

Snow tubing is also available at Lincoln Peak Thursday through Sunday from 10 a.m. to 5 p.m. and on Wednesday and Saturday at night from 6–9 p.m.

Ice skating rinks are at Tucker Hill Lodge, Sugarbush Inn, Sugarbush Health and Racquet Club or the Skatium next to Grand Union in Waitsfield.

Mad River Flick (426-4200) has first-run movies, plus something at the concession stand most movie theaters don't offer, beer and wine.

For the perfect way to unwind, head to **Mad River Massage** (496-5638) on Rte. 100 just south of the intersection with Rte. 17 and get the kinks kneaded out of your body. While you are there, explore their unique gift store with potions, lotions, aroma therapy candles and hand-crafted jewelry.

Waitsfield and Warren have **art galleries**, **country stores** and **antique and collectible shops** that are fun for browsing and buying. Most shops in tiny Warren Village are within easy walking-distance of each other.

Getting there and around

Getting there: Sugarbush is off Rte. 100, about 20 miles south of Waterbury. Burlington airport is about an hour away. Amtrak offers train-ski-lodging packages, with daily service from New York, Philadelphia and Washington, D.C. For information and packages, call (800) 237-7547; (800) 872-7245 for train only.

Getting around: The valley offers daily public buses that run from Waitsfield, to Warren as well to the Sugarbush base areas and Mad River Glen. Schedules can be obtained from your lodging or online at www.madrivervalley.com/transportation. For a one-time visit to town it's okay, but for more frequent visits, bring or rent a car.

Mount Snow/Haystack

Vermont

Summit elevation: 3,600 feet
Vertical drop: 1,700 feet
Base elevation: 1,900 feet

Address: Route 100,
Mount Snow, VT 05356
✆ **Area code:** 802
Ski area phone: 464-3333
Snow report: 464-2151 **Weather:** 464-4131
ⓘ **Toll-free reservations:**
(800) 245-7669 (245-SNOW)
E-mail: info@mountsnow.com
World Wide Web: www.mountsnow.com
Expert:★
Advanced:★
Intermediate:★★★★
Beginner:★★★★
Never-ever:★★

Number of lifts: 23–3 high-speed quads,
1 quad, 10 triples, 4 doubles, 2 surface lifts,
3 magic carpets
Snowmaking: 75 percent
Trail acreage: 756.5 acres
Uphill capacity: 36,252 per hour
Snowboarding: Yes, unlimited
Bed Base: 10,000
Nearest lodging: Base area, condos, hotel
Resort child care: Yes, 6 weeks to 6 years old
Adult ticket, per day: $49-$55 (2000/01)

Dining:★★★★
Apres-ski/nightlife:★★
Other activities:★★

For those living in the Northeast's major metropolitan areas, Mount Snow, with a summit elevation of 3,600 feet, is the closest big-mountain resort. Its proximity to major metropolitan centers means the resort attracts crowds on weekends and holidays. During these times, smart skiers and riders head to nearby Haystack, where Mount Snow's ticket also is valid. As the crow flies, Haystack is 2.5 miles from Mount Snow's southern end, but by car, it's 5 miles up Handle Road, which runs parallel to Rte. 100. Of note, the two resorts are not connected by trails or lifts, and Haystack is only open on weekends and holidays.

Mount Snow's height allows it to live up to its name. When nature fails, the resort, like its American Skiing Company cousin Killington, makes prodigious amounts of snow. Although it's big, Mount Snow is also surprisingly flat. Almost all the runs spilling down the front side from the summit are beginner or intermediate trails, and it's possible to ski top to bottom on the well-groomed runs without breaking a sweat. Not a favorite mountain for experts, Mount Snow is a mecca for intermediates. Those who have always struggled in the bumps or trees might find the resort's terrain a great place to improve these skills.

Mountain layout–Skiing

◆◆ **Expert** ◆ **Advanced:** Aggressive skiers and snowboarders looking for a shot of adrenaline should head straight for the North Face area, a group of isolated steeper runs, some of which are allowed to bump up. With a 37-degree pitch, Ripcord is the steepest, but Jaws, Plummet, Free Fall and Fallen

Timbers also provide fine steep turns. The steep glades at The Plunge, Epiphany and The Trials will challenge any expert. On the opposite side of Mount Snow, the Sunbrook area has mostly cruisers, but Beartrap, the one advanced run, is a haven for bump skiers, in part because of its sunny face and snowmaking coverage. Beartrap has its own double lift, and the resort pumps out loud music from 900-watt speakers to get you in the spirit.

At Haystack, advanced skiers and snowboarders should head for The Witches, a separate area with trails named Merlin, Wizard and Warlock's Woods.

■ **Intermediate:** Other than the North Face, the rest of Mount Snow is a cruiser's delight. You can carve hero turns down just about any trail on the mountain. Be sure not to miss Snowdance, a trail as wide as a football field is long off the Canyon Express chair lift. The Sunbrook area, located off the south side of the summit, is an ideal spot for lower intermediates. With its southern exposure, it's also a great place for catching rays. Although the resort's glades are all marked with black diamonds, Claim Jumper and Sap Tapper aren't steep and are good places for skiers and riders to learn or improve their tree skiing.

At Haystack, stick to the Hayfever lift (for time reasons if nothing else; the Barnstormer triple chair is long). Last Chance usually has some good bumps to warm up on, and after a little practice, the intermediate skier or rider will be ready to try The Witches.

●● **Beginner** ● **Never-ever:** First-timers can start at the Launch Pad area outside the Perfect Turn® Discovery Center on the right side (looking up the mountain) of Mount Snow's main base area. This area has its own lifts: two Magic Carpets, a rope tow and a triple chair. From the summit, beginners will feel comfortable on Deer Run and Long John, two trails that make wide traverses of the mountain. At the south end of the resort is Carinthia, which offers long mellow runs for advanced beginners, lower intermediates and anyone else who wants to have a playful cruise. There are enough zigs, zags and small drops to keep a skier awake. But snowboarders flock to this area and can fly by slower skiers, unnerving those who are still learning the sport.

At Haystack, beginners can start on the Skidder handle tow and graduate to beginner/advanced-beginner trails such as Last Chance and Outcast.

 Mountain layout–Snowboarding

Mount Snow and Haystack both have great trails for boarders of all levels, as well as four excellent terrain parks of varying difficulty. The real center for riders is Carinthia. Terrain parks here include Inferno, Mount Snow's longest terrain park with a double-diamond rating, and the more mellow El Diablo, site of the Palmer Boardercross course, open when snow conditions permit. Get pumped for big air over huge tabletops at Inferno. For more jibbing action, hit the hip. Following that are a kinked rail, straight rail and two more tabletops. The Superpipe is located at the bottom right of Inferno. If you can't hang with the big dogs, head back to the main face. Un Blanco Gulch, located on the Canyon Trail, has smaller, yet substantial features, perfect for intermediate riders. The Grommet terrain park, on Cooper's Junction, is designed for those 12 and younger to let them get their taste of jumps and hits. Teens and adults only are allowed in Grommet when accompanied by a child.

Mountain rating

The emphasis is definitely on the intermediate level. Advanced skiers and riders can try some of the relatively tough runs on the North Face, but if you are an expert, don't come out of your way to ski these; they're not that tough. Beginners, get ready to improve; this mountain has just your kind of terrain.

Cross-country

The Mount Snow Valley has four major ski touring centers. The largest is **Hermitage Cross-Country Touring Center** (464-3511), on Coldbrook Road in Wilmington, with 50 km. of trails that form a circle from the warming hut to Mount Snow and back. **Timber Creek** (464-0999) and the **White House of Wilmington Cross Country Ski Center** (464-2135) offer more than 60 km. of trails skewed toward the intermediate Nordic skier. Advanced cross-country skiers can ski the one-way, 2.5-mile Ridge Trail connecting the Haystack and Mount Snow summits. The Ridge Trail fee is $10, which includes a lift ride to the summit.

 ## Lessons (2002/03 prices)

Lessons and equipment rentals for skiers and riders age 13 and older are offered out of the Perfect Turn® Discovery Center, located on the north side of the main base area at Mount Snow.

Group lessons: The Perfect Turn® instruction program offers several levels of clinics. For lower intermediates and higher, the clinics have a maximum of six people and normally last two hours. Skiers and riders watch a short video that demonstrates various levels of ability, then place themselves into the proper clinic. Morning and afternoon sessions are offered and cost $35.

Never-ever package: Learn-to-Ski or Snowboard for first-timers is a half-day program employing the Guaranteed Learning Method, meaning the resort guarantees new skiers and riders that they will be able to ride a lift, turn and stop by the end of the clinic. The package for Levels 1, 2 and 3 includes lessons, equipment and beginner lift ticket and costs $80 per session. Reservations are required.

Private lessons: $80 an hour. Private lessons at Haystack cost $60 an hour.

Special Programs: Women's programs, adaptive program, family ski/snowboard clinics and senior programs are available. There are also separate clinics available for advanced skiers and snowboarders. Call the resort.

Child care (2002/03 prices)

Child care is open 8 a.m.-4:30 p.m. on weekends and holidays.

Ages: 6 weeks to 6 years.

Costs: $65 for a full day with lunch; $320 for five days. Discovery Camp, an introductory ski program for 3-year-olds registered in full-day childcare, costs an additional $20 with rentals.

Reservations: Required; call (800) 889-4411 or 464-4152.

Babysitting: Mount Snow Child Care has a few babysitters who will come to your vacation home, condo or hotel room. Cost is $10/hour for one child, $1/hour for each additional child (rates do not apply New Year's Eve); call (800) 889-4411 or 464-4152. Baby on the Go (464-5475) rents baby needs, such as cribs, strollers, car seats and high chairs. Delivery and set-up are available at an additional charge.

Children's lessons: Perfect Kids programs are available for ages 4-12. Ages 4-6 enroll in Snow Camp. The full-day cost is $87, including lessons and lunch, but no equipment. Ages 7–12 enroll in Mountain Camp or Mountain Riders. The full-day cost is $72 for lessons and lunch but no equipment. Lifts are covered while kids are in lessons, but half-day enrollees will need to buy a lift ticket if they want to continue on their own. Half-day costs are $52 for Snow Camp and $38 for Mountain Camp or Mountain Riders.

Lift tickets (2001/02 prices)

	Adult	Junior (6-12)
One day*	$58	$37
Three days*	$154 ($51/day)	$104 ($35/day)
Five days*	$246 ($49/day)	$165 ($33/day)

*Note: Prices are rounded to the nearest dollar to include the 5% Vermont sales tax.

Who skis free: Children ages 5 and younger. Children 12 and younger ski free when their parent buys a three- to five-day midweek lift ticket.

Who skis at a discount: Ages 65 and older ski for junior prices; ages 13–18 pay $132 (includes tax) for three days; $176 (includes tax) for five days.

Mount Snow tickets also are valid at Haystack. Tickets to ski Haystack alone cost about $40 for adults (older than 13) and $30 for juniors/seniors a day. Haystack only is open weekends and holidays.

Mount Snow/Haystack is one of the American Skiing Company resorts, most of which are in the Northeast. For a description of discount programs that give benefits at all the resorts, see the Lift Ticket section in the Sunday River chapter.

Accommodations

Condo projects and a lodge at the base area have shuttle service to the slopes. Most of the other lodging lines Rte. 100 between the slopes and Wilmington,, with some tucked on side roads back into the foothills.

Rates vary, depending on season and the size of the unit. Per-person rates start at about $132 for two-day weekend packages; five-day midweek packages (Sunday through Thursday nights) are a bargain—some as low as $35 per person per day. A new one-night package combines a night in a hotel with a day of skiing starting at $44 a day (another bargain).

For a **vacation planner** with descriptions of most area properties, write: Mount Snow, Rte. 100, Mount Snow, Vermont 05356, or call (800) 245-7669 (245-SNOW).

Condominiums

Rates are based on the size of the unit and number of bathrooms. They start at about $250 on the weekends; half that midweek.

The Mount Snow Condominiums (800-451-4211 or 464-7788; $$$–$$$$) are at the base of the lifts, but only the Seasons complex is actually ski-in/ski-out. Seasons' condos are the most highly recommended with an athletic center, indoor pools, saunas and hot tubs. Two-bedroom/two-bath units cost around $800 for a weekend. Call (800) 245-7669 for information on all condos near the base area (shuttle service to the slopes).

Timber Creek Townhomes (800-982-8922 or 464-1222; $$$$) are luxury condos across Rte. 100 from the ski area. They have a fitness center and 18 km. of cross-country trails just outside. Shuttlebuses run between the complex and the ski area.

Greenspring at Mount Snow (800-247-7833 or 464-7111; $$$-$$$$) are upscale condos a mile from the slopes. This complex has the best athletic center in the area.

As an ASC resort, Mount Snow also has a **Grand Summit Resort Hotel & Conference Center** (464-6600 or 800-845-7690; $$$–$$$$) a ski-in/ski-out full-service resort hotel with 200 rooms in the Main Base Area.

Inns

Snow Lake Lodge (800-451-4211 or 802-464-7788; $$–$$$) is a sprawling 92-room mountain lodge near the base of Mount Snow. While still fairly basic, the lodge does have a fitness center, sauna, indoor hot tub, outdoor Jacuzzi and aprés-ski entertainment. The Sundance lift is a 300-yard walk or a free shuttle ride away. The lodge is excellent with children.

The Inn at Sawmill Farm (802-464-8131; $$$$), is one of the nation's top country inns. Secluded in a renovated dairy barn and outbuildings, the inn coddles guests with spacious rooms decorated in a country chic style. Fresh flowers, wood-burning fires, meticulous service and an excellent dining room complete the picture. The inn is not suitable for children, nor does it take credit cards.

Less than a quarter-mile from Mount Snow, the **Yankee Doodle Lodge** (800-388-5591 or 802-464-5591; $$$$) is family-friendly and comes highly recommended by the locals.

The **Lodge at Mount Snow** (800-451-4289 or 802-464-5112; $$$$) is on Rte. 100 near the entrance to the resort and has midweek packages with free lodging for kids 12 and younger.

Andirons Lodge (800-445-7669 or 802-464-2114; $$), on Rte. 100 in West Dover, is just two miles from the lifts. While somewhat short on hospitality, this motel offers low-cost lodging in simple paneled rooms with double beds; some have additional twin beds. There is an indoor pool, a sauna and a newly refurbished game room called the Billiard Sanctuary. The attached Dover Forge restaurant serves affordable meals.

Nordic Hills Lodge (800-326-5130 or 802-464-5130; $$$$), on 179 Coldbrook Road in Wilmington, has cable TV. Rates include breakfast and dinner.

Gray Ghost Inn (800-745-3615 or 802-464-2474), on Rte. 100, West Dover, is a large country inn operated by a British couple. Many rooms have smaller beds or bunk beds for children. Rates include breakfast.

Trail's End (800-859-2585 or 802-464-2727; $$–$$$), Smith Road, Wilmington. This inn has 15 country-style rooms. Meals are served family-style at three round tables, so visitors probably will return home with new friends.

Old Red Mill (800-843-8483 or 802-464-3700; $–$$), Rte. 100 in Wilmington, was created from a former sawmill and is one of the bargains in the region. Rooms are small, only about 7 by 12 feet with a double bed, but all have TV. Larger rooms are available for families. The common areas are rustic.

Horizon Inn (800-336-5513 or 802-464-2131; $–$$$), Rte. 9 in Wilmington, has an indoor heated pool, whirlpool, sauna and game room.

Best Western—The Lodge at Mount Snow (800-451-4289 or 802-464-5112; $$$$), at the base of Mount Snow, has midweek packages that include free lodging for kids 12 and younger.

The White House of Wilmington (464-2135; $$–$$$), Rte. 9, Wilmington, is an upscale, romantic 23-room inn serving breakfast and dinner. An Editor's Pick by the Yankee Travel Guide, the inn has an indoor pool.

Bed & Breakfasts

Mount Snow also has a group of charming and elegant bed-and-breakfast establishments with rates starting at about $125 per night on weekends and $70 midweek. These B&Bs are smaller, most with fewer than 15 rooms.

The Doveberry Inn (800-722-3204 or 464-5652; $$) on Rte. 100, West Dover is run by Michael and Christine Fayette, both culinary-school-trained chefs. This inn is not suitable for young children.

Dining: $$$–Entrees $20+; $$–$10-20; $–less than $10.

Accommodations: (double room) $$$$–$200+; $$$–$141-$200; $$–$81-$140; $–$80 and less.

West Dover Inn (800-732-0745 or 464-5207;$$), Rte. 100, West Dover, is an historic country inn built in 1846. It has 12 elegant rooms furnished with antiques, hand-sewn quilts and color TVs, as well as two suites with fireplaces and whirlpool tubs.

Deerhill Inn (800-464-3100; $$–$$$$), Valley View Road, in West Dover, is a chef-owned romantic hillside inn with panoramic views of Mount Snow and Haystack.

The Red Shutter Inn (800-845-7548 or 464-3768; $$–$$$) is on Rte. 9, Wilmington. This 1894 country home has been converted into an elegant country inn with nine guest rooms.

The Nutmeg Inn (464-3351; $$–$$$) is on Rte. 9W, Wilmington. Built in the 1770s as a home, this inn is decorated with country accents and quilts and has 10 rooms and three fireplace suites.

The Orchard Inn (464-7147; $) on Rte. 100 just north of Wilmington, has seven rooms. The restaurant, Piero's Trattoria, serves the most authentic Italian cuisine in the valley.

The Inn at Quail Run (800-343-7227 or 464-3362; $$$$) is recommended by locals and welcomes both children and pets. Its brunch is considered the best in the valley.

Dining

The top dining experience (and the most expensive) is the **Inn at Sawmill Farm** (464-1130; $$$–$$$$), which holds a Wine Spectator Grand Award.

The Hermitage (464-3511; $$–$$$) serves excellent meals at less stratospheric prices. A very large dining room has the world's largest collection of hanging Delacroix prints. The wine cellar has 30,000 bottles of 2,000 different labels. All game birds and venison are raised on the premises, and the jams, jellies and maple syrup are homemade.

For other fine dining try **Betty Hillman's Le Petit Chef** (464-8437; $$–$$$), **Two Tannery Road** (464-2707; $$$), and **Gregory's** (464-5207; $$–$$$), next to the West Dover Inn. **Doveberry Restaurant** (464-5652; $$$) is small and intimate with husband-and-wife chefs, culinary school graduates who have worked in Nantucket and San Francisco. The menu is Northern Italian. **The Deerhill Inn and Restaurant** (800-626-5674 or 464-3100; $$$), on Valley View Road, in West Dover, features award-winning American cuisine and a strong wine list.

Fennessey's (464-9361; $$) serves up consistently good food at reasonable prices according to locals. **The White House** (464-2135; $$) serves a great Sunday brunch with a 30-foot buffet table. Dinners are excellent and are served in a nice setting overlooking Wilmington. Locals tell us **The Inn at Quail Run** (464-3362; $$) serves the best brunch in the valley.

The Roadhouse (464-5017; $$) is normally packed. It serves the basic stuff skiers love, such as steak, chicken, ribs, swordfish and trout, in large portions. **Dot's of Dover** (464-6476; $) in the Mountain Park Plaza next to the movie theater, serves breakfast, lunch and dinner daily, plus an excellent Sunday brunch. The chili has won awards, and it gives you your O.J. in a jar. The ownership also serves dinner daily at **Dot's Restaurant**, on Rte. 9, in Wilmington (464-7284; $).

For economical eats, try **Poncho's Wreck** (464-9320; $$), a local institution with an eclectic dining room serving Mexican food, steaks, lobsters and fresh fish. **Anchor Seafood** (464-5616; $$), specializes in surf and turf. **Alonzo's Pasta & Grille** (464-0123; $$) at Crafts Inn in Wilmington is another local favorite. **Cafe Tannery** (464-2078; $-$$) offers lighter fare such as burgers, burritos and salads and does take-out.

The Vermont House (464-9360; $-$$) on Wilmington's main street, serves good food for cheap prices and is one of the locals' favorites. Head to **Deacon's Den** (464-9361; $) after skiing for pizza, burgers and sandwiches. **TC's Tavern** (464-9316; $–$$) has inexpensive family fare. For Chinese food, try **First Wok** (464-5861; $-$$) in the Mountain Park Plaza, West Dover.

For groceries, head to Shaw's on Rte. 9 in Wilmington, east of Rte. 100.

 ## Après-ski/nightlife

The **Snow Barn** features live music most weekends, sometimes with up-and-coming national acts. It has a separate area for pool and other games, with a central stone fireplace and a pizza window. Both Snow Barn and **Deacon's Den** usually have cover charges.

Après-ski at **Cuzzins** is a wild affair where the DJ gets folk up and dancing on the tables. The line is long, but the fun is worth it. **Walt's Pub,** at the Snow Lake Lodge, has a quiet, family-style atmosphere with "unplugged" music on Saturday nights and Pub Night on Mondays, featuring a special beer on tap and 10 cent wings.

One of the most popular nightspots, the **Silo**, is actually in a converted grain Silo (in the Silo Family Restaurant on Rt. 100). It caters to a young crowd and has practically a monopoly on nightlife for the snowboarding set. Locals head to the Silo every evening for 10-cent wings from 4-6 p.m. Downstairs is a smoke-filled cigar bar for aficionados. The **Dover Bar & Grille** (464-2689), across Rte. 100 from the Silo, is another local hangout.

 ## Other activities

The Mount Snow Valley is reportedly the busiest area for **snowmobiling** in Vermont. Try High Country Snowmobile Tours (464-2108 or 800-627-7533), which operates from the base of Mt. Snow, Wheeler Farm snowmobile tours (464-5225) in Wilmington and Stizmark (464-3384). **Dog-sledding** is available through Snow Doggin' (464-1100 ext. 4618). Adams Farm (464-3762) in Wilmington offers sleigh rides.

Mount Snow runs a lift-served tubing hill open Friday and Saturday evenings. Rates are $18 per four-hour session or $13 for those with lift tickets.

A **movie theater**, in the Mountain Park Plaza on Rt. 100 in West Dover, shows first-run movies. The **Snowseum** in the main base area covers the history of skiing through Mount Snow's eyes using old equipment and photos. The Grand Summit Resort Hotel now has a **spa** offering massage therapy, facials and body treatments. Reservations are required; call 464-6600, ext. 6005. **Shopping**: Wilmington Village has a few quaint shops, but this is not a major activity at Mount Snow.

 ## Getting there and getting around

By air: The closest airports are in Albany, N.Y. and Hartford's (C.T.) Bradley International, both less than a two-hour drive.

By car: Mount Snow is the closest major Vermont ski resort to New York and Boston. It is on Rte. 100, nine miles north of Wilmington.

Getting Around: A car isn't completely necessary, but it is pretty helpful, especially at night. During the day, take shuttle buses to and from the lifts; at night, take the MOOver, a free shuttle that serves much of the Mount Snow Valley from the resort down into Wilmington. It runs late on weekends. You can't miss it: The buses are painted like Holstein cows.

Okemo Mountain

Vermont

Summit elevation:	3,344 feet
Vertical drop:	2,150 feet
Base elevation:	1,194 feet

Address: 77 Okemo Ridge Road
Ludlow, VT 05149-9708
☎ **Area code:** 802
Ski area phone: 228-4041
Snow report: 228-5222
Fax: 228-4558
ⓘ **Toll-free reservations:**
(800) 786-5366 (800-78-OKEMO)
E-mail: info@okemo.com
Internet: www.okemo.com

Expert: ★
Advanced: ★
Intermediate: ★★★★★
Beginner: ★★★
Never-ever: ★★

Number of lifts: 16—4 high-speed quads,
4 quads, 3 triple chairs, 5 surface lifts
Snowmaking: 95 percent
Skiable acreage: 554 acres
Uphill capacity: 27,250 per hour
Snowboarding: Yes
Bed Base: 10,000
Nearest lodging: Slopeside, condos
Resort child care: Yes, 6 weeks and older
Adult ticket, per day: $57–$62 (02/03 prices)

Dining: ★★★
Apres-ski/nightlife: ★★
Other activities: ★★

For cruising, it's hard to beat Okemo, one of Vermont's friendliest, best-run family resorts. Rising more than 2,150 feet above the town of Ludlow, a bustling Vermont village with roots that extend beyond the ski industry, Okemo was laid out with ribbons of mostly intermediate trails streaming down it, as if the resort planners dumped maple syrup on the summit and put trails wherever it flowed. The trails have few intersections, so you don't have to have one foot on the brake as you cruise down.

Adding to that cruising feel is the snow quality. Okemo covers 95 percent of its terrain with manmade snow, groomed until it feels like brand new wall-to-wall carpeting. "Hero snow," some call it. A few laps off the Northstar Express Quad on blue runs such as World Cup, and you may start to feel as if you could, well, ski on the World Cup.

Owned by Tim and Diane Mueller, Okemo also has a homey feel to it. The Muellers are hands-on owners and can often be found loading lifts or busing trays in the cafeteria on busy weekends. Everyone smiles, says good morning, and asks how your day is going. Everyone, that is, except the grumpy guy who woke up late and had to park in what feels like the next state. Okemo's main base area has limited parking. Once on the mountain, you have to take one of two lifts to get to the more wide-open terrain on the mountain proper. On busy weekends, these two lifts are a bottleneck.

But the new Jackson Gore expansion should ease this crowding. Okemo began construction on Jackson Gore during the spring of 2002 and this year will open 6 new trails, along with a new high-speed quad chairlift. Upon completion, the expansion will comprise 16 new trails (half of which will be intermediate and advanced), along with four lifts, a gondola and the

Jackson Gore Inn, which will have a cafeteria, sit-down restaurant, shops and 117 new residential units, to name a few amenities. The goal is for Jackson Gore to look and feel like a Vermont-style base village. The architecture will have a Colonial feel and look. With the addition of Jackson Gore, Okemo now has five-mountain areas: Jackson Gore, Solitude, Northeast Summit/Glades, South Face and South Ridge

Mountain layout–Skiing

The mellow skiing and most of the beginning ski school action take place on the gentle rise served by two sister lifts, South Ridge Quads A and B. These two quads also provide access to several clusters of condos and townhouses slopeside as well as serving as the gateway to the rest of Okemo's lift system from the Base Lodge. There can be a slight logjam at these two lifts, but once up on the mountain you can ski to a triple chair, a fixed quad or a high-speed quad, all of which take skiers to the upper trails.

The Northstar Express is always the most popular on weekends and holidays and savvy Okemo skiers and riders know that. Instead, they choose to ride the Black Ridge Triple to the Green Ridge Triple and save time (and sneak in a few additional runs). Both Green Ridge and Northstar unload by the Summit Lodge. Another best-kept secret is to ride the Sachem Quad to the Glades Peak Quad and head to the South Face Area of the mountain in the morning and enjoy the glades and long cruisers. You can catch the bright sunshine and are sure to get first tracks in that area of the mountain. Or, take the Black Ridge triple chair to the Green Ridge triple to access the summit area. Okemo's new Jackson Gore area will feature six new trails, complete with snowmaking and one new high-speed quad chairlift. Many of the trails will have sweeping turns and undulations, reminiscent of classic New England trails. Trail names such as Quantum Leap, Sunset Strip, Escape, Limelight and Blue Moon will be found in the new Jackson Gore area. We're told Quantum Leap will challenge any expert!

◆◆ **Expert** ◆ **Advanced:** There are no true double-black trails on the mountain. Outrage and Double Black Diamond are both gladed and not particularly precipitous, but enjoyable and challenging with proper snow conditions. The best challenges for seasoned experts are the glades that have been opened recently to skiers. Forest Bump is 16 acres of tree skiing off the Rimrock trail. Loose Spruce and Stump Jumper provide tight and not-so-tight glades just to the right of the South Face high-speed quad. The other way that Okemo created above average skiing conditions is with bumps. Wild Thing, Blind Faith and Punch Line are often left to bump up, but when they are groomed with the bumps cut down, they are delightful cruising runs. Elsewhere on the mountain, you can often find manmade bumps on Sel's Choice and the Ledges. If air is what you desire, head to the terrain park on Nor'Easter or try the beginner terrain park in front of the Sugar Shack.

■ **Intermediate:** Overall, the pitch on this mountain is so consistent and the trails are so similarly cut, a skier would be hard pressed to describe the difference between Dream Weaver at one side of the mountain and Sidewinder on the opposite side. This is not a negative, just a fact of life on this mountain. At Okemo, intermediates should choose their trails based on crowds. Our experience has been that while a cruise down groomed Punch Line and Blind Faith may be crowded, wide arching turns can be made down Upper and Lower Tomahawk and Screamin' Demon without another skier in sight. As its name implies, the Solitude area is often the least crowded and has a bounty of intermediate terrain. Heaven's Gate to Screamin' Demon is a favorite.

●● **Beginner:** The 4.5-mile Upper (and Lower) Mountain Road is the easiest route from the top. But beginners can ski virtually anywhere that is marked intermediate on this mountain. The Green Ridge triple and the Solitude Peak high-speed quad have many runs for beginners. The trails are wide enough to allow traverses, and the pitch is mellow enough for them to maintain control. The gentle and undulating Sachem and Kettle Brook trails have tunnels to glide through.

● **Never-ever:** Okemo has a learning area near the base lodge, served by two quads and two surface lifts. Riding the surface lifts is free. Unfortunately, the first beginner lessons take place in an area that is crisscrossed by more advanced skiers moving between lifts and condos. Fortunately, the children's learning area is tucked away from other skiers. Beginners are also transported to the Morning Star and Solitude Peak areas, away from the crowds, on peak weekends and holidays.

Mountain layout–Snowboarding

Okemo has a large snowboarding community not confined to the young and restless. Gray-haired ski patrollers and instructors foster a pro-boarding attitude. Most of Okemo's riders hang out at The Zone, a terrain park with a huge excavated superpipe. Because the pipe is excavated, it opens early in the season, so even before the whole mountain is open, you can be hitting its 17-foot high walls, and with a 420-foot length, you're sure to feel good about a few hits. A sound system cranks out tunes at 900 watts here, and there's a surface lift for quick access to this park. If you find this pipe too crowded, there's another superpipe, which opens later when the snow's better, at the Nor'easter Terrain Park. This park has plenty of hits of all sizes as well as a couple of rails for sliding. One word of caution, Sel's Choice, which leads into the Zone, can have some nasty moguls. You can skirt around it on Lower Arrow.

Extreme free-riders should head elsewhere but cruisers will love straight-lining this place. When playing in the double-diamond Forest Bump glades off the South Face quad, keep your speed up, because it dumps into the oh-so-flat Catnap trail.

Mountain rating

If you're an expert or advanced skier, Okemo won't offer enough of a challenge unless you yearn for bumps or glades. But beginners and intermediate skiers and snowboarders will think they've died and gone to heaven. Never-evers might want to look for another resort with a separate learning area, but Okemo is designed to bring never-evers up onto the mountain very quickly. This mountain can be a great ego boost to every skier.

Cross-country and snowshoeing

The **Okemo Valley Nordic Center** (288-1396), set along the Black River, only a half-mile from Okemo Mountain, has fine facilities with 28 km. of trails, a rental and repair shop and a restaurant. Instruction is available. It also has 10 km. of dedicated snowshoe trails. Changing rooms with showers are available. The center is open from 8 a.m.-4 p.m. on weekends and holidays; Monday through Friday, it opens at 9 a.m.

Lessons [2002/03 prices]

Group lessons: $30 for a 1.75-hour lesson. Seniors pay $15.
Never-ever package: For skiing or snowboarding, packages include lesson, rental equipment and beginner lifts, and cost $50 for ages 7–12 and $59 for

adults. Second lesson, same day, is $25. First Tracks is available in a two-day option for $109 for adults, $95 for juniors.

Private lessons: $75 per hour, each additional hour is $65, and each additional skier is charged $40 per hour.

Special programs: Upper-level groups concentrate on various subjects, such as moguls, black diamonds, parallel turns or learning how to use shaped skis. Okemo also has an Adaptive Program for skiers and riders with disabilities (advance reservation required). Women's Ski Spree is a multiday indulgence for women of all abilities. Cost is $550 for the five-day program, $389 for the three-day.

Child care (2002/03 prices)

Ages: 6 weeks to 8 years at the Penguin Playground Day Care Center
Costs: $65 for a full day with lunch. Half days are $43. Sunday morning, 8 a.m.-1:30 p.m., $55, with lunch. Special Mini Stars lessons are available for kids ages 3-4 and are taught by professional Okemo instructors for $22 per session.
Reservations: Recommended; call 228-1780.

Note: Every Saturday evening from January through March, Okemo has Kids Night Out, an evening child care program for ages 5-12. It costs $35 for the four-hour session per child, or $60 for up to three children. Okemo also sells an unlimited season child-care pass for $1,425; Mini Stars add-on is $400.

Children's lessons: Children ages 4-7 enroll in Snow Stars. The program is $80 for a full day with lunch, $50 for a half day; multiday discounts are available. Okemo has Snow Star riders at the same prices for ages 5-7 who want to learn to snowboard. Small-sized boards are available for rent at an extra cost. Young Mountain Explorers and Young Riders, ages 7-12, have supervised lesson programs for $70 a day or $135 for two days (lift ticket is additional) with discounts for additional days. Teens, ages 13-16, have their own lessons, Get Altitude, $32 for a 1.75-hour lesson, either morning or afternoon. A one-hour Parent & Tot program allows kids to learn with Mom and Dad for $75. The instructor will leave parents with tips on helping their child improve on the slopes.

Lift tickets (2002/03 prices)

	Adult	Young Adult (13-18)	Junior (7-12)
One day: weekend/holiday	$62	$53	$40
One day: midweek	$57	$49	$375
Three days: *weekend/holiday	$156/$174	$133/$147	$101/$111
Five days	$304/$270	$202/$230	$154/$165

Who skis free: Children ages 6 and younger, or those riding beginner surface lifts.

Who skis at a discount: Ages 65-69 ski for Young Adult rates; ages 70 and older ski for Junior rates.

Sunday morning discount: The Sunday Solution is available every Sunday as well as Jan. 20 and Feb. 17, 2003: Ski from 8 a.m.-1:30 p.m. for $50 adult; $43 young adult and $31 junior/super-senior (ages 70+) and hit the road before the rest of the traffic.

Note: All listed prices include Vermont sales tax.

Accommodations

Okemo has many **slopeside condos and townhouses** (800-786-5366). Per-person rates vary widely depending on proximity to the slopes and size, but a range would be $375–$850 off-mountain to $450-$1,000+ slopeside for a five-night ski week. Kids ages 12 and younger stay free at Okemo Mountain Resort condos. As always, ask about packages.

The Okemo/Ludlow area, including Chester, Springfield, Weston, Plymouth and Proctorsville, has more than 50 country inns, B&Bs and motels. **The Governor's Inn** (228-8830 or 800-468-3766; $$-$$$$) is located right on Main Street and is one of Ludlow's nicest lodges. All rooms have private baths and are furnished in Victorian fashion, complete with puffy comforters. Rates include breakfast only or breakfast and dinner. The six-course dinners are preceded by hors d'oeuvres in the den. Right at the base of Okemo's Mountain Road is the **Andrie Rose Inn** (228-4846 or 800-223-4846; $$$-$$$$), considered one of the most romantic inns in Vermont. Most rooms have Jacuzzis, and the suites have fireplaces. The inn also has well-appointed family suites.

The Echo Lake Inn (824-6700 or 800-356-6844; $$–$$$$), north on Rte. 100, is a rambling New England inn with an excellent dining room and cozy public rooms. Presidents Coolidge and McKinley slept here. Rates with breakfast only or with breakfast and dinner are available. **The Inn at Water's Edge** (228-8143; $$$-$$$$) north on Rte. 100 on the shores of Echo Lake, opened in the fall of 1999. The owners completely refurbished a 150-year-old Victorian home and made a romantic inn with eleven small rooms complete with antiques, private baths and Jacuzzis. Rates include breakfast, dinner served fireside and afternoon tea. After dinner, relax in the traditional English pub. Of note, the inn caters to couples, and children are discouraged.

The Hawk Inn and Mountain Resort (672-3811 or 800-685-4295; $$$$) has luxury country inn and townhouse facilities. This complex features indoor/outdoor pool, sauna, Jacuzzis, sleigh rides and fine dining. Rates include breakfast. **The Castle** (226-7361; $$$$) is a gracious, turn-of-the-century former Governor's mansion. New owners have painstakingly preserved the old-world standard for luxury and ambiance and have furnished the entire mansion with period furniture. The food is exception and the dining room is extremely romantic. The **Cavendish Pointe Hotel** (226-7688 or 800-438-7908; $-$$) offers the full service of a 70-room country-style hotel, restaurant, indoor pool, lounge and game room. The hotel is on Rte. 103, two miles from Okemo.

The **Best Western Colonial Motel** (228-8188; $$-$$$) offers very affordable lodging within walking distance of Ludlow's shopping, nightlife and dining. **Happy Trails Motel** (228-9984 or 800-228-9984; $-$$$) in Ludlow offers great bargains with a good hot tub.

Dining

On mountain, don't miss **Gables** ($-$$) in the Solitude Day Lodge. This ski-in/ski-out restaurant is now run by the New England Culinary Institute and puts typical ski lodge fare to shame. Lunch delicacies include Tuscan bruschetta, butternut squash ravioli, and portobello mushroom sandwiches. Prices are reasonable, and the restaurant already has a steady following. Hours are 11 a.m. to 3 p.m.

Upscale restaurants that serve dinner in the area include the **Echo Lake Inn** (228-5585; $$–$$$) north of town, where Chef Kevin Barnes has been creating gourmet delicacies for over a decade, and **The River Tavern Restaurant** at the Hawk Inn and Mountain Resort (672-3811; $$–$$$), which serves delicious meals. The tortilla crusted lamb chops with tart cherry chipotle sauce are wonderful and reminiscent of a European gourmet platter. A must visit is the **Old Town Farm Inn** (888-232-1089, $-$$$), a charming, family friendly, restored 1861 Vermont farmhouse, in Chester. What really makes the Old Town Farm Inn unique is the Japanese dinners prepared by owner, Chef Michiko Yoshida-Hunter, a sixth-generation chef. Everything is made to order, so be sure to allow plenty of time for a leisurely meal. Bring your own bottle.

The following restaurants are not as upper crust, but serve excellent affordable meals perfect for families. **Nikki's** (228-7797; $-$$) at the foot of the Okemo Mountain access road has a very good reputation and is a favorite among locals. Nikki's is moderately expensive, but its Osso Bucco con Orechiette or steamed whole Maine lobster are excellent. **Willie Dunn's Grille** (228-1387; $$) at the Okemo Valley Golf & Nordic Center offers superb affordable meals. The Shrimp Puttanesca with capers and olives in a red sauce is excellent. **Sam's Steakhouse,** (228-5622; $$),on Rte. 103 just east of Ludlow, serves a filet mignon so tender it can be cut with a butter knife, as well as seafood, chicken, sinful desserts and an incredible salad bar.

D.J.'s Restaurant (228-5374; $-$$) gets high marks from locals for its prime rib, steak, seafood, pasta and fabulous salad bar. **Cappuccino's** (228-7566; $) also gets raves for chicken and pasta specials as well as beef, pork, veal and vegetarian meals.

The Combes Family Inn (800-822-8799; $$$) serves a single-entrée dinner at 7 p.m. each evening. Call for the day's menu and to make reservations. **The Ludlow Cooking Company** (226-7251; $) in town also has sandwiches, deli items, rich desserts, and something handy for condo dwellers: meals to go, mostly of the Italian variety, but also great homestyle stuffed cabbage for any homesick Polish skiers. **A State of Bean** (228-2326; $) at the base of the access road has over-stuffed chairs and couches, and serves fresh-baked muffins and pastries, homemade soups, sandwiches, salads, desserts and, of course, a variety of coffee drinks. North of Ludlow on Rte. 103 is **Harry's** (259-2996; $-$$), an understated place that has a high repeat business because of its moderate prices and international cuisine. Try the burrito if you want the best (and most!) food for the least money.

In nearby Chester, stop and have a meal at **Raspberries and Thyme** (875-4486; $-$$). Breakfast and lunch are always good. Dinner is served Wednesday to Sunday. On Main Street in Ludlow, **Cafe at deLight, Trappers** and **The Hatchery** are the locals' recommendations for breakfast. **Christopher's** (228-7822) and **Wicked Good Pizza** (228-4131) have good pie (pizza pie, that is). **Goodman's American Pie** (228-4271), on Main Street, serves wood-fired pizza. **Al Dentes** (228-7400; no reservations; $) serves affordable pasta specials.

Après-ski/nightlife

For après-ski on the mountain, try **Sitting Bull Lounge,** with a wide-screen TV, après-ski parties, $1 draft beer day on non-holiday Wednesdays and live music on weekends; **Gables** with its gourmet appetizers or hot cider with Wild Turkey. Locals say **The Loft**, a popular après spot, serves the best wings in town. Down the mountain, head to **Willie Dunn's Grille**, at the Okemo Valley Golf & Nordic Center, or Archie's Steakhouse for its chicken wings and draft beer specials.

Later in the evening, **The Pot Belly** has country rock, '60s and '70s classics with a great bar and a big TV. Watch out when ordering their wines by the glass—they simply recork any leftover bottles each night and save them for the next day, so only order the wine if you can see them open a new bottle. **The Black River Brewing Company**, now located on Rte. 103

outside Ludlow, is one of the best deals in town. The home-brew is good and other local microbrews are available.

Other activities

The Okemo Valley Golf Club has opened a new indoor **Golf Operations Center** (228-1396) that features a 4,200-square-foot indoor practice area, a large putting practice area, indoor golf swing stations, a full swing golf simulator and a pro shop. Golf clinics are offered year round. **Ice skating** is free under the lights at Dorsey Park, but you need your own skates.

Shopping: Ludlow also has a wide array of specialty shops with clothing, antiques and gifts. One of the best browsing stores in the Northeast, the **Vermont Country Store**, is in nearby Weston on Rte. 100. It's full of useful little items that are hard to find elsewhere, such as pant stretchers (wire frames that help natural-fiber pants dry without wrinkles) and Vermont Bag Balm, which helps heal sore cow udders and chapped hands. **The Green Mountain Sugarhouse**, three miles from Ludlow on Rte. 100, is the spot to get those Vermont maple syrup gifts. In downtown Ludlow, don't miss **Chapter 14**, which mixes books with women's clothing, jewelry and an eclectic gallery upstairs, or **Blue Sky Trading Company** for jewelry and gifts.

Getting there and getting around

By air: Colgan Air/US Airways Express offers four flights a day from nearby Rutland (25 miles away) to Boston, but the airport sometimes closes in bad weather. The nearest major airports are Burlington, Vt.; Manchester, N.H.; or Hartford, Conn., all about two hours away.

By car: Okemo is in south-central Vermont on Rte. 103 in Ludlow, about two hours from Albany, N.Y.; three hours from Boston; and 4.5 hours from New York City.

By train: Amtrak has service from New York's Penn Station to Rutland, 25 miles to Okemo. Thrifty has a car rental office at the train station in Rutland.

Getting around: We recommend a car. But unless you are staying on-mountain, beware, parking at Okemo can be a bear. You will most likely end up parking far down the mountain and taking a shuttle to the base area. If you're staying in town, use the free Village Shuttle, which operates four routes through Ludlow and Proctorsville on weekends and holidays, from 7:30 a.m.-5:30 p.m. An on-mountain shuttle runs daily mid-December through March connecting all on-mountain properties with the base area and the Nordic Center.

Smugglers' Notch

Vermont

Summit elevation: 3,640 feet
Vertical drop: 2,610 feet
Base elevation: 1,030 feet

Address: 4323 Vermont Rte. 108 South
Smugglers' Notch, VT 05464-9537
☎ Area code: 802
Ski area phone: 644-8851
Snow report: 644-1111
**ⓘ Toll-free reservations and
information:** (800) 451-8752
Toll-free from the United Kingdom:
0800-169-8219
E-mail: smuggs@smuggs.com
Internet: www.smuggs.com/
Expert:★★★★
Advanced:★★★★
Intermediate:★★★
Beginner:★★★★
Never-ever:★★★★★

Number and types of lifts: 8–6 double
chairs, 2 surface lifts
Acreage: 264 acres marked trails; access to
750 acres of woods
Snowmaking: 62 percent
Uphill capacity: 7,400 per hour
Snowboarding: Yes
Bed base: 1,200; 565 condominiums
Nearest lodging: walking distance, condos
Resort child care: Yes, 6 weeks and older
Adult ticket, per day: $54 (02/03)

Dining:★★
Apres-ski/nightlife:★
Other activities:★★★

Smugglers' Notch has earned bragging rights as the best family resort in North America. In fact, it's the only North American resort that guarantees your family will have fun. If any family member participates in one of the resort's programs and doesn't have fun, Smugglers' will refund the entire program portion of that family member's stay. One of our staff members put that guarantee to the test: Her boyfriend's 16-year-old daughter hadn't skied in several years because she decided it wasn't fun anymore, but after her lesson here, she couldn't be dragged off the mountain. And her skiing improved dramatically in one day!

The family market has been the resort's focus for the past decade and the dividends have been exceptional. *Family Circle, SKI, Skiing, Travel & Leisure, FamilyFun and Better Homes and Gardens magazines* and *AOL's Family Travel Network* and even the United Kingdom's *Good Skiing and Snowboarding Guide* have all given Smugglers' #1 ranking for family vacations. The commitment to families is total: pedestrian-friendly village with stores, restaurants, an outdoor ice rink, sledding hill, indoor pool, saunas, steam baths, outdoor tennis, massage, crafts classes, sleigh rides, movies, parties for kids and adults and the largest licensed day-care facility in New England. The new 5,400 Treasures Child Care Center, scheduled to open in December, has remote access cameras, heated snowmelt walkways, radiant floor heating, and ski-in/ski-out convenience. There's also a 4,000-square-foot outdoor playground. Smugglers' even offers a study hall for youngsters ages 7-17 who need to keep up with classwork while on vacation. The popular Club Smugglers' package includes lodging, lift tickets and daily group lessons; choose from alpine, snowboard, cross-country, ski board, telemark or snowshoe. You can add day care and special activities to the package. Once families arrive and pick up their welcome packets, most will never have to deal with additional payments except meals.

If you're an advanced or expert skier, Smugglers' is a well-kept secret. Its 2,610 vertical feet places second behind Killington for Vermont's longest vertical descent. Smugglers' has three mountains, one of which, Madonna Mountain, gives a 2,130-foot drop off one chair. You normally will have this mountain almost to yourself, and the steeps, bumps, glades and unofficial woods skiing and riding will keep you satisfied for a week-long vacation. Granted, the lift system is old and seems to creep up the mountain, but the time on the flanks of Sterling and Madonna is worth every minute of lift time, and the lift has been reconditioned and lowered, to screen chairs from the wind. Also new this season is the Top of the Notch warming house at the summit of Sterling Mountain.

Incidentally, the area was named for the smugglers and bootleggers who brought in forbidden English goods during the War of 1812 and booze during Prohibition, storing the contraband in caves between Madonna Mountain and Mt. Mansfield, the latter one of the peaks at Stowe. Though Rte. 108 passes Smugglers' and continues through the notch to Stowe, it is closed in winter.

Mountain layout–Skiing

◆◆ **Expert** ◆ **Advanced:** The real challenge is from the top of Madonna Mountain. Smugglers' lays claim to the East's only triple-black-diamond trail, The Black Hole, which is in the woods next to Freefall. Smugglers' doesn't usually overhype its skiing, but this tight, steep, gladed run is no tougher than what you'll find at nearby Stowe Mountain Resort or Jay Peak Resort. Four legitimate double-black-diamond trails also beckon. The icefalls, ledges and stumps on Upper Liftline will make even true experts hold their breath. Freefall is just that: The turns come quickly and you drop 10 to 15 feet with each turn. Upper F.I.S. sports a 41-percent gradient, and with the addition of top-to-bottom snowmaking it has become a tad more civilized than in the past.

If you're hooked on glades, you'll want to check out Doc Dempsey's. It lost some trees in the ice storm a few years ago, which just gives it more character: It's become a winding, narrow New England trail dotted with groves of trees, and the bumps in spring make it extra fun. We just wish it were longer. If the top of Doc's is closed because of lack of snow, follow Catwalk to Upper F.I.S., take about two turns and drop into the set of tracks on skier's right, bypassing the cliff band at the top of Doc's. Another quick adrenaline rush is Highlander Glades on Sterling Mountain. Tree skiers will be awed by the amount of uncut terrain within the resort's boundaries: Keep an eye out for locals who might share their secret stashes. (Smugglers' off-trail policy requires you enter and exit from open trails; you are solely responsible for yourself). An unofficial easy glade that makes for a great first foray into the woods for kids is off the top of the Practice Slope Extension. In all, five new glades have been opened.

The best bump runs are F.I.S., the middle portion of Upper Liftline, Smugglers' Alley and Exhibition. The snow on Madonna Mountain takes longer to soften, so warm up on Sterling and head to the Madonna 1 chair after 11:30 a.m. or so.

■ **Intermediate:** Fifty-three percent of the trails are rated intermediate, and many are well suited to recent ski-school grads. Intermediate runs are concentrated on Madonna and Sterling peaks. Two favorite routes for lower intermediates who want to get a sense of big-mountain skiing are off Sterling: Upper Rumrunner to Lower Rumrunner, and Upper Rumrunner to Black Snake to the bottom of Treasure Run to Lower Exhibition. The views are spectacular both ways.

For advanced intermediates who want to test their mettle, try Chute on Sterling Mountain. It's a short advanced run that's steep with some bumps and stumps, especially in the spring, but the 15 to 20 turns it takes to get down make it perfect in case you decide you're in over your head.

●● **Beginner** ● **Never-ever:** The third mountain at Smugglers' is Morse, with 17 trails ranging from beginner to expert. It is the ski schooler's mountain. You won't find any hotshots here. Morse also is home to Mogul Mouse's Magic Lift, a half-speed double chair especially kind to beginners and young children. From the top of the lift winds the Magic Learning Trail, with nature stations, exploration paths and ski-through "caves." Morse Bowl is served by the Highlands double chair and has five trails for beginners and advanced beginners and a separate base lodge.

Moutain layout–Snowboarding

Prohibition Park on Madonna has a 400-foot Superpipe with a 17-foot radius as well as multiple hits, spines and rolls, and piped-in music. The Night School of Boarding meets three nights a week at Sir Henry's Hill & Fun Park at the base of Morse Mountain. The three-hour sessions are open to novices ages 6 and older. New this year is a Bombardier Super Half Pipe Grinder for grooming. Meadowlark trail from the upper base lodge back to village has a gentle grade, if the snow is fast, it's fine; if its spring and sticky take the shuttlebus. Three, open-to-anyone pipe jams are held during the season. A new snow deck park, next to Teen Alley, will operate all winter.

Mountain rating

Smugglers' is good for all types of skiers and boarders. Kids swarm over Morse Mountain, center of ski school classes, après-ski bonfires and hot chocolate, making it a magnet for those who revel in a family atmosphere. Experts and advanced skiers/riders should head to Madonna Mountain. Intermediates can cruise down Sterling. Smugglers' has no high-speed quads or triple chairs, which sometimes contributes to long waits at the lift loading area on weekends and holidays. The trade-off is that the trails are not congested.

If you're a day visitor of intermediate skiing ability or better, don't turn in to the main village. Continue up the hill to the top parking lot. Here you'll find fewer cars and a short walk to a point where you can ski to the lifts on Sterling and Madonna. Best of all, you can ski back to your car at day's end.

Cross-country and snowshoeing

More than 23 km. (about 14 miles) of scenic, groomed and tracked, cross-country skiing trails, plus 20 km. of dedicated snowshoe trails, are on site. **The Nordic Ski and Snowshoe Adventure Center** offers rentals, lessons, backcountry and night tours as well as snowshoe rentals and tours.

Lessons (2002/03 prices)

Snow Sport University (Smugglers' ski school) Director Peter Ingvoldstad has been acclaimed as one of the most innovative teachers in the country. Lessons are included with most Ski/Snowboard Week packages.

Group lessons: One-and-one-half hours, $36.

Never-ever package: The First Timer One-Day Package is $59 and includes a 1.5-hour coaching session, rentals and lift ticket valid on Morse Mountain on Saturdays and Sundays. A three-day package costs $118.

Private lessons: $70 per hour.

Special programs: Classes on style, terrain tactics, halfpipe tricks, family tours, night snowboarding lessons and programs for skiers 55 and older.

Racing: The race course is located on Lower Liftline on Madonna Mountain. On Saturdays and Sundays, Smuggs' has a free family fun race with prizes.

Child care (2002/03 prices)

Ages: 6 weeks-6 years old.

Costs: $66 per day or $330 for five days.

Reservations: Make them when you book your vacation, either with your travel agent or by calling the toll-free number listed in the fact box.

Note: Treasures Child Care is a major reason why *Family Circle* magazine chose Smugglers' as the top family resort for three years running. The facility is staffed with professional caregivers who may also be hired for evening babysitting.

Every night except Monday, Friday and Sunday, the center has Parents' Night Out, with dinner and activities for ages 3–12, at $25 per child, so Mom and Dad can have some fun on their own.

Children's lessons: Kids and teens are divided into the following age groups: 3–5, 6–10, 11-14 and 15–17. The teen program allows that age group to meet new friends with whom they can hang out at the supervised evening teen activities.

Lesson registration now is done when you make your initial reservations so getting rental equipment is probably the only remaining hassle you will encounter after resort registration; however, the new Three Mountain Equipment Rental shop doubles the floor space of the previous one which makes the rental process a little easier than it was before. Still, if possible, try to pick up rental equipment the afternoon before lessons start. Once kids are assigned to a class, forms are filled out, clothes tucked away and ski boots are pulled on, the instructors get the kids busy with coloring books and games, and young children are given their own trail map and journal in which they can record their ski or snowboard progression. That's a good time for parents to get lost.

Smugglers' has a "Mom & Me/Dad & Me" program that teaches parents how to teach their youngsters to ski. These lessons, essentially specialized private lessons, are for children aged 2 or older and a parent of at least intermediate skiing ability. Parents are taught games to make learning fun, and safety tips such as how to ride the lift with kids.

Young Boy Scouts who are guests at Smugglers' can earn merit badges in alpine and cross-country skiing.

Discovery Dynamos is full-day for kids 3–5 for all ability levels and encourages confidence. It costs $69 a day (lunch included) on the Club Smugglers' package with multiday rates available. Adventure Rangers for ages 6–10 has discovery programs and snow treks for $69 a day on the Club Smugglers' package. Mountain Explorers for the 15–17 group lets teens cruise in groups for $36 a day.

Special programs: All Mountain All Terrain Camp and the Future Stars Ski Racing Camp, both for teens, are scheduled Dec. 27-30 and Feb. 17-20.

Lift tickets (2002/03 prices)

	Adult	Youth (7-18)
Anyday	$54	$38
Multiday	*	*

Who skis free: Ages 6 and younger and 70 and older.
Who skis at a discount: Those 65–69 ski for $38 anytime.
Note: *If you're staying for more than one day here, the wise move is to buy a lodging package that includes tickets and lessons.

 ## Accommodations

At Smugglers' the primary and desirable place to stay is in the **Resort Village**, with plentiful lodging within walking distance of the lifts. Prices start at $595 per adult and $495 for youth for a five-day Club Smugglers' package, including lifts and lessons (packages for fewer days can be arranged). Children aged 6 and younger ski and stay free. Packages also include a welcome party, use of the pool and hot tub, family game nights, outdoor ice skating, family sledding parties, a weekly torchlight parade with fireworks finale and a farewell party. Showtime Theatre, nightly teen activities and adult entertainment (don't get overwrought; it's clean adult fun) are also available. Condos at Smugglers' are spacious, clean and family-furnished.

Smugglers' central check-in area is designed around the concept that once you check in, you have everything you need—lift tickets, instruction vouchers, rentals and day care. Computers at the front desk are tied to key areas such as the rental shop to make the resort very guest-friendly. We give Smugglers' credit for continuing to improve the check-in system. The lines in the check-in area have been greatly alleviated thanks to online preregistration for many activities and the addition of an auxiliary desk for property owners, which takes them out of the line.

Dining

You never have to leave the Village to eat. For home-baked breakfast treats and giant cookies, try **The Green Mountain Deli and Sweet Shoppe** (ext. 1141; $) with fresh-roasted coffee, espresso or cappuccino. Lunch favorites include chili in a bread bowl, spinach salads and made-to-order deli sandwiches. The **Riga-Bello's Pizzeria** (ext. 1142; $–$$) offers daily specials, pizza, salads, calzones and stuffed breads with meat and vegetable fillings—for eating there, taking out or delivery to your condo. The **Mountain Grille** (ext. 1247; $–$$), with a view of the slopes, is open continuously for breakfast, lunch and dinner, including light fare entrées. Kids on the FamilyFest Package get two free kids' meals from a special buffet of family favorites like hot dogs, chicken, potatoes and macaroni and cheese at the Mountain Grille when parents order a meal.

The **Hearth and Candle** (644-8090 $–$$$) is a privately operated restaurant in the Village with a friendly, though more formal, atmosphere. Families are served in the cozy Hearth Room, and couples desiring a quiet atmosphere are escorted upstairs to the adults-only Birch Room. Entrées range from steak and pasta to exotic preparations of fish and game.

Restaurants dot the route between the resort and Jeffersonville, five miles away. Some examples: Across from the entrance to the Village Center is the ever funky **Cafe Banditos** (644-8884; $–$$) with low-cost Mexican food, hickory-smoked chicken and ribs and a children's menu. The **Three Mountain Lodge** (644-5736; $$) serves eclectic dining in a classic log-lodge atmosphere. The night we were there, an acoustic blues guitarist provided entertainment. **Angelina's** (644-2011; $–$$) in Cambridge has great pizza, with a thin crust that's crispy on the bottom and soft on the top and loaded with sauce. Our kids, who consider themselves pizza connoisseurs, gave it an 8 out of 10.

Dining: $$$-Entrees $20+; $$-$10-20; $-less than $10.
Accommodations: (double room) $$$$-$200+; $$$-$141-$200; $$-$81-$140; $-$80 and less.

The Hungry Lion (644-5848), at the Smugglers' Notch Inn, five miles away, is a popular family restaurant that offers daily specials, vegetarian dishes, homemade breads and desserts, and a "cubs" menu. **Dinner's Dunn** (644-8219; $–$$) at The Windridge Bakery meets all appetite styles with simple soups and homemade breads baked in an old oven that's part of the decor, to traditional chicken and beef favorites. It's open for breakfast and lunch.

Après-ski/nightlife

Smugglers' has great nightlife. It's family oriented, but even our childless staffers who have visited here end up having more fun than they initially imagined. Activities provide fun for all ages; for example, a family sledding party on lighted Sir Henry's Hill, evening snowmobile tours, big screen movie night, bingo blast and a pizza-and-ice-cream-sundae party.

For more traditional fun, try **The Mountain Grille** for après-ski and nighttime entertainment such as karaoke on Tuesdays and dancing to DJ music on Saturdays. A magician entertains on Wednesdays. Teens 16 and older have the **Outer Limits Teen Center** with music videos, snacks, and dancing. Younger teens have **Teen Alley**, geared to ages 13-15. Amenities here include Internet access, Playstation 2, X Box and video games as well as music and a dance floor, all in a casual, club-like setting. The new Snow Deck park is just outside. Both teen centers are supervised, but no parents are allowed. Teens also enjoy the **FunZone**, an indoor playground for guests of all ages that includes miniature golf, basketball hoops, and inflatable attractions like a 22-foot giant double-lane slide and a padded jousting ring.

Other activities

Smuggs' has added day trips to its activity roster. These include a Wednesday trip to Montréal that takes in numerous city highlights; A Taste of Vermont tour on Thursday, which includes Ben & Jerry's Ice Cream Factory, Cold Hollow Cider Mill, Lake Champlain Chocolates, Cabot Creamery Annex and the Trapp Family Lodge.

Don't miss a visit to the **Boyden Valley Winery**, 8 miles down the road in Cambridge. This fourth-generation Vermont farmer makes award-winning wines using Vermont apples and berries and his own grapes and maple syrup. Tours and free wine tastings will convince you to buy a case of each and you'll find Vermont specialty products, an artisans' gallery, handmade furniture and gift baskets. You won't leave empty-handed!

If you want handmade Vermont crafts, you also can make your own. Smugglers' has an unusual activity, **Artists in the Mountains**. Local artisans teach classes in traditional New England crafts, such as tin punching, basket weaving, stenciling and dried flower arranging. The classes include materials and cost $35–$40.

As already noted, there are kids' parties, karaoke, sleigh rides, snowshoeing, sledding, a swimming pool, hot tubs, and ice skating.

Getting there and getting around

By air: Burlington International Airport is 40 minutes away. Shuttles are available (24-hour notice required; book it when you book lodging).

By car: Smugglers' Notch is on Rte. 108 near Jeffersonville in northwest Vermont.

Getting around: Everything is within walking distance at the resort or ride the free resort shuttle. If you want to visit some of the restaurants in or on the way to Jeffersonville, you'll need a car. A local taxi service also is available.

Stowe

Vermont

Summit elevation: 3,640 feet
Vertical drop: 2,360 feet
Base elevation: 1,280 feet

Address: 5781 Mountain Rd.
Stowe, VT 05672
☎ Area code: 802
Ski area phone: 253-3000 or 800-253-4754
Snow report: 253-3600
ⓘ Toll-free reservations:
(800) 247-8693 (24-STOWE);
for slopeside lodging only, (800) 253-4754
Advance Ticket Sales: 888-253-4TIX
Fax: 253-3406
E-mail: info@stowe.com
Internet: www.stowe.com; www.ridestowe.com;
www.13pitch.com
Expert: ★★★★
Advanced: ★★★★
Intermediate: ★★★★
Beginner: ★★★★
Never-ever: ★★★

Number and types of lifts: 11–1 high-speed
quad, 1 eight-passenger gondola, 1 triple,
6 doubles, and 2 surface lifts
Skiable acreage: 480 acres
Snowmaking: 73 percent
Uphill capacity: 12,326 per hour
Snowboarding: Yes
Bed base: 5,000+
Nearest lodging: Slopeside, hotel
Resort child care: Yes, 6 weeks and older
Adult ticket, per day: $58 (01/02)

Dining: ★★★★
Apres-ski/nightlife: ★★
Other activities: ★★★

The skiing and riding at Stowe Mountain Resort is spread across two peaks: Mt. Mansfield, the highest in Vermont at 4,395 feet, and Spruce Peak. The first sight of towering Mt. Mansfield, with its snow-capped summit above treeline, is breathtaking. Stowe has an undeniable blue-blood lineage as one of the oldest and most distinguished Eastern ski resorts. Its ski patrol, founded in 1934, is one of the oldest in the United States, and its winter carnival is the longest-running such event in the nation.

Stowe has made a concerted effort to retain its long, narrow, twisting runs cut close into the surrounding forests; runs that are an important part of making Stowe a classic New England ski experience. Ski publications repeatedly bestow various accolades on the resort, giving it top marks for overall experience, for its adventure, backcountry and vintage eastern flavor and for its tree skiing. Stowe's lodging and dining also have received repeated recognition from national publications.

Stowe's best-kept secret is its tree skiing. It's best-kept because the resort has an official policy of not acknowledging its unofficial trails, glades and out-of-bounds terrain. Also the locals are extremely reluctant to share their secret stashes with outsiders and we don't blame them one bit. If you decide to ski or ride on unofficial terrain, you are responsible for your own safety.

The town of Stowe, with its charming, white-steepled church and main street lined with historic buildings, is about seven miles away from the ski area. To truly enjoy all this area has to offer, you need a car.

Mountain layout–Skiing

◆◆ **Expert:** Part of the legend of Stowe revolves around its Front Four, and the fact that it features some of the steepest and most difficult runs in skidom. Having descended the Front Four is a badge of honor for Northeast skiers and deservedly so, given the nature of Goat, Starr, Liftline and National. Besides being steep, the headwalls are frequently draped with vintage New England hardpack, and the trails are liberally moguled. Experts who are gunning for all four should begin with National and Liftline. The resort's winch cats allow groomers to prepare these two from time to time, so this is a good place to get used to the considerable steepness of the Front Four. Starr is not groomed, and the view from the top of this run, as it disappears in a steep dive toward the base lodge area far below, is one you won't forget. If you haven't met your match by this time, then you're ready for Goat, a moguled gut-sucker no more than three to five bumps wide.

Expert tree skiers will want to start in the woods off Bypass, where there's a steep, tight drop-in that opens into perfectly spaced trees. Once you dump out on Nosedive, you'll find plenty of places to slip into the woods. Skiers are known to hike the Chin (4,395 feet) and put their mettle to the test on its out-of-bounds terrain, but we suggest you hook up with someone who's familiar with the area. The cliff bands and tight chutes are really nasty stuff, plus you can easily end up on the backside of the mountain with no clue how to return to civilization.

◆ **Advanced:** A very nice section of glade skiing through well-spaced trees is just off the top section of Nosedive. Chin Clip from the top of the gondola is long, moguled, and moderately narrow, but it does not have quite the steep grade that the Front Four boast.

■ **Intermediate:** This group can enjoy nearly 60 percent of the trails, including much of Spruce Peak. At Mt. Mansfield, ski to the right or left of the Front Four. Advanced-intermediates will probably want to chance the tricky top part of Nosedive for the pleasure of skiing the long, sweeping cruiser that beckons further down. Going left from the top of the FourRunner Quad, take Upper Lord until it leads you to a handful of long excellent intermediate runs all the way to the bottom in Lower Lord, North Slope, Standard and Gulch.

From the quad, reaching the intermediate skiing under the gondola presents a problem. The connection between these two parts of the mountain is not convenient unless you are willing to take a run down Nosedive, rated double-black at its top. (Yes, it's narrow with big moguls, but there's enough room to pick your way down. We got our advanced-intermediate staff member down it before she realized its rating.) If you don't want to chance Nosedive, it's a hike from the quad area over to the gondola, or you can take the green-circle Crossover trail toward the bottom of the mountain, which allows you to traverse directly across the Front Four to the gondola base. If you want to work your way back from the gondola to the quad, take the Cliff Trail, which eventually hooks up with Lower Nosedive and dumps you at the base of the high-speed chair.

If you feel as though you need a little elbow room after too many tight New England trails, try Perry Merrill or Gondolier from the gondola, or cut turns about as wide as you want down Main Street on Spruce Peak, across the base parking lot. Upper Spruce Peak is like skiing was in the old days, which means "no snow from heaven, no skiing." The Big Spruce double is an old and cold lift. When the snow is good and the wind isn't blowing, though, the mountain is a cruiser's delight, and powder days are a real treat.

Intermediates may also enjoy Stowe's night skiing. The upper portion of Perry Merrill and about 85 percent of Gondolier are lit Thursday through Saturday until 9 p.m. The ride up is in the warm gondola.

●● **Beginners:** One route we would recommend to all levels is the 4-mile-long, green-circle Toll Road, which starts at the top of the FourRunner quad. This is a marvelous trail for lower-level skiers, but the more proficient probably will enjoy it too—more for its beauty than for its challenge. You will pass through a canopy of trees, where you can hear only quiet sounds, such as birds chirping or snow plopping from the branches. A little later you'll find the small wood-and-stone Mountain Chapel, where on Sundays at 1 p.m. you can attend an informal church service. You just won't find this type of intimate ski trail out West.

● **Never-evers:** First-timers should start at Spruce Peak base area, then work up to the runs off the Toll House chair (Chair 5), then advance to Chair 4.

Mountain layout–Snowboarding

Stowe has been a leader in the growth and development of snowboarding in the United States. In fact, it's now Jake Burton Carpenter's home mountain.

The resort's terrain park on Tyro is a great place to find Burton employees and riders, who hang here in their free time.

Last year, the Tyro terrain park was ranked among the best our rider had visited. Most of the hits and a good quarterpipe were located on the top section. On the lower half, you have to choose between the halfpipe, which requires a bit of a traverse from Tyro, and Jib Nation, where most of the rails are located. Stowe has a halfpipe on the lower section of North Slope.

Beginning tricksters and those looking to try new moves should head to the Midway Mini Park, near the midway Lodge. Snowdeck rentals are free, and the park has small terrain features and rails. Demos are often staged here.

On the mountain trails, beginners should focus on Lower Spruce, then head over to Mt. Mansfield for long carving runs on Gondolier, Perry Merrill and Sunrise. As the day progresses, advanced riders should move from Liftline and Nosedive to Hayride and Centerline, then North Slope. Freeriders will really like this mountain. Nosedive takes you into some nice tree riding. There's also good hikeable terrain off the gondola. Avoid the Tollhouse lift, it's way too long, even for an expert.

Cross-country and snowshoeing

Stowe has one of the best cross-country networks in the country. Four touring areas all interconnect to provide roughly 150 groomed km. of trails, and an additional 110 km. in the backcountry, plus a slew of trails for snowshoeing.

The Trapp Family Lodge (253-5719; 800-826-7000) organized America's first touring center and has 55 km. groomed and machine-tracked trails that connect to another 100 km. in the Mt. Mansfield and Topnotch Resort networks. Trapp's also has 45 km. of backcountry trails. The fee is $12 a day for adults, $2 for children, free for those younger than 6. Rentals and instruction are available.

The Edson Hill Touring Center (253-7371) has about 50 km. of trails with 35 km. trails groomed. Elevation varies from 1,400 to 2,100 feet. The fee is $10 a day for adults, $5 for children, ages 6 and younger are free. **Stowe Mountain Resort** (253-3000) has 80 km. of trails, 35 km. of which are groomed. The daily fee is $12 for adults and $8 for children. **The Topnotch Resort** (253-8585) has 20 km. of trails, most of which are groomed and tracked. Trail fee is $10 for adults, $6 for children.

Snowshoe rentals and guided tours are available at Umiak Outdoor Outfitters (253-2317).

Lessons (2002/03 prices)

Telephone extension for the ski school is 3680 and 3681.
Group lessons: $35 for 90 minutes.

Never-ever package: Stowe for Starters includes up to two 90-minute group lessons and a Spruce Mountain lift ticket for $72. Offered at Spruce Peak only.

Private lessons: $85 an hour, with multihour and multiperson discounts.

Special programs: The Women in Motion all-day program costs $60 per day for one to three days and includes a lesson (off-piste, bumps, racing, etc.), rental of the newest demo equipment and lunch. Tele Tuesdays is a series of one-day clinics on Telemark skiing.

Lift tickets (2002/03 prices)

	Adult	Child (6-12)
One day (01/02)	$58	$36
Three days	$146 ($171/holiday)	$95 ($104/holiday)
Five days	$222 ($285/holiday)	$145 ($173/holiday)

Who skis free: Children ages 5 and younger with paid parent or guardian.

Who skis at a discount: Ages 65 and older ski for the same price as children. Multiday, non-holiday tickets can be bought by phone, three days in advance.

Note: Non-holiday night skiing is $20 for adults and $16 for children. A twilight ticket, valid from 1 to 9 p.m., is $42 for adults, $30 for children. All prices include Vermont sales tax.

Child care (2002/03 prices)

Ages: 6 weeks through 6 years.
Costs: Full day with lunch is $70. Half day with snack is $50. Children ages 3 and older can have an optional ski lesson for an additional $20.

Reservations: Required; call 253-3000, Ext. 3686. The Cubs child-care center is located at the base of Little Spruce. It's fully licensed by the state of Vermont and has separate crib and nap rooms. Parents must provide formula and food for infants. Toddlers are served lunch and offered snacks throughout the day. A beeper rental is $5 per day.

Children's lessons: Headquartered at Spruce Peak, full-day programs through the Adventure Center for skiing (ages 3-12) and snowboarding (ages 6-12) are $89, with lunch. Kids Super Start, for children ages 3-12 years old, costs $50.

Accommodations

When staying at least three days, ask about the Stowe Vacation Program. Extras include night skiing, extra half days, lessons, etc. Your lift tickets will be waiting for you along with your room key, so there's no need to stop at the ticket window on your way to the trails the next morning. Call (800) 247-8693 (24-STOWE).

When the Trapp Family's life was dramatized in *The Sound of Music,* their everlasting fame was guaranteed. **The Trapp Family Lodge** (253-8511 or 800-826-7000; $$$$), which they established near Stowe upon arriving in the United States, is a legend in its own right. Although the original building burned down in the late 1970s, it was rebuilt. It is still in the family and is the most popular and one of the more upscale places to stay in the area. This is a self-contained resort with an excellent cross-country center. The collection of restaurants is among the best in the area, and a modern pool and fitness center provide excellent amenities.

Make reservations early because this lodge is normally full throughout the season (Christmas reservations should be made about a year in advance). Rates include breakfast and dinner.

Not as famous as the Trapp Family Lodge, but much closer to the lifts and the town, **Topnotch at Stowe Resort & Spa** (253-8585 or 800-451-8686; in Canada 800-228-8686; $$$$) boasts an excellent fitness center and spa. Topnotch has rooms and condos, along with excellent meeting facilities. It also has the only indoor tennis courts in Stowe.

The Inn at the Mountain (800-253-4754 or 253-3000; $$–$$$$) is part of the Stowe Mountain Resort. This beautiful inn and the surrounding condominiums (available through the same telephone number) are the only ski-in/ski-out facilities. The flavor is country New England. The modern Fitness Center across the parking lot is free to all guests. The Fireside Tavern is the perfect place to unwind after a day on the slopes. Room and condo unit rates include breakfast and dinner

The best family accommodations in Stowe are at the **Golden Eagle Resort** (253-4811 or 800-626-1010; $$–$$$). This sprawling complex has more than a dozen buildings and facilities, from motel rooms with kitchenettes to apartments. The complex has one of the best fitness centers in town with an indoor pool. It is unpretentious and affordable. Because there are dozens of pricing options, the best bet is to contact the property and explain your needs.

The Stoweflake Mountain Resort and Spa (253-7355 or 800-253-2232; $$$–$$$$), down the road a bit from the Golden Eagle, recently added a spa and sports club as well as a new wing of deluxe rooms with fireplaces and mountain views. Rates include breakfast and dinner. The Stoweflake also manages a nice group of townhouse condominiums with studio to three-bedroom units.

Ye Olde England Inne (253-7558; 800-477-3771, toll-free in the U.S. and Canada; 800-962-684 toll-free from the U.K.; $$–$$$$), is on the Mountain Road. Bigger than a country inn and smaller than a full-fledged hotel, it has an English country motif and lavish Laura Ashley touches. The Bluff House, perched on the hill behind the inn, has luxury suites with unobstructed views over the valley. Room rates include breakfast.

Green Mountain Inn (253-7301 or 800-253-7302; $$–$$$), on Main Street, is a charming old inn with a super location in the middle of town. The wide-planked floors are pine, as is the furniture, with many antique, four-poster canopied beds. Rooms that front on the street may be noisy for light sleepers; delivery trucks start to rev their engines at the nearby stop light at about 6 a.m. The hotel has an annex, located off the main road; most rooms there have whirlpool tubs. Rates include breakfast.

Ten Acres Lodge (253-7638 or 800-327-7357) is on Luce Hill Road. This country inn was converted from an 1840's farm house. Rooms vary in size; those in the main lodge are relatively simple, but the common areas are beautiful. Eight modern units, called the Hill House, are tucked into the woods behind the old farmhouse. These all have fireplaces in the rooms and share an outdoor hot tub. Rates include breakfast.

The Gables Inn (253-7730 or 800-422-5371; $$–$$$$), on Mountain Road, is a real lived-in house, which helps everyone have a good time. Breakfasts are among the best in Stowe, and guests wouldn't think of eating anywhere else for dinner. Rates include two meals.

The newly built **Stone Hill Inn** (253-6282; $$$$) is an exquisitely luxurious getaway designed for romance and comfort; no kids allowed. Each of the nine rooms has a king-size bed, a cozy sitting area, a fireplace in the bedroom *and* in the bathroom and a Jacuzzi for two. Prices include breakfast, evening hors d'oeuvres and unlimited soft drinks.

The Round Hearth at Stowe (253-7223; $) is a ski dorm that's popular with youth groups.

Dining: $$$-Entrees $20+; $$-$10-20; $-less than $10.

Accommodations: (double room) $$$$-$200+; $$$-$141-$200; $$-$81-$140; $-$80 and less.

Dining

Stowe has long been famous for its cuisine. **Ten Acres** (253-7638) and **Mes Amis** (253-7751; $$$) are considered by most to be the top gourmet spots around. Many locals consider the innovative fine dining offered at **Blue Moon Café** (253-7006; $$–$$$) the best in the area.

The **Trapp Family Lodge** (253-8511; $$–$$$) puts on an excellent Austrian-style meal for a fixed price of about $36. There normally is a choice of about a dozen entrées.

For alternatives that aren't budget-busters, try **Miguel's Stowe Away** (253-7574; $–$$) or the **Cactus Café** (253-7770; $–$$) for Mexican food, **Restaurant Swisspot** (253-4622; $–$$) for fondues and decadent Swiss chocolate pie, and **Gracie's** (253-8741) for great burgers and meat loaf. **The Shed** (253-4364; $–$$) has a microbrewery and is a great spot for steaks and prime rib. **Foxfire** (253-4887; $–$$) has good Italian food, as does **Trattoria La Festa** (253-8480; $$). **The Whip Bar and Grill** (253-7301; $$), in the lower level of the Green Mountain Inn, is a good place for a light dinner or sandwiches. **Mr. Pickwicks Polo Pub** in the Ye Olde England Inne (253-7558; $$) serves excellent game.

The **Fireside Tavern** (235-3000; $$), in the Inn at the Mountain, at the base of the Toll House lift, serves moderate continental cuisine as well as hearty lunches.

On-mountain, there are several choices for lunch and snacks. The **Midway Café** in the Midway Lodge has fresh-baked pastries and muffins and gourmet coffee. The **Cliff House Restaurant** at the gondola top has a nice upscale atmosphere and great views. You can check your email at **The Web Cafe**, in the Octagon.

A breakfast favorite is **McCarthy's,** next to the movie theater, adjacent to the Baggy Knees complex. Also the breakfast at **The Gables** shouldn't be missed, especially on weekends.

 ## Après-ski/nightlife

The ingredients that make the perfect après-ski spot are all there in just the right measure at the **Matterhorn Bar**. On the mountain road, this raucous little roadhouse is packed and rollicking after the lifts close. There's a dance floor, a disc jockey, loud music, a rectangular bar that makes for easy circulation, pool tables, big-screen TV. More low-key après-ski at the mountain is in the **Fireside Tavern** at the Inn at the Mountain.

The **Rusty Nail** is the "in" spot for dancing and live music, frequently blues. **The Seed** brews its own beer. **Mr. Pickwick's** at Ye Olde England Inne gets a good pub crowd with its 150-plus different beers, and the bar at **Miguel's Stowe Away** seems to be a singles meeting place.

 ## Other activities

Indoor tennis can be played at the Topnotch Racquet Club on the Mountain Road. Four Deco Turf courts are available as well as lessons for hourly fees. In the Village, Jackson Arena has an Olympic-size **ice skating** rink (253-6148). **Swimming** open to the public can be found at the Golden Eagle Resort (253-4811), Mountaineer Inn (253-7525), Salzburg Inn (253-8541), Topnotch Resort & Spa (253-9649) and the Town & Country Motor Lodge (253-7595). The **Vermont Ski Museum** has relocated to Main Street in Stowe Village.

Rent **snowmobiles** at Nichols Snowmobiles (253-7239) or from Farm Resort (888-3525). The Sterling Ridge Inn (644-8265), in Jeffersonville, offers snowmobile tours of Smugglers' Notch. **Horse-drawn sleigh rides** take place at Edson Hill Manor (253-7371), Stowehof Inn (253-9722), Pristine Meadows (253-9901), Charlie Horse (253-2215), Stoweflake (253-7355), the Trapp Family Lodge (253-8511) and Topnotch (253-8585). Stowe also has **horseback riding** at Edson Hill Manor (253-7371) and Stowehof Inn (253-9722).

Ben and Jerry's ice cream factory (244-5641) is just down the road in Waterbury and has tours that include samples. Winter is not nearly as busy as summer, so it's a good time to visit. **The Cabot Cheese Factory** (563-2231) is also open.

Stowe has over a hundred **shops** and **art galleries** for browsing, most in town. Shaw's General Store is a century old and was the town's first ski shop. Other unusual shops are Moriarty Hats & Sweaters, for knitted goods, and the Stowe Craft Gallery for handcrafted, contemporary works. At the Cabot Annex complex, in Waterbury, you can purchase a wide variety of Vermont specialty foods. The complex also is home to Lake Champlain Chocolates (Yum!), Vermont Teddy Bears and Mesa International, which sells home furnishings.

Special events include the Stowe Winter Carnival in January, the country's oldest winter party; the Mountain Adventure Fest Tour de Stowe cross-country races as well as the Stowe Derby—the country's oldest combination downhill/cross-country event, both held in February; a Sugar Slalom race with maple-sugar-on-snow at the finish line and the Stowe Snow Beach Party, both in April.

Getting there and getting around

By air: Numerous flights arrive at the Burlington International Airport, which is 45 minutes from Stowe. Most hotels have a transfer service; you can also rent a car. The Stowe Area Association provides discounts on flights and rental cars when you make your hotel reservations.

By train: A romantic trip aboard Amtrak's Vermonter offers private berths, cocktail-bearing attendants and the incomparable sensation of watching the moonlit landscape of New England whirl past your window to the lonely call of the train whistle. You arrive in Waterbury, 15 miles from Stowe, early in the morning (the Stowe trolley meets each daily arrival and departure). Reservations required. The Stowe Area Association offers 10 percent off Amtrak tickets with no date restrictions.

By car: Distance from Boston is about 205 miles; from New York, 325 miles. The resort is a few miles north of Waterbury Exit 10 on I-89.

Getting around: You can manage without a car, but we recommend one. We realize that this will only contribute to increased street congestion, but the alternative is the Town Trolley, which runs between the village of Stowe and Mt. Mansfield. It provides, in the words of a British journalist who begged a ride back into town with us, "an epic voyage." The trolley. Makes. A lot. Of stops. Between town. And. The. Mountain. It costs $1 per single ride and $5 for a week-long pass. It is fine for *short* jaunts and operates until 11 p.m.

Dining: $$$-Entrees $20+; $$-$10-20; $-less than $10.
Accommodations: (double room) $$$$-$200+; $$$-$141-$200; $$-$81-$140; $-$80 and less.

Stratton Mountain & Bromley
and the Manchester area
Vermont

Stratton Facts

Summit elevation: 3,875 feet
Vertical drop: 2,003 feet
Base elevation: 1,872 feet
Address: RR1 Box 145,
Stratton Mountain, VT 05155
☎ **Area code:** 802
Ski area phone: 297-2200
Snow report: 297-4211
ⓘ **Toll-free reservations:**
(800) STRATTON (787-2886)
Fax: 297-4300
E-mail: skistratton@intrawest.com
Internet: www.stratton.com
Number and types of lifts: 13–
1 twelve-passenger gondola, 4 six-passenger
high-speed chair, 4 quads, 1 triple,
1 double, 2 surface lifts
Skiable acreage: 583 acres
Snowmaking: 85 percent
Uphill capacity: 29,550 per hour
Snowboarding: Yes, unlimited
Bed base: 8,000 in region
Nearest lodging: Slopeside
Resort child care: Yes, 6 weeks and older
Adult ticket, per day: $36-$62 (01/02 prices)

Expert:★ **Advanced:**★★★
Intermediate:★★★★
Beginner:★★★★
Never-ever:★★★★

Bromley Facts

Summit elevation: 3,284 feet
Vertical drop: 1,334 feet
Base elevation: 1,950 feet
Address: P.O. Box 1130,
Manchester Center, VT 05255
☎ **Area code:** 802
Ski area phone: 824-5522
Snow report: 824-5522
ⓘ **Toll-free reservations:** (800) 865-4786
Internet: www.bromley.com
Number and types of lifts: 10–1 high-speed
quad, 1 quad, 4 doubles, 4 surface lifts
Skiable acreage: 300 acres
Snowmaking: 84 percent
Bed base: 8,000 in region
Uphill capacity: 9,045 per hour
Snowboarding: Yes, unlimited
Nearest lodging: Slopeside
Resort child care: Yes, 6 weeks and older
Adult ticket, per day: $36-$52 (02/03 prices)

Expert:★ **Advanced:**★
Intermediate:★★★★
Beginner:★★★★
Never-ever:★★★★

Manchester Region
Dining (in region):★★★★★
Apres-ski/nightlife (in region):★★★
Other activities (in region):★★★

Manchester is a hub for skiing in southern Vermont. The town itself, made over as the quintessential Vermont village, complete with white-spire churches, manorial hotels, gourmet dining and antique and craft shops, as well as factory outlets and Orvis fly fishing on the Battenkill River, could take up another entire chapter. Instead, we focus in this chapter on the areas closest to the ski areas.

Stratton, 20 miles from Manchester, is the largest resort in the region and also the chicest. With a car-free base village full of stylish shops, gourmet restaurants, slope-side condos and even a Bavarian-looking clock tower, Stratton does indeed feel like Vail. The cobblestone walkway through the village is even heated. Intrawest just keeps making Stratton bigger and better. New this year are two more six-passenger, high-speed chairs. One services the Sun Bowl; the other goes from the top of the Sun Bowl to the mountain's summit.

Bromley, six miles east of Manchester, is more of a no-nonsense, function-over-fashion ski resort. Its base area consists of a lodge. Period. Nearby are a hotel, some condos and a few private homes but no stores or restaurants. People come to Bromley to ski, ride and hang out with their friends and families on its usually sun-drenched slopes. Although significantly smaller than Stratton, Bromley has trails for everyone, from gentle beginner runs that wind down the mountain through the woods to expert pistes with shots through the trees.

Stratton

Mountain layout–Skiing

One of few eastern resorts with its own base village, Stratton caters to a tony down-country clientele who want convenient amenities and manicured slopes. Excellent grooming on the mostly intermediate terrain makes Stratton one of America's best ego-inflating resorts. Experts can find some good challenges, but don't expect to be pushed; come here to get pampered, and feel good about your skiing.

◆◆ **Expert** ◆ **Advanced:** The pitch for cruising here is nice enough that no expert or advanced skier will complain. Ducking from the trees onto the groomed provides a nice change of pace. For the more challenging terrain, head straight to the summit on the gondola. Polar Bear, Grizzly Bear and Upper Tamarack, all served by the Ursa Express six-passenger chair, are narrow runs in fine New England tradition with good vertical. Upper Kidderbrook to Freefall provides another good advanced cruiser on the Sun Bowl side. Upper Standard, right under the gondola, starts steep but mellows at the bottom. Upper Spruce is the easiest of the double-diamond trails with tempting glades to the right, but none of the double diamonds is really worth of that rating. For bumps, head to World Cup.

■ **Intermediate:** The upper mountain has some steeps for advanced intermediates. Upper Lift Line to Lower Lift Line, the longest fall-line trail on the mountain, is made for big giant-slalom turns, and Upper Drifter to Lower Drifter is the same. Racers from the Stratton Mountain School are often carving turns on these trails, as well as North American, off the Ursa Express. The Sun Bowl chair has excellent cruisers down Rowley's Run and Sunriser. On the lower mountain, Yodeler is a good warm-up run.

●● **Beginner:** Stratton has a Ski Learning Park with 10 gentle trails and its own lift. This park includes a terrain garden, where the mountain staff sculpts bumps and rolls, so beginners can practice their balance and independent leg action. A long top-to-bottom trail, West Meadow to Lower Wanderer, makes beginners feel like champs. In the Sun Bowl area head to Lower Middlebrook. The other beginner trails, 91, Big Ben and Main Line, are only reached from intermediate trails.

Mountain layout–Snowboarding

Stratton, one of the pioneers in snowboarding, demonstrates its commitment to the sport with numerous terrain parks filled with many tricking features and by hosting the annual U.S. Open. Indeed, no matter where you go here, there's bound to be a park nearby. Suntanner Park has the highest visibility and gets the most traffic. It's also home to the Superpipe. Although the trail map boasts two halfpipes, the top one is just a small, one-hitter; the bottom one is the real deal. It's found just beyond the Vermont Diner, which pumps out tunes to get pipe riders in the groove. Suntanner also has tabletops, hips, a spine and a variety of rails. You have to pick and choose your hits, as they're not all in succession.

East Byrneside Park, on the other side of the gondola from Suntanner, has rails, a three-way tabletop and hit. Take the Janeway Juction, far rider's left, to East Meadow, a a beginner freestyler's park. Although the upper section only has a few rollers and a small spine, the lower section is set up bordercross style, with rollers, banked turns and a jump at the end. Our rider found it small and not well maintaineed, but still fun.

If you time your visit to Stratton to about a week before the U.S. Open, head to the Sunriser Supertrail on the other side of the mountain to check out what the competitors trick off. This park and pipe are built about a week before the Open and aren't maintained afterwards. Features here include two big tabletops, a hip, a few straight rails and an S rail, finishing with a big quarterpipe. The huge U.S. Open Superpipe, located under the Sunrise Express chair, is also used by the Ross Powers Snowboard Camp for training a week after the Open.

Take a run down Lower Downeaster and look for Eclipse. This open glade is good for fast cruising and is also a good intro to tree riding. Moondance and Shred Wood Forest are both excellent double-diamond glades with good snow and some good steeps. Stratton also has single-black and blue glades. With good snow, killer glades and rippin' parks, our rider didn't even venture onto the trails.

Lessons (2002/03 prices)

Stratton has an on-mountain Adventure Center where you can try telemark skis, a snowboard, Snowblades or freeride skis designed for fun and tricks, especially in the halfpipe and other places frequented by snowboarders. Begin at Village Rentals in the Village Lodge in the Courtyard. From here, you'll be sent onto the mountain to the rental tent to pick up your equipment, then finally up to the Ski & Snowboard School. Give yourself plenty of time or you'll miss your lesson.

Group lessons: $32 for 1.75 hours.

Never-ever package: $95 includes beginner lift ticket, lesson and equipment; $83 for children ages 7–12.

Private lessons: : $75 per hour

Special programs: Stratton has women's ski and snowboard camps during the season designed to boost confidence and enhance strength, style and technique.

Child care (2002/03 prices)

Stratton: 6 weeks to 5 years. The Childcare Center in the Village Lodge is open 8 a.m. to 5 p.m., and drop-off is under the upper parking deck. A full day costs $95, lunch and snack included; half-day costs $50. Reservations required; call (800) 787-2886 (800-STRATTON).

Children's lessons: Little Cub snow school programs for ages 4–6 run full- ($95) and half-days ($50). The program for age 7–12 is all day and costs $115.

Lift tickets (2001/02 prices)

(weekend/weekday)	Adult	Child (7-12)	13-17 and 65-69
One day	$62/$57	$45/$45	$55/$50
Three days	$143/$129	$95/$83	$115/$109
Five days	$185/$178	$147/$142	$162/$174

Who skis free: Children younger than age 7.
Who skis at a discount: Those 70 and older ski for children's prices.
Stratton and Okemo have joined forces on a multiday lift ticket plan that permits skiing or riding at either resort. For details, call either resort.

Bromley

Intimate in atmosphere and size, Bromley is perfect for those who prefer not to sweat when skiing. There is some advanced stuff, but most of the 43 trails come down blue from the summit, leading into gentle cruising greens; perfect practice runs for intermediates and beginners but hardly deserving of names like Shincracker.

◆◆ **Expert** ◆ **Advanced:** When it is open, The Plunge provides gladed thrills. Pick your own level of difficulty. Even the best will find challenges. A few seasons ago, Bromley added some black runs to the mountain's steeper east side. Short and sharp with a double fall line, the longest of these challenging runs—Stargazer, Havoc and Blue Ribbon—bring you down to the Blue Ribbon Quad. There is more tree skiing between Pabst Peril and Avalanche.

■ **Intermediate:** This is a perfect mountain for every level of intermediate. The mellower trails are to the right of the high-speed quad (looking down the mountain). The black-diamond trails offer advanced-intermediate skiers excellent challenge.

●● **Beginner:** A good beginner area with a closed-in never-ever section of the mountain.

Mountain Layout-Snowboarding

The Snowboard Heaven, on the Lord's Prayer run, has all the right stuff: pipe, rolls and jumps, as well as its own T-bar and loud music. The halfpipe is big, and the resort boasts it's the steepest in Vermont. A second terrain park geared to novices is on the Plaza trail. It has hips, jumps, rolls, tabletops, etc. Occasionally, a boardercross is also built on Plaza.

Lessons (2002/03 prices)

Group lessons: $35 for a 1.75-hour lesson.
Never-ever package: The Beginners Circle and Snowboard Starter programs are for ages 15 and older. The $65 cost includes a 1.75-hour lesson, equipment and a beginner's lift ticket. The two-days cost $99.
Private lessons: $70 per hour, $35 per extra person. Multiple-hour discounts available.

534 • Stratton Mountain & Bromley – Vermont

Child care [2002/03 prices]

The Bromley Kids' Center accepts children ages 6 weeks to 6 years. Half day $28, full day $49. Call 824-5522 for reservations and information.

    Children's lessons: The Mighty Moose Club (3–5 years) includes playtime, skiing sessions and equipment for $50, half day; $91 full day. Pig Dog Pups (5-6 years) and Pig Dog Mountain Club (7–12 years) includes lift tickets, lessons and lunch but no rental equipment for $80 per day; $91 with equipments.

Lift tickets [2002/03 prices]

	Adult	Child (7-14)	Teen (13-17)
One day*	$52/$52/$46	$35/$35/$32	$45/$45/$38
Two days*	$92/$86/$73	$63/$58/$55	$80/$76/$68

* Weekend price, holiday price, weekday price

    Who skis free: Children ages 6 and younger ski free everyday; ages 70 and older ski free on weekends and holidays.

    Who skis at a discount: Ages 65–69 ski for $35/$32 (02/03 rates).

Cross-country

The Manchester area offers an excellent series of trails.

    Hildene (362-1788) in Manchester Village has 15 km. of trails through the pine-covered estate of Robert Todd Lincoln. There is a warming hut in the carriage barn, with rentals, trail tickets and light refreshments.

    Nordic Inn (824-6444), just east of Peru, has trails that wander into the Green Mountain National Forest.

    The Stratton Ski Touring Center (297-4114) at the Sun Bowl has 20 km. of tracked cross-country trails and 50 km. of backcountry skiing. Lessons and guided tours are available.

    Beginner terrain and great views are available at the **Nordic Center** at the Stratton Mountain Country Club. Stratton offers Tubbs snowshoe rentals at both its country club and its mountain summit. Stratton also has backcountry Nordic skiing, and moonlight tours available; call for prices and details.

    Viking Ski Touring Center (824-3933) in Londonderry provides 30 km. of groomed trails through woods and open fields, best suited for intermediates, but with some advanced trails, too. This is one of the oldest cross-country centers in North America.

    Porc Trails (824-3933) are a series of ungroomed trails maintained by the West River Outing Club of Londonderry. If you intend to use them, make sure someone knows where you are and when you intend to return because the trails are not patrolled daily. Call for directions and parking locations.

Accommodations

The town of Manchester is a tourism mecca with accommodations from giant resorts and B&Bs to a slew of lesser-priced roadside motels. The Manchester and Mountains Chamber (362-2100) and the **Londonderry Chamber** (824-8178) can help with arrangements. The hotels and B&Bs listed below are near the ski areas.

    At Stratton: Lift and lodging packages (midweek, non-holiday) begin at $49 per person, per day, based on double occupancy. The new **Long Trail House** units will comfortably house a family for an extended stay, with an outdoor heated pool, hot tubs and underground

www.resortspace.com   Telephone area code: 802

climate-controlled parking. The **Village Lodge** (297-2500) is smack in the middle of Stratton and is the premier property for location: Walk out your door and you are 100 yards from the gondola. It has no pool, dining room, or lounge; for those, take the shuttle to its larger sister hotel, the **Stratton Mountain Inn** (297-2500). The **Liftline Lodge** (297-2600; $–$$) provides Stratton's most economical lodging on the mountain and has many of the resort's restaurants. Stratton Reservations has plenty of condos all within easy reach of the slopes. For reservations at any of Stratton's lodges, call (800) 787-2886 (800-STRATTON). Note: Stratton Mountain packages offer great discounts. Children younger than age 6 stay and ski free anytime. Children 12 and younger stay free in the same room with their parents.

At **Bromley**: Slopeside lodging is available at the **Bromley Sun Lodge** (824-6941; $–$$$), with packages starting at $59 per night, double occupancy. Condos and private homes (up to 4 bedrooms) are either slopeside or fed by a shuttle to the base lodge.

Between Bromley and Magic Mountain, on Rte. 11, try the **Swiss Inn** (824-3442 or 800-847-9477; $–$$). It has basic rooms but a wonderful restaurant. For an upscale B&B experience, call **The Macartney House** (824-6444 or 800-498-6445; $$–$$$). Both are convenient to the Green Mountain National Forest with 26 km. of cross-country trails. **The Londonderry Inn** (824-5226; $–$$), on Rte. 100, has 25 individually decorated rooms.

These property management companies deal with condos throughout the area: **Alpine Rentals** (800-817-4562, 824-4562), **Bondville Real Estate** (800-856-8388; 297-3316) or **Winhill Real Estate** (800-214-5648, 297-1550).

Dining

Dining in the region surrounding the three ski areas is excellent and eclectic. Those looking for a quaint and romantic atmosphere can find it, and those searching for family bargains will not be disappointed.

At **Stratton Mountain: Season's** (297-2600; $$), in the Liftline Lodge, has great crabcakes. **Cafe on the Corner** (297-2600; $), also at the Liftline Lodge, has a good breakfast and nice lunch sandwiches. **Sage Hill Restaurant** (297-2500; $$$), in the Stratton Mountain Inn, has great views and a good kitchen. The lunch and dinner menus are creative, well prepared and wonderfully presented. Great Italian food seems to be the main theme on the mountain with **Mulberry Street** (297-3065; $$) serving basic pastas and pizzas and the cozy **La Pista** (297-2343; $$) featuring trendy Italian cooking.

Mulligan's (297-9293; $$) serves moderately priced, basic American fare with a good kids' menu in a loud, TV-in-every-corner atmosphere. **Cider's** (formerly The Roost; 297-4492; $), right at the base of the slopes, gets rave reviews from families for great breakfasts.

Out Back at Winhall River (297-3663; $$$), just south of the access road, has phenomenal lobster bisque together with other casual fare. Tell the kitchen to go slow on the salt and order red wine by the bottle rather than by the glass. **The Three O'Clock Inn** (824-6327; $$$) serves gourmet fare in an old restored farmhouse in South Londonderry.

The Frog's Leap Inn (824-3019; $$$), in Londonderry, serves creative meals by candlelight. **The Garden Cafe** (824-9574; $$$), at the junction of Rtes. 11 and 100 in Londonderry, has been serving upscale meals for more than 15 years. **The Three Mountain Inn** (800-532-9399 or 874-4140; $$$), in Jamaica, has an intimate and elegant dining room and a menu that changes daily.

For fondues and other Swiss/German entrées, head to the **Swiss Inn** (824-3442; $$). **Foggy Goggle** (827-1300; $$) has steak and seafood in a tavern atmosphere.

Dining: $$$-Entrees $20+; $$-$10-20; $-less than $10.
Accommodations: (double room) $$$$-$200+; $$$-$141-$200; $$-$81-$140; $-$80 and less.

The **Red Fox** (297-2488; $$-$$$), in Bondville, was recommended by about every local for Italian food. **The Noodle Room** (824-4122; $$) has lots of pasta, but doesn't take credit cards. **Johnny Seesaw's** (824-5533), just down the road from Bromley in Peru, serves enormous portions. **Jake's Cafe** (824-6614; $) serves pizzas and sandwiches.

 ## Après-ski/nightlife

At Stratton, après-ski is on the deck of **Grizzly's** with entertainment almost every weekend, in **Mulligan's** with its 50 different types of beer or **The Tavern** in the Stratton Mountain Inn. In the evenings, the action on the mountain continues in the **Green Door Pub** in Mulligan's, with live entertainment on weekends, and at **Snyders,** a tap room in Cider's, with live music. Off the mountain, try the locals' hangout, **Red Fox** in Bondville, for live music Fridays and dancing. The **Foggy Goggle,** also in Bondville, is rockin' on the weekends with live bands and free pizza from 4–5 p.m. daily. If you're into the cigar and martini crazes, head to **Mulberry Street.**

 ## Other activities

The **Stratton Sports Center** has indoor tennis, racquetball, indoor pool, hot tubs, saunas, fitness center, tanning salons and massages. The **Moonlight Snowshoe Tour** goes from the the Country Club Nordic Center, over the gentle golf-course terrain, with a stop at the Pearl Buck Stone House for hot chocolate by the fireplace.

For kids, Stratton offers **mini-snowmobile** rides to kids in the base area. New this season is the **Junior Off-Road Driving School** with mini-repilca Land Rovers, for children ages 4-12.

A run-down **movie theater** in Manchester has two screens. For **ice skating**, head to the Riley Rink (362-0150) in Manchester. **Sleigh rides** are offered by Horses for Hire (297-1468) in Rawsonville, just south of Bondville on Rte. 30, Karl Pfister's Sleigh Rides (824-6320) in Landgrove, near Bromley, Sun Bowl Ranch (297-9210) at Stratton and Taylor Farm Sleigh Rides (824-5690) in Londonderry.

Shopping: This is a major non-ski activity in the Manchester region. About 40 factory outlet stores, including Coach, Brooks Brothers, Cole Hahn and Garnet Hill, are spread throughout Manchester, along with boutiques and shops with handcrafted regional gift items and unusual clothing.

 ## Getting there and getting around

By air: Manchester is about 90 minutes from the Albany, N.Y. airport and requires a car for easy access.

By car: Manchester Center is at the intersection of Rtes. 7A and 30 in southwestern Vermont, about 140 miles from Boston and 235 miles from New York City. Stratton is on Rte. 30 about 20 miles east of Manchester. Look for the Stratton Mountain Road from Rte. 30. If you're heading straight for Stratton from I-91, take Exit 2 at Brattleboro, follow signs to Rte. 30, then drive 38 miles to Bondville and the Stratton Mountain Road. Bromley is six miles from Manchester traveling on Rte. 11, eight miles west of Londonderry.

Getting around: Bring a car.

Snowshoe Mountain

West Virginia

Summit elevation:	**4,800 feet**
Vertical drop:	**1,500 feet**
Base elevation:	**3,200 feet**

Address: 1 Snowshoe Drive, Snowshoe, WV, 26209

Area code: 304

Ski area phone: 572-1000

Snow report: 572-4636; (800) 258-0330

Reservations: 877-441-4386 or 572-5252

Fax: 572-5664

E-mail: info@snowshoemtn.com

Internet: www.snowshoemtn.com

Expert:★

Advanced:★★

Intermediate:★★★★★

Beginner:★★★★

Never-ever:★★★★

Number and types of lifts: 14–2 high-speed quads, 2 quads, 7 triples, 3 surface lifts

Acreage: 224 acres

Snowmaking: 100 percent

Uphill capacity: 22,900 per hour

Snowboarding: Yes

Bed base: 1,500 condominium units; 285 hotel/inn rooms

Nearest lodging: Slopeside

Resort child care: Yes, 12 weeks and up

Adult ticket, per day: $44–$53 (02/03 prices)

Dining: ★★★★

Apres-ski/nightlife: ★★

Other activities: ★★★

"Northern exposure with southern hospitality" is the way Snowshoe Mountain folks like to describe themselves. This southern ski area gets nearly 200 inches of annual snowfall, so you've got to admit they have a point. The vast majority of the nearly half million skiers who come here annually live well south of the Mason-Dixon line, but others are discovering it. In actuality, this Intrawest-owned resort encompasses three areas: Snowshoe, Silver Creek and The Western Territory.

Snowshoe, is an "upside down" resort: The base facilities are at the summit. A mountaintop village has been under construction for several years, and a new lodge, condominiums, restaurants, shops and other base village facilities have been, and continue to be, added. It's the most elaborate and extensive resort in the South, and a vast majority of the skiing/riding is aimed at intermediates.

The Silver Creek area is less crowded, and the slopes are wider and better designed than at the Snowshoe area, but the skiing is less challenging. It's a terrific family area, with night skiing, a terrain park and snow tubing.

The Western Territory has two expert runs served by a high-speed quad. Though the areas are separate, a shuttle bus efficiently transports skiers the short distance between them, and one lift ticket is good at all.

Mountain layout–Skiing

◆◆ **Expert** ◆ **Advanced:** To reach The Western Territory, site of the expert terrain, you must cross the street. Literally. It's located across the access road from Snowshoe. Given the predominance of southern, once-a-year ski-weekers among the clientele, this section is usually least crowded, but it consists of just two runs, Cupp Run and Shay's Revenge, which take advantage of Snowshoe's total vertical drop. Both trails are worthy of their black-diamond rating. At moments along Cupp, nifty little places can be found to zip into the trees, and one section of Shay's is significantly steep and often bumps up.

Silver Creek has two trails marked black, Flying Eagle and Bear Creek. While these have short sections that present some pitch, competent intermediates can handle them.

■ **Intermediate:** More than one-third of the runs here are rated in the blue-square realm. At the Snowshoe area, the best runs are Ball Hooter and Skip Jack, which lead down to the Ballhooter (why the run is denoted in two words and the lift in one word is anybody's guess) and Grabhammer chairs, respectively. Traffic can be a problem here, as these lie at the heart of the hill. Another interesting, less-traveled option is the Upper Flume/J Hook/Lower Widowmaker route, which is found to skier's far right off the Widowmaker chair and combines easy with intermediate sliding on both narrow and wide trails.

At Silver Creek, Fox Chase-to-Laurel Run offers the most extended blue-rated run. Cascade and Slaymaker-to-Spur also present good cruising, but none is particularly long.

●● **Beginners:** The resort caters to green-level skiers and riders. At the far left, off Snowshoe's top ridge, Northern Tract is a comfortably isolated group of a half-dozen easy trails that gives green-trail skiers their own lift-served real estate off the Powderidge chair. These trails are wide enough to be reassuring, but meander a bit to lend texture.

Silver Creek's green-rated runs are generally short but very welcoming, presenting a good place for never-evers to begin the transition to more general terrain. Cubb Run gently hugs the far right edge of the area and allows access to three chairlifts.

● **Never-ever:** The good news is that the Skidder area for never-evers is located just a few steps from the Shavers Center, home to the ski school and rental shop. The bad news is that it's laid out laterally on the ridge top and can become a bit frenzied and turbulent with skiers and riders passing through en route to other parts of the hill. The terrain itself is conducive to learning: short, wide and gentle.

 ## Mountain layout–Snowboarding

Snowshoe has embraced riders with open arms. At Silver Creek, the Ruckus Ridge Mountaineer Terrain Park is a very popular attraction with both riders and freeskiers. The park includes a 450-foot halfpipe that the resort boasts to be "the largest all-snow halfpipe in the region." At least a dozen features fill the park, including berms, tabletops, banks and various jumps. It runs top-to-bottom on the Mountaineer trail which, although rated black diamond, isn't significantly steep.

The resort's terrain is generally snowboarder-friendly, with a minimum of crossover trails and relatively few spots that require unstrapping and pushing. Riders can add some texture to the general cruising nature of the main mountain by taking the short detour onto the Knot Bumper/Glades combination off the Ballhooter chair. The resort stages a variety of competitions and other events throughout the season.

Mountain rating

Snowshoe does very well by its core customers: Southerners who ski once or twice for a week-long vacation or long weekends each season, and families who come from the Washington, DC, and Baltimore areas or from Virginia cities. The terrain is largely approachable with superb snowmaking and snow grooming that allows low-intermediates and intermediates to have a good time. The Silver Creek area presents an excellent venue for families, especially those with younger children, with its combination of single-facility, ski-in/out lodging, night skiing, terrain park and snow tubing. Pickings are slim for the true advanced and expert skier.

 ## Cross-country and snowshoeing

The resort's cross-country skiing operates out of the **Snowshoe Outdoor Adventure Center** (572-5477), between Snowshoe and Silver Creek. The trail system covers 40 km. along the Cheat Mountain Ridge Trail, as well as through the nearby backcountry. The center is fully equipped with rentals and offers instruction.

The **Elk River Inn** (572-3771), in Slatyfork about 5 miles from the bottom of the Snowshoe access road, has a touring center and immediate access to 5 km. of adjacent groomed trails. Another 35 km. can be accessed nearby. The Inn offers ski rentals and will give instruction by appointment.

 ## Lessons (2002/03 prices)

The Snowshoe Ski and Snowboard School operates out of the Shavers Center in the main resort complex, and out of a building adjacent to the Silver Creek Lodge on the Silver Creek side.

Group Lessons: Two-hour, adult group lessons for ages 13 and up (skiing or snowboarding) for Levels 1-4 are scheduled daily at 10 a.m. and 2 p.m. and cost $30. Multi-day lesson packages are available for $25/day. Two-hour afternoon ski clinics are offered daily for adults skiing at Levels 6-9 at 1:30 p.m. for $35 each. Similar sessions are offered for more advanced snowboarders.

Never-ever packages: Magic Trax is specifically designed for first-time skiers and is available during non-holiday periods. It utilizes Rossignol Short Cut skis. A two-hour session costs $30. Equipment rentals and beginner-area ticket are included.

Private Lessons: All-day costs $325, plus $100 for each additional person. Half-day is approximately $175, plus $75 per extra person. One-hour sessions are offered at 8:30 a.m. , 12:15 p.m. and 3:30 p.m. at a rate of approximately $75 per person, plus $35 per additional participant.

 ## Child care (2002/03 prices)

Ages: 12 weeks-10 years.
Costs: Ages 2-10, $45 per day, 8 a.m.-5 p.m., including lunch; $20 per half-day, 8 a.m.-12 p.m. or 1 p.m.-5 p.m., without lunch; or $5 per hour. Younger than age 2, $60 per day, $24 per half-day or $6 per hour.

The Kids' Night Out program is offered Mondays, Wednesdays and Saturdays from 6-9 p.m. for ages 5-12 for $35 and includes arts and crafts, snowshoeing, bonfires, story telling, and other indoor and outdoor activities.

Children's lessons: Full-day and half-day ski and snowboard programs are offered for ages 3-12, with groupings broken into ages 3-4 and 5-12, based also on ability level. Full-day programs run from 9:30 a.m.-4 p.m. Ages 3-4 cost $70 per day, or $67 per day for a multi-day package; ages 5-12 cost $65 and $62 respectively. Half-day sessions run from 9:30 a.m.-12 p.m. and 1:30-4 p.m. The fees for ages 3-4 are $45 per day and $43 per day for multi-day packages; for ages 5-12, fees are $40 and $38 respectively. These rates do not include lift tickets or equipment rental, but all-day sessions do include lunch.

Lift tickets (2002/03 prices)

Snowshoe provides a variety of pricing modes. Below we quote prices for weekends.

	Adult	Junior (7-12)	Student/Sr. (65-69)
One day	$53	$35	$48
Multi-day	$44	$29	$35

Who skis free: Children 6 and younger.

Who skis at a discount: Seniors 70 and older ski for $27 for one day; $26 for multi-day. Weekdays cost $45 for adults, $30 for juniors, $36 for students with ID and seniors (65–69).

Note: Snowshoe sells tickets for night skiing, 4:30-10 p.m. for $27 adult, $19 junior, $23 student/seniors (65–69). There is a Twilight Skiing pass valid 12:30–10 p.m. and an Extended Day ski pass good 8:30 a.m.–10 p.m.

Accommodations

Intrawest is in the process of creating one of its signature base villages (in this case, at the mountain's top) at Snowshoe. The resort holds a vast array of housing of all types, including some 1,500 condominium units and, at the base of the access road, a nice but basic motel. Call 877-441-4386 or 572-5262.

Rimfire Lodge ($$-$$$$), one of the newest facilities, is set in the heart of the pedestrian village. It has hotel rooms, plus studio, one- and two-bedroom units. Typical of Intrawest properties, accommodations are comfortable, but smaller units can be a bit cramped. Most units have kitchens, all have gas-fired fireplaces, and guests get the advantage of underground parking. The intra-resort shuttle stops at the door.

Highland House ($$-$$$$) overlooks the Ballhooter lift and is the resort's latest expansion. Units run the gamut from hotel rooms and so-called deluxe hotel rooms to two-bedroom condos with a den.

Allegheny Springs ($$-$$$$) is the newest and poshest lodging in the village. It has fresh-water thermal pool in the courtyard, as well as a full-service restaurant and a day spa.

Silver Creek Lodge ($$-$$$$) is the 240-unit, self-contained base facility at Silver Creek. Accommodations range from studios to four-bedroom condos, plus a penthouse. This is an ideal site for families with young children, as the tubing hill, night skiing, terrain park, kids' ski school, child care, rental shop, pool and other amenities are right there.

Spruce Lodge ($-$$) is the on-hill no frills lodge, offering double rooms, some with bunk beds. It's low-budget, but located smack in the middle of things.

Inn at Snowshoe ($-$$) sits at the base of the access road, six miles from the summit village. A 150-room hotel, it has some one-bedroom suites.

Off the mountain, the area boasts a handful of nice B&B's. The **Elk River Inn** (572-3771; $-$$) comprises a 10-room inn, a five-room farmhouse with three shared baths and kitchen, and five kitchen-equipped cabins. It's five miles from the access road and offers breakfast, an excellent restaurant and on-site Nordic skiing, as well as its own snowboard shop. The **Morning Glory Inn** (572-5000; $-$$$) is brand new and located just 3 miles from the access road. It has six large bedrooms with oversized Jacuzzi-tub bathrooms, a large, homey public living room and a full breakfast that's substantial and homemade. The **Brazen Head Inn** (339-6917; $-$$$), 7 miles north of the mountain on US Rte. 219, offers comfortable B&B lodging and dining. The 20-room roadside lodge also offers daily dining and features an Irish style pub.

Dining

On-mountain, the number of eateries is expanding rapidly. **The Red Fox** (572-1111; $$-$$$) remains the long-standing benchmark for on-mountain fine dining. It features Mountain Alpine cuisine, which consists of a lot of meat and wild game specialties, presented with an unusual combination of European-style service and American/mountain casual ambiance.

The **Junction Restaurant** (572-5800; $$) is one of the newer entries, a result of the base village expansion. The decor hearkens back to West Virginia logging boom times and the heyday of Shay steam locomotives, with memorabilia from the nearby Cass Scenic Railroad. The food is classic American fare and reasonably good. The **Foxfire Grill** (572-5555; $$-$$$), another new entry in the Rimfire Lodge, features live blues and barbecue, as well as burgers. For something simpler and faster, **The Cheat Mountain Pizza Company** (572-5757; $-$$) serves pretty good pizza, from plain to gourmet, as well as salads, calzones and other Italian fare. One meal that's fun and recommended is the terrific waffle breakfast at **The Boathouse** (572-1000; $), a rustic day lodge set at the base of the Ballhooter Lift. Lunch is also available.

Off mountain, the **Restaurant at the Elk River Inn** (572-3771; $$$) serves a changing menu of truly gourmet regional and international dishes, superb desserts and a nice selection of local microbrews. Reservations are recommended.

 # Après-ski/nightlife

A surprising amount of activity goes on here after dark, including night skiing. If you're looking for a bar scene or club, you can easily find it. **The Connection** is the hottest spot on the mountain. Yes, it's located in the Shavers Centre base facility, so there's nothing exotic about it, but the upstairs club scene really does rock. Live bands and a DJ are a regular feature, plus there's pool, foosball, some video games and a large-screen TV. The partying usually lasts well into the night. A particular favorite of ours is the **Comedy Cellar Bar** (572-5440 for performance info), squirreled away in the basement of the almost dorm-like Mountain Lodge. The bar itself is small and intimate and open nightly Tuesdays-Saturdays at 9 p.m.. Local Roy Riley (not a bad performer himself) shares the small stage with one or two pros who frequent the national circuit for a full evening of stand-up comedy. It's definitely adult entertainment, and it's lots of fun.

Rosa's Cantina, found a bit out of the way at the top of the Widowmaker lift, serves unremarkable burgers and Mexican fare, but somehow manages to have one fine bar. Gregarious bartenders, good brew and an altogether very friendly, locals' atmosphere make it a good spot for a drink. The **Foxfire Grill**, although new, manages to generate a nice sense of atmosphere and frequently offers local, live, foot-stomping music. If you're staying over on the family-oriented Silver Creek side, you have two choices right in Silver Creek Lodge. The **Bear's Den** is on the second floor, a fine spot to take in a quiet beer or hot drink on a cold day. At the **Red Oak Pub**, you can quench your thirst while playing billiards or fooseball.

Other activities

Snowshoe Resort has just recently begun to offer snowmobile touring. **Mile High Snowmobiling Tours** is located near the Cross Country Ski Center, and reservations can be made at the Adventure Center in the base village. The cost for a one-hour tour is $50 per driver, plus $15 per passenger. Another relatively new

Dining: $$$-Entrees $20+; $$-$10-20; $-less than $10.
Accommodations: (double room) $$$$-$200+; $$$-$141-$200; $$-$81-$140; $-$80 and less.

offering is a **Sunrise Country Hut** dinner. You can only get there by snowmobile or all-terrain vehicle (it's a two-mile ride), and you get a good country meal (steak, salmon or chicken; wine included) in a beautiful, isolated setting for $75 per person.

While at the Adventure Center, you can also sign up for a **dogsledding** outing. The cost is $49 per couple. Two **horse-drawn sleigh ride** options are available. A short ride on the Skidder beginner slope (great for small children) costs but $5. One-hour ride will run you $60 for two passengers; one or two other passengers over age 12 can join you for $10 each.

The tubing hill at **Ruckus Ridge Adventure Park** is found at Silver Creek. The cost runs $12 per person for two hours, or $15 for an all-day pass.

Shopping: Nobody is going to mistake this place for a shopper's paradise. The expanding base village represents an attempt to bring in some interesting retail, but it's minimal at best. We like **The Chocolate Factory** (572-1289) because, well, who doesn't love a store that sells chocolate? **The Red Fox Mercantile**, at The Red Fox Restaurant is also interesting for its proprietary sauces and such. You can also pay premium prices for high-quality clothing and accessories here. **The General Store** sells provisions for your condo, but beware the high-elevation prices. If you're heading to a condo, best to pack in supplies from your local supermarket, then add absolute necessities, or must-be-fresh stuff here. It also rents videos and VCRs, sells gas and makes some pretty good sandwiches.

Getting there and getting around

By car: You're going to end up driving here, even if you fly, since the nearest sizable airport is nearly two-and-a-half hours away. The resort is located on Rte. 66 off Rte. 219, about 45 miles south of Elkins, W.V. It's rather remote no matter from which direction you approach. From the south or the west, exit I-64, at White Sulphur Springs, then take Hwy. 92 and 39 to Marlinton, until you see the Snowshoe signs. From the north, exit I-79 at Weston (Hwy. 33 at exit 99), go to Elkins, then south on Highway 219. From the East, it's I-81 to Staunton, Rte. 42/39 west to Rte. 28 south; or, from Harrisonburg, Va., take Rte. 33 west to Rte. 28 south.

By plane: Roanoke, Va., airport is approximately 3 hours from the resort, and is served by US Airways, Delta, American and United Airlines. Yeager Airport in Charleston, W.V., about 3.5 hours away and served by US Airways, United Express and Delta's Comair. Closest is Greenbrier Valley Airport in Lewisburg, W.V., approximately 1.5 hours from Snowshoe, which is only served by US Airways but offers the Greenbrier Valley Airport Shuttle (536-1193) for those who choose not to drive.

Getting around: As long as you're on the mountain, the shuttle bus will reliably get you where you need to go. If you want to go off-mountain, you're going to need that car. Parking is a bit chaotic; however, Rimfire Lodge has underground parking.

Index

downhill and cross-country resorts alphabetically